THE HUMANITIES IN WESTERN CULTURE

VOLUME 1

THE HUMANITIES IN WESTERN CULTURE

A Search for Human Values

TENTH EDITION
VOLUME 1

ROBERT C. LAMM
ARIZONA STATE UNIVERSITY, RETIRED

Boston, Massachusetts   Burr Ridge, Illinois   Dubuque, Iowa
Madison, Wisconsin   New York, New York   San Francisco, California   St. Louis, Missouri

McGraw-Hill

*A Division of The **McGraw·Hill** Companies*

THE HUMANITIES IN WESTERN CULTURE: VOLUME 1

This book is printed on acid-free paper.

10 CK/CK 9 0 9 8 7

ISBN 0-697-25427-5

Publisher *Rosemary Bradley*
Senior Developmental Editor *Deborah Daniel*
Associate Marketing Manager *Kirk Moen*
Editor *Ursula Sadie*
Designers *Barbara Mercer and Richard Foenander*
Picture Researcher *Carrie Haines*
Maps by Oxford Illustrators

Library of Congress Catalog Card Number: 95-76177

http://www.mhcollege.com

Front cover Pont du Gard, near Nîmes, France. Ca. 20–10 BC. Height 180' (275 m). Photo: Spectrum, London.

Spine Statuette of a youth, "Mantiklos dedicated me. . . ." Ca. 700–680 BC. Bronze, height 8" (20.3 cm). Museum of Fine Arts, Boston (Francis Bartlett Donation).

Back cover *Sacrificial Scene*, votive tablet from the cave of Pitsa near Corinth. Ca. 540 BC. Paint on wood, height 6" (15.2 cm). National Archaeological Museum, Athens.

Half-title Rhyton in the Form of a Lion-Griffin. Persian. 5th century BC. Gold, height 6¾" (17.1 cm). Metropolitan Museum of Art, New York (Fletcher Fund, 1954).

Frontispiece *The Abbot Mena, Protected by Christ*, from Egypt. Coptic. 5th century. Painted icon. Louvre, Paris. Photo: R.M.N., Paris.

Prologue Tutankhamen's treasure, detail of a large wooden coffin showing Isis. New Kingdom. Ca. 1350 BC. Gilded wood. Egyptian Museum, Cairo. Photo: Dagli Orti, Paris.

Unit Opener Illustrations

Unit 1 Queen Hatshepsut, architectural detail of the Mortuary Temple of Queen Hatshepsut, Deir-el-Bahri (Thebes), Egypt. New Kingdom, 18th dynasty. Ca. 1480 BC. Photo: Spectrum, London.

Unit 2 Statuette of a youth, "Mantiklos dedicated me. . . ." Ca. 700–680 BC. Bronze, height 8" (20.3 cm). Museum of Fine Arts, Boston (Francis Bartlett Donation).

Unit 3 Pont du Gard, near Nîmes, France. Ca. 20–10 BC. Height 180' (275 m). Photo: Spectrum, London.

Unit 4 *St. Michael*, St Mark's, Venice. 10th century. Enameled gold plaque. Photo: Werner Forman, London.

Unit 5 Duccio, *Rucellai Madonna*, detail, after restoration, 1989. 1285. Tempera on wood, 14' 9" × 9' 6" (4.5 × 2.9 m). Galleria degli Uffizi, Florence. Photo: Dagli Orti, Paris.

Complete Contents

Expanded Contents

UNIT 3
Rome: The International Culture   231

8   A Thousand Years of Rome   233

Maps

Listening Examples

Preface

Welcome to the tenth edition of a text that first appeared over forty years ago with multiple authors and entitled *The Search for Personal Freedom*. The original title continued through the seventh edition, after which the undersigned became the sole author of what is now *The Humanities in Western Culture*.

This is a two-volume text for the integrated humanities: the arts of literature, painting, music, sculpture, photography, architecture, and film, and the discipline of philosophy. Although philosophy is not an "art" in the strictest sense, the major philosophical ideas so consistently permeate each of the arts that they are, of necessity, interwoven throughout the book. The components of the humanities—philosophy and the arts—are presented not as separate technical disciplines but as interrelated manifestations of human creativity. Moreover, they are studied within the context of important developments in science, technology, economics, and politics. This is, in sum, a book about people and about "art's eternal victory over the human condition" (André Malraux).

In order to understand better why we are the way we are, our studies are centered on our cultural legacy—from Mesopotamia, Egypt, Greece, and Rome to the present day. Throughout the book the accomplishments of the past are considered not as museum pieces but as living evidence of enduring responses to the perplexities of life. These achievements have become, in our day, a basic part of our attempts to make sense of the universe.

The text is arranged chronologically and divided into nine major units in two volumes. Because artists naturally respond to the issues of their own time, each unit is prefaced by an overview of the social, scientific, religious, and philosophical climate of the period. Forming the core of this text are the primary sources, the art works themselves—many of them complete works rather than fragments: plays, poetry, short stories, entire sections of large works, hundreds of art illustrations, and numerous musical examples. Introduced with appropriate commentary, the selections are followed by practical exercises and questions. Additionally, there are maps, graphs, time charts, and, at the end of each volume, a glossary of important terms in philosophy and the arts. There is more than enough material for a two-semester course based entirely on the text; alternatively, the book can be used as a central text embellished by additional primary sources.

Because each major culture is distinct and merits its own special study, this is an examination of the evolution of Western civilization and its place in American culture. It is perhaps more multicultural than any other civilization because it has been more open to outside influences and ideas. Western culture—the humanities in particular—derives not just from the Mesopotamian, Egyptian, Graeco-Roman, and Germanic heritage. It has been influenced, altered, and/or enlarged over thousands of years by virtually every culture in the world. With its diverse origins Western humanities is an especially rewarding study in what is undoubtedly the most multicultural nation on earth. From colonial times onward, the United States has been a gathering of immigrants. Whether political refugees or seekers after a better life, people from all parts of the globe have been coming here for over three centuries, and will continue coming. What was once dubbed a "melting pot" culture is actually a rich and unique civilization. Whatever one's ancestry, there is something singular and special about being an American and, to cite only one example, we see it writ large at every session of the Olympic Games.

The presence of numerous non-Western immigrants in a rapidly changing population strongly reinforces the necessity of studying the cultural heritage of the West. Many immigrants are, after all, attracted to Western civilization because of the educational and vocational opportunities and the high standard of living, all of which have derived from the economic, political, and scientific development of Western nations. This does not imply, however, that newer citizens must leave their culture behind: far from it. It is most important to go on to study other major cultures plus what is currently called "global humanities," for global considerations are among the conspicuous realities of the late twentieth century. However, the author is convinced that most students, whether native-born or recent arrivals, would derive greater benefits from studying other cultures after they have acquired a better understanding of the Western heritage. Establishing a frame of reference seems the most practical and efficient way of comprehending cultural developments around the globe, most of which have been influenced by Western civilization.

In this new edition there are many changes in both content and style; a humanities textbook is, or should be, a living document that adjusts to the ever-changing world. New facts about the past are continually emerging, while today's world changes so rapidly as to leave us grasping for comprehension, not to mention gasping for breath.

The biggest change in this book is the addition of many feature boxes that, variously, focus on interesting ideas, other cultural influences, and significant events. There are more and better color illustrations and improved maps. In Volume 1 the chapter on Greek music has been integrated into the chapters on art and philosophy. Added to the art chapters are descriptions and color illustrations of the art and craft of jewelry. Aristophanes' *Lysistrata* is given in a different translation, as is Aristotle's *Poetics*. The unit on the Middle Ages includes additional material on Islamic arts plus a selection from Christine de Pisan, an important writer and early feminist. There is, in fact, increased coverage throughout of some notable contributions of women, especially in art and literature.

The Literary Selections in Volume 2 now include poems and short stories from South Africa, Germany, Greece, Egypt, France, Israel, and Ghana. Other additions include consideration of the religions other than Christianity, Judaism, and Islam that have become increasingly important in American life. These include Hinduism, Buddhism, and Zen Buddhism. The multiplicity of religious beliefs has, of course, added to the multiplicity of American life and culture.

What has not changed is the reading level of the text. After abundant input from users, reviewers, editors, and other interested parties, the author has concluded that writing down to students benefits no one. A watered-down text is manifestly unfair not only to students, but to teachers and higher education in general. Textual clarifications have been added as deemed necessary and the glossary has been substantially enlarged to better support the meaningful utilization of technical terminology. Much of the book has been reorganized with more precise heads and subheads that should contribute to the clarity of the text. The spelling of a number of the Greek proper names has been altered to reflect the most common usage, although a twenty-four-letter alphabet in which thirteen letters differ from the Latin ones can never be totally standardized. Overall, the author has endeavored to compose lucid material that is both accurate and consistently interesting, even entertaining, bearing in mind that the Greeks demanded of their dramas both enlightenment and entertainment. It should surprise no one that much of the content is challenging, for it concerns difficult and abstract concepts. What is most important, however, is that this material represents an essential aspect of what it means to be prepared to live and even flourish in a complex world of ceaseless change.

Robert C. Lamm

ACKNOWLEDGMENTS

This book could not have been written without the expertise and diligence of a reference librarian, photographic associate, and in-house editor, namely Katy Lamm.

I also wish to thank the following professors whose careful reading of the manuscript proved invaluable for this tenth edition: Bernard R. Conroy, Harold Washington College; Rick Davis, Ricks College; Michael G. Davros, Oakton Community College; Stanley J. Kozikowski, Bryant College; George Rogers, Stonehill College; Patrick Schmitt, Pasco-Hernando Community College; and Diane M. Snow, Brigham Young University.

SUPPLEMENTS FOR THE INSTRUCTOR

The integrated teaching package of ancillary materials is available to instructors using *The Humanities in Western Culture*. Please contact your Brown & Benchmark sales representative or call 800–338–5371 to obtain these supplements, or to ask for further details.

Instructor's Resource Manual and Test Item File

The Instructor's Resource Manual is designed to assist instructors as they plan and prepare for classes. Included are chapter summaries, learning goals, lists of key terms, discussion topics, essay questions, and ideas for optional activities. The revised test item file appears at the end of the Instructor's Manual and contains chapter specific objective-type test questions that may be photocopied and used for quizzes or tests. Also included is a list of videotapes, recordings, videodiscs, and their suppliers.

MicroTest III

The questions in the test item file are available on MicroTest III, a powerful yet easy-to-use test generating software available for DOS, Windows, and Macintosh. MicroTest III allows instructors to generate tests and quizzes, and customize questions, headings, and instructions.

Call-in/Mail-in/Fax Service

Instructors may use Brown & Benchmark's convenient call-in/mail-in/fax service to generate tests. Select questions from the test item file at the end of the Instructor's Manual. Then call 800–338–5371, or mail your selections to Educational Resources at Brown & Benchmark Publishers, 25 Kessel Ct., Madison, WI 53711, or fax your request to Educational Resources at 608–277–7351. Within two working days of receiving your order, Brown & Benchmark will send by first-class mail (or fax) a test master, a student answer sheet, and an answer key for fast and easy grading.

Three Audiocassettes

Two sixty-minute cassettes (one each for Volumes 1 and 2) and one ninety-minute cassette (for Brief) contain the core Listening Examples from the text, a total of thirty-eight musical selections. Instructors may obtain copies of the cassettes for classroom use by calling 800–338–5371. Individual cassettes may be purchased separately, or, upon request, cassettes can be packaged with corresponding texts.

Instructor's Set of Compact Discs

This is from *Listener's Guide to Musical Understanding*, seventh edition, by Leon Dallin. An instructor's set of four CDs includes thirty-seven of the Listening Examples in the text as well as additional musical selections.

Slides

A set of fifty high-quality color slides correlated to Volumes 1 and 2, or a museum-specific videodisc, is available free to qualifying adopters.

Videos

Qualifying adopters may select video(s) from the Brown & Benchmark video catalog.

Humanities Transparencies Set

A set of seventy-three acetate transparencies is available with *The Humanities in Western Culture*. The set includes illustrations of art elements and principles; architectural styles; media; maps; musical forms, instruments, and selected musical scores.

Technology Products

Culture 2.0

Developed by Cultural Resources, Inc., Culture 2.0 © takes interdisciplinary humanities students on a fascinating journey into humanity's cultural achievements via Hypercard © software. Available for purchase in either IBM PC or MAC formats, this seven-disk program gives students access to essays, almanacs, and visual and musical examples. For each time period, categories include history, politics, religion, philosophy, art, and music, which provides an interactive Socratic method of learning for students. Culture 2.0 also features note-taking capabilities, report capabilities, and a student workbook for more guided learning. Contact your Brown & Benchmark sales representative or call Educational Resources at 800–338–5371 for ordering and purchase information.

Explore the Humanities!

Currently under development by Brown & Benchmark, this CD-ROM series will soon be available for purchase. *Explore the Humanities!* provides you and your students with a fully interactive exploration of many of the arts, ideas, and societies discussed in *The Humanities in Western Culture*. For further details, call your local Brown & Benchmark sales representative.

An Introduction to Integrated Humanities

Each of the [artistic] masterpieces is a purification of the world, but their common message is that of their existence and the victory of each individual artist over his servitude, spreading like ripples on the sea of time, implementing art's eternal victory over the human situation.

André Malraux

Everyone is capable of living a more rewarding life, which is reason enough for studying the humanities. From cave art to the present, the arts and ideas of human beings are beacons of hope, truth, and beauty for a world that needs to pay far more attention to the humanities, to the arts that teach us "nothing except the significance of life," in the words of twentieth-century American author Henry Miller. In our integrated approach to the humanities, we examine literature, painting, music, sculpture, philosophy, and architecture not as separate disciplines but as marvelous varieties of human creativity. Nor do we study the arts and artists in isolation. Artists are individuals, coping with the stress and strain of everyday life and, perhaps more than other people, influenced by the ideas and values of their society. "Artists are," observed composer Ned Rorem, "like everyone else, only more so."

The focus of our study of the humanities is the belief that the quality of life can be enhanced and that this enrichment is available to all. Unlike Middle East oil reserves, the reservoir of Western (or any other) culture is limitless; the more we draw from it the more there is to draw upon. The only deposits necessary are time and effort. The process amounts to addition or even multiplication; no one has to discard a collection of rock records to listen to Beethoven nor exchange Cowboy Art for Rembrandt.

This prologue is an introduction to the significance of the artist as an individual, the necessity of art, and the primacy of human values. Fundamental to cultural development are values such as truth, beauty, love, justice, and faith. Our investigation of how other cultures developed their value systems is chronological, a "return to the past" to see how the Egyptians, Greeks, and later civilizations handled their problems. What questions did they ask? What solutions did they try? We explore earlier cultures from the vantage point of our own world, studying earlier achievements not as museum pieces but as living evidence of enduring responses to life's perplexities. This priceless legacy is central to our attempts to make sense of the world and of our lives. Some will ask why we look to the past to prepare for the future. Where else can we look?

WHY STUDY THE HUMANITIES?

We explore the humanities not just to acquire facts about past eras but to try to understand those cultures: their questions, answers, and values. We can see the qualities they prized in their art and philosophy, and in their social and political institutions. We examine all of these areas to learn what they did; more importantly, we are concerned with why and how their cultures evolved in certain unique ways. Culture can be defined as what remains after a particular society has vanished. What is left behind is much more than artifacts. The creations of other cultures reveal their visions, their hopes, their dreams.

This is a text for the integrated or interdisciplinary humanities, the interrelationships of the arts, philosophy, and social and political ideas and institutions. Life is itself interdisciplinary. Using the interdisciplinary approach we study the "lives" of other civilizations to see how their values are manifested in just about everything they did, made, or thought. Whatever we learn from other cultures leads inevitably to a fuller understanding of civilization in general and of our own culture in particular.

Each of us has the option of accepting value systems from institutions or other persons, or we can generate a personal set of beliefs and values. The acquisition of an informed set of personal values is, of course, a lifelong project. The knowledge and understanding of other cultures and of ourselves are certainly their own reward, but there are additional advantages. If "the unexamined life is not worth living," as Socrates said, then self-knowledge would seem to be an acquired virtue. The greater our understanding of what is going on in our lives, the more likely we are to be aware of our options and thus of opportunities to improve the quality of life.

We can achieve the freedom objectively to examine alternatives and possibly make better choices. This freedom is not conditioned absolutely by political, social, and

economic considerations, although these factors can help or hinder. One can imagine a political prisoner of a totalitarian state whose knowledge and informed personal values allow a free and independent spirit in the most squalid of surroundings. The prisoner's goals, in this case, are not those of going somewhere or of acquiring material things, but of being a particular person. Those who, in the phrase of American essayist and poet Thoreau, "lead lives of quiet desperation" are at the mercy—intellectually and spiritually—of unknown forces over which they have no control. With no knowledge, no understanding, there is no way to determine whether there are one, two, or more viable choices. All of us have to accept the "slings and arrows of outrageous fortune" (Shakespeare) when we have no alternative. The trick is to be so aware of what is going on in our society and in our lives that we can, at least some of the time, select viable options that will help improve the quality of life. It is worth our while—worth our lives in fact—to study cultures of the past and present, and to make conscious cultural choices.

Western Civilization

As proclaimed by the title, this book is primarily—but not exclusively—concerned with Western civilization and its monumental contributions to world culture: its art, literature, performing arts, philosophy, science, and technology. Because it has had great complexity and influence and because it is our very own heritage, Western civilization commands our full attention. Light years from being monolithic, Western civilization is multicultural, having assimilated elements of every advanced culture in the world from ancient Mesopotamia and Egypt to modern India and China.

> All important cultures have ingenuities of their own. They are all marvelous manifestations of the power of the mind. But our own culture—Western civilization— is the most intellectual of all. More than the others, it is the product of systematic thought. The whole world uses its inventions. Its [science and] scientific methods . . . have been adopted by other civilizations and are transforming them.[1]

That the preeminence of Western culture is the result of systematic thought is only part of the equation. By asking, "systematic thought about what?" we can find the key to Western dominance in science.

> Dear Sir
> Development of Western Science is based on two great achievements; the invention of the formal logical

system (in Euclidean geometry) by the Greek philosophers, and the discovery of the possibility to find out causal relationship by systematic experiment (Renaissance). In my opinion one has not to be astonished that the Chinese sages have not made these steps. The astonishing thing is that these discoveries were made at all.[2]

Yes, these discoveries are astonishing, for they led to the preeminence of the West in empirical science and technological advances. But there is more. The social and political values of the West have also had worldwide influence, ranging from the thought of Solon, Plato, and Aristotle to Cicero, Dante, Voltaire, John Locke, Thomas Jefferson, and Martin Luther King, Jr. Though immigrants from Asia, and Africa, for example, cannot readily perceive Western culture as "theirs," the fact is that their own cultures have adopted much of Western culture, and only partly because of colonialism. The adoption in various degrees of Western technology, science, political, and economic systems by the rest of the world speaks for itself. The further fact that Western civilization was, in general, created by what some have called "dead white men" alters nothing for we cannot rewrite history. The Greeks invented democracy, speculative philosophy, and formal logic, and Renaissance innovators invented and developed the experimental scientific method. The list of Western inventions is virtually endless: the incandescent light bulb, telephone, automobile, airplane, computer, space flight, and, yes, nuclear fission and fusion. The power eventually attained from nuclear-fusion power plants may even save the world from its manifold excesses.

The Culture-Epoch Theory

One begins to understand a culture by learning how that culture developed and what it means to us. We consider the past using a simplified version of the culture-epoch theory of cultural formation. Except for a smattering of political-military history, many of us are neither concerned nor knowledgeable about our cultural heritage. The culture-epoch theory helps overcome that deficiency: it stresses the critical fact of ceaseless change; it weaves cultural and intellectual history into a historic tapestry; and it emphasizes evolutionary processes in the course of history. The theory is neither more nor less "true" than other concepts of cultural evolution; for our purpose, in an interdisciplinary context, the theory works.

According to the culture-epoch theory, a culture is founded upon whatever conception of reality is held by the great majority of its people over a considerable period of time. Most people may not be aware of any concept of reality or, more likely, take it so much for granted that they don't know it is a human idea, held on faith. Thus, for most people at the time this is written, a typewriter is real, a physical tree is real, and all things that can be seen, heard, smelled, felt, or tasted are real.

1. Gilbert Highet, *Man's Unconquerable Mind* (New York: Columbia University Press, 1954), p.14.
2. Albert Einstein, Letter to J. E. Switzer, 23 April 1953. In D. J. de S. Price, *Science Since Babylon* (New Haven: Yale University Press, 1962), p.15n.

Scientists, philosophers, and theologians have given us different concepts of reality that have, at various times in history, come to be widely held. These thinkers contemplated the millions of forms of life, many of them similar yet each one different; they examined the forms of earth, air, fire, and water; they wondered about the processes of change by which a tree today may, at some time in the future, disintegrate into earth and reappear in some totally alien form. They watched such non-tangible things as sunlight and air becoming leaf and branch. Pondering these things, they came inevitably to the ultimate question: "What is the nature of reality?"

To reach an answer, they usually focus on a few profound inquiries, some of which may be given here. For example, they might say, "We see change all around us. We see grass eaten and turn into cow. We see cow eaten and turn into human. We see humans disintegrate and become earth. If all these changes can take place, what are the universal elements of which all things are composed?" Or they might say, "We see an individual human, Jane Doe, as baby, as youth, as adult, as frail old woman, as corpse. From one moment to the next, she is never the same, yet she is always the same, Jane Doe, a distinct being. Can it be that nothing is permanent, that reality is a process rather than a thing or group of things? If we have change, then, how does the process take place? And more to the point, we know that we live in a world of constant change, but what force directs the process?"

"Nonsense," retorts another group of thinkers. "Anything in a constant state of flux cannot be real. Only that which is permanent and unchanging is real. What, then, in the universe is permanent, unchanging in itself, yet can transform itself, manifest itself, or produce from itself the countless forms we see around us?" The responses to basic questions such as these are various concepts of reality.

Based on the idea of reality accepted as "true," specialized thinkers build different thought-structures that underlie visible institutions. These include a philosophy of justice from which particular forms of law and government spring; a philosophy of education that dictates the nature and curriculum of our schools; a religious philosophy that becomes apparent in churches and creeds, in synagogues, mosques, and temples; and an economic philosophy that is manifested in the production and distribution of goods and services. There are, of course, other philosophies and institutions, but these are some that affect our daily living.

A culture may be said to be "complete" and "balanced" when its underlying philosophies and its institutions are in harmony with its concept of reality, but by the time such a pattern is established, there are new forces already at work to undermine it. The wreckers are new critics who note inconsistencies within the idea of reality itself, who question postulates and detect contradictions.

From these innovative thinkers (philosophers, scientists, theologians) emerges a new idea of reality so convincing that it cannot be brushed aside. Once the new reality is generally accepted, the whole cultural structure finds itself without foundation. Law and justice of the old culture are no longer appropriate; educational philosophies are unsatisfactory; religious beliefs must be adjusted or even discarded; old ways of making and distributing things no longer suffice. Over a stretch of time, the culture is plunged into a period of chaos, the first step in the formation of a new epoch.

Periods of Chaos

A notable example of a chaotic period is the Early Middle Ages (ca. 400–800), once called the Dark Ages. The relative stability of the Graeco-Roman era of 480 BC to AD 180 began to disintegrate following the reign of Marcus Aurelius, though the Greek ideal of the individual as reality was superseded by the Roman view that reality was the state without seriously disturbing the cultural balance. Both the Greek and the Roman were secular societies with a general respect for law and justice, a stable social order, and reasonably effective government. Rome's decline was very gradual. Government, the economy, and the rule of law began to unravel and both the rise of Christianity and the barbarian invasions helped finish off a weary and decadent civilization. Most of western Europe soon found itself deep in a period of chaos. Graeco-Roman civilization was not totally destroyed—as demonstrated by the classically inspired Renaissance—but the stage was set for a new idea of reality through which order would be restored.

Periods of Adjustment

Out of the turmoil and confusion of chaotic periods of past cultures emerge periods of adjustment. At these times innovative artists and thinkers—whether painters, scientists, writers, composers, or philosophers—make important contributions that can suggest innovative lines, shapes, or patterns for a new culture.

No one needs to know all about new ideas of reality. In our own time, for example, artists (in particular) may or may not understand Einstein's theories of relativity. As sensitive persons, they generally feel the tensions caused by Einstein's work and its implications. Because they are creators, artists feel compelled to explore the impact that theories, ideas, and events have on their society and to examine or invent new experiences and relationships.

Many people experience the tension and turmoil in periods of chaos and adjustment, but artists tend actively to respond to the chaos and confusion. They explore conflicts within their culture and create new structures and designs; they synthesize the elements of dissension and give fresh meaning to experience. Some works of art are so outstanding that they become symbols of the new age. The Parthenon, for example (see fig. 7.35), still symbolizes the Golden Age of Athens.

At some point another element of the population—we may call them intellectuals—enters the picture. They are people like ourselves, college students and faculty, government officials, business executives, and others who have been troubled by the tensions and conflicts of the time. Still laboring in the period of adjustment, they become aware of fresh meanings and patterns produced by artists and other innovators. They begin reshaping these designs into new philosophies of government, justice, education, economics, and the like. Through their work, order slowly emerges out of chaos. Based on the idea of the Christian God as the ultimate reality, the period of adjustment of the medieval world saw the expansion of the power of the Church of Rome, the rise of universities, and the growth of cities (plus other factors) that coalesced in the thirteenth century into the period of balance of the High Middle Ages.

Periods of Balance

Order is the hallmark of periods of balance. At this point the idea of reality, the philosophies underlying the basic institutions, and the institutions themselves are all in harmony. Life must be very satisfying early in a period of balance with everything tidy and orderly. But new and challenging ideas are already stirring. Probably no one in thirteenth-century Europe perceived the era as a period of balance. Certainly no one foresaw that the balance would be upended by forces leading to stronger national states, the revival of humanism, and the rediscovery of Greek philosophy.

But change is the only constant. At the beginning of this century, for example, some physicists were convinced that the ultimate discoveries had been made with little left to do but some tidying-up. Yet Albert Einstein was just then formulating theories that would overthrow previous knowledge in physics. Exactly when people become certain of virtually everything during a period of balance, new ideas are already fermenting that will dump the apple cart into a new period of chaos.

A word of caution is needed here. This systematic description of an epoch makes it appear that artists function only in a time of chaos or adjustment, or that philosophers quit philosophizing until their proper time comes around. Of course this is not true. While any epoch can be divided roughly into the three periods described above, all functions occur with greater or lesser impact throughout the entire time period.

A COMMON BASIS FOR UNDERSTANDING THE ARTS

In the humanities we take art seriously. As Aristotle observed, "Art is a higher type of knowledge than experience." As previously indicated in the description of a culture-epoch, eminent artists help to create patterns for a way of life. "The object of art is to give life a shape," said the twentieth-century French dramatist Jean Anouilh. The Parthenon, Chartres cathedral, Augustine's *The City of God*, Beethoven's Ninth Symphony, Michelangelo's *David* and Sistine Chapel ceiling are only a few examples of art works that have affected life in the Western world.

One might ask what area of the universe is the darkest, the most unknown. The universe itself? Einstein once said that the most incomprehensible fact about the universe is that it is so comprehensible. No, the most bewildering portion of the universe is yourself. As a member of the human race you are (or should be) asking yourself such questions as "Who am I?", "What am I?", "Why am I here?" It is the artist who persists in reacting to these questions, who seeks answers from within, and who discovers answers that strike responsive chords in the rest of us. As Henry Miller said, "art teaches nothing, except the significance of life."

A Shakespearean scholar once remarked that Shakespeare, in his plays, had made discoveries as important as those made by a scientist. Such an assertion seems, at first, to be an overreaction to the dominance of science in today's world. Consider, however, the playwright's treatment of love and hate in *Romeo and Juliet*, good and evil in *King Lear*, and murder and revenge in *Macbeth*. As enacted on stage, these aspects of the human condition constitute artistic truths. This idea of discoveries by Shakespeare or any other artist can provide a basis for a better understanding of the arts. In this respect, as the French poet and playwright Jean Cocteau observed, "art is science in the flesh."

The physical world is explored by the sciences; the social sciences make discoveries about the behavior and activities of people in various groups; the arts and humanities probe the inner meaning: humanity's hopes, fears, loves, delights as individuals act and react within a social context. "All art is social," historian James Adams noted, "because it is the result of a relationship between an artist and his time." Art is also exploration, and the discoveries made can be expressed as concepts and percepts. Concepts are intangible ideas such as friendship, beauty, truth, and justice. What we perceive with our senses are percepts: line, taste, color, aroma, volume, pitch, and so forth. Artists express concepts by the unique manner in which they choose to arrange the percepts, that is, the sense-apparent objects and materials. Obviously this kind of vivid creativity can never be done by committee. "Art is the most intense mode of individualism that the world has known," said nineteenth-century Irish writer Oscar Wilde.

Differences and Similarities

Because of variations in media and modes of expression, the arts differ from one another in a variety of ways. Certainly a time-art such as music, which exists only as long as it is heard, differs from a space-art such as painting, which uses visual symbols as its means of expression. Both arts are separated from literature, a word-art that depends upon fully developed literacy. The differences between Beethoven's Fifth Symphony, the *Mona Lisa*, and *Hamlet* are obvious; not so obvious are their similarities. "Painting," wrote nineteenth-century American poet and essayist Emerson, "was called silent poetry, and poetry speaking painting. The laws of each art are convertible into the laws of any other." As early as the fourteenth century Dante called sculpture "visible speech." The common basis of all the arts is the exploration, by means of sensory percepts, of the emotions, mind, and personality of human beings; their common goal is to speak directly to our inner being. As Emerson also wrote: "Raphael paints wisdom; Handel sings it; Pheidias carves it; Shakespeare writes it."

The artist deals subjectively with all materials while drawing upon a singular store of personal experience. Artistic production depends as much on the background and personality of the artist as it does upon the raw material of experience. It therefore follows that each artist is unique and that the artist's production is necessarily unique. To illustrate, let us examine the treatment two literary artists make of the same theme: the emptiness of the life of a woman who, herself, is virtually a complete blank, but who moves from man to man, living only as a reflection of each man. Read Dorothy Parker's "Big Blonde" and Anton Chekhov's "The Darling," both short stories. Though the experience is very similar in the two stories, the end result is quite dissimilar and the reader's experience is also different. The reader might protest: "But one of them must be right about this woman and one must be wrong." Actually, both Parker and Chekhov are right—both stories have the ring of truth—and any other artist treating the same material with a different insight would also be right. The discovery of multiple truths is a personal matter and the corollary is that the realm of truth in personality, that prime area where the arts are focused, is inexhaustible. Anyone who understands any work of art grows with each facet of experience shared with the artist. Our boundaries are expanded as we add the artist's experiences to our own.

> Thanks to art, instead of seeing one world, our own, we see it multiplied and, as many original artists as there are, so many worlds are at our disposal.
>
> André Malraux

SUMMARY

The humanities include, but are not limited to, the arts of literature, painting, music, sculpture, architecture, and dance, and the discipline of philosophy that permeates all the arts and finally unites them all. The arts, taken together, are a separate field of human knowledge with their own area of exploration and discovery, and with a method of their own. So these volumes will concentrate on some of the most significant artistic productions of each of the major periods of Western civilization. Each unit begins with an overview of the social, scientific, religious, and philosophic climate of the period in which the artists were working, for artists usually accept the scientific and social world-picture of their time. Following these introductory discussions, attention turns to the arts themselves to reveal answers to the great questions of humankind—the new patterns, structures, and meaning that artists found for life in their time. This procedure enables the student to trace the development and changes of the problems that plague us so sorely in our own time. Equipped with knowledge of the great answers found in the past that still shape the way we live today, having come to know the exalted expressions of humanity revealed at their fullest, each individual can work to develop an informed set of values and a freedom to be the person he or she would like to be.

Not everyone will derive the same kind or degree of satisfaction from a particular art form, but the educated person is obliged to know that "there is something in it," even if that "something" is not deeply moving. And perhaps, with deeper acquaintance and wider knowledge, that "something" will become clearer and of greater value. "I don't get it" is no refutation of either Einstein or Bach.

We have made the assertion that the artist is an explorer and discoverer in the realm of the human personality. The artist uses the methods of intuition and composition. The artist's raw material lies in the human personality and in human experience, with their vast and unknown reaches, their disrupting conflicts. The artist gives form to the component elements of personality and experience, and in so doing generates an artistic truth. No matter whether we speak of literature, painting, sculpture, music, or any of the other arts, this concept of creating form out of chaos is the common basis and foundation for all aesthetics.

Ancient
River-Valley
Civilizations

Prehistory

(most dates approximate)

PALEOLITHIC AGE
40,000 BC
18,000 BC

30,000–20,000 *Venus of Willendorf*, Austria
18,000–15,000 Last Ice Age
13,000 Lascaux cave paintings, France

MESOLITHIC AGE
10,000 BC

10,000 Invention of bow and arrow, first domestication of wheat and barley

NEOLITHIC AGE
8000 BC

8000 Domestication of animals, development of agriculture, pottery, weaving, permanent houses, settlements, fortifications, warfare

Mesopotamia   Egypt

5000 BC

5000 Infiltration of Semites from west and north, non-Semites from east; fusion
3500–3000 Sumerian Protoliterate Period. Infiltration of Sumerians (origin?) and fusion with resident population; invention of written language

5000–3100 Pre-Dynastic Period
4200 Invention of solar calendar
3500 Development of religion: sun worship
3100–2700 Dynasties I and II. Development of hieroglyphics and central administration

BRONZE AGE
3000 BC

3000–2350 Sumerian dynasties
2700 Reign of Gilgamesh, king of Uruk
2500 First dynasty of Ur
2350–2100 Akkadian Period
2350 Sargon the Great
2050–1900 Third dynasty of Ur (Neo-Sumerian Period), Gudea of Lagash

2686–2181 Old Kingdom, dynasties III–VI. Highly centralized political theocracy; strong artistic development
2590–2514 Pyramid Age
2260–2130 First Intermediate Period, dynasties VII–X
2134–1786 Middle Kingdom, dynasties XI–XII. Expansion and prosperity; refinement of arts

2000 BC

2000 *The Epic of Gilgamesh*
1900–1500 First dynasty of Babylonia
1792–1750 Hammurabi and Law Code
1500–1100 Kassite Period, status quo
1076–612 Assyrian Empire
884–859 Assurnasirpal II, capital of Nimrud
722–709 Sargon II, capital of Khorsabad
669–626 Assurbanipal, capital at Nineveh

1780–1550 Second Intermediate Period: Hyksos, dynasties XIII–XVII
1570–1085 New Kingdom (Empire), dynasties XVII–XX
1379–1362 Akhenaton (Amarna Period)
1085–664 Post-Empire Period, dynasties XXI–XXV

IRON AGE
1000 BC

625–539 Chaldean (Neo-Babylonian) Empire
604–562 Nebuchadnezzar II
586–539 Babylonian Captivity of Israelites
539–331 Persian Empire
539–530 Cyrus the Great
521–485 Darius I
(490–479 Persian invasions of Greece)
485–465 Xerxes I
331 Alexander the Great conquers Persian Empire

670 Assyrian conquest of Egypt
663–525 Saite Period, dynasty XXVI; cultural renaissance
525 Persia conquers Egypt
525–343 Persian kings, Egyptian dynasties XXVII–XXX
343–332 Persian kings
332 Alexander the Great conquers Egypt
332–311 Macedonian kings
311–30 The Ptolemies
51–30 Cleopatra VII

1 BC

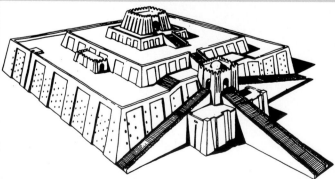

Reconstruction of the ziggurat at Ur. Sumerian, Third Dynasty of Ur. Ca. 2150–2050 BC. Height ca. 90' (27.4 m).

Egyptian columns. From left to right: bud, foliated, palm leaf, papyrus blossom, reed bundle, lotus.

CHAPTER 1

The Emergence of Early Culture

PREHISTORY

Archaeologists have prosaically labeled the periods before the invention of writing according to weapons or tools used, thus the Stone Age, Bronze Age, Iron Age. There are three phases of the extended Stone Age: the Paleolithic (Gk., *paleos*, "old"; *lithos*, "stone"), the Mesolithic ("middle stone"), and Neolithic ("new stone"). The Paleolithic era began about 40,000 BC at about the time that *Homo sapiens* ("the one who knows," meaning "who thinks") had evolved from proto-humans while also deposing Neanderthals.

Human history began with *Homo sapiens*, who invented art during the Paleolithic, domesticated wheat and barley during the Mesolithic, and developed written language and civilization during the Neolithic. Most of what we would call Paleolithic art is today found in the caves at Altamira in Spain and at Lascaux (fig. 1.2) and other caves in southern France. Permanently closed to the public twenty-one years after their discovery in 1940, the Lascaux caves contain paintings that are still remarkably fresh today because there are no visitors bringing in outside contaminants. The spectacular Hall of Running Bulls (figs. 1.1 and 1.3) is filled with art but no one knows why these artists decided to paint all these images. They made no attempt to highlight or frame any of the animals nor, apparently, were they concerned about overpainting earlier work. Standing in this hall is an uncanny experience; while studying the paintings one feels the presence of creative forces applied to those walls many thousands of years ago.

Considerably older than the Lascaux paintings is the so-called Venus of Willendorf (fig. 1.4), at present the first known portrayal of a human being. Very likely a fertility

---

1.1 Hall of Running Bulls, Lascaux, near Montignac, France. Ca. 13,000 BC. Paint on limestone rock walls, individual bulls ca. 13–16' (4–5 m) long. Archiv für Kunst und Geschichte, Berlin.

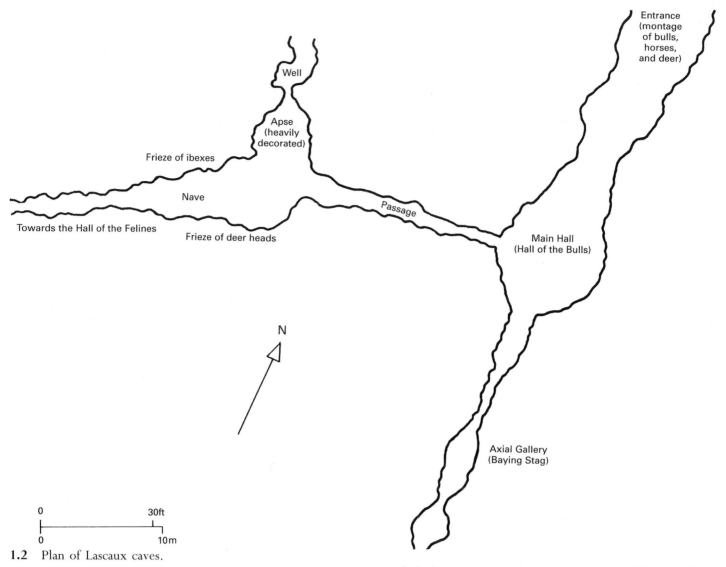

1.2   Plan of Lascaux caves.

1.3   Bull. Paint on limestone rock wall, Lascaux.
Ca. 13,000 BC. 18′ (5.5 m) long. Photo: Colorphoto Hans
Hinz, Basel.

symbol, this ancient statuette has exaggerated female characteristics but no face, possibly indicating a general statement about childbearing and motherhood. Several hundred female figures have been found but no male figures, thus confirming the fertility thesis. Calling what is possibly an early representative of the goddess religion "Venus" is, of course, a misnomer but the label makes a certain amount of sense in today's world.

Trying to learn anything at all about the history of humankind during the prehistoric period is a difficult, complex, and frustrating endeavor. Although archaeologists and anthropologists, among others, can discover objects and unearth ruins all are hard pressed to determine "Why?" Why did artists paint in caves? Why did artists carve representations of nude women? Why was Stonehenge built and why did the people living there continue building for hundreds of years (fig. 1.5)? Stonehenge was probably a Neolithic shrine, but for what purpose? For what gods? It is positioned to align with the summer solstice, indicating that its designers possessed certain astronomical and mathematical skills. How extensive were these skills? Were they

1.4 Venus of Willendorf, from Lower Austria.
Ca. 30,000–20,000 BC. Limestone, height 4½" (11.4 cm).
Naturhistorisches Museum, Vienna.

1.5 *Below* Stonehenge, Salisbury Plain, England.
Ca. 2200–1400 BC. Stone, diameter of circle 97' (29.6 m),
height of tallest monoliths 13'6" (4.1 m). Photo: Skyscan
Balloon Photography, Cheltenham.

exercised by a priesthood? Was there a priesthood?

The questions raised by these ancient art works are
endless, but so is the fascination of exploring them. Not
until we advance to the Neolithic Age and the invention of
writing and civilization do we begin to get some answers
and, even then, so many explanations are incomplete and
subject to speculation.

MESOPOTAMIA: THE LAND BETWEEN THE RIVERS

The roots of Western civilization are found in the Near and
Middle East in such widely separated sites as Jericho in
Palestine, Çatal Hüyük in southern Turkey, and the Sumer
area in southern Mesopotamia (Gk., "land between the
rivers"). A new way of life evolved in all these locales but
we shall concentrate on Sumer, which has been studied
longer and in greater depth than other Neolithic cultures.
Beginning around 8000 BC in the fertile valleys of the Tigris
and Euphrates rivers (map 1.1), there gradually appeared
a series of innovations: pottery, weaving, permanent
houses (rather than tents), organized communities, the

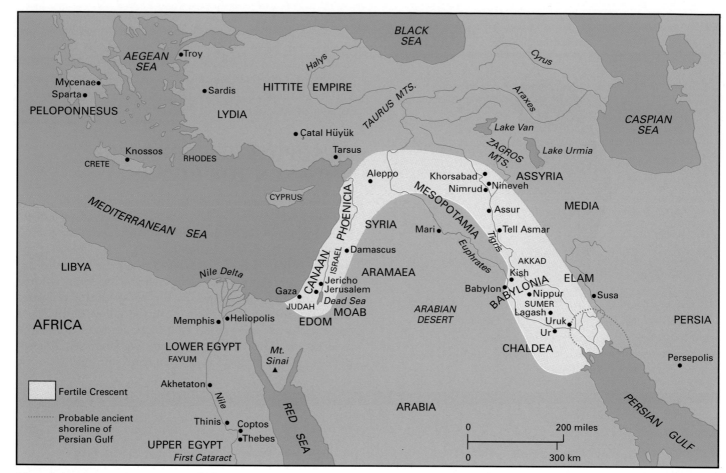

Map 1.1   Ancient Near East and the Fertile Crescent.

buying and selling of crops and goods, calendar fashioning, mathematics, and, most important, writing. What prompted this startling surge of new ideas?

Culture: Cultivation

The answer, in a word, is agriculture. For millennia, nomadic tribes had followed the seasons as they hunted game and gathered edible plants and fruit. At some point the puzzle of propagation was solved and the connection made between seeds and germination, mating and gestation. The resulting planting, harvesting, and animal husbandry enabled tribes to produce more food than was needed, a surplus that normally freed them from the precarious existence common to all hunting/gathering societies. Drought, floods, and storms have always plagued farmers but nomadic hunters are totally at the mercy of a capricious nature.

Stone Age people apparently continued to hunt and gather while cultivating some crops. In about 8000 BC, however, some Mesopotamian tribes settled into permanent villages, where they became wholly dependent on their animals and crops. The innovations that had freed nomads from famine now actually imprisoned agricultural societies. However, returning to the previous existence was never an option. Whatever the endeavor, advancing technology takes a society in one direction only. In today's world a retreat to a horse and buggy, 78 r.p.m. records, or black-and-white television with a 9-inch (23-cm) screen is, quite simply, unthinkable for most of us.

The establishment of permanent agricultural communities marked the beginning of "culture," which originally meant cultivating the soil. As the Mesopotamian communities flourished, they developed a higher civilization than that of Neolithic nomads, a culture as we understand the meaning of the term: socially transmitted behavior patterns, beliefs, institutions, arts, and other human creations.[1] All of this was a direct consequence of settling down to cultivate the land.

Consider the ramifications of creating a new agricultural community. Permanent dwellings become necessary for a population no longer on the move (domestic architecture, pottery, and other household items).

---

1. The concept of culture was first explicitly defined in 1871 by British anthropologist Edward B. Tyler as "that complex whole which includes knowledge, belief, art, morals, law, custom and any other capabilities and habits acquired by man as a member of society." As opposed to genetically endowed behavior, culture always entails learned behavior.

Cultivated land is divided into "your land" and "my land," and properly identified, measured, and recorded (surveying, maps, mathematics, and writing). Because privately owned lands were now at stake, villages organized for defense against those who chose to steal rather than plant (community organization, village fortification and defense). The spring floods upon which most agriculture depended must be anticipated, measured, recorded and, in time, somehow controlled and exploited (development of a calendar, study of the heavens to learn the wishes of the gods, invention of dams and the water wheel, development of irrigation, and ever more writing and recording).

Inevitably, farmers grew too much of one crop and not enough of another; this led to the bartering of grain and, later, to full-fledged commerce as crops, animals, and household goods were bought and sold. This commercial activity necessitated a legal system to stabilize the new world of agriculture, manufacturing, and trade. Further, the buying and selling of goods worked most efficiently when concentrated in financial centers, stimulating the

development of commercial hubs. This, in turn, helped promote commerce. As commerce increased, villages grew into towns that became cities and then city-states as urban developments interacted with the surrounding countryside.

It was in Sumer that a loose confederation of city-states consolidated political and economic power into one of history's earliest ruling dynasties. Sumer lay in the eastern arc of the Fertile Crescent, that broad belt of productive land extending north-westward from the Persian Gulf and curving down the Mediterranean coast almost to Egypt (map 1.1). This was a settlement zone but also one of transit in which the ebb and flow of people and ideas enriched—and disrupted—the growth of civilization.

SUMERIAN PERIOD, 3000–2350 BC

No one knows why a high civilization began in Sumer and, at about the same time, in Egypt. In prehistoric times both centers formed part of a larger cultural region: Mesopotamia was at first indistinguishable from northern Syria, and southern Mesopotamia (Sumer) was linked with Persia (map 1.2). Similarly, Egypt shared its early

Map 1.2 Early Mesopotamia.

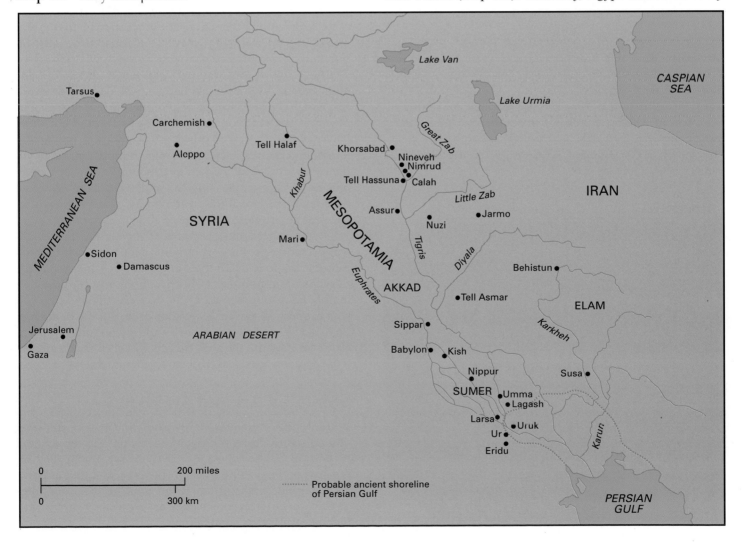

predynastic culture with neighboring Libya, Nubia, and possibly the Sudan. And then came the cultural burst that detached Sumer and Egypt from their surroundings, as it established their place in history.

The mystery is compounded because the origin of the Sumerians is also unknown. Migrating into the river valley around 4500 BC, they amalgamated with the resident population and by about 3000 BC had established themselves as the dominant class. They (or the neighboring Subarians) have been credited with inventing the first written language, a system called **cuneiform** (KYOO-nay-uh-form, "wedge") writing (fig. 1.6). Cuneiform was used initially to record the behavior of the rivers and the astronomical events that provided clues to the return of the life-giving floods.

Early Religion

Predicting annual inundations was only one of the reasons for studying the stars. Primitive religions characteristically attribute natural phenomena—floods, storms, earthquakes—to unseen gods; more advanced cultures study the heavens for clues to superhuman powers involved with the

---

1.6   Clay tablet with cuneiform text, probably from Jemdet Nasr, Iraq. Sumerian. Ca. 3000 BC. 3¼ × 3¼" (8 × 8 cm). British Museum, London.
Written with a wedge-shaped stylus, the lines are read from right to left. The text, probably in Sumerian, concerns the issue of several kinds of rations including the name of the recipient. The "cowboy hat" symbol signifies "day"; the "face" character is a numeral.

creation and governance of the universe. Sumerian beliefs reflected the abundant concerns of everyday life: storms, catastrophic floods, earthquakes, and endless raids by hostile neighbors. Their religion, consequently, was quite self-centered and practical, emphasizing sheer survival in a hostile world.

Mesopotamian gods were considered powerful and immortal but otherwise much like human beings writ large: frivolous, selfish, quarrelsome, sometimes petty, often childish. The gods were arranged in a hierarchy, making this the first systematic **polytheistic** religion. An (or Anu) was a sky god and head of the pantheon (Gk., "all the gods"). Enlil was "Lord Breath," god of the atmosphere. Inanna (or Inini) was "Queen of Heaven," the planet Venus, daughter of the moon god, and spouse of Anu; her name was subsequently changed to the more familiar Ishtar.

All these gods were derived from the deities of nomadic societies in which men were the dominant sex, mainly because of their greater size and strength. Men maintained their dominance as nomadic life evolved into agricultural communities, even though one would expect the goddess of fertility to be the prime deity. By contrast, the fertility goddess was dominant in a Minoan agricultural society that had no nomadic prehistory (see p. 53).

Ascertaining the will of these fractious gods was an overriding concern of the believers and thus was born astrology, later transformed into the science of astronomy. Through prayer, incantations, and magic, the Sumerians attempted to keep the gods happy or at least tolerant and forgiving. The gods would help individuals in distress but never at the time of death. Male-dominated societies have generally accepted this death orientation, unlike life-affirming cultures such as Minoan civilization, in which the sexes are virtually equal in cooperation and responsibilities. In Sumer, pleasing the gods was more desirable than leading a good life—a pragmatic point of view that did little to promote or improve ethical behavior.

The king was chief servant of the gods and their earthly representative; his government presumed that the gods were in charge and that they occupied large areas set aside as sacred communities. Collective labor was employed on temple lands but the rest of the city was divided into private properties. Because sky gods made up the pantheon, their worship should be from temples atop hills or mountains; the closer to the gods the more likely were the deities to be content—and less likely to torment helpless humans.

Sumerian Art and Architecture

With no hills, much less mountains, in the vast and level deserts surrounding the river valleys, the Sumerians had no natural temple sites nor were there any practical building stones. They solved the problem by erecting massive artificial hills made of sun-dried mud bricks. These **ziggurats** were towers constructed as terraced pyramids with inclined walkways connecting each terrace. The ziggurat

1.7 Ziggurat at Ur (partially reconstructed), Iraq. Sumerian, Third Dynasty of Ur. Ca. 2150–2050 BC. Sun-dried mud brick faced with baked brick, height ca. 90' (27.4 m). Three stairways to the top of 100 steps each. Photo: Hirmer, Munich.

at Ur (fig. 1.7) dates from the Neo-Sumerian Period. It is a refined version of the earliest known ziggurat, which was built a thousand years before at Uruk, reputedly the oldest city in the world. The Ur ziggurat has three stairways, 100 steps each, that converge on the first platform; other stairways ascended to the second and then to a third level on which stood the temple of the god.

Dating from around the reign of a legendary ruler called Gilgamesh, an assemblage of marble statuettes depicts, probably, common people, priests, and a king and queen; all await the descent of Dumuzi, another legendary king of Uruk who became a god called the "shepherd" because he was god of the pasture (fig. 1.8). After

1.8 Statuettes of worshipers from Tell Asmar, Iraq. Sumerian. Ca. 2700–2600 BC. Marble and black shell inlay, height of tallest figure 30" (76.2 cm). Iraq Institute, Baghdad, and Oriental Institute, Chicago (Neg. 1151).

deification Dumuzi personified the vegetation that dies in the fall. His death occurred annually, of course, reflecting the cycle of flowering spring and fall desiccation that preoccupied all agricultural societies. The cylindrical shapes of these statuettes is typically Mesopotamian—totally different from uniformly rectangular Egyptian sculptures.

The elegant bull-headed lyre of the Queen of Ur suggests a splendid, luxurious court (fig. 1.9). Only the wood and strings have been restored; all else is original: gold-

1.9 Bull-headed lyre, from the Tomb of Queen Puabi, Ur, Iraq. Sumerian. Ca. 2685 BC. Wood inlaid with gold, lapis lazuli, and shell, height ca. 17" (43.2 cm). University Museum, University of Pennsylvania, Philadelphia (Neg. #T4–29c2).

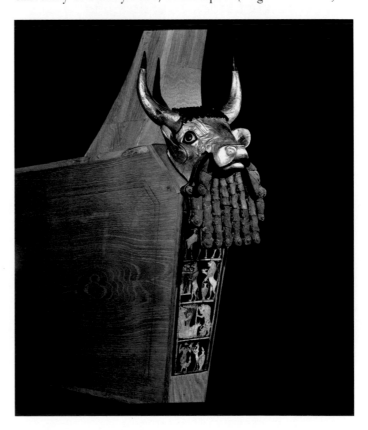

1.10 Soundbox panel of the bull-headed lyre from the Tomb of Queen Puabi, Ur, Iraq, detail of fig. 1.9. Ca. 2685 BC. Bitumen base with shell inlay, height 13" (33 cm). University Museum, University of Pennsylvania.

1.11 *He-Goat and Flowering Tree* (offering stand for fertility god), from Ur, Iraq. Sumerian. Ca. 2500 BC. Wood overlaid with gold, silver, lapis lazuli, shell, and red limestone, height 20" (50.8 cm). British Museum, London.

decorated posts, bull's head with **lapis lazuli** beard, and four narrative scenes. A consistent symbol of Mesopotamian royal power, the bearded bull is intensely alert as if straining to hear the music of the lyre. The top scene of the sound-box panel (fig. 1.10) shows a naked man wrestling two bearded bulls, all with blank expressions. In the bottom scene a scorpion man is attended by a goat carrying libation cups. Both the top and bottom scenes are from the Gilgamesh epic (see below). The two middle scenes may be from some still unknown animal fables.

The strange and fascinating *He-Goat and Flowering Tree* (fig. 1.11) is a masterful example of sculpture created by adding elements instead of cutting them away. As alive and alert as the bearded bull, the goat peers intently through the decorative branches of a symbolic tree. An age-old emblem of male sexuality, this is undoubtedly a fertility symbol.

In addition to their distinctive art and architecture, the Sumerians made important contributions to writing, law, and religion. They also established the foundations of mathematics, science, and engineering. In arithmetic they created multiplication, division, and square and cube roots. They used a 10-base (decimal) system of mathematics plus a 60-base system from which they were the first to derive 60 seconds to a minute and 60 minutes to an hour. In geometry they used the 60-base system to mark out a circle of 360 degrees.

The Epic of Gilgamesh

The most significant Sumerian literary work was *The Epic of Gilgamesh*, the first story in world literature to have a protagonist with a name and personality. This is also the earliest written record of the discovery of death, which Gilgamesh strongly suspects means total extinction but which his contemporaries, still rooted in simple notions, assume to be another form of existence. Originally sketched by the Sumerians, reworked by the Akkadians, and shaped into final form by the Babylonians, *The Epic of Gilgamesh* is the story of a debauched half-historical, half-legendary king whom the gods propose to chastise. To humble the arrogant monarch they create a foil: Enkidu of the strong limbs and simple heart. Before he encounters Gilgamesh, the gods civilize Enkidu by providing him with a courtesan to instruct him in the erotic arts. This humanizing process enables Enkidu to overcome his brutish nature and gain worldly wisdom. As the gods intended, Enkidu and Gilgamesh meet in combat, ending in a draw, as a chastened Gilgamesh joins his new-found comrade in a string of exciting adventures. Inevitably, a misadventure provokes the wrath of the gods and Enkidu dies in the arms of a bereft Gilgamesh, who is left alone to face the meaning of life—and death.

But the story does not end there. Learning that the great flood's legendary hero, Utnapishtim, possesses the secret of eternal life, Gilgamesh tracks him down and finds the thorny plant that guarantees immortality, exactly as revealed to him by the hero. Ecstatic over his precious discovery, Gilgamesh celebrates by bathing in a nearby pool. At that moment "a serpent snuffed [put out] the fragrance of the plant; it came up from the water and carried off the plant. Going back it shed its slough." Considered immortal because of its annual sloughing off of skin, the snake steals immortality from Gilgamesh. "Thereupon Gilgamesh sits down and weeps, His tears running down over his face." This is the truly final loss, confirming the dark

Mesopotamian suspicion that life only seems to be hopeful, happy, and bright. Ultimately the truth is learned, usually the hard way: life ends in nothingness.

The following selections tell of a great flood. This may have been the famous deluge that inundated Mesopotamia around 2900 BC, or, it may be a creation **myth**. Whatever the intention, there are interesting parallels with the flood described in Genesis, chapters 6–8. This is understandable for "The biblical accounts are themselves based on some form of the Gilgamesh epic: Sumerian, Babylonian, or Assyrian, either brought in by Abraham from Ur of the Chaldees or experienced in Jewish exile in Babylonia."[2]

LITERARY SELECTION 1

The Epic of Gilgamesh
From Tablet XI

The story is told to Gilgamesh by Utnapishtim, who relates how he was instructed by the gods.

Tear down this house, build a ship!
Give up possessions, seek thou life.
Forswear worldly goods and keep the soul alive!
Aboard the ship take thou the seed of all living things.
The ship that thou shalt build,
Her dimensions shall be to measure.
Equal shall be her width and length.
On the fifth day I laid her framework.
One whole acre was her floor space,
Ten dozen cubits the height of each of her walls,   10
Ten dozen cubits each edge of the square deck.
I laid out the contours and joined her together.
I provided her with six decks,
Dividing her thus into seven parts.
Her floor plan I divided into nine parts.
I hammered water-plugs into her.
I saw to the punting poles and laid in supplies.
Bullocks I slaughtered for the people,
And I killed sheep every day.
Must, red wine, oil, and white wine   20
I gave the workmen to drink, as though river water,
That they might feast as on New Year's Day.
On the seventh day the ship was completed.
The launching was very difficult,
So that they had to shift the floor planks above and
          below,
Until two-thirds of the structure had gone into the water.
Whatever I had I laded upon her:
Whatever I had of silver I laded upon her;
Whatever I had of gold I laded upon her;
Whatever I had of all the living things I laded upon her.   30
All my family and kin I made go aboard the ship.
The beasts of the field, the wild creatures of the field,
     All the craftsmen I made go aboard.
I watched the appearance of the weather.

2. Philip R. Wiener, editor in chief, *Dictionary of the History of Ideas*, Volume III (New York: Charles Scribner's Sons, 1973, pp. 279–80). Source: James B. Pritchard, ed., *Ancient Near Eastern Texts Relating to the Old Testament* (Princeton: Princeton University Press, 1950), pp. 42, 72, 109.

The weather was awesome to behold.
I boarded the ship and battened up the entrance.
With the first glow of dawn,
A black cloud rose up from the horizon.
For one day the south-storm blew,
Gathering speed as it blew, submerging the
    mountains,   40
Overtaking the people like a battle.
No one can see his fellow,
Nor can the people be recognized from heaven.
The gods were frightened by the deluge,
And, shrinking back, they ascended to the heaven of
    Anu.[3]
The gods cowered like dogs
    Crouched against the outer wall.
Ishtar cried out like a woman in travail,
The sweet-voiced mistress of the gods moans aloud:
"The olden days are alas turned to clay,   50
Because I bespoke evil in the Assembly of the gods.
How could I bespeak evil in the Assembly of the gods,
Ordering battle for the destruction of my people,
When it is I myself who give birth to my people!"
Six days and six nights
Blows the flood wind, as the south-storm sweeps the
    land.
When the seventh day arrived,
    The flood-carrying south-storm subsided in the battle,
Which it had fought like an army.
The sea grew quiet, the tempest was still, the flood
    ceased.   60
I looked at the weather: stillness had set in,
And all of mankind had returned to clay.
The landscape was as level as a flat roof.
I opened a hatch, and light fell upon my face.
Bowing low, I sat and wept,
Tears running down my face.
I looked about for coast lines in the expanse of the sea:
In each of fourteen regions
    There emerged a region-mountain.
On Mount Nisir the ship came to a halt.   70
Mount Nisir held the ship fast,
    Allowing no motion.
One day, a second day, Mount Nisir held the ship fast,
    Allowing no motion.
A third day, a fourth day, Mount Nisir held the ship fast,
    Allowing no motion.
A fifth, and a sixth day, Mount Nisir held the ship fast,
    Allowing no motion.
When the seventh day arrived,
I sent forth and set free a dove.   80
The dove went forth, but came back;
Since no resting-place for it was visible, she turned
    round.
Then I sent forth and set free a swallow.
The swallow went forth, but came back;
Since no resting-place for it was visible, she turned
    round.

Then I sent forth and set free a raven.
The raven went forth and, seeing that the waters had
    diminished,
He eats, circles, caws, and turns not round.
Then I let out all to the four winds
    And offered a sacrifice.   90
I poured out a libation on the top of the mountain.

The "Standard of Ur"

The so-called "Standard of Ur" was found in a tomb in the royal cemetery at Ur (figs. 1.12 and 1.13). Though these two panels form the front and back of a musical instrument, they are described as they appear in the figure, i.e., as upper and lower panels. The upper "war" plate shows, in the top register, the king alighting from his carriage to receive captives. In the center a line of lancers in heavy cloaks faces vanquished enemies on the right. The four chariots in the bottom register drive across the bodies of fallen warriors.

STUDY QUESTIONS

1. **a.** Imagine living with a tribe of nomads with all edibles either gathered or hunted. As you follow the seasons in search of food, what would you carry with you? What would constitute "excess baggage," i.e., things neither useful nor needed?
   b. Now, imagine that you are raising crops and breeding animals. In what ways would your life differ from that of the nomads? What possessions would you have that were previously impractical? How different would your relationships be with your neighbors and with your community?
2. The Latin poet Lucretius claimed that, because early civilizations were unable to account for natural phenomena (particularly the more terrifying aspects), they ascribed such things to the gods. In those terms, what does the nature and behavior of the gods in the Sumerian pantheon suggest about the environment in Mesopotamia? (Environment includes climate, topography, and geography.)
3. Consider the environment in your own area and then invent an appropriate pantheon. Describe the nature and functions of your newly created gods and goddesses.
4. What were the lasting contributions that the Sumerians made to civilization?

3. The highest heaven in the Mesopotamian conception of the cosmos.

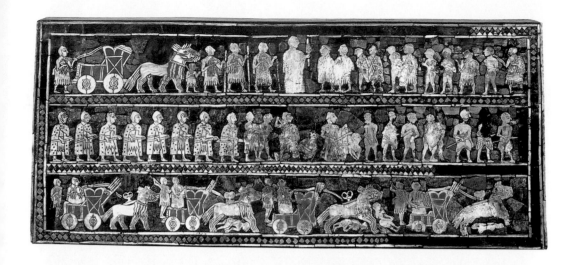

1.12 The Standard of Ur, from Iraq. Sumerian, Early Dynastic II. Ca. 2600–2400 BC. Bitumen base inlaid with shell, red limestone, and lapis lazuli, height of each panel 8" (20.3 cm). British Museum, London.

The lower "peace" panel highlights a banquet scene: the court drinks with the king to the sound of apparently stirring music (judging from the far right figure). In the center row servants are leading animals and holding fish, which may be a depiction of food preparation in a lower part of the palace. The bottom register probably illustrates the spoils of war.

1.13 *Overleaf* The Standard of Ur, detail of war scene in fig. 1.12a.

ANCIENT BREW

A Sumerian tablet of ca. 3500 BC is inscribed in cuneiform with a recipe for "wine of the grain." No one knows who invented beer but the Sumerians (or Egyptians?) were apparently the first (ca. 6000 BC) to make barley better for brewing by germinating barley grains, thus developing enzymes that change starch into fermentable sugars, a process called malting. Because beer turns up so often in Sumerian and Babylonian tablets we can assume that Mesopotamians liked their beer and also liked variety, as attested to by a list of nineteen different kinds of beer. We know also that Ninkasi was the goddess of intoxicating drink but, in these strongly male-dominant societies, we don't know why a mere goddess ruled over beverages as important as beer and wine.

AKKADIAN PERIOD, 2350–2150 BC

The first Sumerian period ended when the city-states fell to Semitic barbarians from the north, the Akkadians, some of whom had probably served the Sumerians as mercenaries. The Akkadians introduced the new concept of a divine monarchy supported by force of arms, which eventually caused the collapse of the Sumerian social order that had, among other things, protected the free peasants. In time, competition with, and the expansion of, large estates reduced the by then debt-ridden peasants to serfdom: the perennial battle of haves and have-nots. New rulers then settle down into the same pattern of inequalities; peasants are crushed and the whole process restarts, leading to takeovers by the Babylonians, the Assyrians, and the Persians.

The dynamic ruler of the Akkadians was Sargon the Great, the first notable military conqueror in history. The bronze head from Nineveh (fig. 1.14), very likely representing Sargon, expresses a new idea in sculpture: a dignified and powerful monarch. Bound in the Sumerian fashion, the hair is plaited, wound around the head, and gathered in a tight bun. This is a ruler in absolute control.

The Akkadians refined Sumerian art and the quality of life but could not convince the Sumerians that they were kinfolk rather than rank outsiders. Sargon and his successors even called themselves kings of Sumer and Akkad, but the Sumerians continued to fume under "foreign" domination and eventually regained political control. A major factor in the fall of Akkad was a volcanic eruption followed by centuries of a drought that turned their verdant land into a desert, from Egypt and Akkad all the way to India.

NEO-SUMERIAN PERIOD, 2050–1900 BC

After the fall of the Akkad dynasty in about 2100 BC, Gudea, ruler of the city of Lagash, united the Sumerians in a renaissance of Sumerian culture. About twenty statues of Gudea have survived, possibly indicating a popular king or an expert in public relations—or both. For Gudea's statues (fig. 1.15) Sumerian sculptors used **diorite**, an exceptionally hard stone, which may also account for the large number of surviving statues. All the statues are similar to this one, portraying the ruler as both devout and wise, a carefully crafted image of composed serenity.

At some time during the waning of this period, according to the Bible, Abraham led the Hebrews from the Sumerian city of Ur of the Chaldees toward an eventual occupation of the Land of Canaan, later called Palestine. The emigration of the Hebrews (see pp. 303–6) may have been prompted by the Babylonian invasion of Sumer.

1.14 *Above* Head, from Nineveh, Iraq. Akkadian. Ca. 2350–2150 BC. Bronze, height 12" (30.5 cm). Iraq Museum, Baghdad. Photo: Hirmer, Munich.

1.15 *Right* Gudea of Lagash, from Iraq. Neo-Sumerian. Ca. 2050 BC. Diorite, height 29" (73.7 cm). British Museum, London.

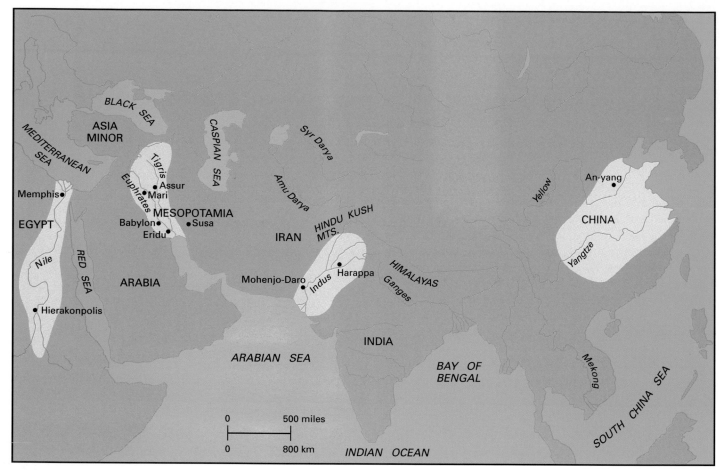

Map 1.3   Ancient river-valley civilizations.

OLD BABYLONIA, 1900–1500 BC

Although the Sumerians and Akkadians had coexisted through the Sumerian revival, the invading Babylonians (originally called Amorites) found a divided land so exhausted from constant friction that opposition was nonexistent. The Sumerians and Akkadians couldn't even get together long enough to fight off a truly foreign invader. Nomads from the Arabian desert, the Babylonians established a powerful state centered on their royal city of Babylon. Excavations at Mari, in the middle Euphrates valley, have revealed an enormous palace of nearly 300 rooms containing thousands of tablets from the royal archives. Chief among the royal correspondents was Hammurabi (ca. 1792–1750 BC), who consolidated the territories of Sumer and Akkad into a powerful Babylonian kingdom.[4]

A striking characteristic of all Mesopotamian cultures was the large number of land-owning merchants and farmers. With its potential for chaos this situation needed a structure that regulated private property, trade, and other business affairs. Legal standards had been developed in the past but none so practical as Hammurabi's Code of Laws

that established the rule of law from the Persian Gulf to the Mediterranean Sea (fig. 1.16). Consisting of a rather poetic prologue and epilogue, the code has a central section that lists 282 regulations dealing with perjury, theft, land tenure, licensed drinking, commerce, marriage and divorce, inheritance, adoption, medical treatment, construction, and the hire of livestock, laborers, and slaves. Oddly enough there is no reference to taxation. In common with earlier codes, the basic principle was "retaliation in kind" or, as expressed by the Hebrews, "an eye for an eye, a tooth for a tooth." As a combination of contemporary tribal practices and of more enlightened provisions for justice, the code did replace some (not all) "retaliation in kind" with fines and money compensation to aggrieved parties. Most important, it worked.

Hammurabi summarized, in the code's prologue, his contribution to the people after he "pronounced the majestic name of Babylon and decreed the extension of its power over the whole universe" so that "I might bring order to my people and so that I might free them from evil and wicked men, that I should defend the weak from the oppression of the mighty." Although self-serving and verging on purple prose, these words do have a noble intent. Establishing order, protecting society, and making all equal before the law are worthy goals in any society.

---

4. The reference to Old Babylonia is modern hindsight; there was a later kingdom called Neo-Babylonia.

STUDY QUESTIONS

1. Compare the portraits in figures 1.14 and 1.15. How do they differ and how are they similar? Considering the visual evidence, what can you deduce about the two rulers?
2. Why was Hammurabi's Code of Law so significant? Before responding to the question, try to imagine what life would be like if you lived in an area in which each community had its own laws. How might this situation affect commerce, trade, and other activities?

1.16 Stele of Hammurabi (upper portion), from Iraq. Babylonian. Ca. 1760 BC. Basalt, height of entire stele 7'4" (2.24 m). Louvre, Paris. Photo: R.M.N., Paris.
The Code of Law is inscribed on the lower portion of the stele. Above the code the king is standing before a divinity who is probably Shamash, the sun god, regarded as the lawgiver.

ANCIENT CHINA

Sometime around 5000 BC the hunter-gatherers of the Yellow River valley and those living on the southeastern China coast shifted to an agricultural way of life, as people in Mesopotamia and Egypt had earlier (map 1.3). Early farming methods (ca. 5000–2500 BC) were so primitive that whole villages had to be moved as the soil became exhausted. Improved techniques after 2500 BC set the stage for the Shang Dynasty (ca. 1525–1027 BC), the first Chinese civilization, whose achievements included an advanced writing system, a sophisticated bronze metallurgy (fig. 1.17), the first Chinese calendar, and a proliferation of cities. Contrary to older beliefs about Near Eastern influences, recent evidence suggests that the Chinese developed their agriculture and invented their civilization with little outside help. During this early period they also developed their characteristic ancestor worship, a belief that the dead can influence the world of the living. This tradition persists today in China despite the antireligious campaigns of the Communist regime.

1.17 Ceremonial vessel, from China. Late Shang Dynasty. Ca. 1000 BC. Bronze, height 20⅟₁₆" (51cm). Freer Gallery of Art, Smithsonian Institution, Washington, D.C. (Accession No. 30.26 AB).

THE ASSYRIAN EMPIRE, 1076–612 BC

After lackluster nomads (Kassites from Iran) had ruled Babylonia in a reasonably benign manner from ca. 1500 to 1100 BC, a far more warlike power emerged in the north. The first militaristic state in history, Assyria was to become, in the words of one of its kings, "Lord of the World," the most powerful and ruthless of all Near Eastern empires.

Assyrian art and architecture served the king, glorifying the monarch as a mighty hunter and implacable warrior (fig. 1.18). The intent was to intimidate any foes foolish enough to resist Assyrian military might. The enormous palace of Assurnasirpal II (uh-soor-NAS-ir-pall; 883–859 BC)[5] at Nimrud (ancient Kalkho), was the administrative center of a garrison state that extended from the Tigris to the Nile and from the Persian Gulf to Turkey (map 1.4). Erected in the Mesopotamian tradition of clusters of rooms surrounding courtyards, the palace walls were covered with elaborate reliefs of warring, hunting kings (much like the scene in fig. 1.18), which were veritable symphonies of violence and death. The palace entrance was flanked by huge

1.18 Lion Hunt of Assurbanipal (uh-soor-BAH-nee-pall), from the Palace of Assurbanipal, Nineveh, Iraq. Assyrian. Ca. 668–630 BC. Gypsum, height ca. 23" (58.4 cm). British Museum, London.

figures of human-headed, winged bulls carved both in relief and in the round (fig. 1.19). Designed to ward off evil spirits, the bulls are depicted at rest (frontal view) and in motion (side view), an illusion furthered by the fifth leg. This combination of fine attention to detail, sweeping wings, and sheer size communicates an awesome vigor symbolizing

Map 1.4 The Assyrian Empire.

5. These and subsequent royal dates are reigning periods.

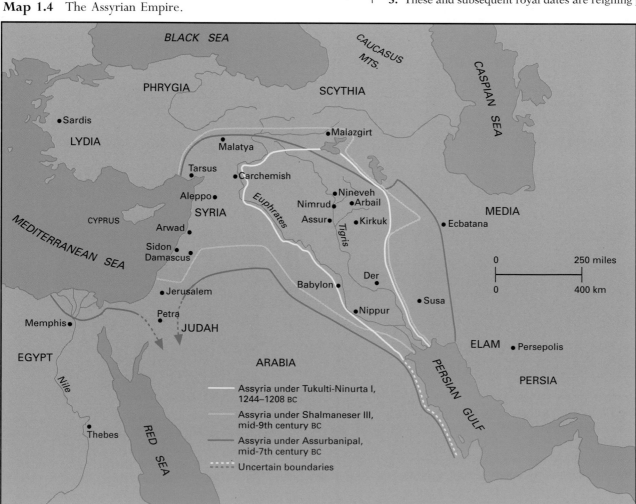

1.19 Winged human-headed bull from Nimrud, Iraq. Assyrian period of Assurnasirpal II. 883–859 BC. Alabaster, height 10'4" (3.15 m). British Museum, London.

the invincibility of Assyrian might. Assurnasirpal II's standard policy guaranteed fear of him and his army. Upon capturing an enemy town his soldiers rounded up surviving inhabitants, cut off their hands and feet, and piled them in the town square to bleed to death.

During the reign of Sargon II (721–705 BC) innovative Assyrian sculptors created immensely powerful solitary figures of divinities, kings, and heroes. The "genius" (person of great influence) illustrated in figure 1.20, thought to be Gilgamesh himself, is a huge model of massive strength, impressive and intimidating. This is how conquered enemies were supposed to view their new masters.[6]

The Assyrian Empire reached the pinnacle of its power during the reign of Sargon II. Because mass murder frequently stiffened enemy resistance, the Assyrians initiated an alternative policy: control dissent by removing entire populations from their homes and scattering them throughout the empire. It was Sargon II who dispersed the population of Israel—the "ten lost tribes of Israel."

Assyrian power gradually waned shortly after the conquest of Israel. Sennacherib's (sen-NAC-ur-ib) sack of Babylon in 689 BC and the conquest of Egypt in 670 BC

6. "The Assyrians were fierce, well-disciplined and cruel. Their cruelty was calculated, at least in part, to terrorize real and potential enemies, for the Assyrians boasted of their brutality." Donald Kagan, et al., *The Western Heritage* (New York: Macmillan Publishing Co., Inc., 1979), p. 22.

1.20 *Propitiatory Genius of a Hero* (Gilgamesh), from Iraq. Assyrian. Reign of Sargon II. 722–705 BC. Alabaster, height 13'10½" (4.23 m). Louvre, Paris. Photo: R.M.N., Paris.

were the last major successes of the Assyrian juggernaut. A coordinated effort of Babylonians, Medes (from northern Persia), and Palestinians decisively defeated the Assyrians in 612 BC, resulting in the destruction of all their major cities, especially the royal city of Nineveh. The end was spectacular. No other ancient empire collapsed so swiftly nor was devastated so completely. The empire simply disappeared, confirming the biblical saying that those who live by the sword shall perish by the sword.

Keeping in mind that the writer of the following was a Hebrew prophet and that Assyria was the hated enemy, this Old Testament account of the fall of Nineveh is appropriately impassioned:

> ¹Woe to the bloody city,
>   all full of lies and booty—
> no end to the plunder!
> ²The crack of whip, and rumble of wheel,
>   galloping horse and bounding chariot!
> ³Horsemen charging,
>   flashing sword and glittering spear,
> hosts of slain,
>   heaps of corpses,
> dead bodies without end—
>   they stumble over the bodies!
>
> ⁷Wasted is Nineveh; who will bemoan her?
>   whence shall I seek comforters for her?
>
> ¹⁸Your shepherds are asleep,
>   O king of Assyria;
>   your nobles slumber.
> Your people are scattered on the mountains
>   with none to gather them.
> ¹⁹There is no assuaging your hurt,
>   your wound is grievous.
> All who hear the news of you
>   clap their hands over you.
> For upon whom has not come
>   your unceasing evil?
>
> Nahum 3:1–3, 7, 18–19

THE CHALDEAN (NEO-BABYLONIAN) EMPIRE, 625–539 BC

The Chaldeans were a Semitic desert race from, perhaps, the Syrian area. They had settled in and around Babylon even before forming the alliance with the Medes that helped destroy Assyria. As the last upholder of Mesopotamian culture, the newly rebuilt Babylon was little more than a sumptuous museum in which older traditions, mostly Sumerian, were collected and preserved. Innovation was virtually unknown in a Babylonia that had shut itself off from the outside world as it contemplated past glories.

With the accession of Nebuchadnezzar II (neb-oo-kud-NEZ-ar, also spelled Nebuchadrezzar; 605–562 BC) to the throne, the legendary might of Sumer and Assyria was recalled in a monumental architecture and in a series of military expeditions that consolidated Babylonian power. A vigorous and brilliant commander, Nebuchadnezzar drove the Egyptians from Palestine, conquered Jerusalem in 586 BC, and exiled many Jews to Babylon. Jeremiah had advised cooperation with Babylon, reasoning that it was better to yield to a Semite foe than join a weak and faithless Egypt. The Jews ignored his sensible counsel and revolted, with predictable results. The king of Judah was blinded, his children and nobles killed and

> ¹²Nebuzaradan, the captain of the bodyguard who served the king of Babylon, entered Jerusalem. ¹³And he burned the house of the Lord and the king's house and all the houses of Jerusalem.
>
> Jeremiah 52:12–13

According to Jeremiah (52:27–30) 4,600 Jews were carried into what they called their **Babylonian Captivity** (586–538 BC). Though Jeremiah stated that "Judah was carried captive out of its land," it was mostly artisans and other skilled workers who were carted off. Many of the poorer class were left behind to continue the traditions of their people as best they could.

Nebuchadnezzar continued to build in Babylon in the grand manner, including an enormous ziggurat 295 feet (90 m) high and named Entemenanki ("Temple of the Foundation of Heaven and Earth") that may have been the biblical Tower of Babel. The Hanging Gardens he constructed for his Median wife became one of the wonders of the ancient world.

One of the more dazzling designs was for the glazed brick Ishtar Gate (fig. 1.21). The Mesopotamians had a special talent for portraying animals, an ability especially evident in this monumental work. Embellished with lions, bulls, and a kind of griffin, the gate stood at the end of the main processional entrance to the opulent capital city.

Despite the size and the splendor of its cities the Babylonian Empire was quite fragile. After the death of Nebuchadnezzar in 562 BC its decline was swift, ending, according to the Bible, with the death of Belshazzar in 539 BC. Biblical scholars cannot confirm Belshazzar's existence or even his name, but the Old Testament account of his demise effectively dramatizes royal decadence and Babylon's precipitous fall.

> ¹King Belshazzar made a great feast for a thousand of his lords, and drank wine in front of the thousand.
> ²Belshazzar, when he tasted the wine, commanded that the vessels of gold and of silver which Nebuchadnezzar his father had taken out of the temple in Jerusalem be brought, that the king and his lords, his wives, and his concubines might drink from

1.21 The Ishtar Gate (restored), from Babylon, Iraq. Reign of Nebuchadnezzar II. Chaldean. 604–562 BC. Glazed brick, height 48' (14.6 m). Staatliche Museen, Berlin. Photo: B.P.K., Berlin (Klaus Göken).

them. ³Then they brought in the golden and silver vessels which had been taken out of the temple, the house of God in Jerusalem; and the king and his lords, his wives, and his concubines drank from them. ⁴They drank wine, and praised the gods of gold and silver, bronze, iron, wood, and stone.

⁵Immediately the fingers of a man's hand appeared and wrote on the plaster of the wall of the king's palace. ⁶Then the king's color changed and his thoughts alarmed him; his limbs gave way and his knees knocked together.

¹³Then Daniel was brought in . . . [and] ¹⁷answered before the king "I will read the writing to the king and make known to him the interpretation.

²⁵"And this is the writing that was inscribed: MENE, MENE, TEKEL, and PARSIN. ²⁶This is the interpretation of the matter: MENE, God has numbered the days of your kingdom and brought it to an end; ²⁷TEKEL, you have been weighed in the balance and found wanting; ²⁸PERES, your kingdom is divided and given to the Medes and Persians."

³⁰That very night Belshazzar the Chaldean king was slain.

Daniel 5:1–6, 13, 17, 25–28, 30

Internal strife, decadence, and degeneracy took their toll, leaving no opposition to the conquering Persians. The Assyrian Empire had gone down fighting; Babylon, the last of twenty-five centuries of Mesopotamian kingdoms, expired with scarcely a whimper.

THE PERSIAN EMPIRE, 539–331 BC[7]

The Persians migrated from somewhere east of the Caspian Sea into the high plateau country north and east of the Persian Gulf. Apparently closely related to the Medes who lived farther north, they spoke an Indo-Iranian language, as did the Medes.[8] Under the remarkable leadership of Cyrus the Great (539–530 BC), the Persians first absorbed the Medes and then moved against the Lydian kingdom ruled by the legendary Croesus (KREE-sus). Croesus had already formed alliances with Egypt and Sparta in anticipation of a preventive war against Persia, but he was uncertain about success until he consulted the Delphic Oracle. According to the Greek historian Herodotos (484–425 BC), the oracle predicted that a Lydian attack would destroy a great army. That did indeed ensue—but the vanquished army was commanded by Croesus.

With the conquest of Egypt in 525 BC by Cyrus's son Cambyses (kam-BYE-sez), the Persian Empire expanded rapidly, eventually extending from Greece to the Himalayas and from southern Russia to the Indian Ocean, the greatest empire the world had yet seen (map 1.5). Like the later Romans, the Persians allowed subjugated peoples to retain their own customs, laws, and religion. The Hebrews, for example, were allowed to worship Jahweh (or Yahweh) and those in Babylon were encouraged to return to Jerusalem, though few chose to do so. For the pragmatic Persians such tolerance was eminently sensible, enabling the government to collect tribute from the far-flung empire without unduly annoying the populace.

One of the major Persian achievements was an elaborate network of imperial roads that formed the best highway system prior to Roman roads. The Royal Road extended some 1,600 miles (2,580 km) from the Persian Gulf to Asia Minor, connecting the empire's principal cities of Susa and Sardis. By using a series of relay riders the "king's messengers" could travel the entire Royal Road in a week. According to Herodotos, "Nothing mortal travels as fast as these Persian messengers. Not snow, nor rain, nor heat, nor gloom of night stays these couriers from the swift completion of their appointed rounds" (*Histories*, VIII).[9]

Although the Persian king did not employ Assyrian terrorist tactics, he was still an absolute monarch whose

7. As the successor to a long progression of Middle Eastern civilizations, the Persian Empire is considered both here and on pp. 73–4, where a discussion of the empire's conflict with Greek civilization is included.
8. With only a few exceptions, all inhabitants of modern Europe speak languages derived from ancient tongues brought from Eurasia (Ukraine or east of there) by Bronze Age conquerors. The term Indo-Iranian identifies various language branches as spoken in Europe, Iran, and northern India. These include Greek, Latin, Sanskrit, Persian, Celtic, and the Germanic languages. The name Iran (used after AD 600) means "land of the Aryan."
9. From which the U.S. Postal Service derived its motto.

Map 1.5   The Empires of Persia.

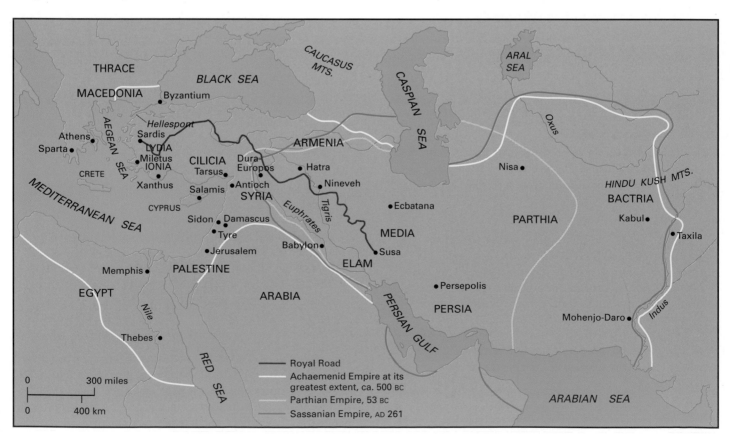

authority was tempered only by some power sharing with his nobles. From the admittedly biased Greek point of view, Cyrus, Darius, and Xerxes were oriental despots and the Persian army a mighty but mindless machine. Some claim that the Persian Empire was quite liberal and humane, but the many insurrections throughout its history testify to the heavy yoke of the man called the King of Kings.

Persian culture was as derivative and eclectic as that of their Roman contemporaries. With nothing original to contribute they adapted their art and architecture from Mesopotamian, Egyptian, Lydian, Palestinian, and Greek models. Probably the most characteristic expression of their culture was their architecture. They copied the raised platform and terraced building style of Babylon and Assyria, adding winged Assyrian bulls and glazed Babylonian bricks. They chose forests of **columns** in the Egyptian manner but with Greek **fluting** and **capitals**. Most importantly, their architecture was wholly secular. Because their new religion of Zoroastrianism (see below) required no priests, rituals, statues, or temples, they concentrated instead on building elaborate palaces.

The Great Palace of Darius and Xerxes at Persepolis (fig. 1.22) was destroyed by Alexander the Great but enough remains of this enormous complex to give some idea of its magnitude. The view shown is of the eastern stairway in front of the Audience Hall, with the Gate of Xerxes on the left. The Great Hall was 250 feet square (23.2m²). It could hold 10,000 people and originally had 100 stone columns, each 40 feet (12.2 m) high and all brightly painted. This was the first use of interior columns in the Mesopotamian world. Though influenced by Egyptian examples, these columns are more closely patterned after Greek models and were probably designed and constructed by Greek artisans. They are topped by a series of complicated capitals composed of the forequarters of lions, bulls (fig.

1.22 East staircase of the Audience Hall of Darius and Xerxes, Great Palace, Persepolis, Iran. Persian. Ca. 500 BC. Stone. Photo: Rainbird/Robert Harding, London.

1.23 Bull capital, Persepolis. Ca. 500 BC. Photo: Boudot-Lamotte, Paris.

1.24   Medes and Persians of the palace guard, east staircase
of the Audience Hall, Persepolis. Ca. 500 BC. Stone relief.
Photo: B.P.K., Berlin (Dietlinde Karig).

1.23) or human-headed bulls. The low reliefs show Persian
guards standing at attention—a security guard in stone
(fig. 1.24). The influence here is clearly Assyrian but nowhere
in the palace are there kings slaughtering enemies or helpless animals. Persian kings preferred tidy and efficient
administration of their vast empire without blatant
intimidation in the Assyrian manner.

Persian culture was highly refined. An example of the
luxury enjoyed by the upper class is a drinking horn in-
geniously combined with a fantastic lion-griffin (fig. 1.25).
The details are sharp and precise: tongue, teeth, sharp claws,
tiny tufts of hair. Characteristic of the Persian style are
such stylistic conventions as the figure-eight shoulder
muscle and the tulip-shaped muscle on the foreleg.

PERSIAN MAGIC

The English word "magic" is derived from Magi, the
priestly hierarchy of Zoroastrianism. Like the Brahmans of India the Magi were members of the highest
caste and keepers of the cult. Supposedly "wise in the
things of God," a **Magus** probably functioned as both
priest and scribe. A branch of the clan moved to Babylon
where they specialized in casting horoscopes, telling fortunes, and interpreting dreams, which qualified them
as practitioners of magic, to use the word in its modern
meaning. Three Persian Magi appear in the **Gospel** of
Matthew as the "wise men from the East" who came
to worship the infant Christ.

1.25   Rhyton in the Form of a Lion-Griffin. Persian. 5th century BC. Gold, height 6¾" (17.1 cm). Metropolitan Museum of Art, New York (Fletcher Fund, 1954).

Zoroastrianism

Perhaps the most important contribution of the illustrious Persian culture was a new religion. A prophet named Zoroaster (Gk.; Zarathustra in Persian) was both a reformer of traditional folk religion and the creator of a new faith. Born sometime in the seventh century BC (660?), he was the first exponent, according to some scholars, of an ethical, **monotheistic** religion. Other scholars contend that Zoroastrianism was a **dualistic** religion, albeit ethical. Which is it? Examining the evidence may supply some answers, but, as in all religions, final explication rests with each interpreter.

In the *Gathas,* his only surviving authentic work, Zoroaster declares that Ahura Mazda (also called Ormazd) is the principle of truth and also the Holy Spirit, the

Creating Word that existed before the world was born, the Word that brought all forms of life into being, boding good for all species, particularly the human race. In order that people might, through struggle, appreciate the true meaning of goodness, a twin of the Holy Spirit—Ahriman the Evil One—was created. It is unclear whether Ahriman was invented by Ahura Mazda (Ormazd) or created simultaneously as the evil twin of Ormazd, and thus the scholarly disagreement about monism and dualism. In any event, all life became a contest between good and evil, truth and error, light and darkness.

In its original form Zoroastrianism was a personal religion with no place for rituals, priests or temples. The emphasis was on practical moral living without extremes such as celibacy or cloistered seclusion; anyone could seek the good and the true. The ethical life was dedicated to the active realization of a just society finally freed from evil.

An elaborate **eschatology** looked forward to the coming of the Saoshyans or Savior, who would resurrect the dead for judgment. The righteous would then pass to heaven and the wicked to hell to suffer physically for their sins. In another passage Zoroaster described the just as residing in the House of Song while the unjust are doomed to the House of the Lie.

According to Zoroastrianism the conflict between good and evil would not last forever. Ultimately Ahura Mazda would overcome Ahriman. Not even those condemned to the House of the Lie would stay there forever. The final victory of Ahura Mazda and the destruction of Ahriman would usher in the *Fraskart*, the ultimate "making excellent" or rehabilitation of Ahriman's followers.

The new faith was so far beyond the capacity of the common people that, over time, its abstractions were minimized and emphasis placed on sacrifice, liturgy, and priestly mediation—the very paraphernalia Zoroastrianism had tried to eradicate. Ishtar, the ancient Mesopotamian fertility goddess, returned to the pantheon where she was joined by Mithra, god of light and new Persian deity. Thus, in time, a religion that had protested against polytheism and empty formalism took on some of the characteristics of the old beliefs it had sought to supplant. Having readily gained the support of the Persian rulers, the new faith later became influential in Mesopotamia, Asia Minor, and Egypt. Much that was new and vital in Zoroastrianism can be detected in subsequent religious movements.

Zoroastrianism languished after the destructive invasion of the Middle East by Alexander the Great and nearly foundered 1,000 years later during the seventh-century Muslim conquest of Persia. Preserved by a mass migration to India and subsequently revived through scholarly Parsee leadership, Parsism (Zoroastrianism) is still practiced in India by the descendants of Persian exiles.

STUDY QUESTIONS

1. How would you characterize Persian conquest and rule of the largest empire prior to the Romans? What did the Persians seem to learn (positive and negative) from earlier kingdoms and empires?
2. Compare Persian Zoroastrianism with the polytheism of Mesopotamia. What changed? Why?
3. What are the elements in Zoroastrianism that seem to have influenced Judaism, Christianity, and Islam?

SUMMARY

Part of the history of Western civilization begins in Mesopotamia with the early agricultural settlements there. When nomads settled down to farm, everything changed, with one invention following upon another: animal husbandry, pottery, weaving, permanent houses, communities, fortifications, mathematics, a calendar, and writing. In due course came trade, manufacturing, law, and all the other complexities of civilization—including warfare.

The Sumerian Period (3000–2350 BC) saw the development of organized polytheism and ziggurats with temples on top; advances in mathematics, writing, and astronomy; and the first major literary work, *The Epic of Gilgamesh*.

Under Sargon the Great the Akkadians assumed political control of Sumerian culture (2350–2150 BC) and refined and improved their art forms. Continually unhappy under Akkadian domination, the Sumerians regained control under Gudea of Lagash (Neo-Sumerian Period, 2050–1900 BC).

The incessant internecine strife of Sumerians and Akkadians left them vulnerable to the Amorites, opportunistic nomads from the Arabian desert, who established the Babylonian Empire (1900–1500 BC), centered on the royal city of Babylon. Chief among the royal rulers was Hammurabi, whose legal code confirmed the rule of law throughout the empire.

Other desert nomads, the Kassites, established a rather benign rule in Babylon (1500–1100 BC), maintaining the culture but doing little to improve life or art. The Kassites were conquered in turn by Assyria, the first militaristic state in history (1076–612 BC). Entirely at the service of the king, Assyrian art had essentially two themes: power and conquest. Ruthless in their warring and ruling, the Assyrians stressed their brutality as a warning to potential dissidents. Assyria's enemies were equally pitiless when the end came, destroying everything Assyrian.

The Assyrians were demolished mainly by the Medes and the Chaldeans, the latter a Semitic desert tribe that reestablished the Babylonian Empire, known today as the Chaldean (Neo-Babylonian) Empire (625–539 BC). Under Nebuchadnezzar II Babylon bloomed briefly as a kind of museum of past glories, the final flowering of a Mesopotamian culture that had begun 2,500 years before.

Last of the ancient Near Eastern powers, the Persian Empire (539–331 BC) was also the greatest that the world had yet seen. Persian culture was eclectic: it incorporated a variety of ideas and styles in art and architecture from other civilizations. This was a highly sophisticated society with an efficiently governed empire that had a truly "international" concern for the diverse cultures it embraced. The Persians' strikingly original contribution, Zoroastrianism, was arguably one of the great world religions.

A culture that began in the Land between the Rivers in about 3000 BC succumbed, finally, to a European power in 331 BC. Not until the expansion of Islam, 1,000 years later, would the Near or Middle East again figure prominently in world affairs.

CULTURE AND HUMAN VALUES

For the average Mesopotamian life was a matter of survival in the here and now. There was some personal freedom but, on the whole, people were at the mercy of forces beyond their control, from raging rivers to warring kings. The gods were believed to be fractious and enemies seemed always at the gates. Ultimate reality was understood as nothing more than the visible world with its constant imperfections and occasional terrors.

None of the Mesopotamian cultures seems to have achieved any appreciable period of balance. Each historical era was mainly one of adjustment, from Sumerians to Akkadians, to Sumerians, Babylonians, and all the rest. There was a chronic proclivity to stagger from one crisis to another without falling totally into chaos but also without rising to a plateau of stability.

If we are to believe ancient Egyptian and Greek writers, Mesopotamia's long and troubled history reveals little concern about ideals such as the true, the good, or the beautiful. We are told that neither its polytheistic religions nor its authoritarian governments inspired any urge toward personal excellence. Pleasing the gods was supposedly more important than living a good life. To a certain extent the ancient writers were probably right, but that is not the whole story. The extant art and architecture alone testify to the notable accomplishments of the several cultures, as do their contributions to writing, law, religion, mathematics, and astronomy—all of this in the face of drought, floods, war, and other disasters. Moreover, there is nothing in Egyptian literature, for example, that compares with *The Epic of Gilgamesh*. Theirs is a remarkable record of human resilience, ingenuity, and creativity, an abiding confirmation of the hardiness of the human spirit.

No
fastly cor
natured
their ow
Their se
certain,
skilled i
Th
exalted
or Amor
ers of na
inally g
of Osiri
Osiris,
brother
and sist
The rise
ed to th
headed
avenged
Th
later de
into a
risen, s
victory
triump
T
general
pictogr
glyphs.
key to
hierogl
W
very slc
BC. In a
doms
miles [
united
but his
("two
of the
enemy
comra
repres
holdin
ing ou
agricu
symbc
this ea
been s
as if v

2.

CHAPTER 2

Egypt: Land of the Pharaohs

ONE PEOPLE, ONE LANGUAGE

As the first truly national state (one people, one language), Egypt had a far more consistent and unified development than did the quarreling, warring city-states of Mesopotamia. Egypt was, in fact, virtually the antithesis of Mesopotamia, largely because of its geography and climate. Mesopotamian cities lay exposed on the broad plain between the rivers with no naturally defensible sites. Egypt was protected on the north by the Mediterranean, by cataracts and mountains on the south, and on the east and west by the trackless Sahara. A 750-mile (1,200-km) strip of richly fertile land averaging 10 miles (16 km) in width, this was the "gift of the Nile." No wonder Greek writer Herodotos defined Egypt as "all the country covered by inundations of the Nile" and Egyptians as "all men who drink Nile water" (*Histories,* II; map 2.1).

The Nile valley produced two crops a year, an agricultural prosperity unmatched in the ancient world. How could a land that was 97 percent desert outproduce all other regions? The answer is supplied by the mighty river that flowed from south to north carrying the mingled waters of the White and Blue Niles. Originating in the African lakes far to the south, the White Nile bore a generous supply of decayed vegetable matter. The Blue Nile flowed from the Abyssinian (Ethiopian) Plateau, carrying soil rich in potash. The fortuitous combination formed a nearly perfect organic fertilizer. Herodotos marveled, "They obtain the fruit of the field with less trouble than any other people in the world." The climate was dry and consistently sunny, with little likelihood of such natural catastrophes as the earthquakes, fierce storms, and raging floods that so bedeviled the people of Mesopotamia. No other area was so sedately stable as the land of the mighty Nile, with its life-giving and predictable patterns of flood and retreat. Naturally enough, Egyptians viewed nature's laws and those of their living god, the king (later called pharaoh), as immutable, and the afterlife as a continuation of the good life in their splendidly affluent valley (see chapter opener opposite).

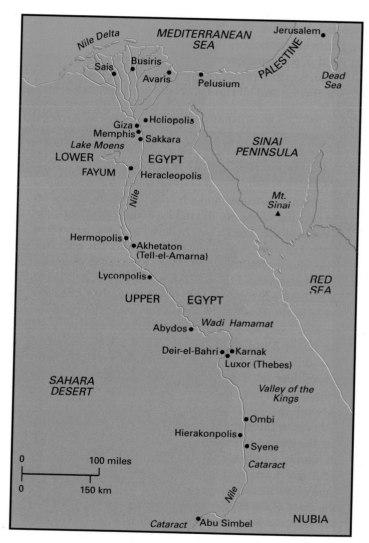

Map 2.1   Ancient Egypt.

Opposite   Banquet, from the tomb of Netamun, Thebes, detail. Ca. 1400 BC. Painted stucco, height of full figures ca. 25" (63 cm). British Museum, London. Photo: E.T. Archive, London.

THE

Egypt
Consi
peopl
deper
becau
ed no
entai
princ
truth
prep;
beyo
fund;
morb
was t
on h

2.2   Sphinx, Giza, oblique view. Old Kingdom, 4th Dynasty. Ca. 2540–2514 BC. Length 840′ (256 m), original height 75′ (23 m). Top of the Great Pyramid of Khufu, Giza. Old Kingdom, 4th Dynasty. Ca. 2590–2568 BC. Original height 482′ (147 m). Photo: Spectrum, London.

2.3   Sphinx, frontal view. Photo: Spectrum, London (Carolyn Clarke).

OLD KINGDOM, 2686–2181 BC, DYNASTIES III–VI

Little is known of the first two Egyptian dynasties, but the third dynasty is so well documented that scholars have dated the Old Kingdom, the first major division of Egyptian history, from that time. It was, however, the fourth dynasty that invented the enormous tombs that launched the brief but monumental Pyramid Age of the Old Kingdom.

In the fifth century BC, when Herodotos beheld the 2,000-year-old Sphinx and the great pyramids he was as awed by their antiquity as by their overwhelming size (figs. 2.2 and 2.3). The **Sphinx**, which combines the body of a lion with the head of the Pharaoh Khafre (fl. 2869 BC?), is the largest surviving colossus and a majestic symbol of royal power. It was not built but carved out of the sedimentary bedrock. The prodigious amount of excess stone was presumably used to build a solar temple under the paws of the beast, with the remainder going into Khafre's pyramid. The Sphinx is believed to represent Khafre as Horus, protector of kingship, while the solar temple is early evidence of a transition from Horus the sky god to Amon-Re the sun god.

The Great Pyramid of Khufu occupies over 13 acres (5.27 ha); 756 feet square (231 m²), it has a volume of 91 cubic feet (2.57 m³). The largest of the three major pyramids,[3] it contains about 250,000 stones, each weighing over 2 tons. Consisting of pyramid, temple, and imitation palace, the pyramid complex represented a funerary cult place and an eternal palace (fig. 2.4). With a shape pointing heavenward, the pyramid linked kingship and the cosmos, while also representing the primeval mound upon which the universe had supposedly been created.

The massiveness of the pyramids was intended, in part, to foil grave robbers searching for the treasure that accompanied each king to the afterlife. They were, however, conspicuous targets, to put it mildly, and all were robbed. Later attempts to hide, disguise, or otherwise protect pharaonic tombs were equally futile; only Tutankhamen's treasure survived relatively intact.

The Pyramid Age lasted less than four centuries, a brief period by Egyptian standards. By contrast, other forms of Egyptian art and architecture followed conventions of style and form that endured throughout Egypt's long history. What are stylistic conventions? An art "convention" is a consistent way of seeing and depicting things in a manner generally accepted and understood. Conventions are, in other words, commonly held values that have been given form.

The bodily proportions used in the Palette of Narmer (fig. 2.1) were refined in the *Portrait of the Court Official Hesira* (fig. 2.5). There is more subtlety here and the proportions are made more heroic with broad shoulders, narrow hips, and noble raised head. The stylized frontal view of body and eyes with face and legs in profile has been

3.   There is a total of eighty pyramids.

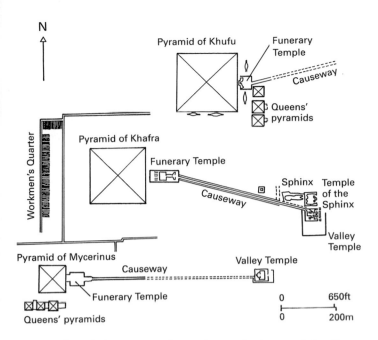

N

Pyramid of Khufu

Funerary Temple

Causeway

Queens' pyramids

Workmen's Quarter

Pyramid of Khafra

Funerary Temple

Causeway

Sphinx

Temple of the Sphinx

Valley Temple

Pyramid of Mycerinus

Causeway

Valley Temple

Funerary Temple

Queens' pyramids

0   650ft

0   200m

2.4 Plan of Giza pyramid complex and section of the Great Pyramid of Khufu.

2.5 *Right Portrait of the Court Official Hesira,* from the tomb of Hesira at Sakkara. Old Kingdom, 3rd Dynasty. Ca. 2750 BC. Wood, height 3'9" (1.15 m). Egyptian Museum, Cairo. Photo: Marburg.

developed into a classical model which was to remain valid for literally millennia. The proportions may change over the centuries but the conventions remain. This arrangement shows key body parts in their most telling and easily understood view, the way artists know (in their mind's eye) rather than how they actually see the parts. Further, by avoiding specific settings and placing boldly two-dimensional figures on a frontal plane, artists emphasized the timeless character of Egyptian art.

When depicting royalty Egyptian sculpture displayed an impassive calm and enduring serenity that suggested their eternal existence. The statue of *Mycerinus and His Queen* (fig. 2.6) shares qualities (conventions) common to every Egyptian sculpture of human figures. Egyptian sculptors took a cubic view of the human form and prepared the statue by drawing front and side views on the faces of a rectangular block, then working inward until the angular views met. The resulting image is one of startling clarity that demands a 90-degree change of position for a different perspective. Egyptian statuary has a monumental frozen quality best observed from directly in front or squarely from each side. Symbolizing the total control of the god-ruler, this immobility is a visual counterpart of Egyptian belief in immutable laws that govern people and nature. Also characteristic of Egyptian portraiture is the rectangularity of the figures, as if they were standing within a

2.6 *Mycerinus and His Queen,* from Giza. Old Kingdom, 4th Dynasty. Ca. 2599–2571 BC. Slate schist, height 4'6½" (1.38 m). Museum of Fine Arts, Boston (Shaw Collection).

rectangular box that reinforces the impression of composed immobility. The rigidity of the figures is heightened by leaving as much stone intact as possible, e.g., in the webbing that binds the tense arms and clenched fists to the figure. Sculptors deliberately avoided making openings in the stone by carving what amounted to very high reliefs. In this example, the queen, conveyor of property through the female line, clasps her husband's waist and touches his left arm to symbolize the transfer of power to the pharaoh.

Egyptian portraiture conventions required formal depictions of high-ranking persons such as the pharaoh but less exalted personages were portrayed more realistically. The celebrated statue of an unnamed scribe (fig. 2.7) clearly follows three-dimensional conventions but lacks the air of a pharaoh's divine authority. It is therefore more realistic, particularly in the steady gaze of the polished stone eyes. The artist accepted the conventions but moved beyond the formula to create this powerful image.

2.7   *Seated Scribe*, from Sakkara. Old Kingdom, 5th Dynasty. Ca. 2500 BC. Painted limestone, height 21" (53.3 cm). Louvre, Paris. Photo: R.M.N., Paris.

MIDDLE KINGDOM, 2135–1786 BC, DYNASTIES XI–XII

Between the Old and Middle Kingdoms there was a hiatus later called the First Intermediate Period (2260–2130 BC; dynasties VII–X). Apparently not even stable, conservative Egypt could sustain more than five centuries of peace and prosperity. A constantly expanding bureaucracy, the growing power of priests, and rebellious local officials all weakened the central authority. For over a century there was civil unrest, political instability (historian Manetho facetiously remarked that the seventh dynasty consisted of seventy kings in seventy days), and invasions by desert barbarians.[4] However, the next four dynasties stabilized the political situation and led Egypt to renewed peace and prosperity. Politically there was considerable local authority that, when coupled with a strong middle class and a weaker but stable central government, made the twelfth dynasty the closest to a democratic state that the Egyptians ever achieved. This was the affluent society of the Middle Kingdom with the highest standard of living yet achieved in the ancient world.

The major art forms of the age followed the canons of the Old Kingdom but with a new refinement and mastery of the material that carried over into the New Kingdom, the last splendid period of Egyptian power and influence. In the scene from the Sarcophagus of Queen Kawyt (fig. 2.8), the queen is seated on a throne holding a cup to her lips with her right hand and a mirror in her left. A maid ties the curls of her wig while a manservant pours her a drink. His words wishing her well appear in the hieroglyphs between them. The composition is spacious, uncluttered, and incised with elegant lines, as in the adroit hands of the woman dressing the wig. Note the convention of ignoring **perspective** and scaling figures according to importance.

The decorative arts, too, flourished in this era. Jewelry is one of the oldest of these, dating back more than 7,000 years to the earliest civilizations in Mesopotamia and Egypt. Making fine jewelry was long an Egyptian specialty but the jewelers of the Middle Kingdom surpassed their predecessors (fig. 2.9). The exquisite necklace is made of gold, lapis lazuli (purple with gold specks), carnelian (red), and turquoise (light blue to darker greenish blue). The pectoral (fig. 2.10) is primarily of gold-inlaid green feldspar and lapis lazuli with carnelian highlights. The facing falcons symbolize Horus the sky god while the kneeling girl presumably represents the recipient of "one of the supreme masterpieces of Egyptian jewelry" (Metropolitan Museum of Art). The necklace was presented to Princess Sit-Hathor-Yunet by her royal father, Sesistris II (reigned ca. 1897–1878 BC).

---

4.   Neither the First nor even the Second Intermediate Period was as chaotic and disruptive as most of the political upheavals in Mesopotamia. They were more like ripples on a calm sea but seemed, to the Egyptians, to be very troublesome just because the sea was usually so serene.

2.8 Sarcophagus of Queen Kawyt, detail, from Deir-el-Bahri (Thebes). Middle Kingdom, 11th Dynasty. Ca. 2100 BC. White limestone, life-size. Egyptian Museum, Cairo. Photo: Hirmer, Munich.

2.9 Necklace of drop and ball beads, from the Treasure of Lahun. Middle Kingdom, 12th Dynasty. Ca. 1880 BC. Gold, carnelian, lapis lazuli, turquoise, green feldspar, amethyst, and garnet, length 32" (80 cm). Metropolitan Museum of Art, New York (Rogers Fund and Henry Walters Gift, 1916, 16.1.3.)

2.10 Pectoral, detail of fig. 2.9. 3¼ × 1¾ (8.2 × 4.5 cm).

BEAUTIFICATION

All the Middle Eastern cultures used cosmetics but the Egyptians also exported cosmetics throughout the ancient world. Egyptian women painted their lashes, eyelids, and eyebrows black with kohl, a paste made with soot and antimony. This was standard practice in the Middle East; kohl not only beautified eyes but also protected them from flies and the fiery sun. (The palettes on which eye makeup was ground inspired ceremonial palettes—see fig. 2.1—that were decorated with reliefs.) Henna was used to dye hair, nails, palms, and the soles of the feet. The Egyptians compounded various raw materials (some imported) to produce perfumes, creams, and lotions. Rouges and lipsticks (red ochre), bath oils, and teeth-cleaning abrasives were used by the upper classes of both sexes. Among these materials were almond, olive, and sesame oils, thyme, oregano, rosewater, saffron, myrrh, frankincense, and spikenard, an aromatic plant imported from India. The ancient Egyptian word for the scent of a perfume was always combined in a form meaning "fragrance of the gods," implying a religious function. Many cosmetic materials used throughout the Middle East began as adjuncts to religious rites before becoming, so to speak, secularized.

STUDY QUESTIONS

1. What does "gift of the Nile" mean? What did the Nile "give" that the Tigris and Euphrates rivers failed to provide? Why? NOTE: Some Study Questions in this book require the use of other sources, particularly those listed in the bibliographies.
2. If environment influences mythology, as it indeed does, how might this apply to the Egyptian pantheon? Why, for example, were Amon-Re and Osiris two of the most important gods?
3. What is a theocracy? Explain how Egyptian government functioned. Why was the Nile so crucial to the concept of a theocratic state?
4. What does jewelry tell us about a culture? Using supplemental sources, consider several pieces of jewelry from the Old, Middle, and New Kingdoms. How do they differ? What do they have in common?

NEW KINGDOM (EMPIRE), 1570–1085 BC, DYNASTIES XVIII–XX

The disruption that ended the Middle Kingdom was more serious and more protracted than that of the earlier Intermediate Period. This was the Second Intermediate Period (1780–1550 BC, dynasties XIII–XVII), marked by the invasion of the Hyksos (Egyptian, "rulers of foreign lands"). These Syro-Palestinians unwittingly set the stage for the emergence of the Egyptian Empire. Though little is known about Hyksos domination, it appears that they introduced the horse and war chariot to their hostile hosts and that the culture was stable despite the belligerent Egyptian reaction. The greatest damage was psychological because the Hyksos were barbarian intruders who wounded Egyptian pride, but who acted also as a catalyst, spurring eighteenth-dynasty rulers to imperial conquests.

At first the New Kingdom pharaohs were neither land-hungry nor bound for glory. Detesting anything foreign, especially alien domination, they first occupied adjoining areas in order to create buffers against hostile incursions. Later—human nature being what it is—conquest became an end in itself, enlarging pharaonic power and glory and producing a bonanza of additional taxes.

Government in the New Kingdom was even more autocratic than it had been in the Old Kingdom. Military might rather than national unity formed the basis for the rule of the pharaoh, a title now associated with the ruler's person. ("Pharaoh" means "great house," a term originally applied to the king's court and residence.) Local authority declined to its lowest level, leaving the pharaoh with consolidated control over an expanding empire.

Temples and Worship

Egyptian temples were the first structures in the ancient world to be built entirely of stone and the first to exploit the **post and lintel construction** that other cultures had used on a small scale. Their imposing, thickly columned temples were visual symbols of the wealth of the pharaohs and the power of the gods, not to mention the authority of the priests who served the gods. The Temple of Amon at Karnak (fig. 2.11) was the seat of the throne of Amon and the center of religious administration. The view is of the main entrance, which was approached from the Nile and then through the avenue of ram-headed sphinxes (fig. 2.12) to Pylon I, thus following the solar path of Amon-Re. With 134 massive columns in the Great Hall alone, this was the most extensive temple in Egypt and one of the largest sanctuaries in the ancient world.

As symbols of divine and royal authority, Egyptian temples were usually built on the flat banks of the Nile, the eternal source of Egyptian power. Constructed below limestone cliffs at Thebes on the west bank of the Nile, the

2.11 Avenue of the Rams and Temple of Amon, Karnak.
New Kingdom, dating from the 20th century BC but
constructed mainly from the 16th to 12th centuries BC.
Photo: Spectrum, London.

2.12 Ram-headed sphinxes, Temple of Amon, Karnak.
Photo: Spectrum, London.

2.17 *Above* Portrait head of Queen Nefretete. New Kingdom, 18th Dynasty. Ca. 1370 BC. Painted limestone, height 20" (50.8 cm). Staatliche Museen, Berlin. Photo: Hirmer, Munich.

incredible haste, not to mention expense. Financing was made possible only by pouring all the nation's resources into the coffers of the king and his god.[5]

Akhenaten's death signaled a sea change. What prompted this to happen so rapidly

> was doubtless the chaos caused by the economic consequences of Akhenaten's religious reforms that brought about a complete reversal to the old order as soon as he was dead. The recollection of the misery of such times was strong enough to bring upon him the odium of later generations.[6]

The naturalistic Amarna style ended with the reign of Akhenaten's son-in-law Tutankhamen (toot-ahng-KAH-mun; 1347–1338 BC). Though he was a minor king, ruling for only nine years, his tomb contained a marvelous array of treasures. Discovered in 1922, the collection was relatively intact, making "King Tut" a household name. Figure 2.18 reveals a richly colored scene of the young king and his wife. The loose-limbed figures are portrayed in an intimate setting with a certain sweetness that was unusual in the Amarna style. The presence of the sun disk at the top is puzzling; Amon-Re was supposedly restored by this time.

The Golden Coffin of Tutankhamen (fig. 2.19) is perhaps the most famous and justly acclaimed creation of the art of goldsmithing, one of an ensemble of coffins that totaled about 450 pounds (204 kg) of gold. The cover of the coffin is a sensitive portrait of a youthful king who was about nineteen when he died. In figures 2.17, 2.18, and 2.19 one sees clear evidence of the grace and beauty so characteristic of the Amarna style.

The artistic backlash against the Amarna Period was strong and, given Akhenaten's unpopularity, predictable. The reaction skipped the New Kingdom's ornamental style and the Middle Kingdom classic style, moving back twelve centuries to the static formal style of the Old Kingdom. The style then remained about the same until the gradual decline of Egyptian power after 1085 BC. Falling, in succession, to the Cushites, Assyria, Persia, and Alexander the Great, Egypt became, in 30 BC, an important Roman province. The fall from power, however, cannot diminish Egypt's magnificent achievements over an incredible span of 1,600 years. No other people have had a longer or more distinguished record.

2.18 Throne with Tutankhamen and Queen, from the Valley of the Kings, detail of the back. New Kingdom, 18th Dynasty, Late Amarna period. Ca. 1352 BC. Wood plated with gold and silver, inlays of glass paste, ca. 12 × 12" (30.5 × 30.5 cm). Egyptian Museum, Cairo. Photo: Robert Harding, London (Richard Ashworth).

5. I. E. S. Edwards et al., eds, *The Cambridge Ancient History*, 3rd ed., vol. II, part 2 (London: Cambridge University Press, 1970), p. 53.
6. Ibid., p. 54.

2.19 The Golden Coffin of Tutankhamen, from the Valley of the Kings. New Kingdom, 18th Dynasty, Late Amarna period. Ca. 1352 BC. Gold inlaid with carnelian, lapis lazuli, and turquoise. Egyptian Museum, Cairo. Photo: Robert C. Lamm, Scottsdale.

STUDY QUESTIONS

1. Explain the forces that impel a military state to ever more conquests. You should expand your discussion beyond the army and officer corps to include merchants, contractors, those who needed workers, patriots, and so on.
2. For a fascinating term project, see what a selection of historians and Egyptologists have to say about Akhenaten and his innovations.
3. What were the outstanding achievements of Egyptian civilization? What seems admirable? Incomprehensible? What do we owe to its culture?

THE RECENT PAST

Civilizations dating back to 3000 or 4000 BC may seem alien, even peculiar, and not relevant to our world. This apparent remoteness is lessened, however, if we reflect on what we share with the past. Consider, for example, an invention that, given the tens of thousands of years that *Homo sapiens* has roamed this planet, occurred a very short time ago—less than 6,000 years. This is the creation of written language as independently invented by the Mesopotamians, Egyptians, Chinese, and Maya of Central America. Written translatable languages are the common thread connecting such disparate personalities as Hammurabi, Hatshepsut, Confucius, the Buddha, Julius Caesar, Cleopatra, Muhammad, Queen Elizabeth I, William Shakespeare, Abraham Lincoln, and Margaret Thatcher. All use one or more versions of written communication that connects literate cultures throughout recorded history and around the world.

SUMMARY

Egypt was the first national state, the ancient world's most homogeneous society. With only two significant interruptions, her history extended from the first dynasty of about 3100 BC until a final slow decline after the fall of the New Kingdom in 1085 BC. This power, prosperity, and continuity were a direct result of the relative security and consistent agricultural affluence of this "gift of the Nile." Artistic styles evolved a bit but the basic conventions remained the same throughout Egyptian history, prompting Plato to remark that Egyptian art had not changed "in ten thousand years" (*Laws*, 656D–E).

The artistic conventions were perfected during the Old Kingdom (2686–2181 BC): a cubic view of standing or seated rulers that conveyed immutability. This was an expression of the theology that the pharaoh and the state were one: divine and indivisible.

After an era of instability (First Intermediate Period, 2260–2130 BC) the eleventh dynasty established the less autocratic Middle Kingdom (2135–1786 BC). This was the classical period of Egyptian civilization, reflecting new levels of affluence and corresponding artistic achievement, possibly indicating that achievement and affluence are interrelated. Artists continued and refined the creation of fine jewelry, furniture, pottery, and other household items. In their reliefs and paintings, artists pictured their subjects not as they saw them but as they intellectually knew them. The emphasis was still upon the timelessness that characterized Egyptian art but with a new command of elegant line and spacious composition.

The invasion of the Syro-Palestinian Hyksos was a serious and long-lasting blow to Egyptian pride (Second Intermediate Period, 1780–1550 BC). After the seventeenth dynasty expelled the invaders, the eighteenth dynasty of the New Kingdom (1570–1085 BC) began the imperial period with a series of military campaigns designed to prevent any subsequent foreign menace.

Some of the famous surviving buildings were constructed during the imperial (New Kingdom) period. These include the mortuary temple of Queen Hatshepsut, the Temple of Amon at Karnak, and the Temple of Amon-Mut-Khonsu at Luxor.

A daring pharaoh of the eighteenth dynasty introduced a new religion while attempting to eradicate the old religion and depose its priests. Egyptologists still debate the motives of Amenhotep IV, who changed his name to Akhenaten and decreed that the nation would worship one God, Aten the sun disk, whose sole earthly representative was the pharaoh himself. This was the Amarna period, when artistic styles became more naturalistic than at any other time in Egyptian history.

With all revenues funneled into the royal treasury for maintaining the pharaoh and his god and for the new capital of Akhetaten at Tell-el-Amarna, the economic consequences were disastrous. Following his death, the new city was immediately abandoned as the nation returned to its traditional religion. Attempts to eradicate Akhenaten and Aten from Egyptian history had no more success than Akhenaten had had in trying to erase Amon-Re's religion.

The years of declining power after 1085 BC put an end, finally, to several millennia of Egyptian civilization—a record of accomplishments that remains unique in the annals of humankind.

CULTURE AND HUMAN VALUES

Each of the Three Kingdoms can be seen as an extended period of balance. There seem to be just two periods of adjustment: between the Old and Middle Kingdoms and between the Middle and New Kingdoms. Once the nation had a central government, the society was so structured and stable that it could weather almost any disruption, at least until after 1085 BC with the sporadic civil wars and, later, the arrival of foreign invaders.

Egyptian life was generally safer and more pleasant than life in Mesopotamia but the great mass of people functioned as cogs in the splendid state machine. A rigid class structure allowed virtually no social mobility, although under the law there was some equality of treatment despite differences in class. All too often we in the modern era take our freedom and social mobility for granted and thus tend to look critically at an ancient culture as rigid as that of Egypt. This, however, was the most stable society in the ancient Mediterranean world; people knew exactly where they stood in the scheme of things. Further, because of their extensive trade throughout the then known world, the Egyptians knew how much better off they were than any other people. Their land was remarkably productive, their religion was comforting and even inspiring, and their god-king was always on his throne. In both material and spiritual terms this was, for much of its long history, a balanced society, comfortable with itself.

One aspect of Egyptian culture that is of particular interest today is its indifference to the color of a person's skin. There is still some speculation about whether Queen Nefretete, Cleopatra or any other Egyptian was white, brown, or black. We do know that Cleopatra was Greek but, as Egyptologists have repeatedly asserted, there is no way of knowing about the others because skin pigmentation was not a major consideration in that ancient world.

Egyptian cultural achievements were truly monumental and influenced Minoan, Mycenaean, Greek, and Roman civilizations. Further, Egyptian religion had a significant ethical component called *maat*, which translates as a synthesis of four ideas: order, truth, justice, and righteousness. A quality not of people but of the world, *maat* symbolized the established moral order of the universe that functioned as a kind of natural law. Acting in accordance with that natural order encouraged harmony with the gods. For peasants this entailed working hard and honestly; for officials it suggested dealing justly. A concern for *maat* coupled with the highest standard of living in the ancient world helped make Egyptian life cheerful and confident for all and—for the wealthy—wonderfully elegant.

Greece: Birthplace of Western Civilization

Greece

(most dates approximate)

	People and Events	Art and Architecture	Literature	Philosophy and Science
BRONZE AGE **3000–1100 BC**	**3000–2000** Early Helladic (mainland) culture; Early Cycladic culture in Aegean **2000–1700** Mycenaeans enter Greece **2000–1100** Minoan civilization on Crete **1550–1100** Mycenaean civilization **1260–1150** Trojan War	**3000–2000** Helladic and Cycladic figurines **1700–1380** Minoan Late Palace Period: frescoes, pottery, jewelry	**1750–1600** Minoan Linear A script **1600–1100** Minoan-Mycenaean Linear B script	
DARK AGE **1100–900 BC**	**1100–800** Dorian invasions of mainland **1100–950** Ionian migrations to Asia Minor **900–** Dorian migrations to Aegean islands and Asia Minor	**1100–900** Loss of writing		

The Citadel, Mycenae, plan.

	People and Events	Art and Architecture	Literature	Philosophy and Science
GEOMETRIC PERIOD **900–700 BC**	**800** Aristocracies begin to replace kingships **776** First Olympic Games	**900–750** Furniture, textiles, glassware, figurines, but mostly pottery	**750–700** Homer: *Iliad* and *Odyssey*	
ARCHAIC PERIOD **700–480 BC**	**750–550** Colonization by city-states **621** Draco's law code, Athens **600** Coinage introduced **594** Constitutional and economic reforms by Solon of Athens **546–527** Pisistratos: third great reformer in Athens **546** Persian conquest of Greeks in Asia Minor **507** Democratic constitution of Cleisthenes **490** First Persian invasion; Battle of Marathon	**660** First life-size statues **620–500** Attic black-figure pottery **600** Early Doric temples **580–500** *Kouros* and *kore* figures **530–400** Attic red-figure pottery	**700** Hesiod: *Theogony* **600** Sappho: lyric poetry; Aesop: *Fables*	**Thales** 636–546 Ionian philosopher **Anaximander** 610–546 Ionian philosopher **Pythagoras** 582–507 philosopher and mathematician **Herakleitos of Ephesos** 535–475 Ionian philosopher
CLASSICAL PERIOD **480–400 BC**	**480–479** Second Persian invasion; Battles of Thermopylai, Salamis, and Plataea **460–430** Golden Age of Athens (Age of Pericles) **431–404** Peloponnesian War	**490–430** Pheidias, sculptor: Parthenon frieze and metopes **480–470** Severe Style of early classicism: *Critios Boy* and *Delphi Charioteer* **480–407** Myron: *Discobolus* **460** Bronze sculpture of *Poseidon* **447–405** Buildings on Acropolis, Athens: Parthenon, Propylaea, Temple of Athena Nike, Erechtheion **fl. 430** Polykleitos: sculptor and initiator of the "canon"	**Aeschylus** 525–456 dramatist: *Oresteia* **Sophocles** 496–406 dramatist: *Antigone, Oedipus* **Herodotos** 484–425 "father of history" **Euripides** 480–406 dramatist: *Medea, Trojan Women* **Thucydides** 471–399 *History of the Peloponnesian War* **Aristophanes** 450–380 dramatist (Old Comedy): *Lysistrata*	**Empedocles** 495–435 philosopher and scientist **Protagoras** 481–411 sophist **Socrates** 469–399 philosopher and "gadfly of Athens" **Hippocrates** 460–377 physician **Democritos** 460–362 atomic theory **Plato** 427–347 philosopher, writer, and teacher
LATE CLASSICAL PERIOD **400–323 BC**	**395–340** Warfare among Greek leagues **384–322** Demosthenes: Athenian orator and statesman **338** Battle of Chaeronea; Philip of Macedon controls city-states **336–323** Reign and conquests of Alexander the Great	**350** Theatre at Epidauros by Polykleitos the Younger **fl. 340** Praxiteles of Athens, sculptor: *Aphrodite of Knidos* **4th c.** Lysippus, sculptor: *Apoxyomenos*	**Xenophon** 434–355 historian and general	**399** Trial and death of Socrates **387** Plato founds Academy near Athens **Aristotle** 384–322 philosopher and teacher, founded Lyceum in Athens in 335
HELLENISTIC AGE **323–30 BC**	**323–30** Despotism dominant form of government **148** Macedonia becomes Roman province **146** Romans level Corinth **86** Sulla sacks Athens	**230–220** *The Dying Gaul* **190** *Nike of Samothrace* **180** Atlar of Zeus, Pergamon **174** Work begins on Temple of the Olympian Zeus, Athens **120** *Aphrodite of Melos*	**Menander** 342–291 New Comedy dramatist **300** Founding of library at Alexandria	**Epicurus** 342–270 philosopher **Zeno the Stoic** 335–263 **Euclid** fl. 300 mathematician and physicist **Archimedes** 289–212 mathematician **Eratosthenes** 276–195 mathematician and astronomer

CHAPTER 3

The Aegean Heritage, ca. 3000–1100 BC

Historians sometimes refer to the great leap that propelled Western culture forward as the "miracle of Greece." Miracle implies something that can't be explained, but, by examining what these people valued, we can begin to understand their spectacular achievements. They prized individualism, rationalism, justice, beauty, and the pursuit of excellence and thereby created a remarkable civilization.

As we have seen in Egypt and Mesopotamia, climate, topography, and geography shape cultures in particular ways and Greece is no exception. The early Aegean cultures, while important in and of themselves, were also crucial preludes to the rise of Greece. There were three Aegean cultures: the Cycladic (KYE-kla-deek) of the Aegean Islands; the Minoan (mi-NO-un) of Crete; and the Late Helladic of the Mycenaeans (my-se-NEE-uns) on the Greek mainland. All three cultures enjoyed a maritime climate that was apparently more energizing than that of the landlocked agricultural lands of the Middle East. Whether living on the islands or the mainland, the Aegean peoples had solid assets that included sufficient agricultural resources, a temperate maritime climate, and, most important, ready access to the sea. With about 1,000 islands dotting the Aegean, sailors were never out of sight of land (a vital factor in the days of rudimentary navigation); even on the mainland no one was more than a few hours' ride from the sea. Homer's "wine-dark sea" helped shape the destinies of the Aegean cultures and, later, that of classical Greece (map 3.1).

The Greek lands consisted of narrow valleys guarded by steep mountains, slender coastal plains, and the multitude of islands studding the Aegean Sea. There was no single land mass to be controlled, as pharaoh ruled the Nile valley; nor were the Aegean lands subject to the extremes of continental weather that so frequently afflicted Mesopotamia. The sea, for the Aegean people, was a kind of golden bowl that nourished the development of their civilizations. A temperate climate, security against invasion, rich fishing grounds, and multiple highways for trade and travel—the sea provided it all. Frequent voyages to foreign ports exposed sailors, merchants, and tourists to a wide world of different ideas and customs, making these travelers more cosmopolitan than their Near Eastern contemporaries, most of whom never left home.

Several constants seem to run through all cultures. Seaports are, by their nature, urban centers, cities are more open to change than rural areas. This leads to a quite consistent equation: the farther people are from a seacoast, the more resistant they will be to change and new ideas. Conversely, sailors, traders, and other travelers are generally more open to innovative notions and unusual customs than those who habitually stay home, especially farmers. As a consequence, civilizations are shaped mostly by developments in urban living, commerce, trade, and travel. Considering all these factors, it is hardly surprising that Aegean civilizations reached such high levels.

CYCLADIC CULTURE, CA. 3000–2000 BC

In the Aegean Sea north of Crete lies a group of islands called the Cyclades, so-named because they "cycle" around the sacred birthplace of Apollo and his twin sister Artemis. A minor Neolithic culture flourished here, but little remains beyond some remarkable marble idols, if that is what these figures were. Strangely modern, they are characterized by a rectangular angularity and an abstract simplicity. They include heads and, primarily, standing nude female figures, all carved of pristine white Parian marble. Ranging in height from several inches to nearly life-size, these figurines have been found in tombs throughout the Aegean.

Unlike the earliest known sculptures that were bulbous figures with the large belly and swollen breasts of a fertility goddess (see fig. 1.4), most Cycladic sculptures were slim, almost virginal figurines with subtle sexual characteristics (fig. 3.1). All the sculptures have sharply defined noses and traces of pigment outlining the eyes and mouths. The female figurines are delicately made with the arms folded across the midriff. No one knows what these artistic conventions mean because no trace of Cycladic writing survives. But the figures seem to be abstracted versions of the artists' perceptions; they are not portraits but possibly images of the earth goddess of Paleolithic and Neolithic cultures.

Because the Cycladic figures and the entire Minoan and Mycenaean civilizations were discovered during the

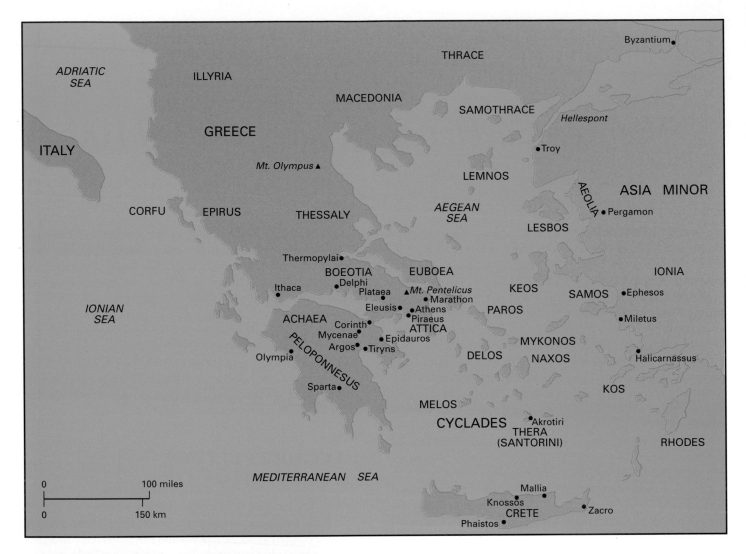

Map 3.1 Ancient Greece.

3.1 Cycladic figurine. Ca. 2500 BC. Marble, 22 × 5¼" × 3¼" (55.9 × 13.3 × 8.3 cm). Seattle Art Museum (Norman and Amelia Davis Classical Collection). Photo: Paul Macapia.

past century or so, we have no way of knowing the full extent of their influence on later Greek culture. We can only suggest that because of their proximity, the intensely curious Greeks knew more about the earlier Aegean civilizations than current evidence indicates.

MINOAN CIVILIZATION, CA. 2600–1100 BC

> One of the great islands of the world in midsea, in the winedark sea, is Krete: spacious and rich and populous, with ninety cities and a mingling of tongues . . . and one among their ninety towns is Knossos. Here lived King Minos whom great Zeus received every ninth year in private council.
>
> Homer, *Odyssey*, Book XIX[1]

The first people who dwelt in Greek lands about whom we have much information were the Minoans, named after the fabled King Minos (MY-nus) who supposedly lived and ruled on the island of Crete. They were probably not truly "Greek"; their language, so far as one can tell, does not seem related to the Indo-Iranian family. (Existing clay tablets in the "Linear A" Minoan script remain undeciphered.) Agrarian people colonized Crete around 6000 BC, very possibly from the culture that produced Çatal Hüyük in Turkey. Minoan culture itself existed from about 2600 till about 1100 BC, and approached its peak around the period 2000 to 1800 BC with the building of the splendid temples at Knossos (KNAWS-us), Phaistos (FEST-os), Mallia (MAH-ya), and Zacro (ZAH-kro).

Although Linear A script remains a mystery we do have considerable knowledge of this culture because of excavations by British archaeologist Arthur Evans (1851–1941) and others. (Active excavations continue at the four temples and other promising sites on Crete and on the island of Thera.) Evans' excavations and reconstructions at Knossos reveal a rich and sophisticated culture that prospered because of a semitropical maritime climate, productive agricultural areas, and, remarkably, an absence of warfare. The Minoans had no traditional enemies and apparently viewed warfare as neither necessary nor desirable. Their trade empire was far more productive than the trophies and territories secured by military aggression. Their ships carried agricultural and manufactured products throughout the eastern Mediterranean and returned to Crete bearing products from many cultures, making them the greatest Mediterranean traders before the Greeks and Phoenicians.

Religion

Minoan religion centered on nature worship, especially the cycle of birth, death, and regeneration that lay at the heart of agricultural societies. The chief deity was an earth goddess derived from peaceful Neolithic societies[2] that lived in what has been characterized as Old Europe.[3] The essential power lay with the queen as the earthly representative of the goddess, the incarnation of the earth mother. Neither a matriarchy nor a patriarchy, this exceptional society is best described as shared responsibilities in a partnership government.

MINOAN WOMEN

According to the available evidence there were no laws or customs in Minoan society that relegated women to subordinate positions. A Minoan wife retained full control of her dowry, which her husband could not use without her permission. Divorce was a right available equally to husband and wife. Further, a wife who proved her husband at fault could reclaim any property given him during the marriage. However, the uniqueness of gender equality in the ancient world is not fully explained by the dominance of the earth goddess. The Minoans were sailors and sailors are usually away from home for long periods of time. What better person to look after their mutual property than the mariner's wife?

A noted architectural historian[4] believes that the consistency of temple orientations and settings confirms the worship of the earth goddess in Minoan society. All major temples are set in enclosed valleys with the north–south axis pointing toward a nearby conical or mounded hill and a more distant notched cleft (saddleback) or a set of double peaks. The paired mountains can be seen as breasts and the saddleback as the female cleft. Visible at all sites, this orientation is particularly noticeable at Knossos and Mallia.

Temples

Until recently archaeologists agreed, more or less, with Sir Arthur Evans, prime excavator at Knossos, that he had uncovered a royal palace and that major buildings at other sites were also palaces. Current best evidence suggests that

1. Robert Fitzgerald, trans. (Garden City, New York: Anchor Books, 1963).
2. Riane Eisler, *The Chalice and the Blade: Our History, Our Future* (San Francisco: Harper & Row, 1987).
3. Marja Gimbutas, *Goddesses and Gods of Old Europe* (Berkeley: University of California Press, 1982). There are about 3,000 Neolithic sites in southeastern Europe and islands of the Aegean and Adriatic seas, some dating back to around 7500 BC. These peaceful agricultural societies apparently influenced Aegean civilizations in the Cyclades, Crete, and Lesbos.
4. Vincent Scully, *The Earth, The Temple, and the Gods* (New Haven, Conn.: Yale University Press, 1979).

3.2   Customs House, Knossos labyrinth, Crete. Labyrinth first constructed in 1930 BC. Abandoned after a fire in 1380 BC. Photo: Scala, Florence.

3.3   Floor plan of the Knossos labyrinth, Crete (after Reynold Higgins).

these buildings were temples and that Evans had made his initial mistake by believing what Homer had to say about King Minos in Book XIX of the *Odyssey*, which is quoted above. Schliemann had found Troy by studying Homer but the poet (and persistent Greek legends) laid a false trail to ancient Crete. There may have been a king, or a king and a queen, but no one knows for sure. No palaces have yet been found but some rooms in the huge temples could have been royal residences.

Unlike, say, Egyptian sanctuaries, Minoan temples were three- to five-story structures that had hundreds of small rooms, rambling corridors and staircases, walls gaily decorated with colorful **murals**, running water, bathtubs, flush toilets, sewage systems, terraces, open galleries, and many light wells that conveyed natural illumination to lower levels. The temples may have functioned not only as religious centers but also as administrative centers for the far-flung trade empire.

Probably the most important temple was the Knossos Labyrinth (fig. 3.2), the vastness of which can only be hinted at in Evans' partial reconstruction. The building

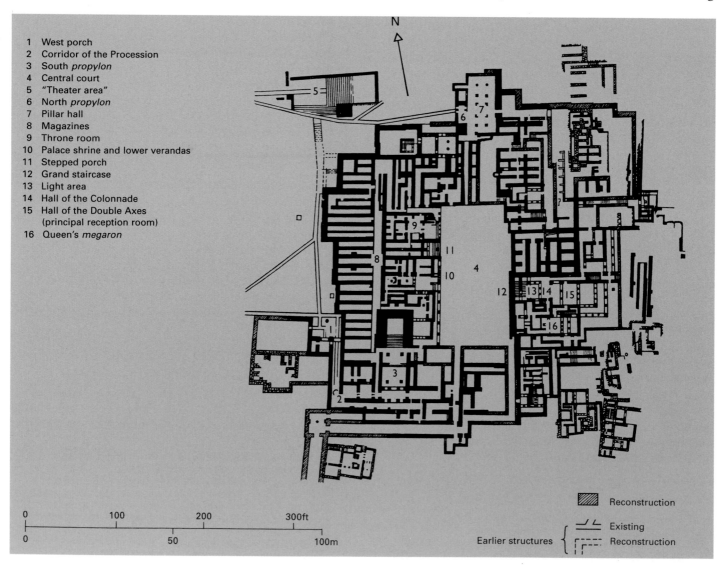

1 West porch
2 Corridor of the Procession
3 South *propylon*
4 Central court
5 "Theater area"
6 North *propylon*
7 Pillar hall
8 Magazines
9 Throne room
10 Palace shrine and lower verandas
11 Stepped porch
12 Grand staircase
13 Light area
14 Hall of the Colonnade
15 Hall of the Double Axes
    (principal reception room)
16 Queen's *megaron*

N

Reconstruction

Existing

Earlier structures { Reconstruction

0   100   200   300ft
0   50   100m

3.4 Throne Room, Knossos labyrinth, Crete. Photo: Ancient Art & Architecture, London.

illustrated stands at the northern end of the palace; Evans called it the Customs House because it was possibly the main checkpoint for visitors arriving by sea 4 miles (6.4 km) to the north. The flaring columns are of wood and apparently symbolized tree trunks. The multiple levels, wandering corridors, and countless rooms (fig. 3.3) possibly inspired the Greek legend of the labyrinth of Minos that was guarded by the fearful Minotaur (half man, half bull—the result of the queen's impregnation by a bull). After Queen Pasiphaë (pus-i-FAH-ee) gave birth to the monster, Minos had it imprisoned in the basement of the palace. The earth-shaking roars attributed to the awesome beast were caused, of course, by the earthquakes that periodically racked Crete.

What Evans called the Throne Room of Minos (fig. 3.4) is a small chamber at ground level containing a simple, high-backed alabaster throne with stone benches around three walls (including the wall with the throne). The fanciful griffin mural is a modern reconstruction based on fragments found in the ruins. A **colonnade** opposite the throne separates this room from an open **atrium** that adds fresh air and light to the intimate and unpretentious setting. Given the female orientation of the religion and the relative equality of the sexes, it is far from certain that a king occupied the throne; it might have been a queen.

Perhaps they alternated, or conceivably a head priestess or priest was the occupant.

The wall decorations in what Evans called the Queen's Megaron are especially elegant. Legendary friends to all sailors, five dolphins frolic contentedly in a seascape mural (figs. 3.5 and 3.6) painted on wet plaster (**fresco**). Brightly illuminated by a light well, the apartment also features bright blue floral designs on the door frames and an adjoining bathroom complete with a bathtub.

3.5 Queen's Megaron (reconstruction), Knossos labyrinth, Crete. Ca. 1600–1400 BC. Photo: Ancient Art & Architecture, London.

3.6 *Opposite* Queen's Megaron (reconstruction), Knossos labyrinth, detail of fig. 3.5. Photo: Ancient Art & Architecture, London.

Minoan Art

Remarkably different from the arts of Mesopotamia and Egypt, Minoan art emphasizes aspects of agriculture and such reflections of the natural world as representations of animals and insects. The warfare and hunting themes that preoccupied the eastern male-dominant cultures are noticeably absent. The playful themes and depictions of the joys of Minoan life also differ from the generally solemn and often fierce art of the other civilizations. One should remember that the eastern cultures emerged from nomadic forebears who struggled to survive, whereas Minoan culture apparently emerged from a comfortable agrarian base with no evidence of a previous nomadic existence.

A culture without a divine monarch has no compelling need for monumental sculpture and indeed none has been found. But typical of diminutive Minoan sculpture is the so-called *Snake Goddess* (fig. 3.7), whether she was a priestess, goddess, or queen. The statue probably relates to goddess worship, for the serpent is a major image in Minoan religion, symbolizing regeneration. Though the rigid frontal pose of this miniature figure suggests an Egyptian influence, the raised arms and the animal on her head (a panther?) help make the mood light and playful. Characteristic of feminine attire at the time, the colorful tiered skirt, tight bodice, and bared breasts appear, to our eyes, very worldly for what is apparently a cult figure.

By about 2400 BC the Minoans had mastered the art of goldsmithing. Gold had always been used in making jewelry because it does not oxidize nor can fire consume it. Further, it is rare (therefore precious), malleable, and, above all, beautiful. One of the most celebrated Minoan creations is the Gold Bee Pendant (fig. 3.8). Two bees are symmetrically placed on opposite sides of a circular honeycomb, leaving a drop of honey on it. Particularly notable is the delicate granulation: minute spherical grains of gold soldered to the gold background. The ancient method left no visible solder between the grains and the gold surface, a sophisticated technology that was not rediscovered until this century. It should be noted that Minoan artisans used magnifying glasses to achieve the fine details in their jewelry and intricate seal stones.

Another Minoan site, Akrotiri, on the island of Thera, was first explored in the 1860s while pumice was being quarried for use in building the Suez Canal and has been extensively excavated since 1967. Buried under ash from a volcanic eruption, this is the Minoan equivalent of Pompeii, a wealthy city with a high standard of living comparable

CIVILIZED LIVING IN INDIA

From about 2500 BC, the Indus city of Mohenjo-Daro had the first known main sewage system to which every house in the city was connected. Brick-lined pipes carried sewage from each home into covered channels that ran along the centers of the main streets to disposal points well away from the city. The sewers took waste from kitchens and bathrooms with indoor toilets. The main drains even had removable covers at crucial inspection points where efficient operation of the system was monitored. The later Minoans and Romans had efficient sewers but not until the seventeenth century (thousands of years later!) did European cities begin using comparable sewage systems.

3.7 *Snake Goddess*, from Knossos labyrinth, Crete. Ca. 1600 BC. Faience, height 17½" (44.5 cm). Archaeological Museum, Heraklion, Crete. Photo: Dagli Orti, Paris.

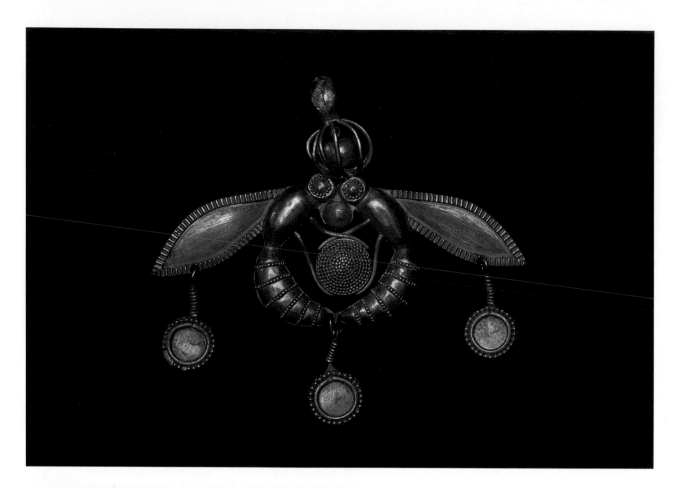

A KILLER VOLCANO

Seventy-five miles (120 km) north of Crete on the island of Thera, a large volcano about 10 miles (16 km) in diameter and possibly 4,500 feet (1,372 m) high erupted violently, covering the island with pumice to a depth of 13 feet (4 m). After minor activity for thirty years, the volcano erupted again in an explosion that was undoubtedly heard throughout the Mediterranean and that buried Akrotiri and the rest of the island under ash over 200 feet (61 m) deep. During this final eruption such massive quantities of pumice, ash, and rocks were ejected that the volcano's cone collapsed into the exhausted magma chamber below. The sea rushed into the fiercely hot caldera, leading to the final calamity, the tsunami that raced outward from the caldera at a probable height of 300 to 400 feet (90–120 m). Because most Minoan settlements were on Crete's northern and eastern shores, virtually the entire culture was washed away by the massive wave. Thera's destruction has traditionally been dated at around 1500 BC but recent studies contradict this. Information from radiocarbon dating of plant remains on Thera, aberrations in the world dendrochronological (tree ring) record, and volcanic debris buried in Greenland's ice suggest that 1628 BC is a more accurate date.[5]

to anything in Crete. The fresco of the *Antelopes* (fig. 3.9), for example, is similar in style and quality to frescoes found at Knossos.[6] The broad sinuous ribbons that outline the bodies give the illusion of being enameled areas in an elegant cloisonné. The contrast of rhythmic curves with open interior space sets up a masterful mobile tension that is both fluid and artful.

The excavations on Thera also contribute to the much-debated theory that this was the legendary Atlantis. According to Plato, the end came with "violent earthquakes and floods; in a single day and night of misfortune . . . the island of Atlantis disappeared in the depths of the sea."[7]

The Minoans rebuilt after the Thera disaster but possibly around 1450 BC the Mycenaeans, a rugged warrior race from the mainland, invaded Crete. With the power of Crete broken the Mycenaean Greeks became the overlords of the Aegean world.

5. According to the *New Grolier Multimedia Encyclopedia*, a 1994 CD-ROM. The earlier date requires reevaluations of all Minoan and Mycenaean chronology. That some of Thera's ash was found in Greenland attests to the magnitude of an eruption that may have been greater than the Krakatoa explosion on 27 August 1883.

3.9 *Antelopes*, from Thera, Greece. Ca. 1500 BC. Fresco, height 8'2½" (2.5 m). National Archaeological Museum, Athens.

MYCENAEAN CIVILIZATION, CA. 1600–1110 BC

From about 1900 BC on tribes from northern Europe had slowly been infiltrating Greece. By about 1600 the invaders had occupied all of the Greek mainland, including the large land mass known as the Peloponnesus (pel-uh-puh-NEES-us) where, at Mycenae, their Great King established his fortified palace. These were warlike people who inevitably came into contact with the Minoans. Their conquest of Crete, however, was more like an occupation in which the invader absorbed much of Minoan culture, though it did replace the Linear A Minoan script with Linear B. In 1953 archaeologist Michael Ventris deciphered the clay tablets in Linear B, proving that the Mycenaeans were true Greeks who spoke a Greek language and worshiped the Greek pantheon of sky gods. The Minoan earth goddess was de-emphasized but continued in Greek mythology as Demeter (de-MEE-ter) and Persephone (per-SEPH-o-nee), enduring symbols of the cyclical regeneration of nature. This male-dominant society created the heritage that was to unite the Hellenes (HEL-uh-neez), as the Greeks called themselves, for it was the Mycenaeans who fought the Trojan War that centuries later became the subject of the Homeric epic poems and the core of the Hellenic tradition.

6. The ongoing excavations at Akrotiri confirm to a considerable degree what some critics called the "highly speculative" nature of the reconstructions of Sir Arthur Evans at Knossos.
7. Most of Thera vanished into the sea leaving behind three very small island remnants.

Homeric Poems

Before them now arose Lord Agamemnon, holding the staff Hephaistos fashioned once and took pains fashioning: it was a gift from him to the son of Kronos, lordly Zeus, who gave it to the bright pathfinder, Hermes. Hermes handed it on in turn to Pelops, famous charioteer, Pelops to Atreus, and Atreus gave it to the sheepherder Thyestes, he to Agamemnon, king and lord of many islands, of all Argos.

Homer, *Iliad*, Book II[8]

Until little more than a century ago much of what anyone knew of the Aegean world was contained in some Greek myths and in Homer's supposedly fictional *Iliad* and *Odyssey*. Helen of Troy, Achilles, Agamemnon, Mycenae, and Troy itself were, according to the experts, figments of Homer's fertile imagination. Then, in 1871, Heinrich Schliemann (1822–90), a wealthy German merchant-cum-archaeologist, startled the world when he announced the discovery of Troy in northwest Turkey, just where his meticulous study of the *Iliad* indicated it should be. He later located what he thought was the palace of Agamemnon at Mycenae and uncovered a wealth of art treasures in and around Mycenae.

The Mycenaeans established themselves in small independent kingdoms with each king occupying a strongly fortified but richly decorated palace. Each ruled through officials who supervised the farmlands, collected taxes in produce, managed religious celebrations, and otherwise acted as the king's deputy. Although all kings were equal they did owe some allegiance to the Great King at Mycenae. As seen in the *Iliad*, a local ruler could challenge the high king—as Achilles (ah-KILL-eez) did with Agamemnon (ag-a-MEM-non)—and not be disciplined or forced to follow the ruler.

Mycenaean trade was mainly between the Greek islands and Asia Minor though Mycenaean influence extended throughout the Mediterranean world. Gold, ivory, textiles, and spices were bartered for the local products; the numerous gold ornaments and cups found in the royal tombs at Mycenae and other palaces attest to substantial royal wealth. Though not as rigid as cultures to the east, this was a male-dominant society that esteemed honor and courage, as evidenced in the Homeric poems. For these Greeks, human worth and dignity lay in total self-fulfillment, usually on the battlefield, where their exploits would bring death, perhaps, but instant fame and renown for generations to come as bards recounted their deeds in song and story.

Another much admired aspect of the Greek character (then and now) was the exercise of a cunning and crafty

8. Robert Fitzgerald, trans. (Garden City, New York: Anchor Books, 1975).

intelligence. The wily Odysseus (o-DIS-ee-us) is the supreme example of this quality. Thus, when Odysseus finally won his way home to his kingdom of Ithaca, he put ashore disguised as a beggar. Here Athena (uh-THEE-nuh; see box 4.1) heard his lying tale. Her response was typical of the Greek attitude:

> "What a cunning knave it would take," she said, "to beat you at your tricks! Even a god would be hard put to it.
>
> "And so my stubborn friend, Odysseus the arch-deceiver, with his craving for intrigue, does not propose even in his own country to drop his sharp practice and the lying tales that he loves from the bottom of his heart. But no more of this: we are both adept at chicane. For in the world of men you have no rival as a statesman and orator, while I am preeminent among the gods for invention and resource."

And a few lines later:

> "How like you to be so wary!" said Athena. "And this is why I cannot desert you in your misfortunes: you are so civilized, so intelligent, so self-possessed."

3.10   Lion Gate, citadel at Mycenae, Greece. Ca. 1250 BC. Limestone, height of relief 9' 6" (2.9 m). Photo: Hirmer, Munich.

Perhaps in our time we cannot readily admire a man who was so smoothly deceitful in gaining his own ends; even in classical Greece the playwright Sophocles (SOF-o-kleez) detested these qualities, as he pictured a despicable Odysseus in the drama *Philoctetes* (fil-OK-ti-teez). For the Greeks of the heroic age, however, this was just one more example of self-fulfillment. Odysseus would have been a fool not to have exploited his keen intelligence, not to mention his cunning.

The King's Citadel

The ruined citadel of the Great King at Mycenae was originally a massive structure whose gigantic stones were placed, according to legend, by a mythical race of one-eyed giants called cyclopes (KY-klo-peas). Located on a broad hilltop site backed by a rugged mountain, what remains of the palace is immediately below the mountain peak. Recurring waves of invading Dorians made fortress architecture a necessity on the Greek mainland. This highly efficient citadel has a ceremonial entrance protected by high walls on three sides (fig. 3.10). The lintel of the ponderous gate is topped by a stone relief of two lions, now headless, flanking a Minoan column symbolizing Mycenaean hegemony in Crete.[9]

After astounding archaeologists with his discovery of Mycenaean civilization, Schliemann continued to amaze everyone as he excavated the royal tombs at Mycenae. They were full of precious jewelry, elaborately decorated weapons, and gold death masks, one of which Schliemann attributed to Agamemnon himself (fig. 3.11). It was soon determined, however, that this Mycenaean had predated the Homeric king by several centuries. Realizing that argument was futile, the undaunted German jokingly renamed his Agamemnon "Schulze." Whatever the appropriate name, the mask from Mycenae is a superb example of the highly developed metal craftsmanship called **toreutics** (tuh-RUE-tiks), the hammering of metals into representational form. The death mask (plus weapons and jewelry) represents a Mycenaean adaptation of the Egyptian funeral practice of burying the illustrious dead with items commensurate with their status in life.

The bronze daggers (fig. 3.12) that Schliemann found in the tombs at Mycenae are striking examples of Minoan metalworking technology as used by Mycenaean artisans. One can immediately see how time has corroded the bronze while scarcely affecting the gold, silver, and niello (a black compound of silver, lead, copper, and sulfur). The gold and silver figures were inlaid in a strip of niello and then engraved to make them sharp and crisp. Note how the figures are adapted to the diminishing space. The papyrus

---

9. Though Mycenae ruled the Minoans there was so much cultural interchange that it is impossible to determine exactly how each culture influenced the development of Greek classical civilization.

3.11   Funeral mask from the royal tombs, Mycenae,
Greece. Ca. 1500 BC. Beaten gold, height ca. 12"
(30.5 cm). National Archaeological Museum, Athens.
Photo: Hirmer, Munich.

3.12 *Left*   Bronze dagger: *Archers and Hoplites Hunting Lions*, from Mycenae. *Left, below* Bronze dagger: *Leopard Attacking Ducks in a Pond*, from Mycenae. 16th century BC. Bronze with gold, silver, and niello incrustations, length of each 9⅜" (23.8 cm). National Archaeological Museum, Athens.

STUDY QUESTIONS

1. **a.** Consider the cultures that developed in ancient Mesopotamia, Egypt, and the Greek lands in the Aegean area. (1) In what ways did climate, topography, and geography affect or condition cultural development in each major area? (2) How and why did people in rural areas react differently from those in urban areas? (3) How and why did seaports differ from inland cities? (4) What conclusions can you draw about the three cultures?
   b. Consider the cultures that developed in New England and in the Deep South during the eighteenth and nineteenth centuries. Then, answer questions (1) to (4) as posed above. What are the similarities between American cultural development and that in the ancient world? Are there any differences? Why or why not?
2. Assume that our world has miraculously grown so peaceful that no nation need maintain any armed forces. What might the total Pentagon budget be spent on and how might this affect American society? Be sure also to consider the short- and long-term effects of the elimination of defense contracts.
3. Using supplemental art books, describe the level of sophistication of Minoan jewelry. Now, consider the technology involved in making the Gold Bee Pendant (fig. 3.8) and other pieces. What does their jewelry tell us about Minoan culture? As a comparison, consider current fashions in American jewelry and what they seem to say about our culture?

designs on the bottom dagger suggest an Egyptian influence, perhaps by way of Crete.

Mycenaean dominance ended sometime around 1200 to 1000 BC but no one knows what brought about the downfall of the Mycenaean world. Whatever happened, the Mycenaean heroes had completed their turn on the stage of history but were later immortalized in the Homeric sagas of the *Iliad* and the *Odyssey*, probably the two greatest epic poems in Western history.

SUMMARY

The Greeks absorbed much of the cultural heritage of Mesopotamia and Egypt while also drawing upon the indigenous cultures of the Aegean civilizations: the Cycladic, Minoan, and Mycenaean. Little is known about the Cycladic civilization except for the abstract sculptures that have survived and imply a form of goddess worship. The Minoans, however, have been extensively documented as a prosperous and

enterprising people who operated the greatest trade empire of their age. Elegant and refined, their culture formed a firm basis for the flowering of Western culture.

The Mycenaeans, conquerors of the Minoans, were a warrior race descended from migrating Dorian tribes that infiltrated from the north. The apex of their civilization was reached with the Trojan expedition of about 1260 BC. Whatever brought down the Great King and his subordinate rulers, posterity inherited the remains of Mycenaean culture and their heroic age as immortalized by Homer.

CULTURE AND HUMAN VALUES

Not enough is known of Cycladic culture to justify any speculation about its cultural evolution but the Minoans have been studied in great detail for over a century. The period of balance of their high civilization lasted, it would appear, from about 2000 to about 1628 BC, when a volcanic eruption devastated their civilization. They may have rebuilt but the Mycenaean invasion of 1450 BC (?) finished it off. There followed a period of adjustment as the Minoans tried to adapt to Mycenaean rule.

The predominant characteristic of Minoan culture was that a good life of security, peace, and possessions was available to much of the population. The economy supported a high standard of living, partly because funds were not diverted to support a standing army. The Minoans built a stable empire based not on military conquest but on peaceful commerce. Vigorous trade also helped in the development of a middle class of artisans and merchants, thus reinforcing political and economic stability. One cannot say enough about the higher quality of life in a society that did not consider warfare a necessary instrument of national policy. Perhaps most importantly, Minoan civilization flowered because of the earth goddess religion and the resulting relative equality of the sexes. Rather than emphasizing such nomadic virtues as strength and courage, the Minoans created a peaceful, joyous, and elegant culture celebrating the pleasures of gracious living.

The period of balance of Mycenaean civilization seems to have begun shortly after the occupation of Crete in about 1450 BC. This was both the high point of Mycenaean culture and, ironically, the beginning of its decline and fall. They had compromised their integrity and honor (the Trojan horse) in the quest for victory at Troy. The price was too high.

For the inhabitants of the Mycenaean city-states ultimate reality was the heroic life—and death—of the noble warrior. An ethical man told the truth, was as good as his word, and kept the faith with king and comrades. First and foremost, he was always prepared to make the ultimate sacrifice, to die fighting for a noble cause, as did Achilles, Hector, and many another warrior.

One can examine the heroic age in several different ways: the actual time period; the Homeric epics; and the view from Athens of the Golden Age. The heroic ideal was something espoused by a noble warrior-aristocrat; Achilles, with all his faults, was the personification of the heroic ideal.

Homer composed the *Iliad* between 750 and 700 BC, nearly four centuries after the Trojan campaign. As with many events of the distant past, time heals, and violence is often romanticized as necessary in the service of a noble cause. (American Civil War buffs, for example, seem to revel in romantic fantasies about Bull Run, Shiloh, and other bloody battlegrounds.) The pain and horror of the Trojan War had faded away; only the heroic ideals were left and no one could better celebrate the valiant heroes of a fabled past than the blind poet.

By the time of the Athenian Golden Age— ca. 460–430 BC—another four centuries had passed and the Trojan adventure was twice removed. Homer and the *Iliad* had become romanticized. (Small wonder that nineteenth-century scholars considered the Trojan campaign the stuff of dreams.) The Athenians accorded the Mycenaean heroes their just due without, however, endorsing war (Ares, the god of war, was never treated as anything other than an inhuman outcast). Odysseus and his comrades were seen as imposing figures of the Hellenic past; they had earned admiration but no one expected emulation.

CHAPTER 4

Early Greece: Preparation for the Good Life

Life in the Greece of the fifth century BC, particularly in Athens, developed a quality that has seldom if ever been equaled. For the first time—and most gloriously—citizens flourished in a political system that allowed individuals the greatest possible freedom compatible with the coherence of the social group. Here, too, there was enough wealth and leisure to allow individuals to develop their capabilities to the fullest. Further, this was a highly competitive society that challenged its people to pursue excellence and willingly honored superior accomplishments.

This chapter traces the development of Greek society from its beginnings to around 480 BC. The focus is necessarily on Athens, where the highest achievements took place and where ideas generated throughout Greece were vigorously discussed and disputed in the marketplace. This was a lively, highly verbal, even brawling culture in which flourished some of the finest flowers of Western civilization.

Let it be said at the outset that there never was, in the ancient world, a nation called Greece. But the people who called themselves Hellenes were united by a common language, religion, and heritage. They lived in independent city-states, each with its own form of government. These states, unlike Mesopotamia or Egypt, were not confined to one geographical location. The mainland of Greece (see map 3.1) forms the tip of the Balkan Peninsula and is joined by a narrow isthmus to a large land mass known as the Peloponnesus. This is the Greek heartland. When Dorian tribes invaded from the north between about 1100 and 800 BC, many mainland Ionians fled to the Aegean Sea's Asian coast and the coastal islands to form a flourishing Greek cultural center. This became known as the Ionian coast that eventually caused the Persian Empire so much grief. Later, in the seventh and sixth centuries BC, land poverty on the mainland encouraged many city-states to send out colonists to develop new lands. As a result, Greek cities were formed from Byzantium (bi-ZANT-e-um; then Constantinople; now Istanbul), to western Mediterranean shores. Important cities included Syracuse in Sicily, Sybaris and Paestum in Italy, and Marseilles in France. Although widely dispersed and frequently at war with each other, the people of these cities shared a common culture (heritage, religion, language) that gave them a sense of kinship as Hellenes. The Hellenes felt that they were different from and better than the "barbarians" (which means non-Greeks), a belief that created unity amid the vast diversity and a pride that helped lead to the remarkable accomplishments of the people known as the Greeks.

THE GEOGRAPHY OF MAINLAND GREECE

The Aegean islands had a relatively benign climate but the mainland was a harder country in which to live. Mountain ranges divided the area, making communication across the countryside extremely difficult; further, the mountains were so eroded that little farmland was available. There were broad and fertile plains in the north but a shorter growing season than in the warmer, sunnier south, where sheep and goats grazed on the mountain slopes and bee-culture was common. The valleys between the mountains offered small plots of arable land on which grew the chief crops of olives and grapes. It was in these valleys that the first villages appeared that would later merge to become city-states.

The climate was milder than that of Mesopotamia but it was not conducive to easy living. Great winter storms roared down from the north bringing torrential rains and, on the mountain peaks, a good deal of snow. Summers were hot and dry but tempered by the ever present sea, which was basic to Greek life. Major cities such as Athens, Argos, and Corinth were seaports and no city, not even Sparta, was far from the sea.

All these factors contributed to the Greek character. People in a hard land must be ingenious and clever to survive. When nature yields little, people must manufacture objects to make a living. Unlike other civilizations, Greek city-states had more artisans and artists than peasants. Finally, the proximity of the sea offered a livelihood for sailors and traders (and pirates). Commerce always

---

Opposite Cossutius, Temple of the Olympian Zeus, Athens. Ca. 174 BC–AD 131. Pentelic marble. Photo: Spectrum, London.

broadens horizons because traders barter not only goods and services but ideas they can carry home. One cannot attribute the character of people to geography and climate alone, yet these factors certainly contributed to the Hellenic personality.

GREEK RELIGION IN THE HEROIC AGE

The worship of the Olympian gods was a complex and fascinating religion. At its most straightforward the religion used mythical gods and goddesses to explain natural forces—for example Poseidon (po-SIDE-on), who controlled the storms that stirred the seas and the quakes that shook the land. At a higher level the Olympians symbolized the most complex of human drives and aspirations—for example Athena, goddess of wisdom and civilized living who represented life lived as an art form (fig. 4.1).

Their religion illustrates a prime Greek characteristic: a special ability to deal with information on both a literal and an abstract level. Zeus was as abstract as the power principle he represented, but he was also the irrepressible seducer of mortal women. Aphrodite symbolized all of love's aspects from love of beauty to maternal love to the joys of erotic love, but her amorous adventures competed with those of Zeus.

This religion had no "revealer," divine or mortal: no Christ, Muhammad, or Buddha. Nor was there a sacred book such as the Talmud, Bible, or Koran. The religion evolved primarily as a collection of myths honored in various ways throughout the Greek world. Consistently imaginative, the myths varied greatly, so that no single version of the history and nature of the gods exists. Hesiod (HEE-see-ud; fl. 8th century BC) in his *Theogony* (thee-OG-uh-nee) had limited success in systematizing the story of the gods. The truth is, Greek religion—all Greek mythology—was probably the most creative collection of mythic literature that the world has ever known.

Vastly simplified, the genealogy is as follows:

> In the beginning was Chaos, composed of void, mass, and darkness. From Chaos emerged a god, Ouranos (YOOR-uh-noss), representing the heavens, and Gaea (JEE–ah), a goddess who represented earth. Among their offspring were the Titans, who personified earthquakes and other earthly cataclysms. Kronos (KRO-nos), a Titan, led a revolt that overthrew his father and took his sister Rhea (REE-uh), also an earth goddess, as his wife. From this union, though not without difficulty, emerged the Olympian gods. The difficulty was that Kronos knew of a prophecy that one of his children would overthrow him; to prevent this, he swallowed all his progeny at birth (Kronos may be thought of as Time that swallows all things). Rhea saved Zeus from being ingested and

> spirited him away to Crete where he grew to manhood. Zeus then led the prophesied revolt and, aided by some Titans, imprisoned his father in the dark cave of Tartarus, but not before Kronos had regurgitated the other children: Demeter (di-MEET-er), Hera (HAY-ra), Hades (also called Pluto), Poseidon, and Hestia. Zeus then took Hera as his wife and from this union arose such gods and goddesses as Apollo, Aphrodite, and Artemis (box 4.1).

Stories about the immortals offer a fascinating range of subjects. We see Zeus pursuing an infinite variety of mortal women; some gods drank copiously and all quarreled constantly among themselves; they had favorites among the mortals, as we saw Athena protecting Odysseus; and everyone used dirty tricks to foil each other's designs for the success of their favorites. How could one revere such an assembly?

Understanding this religion is the key to understanding the Greek character, and particularly their passion for living life to the fullest. Significantly, the Greeks created the gods in their own image. Emphasizing this, Xenophanes of Colophon (zuh-NOFF-uh-neas; 6th century BC) maintained that if oxen, horses, and lions had hands and could paint like men, they would paint their gods as, respectively, oxen, horses, and lions. Black people would worship black gods and Thracians would believe in gods with blue eyes and red hair.

The gods were regarded as a race infinitely superior to human beings in that they were completely powerful, immortal, and always young and beautiful; they had the same characteristics as humans, but in a higher category. If people sometimes showed wisdom and nobility, so did Athena or Apollo (uh-POL-o), but to a vastly superior degree. If mortals were sometimes lustful, Zeus was much more so and, with his power, far more successful. If people were skilled artisans, so was Hephaistos (hay-FYCE-toss); if humans were crafty and skillful, so was Prometheus (pro-MEE-thee-us)—but the skill, wisdom, lust, or whatever quality one may choose of the gods was infinitely beyond that of mortals. Death was a dark oblivion for the Greeks but the gods had life forever, and life in boundless beauty, vigorous youth, and absolute power.

The Gods' Symbolic Roles

Before reviewing actual religious practices, we should consider the symbolic roles of the gods. Representing the power principle, Zeus is amoral, just as power is amoral. At the opposite extreme is Hera, goddess of marriage and domestic order, constantly striving to control and civilize a force that deals in thunderbolts. Athena and Apollo represent the Greek ideals of the arts of civilization and the beauty of intellect. Aphrodite was enthusiastically worshiped by a civilization that viewed the erotic arts as a healthy component of the good life. Superior craftsmanship was also

4.1 "Varvakeion statuette" of Athena, from Athens. 2nd
century AD. Height (including base) 3' 5⅜" (1.05m).
Acropolis Museum, Athens. Photo: Alison Frantz, Princeton.
The helmet and crest-holders are sphinx and pegasi.

highly valued as attested to by the importance of Hephaistos, an artisan elevated to the status of a god. The Greeks even had a god—Hermes—for their peripatetic world of travel, commerce, and trade (and thievery).

Throughout Greek history Ares never received a kind word. He represented violence and destruction and thus had no redeeming virtues. Dionysos, the god of ecstasy, is particularly important and peculiarly Greek. Espousing the virtues of rationality and the life of reason, the Greeks were acutely aware and deeply respectful of the non-rational aspect of humankind. These deep, surging drives had to be understood, acknowledged, and treated with deference.

The Greeks did not distinguish between nature and human nature, believing that nature's laws governed both the physical universe and the moral universe. All mortals and even the gods were subject to what the Greeks called *ananke* (uh–NAHN–key; "what has to be"). This idea of a universal power that is also personal has both a scientific and a religious quality.

The worship of these gods during Mycenaean times and later may help clarify these religious practices, for the formal ceremonies were always feasts. Animals were sacrificed, and part of the meat was burnt upon the fire. The rest was roasted and eaten by those performing the sacrifice. Wine was drunk, with a certain amount poured out first as a libation to the gods. Then the feast proceeded, with the assumption that the god was present as a guest at the meal, and that he or she enjoyed such things as much as mortals.

BOX 4.1   THE GREEK PANTHEON

Zeus and his two brothers seized power from Kronos (Saturn) to originate "The Twelve," the Olympians who figure most prominently in Greek life. (The names in parentheses are Roman but these are only approximations since Greeks and Romans had entirely different attitudes toward their respective gods, and toward most everything else for that matter.)

Zeus (Jupiter, Jove). Leader, god of the thunderbolt, representative of the power principle and womanizer.

Hera (Juno). Long-suffering wife of Zeus, goddess of marriage and domestic stability.

Poseidon (Neptune). God of the sea and earthshaker (earthquakes).

Demeter (Ceres). Sister of Zeus and goddess of agriculture. Mother of Persephone and fertility symbol.

Hades (Pluto, Dis). God of the underworld. Connected with nature myth by his marriage to Persephone who spends half her time on earth (the growing season) and half in the underworld (fall and winter). Thanatos represents death itself.

Pallas Athena (Minerva). Goddess of wisdom, warfare, arts and crafts. Sprang fully-armed from the brow of Zeus. Patron goddess of Athens, representing the art of civilized living.

Phoibos Apollo (Sol). Son of Zeus and Leto, daughter of the Titans Krios and Phoebe. Sun god, archer, musician, god of truth, light, and healing. Represents principle of intellectual beauty.

Artemis (Diana, Cynthia). Sister of Apollo; virgin goddess of the moon and the hunt.

Aphrodite (Venus). Goddess of love and physical beauty. According to one version she was the daughter of Zeus and Dione; an alternate mythic version has her rising from the waves à la Botticelli.

Hephaistos (Vulcan). Lame blacksmith god who made armor for heroes, forged the thunderbolts of Zeus. Much-deceived husband of Aphrodite.

Hermes (Mercury). Son of Zeus and Maia, daughter of Atlas. Messenger and general handyman of Zeus. God of commerce, traders, travelers, and thieves.

Ares (Mars). Son of Zeus and Hera. God of war.

Hestia (Vesta). Virgin sister of Zeus and goddess of hearth and home. Later replaced among the Twelve by Dionysos.

Dionysos (Bacchus). Son of Zeus and mortal woman Semele. Connected, like Demeter, with the principle of fertility and, like Persephone, represented the nature myth by dying in the autumn and being reborn in the spring. The Eleusinian Mysteries were dedicated to all three fertility deities and the festivals of Dionysos were periods of wild, Bacchic rejoicing: scheduled orgies so to speak. Since plays were usually performed at these festivals Dionysos also became god of the **theatre.** He embodies the ecstatic principle as contrasted with the intellectual principle represented by Apollo.

LESSER OLYMPIANS

Eros (Cupid). Eternal child of Aphrodite and Hephaistos. Spirit of love with darts.

Pan (Pan). Son of Hermes, woodland god with goatlike horns and hoofs. Player of the pipes (panpipes).

A Humanistic Culture

There is one further aspect of this religion that was critical in the development of human values; there was no permanent priesthood nor even a priestly class. The Hellenes, unlike the Egyptians, were never subject to priestly dos and don'ts. To us their religious practices seem unstructured, almost casual; there was certainly room for freedom of thought. We will see later that in political organization the Greeks were not oppressed by despots, or at least not for very long. Thus in both religion and politics the Greeks maintained the widest possible latitude for thought, questioning, and experimentation, which, though turbulent and unstable, produced superb humanistic values.

The local variants were many but the general principles of the Olympian religion were practiced throughout ancient Greece. There were always some doubts among the intellectuals but the common people believed in the gods and in the oracles that were consulted for important state decisions. That Apollo's priestess at Delphi or another seer's answers were riddles subject to several interpretations did not shake people's faith in the oracles themselves.

In this bewildering interrelationship of gods and people, what determined an individual's fate? As before, we must rely on Homer, who wrote centuries after the Heroic Age and was himself none too certain of the answer. It was vaguely believed that each person, each hero, had his own *moira* (MOY–ruh), or pattern of life, which he would fulfill. This may be seen as a jigsaw puzzle that the

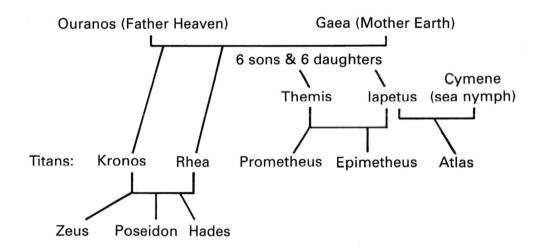

Nemesis. Avenging goddess, the principle of retribution.

Hebe. Goddess of youth and cupbearer to the gods.

Iris. Goddess of the rainbow and sometimes messenger of the gods.

Hymen. Son of Aphrodite and Dionysos; god of the marriage festival.

The Three Graces: Aglaia (Splendor), *Euphrosyne* (Mirth), and *Thalia* (Good Cheer). Embodied the principle of the happy life and always represented as a unit, which is a clear indication of the Greek version of the happy life.

The Nine Muses. Spirits of learning and of the arts. *Clio* (History), *Ourania* (Astronomy), *Melpomene* (Tragedy), *Thalia* (Comedy), *Terpsichore* (Dance), *Calliope* (Epic Poetry), *Erato* (Love Poetry), *Polyhymnia* (Sacred Poetry), and *Euterpe* (Lyric Poetry).

The Erinyes (Furies): *Tisiphone, Megaera* and *Alecto.* Represented pangs of conscience; relentlessly hounded wrongdoers.

The Three Fates allotted to each his/her destiny. *Clotho* spun the thread of life. *Lachesis* wove it into a pattern that determined the kind of life that would be led. *Atropos* cut the thread, terminating existence.

hero's life would piece together, with this complication: the individual never knew what the finished picture would be nor even when it was completed.

Within each person's life there were the three forces of free will, accident, and divine intervention. These worked together—or sometimes in opposition—to determine the course of a person's life, and nothing was ever certain until death finished the picture. (This problem is considered in detail in Sophocles' *Oedipus the King*; see pp. 96–7 and 117–34.) The gods frequently punished anyone whose overweening pride led them to exceed human limits and aim for the realm of the gods. Such *hubris* (HOO–bris) almost certainly brought doom. The gods were not omnipotent, however, because there was a force even more powerful than the gods called *ananke*, "what has to be," or natural law.

4.2   Portrait bust of Homer. Ca. 150 BC. Roman copy, marble. National Archaeological Museum, Naples. Photo: Hirmer, Munich.
Certainly not a likeness, this is an idealized version of how a divinely inspired blind poet should look.

For the most part, in the Heroic Age, a person's character was his or her fate. The people accepted the consequences of what they did because of the kind of person they were. Thus Achilles, despite attempts to outwit his predicted fate, lived his brief life gloriously because he valued personal honor and fame. Odysseus, on the other hand, enjoyed a long and productive life as a daring warrior and as a shrewd and wily Greek with the wit to talk, deceive, and survive.

THE ARCHAIC PERIOD, CA. 750–500 BC

As discussed in the preceding chapter, Mycenaean culture began its decline in the twelfth century BC with the arrival of Dorian invaders from the north. Of the same racial stock as the Mycenaeans, the Dorians were forced south to the Greek mainland because of invasions of their own homeland. The invasions upset everything and produced a long "dark ages" with little cultural development. By the eighth century BC these dark ages moved almost imperceptibly into the Archaic (ar-KAY-ic) times of historic Greece, a period quite well known through Hesiod's poems, *Works and Days*. A farmer in Boeotia, Hesiod once won a poetry contest but apparently knew little else but bad luck. He describes a life of endless tasks with little reward and no future plus a landed aristocracy whose chief occupation was squeezing the small farmer. Justice, so called, was dispensed by these **patricians**, who generally rendered decisions based on the largest bribe. Always reverent toward the gods, Hesiod neither expected nor received either reward or justice, and his plight was the common lot of most of his compatriots.

Homer, too, composed his epic poems during the latter part of the eighth century. Hesiod described his own life and times but Homer's work celebrated the distant glories of the heroic Mycenaeans. We know little about Homer the poet and even less about the man himself (fig. 4.2). Computer analysis confirms that a single poet, whom we call Homer, was the *Iliad*'s composer. Analysis of the adventure tale that is the *Odyssey* is less conclusive, though Homer is the probable poet. Authorship, however, is not the issue. These poems are at the very heart of the Greek heritage. Greek ideals, the idea of superiority over the barbarians, and the overwhelming desire for personal honor were embodied in these works, which came as close to a central religious text as the Greeks ever possessed. Memorized by every student, they were sung and recited at the festivals and games throughout the Hellenic world. The stories were not Homer's inventions but a collection of legends that originated in the songs and recitations of generations of bards and were brought together and transformed into epic tales by the sure hand of a literary genius. The *Iliad* and the *Odyssey* would invigorate and inspire the Greek mind.

Economic and Political Changes

But to return to Hesiod's troubled times. The first problem was the landed aristocracy who, by force and guile, appropriated land from the poor farmers. Lending the farmer money was the most efficient way of acquiring land because the farmer had to use his own person to secure the loan. Failure to pay the debt forfeited his land and the farmer became a slave. But the greatest problem was land poverty, meaning not enough land to support the population.

The inspired solution to land poverty was colonization, with city-states exporting bands of adventurers to found Greek colonies throughout the Mediterranean. The ensuing expansion of the Greek world led to increasing trade among all the Hellenic cities and a swelling flow of wealth into the mother cities. A key factor in the vertical ascent of the lower classes was the large surplus of goods created by Greek artisans. By producing far more goods than they needed the Greeks enlarged their economy and gained leisure time for other pursuits: gymnastics, education, philosophic-scientific investigations, discussions in the **agora**. Trade and manufacturing enabled a prosperous and influential commercial class to emerge as a major factor in urban life. In a city controlled by the aristocracy, farmers were powerless but the new commercial class became a political force to reckon with.

The rise of *tyrants* marked the first of a series of political changes. For us the term suggests a harsh military dictator but among the Hellenes it was just another word for "king." The tyrant seized power and established himself as absolute ruler as long as he could hold office. Maintaining authority required the support of a majority of the population, which he gained with political, judicial, or economic reforms that ensured his continuing popularity. (Unpopular tyrants were sometimes murdered or exiled.) Tyrannical rule thus led, paradoxically, to the early reforms that eventually steered Athens and other cities toward democracy.

THE RISE OF ATHENS

From here on we focus on political developments in Athens, destined to become the most glorious of Greek cities, and where the most significant changes were made under four reformers. Sixth-century Athens had a curious power structure. Determined largely by economic status, three factions waged an unequal battle for power. In descending order of influence, they were the landed aristocracy, the growing commercial class, and the poor farmers eking out a living on marginal land. The political mix was made more complex by four family-clans, originally of the aristocracy, who controlled the individual lives of their members and dominated the city's politics. So long as these four tribes remained powerful their traditions would govern political and economic affairs.

The Reformers

The legendary Draco (DRAY–ko; fl. 621 BC) was the first of the reformers, an early tyrant and publisher of a monumental step toward freedom: the first Greek code of laws. Hesiod and others had complained that only the aristocratic judges knew the laws and that they seemed to make up the rules as they went along. An ordinary citizen involved in litigation was at the mercy of the judges, who generally rendered decisions according to the litigant's economic status, family connections, and the size of the proffered bribe. Draco's Code, though very severe (many crimes were punishable by death), did offer a single standard of justice for all people and, because the law was published, people could know their legal rights. No matter how harsh the laws, their publication was a momentous step toward the development of a rational system of justice devoid of class and privilege.

The second reformer was Solon (SO-lon; ca. 640–558 BC) whose name has become a synonym for a wise lawgiver. A member of the nobility, like Draco, he had traveled extensively and was, moreover, intensely interested in the commercial ventures of the rising middle class. Painfully aware of land distribution injustices and the cruelty of debt-slavery, his first reform freed all slaves who had failed to redeem their land. A man who sought moderation in all things, he was pressured to break up the great estates and distribute the land to the farmers, but he didn't have enough faith in the uneducated masses to take this drastic step. He did, however, encourage everyone to become involved in political affairs. He limited the important governmental offices to the upper classes of aristocrats and merchants but allowed members of the lower class to serve as jurors. Though not as glamorous as public office, jury duty helped educate people in the mechanism of social action. He greatly broadened civic responsibilities by establishing an administrative Council of Four Hundred. Shrewdly anticipating conservative resistance to change and liberal proclivities for tinkering, Solon stipulated that all reforms must remain unchanged and in force for ten years.

Solon encouraged trade and commerce by adopting a much lighter coinage. He also imported skilled artisans, particularly potters, since pottery manufacture was a major industry and a prime export. With his reforms Athens broke away from an economic dependence upon agriculture and evolved into a city whose wealth was generated by manufactured objects independent of natural forces.

Solon was both a pragmatic reformer and, being Greek, an idealist who could foresee the enormous benefits that a just government could bring to Athenian citizens. In the following poem (many Greeks wrote poetry, even politicians) he reviews past injustices caused by bad government and concludes with a vision of what good government could be—and should be.

THE MILKMAID AND HER PAIL

A farmer's daughter had been out to milk the cows, and was returning to the dairy carrying her pail of milk on her head. As she walked along, she fell to musing after this fashion: "The milk in this pail will provide me with cream, which I will make into butter and sell in the market. With the money I will buy some eggs and these, when hatched, will produce chickens, and by and by I shall have a large poultry yard. Then I shall sell some of my fowls and with the money I will buy myself a new gown, which I shall wear to the fair, and all the young men will admire, and want to make love to me. But I shall toss my head and have nothing to say to them." Forgetting all about the pail, and suiting the action to the word, the milk was spilled, and all her fine castles in the air vanished in a moment!

> Do not count your chickens
> before they are hatched.

Aesop, *Fable*, sixth century BC

Samuel Croxall translated the *Fables* in 1722, adding the moral at that time. Aesop's fables have been used to teach ethics, wit, and common sense in schools and other places for 2,500 years.

This city of ours will never be destroyed by the
 planning
  of Zeus, nor according to the wish of the
  immortal gods;
such is she who, great-hearted, mightily
  fathered, protects us,
  Pallas Athena, whose hands are stretched out
  over our heads.
But the citizens themselves in their wildness are
  bent on destruction
  of their great city, and money is the
  compulsive cause.
The leaders of the people are evil-minded. The
  next stage
  will be great suffering, recompense for their
  violent acts,
for they do not know enough to restrain their
  greed and apportion
  orderly shares for all as if at a decorous feast.   10

  They are tempted into unrighteous acts and
  grow rich.

  Sparing the property neither of the public nor
  of the gods,
they go on stealing, by force or deception, each
  from the other,

nor do the solemn commitments of Justice
  keep them in check;
but she knows well, though silent, what happens
  and what has been happening.
  And in her time she returns to extract a full
  revenge;
for it comes upon the entire city as a wound
  beyond healing,
  and quickly it happens that foul slavery is the
  result,
and slavery wakens internal strife, and sleeping
  warfare,
  and this again destroys many in the prime of
  their youth,   20
for from enemies' devising our much-adored city
  is afflicted
  before long by conspiracies so dear to wicked
  men.
Such evils are churning in the home country, but
  of the impoverished,
  many have made their way abroad onto alien
  soil,
sold away, and shamefully going in chains of
  slavery . . .

Thus the public Ruin invades the house of each
  citizen,
  and the courtyard doors no longer have
  strength to keep it away,
  but it overlaps the lofty wall, and though a
  man runs in
  and tries to hide in chamber or closet, it
  ferrets him out.
So my spirit dictates to me: I must tell the
  Athenians   30
  how many evils a city suffers from Bad
  Government,
and how Good Government displays all neatness
  and order,
  and many times she must put shackles on the
  breakers of laws.
She levels rough places, stops Glut and Greed,
  takes the force from Violence;
  she dries up the growing flowers of Despair
  as they grow;
she straightens out crooked judgements given,
  gentles the swollen
  ambitions, and puts an end to acts of
  divisional strife;
she stills the gall of wearisome Hate, and under
  her influence
  all life among mankind is harmonious and
  does well.[1]

1. Richard Lattimore, trans., *Greek Lyrics*, 2nd ed. (Chicago: University of Chicago Press, 1960), p. 46.

Pisistratos (pi-SIS-truh-toss; ca. 605–527 BC), who governed Athens from 546 till his death, was the third reformer. Surpassing Solon's economic reforms, he dismembered the large estates and distributed land to the almost landless peasants. Because economic status usually decided voting privileges and government participation, this single reform broadened the political base and allowed people, already involved in social action by Solon's changes, to assume a larger role in governing the state. He and his sons further increased employment by initiating some great public works, but Pisistratos' most important contribution was his advancement of artistic life. He imported Simonides and Anacreon, two of the finest Hellenic poet-musicians of the time, and commissioned the first scholarly edition of Homer's poems, which may have been the reformer's single greatest contribution. As citizens learned these poems and heard them recited at public functions they gained a sense of common heritage and a feeling of unity *as citizens of Athens*, not as members of a particular family clan. The tyrants of Athens, consciously or unconsciously, were leading the people toward democracy and, by educating them through increased responsibility, making them ready for active participation in a democratic society.

A Democratic Government

Democracy became a reality with the reforms of Cleisthenes (KLICE-the-neez; fl. 507 BC), who sharply curtailed the influence of the four aristocratic tribes who had long dominated Athenian politics. He created ten new "tribes" with membership based on place of residence rather than heredity. First dividing the city into *demes* (neighborhoods), he created artificial units as the basis of a new political structure. Selected at random, the demes were composed of neighborhoods of the shore (people connected with shipping and seafaring trades), the city itself, and the outlying rural areas. No tribe was dominated by any one economic group because the ten tribes that comprised the city-state were themselves a product of the new demes.

With fifty members representing each of the new political tribes, Cleisthenes replaced Solon's Council of Four Hundred with a Council of Five Hundred. The old council had become the voice of the four traditional tribes and Cleisthenes was determined to break their grip on government. Each artificial tribe in the new government nominated a large slate of candidates for the Council from which fifty were then selected by lot, on the theory that any citizen who was nominated—the nomination process eliminated the obviously unfit—was as capable as any other citizen of administering affairs of state. The executive branch of the government consisted of a committee of ten generals elected yearly by the Council and headed by a commander-in-chief, also elected for one year.

Political freedom was something the Athenians had to get used to. When ruled by a despot most people adjust, turn inward, just survive. One of the greatest defects of any tyranny (out of a very long list) is that it stifles not only dissent but productivity and creativity as well. Freedom offers challenge and opportunity; despotism is denial. Herodotos succinctly described what happened in a democratic Athens:

> And it is plain enough that freedom is an excellent thing; since even the Athenians, who, while they continued under the rule of tyrants, were not a whit more valiant than any of their neighbors, no sooner shook off the yoke than they became decidedly the first of all.
>
> *Histories*, V

HERODOTOS, THE "FATHER OF HISTORY"

Much of what we know about the Mediterranean area and the Persian wars is derived from the *Histories* of Greek historian Herodotos. Concerned primarily with the enmity between East and West from about 550 to 479 BC, he wrote in lively detail about the lands, peoples, religions, customs, geography, and history of the Persian Empire and of the Mediterranean peoples. He interviewed witnesses to historic events (and their descendants, as necessary), combining these with extensive visits to many lands to produce a work of insight and wit. His fascinating narrative ends with the Greek victories over the Persians at Salamis and Plataea in 480 and 479 BC that ensured the survival of freedom in the Western world.

Persian Invasions

While Athens was developing its political institutions the mighty Persian Empire was becoming increasingly irritated with the rebellious Greek cities in Asia Minor. Athens supported the Ionian Greeks in their refusal to pay tribute to Darius (da-RYE-us), the Persian king, which gave him all the excuse a despot needs to give rebels a lesson in power and the upstart Athenian democracy some instruction in humility. A pivotal date for the future of Western culture, 490 BC was when the Persians invaded mainland Greece. North of Athens, on the plain of Marathon, the mighty army of a totalitarian state faced a badly outnumbered Athenian force. Led by General Miltiades (mil-TIE-uh-deez), the Greeks, like the wily Odysseus, outwitted the Persians and in a stunning dawn attack drove the humiliated Persians back into their ships. Herodotos reported that the Persians lost more than 6,000 men with only minimal Greek casualties. Free people had turned back the Asian hordes and changed the course of history. Phidippides (fi-DIP-i-deez), the messenger who ran the 22 plus miles (35 km) from Marathon to Athens, symbolized more than news of an incredible victory. Greek pride in Hellenism, in the superiority of their culture over that of the "barbarians," was fully corroborated.

While the vengeful Persians prepared a second invasion the Athenians mined the newly discovered silver deposits at Mount Laurium in Attica that greatly enriched the treasury. Themistocles (the-MIS-tuh-kleez), the Athenian commander-in-chief, sent a delegation to Delphi to ask the Oracle how to combat the Persians and was told by the priestess that they should protect themselves with "wooden walls." Themistocles felt that Athens must defend itself with a strong navy, so, about as wily as Odysseus, he convinced his compatriots that the "wooden walls" were ships. Consequently, the rich silver mines helped build a strong Athenian navy, which became a triumphant military force and the catalyst that turned Athens into a mighty commercial center.

The Persian invasion of 480 was massive. Herodotos estimated the Persian forces at 5,000,000 men—an obvious exaggeration but indicative of the awesome size of the invading horde. Closely attended by a huge navy, the Persian army marched south to the first great engagement, the battle at the pass of Thermopylai (Ther-MOP-a-lye), a Persian victory, but a glorious episode in Greek history. Here, at a narrow pass between the mountains and the sea, 300 soldiers from Sparta (a military state now allied with Athens) under their king, Leonidas (lee-ON-uh-dus), faced the entire Persian army and fought magnificently. When the Spartans were told to surrender or archers would darken the sky with arrows, Leonidas calmly replied that the Spartans would therefore fight in the shade. As often happened in Greek wars, they were betrayed by a traitor who showed the Persians an alternative route through the mountains. The Spartans were surrounded, but, even in the face of such odds, they fought on until all were killed. The inscription later carved on the tomb of the heroic Spartans, in tremendous understatement and compression of meaning, testifies to the spirit of the encounter:

> Go tell the Spartans, thou that passest by,
> That here, obedient to their laws, we lie.
>
> Simonides of Keos

Meanwhile, the Persian fleet sailing down the coast in support of the army had suffered defeats from both Greeks and storms, but it still overwhelmingly outnumbered the ships of Athens and its allies. The Persians sailed to the Bay of Salamis (SAL-a-mise) near Athens while the army moved inexorably toward its goal of sacking that city. Themistocles abandoned the city and all of Attica, moved everyone to the island of Salamis, and gambled everything on a single naval battle. By trickery he enticed the Persian fleet into the Bay of Salamis, where the fleet's very size was a disadvantage; narrow waters made it impossible to maneuver so many ships. Superior Greek sailors in their faster ships taught the Persians a lesson in naval warfare they would never forget. The victory was total. The land war

dragged on for another year, ending with a decisive Spartan victory at the Battle of Plataea (pla-TEE-uh), and the Persian threat was no more.

Greek pride in these victories cannot be overstated. At the time, Persia controlled Egypt, the entire eastern end of the Mediterranean Sea, and all the land as far east as India. Yet a relatively few Greek men, poverty-stricken in comparison to the Persians, had beaten off the totalitarian enemy. The Greeks rightly felt that their cherished freedom, the glory of their honor, and the love they felt for their cities had been decisive factors, as indeed they were. Although the old aristocratic, **oligarchical** party continued to be a force in Athens, the years following the Persian wars marked the complete triumph of democracy in Athens. Suddenly the idea of freedom had worked.

For us in the Western world those ancient wars are monumental landmarks, for the Greek tradition—principally the concept of the worth of the individual— flourished, giving form and substance to the ideas we now hold as of greatest significance. If the Greeks had failed, today's Western world might be a very different place.

GREEK THOUGHT

Systematic speculation about the nature of the universe was a Greek innovation. The Egyptians had made astronomical observations to predict such events as the spring floods upon which their agriculture depended. Babylonian astrologers had studied the stars and made pseudo-scientific predictions about earthly affairs. But pure thought about the nature of things was uniquely Greek. The freedom to think was due, in part, to the loose and relatively non-authoritarian character of a religion that had no mandatory creeds or dogmas and no priestly class.

> It was the Greeks who first conceived a universe something like that we envision today. Their ideas were characterized by a lively skepticism. Once, for example, when Herodotos made a tour of Egypt, he was shown a temple in which priests put out food for the god every night. The food was always gone in the morning, a fact which they presented to Herodotos as proof of the god's existence. "I saw no god," he commented, "but I saw many rats around the base of the statue." It's hard not to like someone who thinks like him.[2]

Further, philosophy is a rational and very personal activity that is perhaps best accomplished in a clearheaded society that cherishes such values as individualism, justice, beauty, and truth.

---

2. Trefil, James, *The Dark Side of the Universe; A Scientist Explores the Cosmos* (New York: Macmillan, 1988), p. 10.

There were other civilizations long before them and contemporary with them, far richer and grander; but only the Greeks *thought*, thought hard and constantly, and thought constantly in human terms. They saw themselves as surrounded on all sides by "barbarians"—which for them meant people who did not live reasonably . . . . Perhaps Nietzsche was right in saying that they felt a constant and terrible pressure of barbarism, not only from around them but from within; and that their civilization was not an effortless growth, but the product of courageous effort sustained by acute tension. They must often have felt like a few sane men living in a world of maniacs and constantly endangered by the infection of madness.[3]

Athenian high civilization was about as flawed as all civilizations have been—and still are. The society that celebrated rationality and high human values was also responsible for the execution of the philosopher Socrates. Its prosperity was built in large part on slavery, but so was that of every Mediterranean society in that faraway world. Nor was there equality of the sexes, again, like most ancient cultures and much of today's world. Male dominance in Athens was at the expense of the women, who were accorded no place at all in the democracy. The women were, however, freeborn and some did assert themselves, as vigorously emphasized by Lysistrata in the comedy bearing her name (see pp. 100 and 134–50). Alone among ancient cultures this society openly pondered its flaws and criticized its achievements.[4]

The Greeks were certainly not the only thinkers, for no one can dispute the importance of the humanistic thought of the Buddha in India, Confucius in China, or countless others in world cultures. Rather, the Greeks thought *systematically* about the cosmos and their relationship to it, which led not only to the invention of philosophy but also to the concurrent invention of pure science, the essence of which is the pursuit of objective knowledge about the world in which we live. This is the significance of the quotation given above from Gilbert Highet; "a few sane men" transformed human society for all time to come.

3. Highet, Gilbert, *Man's Unconquerable Mind* (New York: Columbia University Press, 1954), p. 14.
4. American philosopher Charles Taylor contends that the progression from ancient Greek aristocratic conceptions of politics to a universal respect for human dignity is a progress in understanding that was generated by tensions within the ancient conceptions themselves, with their unarticulated acknowledgment of the humanness of women and slaves. In other words, some Greek intellectuals were aware of the paradoxical nature of Athenian democracy in which one gender participated and the other did not. See Charles Taylor, *Sources of the Self: The Making of the Modern Identity* (Cambridge: Harvard University Press, 1990), p. 106.
5. Benjamin Farrington, *Greek Science* (Baltimore: Penguin Books, 1961), p. 37.

The Ionian Philosophers

The first philosopher-scientists lived in the Ionian city of Miletus (my-LEET-us) where Thales (THAY-leez; ca. 636–546 BC) was their leading thinker. The questions they asked are more important than the answers they found, for the questions are those that constantly return to challenge people's minds. The answers change as our knowledge of the universe expands.

One problem consistently bothered the philosophers of the Ionian (or Milesian) School. They were intrigued by the constant change of everything around them. Soil changed to plant life; plant life changed to animal; wherever they turned they observed movement from one form of existence to another. They postulated that there must be one basic substance accounting for all forms of being, so that the process of change is simply the transformation of the basic element. The first question Thales asked, then, was, What is the single element, the basic stuff of which the universe is composed?

Thales answered that this basic element is water, for all things need water for their existence, and water itself changes to a gas (steam) when heated, or to a solid (ice) when chilled. As these things are true and observable by our relatively coarse sensory equipment, it appeared that all sorts of other changes and transformations that are not sense-apparent could take place in water. Other philosophers, following the line of thought first explored by Thales, argued for earth or air as the basic world-stuff. That his theory was incorrect is not important; it was the question that was critical. In today's world we assume that most people are naturally curious about the universe and everything in it. It is still startling to realize that the Greeks actually invented scientific and philosophical speculation.

The key point is that the Greeks, beginning with Thales, were the first to make informed guesses that were completely **naturalistic** (without reference to supernatural powers). One of the Babylonian creation myths, for example, stated that the world was once all water and that the god Marduk then made a rush mat and piled dirt beside it to construct the dry lands.

> What Thales did was leave Marduk out. He, too, said that everything was once water. But he thought that the earth and everything else had been formed out of water by a natural process, like the silting up of the Delta of the Nile. It is an admirable beginning, the whole point of which is that it gathers into a coherent picture some observed facts *without letting Marduk in.*[5]

A follower of Hippocrates (hy-POK-ra-teas; 460–377 BC), the Greek physician, wrote of the mysterious ailment known as epilepsy (then termed the divine malady):

> It seems to me that the disease is no more divine than any other. It has a natural cause, just as other diseases have. Men think it divine merely because they do not understand it. But if they called everything divine

which they do not understand, why, there would be no end of divine things.[6]

Another Ionian, Anaximander (a-NAKS-uh-man-der; ca. 611–547 BC), a student of Thales, posed the second important question: How do specific things emerge from the basic element? His answer, though seemingly unsatisfactory and vague, is probably more scientifically accurate than those of many of his contemporaries or successors. He rejected physical substances such as water, earth, or air, and simply labeled his basic stuff "the Boundless." This, he suggested, was a form of being we cannot perceive with our senses; that is, it permeates everything and surrounds everything. In specific answer to the question he raised, he asserted that all forms that we can see—trees, living animals, all specific things—are formed by "separating out" of this boundless element. Thus all forms that our senses can know, all physical things, simply congeal out of the non-sense-apparent "boundless" and eventually lose their form and disappear back into it.

Herakleitos (Hair-uh-KLY-toss; ca. 535–475 BC), a later philosopher-scientist from Ephesos on the Ionian coast, extended the speculation of Thales and Anaximander by asking a third major question: What guides the process of change? He granted a basic element from which all particular forms emerged, but he felt there must be some sort of controlling force to keep the process of universal change orderly so that, for example, an elm tree always produces elm trees rather than crocodiles.

A MATTER OF HONOR

Shortly after the battle of Thermopylai

There came now a few deserters from Arcadia to join the Persians—poor men who had nothing to live on and were in want of employment. The Persians brought them into the king's presence, and there inquired of them, by a man who acted as their spokesman, what the Greeks were doing. The Arcadians answered, "They are holding the Olympic games, seeing the athletic sports and the chariot races." "And what," said the man, "is the prize for which they contend?" "An olive-wreath," returned the others,"which is given to the man who wins." Hearing the men say that the prize was not money but a wreath of olive, . . . Tritantaechmes could not forbear from exclaiming before them all, "Good heavens, [General] Mardonius, what manner of men are these against whom you have brought us to fight—men who contend with one another, not for money, but for honor!"

Herodotos, *The Persian Wars*, VIII:26

Herakleitos denied the possibility of *being*, for he felt that the universe was not static but in a process of flow. His basic belief was that nothing *is*; everything is *becoming*. Thus his famous statement that one cannot step into the same river twice. The appearance of the river may be "the same," whatever that may mean, but by the time one has pulled a foot out of the river and immediately plunged it back in, the water has changed, the bank has changed—nothing is exactly the same. The universe, said Herakleitos, was not created in time but existing from all eternity and is ever in flux. Between *now* and *now* it has flowed, changed, varied; it is no longer what it was even though it may seem the same.

Perhaps to illustrate this contention, he chose fire as his basic element. One may watch a blaze in a fireplace for half an hour and say to a companion, "I have been watching that same flame for thirty minutes." Though the flame may seem constant, the burning gas that is the flame is never the same, even for a microsecond. This is the universe envisioned by Herakleitos.

But such a universe needs a guiding force, for the mind finds it perplexing to live with an image of an ever-changing world without some order and direction. So Herakleitos proposed a great **logos** as the guiding force. *Logos* in Greek sometimes means "word."[7] Thus in the Bible the Gospel according to John, originally written in Greek, starts with the sentence, "In the beginning was the Word"—*logos* in Greek. But for John (see pp. 307–8), as for Herakleitos, it obviously had a greater significance than our "word." For Herakleitos it meant, in part, a great Intelligence that permeated the world and somehow guided the constant change of the flame-like element of which all things were composed. This sense of all things "knowing" what shapes they should take, what forms they should assume, is one of the great mysteries of the universe. (How does each maple leaf differ from every other maple leaf in the world, yet take a characteristic shape that can be identified at a glance? How does it "know" the form it must take?)

Herakleitos' theory of a universe ruled by *logos* also concerns the human ordering of the continuously changing world as people think and talk about it. In this sense *logos* can be translated as "reason" or "rational discourse." Nature and *logos* are often deemed one and the same, but Herakleitos' *logos* represents nature's overall rational structure and not the whole of the natural order. For not all natural creatures have reason (*logos*) within them. That cows cannot chat rationally about the universe is only one of many possible examples.

---

6. Farrington, p. 81.
7. *Logos* comes from the root of the Greek verb *lego*, "to say." Its earliest meaning was "connected discourse," but its other (later) meanings included: "argument," "proportion," "reason," "portion," and "rational discourse."

Ionian thought seems reasonable enough in its attempts to explain the element that is One and yet so many, which seems to be always the same and yet so varied. However, the fundamental postulate is one of constant change and, furthermore, all the conclusions reached are based on the testimony of the five senses. We see, hear, taste, feel, or smell the phenomena of the world and the changing nature of all things. The search for a basic element from which it is all made is essentially a quest for "That Which Is Real."

But we can take an entirely different tack in this quest. We can declare, for example, that whatever is real cannot always be changing. The mind can equate permanence with reality and reason that only permanent, unchanging things are real. Furthermore, one can easily prove that our senses cannot be trusted. We know they give us varying reports about the "same" thing. For example, water at a specific temperature as measured by a thermometer will be either "hot" or "cold" depending on the temperature of our hands when touching the water. Perhaps only the "thought process," independent of the senses, can be trusted as a guide to truth. Here is the difference between scientists—people who trust their senses as they can be refined through such instruments as they can make—and pure philosophers, those who depend solely on their minds to lead them to truth. This distinction appeared early in Greek thought.

Pythagoras

Pythagoras (ca. 582–507 BC) was one of the most original and engaging Greek philosophers (fig. 4.3). An Ionian Greek from the island of Samos, he was most influential in Magna Graecia (southern Italy), where he established a religious brotherhood in Crotona. Pythagoras taught that "number" was the essence of all things, in the same sense that other philosophers saw ultimate reality as water, the boundless, or fire. He believed that number was more than symbolic, that all matter was essentially numerical, and that all relationships in the universe could be expressed through number. The first Greek philosopher to reject the geocentric theory that the sun revolved around the earth, Pythagoras relegated the earth to the status of a planet that revolved around the fixed point of a central fire.

In his search for "that which is most real," Pythagoras kept returning to the universality of mathematical relationships. Most famous now is the formula in plane geometry called the Pythagorean theorem: in right-angle triangles the square of the hypotenuse is equal to the sum of the square of the other two sides. Although the triangles can be dissimilar in appearance, one fact about them is true: $AB^2 + AC^2 = BC^2$. In Euclidean geometry this relationship was true before it was ever discovered, and it will remain true with no one left to be aware of it. Here is an "idea" that has no substance, that exists entirely apart from

people's minds. In this numerical relationship we have the pattern for a physical thing. Pythagoras is therefore credited with three major accomplishments: the discovery of pure mathematics, the development of mathematical proofs, and the awareness that form and structure give objects individual identities. These achievements provide the framework for the Eleatic philosophers, especially Plato (see pp. 155–81), upon whom Pythagoras was the single most important influence.

The first to demonstrate a correlation between mathematics and the harmonies of music, Pythagoras discovered that vibrating strings had certain fixed relationships depending on their relative lengths. Building on these musical connections, Pythagoras developed his theory of the relationships among the planets. He pictured the heavenly bodies as revolving from east to west in orderly circular orbits around a central fire. There was, he said,

4.3 Bust identified as a portrait of Pythagoras and placed in the Roman Forum in 343 BC. Marble. Museum, Ostia, Italy. Photo: Canali, Brescia.
The identification is probably correct for what we see here is a religious mystic.

an agreement between nature (the planets) and number (the musical intervals). The predictability of nature, like the musical intervals on a vibrating string, was therefore musical and the wheeling arcs of the celestial globes formed the *"harmonia* of the cosmos": the music (or harmony) of the spheres.

Pythagoras was both a speculative and a practical philosopher, applying his ideas to the religious community that he founded at Crotona. Philosophy was central to a religious way of life that was also intellectual, political, and ethical. Small communities functioned within the larger community, each a social and religious unit as well as a scientific study group. Property was held in common, music and mathematics were integral parts of social life, and there was no discrimination according to gender. Pythagoras may have derived his view of sexual equality from the earlier earth goddess religions in Old Europe and from Minoan culture.

If the sexes were deemed equal, who was in charge? Aesara of Lucania (ee-SAHR-uh; fl. 400 BC), a late Pythagorean philosopher, explained the situation in her *Book on Human Nature.* She said that women bore the responsibility for creating *harmonia* (order and justice; "music" is an alternate translation) in the home and men had the same responsibility in the city.

> Just, harmonious cities require their component parts, households, also to be just and harmonious.
> Therefore, social justice depends on women raising just, harmonious individuals in those households. In the Pythagorean view, women are not peripheral to social justice; they make it possible.[8]

To be sure, not many people today would see this as true sexual equality, but it was a substantial improvement upon views in other Greek city-states.

Perhaps the best-known Pythagorean creed is the doctrine of the transmigration of souls. Pythagoreans believed that souls were reincarnated in a series of lives as they struggled to ascend to an ideal existence in a life of divine bliss. One could approach the ideal only through purification, emphasis upon intellectual activity, and renunciation of fleshly pleasures. Salvation was attained only after a final escape from the cycle of intermediate births.

Affirming a brotherhood of all living things, the Pythagoreans believed in spiritual purification through music and science and physical purification through medicine and gymnastics. They advocated a humane society in which people would live always in harmony and friendship. Eventually they were either killed or forced to flee their communes by hostile neighboring tribes who considered them a threat to established religious practices.

---

8. Mary Ellen Waithe, *A History of Women Philosophers; Vol. 1: Ancient Women Philosophers, 600 BC–AD 500* (Boston: Martinus Nijhoff Publishers, 1987), p. 11.

STUDY QUESTIONS

1. For a culture as rich as that of Greece, a time line is both useful and instructive. Create one by assigning each of the following topics a date (sometimes approximate) or bracket of dates. Then arrange them in chronological order. This will provide an outline of Greek history up to the beginning of the Classical Period (480 BC). Finally, explain the significance of each topic as it contributed to the development of Greek civilization.

   a. Reforms of Cleisthenes
   b. Dorian invasions
   c. Persian wars
   d. Mycenaean culture
   e. Traditional date of the Trojan War
   f. Peak of Minoan culture
   g. Homer and Hesiod active
   h. Volcanic eruption on Thera
   i. Solon's reforms
   j. Linear B script
   k. Early Cycladic culture in the Aegean
   l. First Olympic Games
   m. Introduction of coinage

2. Greek religion functioned at about four levels of belief/disbelief:

   a. Olympians believed in literally at face value.
   b. Gods/goddesses seen as representing aspects of the forces of nature.
   c. Gods/goddesses understood as symbolizing abstract ideas such as power, love, intellectuality, civilized living, and fine craftsmanship.
   d. Gods/goddesses believed to have been invented by people, usually in their own image.

   Explain each level and what each might imply about religious beliefs in general. Then consider other religions and whether or not some or all of these levels are relevant to them. You can include, but need not be limited to, Christianity, Islam, Judaism, Hinduism, and Buddhism.

LITERARY SELECTION 2

The Odyssey

Homer (fl. 9th century BC)

"An epic," said Aristotle, "is a poem about men in action." The action in the *Odyssey* is concerned with getting a husband back to his wife and son and a king returned to his throne. The husband/king is Odysseus, the wife Penelope, the son Telemakhos (tuh-LEM-uh-koss), and the kingdom is the island of Ithaca off the west coast of the Greek mainland.

Odysseus spent ten years fighting at Troy and another ten trying to get home. The story of the wanderer's return is divided, as was the previous *Iliad*, into twenty-four books, one for each letter of the Greek alphabet. (No one knows who first made this division; it wasn't Homer.) There are four interior divisions: (1) The Adventures of Telemakhos, (2) The Homecoming of Odysseus, (3) The Great Wanderings, and (4) Odysseus in Ithaca.

Odysseus is the narrator in the third section as he relates his hazardous journey to the underworld (Book XI). This account is probably based on the oldest story that Homer collected; it has much in common with the underworld story in *The Epic of Gilgamesh*.

Just how Odysseus manages to sail to Hades is deliberately vague but, once there, his encounters with the shades are among the most dramatic in this consistently engrossing epic. Much of the poem is about sailing the seas to faraway lands; Book XI, on the other hand, represents movement in time: figures from the past—Elpenor, Teiresias, his mother (recently dead), heroic mothers and grandmothers, famous heroes—Odysseus in the present; Odysseus as he envisions himself in Hades with Heracles, the hero he most resembles.[9] The translation is by Robert Fitzgerald. Names have been kept as in the original translation but more commonly used transliterations are given in brackets at their first appearance.

Book XI

A Gathering of Shades

"We bore down on the ship at the sea's edge
and launched her on the salt immortal sea,
stepping our mast and spar in the black ship;
embarked the ram and ewe and went aboard
in tears, with bitter and sore dread upon us.
But now a breeze came up for us astern—
a canvas-bellying landbreeze, hale shipmate
sent by the singing nymph with sun-bright hair;
so we made fast the braces, took our thwarts,
and let the wind and steersman work the ship   10
with full sail spread all day above our coursing,
till the sun dipped, and all the ways grew dark
upon the fathomless unresting sea.
                    By night
our ship ran onward toward the Ocean's bourne,
the realm and region of the Men of Winter,
hidden in mist and cloud. Never the flaming

eye of Hêlius [Helius][10] lights on those men
at morning, when he climbs the sky of stars,
nor in descending earthward out of heaven;
ruinous night being rove over those wretches.   20
We made the land, put ram and ewe ashore,
and took our way along the Ocean stream
to find the place foretold for us by Kirkê [Circe].
There Perimêdês and Eurýlokhos [Eurylochus]
pinioned the sacred beasts. With my drawn blade
I spaded up the votive pit, and poured
libations round it to the unnumbered dead:
sweet milk and honey, then sweet wine, and last
clear water; and I scattered barley down.
Then I addressed the blurred and breathless dead,   30
vowing to slaughter my best heifer for them
before she calved, at home in Ithaka [Ithaca],
and burn the choice bits on the altar fire;
as for Teirêsias, I swore to sacrifice
a black lamb, handsomest of all our flock.
Thus to assuage the nations of the dead
I pledged these rites, then slashed the lamb and ewe,
letting their black blood stream into the wellpit.
Now the souls gathered, stirring out of Erebos [Erebus],
brides and young men, and men grown old in pain,   40
and tender girls whose hearts were new to grief;
many were there, too, torn by brazen lanceheads,
battle-slain, bearing still their bloody gear.
From every side they came and sought the pit
with rustling cries; and I grew sick with fear.
But presently I gave command to my officers
to flay those sheep the bronze cut down, and make
burnt offerings of flesh to the gods below—
to sovereign Death, to pale Perséphonê.
Meanwhile I crouched with my drawn sword to keep   50
the surging phantoms from the bloody pit
till I should know the presence of Teirêsias.

One shade came first—Elpênor, of our company,
who lay unburied still on the wide earth
as we had left him—dead in Kirkê's hall,
untouched, unmourned, when other cares compelled us.
Now when I saw him there I wept for pity
and called out to him:
                    'How is this, Elpênor,
how could you journey to the western gloom
swifter afoot than I in the black lugger?'   60

He sighed, and answered:[11]
                    'Son of great Laërtês,
Odysseus, master mariner and soldier,
bad luck shadowed me, and no kindly power;
ignoble death I drank with so much wine.
I slept on Kirkê's roof, then could not see

---

9. Virgil's *Aeneid*, the great Roman epic, is consciously based on Homer's poems. In Book VI of the *Aeneid*, Virgil has Aeneas visit the underworld as a kind of sequel to the visit of Odysseus (see pp. 252–61).
10. The sun god who drove a chariot with four horses across the heavens every day.
11. Elpenor could still speak because he had not yet been cremated.

the long steep backward ladder, coming down,
and fell that height. My neck bone, buckled under,
snapped, and my spirit found this well of dark.
Now hear the grace I pray for, in the name
of those back in the world, not here—your wife   70
and father, he who gave you bread in childhood,
and your own child, your only son, Telémakhos
    [Telemachus],
long ago left at home.

            When you make sail
and put these lodgings of dim Death behind,
you will moor ship, I know, upon Aiaia Island;
there, O my lord, remember me, I pray,
do not abandon me unwept, unburied,
to tempt the gods' wrath, while you sail for home;
but fire my corpse, and all the gear I had,
and build a cairn for me above the breakers—   80
an unknown sailor's mark for men to come.
Heap up the mound there, and implant upon it
the oar I pulled in life with my companions.'
He ceased, and I replied:
               'Unhappy spirit,
I promise you the barrow and the burial.'

So we conversed, and grimly, at a distance,
with my long sword between, guarding the blood,
while the faint image of the lad spoke on.
Now came the soul of Antikleía [Anticleia], dead,
my mother, daughter of Autólykos [Autolycus],   90
dead now, though living still when I took ship
for holy Troy. Seeing this ghost I grieved,
but held her off, through pang on pang of tears,
till I should know the presence of Teirêsias.[12]
Soon from the dark that prince of Thebes came forward
bearing a golden staff; and he addressed me:[13]

'Son of Laërtês and the gods of old,
Odysseus, master of land ways and sea ways,
why leave the blazing sun, O man of woe,
to see the cold dead and the joyless region?   100
Stand clear, put up your sword;
let me but taste of blood, I shall speak true.'

At this I stepped aside, and in the scabbard
let my long sword ring home to the pommel silver,
as he bent down to the sombre blood. Then spoke
the prince of those with gift of speech:
                  'Great captain,
a fair wind and the honey lights of home
are all you seek. But anguish lies ahead;
the god who thunders on the land prepares it,
not to be shaken from your track, implacable,   110
in rancor for the son whose eye you blinded.
One narrow strait may take you through his blows:
denial of yourself, restraint of shipmates.

When you make landfall on Thrinakia first
and quit the violet sea, dark on the land
you'll find the grazing herds of Hêlios
by whom all things are seen, all speech is known.[14]
Avoid those kine, hold fast to your intent,
and hard seafaring brings you all to Ithaka.
But if you raid the beeves, I see destruction   120
for ship and crew. Though you survive alone,
bereft of all companions, lost for years,
under strange sail shall you come home, to find
your own house filled with trouble: insolent men
eating your livestock as they court your lady.[15]
Aye, you shall make those men atone in blood!
But after you have dealt out death—in open
combat or by stealth—to all the suitors,
go overland on foot, and take an oar,
until one day you come where men have lived   130
with meat unsalted, never known the sea,
nor seen seagoing ships, with crimson bows
and oars that fledge light hulls for dipping flight.
The spot will soon be plain to you, and I
can tell you how: some passerby will say,
"What winnowing fan is that upon your shoulder?"[16]
Halt, and implant your smooth oar in the turf
and make fair sacrifice to Lord Poseidon:
a ram, a bull, a great buck boar; turn back,
and carry out pure hekatombs at home   140
to all wide heaven's lords, the undying gods,
to each in order. Then a seaborne death
soft as this hand of mist will come upon you
when you are wearied out with rich old age,
your country folk in blessed peace around you.
And all this shall be just as I foretell.'

When he had done, I said at once,
                 'Teirêsias,
my life runs on then as the gods have spun it.
But come, now, tell me this; make this thing clear:
I see my mother's ghost among the dead   150
sitting in silence near the blood. Not once
has she glanced this way toward her son, nor spoken.
Tell me, my lord,
may she in some way come to know my presence?'

To this he answered:
               'I shall make it clear
in a few words and simply. Any dead man
whom you allow to enter where the blood is
will speak to you, and speak the truth; but those
deprived will grow remote again and fade.'

When he had prophesied, Teirêsias' shade   160
retired lordly to the halls of Death;
but I stood fast until my mother stirred,
moving to sip the black blood; then she knew me
and called out sorrowfully to me:
                'Child,
how could you cross alive into this gloom
at the world's end?—No sight for living eyes;
great currents run between, desolate waters,
the Ocean first, where no man goes a journey
without ship's timber under him.
                  Say, now,

---

12. Odysseus denies her blood (giving her the power to speak)
    until he has spoken with Teiresias.
13. Teiresias, the blind seer, knows everything about the past
    and can also predict the future.
14. Because Helios saw everything below him.
15. Here Teiresias foretells the future.
16. The speaker does not recognize an oar for what it is.

is it from Troy, still wandering, after years,   170
that you come here with ship and company?
Have you not gone at all to Ithaka?
Have you not seen your lady in your hall?'
She put these questions, and I answered her:

'Mother, I came here, driven to the land of death
in want of prophecy from Teirêsias' shade;
nor have I yet coasted Akhaia's [Achaea] hills
nor touched my own land, but have had hard roving
since first I joined Lord Agamémnon's host
by sea for Ilion, the wild horse country,   180
to fight the men of Troy.
But come now, tell me this, and tell me clearly,
what was the bane that pinned you down in Death?
Some ravaging long illness, or mild arrows
a-flying down one day from Artemis?
Tell me of Father, tell me of the son
I left behind me; have they still my place,
my honors, or have other men assumed them?
Do they not say that I shall come no more?
And tell me of my wife: how runs her thought,   190
still with her child, still keeping our domains,
or bride again to the best of the Akhaians?'

To this my noble mother quickly answered:
'Still with her child indeed she is, poor heart,
still in your palace hall. Forlorn her nights
and days go by, her life used up in weeping.
But no man takes your honored place. Telémakhos[17]
has care of all your garden plots and fields,
and holds the public honor of a magistrate,
feasting and being feasted. But your father   200
is country bound and comes to town no more.
He owns no bedding, rugs, or fleecy mantles,
but lies down, winter nights, among the slaves,
rolled in old cloaks for cover, near the embers.
Or when the heat comes at the end of summer,
the fallen leaves, all round his vineyard plot,
heaped into windrows, make his lowly bed.
He lies now even so, with aching heart,
and longs for your return, while age comes on him.
So I, too, pined away, so doom befell me, not   210
that the keen-eyed huntress with her shafts
had marked me down and shot to kill me; not
that illness overtook me—no true illness
wasting the body to undo the spirit;
only my loneliness for you, Odysseus,
for your kind heart and counsel, gentle Odysseus,
took my own life away.'
                                         I bit my lip,
rising perplexed, with longing to embrace her,
and tried three times, putting my arms around her,
but she went sifting through my hands, impalpable   220
as shadows are, and wavering like a dream.
Now this embittered all the pain I bore,
and I cried in the darkness:

17. The son of Penelope and Odysseus.
18. Who spends part of her time in the upper world and part in
    the lower world and is thus the goddess of both fertility and
    death.

                                   'O my mother,
will you not stay, be still, here in my arms,
may we not, in this place of Death, as well,
hold one another, touch with love, and taste
salt tears' relief, the twinge of welling tears?
Or is this all hallucination, sent
against me by the iron queen, Perséphonê[18]
to make me groan again?'
                         My noble mother   230
answered quickly:
                  'O my child—alas,
most sorely tried of men—great Zeus's daughter,
Perséphonê, knits no illusion for you.
All mortals meet this judgment when they die.
No flesh and bone are here, none bound by sinew,
since the bright-hearted pyre consumed them down—
the white bones long exanimate—to ash;
dreamlike the soul flies, insubstantial.
You must crave sunlight soon.
                              Note all things strange
seen here, to tell your lady in after days.'   240
So went our talk; then other shadows came,
ladies in company, sent by Perséphonê—
consorts or daughters of illustrious men—
crowding about the black blood.
                                I took thought
how best to separate and question them,
and saw no help for it, but drew once more
the long bright edge of broadsword from my hip,
that none should sip the blood in company
but one by one, in order; so it fell
that each declared her lineage and name.   250

Here was great loveliness of ghosts! I saw
before them all, that princess of great ladies,
Tyro, Salmoneus' daughter, as she told me,
and queen to Krêtheus [Cretheus], a son of Aiolos
     [Aeolus].
She had gone daft for the river Enipeus,
most graceful of all running streams, and ranged
all day by Enipeus' limpid side,
whose form the foaming girdler of the islands,
the god who makes earth tremble, took and so
lay down with her where he went flooding seaward,   260
their bower a purple billow, arching round
to hide them in a sea-vale, god and lady.
Now when his pleasure was complete, the god
spoke to her softly, holding fast her hand:
'Dear mortal, go in joy! At the turn of seasons,
winter to summer, you shall bear me sons;
no lovemaking of gods can be in vain.
Nurse our sweet children tenderly, and rear them.
Home with you now, and hold your tongue, and tell
no one your lover's name—though I am yours,   270
Poseidon, lord of surf that makes earth tremble.'

He plunged away into the deep sea swell,
and she grew big with Pelias and Neleus,
powerful vassals, in their time, of Zeus.
Pelias lived on broad Iolkos [Iolcus] seaboard
rich in flocks, and Neleus at Pylos [Pylus].
As for the sons borne by that queen of women

to Krêtheus, their names were Aison [Aeson],
    Pherês,
and Amytháon, expert charioteer.

Next after her I saw Antiopê,   280
daughter of Ásopos [Asopus]. She too could boast
a god for lover, having lain with Zeus
and borne two sons to him: Amphion and
Zêthos [Zethus], who founded Thebes, the upper city,
and built the ancient citadel. They sheltered
no life upon that plain, for all their power,
without a fortress wall.
                        And next I saw
Amphitrion's [Amphitryon] true wife, Alkmênê
    [Alcmene], mother,
as all men know, of lionish Heraklês [Heracles],
conceived when she lay close in Zeus's arms;   290
and Megarê [Megara], high-hearted Kreon's [Creon][19]
    daughter,
wife of Amphitrion's unwearying son.
I saw the mother of Oidipous [Oedipus], Epikastê
whose great unwitting deed it was
to marry her own son.[20] He took that prize
from a slain father; presently the gods
brought all to light that made the famous story.
But by their fearsome wills he kept his throne
in dearest Thebes, all through his evil days,
while she descended to the place of Death,   300
god of the locked and iron door. Steep down
from a high rafter, throttled in her noose,
she swung, carried away by pain, and left him
endless agony from a mother's Furies.

And I saw Khloris [Chloris], that most lovely lady,
whom for her beauty in the olden time
Neleus wooed with countless gifts, and married.
She was the youngest daughter of Amphion,
son of Iasos. In those days he held
power at Orkhómenos [Orchomenus], over the Minyai.   310
At Pylos then as queen she bore her children—
Nestor, Khromios [Chromios], Periklýmenos
    [Periclymenus],
and Pêro, too, who turned the heads of men
with her magnificence. A host of princes
from nearby lands came courting her; but Neleus
would hear of no one, not unless the suitor
could drive the steers of giant Iphiklos
from Phylakê [Phylace]—longhorns, broad in the brow,
so fierce that one man only, a diviner,
offered to round them up. But bitter fate   320
saw him bound hand and foot by savage herdsmen.
Then days and months grew full and waned, the year
went wheeling round, the seasons came again,
before at last the power of Iphiklos [Iphiclus],

relenting, freed the prisoner, who foretold
all things to him. So Zeus's will was done.
And I saw Lêda, wife of Tyndareus,
upon whom Tyndareus had sired twins
indomitable: Kastor [Castor], tamer of horses,
and Polydeukês [Polydeuces], best in the boxing ring.   330
Those two live still, though life-creating earth
embraces them: even in the underworld
honored as gods by Zeus, each day in turn
one comes alive, the other dies again.
Then after Lêda to my vision came
the wife of Aloeus, Iphimedeia,
proud that she once had held the flowing sea
and borne him sons, thunderers for a day,
the world-renowned Otos [Otus] and Ephialtês.
Never were men on such a scale   340
bred on the plowlands and the grainlands, never
so magnificent any, after Orion.
At nine years old they towered nine fathoms tall,
nine cubits in the shoulders, and they promised
furor upon Olympos [Olympus], heaven broken by battle
    cries,
the day they met the gods in arms.
                              With Ossa's
mountain peak they meant to crown Olympos
and over Ossa Pelion's forest pile
for footholds up the sky. As giants grown
they might have done it, but the bright son of Zeus   350
by Lêto of the smooth braid shot them down
while they were boys unbearded; no dark curls
clustered yet from temples to the chin.

Then I saw Phaidra [Phaedra], Prokris [Procris]; and
    Ariadnê,[21]
daughter of Minos, the grim king. Theseus took her
aboard with him from Krete [Crete] for the terraced land
of ancient Athens; but he had no joy of her.
Artemis killed her on the Isle of Dia
at a word from Dionysos.
                        Maira, then,
and Klymênê [Clymene], and that detested queen,   360
Eríphylê, who betrayed her lord for gold . . .
but how name all the women I beheld there,
daughters and wives of kings? The starry night
wanes long before I close.
                      Here, or aboard ship,
amid the crew, the hour for sleep has come.
Our sailing is the gods' affair and yours."

Then he fell silent. Down the shadowy hall
the enchanted banqueters were still. Only
the queen with ivory pale arms, Arêtê, spoke,
saying to all the silent men:
                      "Phaiákians [Phaeacians],[22]   370
how does he stand, now, in your eyes, this captain,
the look and bulk of him, the inward poise?
He is my guest, but each one shares that honor.
Be in no haste to send him on his way
or scant your bounty in his need. Remember
how rich, by heaven's will, your possessions are."

Then Ekhenêos [Echeneus], the old soldier, eldest
of all Phaiákians, added his word:

---

19. Creon was king of Thebes after Oedipus was ostracized.
20. See pp. 117–34 for the play *Oedipus* in which Oedipus marries Jocasta, his mother.
21. Ariadne helped lead Theseus from the labyrinth after he had slain the Minotaur.
22. The peace-loving people who welcomed the shipwrecked Odysseus and helped him on his way.

"Friends, here was nothing but our own thought spoken,
the mark hit square. Our duties to her majesty.   380
For what is to be said and done,
we wait upon Alkínoös' [Alcinous] command."

At this the king's voice rang:
                                        "I so command—
as sure as it is I who, while I live,
rule the sea rovers of Phaiákia. Our friend
longs to put out for home, but let him be
content to rest here one more day, until
I see all gifts bestowed. And every man
will take thought for his launching and his voyage,
I most of all, for I am master here."   390

Odysseus, the great tactician, answered:
"Alkínoös, king and admiration of men,
even a year's delay, if you should urge it,
in loading gifts and furnishing for sea—
I too could wish it; better far that I
return with some largesse of wealth about me—
I shall be thought more worthy of love and courtesy
by every man who greets me home in Ithaka."

The king said:
                    "As to that, one word, Odysseus:
from all we see, we take you for no swindler—   400
though the dark earth be patient of so many,
scattered everywhere, baiting their traps with lies
of old times and of places no one knows.
You speak with art, but your intent is honest.
The Argive troubles, and your own troubles,
you told as a poet would, a man who knows the world.
But now come tell me this: among the dead
did you meet any of your peers, companions
who sailed with you and met their doom at Troy?
Here's a long night—an endless night—before us,   410
and no time yet for sleep, not in this hall.
Recall the past deeds and the strange adventures.
I could stay up until the sacred Dawn
as long as you might wish to tell your story."

Odysseus the great tactician answered:

"Alkínoös, king and admiration of men,
there is a time for story telling; there is
also a time for sleep. But even so,
if, indeed, listening be still your pleasure,
I must not grudge my part. Other and sadder   420
tales there are to tell, of my companions,
of some who came through all the Trojan spears,
clangor and groan of war,
only to find a brutal death at home—
and a bad wife behind it.
                              After Perséphonê,
icy and pale, dispersed the shades of women,
the soul of Agamémnon,[23] son of Atreus,

came before me, sombre in the gloom,
and others gathered round, all who were with him
when death and doom struck in Aigísthos' hall.   430
Sipping the black blood, the tall shade perceived me,
and cried out sharply, breaking into tears;
then tried to stretch his hands toward me, but could not,
being bereft of all the reach and power
he once felt in the great torque of his arms.
Gazing at him, and stirred, I wept for pity,
and spoke across to him:
                              'O son of Atreus,
illustrious Lord Marshal, Agamémnon,
what was the doom that brought you low in death?
Were you at sea, aboard ship, and Poseidon   440
blew up a wicked squall to send you under,
or were you cattle-raiding on the mainland
or in a fight for some strongpoint, or women,
when the foe hit you to your mortal hurt?'

But he replied at once:
                              'Son of Laërtês,
Odysseus, master of land ways and sea ways,
neither did I go down with some good ship
in any gale Poseidon blew, nor die
upon the mainland, hurt by foes in battle.
It was Aigísthos who designed my death,   450
he and my heartless wife, and killed me, after
feeding me, like an ox felled at the trough.
That was my miserable end—and with me
my fellows butchered, like so many swine
killed for some troop, or feast, or wedding banquet
in a great landholder's household. In your day
you have seen men, and hundreds, die in war,
in the bloody press, or downed in single combat,
but these were murders you would catch your breath at:
think of us fallen, all our throats cut, winebowl   460
brimming, tables laden on every side,
while blood ran smoking over the whole floor.
In my extremity I heard Kassandra,
Priam's[24] daughter, piteously crying
as the traitress Klytaïmnestra [Clytemnestra] made to kill
    her
along with me. I heaved up from the ground
and got my hands around the blade, but she
eluded me, that whore. Now would she close
my two eyes as my soul swam to the underworld
or shut my lips. There is no being more fell,   470
more bestial than a wife in such an action,
and what an action that one planned!
The murder of her husband and her lord.
Great god, I thought my children and my slaves
at least would give me welcome. But that woman,
plotting a thing so low, defiled herself
and all her sex, all women yet to come,
even those few who may be virtuous.'

He paused then, and I answered: 'Foul and dreadful.
That was the way that Zeus who views the wide world   480
vented his hatred on the sons of Atreus—
intrigues of women, even from the start.
                                        Myriads

---

23. King of Mycenae who was murdered by his wife upon
   returning victoriously from Troy. See the play *Agamemnon*
   on pp. 100–11.
24. Cassandra, the daughter of Priam, king of Troy.

died by Helen's[25] fault, and Klytaïmnestra
plotted against you half the world away.'

And he at once said:
                    'Let it be a warning
even to you. Indulge a woman never,
and never tell her all you know. Some things
a man may tell, some he should cover up.
Not that I see a risk for you, Odysseus,
of death at your wife's hands. She is too wise,   490
too clear-eyed, sees alternatives too well,
Penélopê, Ikârios' [Icarius] daughter—
that young bride whom we left behind—think of it!—
when we sailed off to war. The baby boy
still cradled at her breast—now he must be
a grown man, and a lucky one. By heaven,
you'll see him yet, and he'll embrace his father
with old fashioned respect, and rightly.
                                        My own
lady never let me glut my eyes
on my own son, but bled me to death first.   500
One thing I will advise, on second thought;
stow it away and ponder it.
                        Land your ship
in secret on your island; give no warning.
The day of faithful wives is gone forever.
But tell me, have you any word at all
about my son's life? Gone to Orkhómenos
or sandy Pylos, can he be? Or waiting
with Meneláos [Menelaus][26] in the plain of Sparta?
Death on earth has not yet taken Orestês.'[27]

But I could only answer:
                        'Son of Atreus,   510
why do you ask these questions of me? Neither
news of home have I, nor news of him,
alive or dead. And empty words are evil.'

So we exchanged our speech, in bitterness,
weighed down by grief, and tears welled in our eyes,
when there appeared the spirit of Akhilleus [Achilles],
son of Peleus; then Patróklos' [Patroclus] shade,
and then Antílokhos [Antilochus], and then Aias [Ajax],
first among all the Danaans in strength
and bodily beauty, next to prince Akhilleus.[28]   520
Now that great runner, grandson of Aíakhos [Aeacus],
recognized me and called across to me:

'Son of Laërtês and the gods of old,
Odysseus, master mariner and soldier,
old knife, what next? What greater feat remains
for you to put your mind on, after this?
How did you find your way down to the dark
where these dimwitted dead are camped forever,

the after images of used-up men?'
                                I answered:
'Akhilleus, Peleus' son, strongest of all   530
among the Akhaians, I had need of foresight
such as Teirêsias alone could give
to help me, homeward bound for the crags of Ithaka.
I have not yet coasted Akhaia, not yet
touched my land; my life is all adversity.
But was there ever a man more blest by fortune
than you, Akhilleus? Can there ever be?
We ranked you with immortals in your lifetime,
we Argives did, and here your power is royal
among the dead men's shades. Think, then, Akhilleus: 540
you need not be so pained by death.'
                                To this
he answered swiftly:
                        'Let me hear no smooth talk
of death from you, Odysseus, light of councils.
Better, I say, to break sod as a farm hand
for some poor country man, on iron rations,
than lord it over all the exhausted dead.
Tell me, what news of the prince my son: did he
come after me to make a name in battle
or could it be he did not? Do you know
if rank and honor still belong to Peleus   550
in the towns of the Myrmidons? Or now, may be,
Hellas and Phthia spurn him, seeing old age
fetters him, hand and foot. I cannot help him
under the sun's rays, cannot be that man
I was on Troy's wide seaboard, in those days
when I made bastion for the Argives[29]
and put an army's best men in the dust.
Were I but whole again, could I go now
to my father's house, one hour would do to make
my passion and my hands no man could hold   560
hateful to any who shoulder him aside.'

Now when he paused I answered:
                                'Of all that—
of Peleus' life, that is—I know nothing;
but happily I can tell you the whole story
of Neoptólemos [Neoptolemus], as you require.
In my own ship I brought him out from Skyros
to join the Akhaians[30] under arms.
                                And I can tell you,
in every council before Troy thereafter
your son spoke first and always to the point;
no one but Nestor and I could out-debate him.   570
And when we formed against the Trojan line
he never hung back in the mass, but ranged
far forward of his troops—no man could touch him
for gallantry. Aye, scores went down before him
in hard fights man to man. I shall not tell
all about each, or name them all—the long
roster of enemies he put out of action,
taking the shock of charges on the Argives.
But what a champion his lance ran through
in Eurýpulos [Eurypylus] the son of Télephos [Telephus]!
Keteians   580
in throngs around that captain also died—
all because Priam's gifts had won his mother

---

25. Helen of Troy, wife of Menelaos and sister-in-law of
Agamemnon, whose flight with her lover Paris to Troy
caused, according to legend, the Trojan War.
26. Helen's abandoned husband, brother to Agamemnon.
27. Son of Agamemnon, who will avenge his father's murder by
killing his mother.
28. All were Greek heroes who died at Troy.
29. Men of Argos, i.e., the Greek army.
30. Also referring to the Greek army.

to send the lad to battle; and I thought
Memnon alone in splendor ever outshone him.

But one fact more: while our picked Argive crew
still rode that hollow horse[31] Epeios built,
and when the whole thing lay with me, to open
the trapdoor of the ambuscade or not,
at that point our Danaan lords and soldiers
wiped their eyes, and their knees began to quake,   590
all but Neoptólemos. I never saw
his tanned cheek change color or his hand
brush one tear away. Rather he prayed me,
hand on hilt, to sortie, and he gripped
his tough spear, bent on havoc for the Trojans.
And when we had pierced and sacked Priam's tall city
he loaded his choice plunder and embarked
with no scar on him; not a spear had grazed him
nor the sword's edge in close work—common wounds
one gets in war. Arês in his mad fits   600
knows no favorites.'
            But I said no more,
for he had gone off striding the field of asphodel,
the ghost of our great runner, Akhilleus Aiákidês,
glorying in what I told him of his son.

Now other souls of mournful dead stood by,
each with his troubled questioning, but one
remained alone, apart: the son of Télamon,
Aîas, it was—the great shade burning still
because I had won favor on the beachhead
in rivalry over Akhilleus' arms.   610
The Lady Thetis, mother of Akhilleus
laid out for us the dead man's battle gear,
and Trojan children, with Athena,
named the Danaan fittest to own them. Would
god I had not borne the palm that day!
For earth took Aîas then to hold forever,
the handsomest and, in all feats of war,
noblest of the Danaans after Akhilleus.
Gently therefore I called across to him:
'Aîas, dear son of royal Télamon,   620
you would not then forget, even in death,
your fury with me over those accurst
calamitous arms?—and so they were, a bane
sent by the gods upon the Argive host.
For when you died by your own hand we lost
a tower, formidable in war. All we Akhaians
mourn you forever, as we do Akilleus;
and no one bears the blame but Zeus.
He fixed that doom for you because he frowned
on the whole expedition of our spearmen.   630
My lord, come nearer, listen to our story!
Conquer your indignation and your pride.'

But he gave no reply, and turned away,
following other ghosts toward Erebos
Who knows if in that darkness he might still
have spoken, and I answered?
                But my heart

<hr>

31. The Trojan Horse filled with Greek soldiers which the
    Trojans unwittingly dragged into their city.

longed, after this, to see the dead elsewhere.

And now there came before my eyes Minos,
the son of Zeus, enthroned, holding a golden staff,
dealing out justice among ghostly pleaders   640
arrayed about the broad doorways of Death.

And then I glimpsed Orion, the huge hunter,
gripping his club, studded with bronze, unbreakable,
with wild beasts he had overpowered in life
on lonely mountainsides, now brought to bay
on fields of asphodel.
            And I saw Títyos [Tityus],
the son of Gaia, lying
abandoned over nine square rods of plain.
Vultures, hunched above him, left and right,
rifling his belly, stabbed into the liver,   650
and he could never push them off.
                    This hulk
had once committed rape of Zeus's mistress,
Lêto, in her glory, when she crossed
the open grass of Panopeus toward Pytho.

Then I saw Tántalos [Tantalus] put to the torture:
in a cool pond he stood, lapped round by water
clear to the chin, and being athirst he burned
to slake his dry weasand with drink, though drink
he would not ever again. For when the old man
put his lips down to the sheet of water   660
it vanished round his feet, gulped underground,
and black mud baked there in a wind from hell.
Boughs, too, drooped low above him, big with fruit,
pear trees, pomegranates, brilliant apples,
luscious figs, and olives ripe and dark;
but if he stretched his hand for one, the wind
under the dark sky tossed the bough beyond him.

Then Sísyphos [Sisyphus] in torment I beheld
being roustabout to a tremendous boulder.
Leaning with both arms braced and legs driving,
he heaved it toward a height, and almost over,   670
but then a Power spun him round and sent
the cruel boulder bounding again to the plain.
Whereon the man bent down again to toil,
dripping sweat, and the dust rose overhead.
Next I saw manifest the power of Heraklês—
a phantom, this, for he himself has gone
feasting amid the gods, reclining soft
with Hêbê of the ravishing pale ankles,
daughter of Zeus and Hêra, shod in gold.   680
But, in my vision, all the dead around him
cried like affrighted birds; like Night itself
he loomed with naked bow and nocked arrow
and glances terrible as continual archery.
My hackles rose at the gold swordbelt he wore
sweeping across him: gorgeous intaglio
of savage bears, boars, lions with wildfire eyes,
swordfights, battle, slaughter, and sudden death—
the smith who had that belt in him, I hope
he never made, and never will make, another.   690
The eyes of the vast figure rested on me,
and of a sudden he said in kindly tones:
'Son of Laërtês and the gods of old,

Odysseus, master mariner and soldier,
under a cloud, you too? Destined to grinding
labors like my own in the sunny world?
'Son of Kroníon Zeus or not, how many
days I sweated out, being bound in servitude
to a man far worse than I, a rough master!
He made me hunt this place one time   700
to get the watchdog of the dead: no more
perilous task, he thought, could be; but I
brought back that beast, up from the underworld;
Hermês and grey-eyed Athena showed the way.'

And Heraklês, down the vistas of the dead,
faded from sight; but I stood fast, awaiting
other great souls who perished in times past.
I should have met, then, god-begotten Theseus
and Peirithoös [Peirithous], whom both I longed to see,
but first came shades in thousands, rustling   710
in a pandemonium of whispers, blown together,
and the horror took me that Perséphonê
had brought from darker hell some saurian death's head.
I whirled then, made for the ship, shouted to crewmen
to get aboard and cast off the stern hawsers,
an order soon obeyed. They took their thwarts,
and the ship went leaping toward the stream of Ocean
first under oars, then with a following wind."

Though it is a poem, the *Odyssey* can be viewed as the first novel (extended narrative with complex plot) in Western literature and, according to many authorities, still the greatest. Adventure, romance, fidelity, treachery, sorcery, revenge, love—the range of themes is remarkable. Included are some of the memorable characters in literature: a nymph, sorceress, giants, sirens, cannibals, heroes, dupes, traitors, collaborators, the noble and ignoble. Many events are on a heroic scale but some are very personal and intimate. In one of the most touching little scenes in literature, Odysseus, disguised as a beggar, has finally returned to his palace. Accompanied by a loyal swineherd, Odysseus suggests that Eumaios the swineherd enter the palace first.

> While he spoke
> an old hound, lying near, pricked up his ears
> and lifted up his muzzle. This was Argos,
> trained as a puppy by Odysseus,
> but never taken on a hunt before
> his master sailed for Troy. The young men,
>   afterward,
> hunted wild goats with him, and hare, and deer,
> but he had grown old in his master's absence.
> Treated as rubbish now, he lay at last
> upon a mass of dung before the gates—   10
> manure of mules and cows, piled there until
> fieldhands could spread it on the king's estate.
> Abandoned there, and half destroyed with flies,
> old Argos lay.
>
> But when he knew he heard
> Odysseus' voice nearby, he did his best

to wag his tail, nose down, with flattened ears,
having no strength to move nearer his master.
And the man looked away,
wiping a salt tear from his cheek; but he
hid this from Eumaios [Eumeus].   20

Book XVII

STUDY QUESTIONS

1. Not even a warrior as daring as Odysseus would descend to the underworld just for a new experience. Why visit Hades? Who does he want to meet and what does he expect to learn? What, in fact, does he learn that is useful and practical when he returns to the realm of the living?

2. Until he met Achilles, Odysseus had assumed that the afterlife was to be desired. What, according to Achilles and others, was the true situation? What was lacking that frustrated those who were called the "dimwitted dead" (line 528)?

3. How does the Greek view of existence after death differ from the Mesopotamian version as expressed in the *Epic of Gilgamesh*?

4. If an epic "is a poem about men in action" (Aristotle), why does Homer include the episode of the old dog?

SUMMARY

Introduced in this background chapter were threads that were later woven into the glorious tapestry known as the Athenian Golden Age. The basic strand was the mainland geography that had so much to do with the development of Greek character and the expansion of commerce.

Individualistic to the extreme, the Greeks had no organized religion and, consequently, no hierarchy of priests. Their pantheon of Olympian gods can be viewed as highly imaginative explanations of natural phenomena, as symbols of power, love, intellect, and as the Greeks themselves, writ large.

Our knowledge of early Greece has been obtained in large part from Hesiod and Homer. A commentator on the archaic period, Hesiod spoke as a farmer caught in a losing battle with the aristocracy. Homer sang of the Mycenaeans and the Heroic Age, but he spoke to Greeks of all periods. The Homeric view on women, however, did not appear to carry over to later Greeks. "Altho women suffered disabilities under the patriarchal code, they were not considered inferior or incompetent in the Homeric epic. When Agamemnon and Odysseus sailed to Troy, they had no qualms about leaving their wives to manage their kingdoms in their absence."[32]

The Greeks were highly competitive and this drive seems partially to explain the upward mobility of the land-poor farmer who migrated to a colony to improve his opportunities to get ahead. The rise of trade, a natural consequence of home cities and overseas colonies, was very competitive in the quality of goods and the expansion of markets. A key factor in the vertical ascent of the lower classes was the surplus of goods created by Greek artisans. A society that labors from dawn to dusk just to make ends meet cannot expand its economy or have much time for leisure. By producing far more goods than they needed the Greeks enlarged their economy and gained leisure time for other pursuits.

Athens achieved dominance in large part because of a series of political reforms inaugurated, in turn, by Draco, Solon, Pisistratus, and Cleisthenes. The movement from tyranny to oligarchy to democracy was not smooth by any means but it was headed in the right direction. Actually, the evolution of Athenian democracy was a natural consequence of the individual drive and initiative of a growing middle class of artisans, traders, and businessmen. A good income and some discretionary time made the middle class avid for more of each. To accomplish this they had to get involved in politics, to become part of the government that enacted and administered laws on coinage, trade, and taxes. Of course the four tribes did not meekly submit to political reforms but, given the clout of the new moneyed class, they had no alternative.

With the reforms of Cleisthenes, democratic government was well established, and Athens had convincingly demonstrated her capabilities as a political and economic power. Her military power, however, was put to the test by the Persians.

It is difficult today even to imagine the situation in Athens just before the Battle of Marathon. The might of the Persian armies was unquestioned. Fielded by a powerful totalitarian state and led by skilled professional soldiers, the Persian hordes were known to overrun and destroy everything they attacked. Their strength lay in their enormous numbers and the merciless discipline enforced by their officers. Individual action was inconceivable; mass assaults were the rule. Heavy casualties were expected and were of no consequence. More foot soldiers could always be pressed into service.

When the Athenians confronted the Persian army at Marathon in 490 BC, they felt they could do little more than slow the Persian juggernaut. No one, it seems, believed the Persians could be defeated. But the small Greek force outwitted the Persian invaders and drove them back to their ships in a humiliating retreat.

The Greek victory profoundly shocked and enraged

32. Sarah B. Pomeroy, *Goddesses, Whores, Wives, and Slaves: Women in Classical Antiquity* (New York: Schocken Books, 1975), p. 28.

the Persians. Consequently, the second invasion of Greece—some ten years later—was supposed to redeem the loss of face at Marathon. The army and navy would sweep the land and the sea and the arrogant Greeks would be humiliated. By this time the Greeks were, if anything, even prouder and their military power was considerably greater. The battle at Thermopylai was lost against overwhelming odds but, from then on, the Greeks outfoxed and outfought the enemy and profoundly changed the course of history.

In one form or another the questions posed by the Ionian philosophers are still being asked today. If the Greeks had made only one contribution to Western civilization, the search for *what is* and the introduction of speculative philosophy would have been more than sufficient to earn the gratitude of all humankind. Moreover, their invention of scientific speculation eventually made possible the improvement of the quality of life.

CULTURE AND HUMAN VALUES

The Dorian migrations of ca. 1100–800 BC caused a major step backward into the Greek dark ages. In every sense of the term it was a period of chaos. Then, sometime after 850 BC or so, a long period of adjustment led to a maturing society, but where the adjustment matured into the balance of the Golden Age is difficult to say. From 490 to 480 was very likely the final decade of adjustment, from the victory at Marathon to the triumph at Salamis. Defeating the Persians seemed to provide the inspiration necessary to take a confident stride into classical Greek civilization.

Their military victories gave the Greeks assurance, but it was the development of their values during the archaic period that propelled them into the achievements of the Golden Age. No one can say just why these people were so intensely individualistic and competitive or why they felt compelled to achieve excellence in whatever they did. Nor can we explain how they developed their aesthetic sense as they pursued the ideal of beauty or why they were so passionate about justice. Every one of these values is manifested in some degree in nearly everything they did, said, wrote, or made. The value system in any society is a chicken and egg puzzle. Did justice, for example, come into being because it was a noble theory, or was a particular court decision so objective and so just that it set a precedent? Either is possible and perhaps both; the Greeks were noted for both their idealism and their pragmatism. Perhaps it was a combination of the two that fed the fires of creativity that sparked the achievements of the archaic, classical, and Hellenistic periods.

(NOTE: See summary of Greek culture and values on p. 229.)

CHAPTER 5

Hellenic Athens:
The Fulfillment of the Good Life

ATHENS: THE GOLDEN AGE

> Numberless are the world's wonders but none more
> wonderful than man.
>
> Sophocles

The city of Athens in 461 BC must have been an exciting
place in which to live. It was prosperous and strong and,
though no one knew it at the time, about to enter its Golden
Age, that astonishing era (ca. 460–430 BC) during which
the resident artists, writers, statesmen, and philosophers
would enrich a society based on the value of the individual and on a commitment to truth, beauty, and justice. It
was not a perfect society—far from it—but it did aspire to
perfection. For a fleeting moment life was enveloped in the
lusty embrace of a city-state that dared to compete with
the gods.

Athenian Greeks may have been the most verbal
people in the ancient world. Blessed with a sophisticated
language that was "one of the most exquisite instruments
ever devised by human beings" (Gilbert Highet), they talked,
discussed, argued, and debated everything under the sun:
politics, society, love, and especially philosophy, because
the intellectuals among them were fascinated by the
world of ideas. The Herakleitean belief in constant change
had its supporters, while others contended that reality
could be expressed through numerical relationships, as
Pythagoras had stated. Into this debate now came new ideas
from Elea, a prosperous Greek colony in southern Italy.
Led by Parmenides (par-MEN-uh-deez; born ca. 514 BC),
the Eleatic School refused to accept the Herakleitean idea
that nothing *is* and that the universe is in a constant state
of *becoming*. They based their deliberations on the idea
that whatever is real must be permanent and unchanging.
Turning that statement around may seem more logical:
anything that constantly changes its state of being cannot

be real. Further, they attacked the method of the Ionian
philosophers, who depended entirely upon their five senses for the discovery of truth. The Eleatics were quick to
emphasize that one cannot trust the senses; but if the senses are not reliable as a guide to truth, what is? The Eleatic
philosophers asserted that the mind is the only sure guide.
They pointed to truths established by such geometers as
Pythagoras to support their theory that the mind can arrive
at truth without the aid (or handicap) of the senses. These
thinkers were much like the Pythagoreans, and form a sort
of bridge between Pythagoras and Plato (see pp. 77 and 155).

The development of material philosophy reached its
high point with the Athenian Leucippus and his student,
Democritos (Di-MOK-ruh-toss; ca. 460–370 BC). Democritos
synthesized the attempts of the Ionians to understand the
physical world and developed a theory of this world that
could not be verified until the twentieth century. Using only
the power of his mind he postulated Greek atomic theory,
stating that all matter consists of minute particles called
atoma (Gk. *atomas*: indivisible). These atoms exist in space,
combine and separate because of "necessity," and represent a strict conservation of matter and energy, that is, the
same number of atoms always exists; only the combinations differ. Contemporary nuclear physics confirms a strict
conservation of matter and energy when taken together but
probability replaces necessity when linking cause and effect.
Atoms do exist, of course, and some of them can be split
or fused.

Athenian intellectuals were fascinated with the world
of ideas but average citizens were far more interested in
the tangible world and their place within it. They lived in
a city whose dominant mood, following the Persian wars,
was enthusiastically optimistic, where unlimited opportunities challenged free people in a democratic society. The
Persians had burned the entire city, giving the Athenians
an unprecedented opportunity to rebuild Athens to match
their visions of its greatness. Possibilities for growth and
progress lay everywhere but someone had to point the way.
For development of the human spirit in a free society,
Athenians looked primarily to that unique Greek institution: the theatre.

Opposite   Stone carving of theatrical mask from Ephesos,
Turkey. Ca. 400 BC. Limestone, height ca. 36" (91.4 cm).
Photo: Sonia Halliday, Weston Turville, U.K.
The Graeco-Roman theatre here seated 25,000 spectators.

THE THEATRE:
A GREEK INVENTION

The Greeks created tragedy, comedy, melodrama, mime, ballet, the art and craft of acting, costume and set design, stage machinery, and the theatrical structure itself. All this began with the first formal staging of tragedy during the Athenian Greater Dionysia festival in about 534 BC. Thespis was the name of the actor who led that theatrical troupe and "thespians" is what we sometimes call actors today. The Greater Dionysia was the more important of the two religious festivals held each year in honor of Dionysos, god of fertility and wine and patron of Athenian drama. (Curiously, secular drama evolved out of religious rites twice: in Greece and later in medieval Christian churches.)

Strictly speaking, drama is but one branch of literature, but Greek drama is far more than this. Encompassing poetry, music, dance, and such wide-ranging themes as the nature of truth, beauty, freedom, and justice, Greek theatre represented virtually the whole of that remarkable civilization. Theatres functioned as centers of education, enlightenment, and entertainment, probably in reverse order. No self-respecting Greek would tolerate a boring play, no matter how educational and enlightening. Simply stated, Greek drama can be defined as an alliance of moral passion and entertainment.

The state took full responsibility for every aspect of the festivals from selecting judges to funding and supervising casting and production. A small admission fee partially offset expenses; those too poor to afford even this received the price of a ticket from a "seeing fund." The prime government responsibility, though, was the location, design, construction, and maintenance of the theatre itself.

Theatres and Performances

The climate enabled the Greeks to spend much of their lives out-of-doors, so naturally the theatres were in the open air, with spectators' seats ascending an inward curving hillside. No theatre was ever "built"; it was carved into the side of a hill so that it became part of its environment. Chorus performed in the circular space (**orchestra**) that filled the flat area at the base of the hill. (Chorus was usually thought of as a single actor and was thus a singular noun.) Behind the orchestra and facing the audience was a long, low building (**skene**; SKAY-nuh) with a room at either end (dressing and storage) and a platform (stage) between the rooms.

Because they were important centers for the entire populace of a city-state, theatres were suitably large; seating was for 13,000 at Epidauros (fig. 5.1), 18,000 at Athens, 25,000 at Ephesos (in Turkey). The **acoustics** of these semi-circular stadiums were so fine that actors could be understood fifty rows above the stage. All-male casts wore large masks of easily identifiable character types (which also aided gender distinction; see chapter opener on p. 88).

Violence took place off stage as described (usually) by a messenger though there were some exceptions in the **comedies** of Aristophanes. Each play had a chorus of up to a dozen members that reacted to the action in a variety of ways. Each play used one stage set, while the main stage machinery was the *mekhane* (me-KAY-nee), a crane that transported actors who played gods. This was the celebrated **deus ex machina**, the "god in a machine."

Greek drama was to a considerable degree a musical experience, a unique amalgam for which there is no modern equivalent. Neither opera nor musical play, Greek dramas (both **tragedies** and comedies) moved on their own plane somewhere in between. Chorus was central as it chanted, sang, and danced to the pungent, plaintive sounds of the **aulos** (OW-loss; a double reed-pipe, somewhat like the modern oboe). The instrument of Dionysos, god of the theatre, the aulos was intimately involved in the pace and mood of the drama, commenting, underscoring, highlighting. (Modern stage directions referring to "flute" or "flute-girl" always mean aulos and aulos-player.)[1]

A single set, all-male cast, masks, chorus, music, dance, and off-stage violence were conventions that challenged spectators to use their imaginations to the fullest. What about the imaginations of the playwrights? Did state sponsorship limit what could be said or done? The Greek response to these issues is the key to the eminence and influence of the theatre.

Athens did have some restrictions concerning religion but the stage was the totally uncensored forum of the democracy. The freedom for dramatists to write anything whatever was protected by a society that delighted in the free expression of ideas and the airing of controversial topics. Playwrights, especially the comic dramatists, assaulted politicians, philosophers, civic leaders, and even other dramatists. As might be expected, corruption, hypocrisy, greed, politics, and war were favorite targets.

Compared with our ready access to theatre, the Greeks had limited opportunities to experience the artistry, wit, and wisdom of their playwrights. Athens had only two festivals a year—the Greater Dionysia and the Linaea. Consequently, the festivals were eagerly anticipated and heavily attended. What better way to hear what some of the foremost men of their time had to say? In terms of general interest one can roughly compare the two festivals with the World Series and the Superbowl but with significant differences in impact. The plays generated a year or more of passionate discussions/arguments about the issues, ideas, and controversies presented on stage. Whatever message a writer had to impart to the entire population of the city, drama was the nearly perfect vehicle.

1. Greek plays are no longer performed in their original version because all of the accompanying music has been lost. Over a long period of time those who copied and recopied the manuscripts began omitting the musical notation because they were no longer able to decipher it. The words were transmitted to future generations but the music is gone forever.

5.1 Polykleitos the Younger, Theatre at Epidauros, Greece. Ca. 350 BC.
This view shows the great size (13,000 capacity) typical of Greek theatres.

Aeschylus, 525–456 BC

Though many of their plays have been lost, enough has survived to demonstrate that three of the greatest tragedians in Western history were Greeks, all of whom lived in Athens at about the same time. The first dramatist was Aeschylus (ES-ka-luss), whose life and works were of profound importance in the development of Greek culture, especially the culture of Athens. Though a prize-winning playwright, his tombstone memorializes (at his request) his soldiering at the battle of Marathon. An aristocrat by birth, he synthesized some traditional ideas with those of the most enthusiastic liberals. Critics sometimes accuse Aeschylus of being more of a preacher than a dramatist; all his plays do carry clear messages designed to raise the ethical level of Athenian life. Greek scholar Edith Hamilton points out, however, that he was so instinctive a dramatist that when a suitable dramatic form did not exist, he invented it. Before his time the cast consisted of chorus and one speaking actor. Aeschylus added a second speaking actor, thus introducing true dialogue, real conflict, and the resolution of competing ideas.

Aeschylus wrote about ninety plays of which just seven survive. Of these only the trilogy called the *Oresteia* (o-res-TYE-ya), the story of Orestes, is discussed here. *Agamemnon*, the *Libation Bearers*, and the *Eumenides* (you-MEN-i-deez) make up the trilogy, with the first and third plays included herein. All three are discussed as if they were three acts of a single drama. They relate the story of a system of justice based on tradition, fear, and revenge as it evolved into justice as administered by the law courts of a free society.

Agamemnon: Clytemnestra's Revenge

Agamemnon is a drama of murder, adultery, and revenge. The Greeks have won the Trojan War and Agamemnon is returning to Mycenae in triumph. Awaiting him is Queen Clytemnestra (kly-tem-NES-tra), who is bent on avenging the death of her daughter Iphigeneia (IF-i-je-NY-ya), whom Agamemnon had sacrificed ten years earlier to appease the goddess Diana. Accompanied by a captive Trojan prophetess, Cassandra, in his war chariot, Agamemnon arrives at his citadel, where Clytemnestra and her lover Aigisthos (i-JIS-thos) greet him. The queen encourages her arrogant husband to stride through the Lion Gate on a royal carpet so expensive it was reserved for the gods (figs. 5.2 and 3.10). The play ends shortly after she murders her husband and the Trojan captive and haughtily dismisses her horrified subjects (box 5.1).

TWO WINNERS

Greeks in general and Athenians in particular were the most critical and competitive people in the ancient world. *Arete* (ARE-uh-tay; diligence in the pursuit of excellence) was a creed that applied to everything from pots to temples, music to athletics. The laurel wreath was awarded at the Pythian Games in Delphi for track and field, poetry and music, and sculptures carved to commemorate the victors. In this fiercely competitive society what could be more natural than playwrights vying for the Athenian ivy wreath?

Dramatists competed at two levels; anyone could submit plays but only three finalists were chosen for the three-day festivals. A tragic **trilogy** (three plays on a related theme) was performed each morning followed by a single comedy in the afternoon. The eagerly awaited finale saw the twelve judges issue lists ranking the tragic playwrights and actors, comic playwrights and actors, and the choruses. The victors were crowned with ivy wreaths, and the two top dramatists received the added distinction of a guaranteed appearance at the next festival. Finally, as was the Greek custom, the winners had their names inscribed in stone.

5.2 Entrance to the Palace of Agamemnon at Mycenae, Greece. Ca. 1500–1400 BC. Photo: Robert C. Lamm, Scottsdale.
In the right background is the Argive plain, across which Agamemnon marched home after landing at Tiryns. To the left is the entrance way to the Lion Gate (see fig. 3.10), where Clytemnestra awaited the king.

What does all this mean? The most prevalent image is that of a net or web. The purple carpet is called a web, and Agamemnon has a net thrown over him in his bath so that he cannot escape the murderous blows. Perhaps Aeschylus felt that this net was the old traditionalism, the belief in fate, and the idea of justice as revenge. Chorus is bound up in this web with many speeches against pride, or wealth that breeds pride, or any sort of innovation. Chorus is constrained by ancestral traditions but if they had broken down the palace door they might have also shattered the barrier between themselves and freedom. Curiously, Cassandra tries to inspire them to act, but she, too, is imprisoned by the net. As she enters the palace to meet her known fate, Chorus admonishes her that even slightly delaying her death is a small victory; she can only reply that her time has arrived.

Of all the characters in the play, Clytemnestra alone seems free to act as a human being. True, she blames the curse on the House of Atreus but this only briefly placates Chorus. Her action, however, is destructive, a type of freedom that civilized society cannot tolerate. So, at the end of *Agamemnon* we have two conditions of human existence: Chorus which consults tradition for guidance in life, and Clytemnestra, whose devastating freedom would destroy society. In the remaining two plays the playwright must free one segment and control the other.

BOX 5.1   THE HOUSE OF ATREUS

Like most old Greek families the roots go back to Zeus, in this case through Tantalus, a mortal who was permitted nectar and ambrosia at the table of the gods. To trick the gods and show them as fallible Tantalus hosted a banquet and served them a stew made of his son Pelops. The furious immortals dispatched Tantalus to Hades to suffer eternal hunger and thirst for he was guilty of **hubris** (overbearing pride), the worst of all sins. The family curse continued with the sons of Pelops. Thyestes (thigh-ES-teez) seduced Aerope, his brother's wife; Atreus, in revenge, killed three of Thyestes' four sons (Aigisthos survived) and served them to their father as a meat course. In his *Oresteia* trilogy Aeschylus dramatizes the working out of the curse.

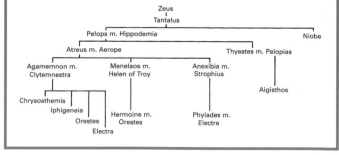

Libation Bearers

The second play, the *Libation Bearers*, is primarily a transition play that brings the problems of vengeance and justice to a head. Apollo has ordered Orestes to avenge his father's murder by killing his mother and her lover. This, interestingly enough, is a directive from the new generation of progressive gods. On the other hand, tribal tradition decrees that anyone spilling kindred blood is hounded to death by the Furies. Caught between contradictory commands, Orestes is damned if he does and damned if he doesn't. But he does commit matricide, is attacked by the Furies and, as the play ends, driven from the stage.

Eumenides

The *Eumenides* may be translated as the "Gracious Ones," and the change of the Furies (the Erinyes; i-RIN-e-eez) to the Eumenides is part of the resolution of the concluding play. The trilogy had begun in darkness in rural Argos and concludes in the sunlit city of Athens where, according to Apollo, Orestes will receive justice.

Chorus (the Furies at this point) laments that they, the older gods, have been shamed and dishonored. If Orestes goes free they predict that children will murder their parents at will, forcing the Furies to blight the land. Athena takes charge by declaring the matter too grave to be decided by ordinary people or by a god. She impanels a jury of citizens to hear the case and render a verdict, a shrewd and civilized solution. A trial by jury transcends the judgment of mortals because juries will, over time, build a body of law that provides a basis for rational, objective judgments.

As defense attorney, Apollo presents the evidence, after which Athena establishes the court, the Areopagus (are-ee-OP-uh-gus; "at the foot of the Acropolis"), and charges it with its duties as the highest court of justice. Her speech, given elsewhere in context, cannot be quoted often enough, for never in the ancient or medieval world and seldom in today's world has there been a clearer statement of how to achieve liberty and justice for all:

> Here reverence
> For law and inbred fear among my people
> Shall hold their hands from evil night and day,
> Only let them not tamper with the laws,
> But keep the fountain pure and sweet to drink.
> I warn you not to banish from your lives
> All terror but to seek the mean between
> Autocracy and anarchy; and in this way
> You shall possess in ages yet unborn
> An impregnable fortress of liberty
> Such as no people has throughout the world.

The jury then returns a tied vote, with Athena casting her ballot for acquittal. Orestes immediately leaves the scene though one-third of the play still remains. Its hero is not Orestes, however, but rather the idea of *justice*. During

BOX 5.2   HOUSE OF CADMOS, FOUNDER OF THEBES

The King of Sidon had a daughter, Europa, who was abducted by Zeus in the form of a bull and carried quite willingly to Crete, where she became the mother of Minos and Rhadamanthys. The King of Sidon sent his sons to search for her. One of them, Cadmos, consulted the oracle at Delphi; she told him to found his own city and forget Europa. He was instructed to follow a heifer and to build his city of Thebes on the heifer's first resting place. First, however, he had to kill a dragon, whose teeth Athena ordered him to sow; armed warriors sprang up, killing each other until just five survived. With the five Cadmos built Thebes and had five daughters and a son. Though Cadmos was a good man misfortune tormented his descendants—none more than Oedipus and Antigone.

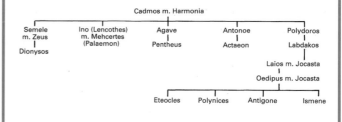

the rest of the play the Furies are transformed into the Eumenides through the strenuous efforts of Athena, goddess of wisdom and persuasion, who convinces them that their new role as defenders of the city will accord them worship and honor.

The universal significance of the trilogy may be described as follows: the people, as represented by Chorus in the *Agamemnon*, are set free simply because their eyes are turned forward rather than backward. No longer will they function under the shadow of tradition and superstition, because each case will be tried using its own evidence and decided according to just laws enacted by human beings.

The *Eumenides* presents the thesis that people must establish the parameters of their own actions, with limits determined by the degree of freedom each can have without compromising the freedom of others. This applies also to the Clytemnestras of the world. Their acts will be brought before the same tribunal and judged by the identical standard. Humanity—at least in Athens of the Golden Age—was encouraged to do so in ways that would serve both the individual and the state.

One further point. The Furies prospered on rule by fear, and it is tempting to discard that aspect of the new order advocated by Aeschylus. However, he has Athena insisting that a certain element of fear is still necessary. Though optimistic about human nature and behavior in a free society, he knew as well as anyone that people act in their own self-interest and that venality and greed cannot be legislated out of existence. To curb these tendencies an inbred fear of punishment must remain, a dread more deeply felt than a purely intellectual respect for law. Some critics have seen the Furies' conversion to the Gracious Ones as a sort of birth of conscience—this should be an ethical conscience that incorporates some degree of fear into a concern for the safety and welfare of society. Perhaps more than any other culture, the ancient Greeks saw men and women both as they were and as they should be.

Athenians revered Aeschylus for the lofty idealism of his dramas and his deep concern for the well-being of his city and its inhabitants. His brief and touching epitaph was written by his younger colleague, the comic playwright Aristophanes (air-i-STOF-uh-neez; his work is discussed later in this chapter):

> Gentle he was in this life,
> Gentle in life beyond.

5.4   Bust inscribed with the name of Pericles, from Tivoli, Italy. Roman copy after a bronze original of 450–425 BC. Marble. Musei Vaticani, Rome. Photo: Alinari, Florence/Art Resource, New York.
The bronze original was possibly by Kresilas and placed on the Athenian Acropolis after the death of Pericles. Though the original work was probably a full figure this copy conforms to the Roman tradition of portrait busts, thus accounting for the feeling that this is an incomplete composition.

THE AGE OF PERICLES, CA. 495–429 BC

The other two major tragic playwrights, Sophocles and Euripides (you-RIP-uh-deez), lived and worked in Athens during its Golden Age, which co-incided with the rule of Pericles. It is best, therefore, to consider the Age of Pericles before discussing the playwrights themselves.

Athenian democracy was most fully realized with the inspired leadership of Pericles (PAIR-i-kleez), truly the best man at the right time. He was first elected general-in-chief in 461 BC and, except for two years when he was voted out of office, he directed Athenian affairs until he succumbed to the plague shortly after the beginning of the Peloponnesian War (431–404 BC) that ended the Golden Age (fig. 5.4)

The population of Attica (Athens and the surrounding territory it governed) at this time has been estimated at about 230,000 people. Of these, 40,000 were free male citizens, the actual voting population that participated in the democracy; 40,000 were women who, at best, were second-class citizens; 50,000 were foreign-born; and 100,000 were slaves. One must remember that Athenian democracy involved only the 40,000 free men. The rest of the free people (the Athenian women) participated on the periphery, and slaves not at all.

It is nevertheless a miracle of history that such a small group of citizens could, in a single century, have produced one great comedy writer, three of the finest writers of tragic drama in the history of literature, and two philosophers whose ideas have helped shape Western civilization for 2,500 years. The continuing influence of their architecture and sculpture, pottery and poetry, cannot be overestimated. Their music and painting are apparently irretrievably lost and, considering that they themselves regarded music as their best developed art and their sculpture as inferior to their painting, this is a terrible loss.

Most significantly, the people of this glorious century achieved a way of life that in its freedom for the individual, coupled with a concern for the welfare of the state as a whole, has been envied (and sometimes emulated) by the Western world ever since. This was the quality of life toward which the dramas of Aeschylus pointed. The Greek ideal is succinctly stated by C. M. Bowra (*The Greek Experience*): "A man served his state best by being himself in the full range of his nobility, and not by sacrificing it to some abstract notion of political power or expediency."

Abstract notions and generalizations about political power and expediency were anathema to a culture that spent much time and effort trying to define itself. The Greeks are known, quite correctly, as idealists who envisioned the world as it should be. They were, however, clear-eyed and literal-minded, seeing themselves and their culture as they really were. Certainly they asked philosophical questions about the nature of justice, freedom, beauty, and love. These are, of course, abstractions but they sought the answers in the concrete reality of the world of here and now. Justice, for example, was literally to be found in the law courts. If justice was not present then injustice had replaced it. If a higher, purer form of justice could be idealized then that was what should be present in the courts. Injustice did not come into being because justice—in the all-too-familiar phrase—"failed to live up to its potential"; justice was either present in the courts or it was not.

This kind of idealistic pragmatism (Gk., *pragmatikos*, "to do business, a thing done") can also be applied to the idea of beauty. After reaching some sort of agreement about ideal beauty (beauty-in-and-of-itself), the proper thing to do is to find beauty in a particular pot, painting, poem, building, song, statue, or whatever. As much as a certain object possesses the attributes of beauty, then it is to that degree that beauty literally resides in the object. The Greeks knew that perfect beauty was not a realistic goal in an imperfect world, but this did not deter them from striving for perfection. As stated before, diligence in the pursuit of excellence (*arete*) was a Greek passion.

Little political change occurred during the Age of Pericles because a reasonably fair and just democratic system was already in place. The quest, then, was for a higher quality of life for the individual and for society. Pericles and some of his compatriots had a vision of Athens as the leading city in the world, in which resided freedom, justice, and beauty. Among other things, he encouraged the free exchange of ideas by reconstructing the marketplace of commerce and ideas (the agora) and literally beautified the city by commissioning the new temples on the Acropolis. Even in their current ruined condition these ancient temples symbolize the Golden Age, some of whose beauty still lingers on atop the Athenian Acropolis.

During the Periclean age the precarious balance between individual aims and the welfare of the state shifted toward greater individualism; there was less concern for Athens and still less for the well-being of other city-states. This was first noticeable in the city's international relations; it converted the Delian League (organized to fight Persia) into what was really an Athenian empire and shifted the treasury from the island of Delos to Athens. It was this treasury that paid for the temples on the Acropolis, leading, predictably, to vigorous protests from League members. The haughty response was that Athens had shouldered the burden of protecting the League and Athens would therefore decide how the League's money was spent.

As a self-anointed international power Athens became increasingly autocratic. The older values of reverence for the state and the gods that had triumphed at Marathon and that Aeschylus had propounded in his plays, faded in the shift toward self-centered individualism. This metamorphosis probably began (or was confirmed) with the teaching of atomists such as Democritos, who argued for total materialism—including the gods, thus removing their spiritual quality—and ascribed all change to pure chance. In this random atomic world with an unpredictable future and gods offering neither guidance nor inspiration the only dependable reality was material pleasure.

Probably taking their cue from the atomists, the sophists (SOF-ists) became the leading teachers of Athens. Their leader was Protagoras (pro-TAG-uh-rus; ca. 481–411 BC), a high-minded thinker whose chief dictum was that "man is the measure of all things." By itself, this is simply a slogan-like restatement of the centrality of human values long espoused by Athenian intellectuals. But there were problems. All is well if humankind is the measure; if an individual is the yardstick then whatever he or she does is proper, with as many yardsticks as there are individuals. The later sophists did indeed move toward this position, teaching that the laws, for instance, were merely a set of opinions; those with different opinions could act on those beliefs. This could lead, of course, to anarchy, one of the extremes cited by Athena in the *Eumenides*. As for religion, Protagoras said, "about the gods I have no knowledge either that they are or that they are not or what is their nature."

Much can be said for sophist philosophy for it introduced a healthy questioning of old traditions and uncritical veneration of the gods. Conversely, complete relativism

THE ENEMY WITHIN

By the second year of the Peloponnesian War Pericles had gathered everyone inside Athens' protective walls while the Spartans ravaged the countryside. The now crowded and unsanitary city was ripe for a menace deadlier even than the enemy at the gates. A four-year epidemic started in 430 BC that, according to Thucydides, killed a third of the population, a psychological toll so destructive it sapped the war effort. At first blaming the Spartans for poisoning the wells, Athenians then accused Pericles, but his sister, his legitimate sons, and finally Pericles himself died of the sickness. What was the disease? The symptoms described by Thucydides most closely match those of scarlet fever but we may never know. We do know that the disease prolonged the war that smashed the Athenian empire and closed a chapter in world history.

ASPASIA AND THE EDUCATION OF WOMEN

Aspasia of Miletus (d. 401 BC) exerted considerable influence on Pericles and on intellectual life in general in Athens. An educated and highly intelligent foreigner, Aspasia was a former hetaera (Gk., *hetaira*, female companion). The hetaerae of ancient Greece were companions—physically, intellectually, and emotionally—to influential men in Athenian society. Well-educated and adept in music, dancing, conversation, and other social graces, they fulfilled a role generally denied to Greek wives who, though undisputed mistresses of their households, were not allowed to partake fully in life outside the home. (Most Greek wives were encouraged to learn the domestic arts of spinning, sewing, weaving, and cooking, but little else.)

Though criticized by some because of her former profession and her political influence, Aspasia established, in Pericles' home, what might be called the first salon. Here she entertained notable artists, philosophers, and political leaders, including the more liberated women of Athens. Some men broke with tradition and brought their wives to Aspasia's dinner parties to participate in discussions about the need for better educated wives to be intellectual companions for their husbands. The brilliant Aspasia was credited by Socrates with teaching Pericles in composing some of his speeches which, according to Plato (*Menexenus*, 236b), included the *Memorial Oration*.

could undermine the cohesion of society and make all thought and action a matter of expediency. The delicate balance between the welfare of the state and that of the individual was indeed shifting in the direction of the individual. It was against this philosophical backdrop that Sophocles and Euripides produced their plays.

Sophocles, ca. 496–406 BC

A contemporary of Pericles, Sophocles was a general, a priest, and the most popular dramatist in Athenian history (fig. 5.5). He is reputed to have written 123 plays and to have won first prize more than twenty times; he was never placed lower than second. Of the seven plays that survived, only *Oedipus the King* (ED-uh-pus, or EED-uh-pus; see complete text on pp. 117–34) is discussed here.

Oedipus the King is a tale of patricide, murder, incest, suicide, and self-mutilation. This is perhaps the best-known of all Greek tragedies, partly because it became the model tragedy in Aristotle's *Poetics* (see pp. 182–7). All the classic elements of tragedy are here: a man of exalted stature is brought low because of a fatal flaw in his personality; the unities of time (a single day) and of place (the exterior of the royal palace at Thebes); the calling forth of the emotions of fear and pity in the spectator; and the final purging or catharsis. One can define catharsis as feeling that the action has worked itself out to its one unavoidable conclusion. In doing so the emotions of pity and fear are purged in the spectator, who is left in peace. The ending, though

A SPARTAN LIFE

The word Spartan is still used to describe something austere, rigorous, disciplined. What was life like in the original Sparta?

The dominant warrior class in this collectivist society was supported by freemen engaged in commerce and crafts and by a large number of slaves (helots) who were owned by the state. The Spartan process began with babies inspected at birth and the weak ones left to die on a mountainside. Military training started at age seven with no clothing permitted until age twelve. Spartans became hoplites (soldiers) at age twenty, lived in military barracks until age thirty and moved into clubs until age sixty, after which those still alive retired from military life. Marriage and robust children were encouraged; a man could spend an evening with his wife but never a whole night. Spartan women received the physical training deemed necessary for producing sturdy babies. The men practiced war, the women raised future soldiers and mothers of soldiers, and the helots did most of the work.

tragic, is right; there is no more to be said or done.

As the play opens the city of Thebes is gripped by a terrible plague that can be lifted, according to the Delphic Oracle, only when the murderer of Laios (LYE-os), the former king, is discovered and punished. Oedipus, the present king, who has married, according to custom, the widowed queen Jocasta (yoe-KOS-ta), swears he will save the city by finding the murderer. He makes this vow in the face of two prophecies, one of which was known to Jocasta and Laios. It was foretold that their son would kill his father and marry his mother (box 5.2). Accordingly, after their son was born, Laios (without Jocasta's consent) had the baby exposed and left to die on the slopes of Mount Cithaeron (KEE-the-ron). The second prophecy, known to Oedipus when he grew up in Corinth as the son of the king and queen there, was that he would kill his father and marry his mother. To avert this he had fled Corinth. During his flight he had an altercation with an old man and his bodyguards at a place where three roads came together. In a fit of rage Oedipus killed the entire group, except a servant who escaped. He then proceeded to Thebes where he freed the city from the plague of the evil Sphinx by solving the riddle: "What walks on four legs in the morning, two legs at noon, and three legs at night?" Oedipus' correct answer was "humankind." Chosen king by a grateful populace, he married Jocasta and fathered four children.

The play is riddled with irony; the audience knows that Oedipus is the murderer he is seeking and that the curse he pronounced on the killer will fulfill itself on him. This expected event comes to pass: Jocasta commits suicide, and Oedipus pierces his eyeballs and exiles himself from the city.

The tragedy ends with the oracles upheld and the gods inflicting a just punishment on the errant king. Taken as a whole, the drama can be interpreted as a clear admonition: the gods are all-powerful and should receive reverence and honor. But was Oedipus only a pawn in a cosmic drama or the agent of his own destruction? Was the king himself a warning to the Athenians?

A common Greek tragic situation is one in which whatever the hero does is wrong. Agamemnon must either kill his daughter or betray his command; Orestes must disobey Apollo or kill his mother; Oedipus must discover the truth or watch his city die.

Whether the hero has erred unknowingly or must err against his will, there could be still another error that justified divine retribution. Consider Agamemnon as he walked upon the purple carpet, colored with a dye so expensive it was reserved for the gods. This was an act of overweening pride guaranteed to incur the wrath of the gods. This was hubris.

Pride was a virtue in ancient Greece. Diligence in the pursuit of excellence (*arete*) could result in impressive achievement and, for the creator, a justifiable feeling of self-esteem. Pride in achievement was expected; the accomplishment somehow enlarged everyone. Pride in onself as

5.5 Portrait bust of Sophocles. Ca. 340 BC. Marble. British Museum, London.

the achiever was another matter because that kind of vanity, that hubris, tended to elevate the one person and demean the many. Far more than vanity, hubris was an overweening pride that was harmful to others. Consider, for example, a film star who received an Oscar for an outstanding performance. And then that Oscar-winner becomes a self-appointed authority on politics and affairs of state or a self-styled expert in the occult and supernatural. In either case the actor has laid claim to expertise totally foreign to the craft of acting. That is hubris.

A careful study of *Oedipus the King* reveals many instances of Oedipus' placing himself above all others as the sole seeker of truth. Though justifiably proud of solving the riddle and saving the city, from the time the play begins he has become the all-knowing savior of Thebes. Hubris—his fatal flaw—led Oedipus to gratuitously attack Teiresias and Creon and to pronounce himself judge and jury in deciding the future of Thebes.

If the fatally-flawed king was indeed self-destructive, was his tragic end a warning to the people of Athens? *Oedipus the King* was produced around the beginning of the Peloponnesian War but it was the *cause* of the war—the Athenian empire itself—that distressed many Athenians. For several decades the empire had been expanding, acquiring riches and power largely at the expense of its commercial and political rivals. That power corrupts and that it is perhaps the ultimate aphrodisiac, are truisms that apply to the majority populist party of middle-class Athenians who lusted after the might of empire. Warnings by Sophocles and others went unheeded by an arrogant populace convinced of Athenian superiority in everything. The ruling populist party fought much of the war with a guns-and-butter philosophy, maintaining a luxurious lifestyle while contending with the "inferior" Spartans.

The size and strength of an empire that many thoughtful citizens had never wanted virtually invited the Spartans to "put out all their strength and overthrow the Athenian power by force of arms" (Greek historian Thucydides). Hubris helped cause the war and hubris was certainly a factor in the final defeat of the haughty city.

fertility rites but the origin of the stop-action choral interludes is unknown. Unlike the tragedians who preferred subtle implications, comic playwrights had every intention of impressing their views on the audience through dialogue and, especially, through barbed and biting choral commentary.

Aristophanes used the stage to attack living persons (such as Socrates and Euripides), but also to fight hypocrisy, corruption, stupidity, greed, and war. In the *Clouds* he depicted Socrates as a sophist who, for a fee, taught either right logic or wrong logic, which did not help matters at the trial, as Socrates pointed out during his *Apology*. The *Wasps* poked fun at lawyers, who could be found, he said, by lifting any rock, while the *Frogs* was a literary satire about Aeschylus and, especially, Euripides, of whom he was sharply critical. In the *Knights* he specified the characteristics of popular politicians: a horrible voice, bad breeding, and a vulgar manner.

Of his eleven extant plays *Lysistrata* best illustrates the theme that concerns us here: the futility of war, particularly the Peloponnesian War that ended Athens' most glorious days. An Athenian woman, Lysistrata, enlists the cooperation of all Greek women (including Spartans) in a simple but wonderfully effective scheme to stop warfare: no sex until the fighting stops. Given a choice between making love and making war, the warriors, with much breast-beating followed by some pitiful pleading, choose the blessings of peace and love. (See the complete play in this chapter.)

The satirical comedies of Aristophanes dealt primarily, and brilliantly, with universal themes—stupidity, for example, never goes out of style—which accounts for their immense popularity throughout antiquity and the many performances in today's world. Some four centuries after the Golden Age the poet Antipater (an-TIP-a-ter) wrote the following epitaph:

> These are Aristophanes' marvelous plays,
> so often crowned with ivy from his deme.
> What Dionysian pages, and how clear
> That ringing voice of comedy edged with charm—
> Heroic dramatist fit to take on Greece,
> Hating the bad and making fun of it.
>
> Alistair Elliot, translator

SUMMARY

The fifth century BC in Athens was truly astonishing. Brief but brilliant, the Golden Age began with the pride of victory over the Persians, with the triumph of democracy, and with the promise of the good life as revealed in the noble plays of Aeschylus. During the early years of Pericles' leadership Athenian citizens realized that good life about as much as it can ever be. It ended in a time of military defeat; a time when the dominant mood was self-serving individualism; a time when Athenians listened no longer to the voice of its most astute philosopher/critic while also ignoring the serious issues in the comedies of Aristophanes.

The loftiest assertion of the human spirit in these exhausted times came at the very end with the trial of Socrates and a glimpse of the philosopher as hero. In the *Apology* (see pp. 161–71 for the complete text) he spoke to the jury as an urbane, civilized man, disdaining high-flown rhetoric on the one hand, and sentiment on the other. Instead, he speaks almost in a conversational tone about his own life and his devotion to his highest ideals for human conduct. The most poignant statement about integrity and justice comes after the vote that condemned him to death:

> And there are many other ways of avoiding death in every danger if a man is willing to say and to do anything. But, my friends, I think that it is a much harder thing to escape from wickedness than from death, for wickedness is swifter than death. And now I, who am old and slow, have been overtaken by the slower pursuer: and my accusers, who are clever and swift, have been overtaken by the swifter pursuer—wickedness. And now I shall go away, sentenced by you to death; and they will go away, sentenced by truth to wickedness and injustice. I abide by my penalty, they by theirs.

LITERARY SELECTION 3

Agamemnon
Aeschylus (525–456 BC)

Throughout this book the thematic relevance of selected literary works is discussed in the body of each chapter—that is, why they were picked for a humanities text. All have great literary merit but selections were not based on merit alone nor necessarily on being the best work of a particular author. The works themselves appear in the Literary Selection sections where they are considered on their own terms as literature. This is why *Agamemnon*, as one example, is discussed in two different places and in two distinctive ways in this chapter.

Before studying this play the reader should reexamine the thematic discussion earlier in the chapter and then review the misfortunes of the House of Atreus in box 5.1. The Greeks had arranged a series of line-of-sight beacons stretching from Troy in western Turkey to the Greek mainland. It is with their imminent flaming that the play begins. The translation is by George Thomson.

CHARACTERS

Watchman
Chorus of Old Men
Clytemnestra
Herald
Agamemnon
Cassandra
Aigisthos
Captain of the Guard

The scene is the entrance to the palace of the Atreidae. Before the doors stand shrines of the gods.

[A WATCHMAN is posted on the roof.]

Watchman: I've prayed God to release me from sentry
　　duty
All through this long year's vigil, like a dog
Couched on the roof of Atreus, where I study
Night after night the pageantry of this vast
Concourse of stars, and moving among them like
Noblemen the constellations that bring
Summer and winter as they rise and fall.
And I am still watching for the beacon signal
All set to flash over the sea the radiant
News of the fall of Troy. So confident　　10
Is a woman's spirit, whose purpose is a man's.
Every night, as I turn in to my stony bed,
Quilted with dew, not visited by dreams,
Not mine—no sleep, fear stands at my pillow
Keeping tired eyes from closing once too often;
And whenever I start to sing or hum a tune,
Mixing from music an antidote to sleep,
It always turns to mourning for the royal house,
Which is not in such good shape as it used to be.
But now at last may the good news in a flash　　20
Scatter the darkness and deliver us.
[The beacon flashes.]
O light of joy, whose gleam turns night to day,
O radiant signal for innumerable
Dances of victory! Ho there! I call the queen,
Agamemnon's wife, to raise with all the women
Alleluias of thanksgiving through the palace
Saluting the good news, if it is true
That Troy has fallen, as this blaze portends:
Yes, and I'll dance an overture myself.
My master's dice have fallen out well, and I　　30
Shall score three sixes for this nightwatching.
[A pause.]
Well, come what will, may it soon be mine to grasp
In this right hand my master's, home again!
[Another pause.]
The rest is secret. A heavy ox has trodden
Across my tongue. These walls would have tales to tell
If they had mouths. I speak only to those
Who are in the know, to others—I know nothing.
[The WATCHMAN goes into the palace. Women's cries are heard. Enter CHORUS OF OLD MEN.]

Chorus: It is ten years since those armed prosecutors
of Justice, Menelaus and Agamemnon, twin-sceptered
in God-given sovereignty, embarked in the thousand　　40

ships crying war, like eagles with long wings beating
the air over a robbed mountain nest, wheeling and
screaming for their lost children. Yet above them
some god, maybe Apollo or Zeus, overhears the sky-
dweller's cry and sends after the robber a Fury.
[CLYTEMNESTRA comes out of the palace and unseen by the elders places offerings before the shrines.]
Just so the two kings were sent by the greater king,
Zeus, for the sake of a promiscuous woman to fight
Paris, Greek and Trojan locked fast together in the
dusty betrothals of battle. And however it stands with
them now, the end is unalterable; no flesh, no wine　　50
can appease God's fixed indignation.
　　As for us, with all the able-bodied men enlisted and
gone, we are left here leaning our strength on a staff;
for, just as in infancy, when the marrow is still unformed,
the War-god is not at his post, so it is in extreme old
age, as the leaves fall fast, we walk on three feet, like
dreams in the daylight.
[They see CLYTEMNESTRA.]
　　O Queen, what news? what message sets light to the
altars? All over the town the shrines are ablaze with unguents
drawn from the royal stores and the flames shoot　　60
up into the night sky. Speak, let us hear all that may
be made public, so healing the anxieties that have
gathered thick in our hearts; let the gleam of good news
scatter them!
[CLYTEMNESTRA goes out to tend the other altars of the city.]
Strength have I still to recall that sign which greeted the
　　two kings
Taking the road, for the prowess of song is not yet
　　spent.
I sing of two kings united in sovereignty, leading
Armies to battle, who saw two eagles
Beside the palace
Wheel into sight, one black, and the other was white-
　　tailed,　　70
Tearing a hare with her unborn litter.
Cry Sorrow cry, but let good conquer!
Shrewdly the priest took note and compared each eagle
　　with each king.
Then spoke out and prefigured the future in these
　　words:
"In time the Greek arms shall demolish the fortress of
　　Priam;
Only let no jealous God, as they fasten
On Troy the slave's yoke,
Strike them in anger; for Artemis[2] loathes the
　　rapacious
Eagles of Zeus that have slaughtered the frail hare.
Cry Sorrow cry, but let good conquer!　　80
O Goddess, gentle to the tender whelp of fierce lions
As to all young life of the wild,
So now fulfill what is good in the omen and mend what
　　is faulty.
And I appeal unto the Lord Apollo,
Let not the north wind hold the fleet storm-bound,
Driving them on to repay that feast with another,

---

2. Artemis is the goddess of the hunt and all wild things. In this
　　context, the hare represents the city of Troy.

Inborn builder of strife, feud that fears no man, it is still
     there,
Treachery keeping the house, it remembers, revenges,
     a child's death!"
Such, as the kings left home, was the seer's revelation.
Cry Sorrow cry, but let good conquer!   90
Zeus, whoe'er he be, if so it best
Please his ear to be addressed,
So shall he be named by me.
All things have I measured, yet
None have found save him alone,
Zeus, if a man from a heart heavy-laden
Seek to cast his cares aside.
Long since lived a ruler of the world,[3]
Puffed with martial pride, of whom
None shall tell, his day is done;   100
Also, he who followed him
Met his master and is gone.
Zeus the victorious, gladly acclaim him;
Perfect wisdom shall be yours;
Zeus, who laid it down that man
Must in sorrow learn and through
Pain to wisdom find his way.
When deep slumber falls, remembered wrongs
Chafe the bruised heart with fresh pangs, and no
Welcome wisdom meets within.   110
Harsh the grace dispensed by powers immortal,
Pilots of the human soul.
Even so the elder prince,[4]
Marshal of the thousand ships,
Rather than distrust a priest,
Torn with doubt to see his men
Harbor-locked, hunger-pinched, hard-oppressed,
Strained beyond endurance, still
Watching, waiting, where the never-tiring
Tides of Aulis ebb and flow: 120
And still the storm blew from mountains far north,
With moorings windswept and hungry crews pent
In rotting hulks,
With tackling all torn and seeping timbers,
Till Time's slow-paced, enforced inaction
Had all but stripped bare the bloom of Greek manhood.
And then was found but one
Cure to allay the tempest—never a blast so bitter—
Shrieked in a loud voice by the priest, "Artemis!"
     striking the Atreidae with dismay, each with his staff
     smiting the ground and weeping.
And then the king spoke, the elder, saying: 130
"The choice is hard—hard to disobey him,
And harder still
To kill my own child, my palace jewel,
With unclean hands before the altar
Myself, her own father, spill a maid's pure blood.

---

3. The reference here is to Ouranus and Kronos, both kings of
   the gods. Zeus led a successful revolt against Kronos so that
   he could become king.
4. This refers to the beginning of the Trojan War when the
   Greek fleet was delayed in the harbor of Aulis. In order to
   appease Artemis and secure favorable winds, Agamemnon,
   "the elder prince," followed the prophecy of the seer, Kalkhas,
   and sacrificed his daughter, Iphigeneia.

I have no choice but wrong.
How shall I fail my thousand ships and betray my
     comrades?
So shall the storm cease, and the men eager for war
     clamor for that virginal blood righteously! So pray for
     a happy outcome!"
And when he bowed down beneath the harness
Of cruel coercion, his spirit veering   140
With sudden sacrilegious change,
He gave his whole mind to evil counsel.
For man is made bold with base-contriving
Impetuous madness, first cause of much grief.
And so then he slew his own child
For a war to win a woman
And to speed the storm-bound fleet from the shore to
     battle.
She cried aloud "Father!" yet they heard not;
A girl in first flower, yet they cared not,
The lords who gave the word for war.   150
Her father prayed, then he bade his vassals
To seize her where swathed in folds of saffron
She lay, and lift her up like a yearling
With bold heart above the altar,
And her lovely lips to bridle
That they might not cry out, cursing the House of
     Atreus,
With gags, her voice sealed with brute force and
     crushed.
And then she let fall her cloak
And cast at each face a glance that dumbly craved
     compassion;
And like a picture she would but could not greet   160
Her father's guests, who at home
Had often sat when the meal was over,
The cups replenished, with all hearts enraptured
To hear her sing grace with clear unsullied voice for her
     loving father.
The end was unseen and unspeakable.
The task of priestcraft was done.
For Justice first chastens, then she presses home her
     lesson.
The morrow must come, its grief will soon be here,
So let us not weep today.
It shall be made known as clear as daybreak.   170
And so may all this at last end in good news,
For which the queen prays, the next of kin and stay of
     the land of Argos.
[CLYTEMNESTRA appears at the door of the palace.]
Our humble salutations to the queen!
Hers is our homage, while our master's throne
Stands empty. We are still longing to hear
The meaning of your sacrifice. Is it good news?
Clytemnestra: Good news! With good news may the
     morning rise
Out of the night—good news beyond all hope!
My news is this: The Greeks have taken Troy.
Chorus: What? No, it cannot be true! I cannot grasp it.   180
Clytemnestra: The Greeks hold Troy—is not that plain
     enough?
Chorus: Joy steals upon me and fills my eyes with
     tears.

Clytemnestra: Indeed, your looks betray your loyalty.
Chorus: What is the proof? Have you any evidence?
Clytemnestra: Of course I have, or else the Gods have
cheated me.
Chorus: You have given ear to some beguiling dream.
Clytemnestra: I would not come screaming fancies
out of my sleep.
Chorus: Rumors have wings—on these your heart has
fed.
Clytemnestra: You mock my intelligence as though I
were a girl.
Chorus: When was it? How long is it since the city fell?   190
Clytemnestra: In the night that gave birth to this
dawning day.
Chorus: What messenger could bring the news so fast?
Clytemnestra: The God of Fire, who from Ida sent forth
light
And beacon by beacon passed the flame to me.
From the peak of Ida first to the cliff of Hermes
On Lemnos, and from there a third great lamp
Was flashed to Athos, the pinnacle of Zeus;
Up, up it soared, luring the dancing fish
To break surface in rapture at the light;
A golden courier, like the sun, it sped   200
Post-haste its message to Macistus, thence
Across Euripus, till the flaming sign
Was marked by the watchers on Messapium,
And thence with strength renewed from piles of heath
Like moonrise over the valley of Asopus,
Relayed in glory to Cithaeron's heights,
And still flashed on, not slow the sentinels,
Leaping across the lake from peak to peak,
It passed the word to burn and burn, and flung
A comet to the promontory that stands   210
Over the Gulf of Saron, there it swooped
Down to the Spider's Crag above the city,
Then found its mark on the roof of this house of Atreus,
That beacon fathered by Ida's far off fires.
Such were the stages of our torch relay,
And the last to run is the first to reach the goal.
That is my evidence, the testimony which
My lord has signaled to me out of Troy.
Chorus: Lady, there will be time later to thank the
Gods.
Now I ask only to listen: speak on and on.   220
Clytemnestra: Today the Greeks have occupied Troy.
I seem to hear there a very strange street-music.
Pour oil and vinegar into one cup, you will see
They do not make friends. So there two tunes are heard.
Slaves now, the Trojans, brothers and aged fathers,
Prostrate, sing for their dearest the last dirge.
The others, tired out and famished after the night's
looting,
Grab what meal chance provides, lodgers now
In Trojan houses, sheltered from the night frosts,
From the damp dews delivered, free to sleep   230
Off guard, off duty, a blissful night's repose.
Therefore, provided that they show due respect
To the altars of the plundered town and are not
Tempted to lay coarse hands on sanctities,
Remembering that the last lap—the voyage home—

Lies still ahead of them, then, if they should return
Guiltless before God, the curses of the bereaved
Might be placated—barring accidents.
That is my announcement—a message from my master.
May all end well, and may I reap the fruit of it!   240
Chorus: Lady, you have spoken with a wise man's
judgment.
Now it is time to address the gods once more
After this happy outcome of our cares.
Thanks be to Zeus and to gracious Night, housekeeper
of heaven's embroidery, who has cast over the towers of
Troy a net so fine as to leave no escape for old or young,
all caught in the snare! All praise to Zeus, who with a
shaft from his outstretched bow has at last brought
down the transgressor!
"By Zeus struck down!" The truth is all clear   250
With each step plainly marked. He said, Be
It so, and so it was. A man denied once
That heaven pays heed to those who trample
Beneath the feet holy sanctities. He lied wickedly;
For God's wrath soon or late destroys all sinners filled
With pride, puffed up with vain presumption,
And great men's houses stocked with silver
And gold beyond measure. Far best to live
Free of want, without grief, rich in the gift of wisdom.
Glutted with gold, the sinner kicks   260
Justice out of his sight, yet
She sees *him* and remembers.
As sweet temptation lures him onwards
With childlike smile into the death-trap
He cannot help himself. His curse is lit up
Against the darkness, a bright baleful light.
And just as false bronze in battle hammered turns black
and shows
Its true worth, so the sinner time-tried stands
condemned.
His hopes take wing, and still he gives chase, with foul
crimes branding all his people.
He cries to deaf heaven, none hear his prayers.   270
Justice drags him down to hell as he calls for succor.
Such was the sinner Paris, who
Rendered thanks to a gracious
Host by stealing a woman.
She left behind her the ports all astir
With throngs of men under arms filing onto shipboard;
She took to Troy in lieu of dowry death.
A light foot passed through the gates and fled,
And then a cry of lamentation rose.
The seers, the king's prophets, muttered darkly: 280
"Bewail the king's house that now is desolate,
Bewail the bed marked with print of love that fled!"
Behold, in silence, without praise, without reproach,
They sit upon the ground and weep.
Beyond the wave lies their love;
Here a ghost seems to rule the palace!
Shapely the grace of statues.
Yet they can bring no comfort,
Eyeless, lifeless and loveless.
Delusive dream shapes that float through the night   290
Beguile him, bringing delight sweet but unsubstantial;
For, while the eye beholds the heart's desire,

The arms clasp empty air, and then
The fleeting vision fades and glides away
On silent wing down the paths of slumber.
The royal hearth is chilled with sorrows such as these,
And more; in each house from end to end of Greece
That sent its dearest to wage war in foreign lands
The stout heart is called to steel itself
In mute endurance against   300
Blows that strike deep into the heart's core:
Those that they sent from home they
Knew, but now they receive back
Only a heap of ashes.
The God of War holds the twin scales of strife,
Heartless gold-changer trafficking in men,
Consigning homeward from Troy a jar of dust fire-
       refined,
Making up the weight with grief,
Shapely vessels laden each
With the ashes of their kin.   310
They mourn and praise them saying, "He
Was practiced well in sword and spear,
And he, who fell so gallantly—
All to avenge another man's wife":
It is muttered in a whisper
And resentment spreads against each of the royal
       warlords.
They lie sleeping, perpetual
Owners each of a small
Holding far from their homeland.
The sullen rumors that pass mouth to mouth   320
Bring the same danger as a people's curse.
And brooding hearts wait to hear of what the night holds
       from sight.
Watchful are the Gods of all
Hands with slaughter stained. The black
Furies wait, and when a man
Has grown by luck, not justice, great,
With sudden turn of circumstance
He wastes away to nothing, dragged
Down to be food in hell for demons.
For the heights of fame are perilous.   330
With a jealous bolt the Lord Zeus in a flash shall blast
       them.
Best to pray for a tranquil
Span of life and to be
Neither victor nor vanquished.
—The news has set the whole town aflame.
Can it be true? Perhaps it is a trick.
—Only a child would let such fiery words
Kindle his hopes, then fade and flicker out.
—It is just like a woman
To accept good news without the evidence.   340
—An old wives' tale, winged with a woman's wishes,
Spreads like wildfire, then sinks and is forgotten.
We shall soon know what the beacon signifies,
Whether it is true or whether this joyful daybreak
Is only a dream sent to deceive us all.
Here comes a messenger breathless from the shore,
Wearing a garland and covered in a cloud
Of dust, which shows that he has news to tell,
And not in soaring rhetoric of smoke and flame,

But either he brings cause for yet greater joy,   350
Or else—no, let us abjure the alternative.
Glad shone the light, as gladly break the day!
[Enter HERALD.]
Herald: O joy! Argos, I greet you, my fatherland!
Joy brings me home after ten years of war.
Many the shattered hopes, but this has held.
Now I can say that when I die my bones
Will lie at rest here in my native soil.
I greet you joyfully, I greet the Sun,
Zeus the All-Highest, and the Pythian King,
Bending no more against us his fatal shafts,   360
As he did beside Scamander—that was enough,
And now defend us, Savior Apollo; all
The Gods I greet, among them Hermes, too,
Patron of messengers, and the spirits of our dead,
Who sent their sons forth, may they now prepare
A joyful welcome for those whom war has spared.
Joy to the palace and to these images
Whose faces catch the sun, now, as of old,
With radiant smiles greet your sovereign lord,
Agamemnon, who brings a lamp to lighten you   370
And all here present, after having leveled
Troy with the mattock of just-dealing Zeus,
Great son of Atreus, master and monarch, blest
Above all living men. The brigand Paris
Has lost his booty and brought down the house of
       Priam.
Chorus: Joy to you, Herald, welcome home again!
Herald: Let me die, having lived to see this day!
Chorus: Your yearning for your country has worn you
       out.
Herald: So much that tears spring to the eyes for joy.
Chorus: Well, those you longed for longed equally
       for you.   380
Herald: Ah yes, our loved ones longed for our safe
       return.
Chorus: We have had many anxieties here at home.
Herald: What do you mean? Has there been
       disaffection?
Chorus: Never mind now. Say nothing and cure all.
Herald: Is it possible there was trouble in our absence?
Chorus: Now, as you said yourself, it would be a joy to
       die.
Herald: Yes, all has ended well. Our expedition
Has been successfully concluded, even though in part
The issue may be found wanting. Only the Gods
Prosper in everything. If I should tell you all   390
That we endured on shipboard in the night watches,
Our lodging the bare benches, and even worse
Ashore beneath the walls of Troy, the rains
From heaven and the dews that seeped
Out of the soil into lice-infested blankets;
If I should tell of those winters, when the birds
Dropped dead and Ida heaped on us her snows;
Those summers, when unruffled by wind or wave
The sea slept breathless under the glare of noon—
But why recall that now? It is all past,   400
Yes, for the dead past never to stir again.
Ah, they are all gone. Why count our losses? Why
Should we vex the living with grievance for the dead?

Goodbye to all that for us who have come back!
Victory has turned the scale, and so before
This rising sun let the good news be proclaimed
And carried all over the world on wings of fame:
"These spoils were brought by the conquerors of Troy
And dedicated to the Gods of Greece."
And praise to our country and to Zeus the giver   410
And thanks be given. That is all my news.
[CLYTEMNESTRA appears at the palace door.]
Chorus: Thank God that I have lived to see this day!
This news concerns all, and most of all the queen.
Clytemnestra: I raised my alleluia hours ago,
When the first messenger lit up the night,
And people mocked me saying, "Has a beacon
Persuaded you that the Greeks have captured Troy?
Truly a woman's hopes are lighter than air."
But I still sacrificed, and at a hundred
Shrines throughout the town the women chanted   420
Their endless alleluias on and on,
Singing to sleep the sacramental flames,
And now what confirmation do I need from you?
I wait to hear all from my lord, for whom
A welcome is long ready. What day is so sweet
In a woman's life as when she opens the door
To her beloved, safe home from war? Go and tell him
That he will find, guarding his property,
A wife as loyal as he left her, one
Who in all these years has kept his treasuries sealed,   430
Unkind only to enemies, and knows no more
Of other men's company than of tempering steel.
[Exit.]
Herald: Such a protestation, even though entirely
   true,
Is it not unseemly on a lady's lips?
Chorus: Such is her message, as you understand,
Full of fine phrases plain to those who know.
But tell us now, what news have you of the king's
Co-regent, Menelaus? Is he too home again?
Herald: Lies cannot last, even though sweet to hear.
Chorus: Can you not make your news both sweet and
   true?   440
Herald: He and his ships have vanished. They are
   missing.
Chorus: What, was it a storm that struck the fleet at
   sea?
Herald: You have told a long disaster in a word.
Chorus: Has no one news whether he is alive or dead?
Herald: Only the Sun, from whom the whole earth
   draws life.
Chorus: Tell us about the storm. How did it fall?
Herald: A day of national rejoicing must not be marred
By any jarring tongue. A messenger who comes
With black looks bringing the long prayed-against
Report of total rout, which both afflicts   450
The state in general and in every household leaves
The inmates prostrate under the scourge of war—
With such a load upon his lips he may fitly
Sing anthems to the Furies down in hell;
But when he greets a prospering people with
News of the war's victorious end—how then
Shall I mix foul with fair and find words to tell you

Of the blow that struck us out of that angry heaven?
Water and Fire, those age-old enemies,
Made common cause against the homebound fleet.   460
Darkness had fallen, and a northerly gale
Blew up and in a blinding thunderstorm
Our ships were tossed and buffeted hull against hull
In a wild stampede and herded out of sight;
Then, at daybreak, we saw the Aegean in blossom
With a waving crop of corpses and scattered timbers.
Our ship came through, saved by some spirit, it seems,
Who took the helm and piloted her, until
She slipped under the cliffs into a cove.
There, safe at last, incredulous of our luck,   470
We brooded all day, stunned by the night's disaster.
And so, if any of the others have survived,
They must be speaking of us as dead and gone.
May all yet end well! Though it is most to be expected
That Menelaus is in some great distress.
Yet, should some shaft of sunlight spy him out
Somewhere among the living, rescued by Zeus,
Lest the whole house should perish, there is hope
That he may yet come home. There you have the truth.
Chorus: Tell us who invented that   480
Name so deadly accurate?
Was it one who presaging
Things to come divined a word
Deftly tuned to destiny?
Helen—hell indeed she carried
To men, to ships, to a proud city, stealing
From the silk veils of her chamber, sailing seaward
With the Zephyr's breath behind her;
And they set forth in a thousand ships to hunt her
On the path that leaves no imprint,   490
Bringers of endless bloodshed.
So, as Fate decreed, in Troy,
Turning into keeners kin,
Furies, instruments of God's
Wrath, at last demanded full
Payment for the stolen wife;
And the wedding song that rang out
To greet the bride from beyond the broad Aegean
Was in time turned into howls of imprecation
From the countless women wailing   500
For the loved ones they had lost in war for her sake,
And they curse the day they gave that
Welcome to war and bloodshed.
An old story is told of an oxherd who reared at his hearth
   a lion-cub, a pet for his children,
Pampered fondly by young and old with dainty morsels
   begged at each meal from his master's table.
But Time showed him up in his true nature after his
   kind—a beast savaging sheep and oxen,
Mad for the taste of blood, and only then they knew
   what they had long nursed was a curse from heaven.
And so it seemed then there came to rest in Troy
A sweet-smiling calm, a clear sky, seductive,
A rare pearl set in gold and silver,   510
Shaft of love from a glancing eye.
She is seen now as an agent
Of death sent from Zeus, a Fury
Demanding a bloody bride-price.

[Enter CLYTEMNESTRA.]
From ancient times people have believed that when
A man's wealth has come to full growth it breeds
And brings forth tares and tears in plenty.
No, I say, it is only wicked deeds
That increase, fruitful in evil.
The house built on justice always   520
Is blest with a happy offspring.
And yet the pride bred of wealth often burgeons
    anew
In evil times, a cloud of deep night,
Specter of ancient crimes that still
Walks within the palace walls,
True to the dam that bore it.
But where is Justice? She lights up the smoke-darkened
    hut.
From mansions built by hands polluted
Turning to greet the pure in heart,
Proof against false praise, she guides   530
All to its consummation.
*[Enter AGAMEMNON in a chariot followed by another
chariot carrying CASSANDRA and spoils of war.]*
Agamemnon, conqueror, joy to our king! How shall my
greeting neither fall short nor shoot too high? Some men
feign rejoicing or sorrow with hearts untouched; but
those who can read man's nature in the book of the
eyes will not be deceived by dissembled fidelity. I
declare that, when you left these shores ten years ago
to recover with thousands of lives one woman, who
eloped of her own free will, I deemed your judgment
misguided; but now in all sincerity I salute you with joy.   540
Toil happily ended brings pleasure at last, and in time you
shall learn to distinguish the just from the unjust
steward.

Agamemnon: First, it is just that I should pay my
    respects
To the land of Argos and her presiding Gods,
My partners in this homecoming as also
In the just penalty which I have inflicted on
The city of Troy. When the supreme court of heaven
Adjudicated on our cause, they cast
Their votes unanimously against her, though not   550
Immediately, and so on the other side
Hope hovered hesitantly before it vanished.
The fires of pillage are still burning there
Like sacrificial offerings. Her ashes
Redolent with riches breathe their last and die.
For all this it is our duty to render thanks
To the celestial powers, with whose assistance
We have exacted payment and struck down
A city for one woman, forcing our entry
Within the Wooden Horse, which at the setting   560
Of the Pleiades like a hungry lion leapt
Out and slaked its thirst in royal blood.
As to your sentiments, I take due note
And find that they accord with mine. Too few
Rejoice at a friend's good fortune. I have known
Many dissemblers swearing false allegiance.
One only, though he joined me against his will,
Once in the harness, proved himself a staunch
Support, Odysseus, be he now alive or dead.

All public questions and such as concern the Gods   570
I shall discuss in council and take steps
To make this triumph lasting; and if here or there
Some malady comes to light, appropriate
Remedies will be applied to set it right.
Meanwhile, returning to my royal palace,
My first duty is to salute the Gods
Who led me overseas and home again.
Victory attends me; may she remain with me!

Clytemnestra: Citizens of Argos, councillors and
    elders,
I shall declare without shame in your presence   580
My feelings for my husband. Diffidence
Dies in us all with time. I shall speak of what
I suffered here, while he was away at the war,
Sitting at home, with no man's company,
Waiting for news, listening to one
Messenger after another, each bringing worse
Disasters. If all his rumored wounds were real,
His body was in shreds, shot through and through.
If he had died—the predominant report—
He was a second Geryon, an outstretched giant   590
With three corpses and one death for each,
While I, distraught, with a knot pressing my throat,
Was rescued forcibly, to endure still more.
    And that is why our child is not present here,
As he should be, pledge of our marriage vows,
Orestes. Let me reassure you. He lives
Safe with an old friend, Strophius, who warned me
Of various dangers—your life at stake in Troy
And here a restive populace, which might perhaps
Be urged to kick a man when he is down.   600
    As for myself, the fountains of my tears
Have long ago run dry. My eyes are sore
After so many nights watching the lamp
That burnt at my bedside always for you.
If I should sleep, a gnat's faint whine would shatter
The dreams that were my only company.
    But now, all pain endured, all sorrow past,
I salute this man as the watchdog of the fold,
The stay that saves the ship, the sturdy oak
That holds the roof up, the longed-for only child,   610
The shore despaired-of sighted far out at sea.
God keep us from all harm! And now, dearest,
Dismount, but not on the bare ground! Servants,
Spread out beneath those feet that have trampled Troy
A road of royal purple, which shall lead him
By the hand of Justice into a home unhoped-for,
And there, when he has entered, our vigilant care
Shall dispose of everything as the Gods have ordained.

Agamemnon: Lady, royal consort and guardian of our
    home,
I thank you for your words of welcome, extended   620
To fit my lengthy absence; but due praise
Should rather come from others; and besides,
I would not have effeminate graces unman me
With barbarous salaams and beneath my feet
Purple embroideries designed for sacred use.[5]
Honor me as a mortal, not as a god.
Heaven's greatest gift is wisdom. Count him blest
Who has brought a long life to a happy end.

I shall do as I have said, with a clear conscience.

Clytemnestra: Yet tell me frankly, according to your judgment.   630

Agamemnon: My judgment stands. Make no mistake about that.

Clytemnestra: Would you not in time of danger have vowed such an act?

Agamemnon: Yes, if the priests had recommended it.

Clytemnestra: And what would Priam have done, if he had won?

Agamemnon: Oh, he would have trod the purple without a doubt.

Clytemnestra: Then you have nothing to fear from wagging tongues

Agamemnon: Popular censure is a potent force.

Clytemnestra: Men must risk envy in order to be admired.

Agamemnon: A contentious spirit is unseemly in a woman.

Clytemnestra: Well may the victor yield a victory.   640

Agamemnon: Do you set so much store by your victory?

Clytemnestra: Be tempted, freely vanquished, victor still!

Agamemnon: Well, if you will have it, let someone unlace

These shoes, and, as I tread the purple, may

No far-off god cast at me an envious glance

At the prodigal desecration of all this wealth!

Meanwhile, extend your welcome to this stranger.

Power tempered with gentleness wins God's favor.

No one is glad to be enslaved, and she

Is a princess presented to me by the army,   650

The choicest flower culled from a host of captives.

And now, constrained to obey you, setting foot

On the sacred purple, I pass into my home.

Clytemnestra: The sea is still there, nothing can dry it up,

Renewing out of its infinite abundance

Unfailing streams of purple and blood-red dyes.

So too this house, the Gods be praised, my lord,

Has riches inexhaustible. There is no counting

The robes I would have vowed to trample on,

Had some oracle so instructed, if by such means   660

I could have made good the loss of one dear soul.[6]

So now your entry to your hearth and home

Is like a warm spell in the long winter's cold,

Or when Zeus from the virgin grape at last

Draws wine, coolness descends upon the house

(For then from the living root the new leaves raise

A welcome shelter against the burning Dog-Star)

As man made perfect moves about his home.

[Exit AGAMEMNON.]

Zeus, perfector of all things, fulfill my prayers

And fulfill also your own purposes!   670

[Exit.]

---

5. The purple dye was extracted from seaweed. It was very rare, therefore very expensive: a color reserved for the gods.
6. Iphigeneia.

Chorus: What is this delirious dread,

Ominous, oracular,

Droning through my brain with unrelenting

Beat, irrepressible prophet of evil?

Why can I not cast it out

Planting good courage firm

On my spirit's empty throne?

In time the day came

When the Greeks with anchors plunged

Moored the sloops of war, and troops   680

Thronged the sandy beach of Troy.

So today my eyes have seen

Safe at last the men come home.

Still I hear the strain of stringless music,

Dirge of the Furies, a choir uninvited

Chanting in my heart of hearts.

Mortal souls stirred by God

In tune with fate divine the shape

Of things to come; yet

Grant that these forebodings prove   690

False and bring my fears to naught.

If a man's health be advanced over the due mean,

It will trespass soon upon sickness, who stands

Next neighbor, between them a thin wall.

So does the vessel of life

Launched with a favoring breeze

Suddenly founder on reefs of destruction.

Caution seated at the helm

Casts a portion of the freight

Overboard with measured throw;   700

So the ship may ride the storm.

Furrows enriched each season with showers from heaven

Banish hunger from the door.

But if the red blood of a man spatters the ground, dripping and deadly, then who

Has the magical power to recall it?

Even the healer who knew

Spells to awaken the dead,

Zeus put an end to his necromancy.

Portions are there preordained,

Each supreme within its own   710

Province fixed eternally.

That is why my spirit groans

Brooding in fear, and no longer it hopes to unravel

Mazes of a fevered mind.

[Enter CLYTEMNESTRA.]

Clytemnestra: You, too, Cassandra, come inside! The merciful

Zeus gives you the privilege to take part

In our domestic sacrifice and stand

Before his altar among the other slaves there.

Put by your pride and step down. Even Heracles

Submitted once to slavery, and be consoled   720

In serving a house whose wealth has been inherited

Over so many generations. The harshest masters

Are those who have snatched their harvest out of hand.

You shall receive here what custom prescribes.

Chorus: She is speaking to you. Caught in the net, surrender.

Clytemnestra: If she knows Greek and not some
  barbarous language,
My mystic words shall fill the soul within her.
Chorus: You have no choice. Step down and do her
  will.
Clytemnestra: There is no time to waste. The victims
  are
All ready for the knife to render thanks   730
For this unhoped-for joy. If you wish to take part,
Make haste, but, if you lack the sense to understand,—
[To the CHORUS.]
Speak to her with your hands and drag her down.
Chorus: She is like a wild animal just trapped.
Clytemnestra: She is mad, the foolish girl. Her city
  captured,
Brought here a slave, she will be broken in.
I'll waste no words on her to demean myself.
[Exit.]
Cassandra: Oh! oh! Apollo!
Chorus: What blasphemy, to wail in Apollo's name!
Cassandra: Oh! oh! Apollo!   740
Chorus: Again she cries in grief to the god of joy!
Cassandra: Apollo, my destroyer! a second time!
Chorus: Ah, she foresees what is in store for her.
  She is now a slave, and yet God's gift remains.
Cassandra: Apollo, my destroyer! What house is this?
Chorus: Do you not know where you have come,
  poor girl?
Then let us tell you. This is the House of Atreus.
Cassandra: Yes, for its very walls smell of iniquity,
A charnel house that drips with children's blood.[7]
Chorus: How keen her scent to seize upon the trail!
Cassandra: Listen to them as they bewail the foul   750
Repast of roast meat for a father's mouth!
Chorus: Enough! Reveal no more! We know it all.
Cassandra: What is it plotted next? Horror
  unspeakable.
A hard cross for kinsfolk.
The hoped-for savior is far away.
Chorus: What does she say? This must be something
  new.
Cassandra: Can it be so—to bathe one who is travel-
  tired,
And then smiling stretch out
A hand followed by a stealthy hand!
Chorus: She speaks in riddles, and I cannot read them. 760
Cassandra: What do I see? A net!
Yes, it is she, his mate and murderess!
Cry alleluia, cry, angels of hell, rejoice,
Fat with blood, dance and sing!
Chorus: What is the Fury you have called upon?
Helpless the heart faints with the sinking sun.
Closer still draws the stroke.
Cassandra: Ah, let the bull[8] beware!
It is a robe she wraps him in, and strikes!
Into the bath he slumps heavily, drowned in blood.   770
Such her skilled handicraft.
Chorus: It is not hard to read her meaning now.
Why does the prophet's voice never have good to
  tell,
Only cry woes to come?

Cassandra: Oh, pitiful destiny! Having lamented his,
Now I lament my own passion to fill the bowl.
Where have you brought me? Must I with him die?
Chorus: You sing your own dirge, like the red-brown
  bird
That pours out her grief-stricken soul,
Itys, Itys! she cries, the sad nightingale.   780
Cassandra: It is not so; for she, having become a bird,
Forgot her tears and sings her happy lot,
While I must face the stroke of two-edged steel.
Chorus: From whence does this cascade of harsh
  discords
Issue, and where will it at last be calmed?
Calamity you cry—O where must it end?
Cassandra: O wedding day, Paris accurst of all!
Scamander,[9] whose clear waters I grew beside!
Now I must walk weeping by Acheron.
Chorus: Even a child could understand.   790
The heart breaks, as these pitiful cries
Shatter the listening soul.
Cassandra: O fall of Troy, city of Troy destroyed!
The king's rich gifts little availed her so
That she might not have been what she is now.
Chorus: What evil spirit has possessed
Your soul, strumming such music upon your lips
As on a harp in hell?
Cassandra: Listen! My prophecy shall glance no longer
As through a veil like a bride newly-wed,   800
But bursting towards the sunrise shall engulf
The whole world in calamities far greater
Than these. No more riddles, I shall instruct,
While you shall verify each step, as I
Nose out from the beginning this bloody trail.
Upon this roof—do you see them?—stands a choir—
It has been there for generations—a gallery
Of unmelodious minstrels, a merry troop
Of wassailers drunk with human blood, reeling
And retching in horror at a brother's outraged bed.   810
Well, have I missed? Am I not well-read in
Your royal family's catalogue of crime?
Chorus: You come from a far country and recite
Our ancient annals as though you had been present.
Cassandra: The Lord Apollo bestowed this gift on me.
Chorus: Was it because he had fallen in love with you?
Cassandra: I was ashamed to speak of this till now.
Chorus: Ah yes, adversity is less fastidious.
Cassandra: Oh, but he wrestled strenuously for my
  love.
Chorus: Did you come, then, to the act of getting child? 820
Cassandra: At first I consented, and then I cheated him.
Chorus: Already filled with his gift of prophecy?
Cassandra: Yes, I forewarned my people of their
  destiny.
Chorus: Did your divine lover show no displeasure?
Cassandra: Yes, the price I paid was that no one
  listened to me.

---

7. She refers to Thyestes' banquet. See box 5.1.
8. Agamemnon.
9. Scamander is a river near Troy; Acheron (AK-e-ron) is one of
the rivers of the underworld.

Chorus: Your prophecies seem credible enough to us.
Cassandra: Oh!
Again the travail of the prophetic trance
Runs riot in my soul. Do you not see them
There, on the roof, those apparitions—children   830
Murdered by their own kin, in their hands
The innards of which their father ate—oh
What a pitiable load they carry! For that crime
Revenge is plotted by the fainthearted lion,[10]
The stay-at-home, stretched in my master's bed
(Being his slave, I must needs call him so),
Lying in wait for Troy's great conqueror.
Little he knows what that foul bitch with ears
Laid back and rolling tongue intends for him
With a vicious snap, her husband's murderess.   840
What abominable monster shall I call her—
A two-faced amphisbaena or Scylla that skulks
Among the rocks to waylay mariners,
Infernal sea-squib locked in internecine
Strife—did you not hear her alleluias
Of false rejoicing at his safe return?
Believe me or not, what must be will be, and then
You will pity me and say, She spoke the truth.
Chorus: The feast of Thyestes I recognized, and
    shuddered,
But for the rest my wits are still astray.   850
Cassandra: Your eyes shall see the death of
    Agamemnon.
Chorus: No, hush those ill-omened lips, unhappy girl!
Cassandra: There is no Apollo present, and so no
    cure.
Chorus: None, if you speak the truth; yet God
    forbid!
Cassandra: Pray God forbid, while they close in for
    the kill!
Chorus: What man is there who would plot so
    foul a crime?
Cassandra: Ah, you have altogether misunderstood.
Chorus: But how will he do it? That escapes me still.
Cassandra: And yet I can speak Greek only too well.
Chorus: So does Apollo, but his oracles are obscure.   860
Cassandra: Ah, how it burns me up! Apollo! Now
That lioness[11]—on two feet pours in the cup
My wages too, and while she whets the blade
For him promises to repay my passage money
In my own blood. Why wear these mockeries,
This staff and wreath, if I must die, then you
Shall perish first and be damned. Now we are quits!
Apollo himself has stripped me, looking upon me
A public laughingstock, who has endured
The name of witch, waif, beggar, castaway.   870
So now the god who gave me second sight
Takes back his gift and dismisses his servant,
Ready for the slaughter at a dead man's grave.
Yet we shall be avenged. Now far away,
The exile[12] shall return, called by his father's
Unburied corpse to come and kill his mother.
Why weep at all this? Have I not seen Troy fall,
And those who conquered her are thus discharged.
I name this door the gate of Hades: now
I will go and knock, I will take heart to die.   880

I only pray that the blow may be mortal,
Closing these eyes in sleep without a struggle,
While my life blood ebbs quietly away.
Chorus: O woman, in whose wisdom is so much grief,
How, if you know the end, can you approach it
So gently, like an ox that goes to the slaughter?
Cassandra: What help would it be if I should put it off?
Chorus: Yet, while there is life there's hope—so people
    say.
Cassandra: For me no hope, no help. My hour has
    come.
Chorus: You face your end with a courageous heart.   890
Cassandra: Yes, so they console those whom life has
    crossed.
Chorus: Is there no comfort in an honorable death?
Cassandra: O Priam, father, and all your noble sons!
[She approaches the door, then draws back.]
Chorus: What is it? Why do you turn back, sick at
    heart?
Cassandra: Inside there is a stench of dripping blood.
Chorus: It is only the blood of their fireside sacrifice.
Cassandra: It is the sort of vapor that issues from a
    tomb.
I will go now and finish my lament
Inside the house. Enough of life! O friends!
I am not scared. I beg of you only this: 900
When the day comes for them to die, a man
For a man, woman for woman, remember me!
Chorus: Poor soul condemned to death, I pity you.
Cassandra: Yet one word more, my own dirge for
    myself.
I pray the Sun, on whom I now look my last,
That he may grant to my master's avengers
A fair price for the slave-girl slain at his side.
O sad mortality! when fortune smiles,
A painted image; and when trouble comes,
One touch of a wet sponge wipes it away.   910
[Exit.]
Chorus: And her case is even more pitiable than his.
Human prosperity never rests but always craves more,
till blown up with pride it totters and falls. From the
opulent mansions pointed at by all passersby
none warns it away, none cries, "Let no more riches
enter!" To him was granted the capture of Troy, and he
has entered his home as a god, but now, if the blood of
the past is on him, if he must pay with his own death for
the crimes of bygone generations, then who is assured
of a life without sorrow?   920
Agamemnon: Oh me!
Chorus: Did you hear?
Agamemnon: Oh me, again!
Chorus:[13] It is the King. Let us take counsel!

---

10. Aigisthos.
11. Clytemnestra.
12. Orestes.
13. To the best of our knowledge, this is the first time in any
Greek play that the chorus-members speak as individuals.
Some translations show the passage as a crescendo through
the seventh speech, then a lapse into a do-nothing attitude.
What does this movement illustrate about the relation of
the people to their tradition-ridden, fatalistic society?

1 I say, raise a hue and cry!
2 Break in at once!
3 Yes, we must act.
4 *They* spurn delay.
5 They plot a tyranny.
6 Must we live their slaves?   930
7 Better to die.
8 Old men, what can we do?
9 We cannot raise the dead.
10 His death is not yet proved.
11 We are only guessing.
12 Let us break in and learn the truth!

[The doors are thrown open and CLYTEMNESTRA is seen standing over the bodies of AGAMEMNON and CASSANDRA, which are laid out on a purple robe.]

Clytemnestra: All that I said before to bide my time
Without any shame I shall now unsay. How else
Could I have plotted against an enemy
So near and seeming dear and strung the snare   940
So high that he could not jump it? Now the feud
On which I have pondered all these years has been
Fought out to its conclusion. Here I stand
Over my work, and it was so contrived
As to leave no loophole. With this vast dragnet
I enveloped him in purple folds, then struck
Twice, and with two groans he stretched his legs,
Then on his outspread body I struck a third blow,
A drink for Zeus the Deliverer of the dead.
There he lay gasping out his soul and drenched me   950
In these deathly dew-drops, at which I cried
In sheer delight like newly-budding corn
That tastes the first spring showers. And so,
Venerable elders, you see how the matter stands.
Rejoice, if you are so minded. I glory in it.
With bitter tears he filled the household bowl;
Now he has drained it to the dregs and gone.

Chorus: How can you speak so of your murdered king?

Clytemnestra: You treat me like an empty-headed
      woman.
Again, undaunted, to such as understand   960
I say—commend or censure, as you please—
It makes no difference—here is Agamemnon,
My husband, dead, the work of this right hand,
Which acted justly. There you have the truth.

Chorus: Woman, what evil brew have you devoured to
      take
On you a crime that cries out for a public curse?
Yours was the fatal blow, banishment shall be yours,
Hissed and hated of all men.

Clytemnestra: Your sentence now for me is
      banishment,
But what did you do then to contravene   970
His purpose, when, to exorcise the storms,
As though picking a ewe-lamb from his flocks,
Whose wealth of snowy fleeces never fails
To increase and multiply, he killed his own
Child, born to me in pain, my best-beloved?
Why did you not drive *him* from hearth and home?
I bid you cast at me such menaces
As make for mastery in equal combat
With one prepared to meet them, and if, please God,

The issue goes against you, suffering   980
Shall school those grey hairs in humility.

Chorus: You are possessed by some spirit of sin that
      stares
Out of your bloodshot eyes matching your bloody hands.
Dishonored and deserted of your kind, for this
Stroke you too shall be struck down.

Clytemnestra: Listen! By Justice, who avenged my
      child,
By the Fury to whom I vowed this sacrament,
No thought of fear shall enter through this door
So long as the hearth within is kindled by
Aigisthos, faithful to me now as always.   990
Low lies the man who insulted his wedded wife
The darling of the Chryseids at Troy,
And stretched beside him this visionary seer,
Whom he fondled on shipboard, both now rewarded,
He as you see, and she swanlike has sung
Her dying ditty, his tasty side dish, for me
A rare spice to add relish to my joy.

Chorus: Oh, for the gift of death
To bring the long sleep that knows no waking,
Now that my lord and loyal protector   1000
Breathes his last. For woman's sake
Long he fought overseas,
Now at home falls beneath a woman's hand
      Helen, the folly-beguiled, having ravaged the city of
      Troy,
      She has set on the curse of Atreus
      A crown of blood beyond ablution.

Clytemnestra: Do not pray for death nor turn your
      anger against one woman as the slayer of
      thousands!

Chorus: Demon of blood and tears
Inbred in two women single-hearted!
Perched on the roof he stands and preens his   1010
Sable wings, a carrion-crow
Loud he croaks, looking down
Upon the feast spread before him here below.

Clytemnestra: Ah now you speak truth, naming the
      thrice-fed demon, who, glutted with blood, craves
      more, still young in his hunger.

Chorus: When will the feast be done?
Alas, it is the will of Zeus,
Who caused and brought it all to pass.
Nothing is here but was decreed in heaven.

Clytemnestra: It was not my doing, nor am I
      Agamemnon's wife, but a ghost in woman's guise,
      the shade of the banqueter whom Atreus fed.

Chorus: How is the guilt not yours?   1020
And yet the crimes of old may well
Have had a hand, and so it drives
On, the trail of internecine murder.

Clytemnestra: What of *him*? Was the guilt not his,
      when he killed the child that I bore him? And so by
      the sword he has fallen.

Chorus: Alas, the mind strays. The house is falling.
A storm of blood lays the walls in ruins.
Another mortal stroke for Justice's hand
Will soon be sharpened.
      Oh me, who shall bury him, who sing the dirge?

Who shall intone at the tomb of a blessed spirit   1030
A tribute pure in heart and truthful?

Clytemnestra: No, I'll bury him, but without mourners.
By the waters of Acheron Iphigeneia is waiting for
him with a kiss.

Chorus: The charge is answered with countercharges.
The sinner must suffer: such is God's will.
The ancient curse is bringing down the house
In self-destruction.

Clytemnestra: That is the truth, and I would be content
that the spirit of vengeance should rest, having
absolved the house from its madness.

[Enter AIGISTHOS with a bodyguard.]

Aigisthos: Now I have proof that there are Gods in
heaven,
As I gaze on this purple mesh in which
My enemy lies, son of a treacherous father,   1040
His father, Atreus, monarch of this realm,
Was challenged in his sovereign rights by mine,
Thyestes, his own brother, and banished him
From hearth and home. Later he returned
A suppliant and found sanctuary, indeed
A welcome; for his brother entertained him
To a feast of his own children's flesh, of which
My father unsuspecting took and ate.
Then, when he knew what he had done, he fell
Back spewing out the slaughtered flesh and, kicking   1050
The table to the floor, with a loud cry
He cursed the House of Pelops. That is the crime
For which the son lies here. And fitly too
The plot was spun by me; for as a child
I was banished with my father, until Justice
Summoned me home. Now let me die, for never
Shall I live to another sight so sweet.

Chorus: Aigisthos, if it was you who planned this
murder,
Then be assured, the people will stone you for it.

Aigisthos: Such talk from the lower benches! Even in
dotage   1060
Prison can teach a salutary lesson.
Better submit, or else you shall smart for it.

Chorus: You woman, who stayed at home and
wallowed in
His bed, you plotted our great commander's death!

Aigisthos: Orpheus led all in rapture after him.[14]
Your senseless bark will be snuffed out in prison.

Chorus: You say the plot was yours, yet lacked the
courage
To raise a hand but left it to a woman!

Aigisthos: As his old enemy, I was suspect.
Temptation was the woman's part. But now   1070
I'll try my hand at monarchy, and all
Who disobey me shall be put in irons
And starved of food and light till they submit.

Chorus: Oh, if Orestes yet beholds the sun,
May he come home and execute them both!

Aigisthos: Ho, my guards, come forward, you have
work to do.

Captain of the Guard: Stand by, draw your swords!

Chorus: We are not afraid to die.

Aigisthos: Die! We'll take you at your word.

Clytemnestra: Peace, my lord, and let no further wrong
be done.   1080
Captain, sheathe your swords. And you, old men,
Go home quietly. What has been, it had to be.
Scars enough we bear, now let us rest.

Aigisthos: Must I stand and listen to their threats?

Chorus: Men of Argos never cringed before a rogue.

Aigisthos: I shall overtake you yet—the day is near.

Chorus: Not if Orestes should come home again.

Aigisthos: Vain hope, the only food of castaways.

Chorus: Gloat and grow fat, blacken justice while you
dare!

Aigisthos: All this foolish talk will cost you dear.   1090

Chorus: Flaunt your gaudy plumes and strut beside
your hen!

Clytemnestra: Pay no heed to idle clamor. You and I,
Masters of the house, shall now direct it well.

STUDY QUESTIONS

1. Book XI of Homer's *Odyssey* is given on pp. 79–86. In this excerpt, Odysseus visits the underworld and, among others, meets the shade of Agamemnon, who found "a brutal death at home—and a bad wife behind it" (line 424 ff.). Compare Homer's story—presumably the accepted version—with the *Agamemnon* by Aeschylus. Homer portrays Agamemnon as a blameless hero who was done in by Aigisthos with the assistance of the "bad wife." Aeschylus, however, depicts Agamemnon as a weak and vain ruler and, rather than just a "bad wife," Clytemnestra becomes the avenging mother of a murdered daughter. Why were these changes made? Did they strengthen the plot? If so, in what ways?

2. Reading through the speeches of Chorus without reference to the other speeches or action of the play can be very revealing. What is your impression of their attitude toward life? Do you find many examples where they speak proverbial wisdom? In the Greeks' early cultural development they were bound by tradition and nature. How does speaking in proverbs illustrate this? Does such use of proverbs bear any relation to this theme?

3. Cassandra is trying to rouse the Chorus to action. Besides the legendary curse of Apollo, which caused everyone to disbelieve her

---

14. That is: you are not Orpheus, whose music caused people to follow him.

prophecies, can you see any other reason why she cannot get these men to act? For example, why, when she is left alone in the chariot, knowing that she faces death as soon as she enters the palace, did she not run away? Certainly Chorus would not stop her.

4. When Chorus reports the death of Iphigeneia, she is spoken of as "swathed in folds of saffron." Later the description is of "Night . . . who has cast over the towers of Troy a net so fine." Still later, Agamemnon walks on a purple "web," or "net." Why did Aeschylus use this image throughout the play? Examine the different levels of significance beyond its literal meaning.

5. Notice that *Agamemnon* has its beginning in the darkness in the country town of Mycenae. The *Eumenides*, the third play of the trilogy, ends in the bright sunlight of Athens. What does this symbolize?

LITERARY SELECTION 4

Eumenides

Aeschylus

The discussion earlier in this chapter outlined the themes and plots of the *Libation Bearers* and the *Eumenides*. Below is the beginning of the text of the *Eumenides* where Athena impanels a jury of citizens to hear the case against Orestes. George Thomson is the translator.

CHARACTERS

Athena
Judges
Apollo
Orestes
Chorus

[Enter ATHENA with the JUDGES, followed by citizens of Athens.]

Athena: Herald, give orders to hold the people back,
Then sound the trumpet and proclaim silence.
For while this new tribunal is being enrolled,
It is right that all should ponder on its laws,
Both the litigants here whose case is to be judged,
And my whole people for all generations.
[Enter APOLLO.]
Chorus: Apollo, what is there here that concerns you?
We say you have no authority in this matter.
Apollo: I come both as a witness, the accused

Having been a suppliant at my sanctuary   10
And purified of homicide at my hands,
And also to be tried with him, for I too
Must answer for the murder of his mother.
Open the case, and judge as you know how.
Athena: The case is open. You shall be first to speak.
[To the CHORUS.]
The prosecutors shall take precedence
And first inform us truthfully of the facts.
Chorus: Many in number, we shall be brief in speech.
We beg you to answer our questions one by one.
First, is it true that you killed your mother?   20
Orestes: I killed her. That is true, and not denied.
Chorus: So then the first of the three rounds is ours.
Orestes: You should not boast that you have thrown me yet.
Chorus: Next, since you killed her, you must tell us how.
Orestes: Yes, with a drawn sword leveled at the throat.
Chorus: Who was it who impelled or moved you to it?
Orestes: The oracle of this God who is my witness.
Chorus: The God of prophecy ordered matricide?
Orestes: Yes, and I have not repented it to this day.
Chorus: You *will* repent it, when you have been condemned.   30
Orestes: My father shall defend me from the grave.
Chorus: Having killed your mother, you may well trust the dead!
Orestes: She was polluted by a double crime.
Chorus: How so? Explain your meaning to the judges.
Orestes: She killed her husband and she killed my father.
Chorus: She died without bloodguilt, and you still live.
Orestes: Why did you not hunt her when she was alive?
Chorus: She was not bound by blood to the man she killed.
Orestes: And am I then bound by blood to my mother?
Chorus: Abandoned wretch, how did she nourish you   40
Within the womb? Do you repudiate
The nearest and dearest tie of motherhood?
Orestes: Apollo, give your evidence. I confess
That I did this deed as I have said.
Pronounce your judgment: was it justly done?
Apollo: Athena's appointed judges, I say to you,
Justly, and I, as prophet, cannot lie.
Never from my prophetic shrine have I
Said anything of city, man or woman
But what my father Zeus has commanded me.   50
This plea of mine must override all others,
Since it accords with our great father's will.
Chorus: Your argument is, then, that Zeus commanded you
To charge Orestes with this criminal act
Regardless of the bond between son and mother?
Apollo: It is not the same, to murder a great king,
A woman too to do it, and not in open
Fight like some brave Amazon, but in such
Manner as I shall now inform this court.
On his return from battle, bringing home   60
A balance for the greater part of good,

She welcomed him with fine words and then, while
He bathed, pavilioned him in a purple robe
And struck him down and killed him—a man and king
Whom the whole world had honored. Such was the
    crime
For which she paid. Let the judges take note.
Chorus: According to your argument Zeus gives
Precedence to the father; yet Zeus it was
Who cast into prison his own father Kronos.
Judges, take note, and ask him to explain.   70
Apollo: Abominable monsters, loathed by gods
And men, do you not understand that chains
Can be unfastened and prison doors unlocked?
But once the dust has drunk a dead man's blood,
He can never rise again—for that no remedy
Has been appointed by our almighty Father,
Although all else he can overturn at will
Without so much effort as a single breath.
Chorus: See what your plea for the defendant means.
Is this not what he did—to spill his mother's   80
Blood on the ground? And shall he then be allowed
To live on in his father's house? What public
Altar can he approach and where find fellowship?
Apollo: The mother is not a parent, only the nurse
Of the seed which the true parent, the father,
Commits to her as to a stranger to
Keep it with God's help safe from harm. And I
Have proof of this. There can be a father
Without a mother. We have a witness here,
This daughter of Olympian Zeus, who sprang   90
Armed from her father's head, a goddess whom
No goddess could have brought to birth. Therefore,
Out of goodwill to your country and your people
I sent this suppliant to seek refuge with you,
That you, Athena, may find in him and his
A faithful ally for all time to come.
Athena: Enough has now been spoken. Are you agreed
That I call on the judges to record
Their votes justly according to their conscience?
Apollo: Our quiver is empty, every arrow spent.   100
We wait to hear the issue of the trial.
Athena: And has my ruling your approval too?
Chorus: Sirs, you have heard the case, and now declare
Judgment according to your solemn oath.
Athena: Citizens of Athens, hear my declaration
At this first trial in the history of man.
This great tribunal shall remain in power
Meeting in solemn session on this hill,
Where long ago the Amazons encamped
When they made war on Theseus, and sacrificed   110
To Ares—hence its name:[15] Here reverence
For law and inbred fear among my people
Shall hold their hands from evil night and day,
Only let them not tamper with the laws,
But keep the fountain pure and sweet to drink.
I warn you not to banish from your lives
All terror but to seek the mean between
Autocracy and anarchy; and in this way
You shall possess in ages yet unborn
An impregnable fortress of liberty   120
Such as no people has throughout the world.

With these words I establish this tribunal
Grave, quick to anger, incorruptible,
And always vigilant over those that sleep.
Let the judges now rise and cast their votes.[16]
Chorus: We charge you to remember that we have
Great power to harm, and vote accordingly.
Apollo: I charge you to respect the oracles
Sanctioned by Zeus and see that they are fulfilled.
Chorus: By interfering in what is not your office   130
You have desecrated your prophetic shrine.
Apollo: Then was my Father also at fault when he
Absolved Ixion, the first murderer?
Chorus: Keep up your chatter, but if our cause should
    fail,
We shall lay on this people a heavy hand.
Apollo: Yes, you will lose your case, and then you may
Spit out your poison, but it will do no harm.
Chorus: Insolent youth mocks venerable age.
We await the verdict, ready to let loose
Against this city our destructive rage.   140
Athena: The final judgment rests with me, and I
Announce that my vote shall be given to Orestes.
No mother gave me birth, and in all things
Save marriage I commend with all my heart
The masculine, my father's child indeed.
Therefore I cannot hold in higher esteem
A woman killed because she killed her husband.
If the votes are equal, Orestes wins.
Let the appointed officers proceed
To empty the urns and count the votes.   150
Orestes: O bright Apollo, how shall the judgment go?
Chorus: O black mother Night, are you watching this?
Orestes: My hour has come—the halter or the light.
Chorus: And ours—to exercise our powers or perish.
Apollo: Sirs, I adjure you to count carefully.
If judgment errs, great harm will come of it,
Whereas one vote may raise a fallen house.
Athena: He stands acquitted on the charge of
    bloodshed,
The human votes being equally divided.
Orestes: Lady Athena, my deliverer,   160
I was an outcast from my country, now
I can go home again and live once more
In my paternal heritage, thanks to you
And to Apollo and to the third, Zeus,
Who governs the whole world. Before I go
I give my word to you and to your people
For all posterity that no commander
Shall lead an Argive army in war against
This city. If any should violate this pledge,
Out of the graves which shall then cover us   170
We would arise with adverse omens to
Obstruct and turn them back. If, however,
They keep this covenant and stand by your side,
They shall always have our blessing. And so farewell!

15. The hill and the court that met on it were called the
    Areopagus.
16. It is understood that the members of the jury are dropping
    their votes into an urn during the next eight speeches.

May you and your people always prevail
Against the assaults of all your enemies!
[Exit.]
Chorus: Oho, you junior gods, since you have trod
          under foot
The laws of old and robbed us of our powers,
We shall afflict this country
With damp contagion, bleak and barren, withering up
          the soil,   180
Mildew on bud and birth abortive. Venomous pestilence
Shall sweep your cornlands with infectious death.
To weep—No! To work? Yes! To work ill and lay low the
          people!
So will the maids of Night mourn for their stolen honors.
Athena: Let me persuade you to forget your grief!
You are not defeated. The issue of the trial
Has been determined by an equal vote.
It was Zeus himself who plainly testified
That Orestes must not suffer for what he did.
I beg you, therefore, do not harm my country,   190
Blasting her crops with drops of rank decay
And biting cankers in the early buds.
Rather accept my offer to stay and live
In a cavern on this hill and there receive
The adoration of my citizens.
Chorus: Oho, you junior gods, since you have trod
          under foot.
The laws of old and robbed us of our powers.
We shall affict this country
With damp contagion, bleak and barren, withering up
          the soil,
Mildew on bud and birth abortive. Venomous pestilence   200
Shall sweep your cornlands with infectious death.
To weep—No! To work? Yes! To work ill and lay low the
          people!
So will the maids of Night mourn for their stolen honors.
Athena: No, *not* dishonored, and therefore spare my
          people!
I too confide in Zeus—why speak of that?—
And I alone of all the Olympian gods
Know of the keys which guard the treasury
Of heaven's thunder. But there is no need of that.
Let my persuasion serve to calm your rage.
Reside with me and share my majesty;   210
And when from these wide acres you enjoy
Year after year the harvest offerings
From couples newly-wed praying for children,
Then you will thank me for my intercession.
Chorus: How can you treat us so?
Here to dwell, ever debased, defiled!
Hear our passion, hear, black Night!
For the powers once ours, sealed long, long ago
Have by the junior gods been all snatched away.
Athena: You are my elders, and therefore I indulge   220
Your passion. And yet, though not so wise as you,
To me too Zeus has granted understanding.
If you refuse me and depart, believe me,
This country will yet prove your heart's desire,
For as the centuries pass so there will flow
Such glory to my people as will assure
To all divinities worshiped here by men

And women gathered on festive holidays
More honors than could be yours in any other
City throughout the world. And so, I beg you,   230
Keep from my citizens the vicious spur
Of internecine strife, which pricks the breast
Of manhood flown with passion as with wine!
Abroad let battle rage for every heart
That is fired with love of glory—that shall be theirs
In plenty. So this is my offer to you—
To give honor and receive it and to share
My glory in this country loved by heaven.
Chorus: How can you, treat us so?
Here to dwell, ever debased, defiled!   240
Hear our passion, hear, black Night!
For the powers once ours, sealed long, long ago,
Have by the junior gods been all snatched away.
Athena: I will not weary in my benedictions,
Lest it should ever be said that you, so ancient
In your divinity, were driven away
By me and by my mortal citizens.
No, if Persuasion's holy majesty,
The sweet enchantment of these lips divine,
Has power to move you, please, reside with me.   250
But, if you still refuse, then, since we have made
This offer to you, it would be wrong to lay
Your hands upon us in such bitter rage.
Again, I tell you, it is in your power to own
This land attended with the highest honors.
Chorus: Lady Athena, what do you offer us?
Athena: A dwelling free of sorrow. Pray accept.
Chorus: Say we accept, what privileges shall we have?
Athena: No family shall prosper without your grace.
Chorus: Will you ensure us this prerogative?   260
Athena: I will, and bless all those that worship you.
Chorus: And pledge that assurance for all time to
          come?
Athena: I need not promise what I will not perform.
Chorus: Your charms are working, and our rage
          subsides.
Athena: Here make your dwelling, where you shall win
          friends.
Chorus: What song then shall we chant in salutation?
Athena: A song of faultless victory—from land and sea,
From skies above let gentle breezes blow
And breathing sunshine float from shore to shore;
Let crops and cattle increase and multiply   270
And children grow in health and happiness,
And let the righteous prosper; for I, as one
Who tends flowers in a garden, cherish fondly
The seed that bears no sorrow. That is your part,
While I in many a battle shall strive until
This city stands victorious against all
Its enemies and renowned throughout the world.
Chorus: We accept; we agree to dwell with you
Here in Athens, which by grace of Zeus
Stands a fortress for the gods,   280
Jeweled crown of Hellas. So
With you now we join in prayer
That smiling suns and fruitful soils unite to yield
Lifelong joy, fortune fair,
Light and darkness reconciled.

Athena: For the good of my people I have given homes in the city to these deities,[17] whose power is so great and so slowly appeased; and, whenever a man falls foul of them, apprehended to answer for the sins of his fathers, he shall be brought to judgment before them, and the dust shall stifle his proud boast.   290

Chorus: Free from blight may the early blossom deck Budding trees, and may no parching drought Spread across the waving fields. Rather Pan in season grant From the flocks and herds a full Return from year to year, and from the rich Store which these gods vouchsafe May the Earth repay them well!

Athena: Guardians of my city, listen to the blessings   300 they bring, and remember that their power is great in heaven and hell, and on earth too they bring to some glad music and to some lives darkened with weeping.

Chorus: Free from sudden death that cuts Short the prime of manhood, blest In your daughters too, to whom Be granted husband and home, and may the dread Fates Keep them safe, present in every household, Praised and magnified in every place!

Athena: Fair blessings indeed from powers that so   310 lately were averted in anger, and I thank Zeus and the spirit of persuasion that at last there is no strife left between us, except that they vie with me in blessing my people.

Chorus: Peace to all, free from that Root of evil, civil strife! May they live in unity, And never more may the blood of kin be let flow! Rather may all of them bonded together Feel and act as one in love and hate!   320

Athena: From these dread shapes, so quick to learn a new music, I foresee great good for my people, who, if only they repay their favors with the reverence due, shall surely establish the reign of justice in a city that will shine as a light for all mankind.

[Enter ESCORT OF WOMEN, carrying crimson robes and torches.]

Chorus: Joy to you all in your justly appointed riches, Joy to all the people blest With the Virgin's love, who stands Next beside her Father's throne! Wisdom man has learnt at last.   330 Under her protection this Land enjoys the grace of Zeus.

Athena: Joy to you also, and now let me lead you in torchlight to your new dwelling place! Let solemn oblations speed you in joy to your home beneath the earth, and there imprison all harm while still letting flow your blessings!

Chorus: Joy to you, joy, yet again we pronounce our blessing, Joy to all the citizens, Gods and mortals both alike.   340

While you hold this land and pay Homage to our residence, You shall have no cause to blame Chance and change in human life.

Athena: I thank you for your gracious salutations, And now you shall be escorted in the light Of torches to your subterranean dwelling, Attended by the sacristans of my temple Together with this company of girls And married women and others bowed with years.   350 Women, let them put on these robes of crimson, And let these blazing torches light the way, That the goodwill of our new co-residents Be shown in the manly prowess of your sons!

[The CHORUS put on the crimson robes and a procession is formed led by young men in armor, with the CHORUS and the escort following, and behind them the citizens of Athens. The rest is sung as the procession moves away.]

Chorus of the Escort: Pass on your way, O powers majestic, Daughters of darkness in happy procession! People of Athens, hush, speak fair! Pass to the caverns of earth immemorial There to be worshiped in honor and glory! People of Athens, hush, speak fair!   360 Gracious and kindly of heart to our people, Come with us, holy ones, hither in gladness, Follow the lamps that illumine the way! O sing at the end alleluia! Peace to you, peace of a happy community, People of Athens! Zeus who beholds all Watches, himself with the Fates reconciled. O sing at the end alleluia!

---

17. This is the transition of the dreadful goddesses from the *Erinyes* (the Furies) to the *Eumenides* (the Gracious Ones).

STUDY QUESTIONS

1. To understand this play one must comprehend the difference in the meaning of the word "justice" as it is first used by the Furies and as it is utilized by Athena in her last speech of the play. That difference in meaning is worth analyzing and discussing. Here are some questions to guide you.

   a. Insofar as the structure of the play and its significance are concerned, why can Orestes leave when only two-thirds of the play is over?
   b. The Furies insist that fear is a necessary part of the idea of justice that people hold. How right are they?
   c. The real turning point of the play occurs when Athena gives her final instructions to the jury (see lines 106–25). What principles are involved in this statement?

> **d.** The actual role of the Eumenides (or Gracious Ones as they are changed from the Furies) is never made entirely clear. From the evidence in the play itself, what seems to be their role in the maintenance of a new type of justice?
>
> **2.** What differences would have been found in the lives of the people of Athens as they changed from the old idea of justice to the new? In what ways did the new idea allow for personal freedom?
>
> **3.** Refer back to Study Question 1 following the text of the *Agamemnon* (see p. 111). Could the *Eumenides* have been written if Aeschylus had stayed with Homer's version of the plot? Why or why not?

LITERARY SELECTION 5

Memorial Oration

Pericles (ca. 495–429 BC)

As you read this eloquent address, you should remind yourself of the questions about human aspirations raised in the plays of Aeschylus. In the *Agamemnon* Chorus railed against great wealth, insisting that the humble life was the best. In the *Eumenides* the question was whether justice should be dispensed by reason or by stern revenge within the family. The playwright examined the conflict between people and an absolute god who ruled through fear.

Further questions in the Greek mind (and our own) could be: must the state protect itself with a standing army?; does a life of cultural pursuits weaken the state? Perhaps the most significant question for their time (and ours) is whether a democracy can function efficiently and effectively. The argument on the other hand is that an absolute government can operate quickly and efficiently, while in a democracy people talk so much that they rarely get anything done. Aristotle later put his finger squarely on the basic problem: "Democracy arises out of the notion that those who are equal in any respect are equal in all respects; because men are equally free, they claim to be absolutely equal" (from *Politics*).

This portion of Pericles' famous oration is taken from *The History of the Peloponnesian War* by Thucydides. Pericles made this address at the public funeral of some Athenian young men who had been killed in the war. Pericles surveyed the waiting throng and said:

Before I praise the dead, I should like to point out by what principles of action we rose to power, and under what institutions and through what manner of life our empire became great. For I conceive that such thoughts are not unsuited to the occasion, and that this numerous assembly of citizens and strangers may profitably listen to them.

Our form of government does not enter into rivalry with the institutions of others. We do not copy our neighbors, but are an example to them. It is true that we are called a democracy; for the administration is in the hands of the many and not of the few. But while the law secures equal justice to all alike in their private disputes, the claim of excellence is also recognized; and when a citizen is in any way distinguished, he is preferred to the public service, not as a matter of privilege, but as the reward of merit. Neither is poverty a bar, but a man may benefit his country whatever be the obscurity of his condition. There is no exclusiveness in our public life, and in our private intercourse we are not suspicious of one another, nor angry with our neighbor if he does what he likes; we do not put on sour looks at him, which though harmless are not pleasant. While we are thus unconstrained in our private intercourse, a spirit of reverence pervades our public acts: we are prevented from doing wrong by respect for authority and for the laws; having an especial regard to those which are ordained for the protection of the injured, as well as to these unwritten laws which bring upon the transgressor of them the reprobation of the general sentiment.

And we have not forgotten to provide for our weary spirits many relaxations from toil; we have regular games and sacrifices throughout the year; at home the style of our life is refined; and the delight which we daily feel in all these things helps to banish melancholy. Because of the greatness of our city the fruits of the whole earth flow in upon us; so that we enjoy the goods of other countries as freely as of our own.

Then again, our military training is in many respects superior to that of our adversaries. Our city is thrown open to the world; and we never expel a foreigner, or prevent him from seeing or learning anything of which the secret, if revealed to an enemy, might profit him. We rely not upon management of trickery, but upon our own hearts and hands. And in the matter of education whereas they from early youth are always undergoing laborious exercises which are to make them brave, we live at ease, and yet are equally ready to face the perils which they face . . . .

If, then, we prefer to meet danger with a light heart but without laborious training, and with a courage which is gained by habit and not enforced by law, are we not greatly the gainers? Since we do not anticipate the pain, although, when the hour comes, we can be as brave as those who never allow themselves to rest; and thus too our city is equally admirable in peace and in war. For we are lovers of the beautiful, yet simple in our tastes, and we cultivate the mind without loss of manliness. Wealth we employ, not for talk and ostentation, but when there is a real use for it. To avow poverty with us is no disgrace; the true disgrace is in doing nothing to avoid it. An Athenian citizen does not neglect the State because he takes care of his own household; and even those of us who are engaged in business have a very fair idea of politics. We alone regard a man who takes no interest in public affairs, not as a harmless but as a useless character; and if few of us are originators, we are all sound judges, of a policy. The great impediment to action is, in our opinion, not discussion, but the want of that knowledge which is gained by discussion preparatory to action. For we have a peculiar power of thinking before we act, and of acting too; whereas other men are courageous from ignorance but hesitate upon reflection. And they are surely to be esteemed the bravest spirits, who, having the clearest sense both of the pains and the pleasures of life, do not on that account shrink from danger. In doing good, again we are unlike others; we make our friends by conferring, not by receiving favors. Now he who confers a favor is the firmer friend, because he would fain by kindness keep alive the memory of an obligation; but the recipient is colder in his feelings, because he knows that in requiting another's generosity he will not be winning gratitude, but only paying a debt. We alone do good to our neighbors not upon a calculation of interest, but in the confidence of freedom and in a frank and fearless spirit.

To sum up: I say that Athens is the school of Hellas, and that the individual Athenian in his own person seems to have the power of adapting himself to the most varied forms of action with the utmost versatility and grace. This is no passing and idle word, but truth and fact; and the assertion is verified by the position to which these qualities have raised the State. For in the hour of trial, Athens alone among her contemporaries is superior to the report of her. No enemy who comes against her is indignant at the reverses which he sustains at the hands of such a city; no subject complains that his masters are unworthy of him. And we shall assuredly not be without witnesses: there are mighty monuments of our power, which will make us the wonder of this and of succeeding ages; we shall not need the praises of Homer or of any other panegyrist, whose poetry may please for the moment although his representation of the facts will not bear the light of day. For we have compelled every land and every sea to open a path for our valor, and have everywhere planted eternal memorials of our friendship and of our enmity. Such is the city for whose sake these men nobly fought and died: they could not bear the thought that she might be taken from them; and every one of us who survive should gladly toil on her behalf.

70

80

100

110

120

1. The chorus of *Agamemnon* cautions against the evils of wealth. We, too, have a proverb about money as the root of evil. How have the Greeks developed since Aeschylus wrote of the earlier populace? How might Pericles have argued with our own proverb?
2. What similarities in terms of purpose and ideals do you see between this oration and Lincoln's "Gettysburg Address" (delivered when our own nation was undergoing the ordeal of a Civil War)? Are the ideals of either any less relevant today?
3. Here Pericles raises the old question about men of words and men of action. Is a compromise between words and action possible?
4. Why does Pericles speak of the individual Athenian when he is making a summary of the government?

LITERARY SELECTION 6

Oedipus the King
Sophocles (496–406 BC)

Clear-cut structure is always important in Greek drama and never more so than in the tragedies of Sophocles. Like most Greek writers, he follows the rule of three, the perfect number: beginning, middle, and end. Below is an outline of the tripartite structure of *Oedipus* followed by a brief explanation:

Prologue; Parodos	exposition
Scene I; Ode I Scene II; Ode II Scene III; Ode III Scene IV; Ode IV	complication
Exodos	resolution

In the Prologue the background to the coming action is supplied by Oedipus, the Priest, and Creon. Next, Chorus enters in the Parodos, singing, dancing, and commenting on the situation. The combination of Prologue and Parodos presents the dramatic exposition, the explanation of the coming struggle: the Theban woes and Oedipus' search for the cause.

In the body of the play, the dramatic complication, each of the four scenes is followed by an ode. The scenes involve dialogue between two or more characters sometimes including Choragos, who is a representative Theban citizen and leader of Chorus. During the odes Chorus sings and dances to paired stanzas (strophes and antistrophes); for the strophe they dance up one side of the orchestra, and down the other side during the antistrophe.

In the final section, or Exodos, the complications are resolved, the consequences revealed, and the characters make their exit. The translation is by Dudley Fitts and Robert Fitzgerald.

CHARACTERS

Oedipus	**Teiresias**	**Shepherd of Laios**
A Priest	**Jocasta**	**Second Messenger**
Creon	**Messenger**	**Chorus of Theban Elders**

The scene. Before the palace of Oedipus, King of Thebes. A central door and two lateral doors open onto a platform which runs the length of the facade. On the platform, right and left, are altars; and three steps lead down into the "orchestra," or chorus-ground. At the beginning of the action these steps are crowded by suppliants who have brought branches and chaplets of olive leaves and who lie in various attitudes of despair. OEDIPUS enters.

Prologue

Oedipus: My children, generations of the living
In the line of *Cadmos*, nursed at his ancient hearth:
Why have you strewn yourselves before these altars
In supplication, with your boughs and garlands?
The breath of incense rises from the city
With a sound of prayer and lamentation.
                              Children,
I would not have you speak through messengers,
And therefore I have come myself to hear you—
I, Oedipus, who bear the famous name.
[To a PRIEST.]
You, there, since you are eldest in the company,   10
Speak for them all, tell me what preys upon you,
Whether you come in dread, or crave some blessing:
Tell me, and never doubt that I will help you
In every way I can; I should be heartless
Were I not moved to find you suppliant here.
Priest: Great Oedipus, O powerful King of Thebes!
You see how all the ages of our people
Cling to your altar steps: here are boys
Who can barely stand alone, and here are priests
By weight of age, as I am a priest of God,   20
And young men chosen from those yet unmarried;
As for the others, all that multitude,
They wait with olive chaplets in the squares,
At the two shrines of Pallas, and where Apollo
Speaks in the glowing embers.
                              Your own eyes
Must tell you: Thebes is tossed on a murdering sea
And can not lift her head from the death surge.
A rust consumes the buds and fruits of the earth;
The herds are sick; children die unborn,
And labor is vain. The god of plague and pyre   30
Raids like detestable lightning through the city,
And all the house of Cadmos is laid waste,
All emptied, and all darkened: Death alone
Battens upon the misery of Thebes.

You are not one of the immortal gods, we know;

Yet we have come to you to make our prayer
As to the man surest in mortal ways
And wisest in the ways of God. You saved us
From the Sphinx, that flinty singer, and the tribute
We paid to her so long; yet you were never   40
Better informed than we, nor could we teach you:
It was some god breathed in you to set us free.

Therefore, O mighty King, we turn to you:
Find us our safety, find us a remedy,
Whether by counsel of the gods or men.
A king of wisdom tested in the past
Can act in a time of troubles, and act well.
Noblest of men, restore
Life to your city! Think how all men call you
Liberator for your triumph long ago;   50
Ah, when your years of kingship are remembered,
Let them not say *We rose, but later fell*—
Keep the State from going down in the storm!
Once, years ago, with happy augury,
You brought us fortune; be the same again!
No man questions your power to rule the land:
But rule over men, not over a dead city!
Ships are only hulls, citadels are nothing,
When no life moves in the empty passageways.
Oedipus: Poor children! You may be sure I know   60
All that you longed for in your coming here.
I know that you are deathly sick; and yet,
Sick as you are, not one is as sick as I.
Each of you suffers in himself alone
His anguish, not another's; but my spirit
Groans for the city, for myself, for you.
I was not sleeping, you are not waking me.
No, I have been in tears for a long while
And in my restless thought walked many ways.
In all my search, I found one helpful course,   70
And that I have taken: I have sent Creon,
Son of Menoikeus [Menoeceus], brother of the Queen,
To Delphi, Apollo's place of revelation,
To learn there, if he can,
What act or pledge of mine may save the city.
I have counted the days, and now, this very day,
I am troubled, for he has overstayed his time.
What is he doing? He has been gone too long.
Yet whenever he comes back, I should do ill
To scant whatever duty God reveals.   80
Priest: It is a timely promise. At this instant
They tell me Creon is here.
Oedipus: O Lord Apollo!
May his news be fair as his face is radiant!
Priest: It could not be otherwise: he is crowned with bay,
The chaplet is thick with berries.
Oedipus: We shall soon know;
He is near enough to hear us now.
[Enter CREON.]
                              O Prince:
Brother: son of Menoikeus:
What answer do you bring us from the god?
Creon: A strong one. I can tell you, great afflictions
Will turn out well, if they are taken well.   90

Oedipus: What was the oracle? These vague words
Leave me still hanging between hope and fear.
Creon: Is it your pleasure to hear me with all these
Gathered around us? I am prepared to speak,
But should we not go in?
Oedipus: Let them all hear it.
It is for them I suffer, more than for myself.
Creon: Then I will tell you what I heard at Delphi.
In plain words
The god commands us to expel from the land of Thebes
An old defilement we are sheltering.   100
It is a deathly thing, beyond cure;
We must not let it feed upon us longer.
Oedipus: What defilement? How shall we rid ourselves
    of it?
Creon: By exile or death, blood for blood. It was
Murder that brought the plague-wind on the city.
Oedipus: Murder of whom? Surely the god has named
    him?
Creon: My lord, long ago Laios was our king,
Before you came to govern us.
Oedipus: I know;
I learned of him from others; I never saw him.
Creon: He was murdered; and Apollo commands us
    now   110
To take revenge upon whoever killed him.
Oedipus: Upon whom? Where are they? Where shall
    we find a clue
To solve that crime, after so many years?
Creon: Here in this land, he said.
                            If we make enquiry,
We may touch things that otherwise escape us.
Oedipus: Tell me: Was Laios murdered in his house,
Or in the fields, or in some foreign country?
Creon: He said he planned to make a pilgrimage.
He did not come home again.
Oedipus: And was there no one,
No witness, no companion, to tell what happened?   120
Creon: They were all killed but one, and he got away
So frightened that he could remember one thing only.
Oedipus: What was that one thing? One may be the
    key
To everything, if we resolve to use it.
Creon: He said that a band of highwaymen attacked
    them,
Outnumbered them, and overwhelmed the King.
Oedipus: Strange, that a highwayman should be so
    daring—
Unless some faction here bribed him to do it.
Creon: We thought of that. But after Laios' death
New troubles arose and we had no avenger.   130
Oedipus: What troubles could prevent your hunting
    down the killers?
Creon: The riddling Sphinx's song
Made us deaf to all mysteries but her own.
Oedipus: Then once more I must bring what is dark to
    light.
It is most fitting that Apollo shows,
As you do, this compunction for the dead.
You shall see how I stand by you, as I should,
To avenge the city and the city's god,

And not as though it were for some distant friend,
But for my own sake, to be rid of evil.   140
Whoever killed King Laios might—who knows?—
Decide at any moment to kill me as well.
By avenging the murdered king I protect myself.

Come, then, my children: leave the altar steps,
Lift up your olive boughs!
                            One of you go.
And summon the people of Cadmos to gather here.
I will do all that I can; you may tell them that.
[Exit a PAGE.]
So, with the help of God,
We shall be saved—or else indeed we are lost.
Priest: Let us rise, children. It was for this we came,   150
And now the King has promised it himself.
Phoibos [Phoebus] has sent us an oracle; may he descend
Himself to save us and drive out the plague.
[Exeunt OEDIPUS and CREON into the palace by the central
door. The PRIEST and the SUPPLIANTS disperse R and L.
After a short pause the CHORUS enters the orchestra.]

Parodos

Chorus:

                                                    Strophe 1

What is God singing in his profound
Delphi of gold and shadow?
What oracle for Thebes, the sunwhipped city?

Fear unjoints me, the roots of my heart tremble.

Now I remember, O Healer, your power, and wonder:
Will you send doom like a sudden cloud, or weave it
Like nightfall of the past?   160

Speak, speak to us, issue of holy sound:
Dearest to our expectancy: be tender!

                                                    Antistrophe 1

Let me pray to Athena, the immortal daughter of Zeus,
And to Artemis her sister
Who keeps her famous throne in the market ring,
And to Apollo, bowman at the far butts of heaven—

O gods, descend! Like three streams leap against
The fires of our grief, the fires of darkness;
Be swift to bring us rest!
As in the old time from the brilliant house   170
Of air you stepped to save us, come again!

                                                    Strophe 2

Now our afflictions have no end,
Now all our stricken host lies down
And no man fights off death with his mind;

The noble plowland bears no grain,
And groaning mothers can not bear—

See, how our lives like birds take wing,
Like sparks that fly when a fire soars,
To the shore of the god of evening.

                                                    Antistrophe 2

The plague burns on, it is pitiless,   180
Though pallid children laden with death
Lie unwept in the stony ways,

And old gray women by every path
Flock to the strand about the altars
There to strike their breasts and cry
Worship of Phoibos in wailing prayers:
Be kind, God's golden child!

                                                    Strophe 3

There are no swords in this attack by fire,
No shields, but we are ringed with cries.
Send the besieger plunging from our homes   190
Into the vast sea-room of the Atlantic
Or into the waves that foam eastward of Thrace—

For the day ravages what the night spares—

Destroy our enemy, lord of the thunder!
Let him be riven by lightning from heaven!

                                                    Antistrophe 3

Phoibos Apollo, stretch the sun's bowstring,
That golden cord, until it sing for us,
Flashing arrows in heaven!
                              Artemis, Huntress,
Race with flaring lights upon our mountains!
O scarlet god, O golden-banded brow,   200
O Theban Bacchos in a storm of Maenads,
[Enter OEDIPUS, C.]
Whirl upon Death, that all the Undying hate!
Come with blinding torches, come in joy!

Scene I

Oedipus: Is this your prayer? It may be answered.
    Come,
Listen to me, act as the crisis demands,
And you shall have relief from all these evils.

Until now I was a stranger to this tale,
As I had been a stranger to the crime.
Could I track down the murderer without a clue?
But now, friends,   210
As one who became a citizen after the murder,
I make this proclamation to all Thebans:
If any man knows by whose hand Laios, son of
    Labdakos,
Met his death, I direct that man to tell me everything,
No matter what he fears for having so long withheld it.
Let it stand as promised that no further trouble
Will come to him, but he may leave the land in safety.

Moreover: If anyone knows the murderer to be foreign,
Let him not keep silent: he shall have his reward from
    me.
However, if he does conceal it; if any man   220
Fearing for his friend or for himself disobeys this edict,
Hear what I propose to do:

I solemnly forbid the people of this country,
Where power and throne are mine, ever to receive that
    man
Or speak to him, no matter who he is, or let him
Join in sacrifice, lustration, or in prayer.
I decree that he be driven from every house,
Being, as he is, corruption itself to us: the Delphic

Voice of Zeus has pronounced this revelation.
Thus I associate myself with the oracle   230
And take the side of the murdered king.

As for the criminal, I pray to God—
Whether it be a lurking thief, or one of a number—
I pray that that man's life be consumed in evil and
    wretchedness.
And as for me, this curse applies no less
If it should turn out that the culprit is my guest here,
Sharing my hearth.
                       You have heard the penalty.
I lay it on you now to attend to this
For my sake, for Apollo's, for the sick
Sterile city that heaven has abandoned.   240
Suppose the oracle had given you no command:
Should this defilement go uncleansed for ever?
You should have found the murderer: your king,
A noble king, had been destroyed!
                                    Now I,
Having the power that he held before me,
Having his bed, begetting children there
Upon his wife, as he would have, had he lived—
Their son would have been my children's brother,
If Laios had had luck in fatherhood!
(But surely ill luck rushed upon his reign)—   250
I say I take the son's part, just as though
I were his son, to press the fight for him
And see it won! I'll find the hand that brought
Death to Labdakos' and Polydoros' child,
Heir of Cadmos' and Agenor's line.
And as for those who fail me,
May the gods deny them the fruit of the earth,
Fruit of the womb, and may they rot utterly!
Let them be wretched as we are wretched, and worse!

For you, for loyal Thebans, and for all   260
Who find my actions right, I pray the favor
Of justice, and of all the immortal gods.
Choragos: Since I am under oath, my lord, I swear
I did not do the murder, I can not name
The murderer. Might not the oracle
That has ordained the search tell where to find him?
Oedipus: An honest question. But no man in the world
Can make the gods do more than the gods will.
Choragos: There is one last expedient—
Oedipus: Tell me what it is.
Though it seem slight, you must not hold it back.   270
Choragos: A lord clairvoyant to the lord Apollo,
As we all know, is the skilled Teiresias.
One might learn much about this from him, Oedipus.
Oedipus: I am not wasting time:
Creon spoke of this, and I have sent for him—
Twice, in fact; it is strange that he is not here.
Choragos: The other matter—that old report—seems
    useless.
Oedipus: Tell me. I am interested in all reports.
Choragos: The King was said to have been killed by
    highwaymen.
Oedipus: I know. But we have no witnesses to that.   280
Choragos: If the killer can feel a particle of dread,
Your curse will bring him out of hiding!

Oedipus: No.
The man who dared that act will fear no curse.
[Enter the blind seer TEIRESIAS, led by a PAGE.]
Choragos: But there is one man who may detect the
    criminal.
This is Teiresias, this is the holy prophet
In whom, alone of all men, truth was born.
Oedipus: Teiresias: seer: student of mysteries,
Of all that's taught and all that no man tells,
Secrets of Heaven and secrets of the earth:
Blind though you are, you know the city lies   290
Sick with plague; and from this plague, my lord,
We find that you alone can guard or save us.

Possibly you did not hear the messengers?
Apollo, when we sent to him,
Sent us back word that this great pestilence
Would lift, but only if we established clearly
The identity of those who murdered Laios.
They must be killed or exiled.
                        Can you use
Birdflight or any art of divination
To purify yourself, and Thebes, and me   300
From this contagion? We are in your hands.
There is no fairer duty
Than that of helping others in distress.
Teiresias: How dreadful knowledge of the truth can be
When there's no help in truth! I knew this well,
But made myself forget. I should not have come.
Oedipus: What is troubling you? Why are your eyes so
    cold?
Teiresias: Let me go home. Bear your own fate, and I'll
Bear mine. It is better so: trust what I say.
Oedipus: What you say is ungracious and unhelpful   310
To your native country. Do not refuse to speak.
Teiresias: When it comes to speech, your own is
    neither temperate
Nor opportune. I wish to be more prudent.
Oedipus: In God's name, we all beg you—
Teiresias: You are all ignorant.
No; I will never tell you what I know.
Now it is my misery; then, it would be yours.
Oedipus: What! You do know something, and will not
    tell us?
You would betray us all and wreck the State?
Teiresias: I do not intend to torture myself, or you.
Why persist in asking? You will not persuade me.   320
Oedipus: What a wicked old man you are! You'd try a
    stone's
Patience! Out with it! Have you no feeling at all?
Teiresias: You call me unfeeling. If you could only see
The nature of your own feelings . . . .
Oedipus: Why,
Who would not feel as I do? Who could endure
Your arrogance toward the city?
Teiresias: What does it matter!
Whether I speak or not, it is bound to come.
Oedipus: Then, if "it" is bound to come, you are bound
    to tell me.
Teiresias: No, I will not go on. Rage as you please.
Oedipus: Rage? Why not!

                        And I'll tell you what I think: 330
You planned it, you had it done, you all but
Killed him with your own hands: if you had eyes,
I'd say the crime was yours, and yours alone.
Teiresias: So? I charge you, then,
Abide by the proclamation you have made:
From this day forth
Never speak again to these men or to me;
You yourself are the pollution of this country.
Oedipus: You dare say that! Can you possibly think you
    have
Some way of going free, after such insolence?   340
Teiresias: I have gone free. It is the truth sustains me.
Oedipus: Who taught you shamelessness? It was not
    your craft.
Teiresias: You did. You made me speak. I did not want
    to.
Oedipus: Speak what? Let me hear it again more
    clearly.
Teiresias: Was it not clear before? Are you tempting
    me?
Oedipus: I did not understand it. Say it again.
Teiresias: I say that you are the murderer whom you
    seek.
Oedipus: Now twice you have spat out infamy. You'll
    pay for it!
Teiresias: Would you care for more? Do you wish to be
    really angry?
Oedipus: Say what you will. Whatever you say is
    worthless.   350
Teiresias: I say you live in hideous shame with those
Most dear to you. You can not see the evil.
Oedipus: It seems you can go on mouthing like this for
    ever.
Teiresias: I can, if there is power in truth.
Oedipus: There is:
But not for you, not for you,
You sightless, witless, senseless, mad old man!
Teiresias: You are the madman. There is no one here
Who will not curse you soon, as you curse me.
Oedipus: You child of endless night! You can not hurt
    me
Or any other man who sees the sun.   360
Teiresias: True: it is not from me your fate will come.
That lies within Apollo's competence,
As it is his concern.
Oedipus: Tell me:
Are you speaking for Creon, or for yourself?
Teiresias: Creon is no threat. You weave your own
    doom.
Oedipus: Wealth, power, craft of statesmanship!
Kingly position, everywhere admired!
What savage envy is stored up against these,
If Creon, whom I trusted, Creon my friend,
For this great office which the city once   370
Put in my hands unsought—if for this power
Creon desires in secret to destroy me!

He has bought this decrepit fortune-teller, this
Collector of dirty pennies, this prophet fraud—
Why, he is no more clairvoyant than I am!

Tell us:
Has your mystic mummery ever approached the truth?
When that hellcat the Sphinx was performing here,
What help were you to these people?
Her magic was not for the first man who came along:
It demanded a real exorcist. Your birds—   380
What good were they? or the gods, for the matter of
      that?
But I came by,
Oedipus, the simple man, who knows nothing—
I thought it out for myself, no birds helped me!
And this is the man you think you can destroy,
That you may be close to Creon when he's king!
Well, you and your friend Creon, it seems to me,
Will suffer most. If you were not an old man,
You would have paid already for your plot.
Choragos: We can not see that his words or yours   390
Have been spoken except in anger, Oedipus,
And of anger we have no need. How can God's will
Be accomplished best? That is what most concerns us.
Teiresias: You are a king. But where argument's
      concerned
I am your man, as much a king as you.
I am not your servant, but Apollo's.
I have no need of Creon to speak for me.

Listen to me. You mock my blindness, do you?
But I say that you, with both your eyes, are blind:
You can not see the wretchedness of your life,   400
Nor in whose house you live, no, nor with whom.
Who are your father and mother? Can you tell me?
You do not even know the blind wrongs
That you have done them, on earth and in the world
      below.
But the double lash of your parents' curse will whip you
Out of this land some day, with only night
Upon your precious eyes.
Your cries then—where will they not be heard?
What fastness of Cithaeron will not echo them?
And that bridal-descant of yours—you'll know it then,   410
The song they sang when you came here to Thebes
And found your misguided berthing.
All this, and more, that you can not guess at now,
Will bring you to yourself among your children.

Be angry, then. Curse Creon. Curse my words.
I tell you, no man that walks upon the earth
Shall be rooted out more horribly than you.
Oedipus: Am I to bear this from him?—Damnation
Take you! Out of this place! Out of my sight!
Teiresias: I would not have come at all if you had not
      asked me.   420
Oedipus: Could I have told that you'd talk nonsense,
      that
You'd come here to make a fool of yourself, and of me?
Teiresias: A fool? Your parents thought me sane
      enough.
Oedipus: My parents again!—Wait: who were my
      parents?
Teiresias: This day will give you a father, and break your
      heart.

Oedipus: Your infantile riddles! Your damned
      abracadabra!
Teiresias: You were a great man once at solving riddles.
Oedipus: Mock me with that if you like; you will find it
      true.
Teiresias: It was true enough. It brought about your
      ruin.
Oedipus: But if it saved this town?
Teiresias:
[To the PAGE.]
                              Boy, give me your hand.   430
Oedipus: Yes, boy; lead him away.
                              —While you are here
We can do nothing. Go; leave us in peace.
Teiresias: I will go when I have said what I have to say.
How can you hurt me? And I tell you again:
The man you have been looking for all this time,
The damned man, the murderer of Laios,
That man is in Thebes. To your mind he is foreign-born,
But it will soon be shown that he is a Theban,
A revelation that will fail to please.
                              A blind man,
Who has his eyes now; a penniless man, who is rich
      now;   440
And he will go tapping the strange earth with his staff
To the children with whom he lives now he will be
Brother and father—the very same; to her
Who bore him, son and husband—the very same
Who came to his father's bed, wet with his father's
      blood.
Enough. Go think that over.
If later you find error in what I have said,
You may say that I have no skill in prophecy.
[Exit TEIRESIAS, led by his PAGE. OEDIPUS goes into the
palace.]

Ode I

Chorus:

                                                                        Strophe 1

The Delphic stone of prophecies
Remembers ancient regicide   450
And a still bloody hand.
That killer's hour of flight has come.
He must be stronger than riderless
Coursers of untiring wind,
For the son of Zeus armed with his father's thunder
Leaps in lightning after him;
And the Furies follow him, the sad Furies.

                                                                   Antistrophe 1

Holy Parnassos' peak of snow
Flashes and blinds that secret man,
That all shall hunt him down: 460
Though he may roam the forest shade
Like a bull gone wild from pasture
To rage through glooms of stone.
Doom comes down on him; flight will not avail him;
For the world's heart calls him desolate,
And the immortal Furies follow, for ever follow.

Strophe 2

But now a wilder thing is heard
From the old man skilled at hearing Fate in the
    wing-beat of a bird.
Bewildered as a blown bird, my soul hovers and can not
    find
Foothold in this debate, or any reason or rest of mind.   470
But no man ever brought—none can bring
Proof of strife between Thebes' royal house,
Labdakos' line, and the son of Polybos;
And never until now has any man brought word
Of Laios' dark death staining Oedipus the King.

Antistrophe 2

Divine Zeus and Apollo hold
Perfect intelligence alone of all tales ever told;
And well though this diviner works, he works in his own
    night;
No man can judge that rough unknown or trust in
    second sight,
For wisdom changes hands among the wise.   480
Shall I believe my great lord criminal
At a raging word that a blind old man let fall?
I saw him, when the carrion woman faced him of old,
Prove his heroic mind! These evil words are lies.

Scene II

Creon: Men of Thebes:
I am told that heavy accusations
Have been brought against me by King Oedipus

I am not the kind of man to bear this tamely.

If in these present difficulties
He holds me accountable for any harm to him   490
Through anything I have said or done—why, then,
I do not value life in this dishonor.
It is not as though this rumor touched upon
Some private indiscretion. The matter is grave.
The fact is that I am being called disloyal
To the State, to my fellow citizens, to my friends.
Choragos: He may have spoken in anger, not from his
    mind.
Creon: But did you not hear him say I was the one
Who seduced the old prophet into lying?
Choragos: The thing was said; I do not know how
    seriously.   500
Creon: But you were watching him! Were his eyes
    steady?
Did he look like a man in his right mind?
Choragos: I do not know.
I can not judge the behavior of great men.
But here is the King himself.
[Enter OEDIPUS.]
Oedipus: So you dared come back
Why? How brazen of you to come to my house,
You murderer!

            Do you think I do not know
That you plotted to kill me, plotted to steal my
    throne?
Tell me, in God's name: am I coward, a fool,

That you should dream you could accomplish this?
A fool who could not see your slippery game?   510
A coward, not to fight back when I saw it?
You are the fool, Creon, are you not? hoping
Without support or friends to get a throne?
Thrones may be won or bought: you could do neither.
Creon: Now listen to me. You have talked; let me talk,
    too.
You can not judge unless you know the facts.
Oedipus: You speak well: there is one fact; but I find it
    hard
To learn from the deadliest enemy I have.
Creon: That above all I must dispute with you.
Oedipus: That above all I will not hear you deny.   520
Creon: If you think there is anything good in being
    stubborn
Against all reason, then I say you are wrong.
Oedipus: If you think a man can sin against his own
    kind
And not be punished for it, I say you are mad.
Creon: I agree. But tell me: what have I done to you?
Oedipus: You advised me to send for that wizard, did
    you not?
Creon: I did. I should do it again.
Oedipus: Very well. Now tell me:
How long has it been since Laios—
Creon: What of Laios?
Oedipus: Since he vanished in that onset by the road?
Creon: It was long ago, a long time.
Oedipus: And this prophet,   530
Was he practicing here then?
Creon: He was; and with honor, as now.
Oedipus: Did he speak of me at that time?
Creon: He never did;
At least, not when I was present.
Oedipus: But . . . the enquiry?
I suppose you held one?
Creon: We did, but we learned nothing.
Oedipus: Why did the prophet not speak against me
    then?
Creon: I do not know; and I am the kind of man
Who holds his tongue when he has no facts to go on.
Oedipus: There's one fact that you know, and you
    could tell it.
Creon: What fact is that? If I know it, you shall have it.
Oedipus: If he were not involved with you, he could not
    say   540
That it was I who murdered Laios.
Creon: If he says that, you are the one that knows it!—
But now it is my turn to question you.
Oedipus: Put your questions. I am no murderer.
Creon: First, then: You married my sister?
Oedipus: I married your sister.
Creon: And you rule the kingdom equally with her?
Oedipus: Everything that she wants she has from me.
Creon: And I am the third, equal to both of you?
Oedipus: That is why I call you a bad friend.
Creon: No. Reason it out, as I have done.   550
Think of this first: Would any sane man prefer
Power, with all a king's anxieties,
To that same power and the grace of sleep?

Certainly not I.
I have never longed for the king's power—only his
    rights.
Would any wise man differ from me in this?
As matters stand, I have my way in everything
With your consent, and no responsibilities.
If I were king, I should be a slave to policy.

How could I desire a scepter more   560
Than what is now mine—untroubled influence?
No, I have not gone mad; I need no honors,
Except those with the perquisites I have now.
I am welcome everywhere; every man salutes me,
And those who want your favor seek my ear,
Since I know how to manage what they ask.
Should I exchange this ease for that anxiety?
Besides, no sober mind is treasonable.
I hate anarchy
And never would deal with any man who likes it.   570

Test what I have said. Go to the priestess
At Delphi, ask if I quoted her correctly.
And as for this other thing: if I am found
Guilty of treason with Teiresias,
Then sentence me to death! You have my word
It is a sentence I should cast my vote for—
But not without evidence!
                        You do wrong
When you take good men for bad, bad men for good.
A true friend thrown aside—why, life itself
Is not more precious!
                        In time you will know this well: 580
For time, and time alone, will show the just man,
Though scoundrels are discovered in a day.
Choragos: This is well said, and a prudent man would
    ponder it.
Judgments too quickly formed are dangerous.
Oedipus: But is he not quick in his duplicity?
And shall I not be quick to parry him?
Would you have me stand still, hold my peace, and let
This man win everything, through my inaction?
Creon: And you want—what is it, then? To banish me?
Oedipus: No, not exile. It is your death I want,   590
So that all the world may see what treason means.
Creon: You will persist, then? You will not believe me?
Oedipus: How can I believe you?
Creon: Then you are a fool.
Oedipus: To save myself?
Creon: In justice, think of me.
Oedipus: You are evil incarnate.
Creon: But suppose that you are wrong?
Oedipus: Still I must rule.
Creon: But not if you rule badly.
Oedipus: O city, city!
Creon: It is my city, too!
Choragos: Now, my lords, be still. I see the Queen,
Jocasta, coming from her palace chambers;
And it is time she came, for the sake of you both.   600
This dreadful quarrel can be resolved through her.
[Enter JOCASTA.]
Jocasta: Poor foolish men, what wicked din is this?
With Thebes sick to death, is it not shameful

That you should rake some private quarrel up?
[To OEDIPUS.]
Come into the house.
                        And you, Creon, go now:
Let us have no more of this tumult over nothing.
Creon: Nothing? No, sister: what your husband plans
    for me
Is one of two great evils: exile or death.
Oedipus: He is right.
                        Why, woman I have caught him squarely
Plotting against my life.
Creon: No! Let me die   610
Accurst if ever I have wished you harm!
Jocasta: Ah, believe it, Oedipus!
In the name of the gods, respect this oath of his
For my sake, for the sake of these people here!
                                        Strophe 1
Choragos: Open your mind to her, my lord. Be ruled
    by her, I beg you!
Oedipus: What would you have me do?
Choragos: Respect Creon's word. He has never
    spoken like a fool,
And now he has sworn an oath.
Oedipus: You know what you ask?
Choragos: I do.
Oedipus: Speak on, then.
Choragos: A friend so sworn should not be baited so,
In blind malice, and without final proof.   620
Oedipus: You are aware, I hope, that what you say
Means death for me, or exile at the least.
                                        Strophe 2
Choragos: No, I swear by Helios, first in Heaven!
    May I die friendless and accurst,
The worst of deaths, if ever I meant that!
        It is the withering fields
            That hurt my sick heart:
        Must we bear all these ills,
            And now your bad blood as well?
Oedipus: Then let him go. And let me die, if I must,   630
Or be driven by him in shame from the land of Thebes.
It is your unhappiness, and not his talk,
That touches me.
            As for him—
Wherever he goes, hatred will follow him.
Creon: Ugly in yielding, as you were ugly in rage!
Natures like yours chiefly torment themselves.
Oedipus: Can you not go? Can you not leave me?
Creon: I can.
You do not know me; but the city knows me,
And in its eyes I am just, if not in yours.
[Exit CREON.]
                                        Antistrophe 1
Choragos: Lady Jocasta, did you not ask the King to go
    to his chambers?   640
Jocasta: First tell me what has happened.
Choragos: There was suspicion without evidence; yet
    it rankled
As even false charges will.
Jocasta: On both sides?
Choragos: On both.
Jocasta: But what was said?

Choragos: Oh let it rest, let it be done with!
Have we not suffered enough?
Oedipus: You see to what your decency has brought
    you:
You have made difficulties where my heart saw none.

                                                Antistrophe 2
Choragos: Oedipus, it is not once only I have told
    you—
    You must know I should count myself unwise
To the point of madness, should I now forsake you—   650
        You, under whose hand,
            In the storm of another time,
            Our dear land sailed out free.
            But now stand fast at the helm!
Jocasta: In God's name, Oedipus, inform your wife as
    well:
Why are you so set in this hard anger?
Oedipus: I will tell you, for none of these men
    deserves
My confidence as you do. It is Creon's work,
His treachery, his plotting against me.
Jocasta: Go on, if you can make this clear to me.   660
Oedipus: He charges me with the murder of Laios.
Jocasta: Has he some knowledge? Or does he speak
    from hear-say?
Oedipus: He would not commit himself to such a
    charge,
But he has brought in that damnable soothsayer
To tell his story.
Jocasta: Set your mind at rest.
If it is a question of soothsayers, I tell you
That you will find no man whose craft gives knowledge
Of the unknowable.
                Here is my proof:

An oracle was reported to Laios once
(I will not say from Phoibos himself, but from   670
His appointed ministers, at any rate)
That his doom would be death at the hands of his own
    son—
His son, born of his flesh and of mine!

Now, you remember the story: Laios was killed
By marauding strangers where three highways meet,
But his child had not been three days in this world
Before the King had pierced the baby's ankles
And left him to die on a lonely mountainside.

Thus, Apollo never caused that child
To kill his father, and it was not Laios' fate   680
To die at the hands of his son, as he had feared.
This is what prophets and prophecies are worth!
Have no dread of them.
                It is God himself
Who can show us what he wills, in his own way.
Oedipus: How strange a shadowy memory crossed my
    mind,
Just now while you were speaking; it chilled my heart.
Jocasta: What do you mean? What memory do you
    speak of?
Oedipus: If I understand you, Laios was killed
At a place where three roads meet.

Jocasta: So it was said;
We have no later story.
Oedipus: Where did it happen?   690
Jocasta: Phokis, it is called: at a place where the
    Theban Way
Divides into the roads toward Delphi and Daulia.
Oedipus: When?
Jocasta: We had the news not long before you came
And proved the right to your succession here.
Oedipus: Ah, what net has God been weaving for me?
Jocasta: Oedipus! Why does this trouble you?
Oedipus: Do not ask me yet.
First, tell me how Laios looked, and tell me
How old he was.
Jocasta: He was tall, his hair just touched
With white; his form was not unlike your own.
Oedipus: I think that I myself may be accurst   700
By my own ignorant edict.
Jocasta: You speak strangely.
It makes me tremble to look at you, my King.
Oedipus: I am not sure that the blind man can not see.
But I should know better if you were to tell me—
Jocasta: Anything—though I dread to hear you ask it.
Oedipus: Was the King lightly escorted, or did he ride
With a large company, as a ruler should?
Jocasta: There were five men with him in all: one was
    a herald,
And a single chariot, which he was driving.
Oedipus: Alas, that makes it plain enough!
                                    But who—   710
Who told you how it happened?
Jocasta: A household servant,
The only one to escape.
Oedipus: And is he still
A servant of ours?
Jocasta: No; for when he came back at last
And found you enthroned in the place of the dead king,
He came to me, touched my hand with his, and begged
That I would send him away to the frontier district
Where only the shepherds go—
As far away from the city as I could send him.
I granted his prayer; for although the man was a
    slave,
He had earned more than this favor at my hands.   720
Oedipus: Can he be called back quickly?
Jocasta: Easily.
But why?
Oedipus: I have taken too much upon myself
Without enquiry; therefore I wish to consult him.
Jocasta: Then he shall come.
                        But am I not one also
To whom you might confide these fears of yours?
Oedipus: That is your right; it will not be denied you,
Now least of all; for I have reached a pitch
Of wild foreboding. Is there anyone
To whom I should sooner speak?

Polybus of Corinth is my father.   730
My mother is a Dorian: Merope.
I grew up chief among the men of Corinth
Until a strange thing happened—

Not worth my passion, it may be, but strange.

At a feast, a drunken man maundering in his cups
Cries out that I am not my father's son!

I contained myself that night, though I felt anger
And a sinking heart. The next day I visited
My father and mother, and questioned them. They
    stormed,
Calling it all the slanderous rant of a fool;   740
And this relieved me. Yet the suspicion
Remained always aching in my mind;
I knew there was talk; I could not rest;
And finally, saying nothing to my parents,
I went to the shrine at Delphi.
The god dismissed my question without reply;
He spoke of other things.
                    Some were clear,
Full of wretchedness, dreadful, unbearable:
As, that I should lie with my own mother, breed
Children from whom all men would turn their eyes;   750
And that I should be my father's murderer.

I heard all this, and fled. And from that day
Corinth to me was only in the stars
Descending in that quarter of the sky,
As I wandered farther and farther on my way
To a land where I should never see the evil
Sung by the oracle. And I came to this country
Where, so you say, King Laios was killed.

I will tell you all that happened there, my lady.
There were three highways   760
Coming together at a place I passed;
And there a herald came towards me, and a chariot
Drawn by horses, with a man such as you describe
Seated in it. The groom leading the horses
Forced me off the road at his lord's command;
But as this charioteer lurched over towards me
I struck him in my rage. The old man saw me
And brought his double goad down upon my head
As I came abreast.
                    He was paid back, and more!
Swinging my club in this right hand I knocked him   770
Out of his car, and he rolled on the ground.
                    I killed him.
I killed them all.
Now if that stranger and Laios were—kin,
Where is a man more miserable than I?
More hated by the gods? Citizen and alien alike
Must never shelter me or speak to me—
I must be shunned by all.
                    And I myself
Pronounced this malediction upon myself!

Think of it: I have touched you with these hands,
These hands that killed your husband. What defilement!   780

Am I all evil, then? It must be so,
Since I must flee from Thebes, yet never again
See my own countrymen, my own country,
For fear of joining my mother in marriage
And killing Polybus, my father.
                    Ah,

If I was created so, born to this fate,
Who could deny the savagery of God?

O holy majesty of heavenly powers!
May I never see that day! Never!
Rather let me vanish from the race of men   790
Than know the abomination destined me!

Choragos: We too, my lord, have felt dismay at this.
But there is hope: you have yet to hear the shepherd.
Oedipus: Indeed, I fear no other hope is left me.
Jocasta: What do you hope from him when he
    comes?
Oedipus: This much:
If his account of the murder tallies with yours,
Then I am cleared.
Jocasta: What was it that I said
Of such importance?
Oedipus: Why, "marauders," you said,
Killed the King, according to this man's story.
If he maintains that still, if there were several,   800
Clearly the guilt is not mine: I was alone.
But if he says one man, singlehanded, did it,
Then the evidence all points to me.
Jocasta: You may be sure that he said there were
    several;
And can he call back that story now? He can not.
The whole city heard it as plainly as I.
But suppose he alters some detail of it:
He can not ever show that Laios' death
Fulfilled the oracle: for Apollo said
My child was doomed to kill him; and my child—   810
Poor baby!—it was my child that died first.

No. From now on, where oracles are concerned,
I would not waste a second thought on any.
Oedipus: You may be right.
                    But come: let someone go
For the shepherd at once. This matter must be
    settled.
Jocasta: I will send for him.
I would not wish to cross you in anything,
And surely not in this.—Let us go in.
[Exeunt into the palace.]

Ode II

Chorus:

                                                Strophe 1

Let me be reverent in the ways of right,
Lowly the paths I journey on;   820
Let all my words and actions keep
The laws of the pure universe
From highest Heaven handed down.
For Heaven is their bright nurse,
Those generations of the realms of light;
Ah, never of mortal kind were they begot,
Nor are they slaves of memory, lost in sleep:
Their Father is greater than Time, and ages not.

                                                Antistrophe 1

The tyrant is a child of Pride

Who drinks from his great sickening cup   830
Recklessness and vanity,
Until from his high crest headlong
He plummets to the dust of hope.
That strong man is not strong.
But let no fair ambition be denied;
May God protect the wrestler for the State
In government, in comely policy,
Who will fear God, and on His ordinance wait.

                                                    Strophe 2

Haughtiness and the high hand of disdain
Tempt and outrage God's holy law;   840
And any mortal who dares hold
No immortal Power in awe
Will be caught up in a net of pain:
The price for which his levity is sold.
Let each man take due earnings, then,
And keep his hands from holy things,
And from blasphemy stand apart—
Else the crackling blast of heaven
Blows on his head, and on his desperate heart;
Though fools will honor impious men,   850
In their cities no tragic poet sings.

                                                  Antistrophe 2

Shall we lose faith in Delphi's obscurities,
We who have heard the world's core
Discredited, and the sacred wood
Of Zeus at Elis praised no more?
The deeds and the strange prophecies
Must make a pattern yet to be understood.
Zeus, if indeed you are lord of all,
Throned in light over night and day,
Mirror this in your endless mind: 860
Our masters call the oracle
Words on the wind, and the Delphic vision blind!
Their hearts no longer know Apollo,
And reverence for the gods has died away.

Scene III

[Enter JOCASTA.]

Jocasta: Princes of Thebes, it has occurred to me
To visit the altars of the gods, bearing
These branches as a suppliant, and this incense.
Our King is not himself: his noble soul
Is overwrought with fantasies of dread,
Else he would consider   870
The new prophecies in the light of the old.
He will listen to any voice that speaks disaster,
And my advice goes for nothing.
[She approaches the altar.]
                          To you, then, Apollo,
Lycean lord, since you are nearest, I turn in prayer.
Receive these offerings, and grant us deliverance
From defilement. Our hearts are heavy with fear
When we see our leader distracted, as helpless
        sailors
Are terrified by the confusion of their helmsman.

[Enter MESSENGER.]
Messenger: Friends, no doubt you can direct me:
Where shall I find the house of Oedipus,   880
Or, better still, where is the King himself?
Choragos: It is this very place, stranger; he is inside.
This is his wife and mother of his children.
Messenger: I wish her happiness in a happy house,
Blest in all the fulfillment of her marriage.
Jocasta: I wish as much for you: your courtesy
Deserves a like good fortune. But now, tell me:
Why have you come? What have you to say to us?
Messenger: Good news, my lady, for your house and
        your husband.
Jocasta: What news? Who sent you here?
Messenger: I am from Corinth.   890
The news I bring ought to mean joy for you,
Though it may be you will find some grief in it.
Jocasta: What is it? How can it touch us in both ways?
Messenger: The word is that the people of the Isthmus
Intend to call Oedipus to be their king.
Jocasta: But old King Polybus—is he not reigning still?
Messenger: No. Death holds him in his sepulcher.
Jocasta: What are you saying? Polybus is dead?
Messenger: If I am not telling the truth, may I die
        myself.
Jocasta:
[To a MAIDSERVANT.]
Go in, go quickly; tell this to your master.   900
O riddlers of God's will, where are you now!
This was the man whom Oedipus, long ago,
Feared so, fled so, in dread of destroying him—
But it was another fate by which he died.
[Enter OEDIPUS, C.]
Oedipus: Dearest Jocasta, why have you sent for me?
Jocasta: Listen to what this man says, and then tell me
What has become of the solemn prophecies.
Oedipus: Who is this man? What is his news for me?
Jocasta: He has come from Corinth to announce your
        father's death!
Oedipus: Is it true, stranger? Tell me in your own
        words.   910
Messenger: I can not say it more clearly: the King is
        dead.
Oedipus: Was it by treason? Or by an attack of illness?
Messenger: A little thing brings old men to their rest.
Oedipus: It was sickness, then?
Messenger: Yes, and his many years.
Oedipus: Ah!
Why should a man respect the Pythian hearth, or
Give heed to the birds that jangle above his head?
They prophesied that I should kill Polybus,
Kill my own father; but he is dead and buried,
And I am here—I never touched him, never,
Unless he died of grief for my departure,   920
And thus, in a sense, through me. No. Polybus
Has packed the oracles off with him underground.
They are empty words.
Jocasta: Had I not told you so?
Oedipus: You had; it was my faint heart that betrayed
        me.

Jocasta: From now on never think of those things again.
Oedipus: And yet—must I not fear my mother's bed?
Jocasta: Why should anyone in this world be afraid,
Since Fate rules us and nothing can be foreseen?
A man should live only for the present day.

Have no more fear of sleeping with your mother: 930
How many men, in dreams, have lain with their
     mothers!
No reasonable man is troubled by such things.
Oedipus: That is true; only—
If only my mother were not still alive!
But she is alive. I can not help my dread.
Jocasta: Yet this news of your father's death is
     wonderful.
Oedipus: Wonderful. But I fear the living woman.
Messenger: Tell me, who is this woman that you fear?
Oedipus: It is Merope, man; the wife of King Polybus.
Messenger: Merope? Why should you be afraid of
     her?   940
Oedipus: An oracle of the gods, a dreadful saying.
Messenger: Can you tell me about it or are you sworn
     to silence?
Oedipus: I can tell you, and I will.
Apollo said through his prophet that I was the man
Who should marry his own mother, shed his father's
     blood
With his own hands. And so, for all these years
I have kept clear of Corinth, and no harm has come—
Though it would have been sweet to see my parents
     again.
Messenger: And is this the fear that drove you out of
     Corinth?
Oedipus: Would you have me kill my father?
Messenger: As for that   950
You must be reassured by the news I gave you.
Oedipus: If you could reassure me, I would reward
     you.
Messenger: I had that in mind, I will confess: I thought
I could count on you when you returned to Corinth.
Oedipus: No: I will never go near my parents again.
Messenger: Ah, son, you still do not know what you
     are doing—
Oedipus: What do you mean? In the name of God tell
     me!
Messenger: —If these are your reasons for not going
     home.
Oedipus: I tell you, I fear the oracle may come true.
Messenger: And guilt may come upon you through
     your parents?   960
Oedipus: That is the dread that is always in my heart.
Messenger: Can you not see that all your fears are
     groundless?
Oedipus: How can you say that? They are my parents,
     surely?
Messenger: Polybus was not your father.
Oedipus: Not my father?
Messenger: No more your father than the man
     speaking to you.
Oedipus: But you are nothing to me!

Messenger: Neither was he.
Oedipus: Then why did he call me son?
Messenger: I will tell you:
     Long ago he had you from my hands, as a gift.
Oedipus: Then how could he love me so, if I was not his?
Messenger: He had no children, and his heart turned to
     you.
Oedipus: What of you? Did you buy me? Did you find
     me by chance?   970
Messenger: I came upon you in the crooked pass of
     Cithaeron.
Oedipus: And what were you doing there?
Messenger: Tending my flocks.
Oedipus: A wandering shepherd?
Messenger: But your savior, son, that day
Oedipus: From what did you save me?
Messenger: Your ankles should tell you that.
Oedipus: Ah, stranger, why do you speak of that
     childhood pain?
Messenger: I cut the bonds that tied your ankles
     together.
Oedipus: I have had the mark as long as I can
     remember.
Messenger: That was why you were given the name
     you bear.
Oedipus: God! Was it my father or my mother who did
     it? Tell me!
Messenger: I do not know. The man who gave you to
     me   980
Can tell you better than I.
Oedipus: It was not you that found me, but another?
Messenger: It was another shepherd gave you to me.
Oedipus: Who was he? Can you tell me who he was?
Messenger: I think he was said to be one of Laios'
     people.
Oedipus: You mean the Laios who was king here years
     ago?
Messenger: Yes; King Laios; and the man was one of
     his herdsmen.
Oedipus: Is he still alive? Can I see him?
Messenger: These men here
Know best about such things.
Oedipus: Does anyone here
Know this shepherd that he is talking about?   990
Have you seen him in the fields, or in the town?
If you have, tell me. It is time things were made plain.
Choragos: I think the man he means is that same
     shepherd
You have already asked to see. Jocasta perhaps
Could tell you something.
Oedipus: Do you know anything
About him, Lady? Is he the man we have summoned?
Is that the man this shepherd means?
Jocasta: Why think of him?
Forget this herdsman. Forget it all.
This talk is a waste of time.
Oedipus: How can you say that,
When the clues to my true birth are in my hands?   1000
Jocasta: For God's love, let us have no more
     questioning!

Is your life nothing to you?
My own is pain enough for me to bear.
Oedipus: You need not worry. Suppose my mother a
slave,
And born of slaves: no baseness can touch you.
Jocasta: Listen to me, I beg you: do not do this thing!
Oedipus: I will not listen; the truth must be made
known.
Jocasta: Everything that I say is for your own good!
Oedipus: My own good
Snaps my patience, then; I want none of it.
Jocasta: You are fatally wrong! May you never learn
who you are!   1010
Oedipus: Go, one of you, and bring the shepherd here.
Let us leave this woman to brag of her royal name.
Jocasta: Ah, miserable!
That is the only word I have for you now.
That is the only word I can ever have.
[Exit into the palace.]
Choragos: Why has she left us, Oedipus? Why has she
gone
In such a passion of sorrow? I fear this silence:
Something dreadful may come of it.
Oedipus: Let it come!
However base my birth, I must know about it.
The Queen, like a woman, is perhaps ashamed   1020
To think of my low origin. But I
Am a child of Luck; I can not be dishonored.
Luck is my mother; the passing months, my brothers,
Have seen me rich and poor.
                              If this is so,
How could I wish that I were someone else?
How could I not be glad to know my birth?

Ode III

Chorus:

                                                Strophe

If ever the coming time were known
To my heart's pondering,
Cithaeron, now by Heaven I see the torches
At the festival of the next full moon,   1030
And see the dance, and hear the choir sing
A grace to your gentle shade:
Mountain where Oedipus was found,
O mountain guard of a noble race!
May the god who heals us lend his aid,
And let that glory come to pass
For our king's cradling-ground.

                                                Antistrophe

Of the nymphs that flower beyond the years,
Who bore you, royal child,
To Pan of the hills or the timberline Apollo,   1040
Cold in delight where the upland clears,
Or Hermes for whom Kyllene's heights are piled?
Or flushed as evening cloud,
Great Dionysos, roamer of mountains,
He—was it he who found you there,
And caught you up in his own proud
Arms from the sweet god-ravisher
Who laughed by the Muses' fountains?

Scene IV

Oedipus: Sirs: though I do not know the man,
I think I see him coming, this shepherd we want: 1050
He is old, like our friend here, and the men
Bringing him seem to be servants of my house.
But you can tell, if you have ever seen him.
[Enter SHEPHERD escorted by servants.]
Choragos: I know him, he was Laios' man. You can
trust him.
Oedipus: Tell me first, you from Corinth: is this the
shepherd
We were discussing?
Messenger: This is the very man.
Oedipus:
[To SHEPHERD.]
Come here. No, look at me. You must answer
Everything I ask.—You belonged to Laios?
Shepherd: Yes: born his slave, brought up in his
house.
Oedipus: Tell me: what kind of work did you do for
him?   1060
Shepherd: I was a shepherd of his, most of my life.
Oedipus: Where mainly did you go for pasturage?
Shepherd: Sometimes Cithaeron, sometimes the hills
near-by.
Oedipus: Do you remember ever seeing this man out
there?
Shepherd: What would he be doing there? This man?
Oedipus: This man standing here. Have you ever seen
him before?
Shepherd: No. At least, not to my recollection.
Messenger: And that is not strange, my lord. But I'll
refresh
His memory: he must remember when we two
Spent three whole seasons together, March to
September,   1070
On Cithaeron or thereabouts. He had two flocks;
I had one. Each autumn I'd drive mine home
And he would go back with his to Laios' sheepfold.—
Is this not true, just as I have described it?
Shepherd: True, yes; but it was all so long ago.
Messenger: Well, then: do you remember, back in
those days,
That you gave me a baby boy to bring up as my own?
Shepherd: What if I did? What are you trying to say?
Messenger: King Oedipus was once that little child.
Shepherd: Damn you, hold your tongue!
Oedipus: No more of that! 1080
It is your tongue needs watching, not this man's.
Shepherd: My King, my Master, what is it I have done
wrong?
Oedipus: You have not answered his question about
the boy.
Shepherd: He does not know. . . . He is only making
trouble. . . .
Oedipus: Come, speak plainly, or it will go hard with
you.
Shepherd: In God's name, do not torture an old man!
Oedipus: Come here, one of you; bind his arms behind
him.

Shepherd: Unhappy king! What more do you wish to
learn?
Oedipus: Did you give this man the child he speaks of?
Shepherd: I did.
And I would to God I had died that very day.   1090
Oedipus: You will die now unless you speak the
truth.
Shepherd: Yet if I speak the truth, I am worse than
dead.
Oedipus: Very well; since you insist upon delaying—
Shepherd: No! I have told you already that I gave him
the boy.
Oedipus: Where did you get him? From your house?
From somewhere else?
Shepherd: Not from mine, no. A man gave him to me.
Oedipus: Is that man here? Do you know whose slave
he was?
Shepherd: For God's love, my King, do not ask me any
more!
Oedipus: You are a dead man if I have to ask you
again.
Shepherd: Then . . . Then the child was from the
palace of Laios.   1100
Oedipus: A slave child? or a child of his own line?
Shepherd: Ah, I am on the brink of dreadful speech!
Oedipus: And I of dreadful hearing. Yet I must hear.
Shepherd: If you must be told, then . . .
                                    They said it was Laios' child;
But it is your wife who can tell you about that.
Oedipus: My wife!—Did she give it to you?
Shepherd: My lord, she did.
Oedipus: Do you know why?
Shepherd: I was told to get rid of it.
Oedipus: An unspeakable mother!
Shepherd: There had been prophecies . . .
Oedipus: Tell me.
Shepherd: It was said that the boy would kill his own
father.   1110
Oedipus: Then why did you give him over to this old
man?
Shepherd: I pitied the baby, my King,
And I thought that this man would take him far away
To his own country.
                        He saved him—but for what a fate!
For if you are what this man says you are,
No man living is more wretched than Oedipus.
Oedipus: Ah God!
It was true!
        All the prophecies!
                        —Now,
O Light, may I look on you for the last time!
I, Oedipus,   1120
Oedipus, damned in his birth, in his marriage
damned,
Damned in the blood he shed with his own hand!
[He rushes into the palace.]

Ode IV

Chorus:

                                                    Strophe 1
Alas for the seed of men.
What measure shall I give these generations
That breathe on the void and are void
And exist and do not exist?

Who bears more weight of joy
Than mass of sunlight shifting in images,
Or who shall make his thought stay on
That down time drifts away?   1130

Your splendor is all fallen.
O naked brow of wrath and tears,
O change of Oedipus!
I who saw your days call no man blest—
Your great days like ghosts gone.
That mind was a strong bow.

                                                    Antistrophe 1
Deep, how deep you drew it then, hard archer,
At a dim fearful range,
And brought dear glory down!

You overcame the stranger—   1140
The virgin with her hooking lion claws—
And though death sang, stood like a tower
To make pale Thebes take heart.

Fortress against our sorrow!

True king, giver of laws,
Majestic Oedipus!
No prince in Thebes had ever such renown,
No prince won such grace of power.

                                                    Strophe 2
And now of all men ever known
Most pitiful is this man's story: 1150
His fortunes are most changed, his state
Fallen to a low slave's
Ground under bitter fate.

O Oedipus, most royal one!
The great door that expelled you to the light
Gave at night—ah, gave night to your glory:
As to the father, to the fathering son.

All understood too late.

How could that queen whom Laios won,
The garden that he harrowed at his height,   1160
Be silent when that act was done?
But all eyes fail before time's eye,

                                                    Antistrophe 2
All actions come to justice there.
Though never willed, though far down the deep past,
Your bed, your dread sirings,
Are brought to book at last.
Child by Laios doomed to die,
Then doomed to lose that fortunate little death,
Would God you never took breath in this air
That with my wailing lips I take to cry: 1170

For I weep the world's outcast.

I was blind, and now I can tell why:
Asleep, for you had given ease of breath
To Thebes, while the false years went by.

Exodos

[Enter, from the palace, SECOND MESSENGER.]
Second Messenger: Elders of Thebes, most honored
    in this land,
What horrors are yours to see and hear, what weight
Of sorrow to be endured, if, true to your birth,
You venerate the line of Labdakos!
I think neither Istros nor Phasis, those great rivers,
Could purify this place of the corruption   1180
It shelters now, or soon must bring to light—
Evil not done unconsciously, but willed.

The greatest griefs are those we cause ourselves.

Choragos: Surely, friend, we have grief enough
    already;
What new sorrow do you mean?
Second Messenger: The Queen is dead.
Choragos: Jocasta? Dead? But at whose hand?
Second Messenger: Her own.
The full horror of what happened you can not know,
For you did not see it; but I, who did, will tell you
As clearly as I can how she met her death.

When she had left us,   1190
In passionate silence, passing through the court,
She ran to her apartment in the house,
Her hair clutched by the fingers of both hands.
She closed the doors behind her; then, by that bed
Where long ago the fatal son was conceived—
That son who should bring about his father's death—
We heard her call upon Laios, dead so many years,
And heard her wail for the double fruit of her marriage,
A husband by her husband, children by her child.

Exactly how she died I do not know: 1200
For Oedipus burst in moaning and would not let us
Keep vigil to the end: it was by him
As he stormed about the room that our eyes were
    caught.
From one to another of us he went, begging a sword,
Cursing the wife who was not his wife, the mother
Whose womb had carried his own children and
    himself.
I do not know: it was none of us aided him,
But surely one of the gods was in control!
For with a dreadful cry
He hurled his weight, as though wrenched out of
    himself,   1210
At the twin doors: the bolts gave, and he rushed in.
And there we saw her hanging, her body swaying
From the cruel cord she had noosed about her neck.
A great sob broke from him, heartbreaking to hear,
As he loosed the rope and lowered her to the ground.

I would blot out from my mind what happened next!

For the King ripped from her gown the golden brooches
That were her ornament, and raised them, and plunged
    them down
Straight into his own eyeballs, crying, "No more,
No more shall you look on the misery about me,   1220
The horrors of my own doing! Too long you have known
The faces of those whom I should never have seen,
Too long been blind to those for whom I was searching!
From this hour, go in darkness!" And as he spoke,
He struck at his eyes—not once, but many times;
And the blood spattered his beard,
Bursting from his ruined sockets like red hail.

So from the unhappiness of two this evil has sprung,
A curse on the man and woman alike. The old
Happiness of the house of Labdakos   1230
Was happiness enough: where is it today?
It is all wailing and ruin, disgrace, death—all
The misery of mankind that has a name—
And it is wholly and for ever theirs.
Choragos: Is he in agony still? Is there no rest for him?
Second Messenger: He is calling for someone to lead
    him to the gates
So that all the children of Cadmos may look upon
His father's murderer, his mother's—no,
I can not say it!
        And then he will leave Thebes,
Self-exiled, in order that the curse   1240
Which he himself pronounced may depart from the
    house.
He is weak, and there is none to lead him,
So terrible is his suffering.
        But you will see:
Look, the doors are opening; in a moment
You will see a thing that would crush a heart of stone.
    [The central door is opened; OEDIPUS, blinded, is led in.]
Choragos: Dreadful indeed for men to see.
Never have my own eyes
Looked on a sight so full of fear.
Oedipus!
What madness came upon you, what daemon   1250
Leaped on your life with heavier
Punishment than a mortal man can bear?
No: I can not even
Look at you, poor ruined one.
And I would speak, question, ponder,
If I were able. No.
You make me shudder.
Oedipus: God.   God.
Is there a sorrow greater?
Where shall I find harbor in this world?   1260
My voice is hurled far on a dark wind.
What has God done to me?
Choragos: Too terrible to think of, or to see.

        Strophe 1

Oedipus: O cloud of night,
Never to be turned away: night coming on,
I can not tell how: night like a shroud!

My fair winds brought me here.
        O God. Again
The pain of the spikes where I had sight,

The flooding pain
Of memory, never to be gouged out.   1270
Choragos: This is not strange.
You suffer it all twice over, remorse in pain,
Pain in remorse.

Antistrophe 1

Oedipus: Ah dear friend
Are you faithful even yet, you alone?
Are you still standing near me, will you stay here,
Patient, to care for the blind?

The blind man!

Yet even blind I know who it is attends me,
By the voice's tone—
Though my new darkness hide the comforter.   1280
Choragos: Oh fearful act!
What god was it drove you to rake black
Night across your eyes?

Strophe 2

Oedipus: Apollo. Apollo. Dear
Children, the god was Apollo.
He brought my sick, sick fate upon me.
But the blinding hand was my own!
How could I bear to see
When all my sight was horror everywhere?
Choragos: Everywhere; that is true.   1290
Oedipus: And now what is left?
Images? Love? A greeting even,
Sweet to the senses? Is there anything?
Ah, no, friends: lead me away.
Lead me away from Thebes.

Lead the great wreck

And hell of Oedipus, whom the gods hate.
Choragos: Your fate is clear, you are not blind to that.
Would God you had never found it out!

Antistrophe 2

Oedipus: Death take the man who unbound
My feet on that hillside   1300
And delivered me from death to life! What life?
If only I had died,
This weight of monstrous doom
Could not have dragged me and my darlings down.
Choragos: I would have wished the same.
Oedipus: Oh never to have come here
With my father's blood upon me! Never
To have been the man they call his mother's husband!
Oh accurst! Oh child of evil,
To have entered that wretched bed—

the selfsame one!   1310

More primal than sin itself, this fell to me.
Choragos: I do not know how I can answer you.
You were better dead than alive and blind.
Oedipus: Do not counsel me any more. This
    punishment
That I have laid upon myself is just.
If I had eyes,
I do not know how I could bear the sight
Of my father, when I came to the house of Death,
Or my mother: for I have sinned against them both
So vilely that I could not make my peace   1320
By strangling my own life.

Or do you think my children,

Born as they were born, would be sweet to my eyes?
Ah never, never! Nor this town with its high walls,
Nor the holy images of the gods.

For I,

Thrice miserable!—Oedipus, noblest of all the line
Of Cadmos, have condemned myself to enjoy
These things no more, by my own malediction
Expelling that man whom the gods declared
To be a defilement in the house of Laius.
After exposing the rankness of my own guilt,   1330
How could I look men frankly in the eyes?
No, I swear it,
If I could have stifled my hearing at its source,
I would have done it and made all this body
A tight cell of misery, blank to light and sound:
So I should have been safe in a dark agony
Beyond all recollection.

Ah Cithaeron!

Why did you shelter me? When I was cast upon you,
Why did I not die? Then I should never
Have shown the world my execrable birth.   1340

Ah Polybus! Corinth, city that I believed
The ancient seat of my ancestors: how fair
I seemed, your child! And all the while this evil
Was cancerous within me!

For I am sick

In my daily life, sick in my origin.

O three roads, dark ravine, woodland and way
Where three roads met: you, drinking my father's blood,
My own blood, spilled by my own hand: can you
    remember
The unspeakable things I did there, and the things
I went on from there to do?

O marriage, marriage!   1350

The act that engendered me, and again the act
Performed by the son in the same bed—

Ah, the net

Of incest, mingling fathers, brothers, sons,
With brides, wives, mothers: the last evil
That can be known by men: no tongue can say
How evil!

No. For the love of God, conceal me

Somewhere far from Thebes; or kill me; or hurl me
Into the sea, away from men's eyes for ever.

Come, lead me. You need not fear to touch me.
Of all men, I alone can bear this guilt.   1360
[Enter CREON.]
Choragos: We are not the ones to decide; but Creon
    here
May fitly judge of what you ask. He only
Is left to protect the city in your place.
Oedipus: Alas, how can I speak to him? What right
    have I
To beg his courtesy whom I have deeply wronged?
Creon: I have not come to mock you, Oedipus,
Or to reproach you, either.
    [To ATTENDANTS.]

—You, standing there:

If you have lost all respect for man's dignity,
At least respect the flame of Lord Helios:
Do not allow this pollution to show itself   1370
Openly here, an affront to the earth
And Heaven's rain and the light of day. No, take him
Into the house as quickly as you can.
For it is proper
That only the close kindred see his grief.
Oedipus: I pray you in God's name, since your courtesy
Ignores my dark expectation, visiting
With mercy this man of all men most execrable:
Give me what I ask—for your good, not for mine.
Creon: And what is it that you would have me do?   1380
Oedipus: Drive me out of this country as quickly as
      may be
To a place where no human voice can ever greet me.
Creon: I should have done that before now—only,
God's will had not been wholly revealed to me.
Oedipus: But his command is plain: the parricide
Must be destroyed. I am that evil man.
Creon: That is the sense of it, yes; but as things are,
We had best discover clearly what is to be done.
Oedipus: You would learn more about a man like me?
Creon: You are ready now to listen to the god.   1390
Oedipus: I will listen. But it is to you
That I must turn for help. I beg you, hear me.

The woman in there—
Give her whatever funeral you think proper:
She is your sister.
                     But let me go, Creon!
Let me purge my father's Thebes of the pollution
Of my living here, and go out to the wild hills,
To Cithaeron, that has won such fame with me,
The tomb my mother and father appointed for me,
And let me die there, as they willed I should.   1400
And yet I know
Death will not ever come to me through sickness
Or in any natural way: I have been preserved
For some unthinkable fate. But let that be.

As for my sons, you need not care for them.
They are men, they will find some way to live.
But my poor daughters, who have shared my table,
Who never before have been parted from their father—
Take care of them, Creon; do this for me.
And will you let me touch them with my hands   1410
A last time, and let us weep together?
Be kind, my lord,
Great prince, be kind!
                     Could I but touch them
They would be mine again, as when I had my eyes.
[Enter ANTIGONE and ISMENE, attended.]
Ah, God!
Is it my dearest children I hear weeping?
Has Creon pitied me and sent my daughters?
Creon: Yes, Oedipus: I knew that they were dear to you
In the old days, and know you must love them still.
Oedipus: May God bless you for this—and be a
      friendlier   1420
Guardian to you than he has been to me!

Children, where are you?
Come quickly to my hands: they are your brother's—
Hands that have brought your father's once clear eyes
To this way of seeing—
                     Ah dearest ones,
I had neither sight nor knowledge then, your father
By the woman who was the source of his own life!
And I weep for you—having no strength to see you—,
I weep for you when I think of the bitterness
That men will visit upon you all your lives.   1430
What homes, what festivals can you attend
Without being forced to depart again in tears?
And when you come to marriageable age,
Where is the man, my daughters, who would dare
Risk the bane that lies on all my children?
Is there any evil wanting? Your father killed
His father; sowed the womb of her who bore him;
Engendered you at the fount of his own existence!
That is what they will say of you.
                          Then, whom
Can you ever marry? There are no bridegrooms for
      you,   1440
And your lives must wither away in sterile dreaming.

O Creon, son of Menoikeus!
You are the only father my daughters have,
Since we, their parents, are both of us gone for ever.
They are your own blood: you will not let them
Fall into beggary and loneliness;
You will keep them from the miseries that are mine!
Take pity on them; see, they are only children,
Friendless except for you. Promise me this,
Great Prince, and give me your hand in token of it.   1450
[CREON clasps his right hand.]
Children:
I could say much, if you could understand me,
But as it is, I have only this prayer for you:
Live where you can, be as happy as you can—
Happier, please God, than God has made your father!
Creon: Enough. You have wept enough. Now go within.
Oedipus: I must; but it is hard.
Creon: Time eases all things
Oedipus: But you must promise—
Creon: Say what you desire.
Oedipus: Send me from Thebes!
Creon: God grant that I may!
Oedipus: But since God hates me . . .
Creon: No, he will grant your wish. 1460
Oedipus: You promise?
Creon: I can not speak beyond my knowledge.
Oedipus: Then lead me in.
Creon: Come now, and leave your children.
Oedipus: No! Do not take them from me!
Creon: Think no longer
That you are in command here, but rather think
How, when you were, you served your own destruction.
*[Exeunt into the house all but the CHORUS; the CHORAGOS
chants directly to the audience.]*
Choragos: Men of Thebes: look upon Oedipus.

This is the king who solved the famous riddle

And towered up, most powerful of men.
No mortal eyes but looked on him with envy,
Yet in the end ruin swept over him.   1470

Let every man in mankind's frailty
Consider his last day; and let none
Presume on his good fortune until he find
Life, at his death, a memory without pain.

STUDY QUESTIONS

1. *Oedipus* is sometimes cited as a forerunner of the detective story. Though most everyone in the audience knew "who done it," the suspense concerns when and how the murderer (Oedipus) will be revealed while the detective (Oedipus) assembles the clues. Step by step, what are the clues that lead inevitably to the terrible truth?

2. Does the murder of Laios reveal a character flaw of both Laios and Oedipus? Consider Oedipus' description in Ode II of the encounter on the road. What is the mutual flaw and how did it contribute to the killing? You need to consider the fact that all Greek "roads" were artificial ruts made of masonry. Laios' chariot was therefore in the only rutted track.

3. Describe how the motif of blindness functions ironically in the play. When does the king truly see what the blind prophet saw so clearly early in the play?

4. Review the discussion of the play earlier in this chapter and decide whether Oedipus was the agent of his own destruction through hubris, through a character flaw, or because the gods willed it so. Or, on the other hand, despite the price he paid, did he ultimately fulfill his destiny as the savior of Thebes?

LITERARY SELECTION 7

Lysistrata

Aristophanes (ca. 450–380 BC)

This was the greatest event in the war, or, in my opinion, in Greek history; at once most glorious to the victors and most calamitous to the conquered. They were beaten at all points and altogether; their sufferings in every way were great. They were totally destroyed—their fleet, army, everything—and few out of many returned home. So ended the Sicilian expedition.

Thucydides, T*he History of the Peloponnesian War,*
Book VIII, section 87

Lysistrata was completed in 411, only two years after the ghastly failure of the Sicilian expedition, and performed in an Athens still enveloped in gloom over the defeat, a city confronting the growing realization that this war could be lost! Aristophanes challenged his Athenian compatriots with a way to end the war with no one the loser. His theme is serious—he hates the destructive stupidity of any war—but his method is comical. This is, in fact, his most serious comedy.

What Aristophanes hoped for was a miracle. *Lysistrata* was not just an amusing entertainment but a playwright's daring solution for an ever more desperate situation. That his fanciful proposal failed to bring the warring cities to their senses is a matter of record. The modern reader might more clearly understand the significance of the Peloponnesian War if we compare it with the Vietnam War in southeast Asia. Whether or not the United States should have fought that war is not the issue here. It is, rather, the mistaken belief that America's troops and resources were more than sufficient to "win" the war, which precisely mirrors the Athenian attitude. The realization that the war had been lost was a very bitter pill—in ancient Athens, and in the United States.

The anti-war theme was nothing new for those who had seen Aristophanes' earlier *Peace* and *The Acharians. Lysistrata* differs from these plays, however, in its depiction of women, whom most Greek men regarded as mere housewives supposedly incapable of understanding the political and military matters of a man's world. But Aristophanes portrays Lysistrata and her comrades-in-revolution as the rational and reasonable sex who not only perceive the world as it is but set out to change it. Throughout the comedy the men are emotional, illogical, vain, and utterly at the mercy of their bodies, but very respectful of honor and war. Except for honor and war these are precisely the negative characteristics that this male-dominated society attributed to women. We can safely assume that this reversal of gender roles captured the undivided attention of the audience.

Also unusual is the dramatist's focus on married love. Athenian men usually had a variety of extramarital outlets: hetaerae, concubines, courtesans, prostitutes, and other men. None of these possibilities exist in *Lysistrata*; there are only wives, husbands, and married love. (Aristophanes had a particular goal in mind, as we shall see.)

Another surprising facet is the unavailability of husbands before the revolution and their instant appearance after the revolt. Wives who complained about absentee husbands off fighting a distant war are suddenly confronted with very available mates. This is, of course, dramatic license. If war and sex are the issues then the latter has to be a possibility.

What *Lysistrata* shared with all Greek comedies was its bawdiness, for the Greeks knew nothing of puritanical constraints. Generally speaking, what was said and done in everyday life was said and done on stage. After all, comedies had originated in Dionysian fertility rites, which accounts for the celebration of such sensual pleasures as dance, food, drink, and sex. Besides, Aristophanes obviously enjoyed writing bawdy plays.

Much of the charm of the Aristophanic style was his skill in shifting between explicit bawdy and hilarious *double entendre.* An audience as literate, verbal, and sophisticated as the Athenians delighted in complex word play: acrostics, double meanings, puns, palindromes, and the like. The word play was extended to the names of some of the actors to indicate their function. Lysistrata means "she who disbands armies"; of the Athenian women, Kalonike (kal-o-NY-kee) means "dried weed" and Myrrhine (MIR-ri-nee) translates as "myrtle-wreath," a standard euphemism for the female genitalia. The name of her eager husband, Kinesias (ki-NEE-si-as), is derived from a well-known verb for sexual intercourse. And yet this is far from being the dramatist's bawdiest play; that distinction belongs to *The Congresswomen* (also called *The Assemblywomen*).

Lysistrata is about sex, which is natural, and war, which the playwright considers unnatural. It does not, however, depict the brutality of war nor does it exalt lust. By excluding references to sexuality except for the marital bond, Aristophanes raised married love to the level of civic virtue. This is why he placed his protagonists on the Acropolis in the heart of the city. His goal is a united city as symbolized by the union of the loving couples, followed by a unified Hellas, and all brought together by Aphrodite, the goddess of love. As the comedy roars to its exuberant conclusion we are reminded that there are other joys that are infinitely superior to war, including festivals, poetry, dancing, and music. If there is a Utopia, it is undoubtedly in Lysistrata's peaceful, festive Athens.

This translation is by Dudley Fitts, who, like most translators, softened many words in translation that, in Greek, are comparable to our well-known Anglo-Saxon words. Fitts noted that he gave the Spartans a Deep-South accent to suggest the Doric intonation of the Spartans. To Athenian ears, accustomed to Ionic Greek, the Dorians sounded semi-civilized at best.

CHARACTERS

Lysistrata	Commissioner
Kalonike	Kinesias
Myrrhine	Spartan herald
Lampito	Spartan ambassador
Chorus	A sentry

Scene: Athens. First, a public square; later, beneath the walls of the Akropolis; later, a courtyard within the Akropolis.

Until the Exodos, the CHORUS is divided into two hemichori: the first, of Old Men; the second, of Old Women. Each of these has its CHORAGOS [leader]. In the Exodos, the hemichori return as Athenian and Spartans. The supernumeraries include the BABY SON of Kinesias; STRATYLLIS, a member of the hemichorus of Old Women; various individual speakers, both Spartan and Athenian.

Prologue

[Athens; a public square; early morning; LYSISTRATA sola.]

Lysistrata: If someone had invited them to a festival—
of Bacchos, say; or to Pan's shrine, or to Aphrodite's
over at Kolias—, you couldn't get through the streets,
what with the drums and the dancing. But now,
not a woman in sight!
                              Except—oh, yes!
[Enter KALONIKE.]
Here's one of my neighbors, at last. Good
morning, Kalonike.
Kalonike: Good morning, Lysistrata.
                              Darling,
don't frown so! You'll ruin your face!
Lysistrata: Never mind my face.
Kalonike,
the way we women behave! Really, I don't blame the
    men   10
for what they say about us.
Kalonike: No; I imagine they're right.
Lysistrata: For example: I call a meeting
to think out a most important matter—and what
    happens?
The women all stay in bed!
Kalonike: Oh, they'll be along.
It's hard to get away, you know: a husband, a cook,
a child . . . Home life can be *so* demanding!
Lysistrata: What I have in mind is even more
    demanding.
Kalonike: Tell me: what is it?
Lysistrata: It's big.
Kalonike: Goodness! *How* big?
Lysistrata: Big enough for all of us.
Kalonike: But we're not all here!
Lysistrata: We would be, if *that's* what was up!
                              No, Kalonike,   20
this is something I've been turning over for nights,
long sleepless nights.
Kalonike: It must be getting worn down, then,
if you've spent so much time on it.
Lysistrata: Worn down or not,
it comes to this: Only we women can save Greece!
Kalonike: Only we women? Poor Greece!
Lysistrata: Just the same,
it's up to us. First, we must liquidate
the Peloponnesians—
Kalonike: Fun, fun!
Lysistrata: —and then the Boiotians.
Kalonike: Oh! But not those heavenly eels!
Lysistrata: You needn't worry.
I'm not talking about eels. —But here's the point:
If we can get the women from those places—   30
all those Boiotians and Peloponnesians—
to join us women here, why, we can save
all Greece!
Kalonike: But dearest Lysistrata!
How can women do a thing so austere, so
political? We belong at home. Our only armor's
our perfumes, our saffron dresses and
our pretty little shoes!
Lysistrata: Exactly. Those
transparent dresses, the saffron, the
perfume, those pretty shoes—
Kalonike: Oh?
                              Not a single man would lift
his spear
Kalonike: I'll send my dress to the dyer's tomorrow!   40

Lysistrata: —or grab a shield—
Kalonike: The sweetest little negligée—
Lysistrata: —or haul out his sword.
Kalonike: I know where I can buy
the dreamiest sandals!
Lysistrata: Well, so you see. Now, shouldn't
the women have come?
Kalonike: Come? They should have *flown*!
Lysistrata: Athenians are always late.
                                           But imagine!
There's no one here from the South Shore, or from
      Salamis
Kalonike: Things are hard over in Salamis, I swear.
They have to get going at dawn.
Lysistrata: And nobody from Acharnai.
I thought they'd be here hours ago.
Kalonike: Well, you'll get
that awful Theagenes woman: she'll be   50
a sheet or so in the wind.
                                  But look!
Someone at last! Can you see who they are?
[Enter MYRRHINE and other women.]
Lysistrata: They're from Anagyros.
Kalonike: They certainly are.
You'd know them anywhere, by the scent.
Myrrhine: Sorry to be late, Lysistrata.
                                    Oh come,
don't scowl so. Say something!
Lysistrata: My dear Myrrhine
what is there to say? After all,
you've been pretty casual about the whole thing.
Myrrhine: Couldn't find
my girdle in the dark, that's all.
                             But what *is*
"the whole thing"?
Kalonike: No we've got to wait   60
for those Boiotians and Peloponnesians.
Lysistrata: That's more like it. —But look!
Here's Lampito!
[Enter LAMPITO with women from Sparta.]
Lysistrata: Darling Lampito,
how pretty you are today! What a nice color!
Goodness, you look as though you could strangle a bull!
Lampito: Ah think Ah could! It's the work-out
in the gym every day; and, of co'se that dance of ahs
where y' kick yo' own tail.
Kalonike: What an adorable figure!
Lampito: Lawdy, when y' touch me lahk that,
Ah feel lahk a heifer at the altar!
Lysistrata: And this young lady?   70
Where is she from?
Lampito: Boiotia. Social-Register type.
Lysistrata: Ah. "Boiotia of the fertile plain."
Kalonike: And if you look,
you'll find the fertile plain has just been mowed.
Lysistrata: And this lady?
Lampito: Hagh, wahd, handsome. She
      comes from Korinth.
Kalonike: High and wide's the word for it.
Lampito: Which one of you
called this heah meeting, and why?

Lysistrata: I did.
Lampito: Well, then, tell us:
What's up?
Myrrhine: Yes, darling, what *is* on your mind, after all?
Lysistrata: I'll tell you. —But first, one little question.
Myrrhine: Well?
Lysistrata: It's your husbands. Fathers of your children.
      Doesn't it bother you
that they're always off with the Army? I'll stake my life,   80
not one of you has a man in the house this minute!
Kalonike: Mine's been in Thrace the last five months,
      keeping an eye
on that General.
Myrrhine: Mine's been in Pylos for seven.
Lampito: And mahn,
whenever he gets a *dis*charge, he goes raht back
with that li'l ole shield of his, and enlists again!
Lysistrata: And not the ghost of a lover to be found!
From the very day the war began—
                                  those Milesians!
I could skin them alive!
                        —I've not seen so much, even,
as one of those leather consolation prizes—.[18]
But there! What's important is: If I've found a way   90
to end the war, are you with me?
Myrrhine: I should *say* so!
Even if I have to pawn my best dress and
drink up the proceeds.
Kalonike: Me, too! Even if they split me
right up the middle, like a flounder.
Lampito: Ah'm shorley with you.
Ah'd crawl up Taygetos on mah knees
if that'd bring peace.
Lysistrata: All right, then; here it is:
Women! Sisters!
If we really want our men to make peace,
we must be ready to give up—
Myrrhine: Give up what?
Quick, tell us!
Lysistrata: But *will* you?
Myrrhine: We will, even if it kills us.   100
Lysistrata: Then we must give up going to bed with our
      men.
[Long silence.]
Oh? so now you're sorry? Won't look at me?
Doubtful? Pale? All teary-eyed?
                             But come: be frank with me.
Will you do it, or not? Well? Will you do it?
Myrrhine: I couldn't. No.
Let the war go on.
Kalonike: Nor I. Let the war go on.
Lysistrata: You, you little flounder,
ready to be split up the middle?
Kalonike: Lysistrata, no!
I'd walk through fire for you—you *know* I would— but
      don't
ask us to give up *that*! Why, there's nothing like it!
Lysistrata: And you?
Boiotian: No. I must say *I'd* rather walk through fire.   100
Lysistrata: What an utterly perverted sex we women
      are!

No wonder poets write tragedies about us.
There's only one thing we can think of.
                                        But you from Sparta:
if you stand by me, we may win yet! Will you?
It means so much!

Lampito: Ah sweah, it means *too* much!
By the Two Goddesses, it does! Asking a girl
to sleep—Heaven knows how long—in a great big bed
with nobody there but herself! But Ah'll stay with you!
Peace comes first!

Lysistrata: Spoken like a true Spartan!

Kalonike: But if—
                    oh dear!
                          —if we give up what you tell us to,   120
will there *be* any peace?

Lysistrata: Why, mercy, of course there will!
We'll just sit snug in our very thinnest gowns,
perfumed and powdered from top to bottom, and those
      men
simply won't stand still! And when we say No,
they'll go out of their minds! And there's your peace.
You can take my word for it.

Lampito: Ah seem to remember
that Colonel Menelaos threw his sword away
when he saw Helen's breast all bare.

Kalonike: But, goodness me!
What if they just get up and leave us?

Lysistrata: In that case
we'll have to fall back on ourselves, I suppose.   130
But they won't.

Kalonike: I must say that's not much help. But
what if they drag us into the bedroom?

Lysistrata: Hang on to the door.

Kalonike: What if they slap us?

Lysistrata: If they do, you'd better give in.
But be sulky about it. Do I have to teach you how?
You know there's no fun for men when they have to
      force you.
There are millions of ways of getting them to see
      reason.
Don't you worry: a man
doesn't like it unless the girl co-operates.

Kalonike: I suppose so. Oh, all right. We'll go along.

Lampito: Ah imagine us Spahtans can arrange a peace.   140
      But you
Athenians! Why, you're just war-mongerers!

Lysistrata: Leave that to me.
I know how to make them listen.

Lampito: Ah don't see how.
After all, they've got their boats: and there's lots of
      money
piled up in the Akropolis[19]

Lysistrata: The Akropolis? Darling,
we're taking over the Akropolis today!
That's the older women's job. All the rest of us

are going to the Citadel to sacrifice—you understand
      me?
And once there, we're in for good!

Lampito: Whee! Up the rebels!
Ah can see you're a good strat*ee*gist.

Lysistrata: Well, then Lampito,
what we have to do now is take a solemn oath.   150

Lampito: Say it. We'll sweah.

Lysistrata: This is it.
—But where's our Inner Guard?
                      —Look, Guard: you see this shield?
Put it down here. Now bring me the victim's entrails.

Kalonike: But the oath?

Lysistrata: You remember how in Aischylos' *Seven*
they killed a sheep and swore on a shield? Well, then?

Kalonike: But I don't see how you can swear for peace
      on a shield.

Lysistrata: What else do you suggest?

Kalonike: Why not a white horse?[20]
We could swear by that.

Lysistrata: And where will you get a white horse?

Kalonike: I never thought of that. *What* can we do?

Lysistrata: I have it!
Let's set this big black wine-bowl on the ground   160
and pour in a gallon or so of Thasian, and swear
not to add one drop of water.

Lampito: Ah lahk *that* oath!

Lysistrata: Bring the bowl and the wine-jug.

Kalonike: Oh, what a simply *huge* one!

Lysistrata: Set it down. Girls, place your hands on the
      gift-offering.
O Goddess of Persuasian! And thou, O Loving-cup!
Look upon this our sacrifice, and
be gracious!

Kalonike: See the blood spill out. How red and pretty it
      is!

Lampito: And Ah must say it smells good.

Myrrhine: Let me swear first!

Kalonike: No, by Aphrodite, we'll match for it!   170

Lysistrata: Lampito: all of you women: come, touch the
      bowl,
and repeat after me—remember, this is an oath—:
I WILL HAVE NOTHING TO DO WITH MY HUSBAND
      OR MY LOVER

Kalonike: *I will have nothing to do with my husband or
      my lover*

Lysistrata: THOUGH HE COME TO ME IN PITIABLE
      CONDITION

Kalonike: *Though he come to me in pitiable condition*
(Oh Lysistrata! This is killing me!)

Lysistrata: IN MY HOUSE I WILL BE UNTOUCHABLE

Kalonike: *In my house I will be untouchable*

Lysistrata: IN MY THINNEST SAFFRON SILK   180

Kalonike: *In my thinnest saffron silk*

Lysistrata: AND MAKE HIM LONG FOR ME.

Kalonike: *And make him long for me.*

Lysistrata: I WILL NOT GIVE MYSELF

Kalonike: *I will not give myself*

Lysistrata: AND IF HE CONSTRAINS ME

Kalonike: *And if he constrains me*

Lysistrata: I WILL BE COLD AS ICE AND NEVER MOVE

---

18. I.e., a dildo.
19. Pericles set aside an enormous sum at the beginning of the
    war for use in an emergency.
20. A white horse was a symbol for coitus.

Kalonike: *I will be cold as ice and never move*
Lysistrata: I WILL NOT LIFT MY SLIPPERS TOWARD
THE CEILING   190
Kalonike: *I will not lift my slippers toward the ceiling*
Lysistrata: OR CROUCH ON ALL FOURS LIKE THE
LIONESS IN THE CARVING
Kalonike: *Or crouch on all fours like the lioness in the
carving*
Lysistrata: AND IF I KEEP THIS OATH LET ME DRINK
FROM THIS BOWL
Kalonike: *And if I keep this oath let me drink from this
bowl*
Lysistrata: IF NOT, LET MY OWN BOWL BE FILLED
WITH WATER.
Kalonike: *If not, let my own bowl be filled with water.*
Lysistrata: You have all sworn?
Myrrhine: We have.
Lysistrata: Then thus
I sacrifice the victim.
[Drinks largely.]
Kalonike: Save some for us!
Here's to you, darling, and to you, and to you!   200
[Loud cries off-stage.]
Lampito: What's all *that* whoozy-goozy?
Lysistrata: Just what I told you.
The older women have taken the Akropolis.
Now you, Lampito,
rush back to Sparta. We'll take care of things here. Leave
these girls here for hostages.
                                        The rest of you,
up to the Citadel: and mind you push in the bolts.
Kalonike: But the men? Won't they be after us?
Lysistrata: Just you leave
the men to me. There's not fire enough in the world,
or threats either, to make me open these doors
except on my own terms.
Kalonike: I hope not, by Aphrodite!   210
After all,
we've got a reputation for bitchiness to live up to.
[Exeunt.]

Parodos: Choral Episode

*[The hillside just under the Akropolis. Enter CHORUS OF
OLD MEN with burning torches and braziers; much
puffing and coughing.]*
Choragos (m): Forward march, Drakes, old friend: never
      you mind
that damn big log banging hell down on your back.
Chorus (m):   Strophe 1
There's this to be said for longevity:
You see things you thought that you'd never see.
      Look, Strymodoros, who would have thought it?
      We've caught it—
                         The New Femininity!
The wives of our bosom, our board, our bed—
Now by the gods, they've gone ahead   220
And taken the Citadel (Heaven knows why!),

Profaned the sacred statuary,
                         And barred the doors,
                              The subversive whores!
Choragos (m): Shake a leg there, Philurgos, man: the
      Akropolis or bust!
Put the kindling around here. We'll build one almighty big
bonfire for the whole bunch of bitches, every last one;
and the first we fry will be old Lykon's woman.
Chorus (m):   Antistrophe 1
They're not going to give me the old horse-laugh!
No, by Demeter, they won't pull this off!   230
      Think of Kleomenes: even he
      Didn't go free
                         till he brought me his stuff.
A good man he was, all stinking and shaggy,
Bare as an eel except for the bag he
Covered his rear with. God, what a mess!
Never a bath in six years, I'd guess.
                         Pure Sparta, man!
                              He also ran.
Choragos (m): That was a siege, friends! Seventeen
      ranks strong
we slept at the Gate. And shall we not do as much   240
against these women, whom God and Euripides hate?
If we don't, I'll turn in my medals from Marathon.
Chorus (m):   Strophe 2
      Onward and upward! A little push,
      And we're there.
      Ouch, my shoulders! I could wish
      For a pair
Of good strong oxen. Keep your eye
      On the fire there, it mustn't die.
         Akh! Akh!
      The smoke would make a cadaver cough!   250
                                        Antistrophe 2
      Holy Herakles, a hot spark
      Bit my eye!
Damn this hellfire, damn this work!
      So say I.
Onward and upward just the same.
(Laches, remember the Goddess: for shame!)
         Akh! Akh!
      The smoke would make a cadaver cough!
Choragos (m): At last (and let us give suitable thanks to
      God
for his infinite mercies) I have managed to bring   260
my personal flame to the common goal. It breathes, it
      lives.
Now, gentlemen, let us consider. Shall we insert
the torch, say, into the brazier, and thus extract
a kindling brand? And shall we then, do you think,
push on to the gate like valiant sheep? On the whole, yes.
But I would have you consider this, too: if they—
I refer to the women—should refuse to open,
what then? Do we set the doors afire
and smoke them out? At ease, men. Meditate.
Akh, the smoke! Woof! What we really need   270
is the loan of a general or two from the Samos
      Command.
At least we've got this lumber off our backs.
That's something. And now let's look to our fire.

O Pot, brave Brazier, touch my torch with flame!
Victory, Goddess, I invoke thy name!
Strike down these paradigms of female pride,
    And we shall hang our trophies up inside.
[Enter CHORUS OF OLD WOMEN on the walls of the
Akropolis, carrying jars of water.]
Choragos (w): Smoke, girls, smoke! There's smoke all
    over the place!
Probably fire, too. Hurry, girls! Fire! Fire!

Chorus (w):   Strophe 1
        Nikodike, run!   280
        Or Kalyke's done
        To a turn, and poor Kratylla's
        Smoked like a ham.
                    Damn
        These old men! Are we too late?
        I nearly died down at the place
        Where we fill our jars:
            Slaves pushing and jostling—
            Such a hustling!
        I never saw in all my days.

                                                   Antistrophe 1
        But here's water at last.   290
        Haste, sisters, haste!
        Slosh it on them, slosh it down,
        The silly old wrecks!
                    Sex
        Almighty! What they want's
        A hot bath? Good. Send one down.
        Athena of Athens town,
            Trito-born! Helmet of Gold!
            Cripple the old
        Firemen! Help us help them drown!
[The OLD MEN capture a woman, STRATYLLIS.]
Stratyllis: Let me go! Let me go!
Choragos (w):   You walking corpses,   300
have you no shame?
Choragos (m):   I wouldn't have believed it!
An army of women in the Akropolis!
Choragos (w): So we scare you, do we? Grandpa,
    you've seen
only our pickets yet!
Choragos (m):   Hey, Phaidrias!
Help me with the necks of these jabbering hens!
Choragos (w): Down with your pots, girls! We'll need
    both hands
if these antiques attack us.
Choragos (m):   Want your face kicked in?
Choragos (w): Want your balls chewed off?
Choragos (m):   Look out! I've got a stick!
Choragos (w): You lay a half-inch of your stick on
    Stratyllis,
and you'll never stick again!   310
Choragos (m): Fall apart!
Choragos (w):   I'll spit up your guts!
Choragos (m):   Euripides! Master!
How well you knew women!
Choragos (w):   Listen to him! Rhodippe,
up with the pots!
Choragos (m): Demolition of God,
what good are your pots?

Choragos (w):   You refugee from the tomb,
what good is your fire?
Choragos (m):   Good enough to make a pyre
to barbecue you!
Choragos (w): We'll squizzle your kindling!
Choragos (m): You think so?
Choragos (w):   Yah! Just hang around a while!
Choragos (m): Want a touch of my torch?
Choragos (w):   It needs a good soaping.
Choragos (m): How about you?
Choragos (w):   Soap for a senile bridegroom!
Choragos (m): Senile? Hold your trap!
Choragos (w):   Just *you* try to hold it!   320
Choragos (m): The yammer of women!
Choragos (w):   Oh is that so?
You're not in the jury room now, you know.
Choragos (m): Gentlemen, I beg you, burn off that
    woman's hair!
Choragos (w): Let it come down!
[They empty their pots on the men.]
Choragos (m): What a way to drown!
Choragos (w):   Hot, hey?
Choragos (m):   Say,
enough!
Choragos (w): Dandruff
needs watering. I'll make you
nice and fresh.
Choragos (m): For God's sake, you sluts,
hold off!

Scene I

[Enter a COMMISSIONER accompanied by four constables.]
Commissioner: These degenerate women! What a
    racket of little drums,   330
what a yapping for Adonis on every house-top!
It's like the time in the Assembly when I was listening
to a speech—out of order, as usual—by that fool
Demostratos, all about troops for Sicily[21]
that kind of nonsense—
                    and there was his wife
trotting around in circles howling
Alas for Adonis!—
                    and Demostratos insisting
we must draft every last Zakynthian that can walk—
and his wife up there on the roof,
drunk as an owl, yowling   340
Oh weep for Adonis!—
                    and that damned ox Demostratos
mooing away through the rumpus. That's what we get
for putting up with this wretched woman-business!
Choragos (m): Sir, you haven't heard the half of it. They
    laughed at us!
Insulted us! They took pitchers of water

---

21. Referring to the disastrous failure of the Sicilian expedition
(416 BC) from which Athens never recovered. It was the
Sicilian fiasco that prompted Aristophanes to suggest his
unique way to end a war neither side could "win."

and nearly drowned us! We're still wringing out our
   clothes,
for all the world like unhousebroken brats.
Commissioner: Serves you right, by Poseidon!
Whose fault is it if these women-folk of ours
get out of hand? We coddle them,   350
we teach them to be wasteful and loose. You'll see a
   husband
go into a jeweler's. "Look," he'll say,
"jeweler," he'll say, "you remember that gold choker
you made for my wife? Well, she went to a dance last
   night
and broke the clasp. Now, I've got to go to Salamis,
and can't be bothered. Run over to my house tonight,
will you, and see if you can put it together for her."
Or another one
goes to a cobbler—a good strong workman, too,
with an awl that was never meant for child's play. "Here,"   360
he'll tell him, "one of my wife's shoes is pinching
her little toe. Could you come up about noon
and stretch it out for her?"
                              Well, what do you expect?
Look at me, for example. I'm a Public Officer,
and it's one of my duties to pay off the sailors.
And where's the money? Up there in the Akropolis!
And those blasted women slam the door in my face!
But what are we waiting for?
                              —Look here, constable,
stop sniffing around for a tavern, and get us
some crowbars. We'll force their gates! As a matter of
   fact,   370
I'll do a little forcing myself.
*[Enter LYSISTRATA, above, with MYRRHINE, KALONIKE, and
the BOIOTIAN.]*
Lysistrata: No need of forcing.
Here I am, of my own accord. And all this talk
about locked doors—! We don't need locked doors,
but just the least bit of common sense.
Commissioner: Is that so, ma'am!
                              —Where's my constable?
                                        —Constable,
arrest that woman, and tie her hands behind her.
Lysistrata: If he touches me, I swear by Artemis
there'll be one scamp dropped from the public pay-roll
   tomorrow!
Commissioner: Well, constable? You're not afraid, I
   suppose? Grab her,
two of you, around the middle!
Kalonike: No, by Pandrosos!   380
Lay a hand on her, and I'll jump on you so hard
your guts will come out the back door!
Commissioner: That's what *you* think!
Where's the sergeant?—Here, you: tie up that trollop
   first,
the one with the pretty talk!
Myrrhine: By the Moon-Goddess,
just try! They'll have to scoop you up with a spoon!
Commissioner: Another one!
                              Officer, seize that woman!
                                             I swear
I'll put an end to this riot!

Boiotian: By the Taurian,
one inch closer, you'll be one screaming bald-head!
Commissioner: Lord, what a mess! And my constables
   seem ineffective.
But—women get the best of us? By God, no!
                                   —Skythians! 390
Close ranks and forward march!
Lysistrata: "Forward," indeed!
By the Two Goddesses, what's the sense in *that*?
They're up against four companies of women
armed from top to bottom.
Commissioner: Forward, my Skythians!
Lysistrata: Forward, yourselves, dear comrades!
You grainlettucebeanseedmarket girls!
You garlicandonionbreadbakery girls!
Give it to 'em! Knock 'em down! Scratch 'em!
Tell 'em what you think of 'em!
[General mêlée; the Skythians yield.]
                              —Ah, that's enough!
Sound a retreat: good soldiers don't rob the dead.   400
Commissioner: A nice day *this* has been for the police!
Lysistrata: Well, there you are.—Did you really think we
   women
would be driven like slaves? Maybe now you'll admit
that a woman knows something about spirit.
Commissioner: Spirit enough,
especially spirits in bottles! Dear Lord Apollo!
Choragos (m): Your Honor, there's no use talking to
   them. Words
mean nothing whatever to wild animals like these.
Think of the sousing they gave us! and the water
was not, I believe, of the purest.
Choragos (w): You shouldn't have come after us. And if
   you try it again,   410
you'll be one eye short!—Although, as a matter of fact,
what I like best is just to stay at home and read,
like a sweet little bride: never hurting a soul, no,
never going out. But if you *must* shake hornets' nests,
look out for the hornets!
Chorus (m):   Strophe 1
   Of all the beasts that God hath wrought
      What monster's worse than women?
   Who shall encompass with his thought
      Their guile unending? No man.

   They've seized the Heights, the Rock, the Shrine—   420
      But to what end? I wot not.
   Sure there's some clue to their design!
      Have you the key? I thought not.
Choragos (m): We might question them, I suppose. But
   I warn you, sir,
don't believe anything you hear! It would be un-Athenian
not to get to the bottom of this plot.
Commissioner: Very well.
My first question is this: Why, so help you God,
did you bar the gates of the Akropolis?
Lysistrata: Why?
To keep the money, of course. No money, no war.
Commissioner: You think that money's the cause of
   war?
Lysistrata: I do.   430

Money brought about that Peisandros business
and all the other attacks on the State. Well and good!
They'll not get another cent here!
Commissioner: And what will you do?
Lysistrata: What a question! From now on, we intend
to control the Treasury.
Commissioner: Control the Treasury!
Lysistrata: Why not? Does that seem strange? After all,
we control our household budgets.
Commissioner: But that's different!
Lysistrata: "Different"? What do you mean?
Commissioner: I mean simply this:
it's the Treasury that pays for National Defense.
Lysistrata: Unnecessary. We propose to abolish war.   440
Commissioner: Good God—And National Security?
Lysistrata: Leave that to us.
Commissioner: You?
Lysistrata: Us.
Commissioner: We're done for, then!
Lysistrata: Never mind.
We women will save you in spite of yourselves.
Commissioner: What nonsense!
Lysistrata: If you like. But you must accept it, like it or
     not.
Commissioner: Why, this is downright subversion!
Lysistrata: Maybe it is.
But we're going to save you, Judge.
Commissioner: I don't *want* to be saved.
Lysistrata: Tut. The death-wish. All the more reason.
Commissioner: But the idea
of women bothering themselves about peace and war!
Lysistrata: Will you listen to me?
Commissioner: Yes. But be brief, or I'll—
Lysistrata: This is no time for stupid threats.
Commissioner: By the gods,   450
I can't stand any more!
An Old Woman: Can't stand? Well, well.
Commissioner: That's enough out of you, you old
     buzzard!
Now, Lysistrata: tell me what you're thinking.
Lysistrata: Glad to.
              Ever since this war began
We women have been watching you men, agreeing with
     you,
keeping our thoughts to ourselves. That doesn't mean
we were happy: we weren't, for we saw how things
     were going;
but we'd listen to you at dinner
arguing this way and that.
                —Oh you, and your big
Top Secrets!—
          And then we'd grin like little patriots   460
(though goodness knows we didn't feel like grinning)
     and ask you:
"Dear, did the Armistice come up in Assembly today?"
And you'd say, "None of your business! Pipe down!",
     you'd say.
And so we would.
An Old Woman: *I* wouldn't have, by God!
Commissioner: You'd have taken a beating, then!
                —Go on.

Lysistrata: Well, we'd be quiet. But then, you know, all
     at once
you men would think up something worse than ever.
Even *I* could see it was fatal. And, "Darling," I'd say,
"have you gone completely mad?" And my husband
     would look at me
and say, "Wife, you've got your weaving to attend to.   470
Mind your tongue, if you don't want a slap. 'War's
a man's affair'!"[22]
Commissioner: Good words, and well pronounced!
Lysistrata: You're a fool if you think so.
                    It was hard enough
to put up with all this banquet-hall strategy.
But then we'd hear you out in the public square:
"Nobody left for the draft-quota here in Athens?"
you'd say; and, "No," someone else would say, "not a
     man!"
And so we women decided to rescue Greece.
You might as well listen to us now: you'll have to, later.
Commissioner: *You* rescue Greece? Absurd.
Lysistrata: You're the absurd one.   480
Commissioner: You expect me to take orders from a
     woman?
          I'd die first!
Lysistrata: Heavens, if that's what's bothering you, take
     my veil,
here, and wrap it around your poor head.
Kalonike: Yes,
and you can have my market-basket, too.
Go home, tighten your girdle, do the washing, mind
your beans! "War's
a woman's affair"!
Choragos (w): Ground pitchers! Close ranks!
Chorus (w):   Antistrophe
          This is a dance that I know well,
               My knees shall never yield.
          Wobble and creak I may, but still   490
          I'll keep the well-fought field.

          Valor and grace march on before,
               Love prods us from behind.
          Our slogan is EXCELSIOR,
               Our watchword SAVE MANKIND.
Choragos (w): Women, remember your grandmothers!
     Remember
that little old mother of yours, what a stinger she was!
On, on, never slacken. There's a strong wind astern!
Lysistrata: O Eros of delight! O Aphrodite! Kyprian!
If ever desire has drenched our breasts or dreamed   500
in our thighs, let it work so now on the men of Hellas
that they shall tail us through the land, slaves, slaves
to Woman, Breaker of Armies!
Commissioner: And if we do?
Lysistrata: Well, for one thing, we shan't have to watch
     you
going to market, a spear in one hand, and heaven knows
what in the other.
Kalonike: Nicely said, by Aphrodite!

---

22. Quoted from *Iliad*, VI, 492; Hector to Andromache.

Lysistrata: As things stand now, you're neither men nor
women.
Armor clanking with kitchen pans and pots—
you sound like a pack of Korybantes!
Commissioner: A man must do what a man must do.
Lysistrata: So I'm told.   510
But to see a General, complete with Gorgon-shield,
jingling along the dock to buy a couple of herrings!
Kalonike: *I* saw a Captain the other day—lovely fellow
he was,
nice curly hair—sitting on his horse; and—can you
believe it?—
he'd just bought some soup, and was pouring it into his
helmet!
And there was a soldier from Thrace
swishing his lance like something out of Euripides,
and the poor fruit-store woman got so scared
that she ran away and let him have his figs free!
Commissioner: All this is beside the point.
                              Will you be so kind   520
as to tell me how you mean to save Greece:
Lysistrata: Of course.
Nothing could be simpler.
Commissioner: I assure you, I'm all ears.
Lysistrata: Do you know anything about weaving?
Say the yarn gets tangled: we thread it
this way and that through the skein, up and down,
until it's free. And it's like that with war.
We'll send our envoys
up and down, this way and that, all over Greece,
until it's finished.
Commissioner: Yarn? Thread? Skein?
Are you out of your mind? I tell you,   530
war is a serious business.
Lysistrata: So serious
that I'd like to go on talking about weaving.
Commissioner: All right. Go ahead.
Lysistrata: The first thing we have to do
is to wash our yarn, get the dirt off of it.
You see? Isn't there too much dirt here in Athens?
You must wash those men away.
                         Then our spoiled wool—
that's like your job-hunters, out for a life
of no work and big pay. Back to the basket,
citizens or not, allies or not,
or friendly immigrants.
                         And your colonies?   540
Hanks of wool lost in various places. Pull them
together, weave them into one great whole,
and our voters are clothed for ever.
Commissioner: It would take a woman
to reduce state questions to a matter of carding and
weaving.
Lysistrata: You fool! Who were the mothers whose
sons sailed off
to fight for Athens in Sicily?
Commissioner: Enough!
I beg you, do not call back those memories.
Lysistrata: And then,
instead of the love that every woman needs,
we have only our single beds, where we can dream

of our husbands off with the Army.
                         Bad enough for wives!   550
But what about our girls, getting older every day,
and older, and no kisses?
Commissioner: Men get older, too.
Lysistrata: Not in the same sense.
                         A soldier's discharged,
and he may be bald and toothless, yet he'll find
a pretty young thing to go to bed with.
                         But a woman!
Her beauty is gone with the first grey hair.
She can spend her time
consulting the oracles and the fortune-tellers,
but they'll never send her a husband.
Commissioner: Still, if a man can rise to the occasion—   560
Lysistrata: Rise? Rise, yourself!
[Furiously.]
Go invest in a coffin!
                         You've money enough.
                                   I'll bake you
a cake for the Underworld.
                         And here's your funeral
wreath!
[She pours water upon him.]
Myrrhine: And here's another!
[More water.]
Kalonike: And here's
my contribution!
[More water.]
Lysistrata: What are you waiting for?
All aboard Styx Ferry!
                         Charon's calling for you!
It's sailing-time: don't disrupt the schedule!
Commissioner: The insolence of women! And to me!
No, by God, I'll go back to town and show
the rest of the Commission what might happen to them.   570
[Exit COMMISSIONER.]
Lysistrata: Really, I suppose we should have laid out his
corpse
on the doorstep, in the usual way.
                         But never mind.
We'll give him the rites of the dead tomorrow morning.
[Exit LYSISTRATA with MYRRHINE and KALONIKE.]

Parabasis: Choral Episode

Choragos (m):   Strophe 1
Sons of Liberty, awake! The day of glory is at hand.
Chorus (m): I smell tyranny afoot, I smell it rising from
the land.
I scent a trace of Hippias, I sniff upon the breeze
A dismal Spartan hogo that suggests King Kleisthenes.
     Strip, strip for action, brothers!
     Our wives, aunts, sisters, mothers
Have sold us out: the streets are full of godless female
rages.   580
Shall we stand by and let our women confiscate our
wages?
Choragos (m):
Gentlemen, it's a disgrace to Athens, a disgrace

to all that Athens stands for, if we allow these grandmas
to jabber about spears and shields and making friends
with the Spartans. What's a Spartan? Give me a wild
    wolf
any day. No. They want the Tyranny back, I suppose.
Are we going to take that? No. Let us look like
the innocent serpent, but be the flower under it,
as the poet sings. And just to begin with,
I propose to poke a number of teeth   590
down the gullet of that harridan over there.

Choragos (w):   Antistrophe 1
Oh, is that so? When you get home, your own mamma
    won't know you!

Chorus (w): Who do you think we are, you senile
    bravos? Well, I'll show you.
I bore the sacred vessels in my eighth year, and at ten
I was pounding out the barley for Athena Goddess; then
    They made me little Bear
    At the Braunonian Fair;
I'd held the Holy Basket by the time I was of age,
The Blessed Dry Figs had adorned my plump
    décolletage.

Choragos (w):
A "disgrace to Athens", am I, just at the moment   600
I'm giving Athens the best advice she ever had?
Don't I pay taxes to the State? Yes, I pay them
in baby boys. And what do you contribute,
you impotent horrors? Nothing but waste: all
our Treasury, dating back to the Persian Wars,
gone! rifled![23] And not a penny out of your pockets!
Well, then? Can you cough up an answer to that?
Look out for your own gullet, or you'll get a crack
from this old brogan that'll make your teeth see stars!

Chorus (m):   Strophe 2
    Oh insolence!   610
    Am I unmanned?
    Incontinence!
    Shall my scarred hand
    Strike never a blow
    To curb this flow-
    ing female curse?

    Leipsydrion!
    Shall I betray
    The laurels won
    On that great day?   620
    Come, shake a leg,
    Shed old age, beg
    The years reverse!

Choragos (m):
Give them an inch, and we're done for! We'll have them
launching boats next and planning naval strategy,
sailing down on us like so many Artemisias.
Or maybe they have ideas about the cavalry.

---

23. A large sum of money, originally contributed by Athens and
her allies and intended to finance an extension of the sea-
war against Persia. Since the failure of the Sicilian
expedition, the contributions of the allies had fallen off; the
fund itself was then being raided by Athenian politicians.
24. A grotto on the north side of the Acropolis, beneath the
walls.

That's fair enough, women are certainly good
in the saddle. Just look at Mikon's paintings,
all those Amazons wrestling with all those men!   630
On the whole, a straitjacket's their best uniform.

Chorus (w):   Antistrophe 2
    Tangle with me,
    And you'll get cramps.
    Ferocity
    's no use now, Gramps!
    By the Two,
    I'll get through
    To you wrecks yet!

    I'll scramble your eggs,
    I'll burn your beans,   640
    With my two legs.
    You'll see such scenes
    As never yet
    Your two eyes met.
    A curse? You bet!

Choragos (w):
If Lampito stands by me, and that delicious Theban girl,
Ismenia—what good are *you*? You and your seven
Resolutions! Resolutions? Rationing Boiotian eels
and making our girls go without them at Hekate's Feast!
That was statesmanship! And we'll have to put up with
    it   650
and all the rest of your decrepit legislation
until some patriot—God give him strength!—
grabs you by the neck and kicks you off the Rock.

Scene II

[Re-enter LYSISTRATA and her lieutenants.]

Choragos (w): Great Queen, fair Architect of our
    emprise,
Why lookst thou on us with foreboding eyes?

Lysistrata: The behavior of these idiotic women!
There's something about the female temperament
that I can't bear!

Choragos (w): What in the world do you mean?

Lysistrata: Exactly what I say.

Choragos (w):   What dreadful thing has happened?
Come, tell us: we're all your friends.

Lysistrata: It isn't easy   660
to say it; yet, God knows, we can't hush it up.

Choragos (w): Well, then? Out with it!

Lysistrata: To put it bluntly,
we're dying to get laid.

Choragos (w):   Almighty God!

Lysistrata: Why bring God into it?—No, it's just as I say.
I can't manage them any longer: they've gone man-
    crazy,
they're all trying to get out.

               Why, look:
one of them was sneaking out the back door
over there by Pan's cave;[24] another
was sliding down the walls with rope and tackle;
another was climbing aboard a sparrow, ready to take off   670
for the nearest brothel—I dragged *her* back by the hair!

They're all finding some reason to leave.
                              Look there!
There goes another one.
                    —Just a minute, you!
Where are you off to so fast?
First Woman: I've got to get home.
I've a lot of Milesian wool, and the worms are spoiling it.
Lysistrata: Oh bother you and your worms! Get back
        inside!
First Woman: I'll be back right away, I swear I will.
I just want to get it stretched out on my bed.
Lysistrata: You'll do no such thing. You'll stay right here.
First Woman: And my wool?
You want it ruined?
Lysistrata: Yes, for all I care.   680
Second Woman: Oh dear! My lovely new flax from
        Amorgos—
I left it at home, all uncarded!
Lysistrata: Another one!
And all she wants is someone to card her flax.
Get back in there!
Second Woman: But I swear by the Moon-Goddess,
the minute I get it done, I'll be back!
Lysistrata: I say No.
If you, why not all the other women as well?
Third Woman: O Lady Eileithyia! Radiant goddess!
        Thou
intercessor for women in childbirth! Stay, I pray thee,
oh stay this parturition. Shall I pollute
a sacred spot?
Lysistrata: And what's the matter with *you*?   690
Third Woman: I'm having a baby—any minute now.
Lysistrata: But you weren't pregnant yesterday.
Third Woman: Well, I am today.
Let me go home for a midwife, Lysistrata:
there's not much time.
Lysistrata: I never heard such nonsense.
What's that bulging under your cloak:
Third Woman: A little baby boy.
Lysistrata: It certainly isn't. But it's something hollow,
like a basin or— Why, it's the helmet of Athena!
And you said you were having a baby.
Third Woman: Well, I am! So there!
Lysistrata: Then why the helmet?
Third Woman: I was afraid that my pains
might begin here in the Akropolis; and I wanted   700
to drop my chick into it, just as the dear doves do.
Lysistrata: Lies! Evasions—But at least one thing's
        clear;
you can't leave the place before your purification.
Third Woman: But I can't stay here in the Akropolis!
        Last night I dreamed
of a Snake.[25]
First Woman: And those horrible owls,[26] the noise they
        make!
I can't get a bit of sleep; I'm just about dead.
Lysistrata: You useless girls, that's enough: Let's have

---

25. The dreamer seems to be anticipating Freud.
26. The owl was sacred to Athena.

no more lying.
Of course you want your men. But don't you imagine
that they want you just as much? I'll give you my word,
their nights must be pretty hard.
                              Just stick it out!   710
A little patience, that's all, and our battle's won.
I have heard an Oracle. Should you like to hear it?
First Woman: An Oracle? Yes, tell us!
Lysistrata: Here is what it says:
WHEN SWALLOWS SHALL THE HOOPOE SHUN
    AND SPURN HIS HOT DESIRE,
ZEUS WILL PERFECT WHAT THEY'VE BEGUN
    AND SET THE LOWER HIGHER.
First Woman: Does that mean we'll be on top?
Lysistrata:
BUT IF THE SWALLOWS SHALL FALL OUT
    AND TAKE THE HOOPOE'S BAIT,   720
A CURSE MUST MARK THEIR HOUR OF DOUBT,
    INFAMY SEAL THEIR FATE.
Third Woman: I swear, *that* Oracle's all too clear.
First Woman: Oh the dear gods!
Lysistrata: Let's not be downhearted, girls. Back to our
        places!
The god has spoken. How can we possibly fail him?
[Exit LYSISTRATA with the dissident women.]

Choral Episode

Chorus (m):   Strophe
I know a little story that I learned way back in school
Goes like this:
Once upon a time there was a young man—and no
        fool—
Named Melanion; and his
One aversion was marriage. He loathed the very
        thought.   730
So he ran off to the hills, and in a special grot
Raised a dog, and spent his days
Hunting rabbits. And it says
That he never never never did come home.
It might be called a refuge *from* the womb.
All right,
        all right,
                all right!
We're as bright as young Melanion, and we hate the
        very sight
Of you women!
A Man: How about a kiss, old lady?
A Woman: Here's an onion for your eye!   740
A Man: A kick in the guts, then?
A Woman: Try, old bristle-tail, just try!
A Man: Yet they say Myronides
On hands and knees
Looked just as shaggy fore and aft as I!
Chorus (w):   Antistrophe
Well, *I* know a little story, and it's just as good as yours.
Goes like this:
Once there was a man named Timon—a rough diamond,
        of course,
And that whiskery face of his

Looked like murder in the shrubbery. By God, he was a
    son   750
Of the Furies, let me tell you! And what did he do but
    run
From the world and all its ways,
Cursing mankind! And it says
that his choicest execrations as of then
Were leveled almost wholly at *old* men.
All right,
      all right,
           all right!
But there's one thing about Timon: he could always
    stand the sight
Of us women.
A Woman: How about a crack in the jaw, Pop?
A Man: I can take it, Ma—no fear!   760
A Woman: How about a kick in the face?
A Man You'd reveal your old caboose?
A Woman: What I'd show,
I'll have you know,
Is an instrument you're too far gone to use.

Scene III

[Re-enter LYSISTRATA.]
Lysistrata: Oh, quick, girls, quick! Come here!
A Woman: What is it?
Lysistrata: A man.
A man simply bulging with love.
                          O Kyprian Queen,
O Paphian, O Kythereian! Here us and aid us!
A Woman: Where is this enemy?
Lysistrata: Over there, by Demeter's shrine.
A Woman: Damned if he isn't. But who *is* he?
Myrrhine: My husband.   770
    Kinesias.
Lysistrata: Oh then, get busy! Tease him! Undermine
    him!
Wreck him! Give him everything—kissing, tickling,
    nudging,
whatever you generally torture him with—: give him
    everything
except what we swore on the wine we would not give.
Myrrhine: Trust me.
Lysistrata: I do. But I'll help you get him started.
The rest of you women, stay back.
[Enter KINESIAS.]
Kinesias: Oh God! Oh my God!
I'm stiff from lack of exercise. All I can do to stand up.
Lysistrata: Halt! Who are you, approaching our lines?
Kinesias: Me? I.
Lysistrata: A man?
Kinesias: You have eyes, haven't you?
Lysistrata: Go away.
Kinesias: Who says so?
Lysistrata: Officer of the Day.
Kinesias: Officer, I beg you,   780
by all the gods at once, bring Myrrhine out.
Lysistrata: Myrrhine? And who, my good sir, are you?

Kinesias: Kinesias. Last name's Pennison. Her husband.
Lysistrata: Oh, of course. I beg your pardon. We're glad
    to see you.
We've heard so much about you. Dearest Myrrhine
is always talking about "Kinesias"—never nibbles an egg
or an apple without saying
"Here's to Kinesias!"
Kinesias: Do you really mean it?
Lysistrata: I do.
When we're discussing men, she always says
"Well, after all, there's nobody like Kinesias!"   790
Kinesias: Good God.—Well, then please send her down
    here.
Lysistrata: And what do *I* get out of it?
Kinesias: A standing promise.
Lysistrata: I'll take it up with her.
[Exit LYSISTRATA.]
Kinesias: But be quick about it!
Lord, what's life without a wife? Can't eat. Can't sleep.
Every time I go home, the place is so empty, so
insufferably sad. Love's killing me. Oh,
hurry!
[Enter MANES, a slave, with KINESIAS' baby; the
voice of MYRRHINE is heard off-stage.]
Myrrhine: But of course I love him! Adore him!—But
    no,
he hates love. No. I won't go down.
[Enter MYRRHINE, above.]
Kinesias: Myrrhine!
Darlingest Myrrhinette! Come down quick!
Myrrhine: Certainly not.
Kinesias: Not? But why, Myrrhine?   800
Myrrhine: Why? You don't need me.
Kinesias: Need you? My God, *look* at me!
Myrrhine: So long!
[Turns to go.]
Kinesias: Myrrhine, Myrrhine, Myrrhine!
If not for my sake, for our child!
[Pinches baby.]
                —All right, you: pipe up!
Baby: Mummie! Mummie! Mummie!
Kinesias: You hear that?
Pitiful, I call it. Six days now
with never a bath; no food; enough to break your heart!
Myrrhine: My darlingest child! What a father *you*
    acquired!
Kinesias: At least come down for his sake.
Myrrhine: I suppose I must.
Oh, this mother business![27]
[Exit.]
Kinesias: How pretty she is! And younger!
The harder she treats me, the more bothered I get.
[MYRRHINE enters, below.]
Myrrhine: Dearest child,   810
you're as sweet as your father's horrid. Give me a kiss.
Kinesias: Now don't you see how wrong it was to get
    involved
in this scheming League of women? it's bad

---

27. Parody of Euripides.

for us both.
Myrrhine: Keep your hands to yourself!
Kinesias: But our house
going to rack and ruin?
Myrrhine: *I* don't care.
Kinesias: And your knitting
all torn to pieces by the chickens? Don't you care?
Myrrhine: Not at all.
Kinesias: And our debt to Aphrodite?
Oh, *won't* you come back?
Myrrhine: No—At least, not until you men
make a treaty and stop this war.
Kinesias: Why, I suppose
that might be arranged.
Myrrhine: Oh? Well, I suppose   820
I might come down then. But meanwhile,
I've sworn not to.
Kinesias: Don't worry.—Now, let's have fun.
Myrrhine: No! Stop it! I said No!
                       —Although, of course,
I *do* love you.
Kinesias: I know you do. Darling Myrrhine:
come, shall we?
Myrrhine: Are you out of your mind? In front of the
    child?
Kinesias: Take him home, Manes.
[Exit MANES with BABY.]
                      There. He's gone.
                          Come on!
There's nothing to stop us now.
Myrrhine: You devil! But where?
Kinesias: In Pan's cave. What could be snugger than
    that?
Myrrhine: But my purification before I go back to the
    Citadel?
Kinesias: Wash in the Klepsydra.
Myrrhine: And my oath?
Kinesias: Leave the oath to me.   830
After all, I'm the man.
Myrrhine: Well . . . if you say so.
                     I'll go find a bed.
Kinesias: Oh, bother a bed! The ground's good enough
    for me.
Myrrhine: No. You're a bad man, but you deserve
    something better than dirt.
[Exit MYRRHINE.]
Kinesias: What a love she is! And how thoughtful!
[Re-enter MYRRHINE.]
Myrrhine: Here's your bed.
Now let me get my clothes off.
                     But, good horrors!
We haven't a mattress.
Kinesias: Oh, forget the mattress!
Myrrhine: No.
Just lying on blankets? Too sordid.
Kinesias: Give me a kiss.
Myrrhine: Just a second.
[Exit MYRRHINE.]
Kinesias: I swear, I'll explode!
[Re-enter MYRRHINE.]
Myrrhine: Here's your mattress.

I'll just take my dress off.
                   But look—
where's our pillow?
Kinesias: I don't *need* a pillow!
Myrrhine: Well, *I* do.   840
[Exit MYRRHINE.]
Kinesias: I don't suppose even Herakles
would stand for this!
[Re-enter MYRRHINE.]
Myrrhine: There we are. Ups-a-daisy!
Kinesias: So we are. Well, come to bed.
Myrrhine: But I wonder:
is everything ready now?
Kinesias: I can swear to that. Come, darling!
Myrrhine: Just getting out of my girdle.
                       But remember now,
what you promised about the treaty.
Kinesias: Yes, yes, yes!
Myrrhine: But no coverlet!
Kinesias: Damn it, I'll be
your coverlet!
Myrrhine: Be right back.
[Exit MYRRHINE.]
Kinesias: This girl and her coverlets
will be the death of me.
[Re-enter MYRRHINE.]
Myrrhine: Here we are. Up you go!
Kinesias: Up? I've been up for ages.
Myrrhine: Some perfume?   850
Kinesias: No, by Apollo!
Myrrhine: Yes, by Aphrodite!
I don't care whether you want it or not.
[Exit MYRRHINE.]
Kinesias: For love's sake, hurry!
[Re-enter MYRRHINE.]
Myrrhine: Here, in your hand. Rub it right in.
Kinesias: Never cared for perfume.
And this is particularly strong. Still, here goes.
Myrrhine: What a nitwit I am! I brought you the
    Rhodian bottle.
Kinesias: Forget it.
Myrrhine: No trouble at all. You just wait there.
[Exit MYRRHINE.]
Kinesias: God damn the man who invented perfume!
[Re-enter MYRRHINE.]
Myrrhine: At last! The right bottle!
Kinesias: I've got the rightest   850
bottle of all, and it's right here waiting for you.
Darling, forget everything else. Do come to bed.
Myrrhine: Just let me get my shoes off.
                   —And, by the way,
you'll vote for the treaty?
Kinesias: I'll think about it.
[MYRRHINE runs away.]
There! That's done it! The damned woman,
she gets me all bothered, she half kills me,
and off she runs! What'll I do? Where
can I get laid?
           —And you, little prodding pal,
who's going to take care of *you*? No, you and I
had better get down to old Foxdog's Nursing Clinic.

Chorus (m):
    Alas for the woes of man, alas   870
      Specifically for you.
    She's brought you to a pretty pass:
      What are you going to do?
    Split, heart! Sag, flesh! Proud spirit, crack!
    Myrrhine's got you on your back.

Kinesias:
    The agony, the protraction!

Choragos (m):   Friend,
    What woman's worth a damn?
    They bitch us all, world without end.

Kinesias:
      Yet they're so damned sweet, man!

Choragos (m):
    Calamitous, that's what I say.   880
    You should have learned that much today.

Chorus (m):
    O blessed Zeus, roll womankind
      Up into one great ball;
    Blast them aloft on a high wind,
      And once there, let them fall.
    Down, down they'll come, the pretty dears,
    And split themselves on our thick spears.
[Exit KINESIAS.]

Scene IV

[Enter a SPARTAN HERALD.]

Herald: Gentlemen, Ah beg you will be so kind
as to direct me to the Central Committee.
Ah have a communication.

[Re-enter COMMISSIONER.]

Commissioner: Are you a man,   890
or a fertility symbol?

Herald: Ah refuse to answer that question!
Ah'm a certified herald from Spahta, and Ah've come
to talk about an ahmistice.

Commissioner: Then why
that spear under your cloak?

Herald: Ah have no speah!

Commissioner: You don't walk naturally, with your tunic
poked out so. You have a tumor, maybe,
or a hernia?

Herald: You lost yo' mahnd, man?

Commissioner: Well,
something's up, I can see that. And I don't like it.

Herald: Colonel, Ah resent this.

Commissioner: So I see. But what *is* it?

Herald: A scroll
with a message from Spahta.

Commissioner: Oh. I know about those scrolls. 900
Well, then, man, speak out: How are things in Sparta?

Herald: Hahd, Colonel, hahd! We're at a standstill.
Cain't seem to think of anything but women.

Commissioner: How curious! Tell me, do you Spartans
    think
that maybe Pan's to blame?

Herald: Pan? No. Lampito and her little naked friends.
They won't let a man come nigh them.

Commissioner: How are you handling it?

Herald: Losing our mahnds,
if y' want to know, and walking around hunched over
lahk men carrying candles in a gale.   910
The women have sworn they'll have nothing to do with
    us
until we get a treaty.

Commissioner: Yes. I know.
It's a general uprising, sir, in all parts of Greece.
But as for the answer—
                Sir: go back to Sparta
and have them send us your Armistice Commission.
I'll arrange things in Athens.
               And I may say
that my standing is good enough to make them listen.

Herald: A man after mah own haht! Sir, Ah thank you.
[Exit HERALD.]

Choral Episode

Chorus (m):   Strophe
    Oh these women! Where will you find
    A slavering beast that's more unkind?   920
      Where a hotter fire?[28]
    Give me a panther, any day.
    He's not so merciless as they,
      And panthers don't conspire.

Chorus (w):   Antistrophe
    We may be hard, you silly old ass,
    But who brought you to this stupid pass?
      You're the ones to blame.
    Fighting with us, your oldest friends,
    Simply to serve your selfish ends—
      Really, you have no shame!   930

Choragos (m): No, I'm through with women for ever.[29]

Choragos (w):   If you say so.
Still, you might put some clothes on. You look too absurd
standing around naked. Come, get into this cloak.

Choragos (m): Thank you; you're right. I merely took it
    off
because I was in such a temper.

Choragos (w):   That's much better.
Now you resemble a man again.
             Why have you been so horrid?
And look: there's some sort of insect in your eye.
Shall I take it out?

Choragos (m):   An insect, is it? So that's
what's been bothering me. Lord, yes: take it out!

Choragos (w): You might be more polite.
            —But, heavens! 940
What an enormous mosquito!

Choragos (m):   You've saved my life.
    That mosquito was drilling an artesian well
in my left eye.

Choragos (w): Let me wipe
those tears away.—And now: one little kiss?

---

28. Parody of Euripides.
29. Parody of Euripides.

Choragos (m) No, no kisses.
Choragos (w):   You're so difficult.
Choragos (m): You impossible women! How you do get
    around us!
The poet was right: Can't live with you, or without you.
But let's be friends.
And to celebrate, you might join us in an Ode.

Chorus (m & w)   Strophe 1
          Let it never be said   950
          That my tongue is malicious:
          Both by world and by deed
I would set an example that's noble and gracious.
          We've had sorrow and care
          Till we're sick of the tune.
          Is there anyone here
          who would like a small loan?
             My purse is crammed,
             As you'll soon find;
And you needn't pay me back if the Peace gets signed!   960
          I've invited to lunch   Strophe 2
          Some Karystian rips—
          An esurient bunch,
But I've ordered a menu to water their lips.
          I can still make soup
          And slaughter a pig.
          You're all coming, I hope?
          But a bath first, I beg!
             Walk right up
             As though you owned the place,   970
And you'll get the front door slammed to in your face.

Scene V

[Enter SPARTAN AMBASSADOR, with entourage.]
Choragos (m): The Commission has arrived from Sparta.
                                        How oddly
they're walking!
                    Gentlemen, welcome to Athens!
How is life in Laconia?
Ambassador: Need we discuss that?
Simply use your eyes.
Chorus (m):   The poor man's right:
                        What a sight!
Ambassador: Words fail me.
But come, gentlemen, call in your Commissioners,
and let's get down to a Peace.
Choragos (m):   The state we're in! Can't bear
a stitch below the waist. It's a kind of pelvic
paralysis.
Commissioner: Won't somebody call Lysistrata? —
    Gentlemen,
we're no better off than you.
Ambassador: So I see.   980
A Spartan: Seh, do you'll feel a certain strain
early in the morning?
An Athenian: I do, sir. It's worse than a strain.
A few more days, and there's nothing for us but
    Cleisthenes,
that broken blossom.
Choragos (m):   But you'd better get dressed again.

You know these people going around Athens with
    chisels,
looking for statues of Hermes.[30]
Athenian: Sir, you are right.
Spartan: He certainly is! Ah'll put mah own clothes
    back on.
[Enter ATHENIAN COMMISSIONERS.]
Commissioner: Gentlemen from Sparta, welcome. This
    is a sorry business.
Spartan: Colonel, we got dressed just in time. Ah
    sweah,
if they'd seen us the way we were, there'd have been a
    new wah   990
between the states.
Commissioner: Shall we call the meeting to order?
                    Now, Lakonians,
what's your proposal?
Ambassador: We propose to consider peace.
Commissioner: Good. That's on our minds, too.
                        —Summon Lysistrata.
We'll never get anywhere without her.
Ambassador: Lysistrata?
Summon Lysis-anybody! Only, summon!
Choragos (m):   No need to summon:
here she is, herself.
[Enter LYSISTRATA.)
Commissioner: Lysistrata! Lion of women!
This is your hour to be
hard and yielding, outspoken and shy, austere and
gentle. You see here   1000
the best brains of Hellas (confused, I admit,
by your devious charming) met as one man
to turn the future over to you.
Lysistrata: That's fair enough,
unless you men take it into your heads
to turn to each other instead of to us. But I'd know
soon enough if you did.
                    —Where is Reconciliation?
Go, some of you: bring her here.
[Exeunt two women.]
                            And now, women,
lead the Spartan delegates to me: not roughly
or insultingly, as our men handle them, but gently,
politely, as ladies should.[31] Take them by the hand,   1010
or by anything else if they won't give you their hands.
[The SPARTANS are escorted over.]
There.—The Athenians next, by any convenient handle.
[The ATHENIANS are escorted.]
Stand there, please. —Now, all of you, listen to me.
[During the following speech the two women
re-enter, carrying an enormous statue of a naked
girl; this is RECONCILIATION.][32]
I'm only a woman, I know; but I've a mind,
and, I think, not a bad one: I owe it to my father
and to listening to the local politicians.
So much for that.
                    Now, gentlemen,
since I have you here, I intend to give you a scolding.
We are all Greeks.
Must I remind you of Thermopylai, of Olympia,   1020
of Delphoi? names deep in all our hearts?

Are they not a common heritage?
                                          Yet you men
go raiding through the country from both sides,
Greek killing Greek, storming down Greek cities—
and all the time the Barbarian across the sea
is waiting for his chance!
                              —That's my first point.
An Athenian: Lord! I can hardly contain myself.
Lysistrata: As for you Spartans:
Was it so long ago that Perikleides
came here to beg our help? I can see him still,
his grey face, his sombre gown. And what did he want?   1030
An army from Athens. All Messene
was hot at your heels, and the sea-god splitting your
      land.
Well, Kimon and his men,
four thousand strong, marched out and saved all Sparta.
And what thanks do we get? you come back to murder
      us.
An Athenian: They're aggressors, Lysistrata!
A Spartan: Ah admit it.
When Ah look at those laigs, Ah sweah Ah'll aggress
      mahself!
Lysistrata: And you, Athenians: do you think you're
      blameless?
Remember that bad time when we were helpless,
and an army came from Sparta,   ·1040
and that was the end of the Thessalian menace,
the end of Hippias and his allies.
                          And that was Sparta,
and only Sparta; but for Sparta, we'd be
cringing slaves today, not free Athenians.
*[From this point, the male responses are less to LYSISTRATA
than to the statue.]*
A Spartan: A well shaped speech.
An Athenian: Certainly it has its points.
Lysistrata: Why are we fighting each other? With all
      this history
of favors given and taken, what stands in the way
of making peace?
Ambassador: Spahta is ready, ma'am,
so long as we get that place back.
Lysistrata: What place, man?
Ambassador: Ah refer to Pylos.

30. The statues were of Hermes, messenger of the gods. Just
      before the Sicilian expedition sailed, anonymous vandals
      mutilated these statues by chiseling off the heads and the
      protuberant phalluses. Athenians considered this an
      unhappy augury for the expedition.
31. Apparently a reference to an earlier occasion when Sparta
      proposed terms to Athens, only to be rejected.
32. Lysistrata has already asked "Where is that goddess of
      Peace?", and it seems reasonable that someone should fetch
      her. But in what form? Some authorities prescribe a nude
      young woman. Still others suggest a statue. The nudity is
      all important, for the abstracted replies of Athenians and
      Spartans alike depend upon their preoccupation with this
      image of Peace.
33. This and the following are sexual equivocations, though the
      places themselves are real. Their only significance here lies
      in the application to the naked Peace (or Reconciliation),
      whether statue or real girl.

Commissioner: Not a chance, by God!   1050
Lysistrata: Give it to them, friend.
Commissioner: But—what shall we have to bargain with?
Lysistrata: Demand something in exchange.
Commissioner: Good idea.—Well, then:
Cockeville first, and the Happy Hills, and the country
between the Legs of Megara.[33]
Ambassador: Mah government objects.
Lysistrata: Over-ruled. Why fuss about a pair of legs?
[General assent. The statue is removed.]
An Athenian: I want to get out of these clothes and
      start my plowing.
A Spartan: Ah'll fertilize mahn first, by the Heavenly
      Twins!
Lysistrata: And so you shall,
once you've made peace. If you are serious,
go, both of you, and talk with your allies.   1060
Commissioner: Too much talk already. No, we'll stand
      together.
We've only one end in view. All that we want
is our women; and I speak for our allies.
Ambassador: Mah government concurs.
An Athenian: So does Karystos.
Lysistrata: Good.—But before you come inside
to join your wives at supper, you must perform
the usual lustration. Then we'll open
our baskets for you, and all that we have is yours.
But you must promise upright good behavior
from this day on. Then each man home with his woman! 1070
An Athenian: Let's get it over with.
A Spartan: Lead on. Ah follow.
An Athenian: Quick as a cat can wink!
[Exeunt all but the CHORUSES.]
Chorus (w):   Antistrophe 1
      Embroideries and
      Twinkling ornaments and
      Pretty dresses—I hand
Them all over to you, and with never a qualm.
      They'll be nice for your daughters
      On festival days
      When the girls bring the Goddess
      The ritual prize.   1080
          Come in, one and all:
          Take what you will.
I've nothing here so tightly corked that you can't make it
      spill.

      You may search my house,   Antistrophe 2
      But you'll not find
      The least thing of use,
Unless your two eyes are keener than mine.
      Your numberless brats
      Are half starved? and your slaves?
      Courage, grandpa! I've lots   1090
      Of grain left, and big loaves.
          I'll fill your guts,
          I'll go the whole hog;
But if you come too close to me, remember: 'ware the
      dog!
[Exeunt CHORUSES.]

Exodos

*[A DRUNKEN CITIZEN enters, approaches the gate,
and is halted by a sentry.]*
Citizen: Open. The. Door.
Sentry: Now, friend, just shove along!
—So you want to sit down. If it weren't such an old joke,
I'd tickle your tail with this torch. Just the sort of gag
this audience appreciates.
Citizen: I. Stay. Right. Here.
Sentry: Get away from there, or I'll scalp you! The
         gentlemen from Sparta
are just coming back from dinner.
*[Exit CITIZEN; the general company re-enters;
the two CHORUSES now represent SPARTANS and
ATHENIANS.]*
A Spartan: Ah must say,   1100
Ah never tasted better grub.
An Athenian: And those Lakonians!
They're gentlemen, by the Lord! Just goes to show,
a drink to the wise is sufficient.
Commissioner: And why not?
A sober man's an ass.
Men of Athens, mark my words: the only efficient
Ambassador's a drunk Ambassador. Is that clear?
Look: we go to Sparta,
and when we get there we're dead sober. The result?
Everyone cackling at everyone else. They make
         speeches;
and even if we understand, we get it all wrong   1110
when we file our reports in Athens. But today—!
Everybody's happy. Couldn't tell the difference
between *Drink to Me* Only and
The Star-Spangled Athens.
                    What's a few lies,
washed down in good strong drink?
[Re-enter the DRUNKEN CITIZEN.]
Sentry: God almighty,
he's back again!
Citizen: I. Resume. My. Place
A Spartan: Ah beg yo', sir,
take yo' instrument in yo' hand and play for us.
Ah'm told
yo' understand the in*tric*acies of the floot?   1120
Ah'd lahk to execute a song and dance
in honor of Athens,
                    and, of course, of Spahta.
Citizen: Toot. On. Your. Flute.
*[The following song is a solo—an aria—accompanied
by the flute. The CHORUS OF SPARTANS begins a
slow dance.]*
A Spartan:
         O Memory,
         Let the Muse speak once more
         In my young voice. Sing glory.
         Sing Artemision's shore,
         Where Athens fluttered the Persians. *Alalai,*
         Sing glory, that great
         Victory! Sing also   1130
         Our Leonidas and his men,
         Those wild boars, sweat and blood

Down in a red drench. Then, then
The barbarians broke, though they had stood
Numberless as the sands before!

O Artemis,
Virgin Goddess, whose darts
Flash in our forests: approve
This pact of peace and join our hearts,
From this day on, in love.   1140
Huntress, descend!
Lysistrata: All that will come in time.
                    But now, Lakonians,
take home your wives. Athenians, take yours.
Each man be kind to his woman; and you, women,
be equally kind. Never again, pray God,
shall we lose our way in such madness.
Choragos (a):   And now
let's dance our joy.
[From this point the dance becomes general.]
Chorus (a):
         Dance, you Graces
                    Artemis, dance
         Dance, Phoibos, Lord of dancing
                    Dance,
         In a scurry of Maenads, Lord Dionysos
                    Dance, Zeus Thunderer
                    Dance, Lady Hera   1150
         Queen of the Sky
                    Dance, dance, all you gods
         Dance witness everlasting of our pact
         Evohi Evohe
         Dance for the dearest
                    the Bringer of Peace
         Deathless Aphrodite!
Commissioner: Now let us have another song from Sparta.
Chorus (s):
         From Taygetos, from Taygetos,
              Lakonian Muse, come down.
         Sing to the Lord Apollo
              Who rules Amyklai Town.   1160

         Sing Athena of the House of Brass!

         Sing Leda's Twins, that chivalry
              Resplendent on the shore
         Of our Eurotas; sing the girls
              That dance along before:

         Sparkling in dust their gleaming feet,
              Their hair a Bacchant fire,
         And Leda's daughter, thyrsos raised,
              Leads their triumphant choir.
Chorus (a & s):
Evohe!
     Evohai!
          Evohe!
               We pass
                    Dancing
                         dancing
                              to greet   1170
Athena of the House of Brass.[34]

| **34.** This famous temple stood on the Acropolis of Sparta.

STUDY QUESTIONS

1. Describe and evaluate the character of Lysistrata. Why did Aristophanes create such an inflexible and hard-nosed heroine? Did he have someone like Aspasia in mind? Consider, also, the evolution of the male attitude toward Lysistrata. What causes this?

2. We know that Lysistrata has a husband but he is not mentioned nor is he present even in the final scene. Why did the playwright use this device and what did he gain by it?

3. The women temporarily dispose of the Commissioner by the mid-point of the play, dealing from then on with only the Choragos of Men and the Chorus of Men. What does this signify? In other words, what does the Commissioner represent? The Chorus of Men?

4. Why does Lysistrata itemize the mutual debts of the Spartans and the Athenians and stress the idea of Greekness?

5. Aristophanes has a three-part message for his audience, of which the first two parts are suggested in the above question. What is the third part of that message and how does he deliver it? You should consider the critical difference between the conventions of tragedy and those of comedy: the way Aristophanes uses his choruses, particularly near the end of the play.

6. The names of various gods and goddesses are invoked throughout the play, particularly that of Zeus by the men. The women refer to Zeus at first but switch to several goddesses. Who are they and what does this symbolize? Why is Athena emphasized only at the very end of the play?

SUMMARY

The achievements of the individuals discussed in this chapter demonstrate what can happen when people have the freedom to excel in a society that values and rewards excellence. First and foremost, the Greeks towered over all other societies in that they thought and thought hard, thereby inventing both philosophy and theoretical science. The Eleatics, particularly Parmenides, saw that whatever was real must be permanent and unchanging, a position that challenged the idea of the individual as the ultimate reality. Democritos, on the other hand, postulated an atomic theory that confirmed the materialistic view of reality and the individual.

The passion for excellence spurred achievements that enriched both the artist and society. With his

Oresteia Aeschylus won the ivy wreath while challenging his fellow citizens with a model of how true justice should work in a court of law. But when Sophocles wrote *Oedipus the King* it was time to alert the populace to what hubris could call down on a man such as Oedipus or a city such as Athens. *The Trojan Women* won a first prize for Euripides while mercilessly exposing the ethical degeneration of the once heroic Greeks. The decline had begun after the death of Pericles and accelerated as the Peloponnesian War dragged on and on.

The Post-Periclean decline was identified and satirized by Aristophanes, whose plays after *Lysistrata* gradually subsided into amusing and popular comedies designed only to entertain a city no longer avid for enlightenment. One can only speculate as to what might have been had the Athenians and the Spartans listened to Lysistrata and ended the war with singing and dancing. The trial and death of Socrates in 399 BC signified the end of the postscript to the Golden Age and the beginning of a world that was to become less and less interested in freedom, truth, and justice.

But we should not overreact. The use of terms such as "degeneration" and "decline" are undeniably appropriate when describing Greece after the Golden Age. However, this was still an exceptional culture that, for centuries to come, was superior to all others. Late classicism and the Hellenistic age are notable for the achievements of Plato, Aristotle, Euclid, Archimedes, and Alexander the Great, to mention only a few celebrated names.

CULTURE AND HUMAN VALUES

In terms of the culture-epoch theory (as discussed in the Prologue), the Periclean Age was the golden moment of a period of balance that extended from the Greek classical period to the beginning of the long decline of the Roman Empire (ca. 480 BC–AD 180). Whatever its flaws, and they were abundant, this Graeco-Roman epoch was distinguished, on the whole, by a rational approach to civilized living in the secular world of the here and now. This achievement is even more remarkable when one considers what followed classical civilization, namely the decline and fall of Rome and the ensuing chaotic times of the early Middle Ages.

A balance was struck during the Periclean age between the rights of the individual and the welfare of the group. An idealistic society that firmly believed in what people *should* be, the Athenians advocated freedom, beauty, truth, and justice as the necessary foundations for the art of civilized living. From that time to ours Athenian achievements in the arts, government, and philosophy testify to the high goals these remarkable people set for themselves.

(NOTE: See summary of Greek culture and values on p. 229.)

CHAPTER 6

Greece: From Hellenic to Hellenistic World

Had Greek civilization never existed . . . we would never have become fully conscious, which is to say that we would never have become, for better or worse, fully human.

W. H. Auden

"The name Greek is no longer a mark of race, but of outlook, and is accorded to those who share our culture rather than our blood," said the Athenian orator Isocrates in 380 BC. By then the Greek city-states no longer dominated the eastern Mediterranean but Greek culture continued its expansion throughout the Mediterranean and even into the vast Persian Empire. What caused the decline of the Greek city-states? Their fervor and pride had enabled them to rout the far larger forces of the Persian Empire because they were, for the first and last time, united against a common foe. Afterwards their pride and belligerent independence caused endless squabbles, culminating in the disastrous war between Athens and Sparta plus assorted allies on both sides. The Persian wars (490–479 BC) inspired confidence but the internecine Peloponnesian War (431–404 BC) left despair and decay in its wake. Not one city-state was strong enough to take control, making a federation impossible. Sparta dominated for a time, followed by Thebes, Athens[1] and Corinth, but always with the tireless Persians in the background manipulating events through bribery and coercion.

In the middle of the fourth century BC, in a backwater of Greek civilization, King Philip of Macedonia began his move toward an empire that was to unite all of Greece. Military strategy achieved some of his objectives but most were realized through a series of wily political and diplomatic moves, accomplished despite repeated warnings by the Athenian orator Demosthenes (De-MOSS-th-neez; fig. 6.1). Upon Philip's assassination in 336 BC, his brilliant young son, Alexander (see chapter opener opposite), a

student of Aristotle's, became king. In one extended and remarkable campaign Alexander brought Greece, Egypt, all of the Persian Empire (including the territory of modern Turkey), and lands as far east as India, into one vast empire. In doing so, he disseminated Greek culture throughout that immense territory.

6.1 Portrait bust of Demosthenes. Roman copy, probably after an original bronze of 280/279 BC. Marble, life-size. Ashmolean Museum, Oxford.
This last great champion of Athenian liberty lived to see Athens free itself from Macedonia after Alexander's death in 323 BC.

Opposite Leochares(?), Portrait bust of Alexander the Great. Ca. 330–325 BC. Marble. Acropolis Museum, Athens. Photo: Scala, Florence.
Alexander, history's greatest military genius, conquered and Hellenized the then known world in just twelve years.

---

1. After ineffectual Spartan rule, Athens underwent a reign of terror under Critias and the Thirty Tyrants, followed by a brief civil war. Democracy was restored in 401 BC. It was the insecure government of a reestablished Athens that tried and condemned Socrates in 399 BC. (See the *Apology* on pp. 161–71 for Plato's account of the trial.)

ANCIENT INDIA

Beginning around 3000 BC, the great Indus civilization developed in the Indus River valley and along the Arabian Sea in what is now Pakistan. Its cities, such as Mohenjo-Daro, were laid out in the gridiron pattern (like many American cities), with underground sewers, huge granaries, and two- and three-story brick houses. The inhabitants used stone, copper, and bronze tools, wore cotton clothing, and utilized sophisticated pottery and cooking utensils. Their arts and crafts were well developed (fig. 6.2) as was their language, a pictograph script that was finally deciphered in 1969.

Led by a warrior aristocracy, barbaric Aryans from the Iranian plateau invaded in ca. 1500 BC, destroying virtually the entire civilization. Much as when the Mycenaeans had invaded Crete, the Aryans brought their pantheon of sky gods into a culture whose religion was probably a fertility cult complete with goddess worship. Most of what we know about the Aryans has been handed down through religious texts—the Vedas, especially the Rig Veda (Sanskrit: "Verses of Knowledge"). The Aryans spread east and south from the river valley, establishing elaborate priestly rituals (Brahmin) and the beginning of the caste system, both of which are central to Hinduism, India's socio-religious system. This is the civilization that fell to Alexander the Great in the late fourth century BC.

6.2   Bust from Mohenjo-Daro. Ca. 2300–1750 BC. Limestone,   height 6⅞" (17.5 cm). National Museum of India, New Delhi. Photo: Scala, Florence.

Alexander apparently intended to establish what amounted to a Greek "league of nations." The conquered peoples would retain a certain amount of autonomy and all of their customs. Greek language and culture would be added throughout the empire so that the entire known world could benefit from Greek accomplishments. Alexander died at the age of thirty-three bemoaning the lack of new worlds to conquer, but he may have been referring to cultural, as well as geographical, conquest

To further his dream of a universal Greek culture Alexander had established many new cities—such as Antioch in Syria and about a dozen Alexandrias stretching as far east as Bactria (present-day Afghanistan)—in which he built libraries, museums, and other centers of civilization. The Alexandria constructed in Egypt supplanted Athens as the cultural center and largest city of antiquity. Established by Ptolemy I (TAHL-uh-me), the first Greek ruler of Egypt, the famous Library at Alexandria was the wonder of the ancient world with over 700,000 manuscripts by Julius Caesar's time (first century BC). Remnants of Alexander's empire survived until 146 BC, when Rome finally conquered the last Achaean League, but Hellenistic art and philosophy were influential throughout most of the Roman period, a span of some seven centuries.

ALEXANDRIAN SCIENCE

Euclid (fl. 300 BC): The acclaimed geometer whose *Elements* (of geometry) was not challenged until a non-Euclidian geometry was devised in the 19th century. Probably instructed by a student of Plato's, he founded and taught at a school of mathematics in Alexandria, Egypt, during the reign of Ptolemy I Soter (323–283 BC). **Aristarchus of Samos** (ar-i-STAHR-kus; ca. 310–230 BC): Originated a sun-centered world system that Copernicus would rely on 1,900 years later to develop his own heliocentric system. **Archimedes** (ar-kuh-MEE-dez; ca. 298–212 BC): Working in Egypt and his native city of Syracuse, he was antiquity's greatest mathematician. He developed fundamental theorems on the gravity centers of plane and solid figures and the weight of a body immersed in a liquid (Archimedes' Principle). He improved the catapult, and invented the compound pulley—a water raising device known as Archimedes' Screw—and a burning mirror to defend Syracuse against the Romans. "Give me a lever long enough," he once boasted, "and a place to stand and I can move the earth." **Eratosthenes of Cyrene** (air-uh-TAHS-thuh-neez; ca. 276–195 BC): Best known for his amazingly close calculation of the earth's circumference, he served as chief librarian of the museum in Alexandria, Egypt.

"Hellenism" is the name of the civilization disseminated throughout the Mediterranean and the Near East in the wake of Alexander's conquests. This was the first great international culture of the West. The language was Greek and the milieu was the city, particularly all those cities named Alexandria. The politics were aristocratic but there was always a measure of participatory democracy. A person's ethnic origins were virtually incidental because the culture was remarkably universal. To become Greek was to be truly educated, the real key to participation in the era's international civilization. Models for educated people throughout the culture were the scholars and scientist-mathematicians of Alexandria and the philosophers Plato and Aristotle, who epitomized the Greek characteristic of thinking and thinking hard.

PLATO, 427–347 BC

Born two years after the death of Pericles, Plato (fig. 6.3) was a young man when Athens lost the Peloponnesian War. He was an ardent student of Socrates. No one can distinguish between the thought of Plato and that of Socrates in Plato's early writings, for most are dialogues with Socrates the principal speaker. Plato probably included much of his own thought in these dialogues, or perhaps he reported the Socratic ideas with which he agreed. Only in the latter part of his life did he speak entirely for himself, as in the *Laws*.

Plato's thought about that-which-is-real is perhaps his most significant contribution to world philosophy. He began with the work of Pythagoras and the Eleatic

6.3 Silanion(?), Portrait bust of Plato. 350–340 BC. Roman copy (one of eighteen) of an original bronze of ca. 427–347 BC. Marble. Glypothek, Munich. Photo: E. T. Archive, London.
Apparently the original was dedicated in the Academy after Plato's death. Though his real name was Aristocles, Plato has always been known by his nickname, which means "the Broad."

Map 6.1 Alexander's Empire, 323 BC.

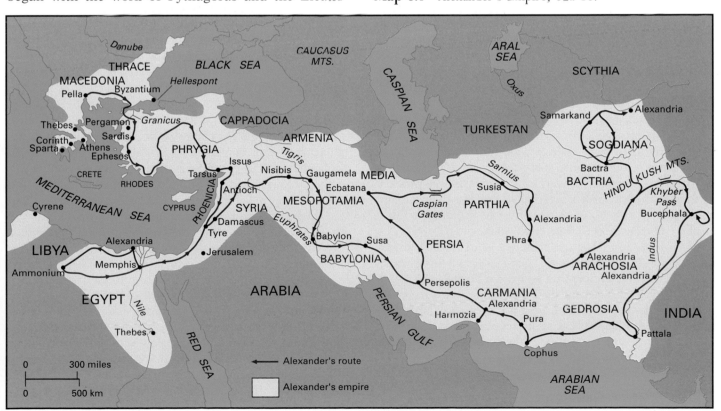

philosophers by accepting permanence and unchangeability as the basic criteria for reality, and the mind as the only way to a knowledge of the real. Thus he denied the reality of all the sense-apparent objects around us: trees, animals, humans, or even abstract concepts such as love or justice. He regarded all sense-apparent things as shadows of the Real, made imperfect by an alliance with material stuff, which is illustrated in "The **Allegory** of the Cave" (p. 179).

Reality

Reality, for Plato, consisted of Ideas (or Forms) of all basic things, Forms that exist beyond the grasp of the senses or even the mind. These Ideas have no physical attributes or material substance; they are the "pure form" of all things we see and know in our earthly existence. These Forms are not, however, ideas-in-the-minds-of-people. Trying to imagine the perfect tree or chair has nothing to do with Plato's Forms. His Ideas[2] exist, are unchanging, and are the source of all things: the eternal Forms of everything in the universe. But the individual thing—what we perceive—is always a distorted or impure shadow of its Form. Because it is involved with matter it is at least one step removed from its Idea.

We can illustrate this by assuming that we have commissioned an architect to design a building. After prolonged wrestling with design problems, the architect suddenly has a flash, a mental image of a perfectly completed structure. "Eureka!" she cries. "This is *it!*" She rushes to the drawing board. But changes have to be made that affect the original concept: practical problems involving heating, cooling, lights, and service areas. The final blueprints reveal a building already substantially different from the original idea. Construction begins. A strike forces the substitution of one material for another. Costs go over budget, necessitating space cutbacks and less expensive finishing materials. Finally the building is complete, existing in its material form for people to use.

When was the structure most real? One can argue that it was most real when it was pure idea and that it became less authentic with every compromise in structure or materials. Certainly the architect sees the final product as a mere shadow of her original vision. For the moment, let us accept this as true: the physical building is but a clumsy manifestation of the "real" idea.

Now, assume that the architect is an eternal creator and the building the universe. The ideas for all things existed in this entity's conception and these Forms exist forever. But they are altered and distorted as they are mixed with material substance: animal, vegetable, mineral. Now, perhaps, we have Plato's belief about true reality, but we must take one more step and subtract the creator. Though Plato spoke of the gods—and sometimes of God—he did not

believe that a creator had originated the Forms; they had existed eternally.

This Platonic version of reality had philosophical repercussions, of which the most significant is the separation of the soul from the body. That is, the belief that a soul that relates to the realm of the essences is imprisoned by a base, material body. This has been a major issue in Christian belief. Augustine, for example, borrowed heavily from Platonism in formulating the first unified Christian theology. Specifically, Plato believed that there was a hierarchy in the realm of ideas that started at the bottom with the essences of plants and animals and ended at the top with the idea of the Good. This is reflected in the image of light or fire encountered in "The Allegory of the Cave". Early Christian theology converted this Good into a concept of God as the highest and best ideal and the goal toward which all Christians should strive.

Arts and Ethics

His concern for the soul led Plato to ponder the role of poetry, music, and the other arts—especially music—in Athenian life. He believed, as did others, that music influenced the will in three ways. It could (1) provoke action; (2) help strengthen character (or conversely, it could undermine it); and (3) suspend normal will power and thus make people unaware of their actions. The emphasis upon ethical imperatives led to the Greek doctrine of **ethos,** with Plato as its most eloquent advocate.

The doctrine of ethos (EE-thos; Gk., *ethos*, "character") is concerned with the ethical, ideal, or universal element in an art work, as distinguished from its emotional appeal. (The Greek word for the latter is *pathos*, which means "suffering.") The doctrine of ethos brought external order into music's domain, for Plato saw an analogy between movements of the soul and musical progressions. He therefore felt that music must transcend mere amusement and set a goal of harmonic education and perfection of the soul. Music's primary role was therefore a pedagogical one that helped build character and promote ethical behavior. The practice of music was necessarily public rather than private, an affair of state rather than of the home. Every melody, rhythm, and musical instrument had its unique effect on the ethical nature of humankind, and therefore upon the ethics of the state. Good music promoted the welfare of the state whereas bad music was harmful to the individual and to society.

All Athenian citizens received musical training until they were thirty and all, regardless of age, sang in a chorus on proper social, political, and religious occasions. Music education was mandatory and universal but prohibited for slaves because it was a mark of nobility and of education reserved for free Athenians.

In the *Republic*, Plato recognized that there should be a balance between music and gymnastics in education but felt that music should precede and dominate

---

2. "Ideas" and "Forms" are used interchangeably because it takes both words to approximate Plato's conception.

gymnastics. Music first ennobles the soul, after which the soul should then build up the body. He included dance (as well as wrestling) in gymnastics and combined poetry with music, because performers usually recited or sang poetry with musical accompaniment. Plato insisted that the latter two should be subject to state control, that is, censorship. By advocating censorship of music and poetry he implicitly acknowledged the power of these arts. Like all Athenians, he had attended performances of tragedies by Aeschylus, Sophocles, and Euripides. One can imagine the waves of powerful emotions that swept over the 18,000 spectators, emotions so intense as to be almost palpable. No wonder Plato was concerned that music and poetry should educate the young to take pleasure in the right things.

In *Laws*, his last work, Plato went beyond his ideas in the *Republic*, adding recreation as a second function of poetry and music. He noted in Book 2 that music education would properly train the emotions in childhood but that this was not enough; many rough spots in growing up disturbed the proper balance. There must be "festivals of the muses, Apollo, and Dionysos" he wrote, so that people might be "put right" by having their emotional balance restored. His idea of the restorative power of poetry and music appears to have much in common with Aristotle's later theory of **catharsis** ("to purify"; see p. 182).

Plato and Aristotle considered the Dorian and Phrygian modes (two of the various Greek musical pitch organizations) ethically superior to the other modes (Lydian and Mixolydian), but, given their preference for rigor and austerity, the Dorian might be considered preeminent because it was strong and dignified. Phrygian was ecstatic and religious and exerted a positive influence on the soul. Lydian was considered piercing and suitable only for lamentations; Mixolydian was intimate and lascivious.[3]

These ethical doctrines also applied to the two national instruments. Restrained and elegant, the lyre was seen as proper for the performance of Dorian melodies. The aulos (see p. 90) was strong and powerful and thus particularly suitable for the emotional intensity of Phrygian melodies. This intensity made the aulos the chosen instrument of Greek comedies and, especially, tragedies.

In sum, the doctrine of ethos was a manifestation of the cult of Apollo and was designed to control the Dionysian power of the aulos and music, poetry, dance and, by extension, tragedy. Tragedy was, of course, an ingenious combination of all these elements. As noted earlier, it was probably the dramatic performances themselves that convinced Plato of the need for imposing rational control over them. But it was in the *Republic* that Plato expanded the idea of rational control to society itself.

3. A rough approximation of the Dorian mode can be made by playing the white keys of the piano from *e* to the next *e* above or below. Phrygian is *d* to *d*, Lydian *c* to *c*, and Mixolydian *b* to *b*.

The *Republic*

Because the Athenian democracy had executed Socrates, Plato sought a definition of true justice, one that would rise above his ironic description of a democracy, which is "a charming form of government, full of variety and disorder and dispensing a sort of equality to equals and unequals alike."

Plato was deeply committed to the idea that all citizens had an obligation to participate in government: "The punishment which the wise suffer who refuse to take part in the government, is to live under the government of worse men." The dialogue called the *Republic* provides a comprehensive view of the Socratic-Platonic ideas of human personality and the nature of government. The *Republic* is not Plato's formation of an ideal state (or Utopia, as Sir Thomas More later called it); it is, instead, an extended dialogue between Socrates and his students about the nature of justice. Not a problem when someone lives alone on an island, justice becomes a critical issue in a populous city-state composed of rich and poor, saints and scoundrels, masters and slaves. So in the *Republic*, discussants formulate a picture of a luxurious city-state (that goes beyond minimal human needs) as they seek the elusive quality—justice—that exists to a greater or lesser degree in the interrelationships of human beings.

Plato believed that men and women were dominated by one of three qualities: appetite, spirit, or intellect. So he divided people into three classes of metal: iron, silver, and gold. Those driven primarily by appetite, iron, were to be the workers, including all who followed commercial pursuits. The silver, people of spirit, formed the auxiliaries or soldier class, who had no property or money to distract them from their duty: protection from foreign enemies and maintenance of order at home. The men and women of intellect, the guardian class of gold, were educated to become the stewards of the state, the rulers, the philosopher-kings.

Education was the key to the formation of this state. The lowest class would receive whatever education they could pick up on their own. The soldier or auxiliary group would train in gymnastics (to give them strong bodies, fit for their duties) and music and poetry (to make them sensitive and considerate). Socrates used the example of the good watchdog to illustrate his point, for such an animal is gentle toward the master and known friends but fierce toward enemies. The soldier class should have such a nature, with their spirits tempered by the study of music. The guardian class would have all of the education of the soldiers as well as studies in reasoning—emphasizing mathematics—and philosophy. After many years of formal education, they were to be subjected to a series of trials and temptations testing their strength of character and ability to make decisions that contributed to the greater good of the state. Selected from the best specimens of both sexes, these educated executives were to be highly original scientific thinkers and persons of impeccable integrity. Finally, at about age fifty, the guardians would be called upon to govern the city as philosopher-kings.

Socrates (as leader of the *Republic* dialogue) advocates strict control of the arts, particularly stories, poetry, and music, so that girls and boys would be educated in a beautiful environment. The highest good would enter into their souls because they were exposed to only the best and most morally uplifting of the arts. This is, once again, the doctrine of ethos. (The idea that the state should control—censor—the arts to maintain high moral standards has provoked arguments on both sides that continue, without resolution, to this day.)

Material possessions would neither encumber nor influence the soldiers or the guardians. Wealth was banished as was poverty. Socrates was convinced that wealth would spoil a person's character and that vested interests affected judgment. On the other hand, poverty could break the human spirit and render men and women unfit to be public servants as soldiers or guardians.

THE HIPPOCRATIC OATH

Frequently called the "father of medicine," the Greek physician Hippocrates (hi-POK-ruh-teez; ca. 460–377 BC) is credited with establishing a distinguished tradition of medical ethics. His oath, which was based on Pythagorean philosophy and the Platonic virtues (and which he probably did not write), has for about 2,400 years been the requisite ethical code for physicians. In 1948 the World Medical Association drew up a modern version which, as amended in 1968, reads as follows:

At the time of being admitted a member of the medical profession:

I solemnly pledge myself to consecrate my life to the service of humanity; I will give my teachers the respect and gratitude which is their due; I will practice my profession with conscience and dignity; The health of my patient will be my first consideration; I will respect the secrets which are confided in me, even after the patient has died; I will maintain by all the means in my power, the honor and the noble traditions of the medical profession; My colleagues will be my brothers; I will not permit considerations of religion, nationality, race, party politics or social standing to intervene between my duty and my patient; I will maintain the utmost respect for human life from the time of conception; even under threat I will not use my medical knowledge contrary to the laws of humanity.

I make these promises solemnly, freely and upon my honor.

By far the largest class, the men and women of iron included workers, farmers, sailors, artisans, merchants, professionals, and entrepreneurs. Their possessions were expressly their own; property held in common was explicitly forbidden. Plato's *Republic* was not communistic. The two small classes of guardians and soldiers—servants of the state—were denied property ownership for economic reasons: to eliminate conflicts between self-interest and public duty by putting a chasm between political power and financial influence. Everyone who did not serve the state (the bulk of the population) worked as individuals of varying degrees of wealth, from a farmer or worker to the owner of a merchant fleet.

At first glance the iron-silver-gold classes of the *Republic* seem as structured as the caste system still prevalent in today's India. But "caste" means something people are born into, above which they can never rise. Most societies have class structures in which the ease or difficulty of vertical movement depends on the rigidity of the society or nation in question. The opportunity for moving across class lines—up or down—was considerably greater in the *Republic* than it is in, say, Britain.

Socrates believed that heredity was a powerful force in shaping a person's character and abilities, and was therefore convinced that most people would find their rightful place in their parents' class. Some would be unfit for this, while others had the ability and ambition to rise above their origins, even from iron to gold. The authorities could identify any girl or boy as worthy of preparation for the highest responsibilities because class mobility was necessary in a state dependent upon an elite of philosopher-kings.

And where does justice come in? Each citizen, of whatever class, has theoretically found a proper niche in society with little inclination or opportunity to interfere with the rights of others. Potters make pots and merchants make profits, police keep the peace, soldiers guard the state, the rulers govern fairly and justly. Citizens are guaranteed equality of educational opportunities irrespective of class or gender. The people of iron may indulge their appetite for money and possessions, those of silver may gratify their spirit with honor and glory, and the men and women of gold may exercise their intellect to the fullest in the responsible governance of the state. Based on the principle of specialization of function according to vocation, justice has been established on a grand scale.

Did Plato believe that his theoretical city-state could really work? Think back to the hypothetical case of the architect and her building. Plato's *Republic* and the completed blueprints for the structure are roughly analogous, but both are already one step removed from the original conceptions of perfect justice and a perfect building. If constructing the building requires compromises in materials and design, what might the problems be if we tried to construct a complex human society? Plato had no illusions. At one point in the *Republic* he introduces the story of a young shepherd boy, "The Ring of Gyges." After Gyges discovers a ring that makes him invisible (and thus not accountable for his actions), he embarks on a successful career of robbery and murder that leads him to the richest and most powerful position in his native land.

Though the "Ring of Gyges" may or may not be an extreme example, Plato believed that no normal human being could maintain an intact virtue when guaranteed immunity from detection. If no one knew what we were doing, would we lower our standards? Do we ever act out of self-interest rather than out of duty? Plato saw that narrow self-interest, greed, envy, and other human failings would be potentially fatal problems in any republic, no matter how perfectly constructed.

As for the nature of justice, Plato and Socrates take the middle ground, the Golden Mean, ever a Greek ideal. Intellect should be in control, so that appetite would be curbed to the point of temperance, spirit limited to the point of courage, and intellect finally become wisdom. Justice would emerge when these conditions were met, meaning that behavior would be ethical and scrupulous and therefore just. These qualities—temperance, courage, wisdom, and justice—were the great Platonic virtues. Christians later added faith, hope, and love to establish the seven cardinal virtues. The difference between the Platonic intellectual virtues and the Christian emotional and spiritual virtues illustrates a fundamental distinction between the aspirations of the two cultures.

ARISTOTLE, 384–322 BC

Aristotle's background differed considerably from that of Plato. Though he studied with Plato at the Academy, his answers to the important questions are quite different, perhaps because of the dissimilarities in youthful experience. Aristotle's father was a physician who was called, early in Aristotle's life, to serve the court of King Philip II at Pella. Perhaps Aristotle's inquiring mind about sense-apparent things, his interest in experimentation, his concern with change rather than permanence, and his refusal to accept the mind alone as a guide to truth came from his father's interest in similar things. In fact, exactly as Plato's thought had its source in Pythagoras and the Eleatics, Aristotle's mature conclusions are rooted in the Ionians.

Aristotle's was one of the most extraordinary minds of all time. The keenness of his intellect, the range of his interests and studies, and the staggering amount of information and speculation in his enormous collection of writings rouse the admiration and awe of all who read his work. Not the least of his distinctions is that he tutored the youthful Prince Alexander of Macedonia (see p. 153) and must have greatly influenced that monarch's brilliant career. After this period of tutoring, Aristotle moved to Athens and founded his own school, the Lyceum. Along with Plato, he was to shape the course of Western thought.

As we have seen, Plato's quest for the permanent, the Idea or Form, rather than the actuality of experience, led

him into a dualism that separates form from substance, soul from body. By contrast, Aristotle, who was profoundly interested in the changing life about him, tried to reconcile the two. The difference can be expressed as follows. When Plato considered the state he wrote the *Republic* and the *Laws*, which were theoretical constructions of an imaginary state. When Aristotle pondered the state, he and his students collected and studied the constitutions of 158 Greek city-states as a prelude to writing the work known as *Politics*.

The extent of Aristotle's writings is astonishing. His speculations range from logic and the proper process of thought through biology, physics, metaphysics, ethics, law and politics, and literary criticism (see his *Poetics* on pp. 182–7). Only two of his ideas concern us here: one is his view of the nature of reality; the other is how life should be lived because of that view.

For Aristotle, the abstract Idea or Form of Plato's teaching could not be separated from the matter or substance by which it was known; the two somehow had to come together as different aspects of the same thing. Thus Plato's "ideal" chair did not exist for Aristotle apart from the actual wood and metal that composed it. A brick is a brick only when the "idea" brick and the clay composing it come together; then the brick is "real." The brick may then become the matter or substance of another "idea," and become house; and the house, in turn, may be substance to the idea of town or city. At every stage, the union of substance and form, of matter and idea, is necessary to constitute "reality"; and there is a progression, upward or downward. The substance that Plato is not concerned with becomes for Aristotle the basis for higher, more complex realities when it is informed by idea or form. Such is the direction of the difference between the two men; Plato's static view becomes more dynamic in Aristotle's teaching.

Aristotle accounts for the process of change (which Plato never satisfactorily explains) in his theory of enteleche (en-TEL-uh-key), which consists of the prefix *en* ("within") and the *telos* ("purpose") and *echaia* ("having"). Thus it is in the nature of things that they have an inner goal, a destiny, to fulfill: the seed becomes plant, for that is its enteleche; the clay becomes brick for its enteleche, but clay can become pot for a different enteleche. The upward movement through increasing complexity is the enteleche of the universe. The cause of the process, drawing all things toward their own perfection, is God, the First Cause, who moved all things without being moved—in Aristotle's phrase, the "Unmoved Mover."

The motive power of Aristotle's God is apparently not love, as Christianity might contend, nor will, as Judaism might argue. Rather there seems to be a cosmic yearning toward perfection, and that perfection is, by definition, God. Aristotle's customary view of the necessity for the union of both form and matter to constitute reality here breaks down (or more kindly, transcends itself?), for such a God must be pure form, with none of the inherent weakness or imperfection of the material world.[4] God is the only instance of pure form separated from matter.

And what about the good life? Aristotle was no ascetic, and he matter-of-factly assumed that everyone had enough material resources to enable them to choose among reasonable alternatives. Given adequate wealth, what does one do? The enteleche of which Aristotle speaks implies that there is a goal, or end, reached when a person or thing is functioning properly—that is, in accord with its inner purposes. When conditions permit, one can attain a highest good—what later philosophers would call a *summum bonum* (Lat. "greatest good"). Thus the enteleche of humans leads them to their own *summum bonum*, the worthy and proper fulfillment of their humanity. Because the human being is, for Aristotle, the "rational animal," that fulfillment is the life of reason. When people are living harmoniously, using their minds, functioning in family and state (for Aristotle also calls us political, that is, social animals), they have achieved their greatest good. Such a life has many implications, two of which concern us here.

One is that such a life will be one of virtue, or excellence. But virtues may fail by being deficient, or by being carried to excess. What one should desire is the middle ground between extremes. Courage, for instance, is a virtue; but deficiency may pervert it into cowardice, or a no less perverted excess becomes foolhardiness or rashness. Generosity is also a virtue but excessive generosity becomes prodigality and wastefulness, while its deficiency becomes stinginess. To mediate between extremes, to discover the "Golden Mean"—which is relative and not an absolute matter—is to achieve virtue.

The other implication, then, is that the finest use of reason is in a life of contemplation. People must have time to read, to talk, to think about the whole idea of excellence, that they may achieve the high-mindedness that is their *summum bonum* (the word that Aristotle uses is "magnanimity"). Such a quality is not to be won in the heat and dust of the marketplace. For although good people can perform their duties as members of society, the life of action cannot compare with the life of contemplation.

THE GREEK PHILOSOPHICAL LEGACY

Plato and Aristotle are generally considered the most influential philosophers in the history of Western culture. Plato's search for knowledge had an astonishing range and depth, embracing physics, metaphysics, mathematics, ethics, politics, religion, literature, music, and art. His influence on Aristotle is incalculable; surely this is the most remarkable teacher-student combination in human history.

Their answers might vary, sometimes considerably, but Plato and Aristotle asked many of the same questions: What are the moral, ethical, and legal bases of life? How, in a democracy, can we define the public good? Where is the line between protecting the individual and guarding the community? What is the good life and how may one achieve it?

Aristotle's influence has perhaps been greatest in the field of logic, particularly his invention of the **syllogism** as a tool for deductive reasoning. That the syllogism was a less than perfect tool for logical deduction was not Aristotle's fault. As Plato's greatest student, he stood alone at the end of the golden age of Greek philosophy. Aristotle followed Plato but not for 2,000 years did anyone follow Aristotle. For centuries he was the unquestioned authority—the philosopher—of medieval scholars, especially the Scholastic philosophers of the High Middle Ages.

Plato's influence was particularly strong during the formation of the early Christian church's theology. There have been revivals of Platonism during the Italian Renaissance, throughout the Age of Reason, and into our own century. That he was also among the finest literary artists of Western civilization is a whole other topic. Perhaps Alfred North Whitehead (1861–1947), the British philosopher and mathematician, best summarized Plato's contributions with his oft-quoted remark: "The safest general characterization of the European philosophical tradition is that it consists of a series of footnotes to Plato."

> ## QUOTATIONS FROM ARISTOTLE
>
> Law is order and good law is good order.
>
> The basis of a democratic state is liberty.
>
> The best political community is formed by citizens of the middle class.
>
> If liberty and equality, as is thought by some, are chiefly to be found in democracy, they will be best obtained when all persons alike share in the government to the utmost.
>
> Plato is dear to me but dearer still is truth.
>
> If happiness is activity in accordance with excellence, it is reasonable that it should be in accordance with the highest excellence.
>
> Education is the best provision for old age.
>
> Neglect of an effective birth control policy is a never failing source of poverty, which, in turn, is the parent of revolution and crime.
>
> One swallow does not make a summer.

---

4. "Such then is the principle upon which depend the heavens and the world of nature. And its life (i.e., the principle, or God) is like the best that we enjoy, and enjoy but for a short time; for it is ever in this state, which we cannot be. And if then God is always in that good state in which we sometimes are, this compels our wonder; and if in a better state, then this compels it yet more. And God is in a better state. We say therefore, that God is a living being, eternal, most good; so that life and a continual eternal existence belong to God; for this is God." (Aristotle, *Metaphysics*, XII, 7.)

STUDY QUESTIONS

1. Identify the essential differences between Hellenic and Hellenistic culture. Then explain how and why these differences developed.
2. In your own words explain what Plato meant by his Ideas (his Pure Forms).
3. Explain the doctrine of ethos and how it worked in Greek education, society, and the arts. Are there any modern parallels? Some claim, for example, that certain kinds of popular music are "satanic" or that it "corrupts the young." In the 1920s and 1930s the accusations were that jazz (swing, dance music) was sinful and corrupted the listeners and dancers. Similar charges have been aimed at rock. Are any of these charges based on objective facts? Is the music to blame or something else? Who makes these charges and what impels them to do so?
4. Plato's concept of reality is based on a static universe while Aristotle's thinking involves an ever-changing universe, which is essentially the difference between the ideas of the Eleatics and the Ionians.

   a. Explain the differences between the ideas of the two philosophers concerning the nature of reality.
   b. How much did Plato and Aristotle believe one could know of reality?
   c. What, for Aristotle, guides the process of change?
   d. It appears that Plato sought permanence whereas Aristotle was prepared to cope with change. If, as has been frequently said, everyone is either a Platonist or an Aristotelian, which are you and how did you arrive at your conclusion?

LITERARY SELECTION 8

Apology

Plato (427–347 BC)

Socrates was tried in 399 BC before a generally hostile jury of 501 citizens on vague charges of impropriety toward the gods and corruption of the young. Long regarded as a suspicious character because of his relentless questioning of fellow Athenians, Socrates, due to a general amnesty, could not be charged for any offenses prior to the defeat of Athens in 404 BC. The unspoken charges were: (1) being the teacher of Alcibiades the traitor (interpreted as a corrupter of youth); (2) associating with the Thirty Tyrants (viewed as possible collaboration); (3) accepting money for teaching argumentation (mistakenly taking him for a sophist); (4) causing political and intellectual unrest. In Plato's account of the trial, Socrates (fig. 6.4) cheerfully admits to causing unrest, contending that the gods had commanded him to search into himself and other men to find the truth. This trial is his apology (or "defense") for his philosophical life. The translation is by F. J. Church and R. D. Cummings.

CHARACTERS

Socrates
Meletus

Scene: The Court of Justice

Socrates: I cannot tell what impression my accusers have made upon you, Athenians. For my own part, I know that they nearly made me forget who I was, so persuasive were they; and yet they have scarcely uttered one single word of truth. But of all their many falsehoods, the one which astonished me most was when they said that I was a clever speaker, and that you must be careful not to let me deceive you. I thought that it was most shameless of them not to be ashamed to talk in that way; for as soon as I open my mouth they will be refuted, and I shall prove that I am not a clever speaker in any way at all—unless, indeed, by a clever speaker they mean a man who speaks the truth. If that is their meaning, I agree with them that I am an orator not to be compared with them. My accusers, then, I repeat, have said little or nothing that is true; but from me you shall hear the whole truth. Certainly you will not   10

6.4 Lysippos, Portrait bust of Socrates. Roman copy of an original bronze of ca. 350 BC. Marble, life-size. Museo Nazionale Romano, Rome. Photo: Alinari, Florence.

hear an elaborate speech, Athenians, dressed up, like
theirs, with words and phrases. I will say to you what I
have to say, without preparation, and in the words which
come first, for I believe that my cause is just; so let none
of you expect anything else. Indeed, my friends, it would
hardly be seemly for me, at my age, to come before you
like a young man with his specious phrases. But there is
one thing, Athenians, which I do most earnestly beg and
entreat of you. Do not be surprised and do not interrupt
with shouts if in my defense I speak in the same way
that I am accustomed to speak in the market-place, at
the tables of the money-changers, where many of you
have heard me, and elsewhere. The truth is this. I am
more than seventy years old, and this is the first time
that I have ever come before a law-court; so your
manner of speech here is quite strange to me. If I had
been really a stranger, you would have forgiven me for
speaking in the language and the manner of my native
country; and so now I ask you to grant me what I think I
have a right to claim. Never mind the manner of my
speech—it may be better or it may be worse—give your
whole attention to the question, Is what I say just, or is it
not? That is what makes a good judge, as speaking the
truth makes a good orator.

I have to defend myself, Athenians, first against the
old false accusations of my old accusers, and then
against the later ones of my present accusers. For many
men have been accusing me to you, and for very many
years, who have not uttered a word of truth; and I fear
them more than I fear Anytus and his associates,
formidable as they are. But, my friends, those others are
still more formidable; for they got hold of most of you
when you were children, and they have been more
persistent in accusing me untruthfully and have
persuaded you that there is a certain Socrates, a wise
man, who speculates about the heavens, and who
investigates things that are beneath the earth, and who
can make the worse argument appear the stronger.
These men, Athenians, who spread abroad this report
are the accusers whom I fear; for their hearers think that
persons who pursue such inquiries never believe in the
gods. Then they are many, and their attacks have been
going on for a long time, and they spoke to you when
you were at the age most readily to believe them, for
you were all young, and many of you were children, and
there was no one to answer them when they attacked
me. And the most unreasonable thing of all is that I do
not even know their names: I cannot tell you who they
are except when one happens to be a comic poet. But
all the rest who have persuaded you, from motives of
resentment and prejudice, and sometimes, it may be,
from conviction, are hardest to cope with. For I cannot
call any one of them forward in court to cross-examine
him. I have, as it were, simply to spar with shadows in
my defense, and to put questions which there is no one
to answer. I ask you, therefore, to believe that, as I say, I
have been attacked by two kinds of accusers—first, by
Meletus and his associates, and, then, by those older

ones of whom I have spoken. And, with your leave, I will
defend myself first against my old accusers; for you
heard their accusations first, and they were much more
forceful than my present accusers are.

Well, I must make my defense, Athenians, and try in
the short time allowed me to remove the prejudice
which you have been so long a time acquiring. I hope
that I may manage to do this, if it be good for you and
for me, and that my defense may be successful; but I
am quite aware of the nature of my task, and I know that
it is a difficult one. Be the outcome, however, as is
pleasing to God, I must obey the law and make my
defense.

Let us begin from the beginning, then, and ask what
is the accusation which has given rise to the prejudice
against me, which was what Meletus relied on when he
brought his indictment. What is the prejudice which my
enemies have been spreading about me? I must assume
that they are formally accusing me, and read their
indictment. It would run somewhat in this fashion:
"Socrates is a wrongdoer, who meddles with inquiries
into things beneath the earth and in the heavens, and
who makes the worse argument appear the stronger,
and who teaches others these same things." That is
what they say; and in the comedy of Aristophanes[5] you
yourselves saw a man called Socrates swinging round in
a basket and saying that he walked the air, and
sputtering a great deal of nonsense about matters of
which I understand nothing, either more or less. I do not
mean to disparage that kind of knowledge if there is any
one who is wise about these matters. I trust Meletus
may never be able to prosecute me for that. But the
truth is, Athenians, I have nothing to do with these
matters, and almost all of you are yourselves my
witnesses of this. I beg all of you who have ever heard
me discussing, and they are many, to inform your
neighbors and tell them if any of you have ever heard
me discussing such matters, either more or less. That
will show you that the other common statements about
me are as false as this one.

But the fact is that not one of these is true. And if you
have heard that I undertake to educate men, and make
money by so doing, that is not true either, though I think
that it would be a fine thing to be able to educate men,
as Gorgias of Leontini, and Prodicus of Keos, and Hippias
of Elis do. For each of them, my friends, can go into any
city, and persuade the young men to leave the society of
their fellow citizens, with any of whom they might
associate for nothing, and to be only too glad to be
allowed to pay money for the privilege of associating
with themselves. And I believe that there is another
wise man from Paros residing in Athens at this moment.
I happened to meet Kallias, the son of Hipponicus, a man
who has spent more money on sophists than every one
else put together. So I said to him (he has two sons),
Kallias, if your two sons had been foals or calves, we
could have hired a trainer for them who would have
made them perfect in the virtue which belongs to their
nature. He would have been either a groom or a farmer.
But whom do you intend to take to train them, seeing
that they are men? Who understands the virtue which

---

5. The *Clouds*. The basket was satirically assumed to facilitate
   Socrates' inquiries into things in the heavens.

belongs to men and to citizens? I suppose that you must have thought of this, because of your sons. Is there such a person, said I, or not? Certainly there is, he replied. Who is he, said I, and where does he come from, and what is his fee? Evenus, Socrates, he replied, from Paros, five minae. Then I thought that Evenus was a fortunate person if he really understood this art and could teach so cleverly. If I had possessed knowledge of that kind, I should have been conceited and disdainful. But, Athenians, the truth is that I do not possess it. 140

Perhaps some of you may reply: But, Socrates, what is the trouble with you? What has given rise to these prejudices against you? You must have been doing something out of the ordinary. All these rumors and reports of you would never have arisen if you had not been doing something different from other men. So tell us what it is, that we may not give our verdict in the dark. I think that that is a fair question, and I will try to explain to you what it is that has raised these prejudices against me and given me this reputation. Listen, then. Some of you perhaps, will think that I am joking, but I assure you that I will tell you the whole truth. I have gained this reputation, Athenians, simply by reason of a certain wisdom. But by what kind of wisdom? It is by just that wisdom which is perhaps human wisdom. In that, it may be, I am really wise. But the men of whom I was speaking just now must be wise in a wisdom which is greater than human wisdom, or else I cannot describe it, for certainly I know nothing of it myself, and if any man says that I do, he lies and speaks to arouse prejudice against me. Do not interrupt me with shouts, Athenians, even if you think that I am boasting. What I am going to say is not my own. I will tell you who says it, and he is worthy of your respect. I will bring the god of Delphi to be the witness of my wisdom, if it is wisdom at all, and of its nature. You remember Khaerephon. From youth upwards he was my comrade; and also a partisan of your democracy, sharing your recent exile[6] and returning with you. You remember, too, Khaerephon's character—how impulsive he was in carrying through whatever he took in hand. Once he went to Delphi and ventured to put this question to the oracle—I entreat you again, my friends, not to interrupt me with your shouts—he asked if there was any one who was wiser than I. The priestess answered that there was no one. Khaerephon himself is dead, but his brother here will witness to what I say. 150 160 170 180

Now see why I tell you this. I am going to explain to you how the prejudice against me has arisen. When I heard of the oracle I began to reflect: What can the god mean by this riddle? I know very well that I am not wise, even in the smallest degree. Then what can he mean by saying that I am the wisest of men? It cannot be that he is speaking falsely, for he is a god and cannot lie. For a long time I was at a loss to understand his meaning. Then, very reluctantly, I turned to investigate it in this manner: I went to a man who was reputed to be wise, 190

6. During the totalitarian regime of The Thirty that remained in power for eight months (in 404 BC), five years before the trial.

thinking that there, if anywhere, I should prove the answer wrong, and meaning to point out to the oracle its mistake, and to say, "You said that I was the wisest of men, but this man is wiser than I am." So I examined the man—I need not tell you his name, he was a politician—but this was the result, Athenians. When I conversed with him I came to see that, though a great many persons, and most of all he himself, thought that he was wise, yet he was not wise. Then I tried to prove to him that he was not wise, though he fancied that he was; and by so doing I made him indignant, and many of the bystanders. So when I went away, I thought to myself, "I am wiser than this man: neither of us knows anything that is really worthwhile, but he thinks that he has knowledge when he has not, while I, having no knowledge, do not think that I have. I seem, at any rate, to be a little wiser than he is on this point: I do not think that I know what I do not know." Next I went to another man who was reputed to be still wiser than the last, with exactly the same result. And there again I made him, and many other men, indignant. 200 210

Then I went on to one man after another, seeing that I was arousing indignation every day, which caused me much grief and anxiety. Still I thought that I must set the god's command above everything. So I had to go to every man who seemed to possess any knowledge, and investigate the meaning of the oracle. Athenians, I must tell you the truth; by the dog, this was the result of the investigation which I made at the god's bidding: I found that the men whose reputation for wisdom stood highest were nearly the most lacking in it, while others who were looked down on as common people were much more intelligent. Now I must describe to you the wanderings which I undertook, like Heraklean labors, to prove the oracle irrefutable. After the politicians, I went to the poets, tragic, dithyrambic, and others, thinking that there I should find myself manifestly more ignorant than they. So I took up the poems on which I thought that they had spent most pains, and asked them what they meant, hoping at the same time to learn something from them. I am ashamed to tell you the truth, my friends, but I must say it. Almost any one of the bystanders could have talked about the works of these poets better than the poets themselves. So I soon found that it is not by wisdom that the poets create their works, but by a certain natural power and by inspiration, like soothsayers and prophets, who say many fine things, but who understand nothing of what they say. The poets seemed to me to be in a similar situation. And at the same time I perceived that, because of their poetry, they thought that they were the wisest of men in other matters, too, which they were not. So I went away again, thinking that I had the same advantage over the poets that I had over the politicians. 220 230 240

Finally, I went to the artisans, for I knew very well that I possessed no knowledge at all worth speaking of, and I was sure that I should find that they knew many fine things. And in that I was not mistaken. They knew what I did not know, and so far they were wiser than I. But, Athenians, it seemed to me that the skilled artisans had the same failing as the poets. Each of them believed 250 himself to be extremely wise in matters of the greatest importance because he was skillful in his own art: and this presumption of theirs obscured their real wisdom. So I asked myself, on behalf of the oracle, whether I would choose to remain as I was, without either their wisdom or their ignorance, or to possess both, as they did. And I answered to myself and to the oracle that it was better for me to remain as I was.   260

From this examination, Athenians, has arisen much fierce and bitter indignation, and from this a great many prejudices about me, and people say that I am "a wise man." For the bystanders always think that I am wise myself in any matter wherein I refute another. But, gentlemen, I believe that the god is really wise, and that by this oracle he meant that human wisdom is worth little or nothing. I do not think that he meant that   270
Socrates was wise. He only made use of my name, and took me as an example, as though he would say to men, "He among you is the wisest who, like Socrates, knows that in truth his wisdom is worth nothing at all." Therefore I still go about testing and examining every man whom I think wise, whether he be a citizen or a stranger, as the god has commanded me; and whenever I find that he is not wise, I point out to him, on the god's behalf, that he is not wise. I am so busy in this pursuit   280
that I have never had leisure to take any part worth mentioning in public matters or to look after my private affairs. I am in great poverty as the result of my service to the god.

Besides this, the young men who follow me about, who are the sons of wealthy persons and have the most leisure, take pleasure in hearing men cross-examined. They often imitate me among themselves; then they try their hands at cross-examining other people. And, I imagine, they find plenty of men who think that they know a great deal when in fact they know little or   290
nothing. Then the persons who are cross-examined get angry with me instead of with themselves, and say that Socrates is an abomination and corrupts the young. When they are asked, "Why, what does he do? what does he teach?" they do not know what to say; but, not to seem at a loss, they repeat the stock charges against all philosophers, and allege that he investigates things in the air and under the earth, and that he teaches people to disbelieve in the gods, and to make the worse argument appear the stronger. For, I suppose, they   300
would not like to confess the truth, which is that they are shown up as ignorant pretenders to knowledge that they do not possess. So they have been filling your ears with their bitter prejudices for a long time, for they are ambitious, energetic, and numerous; and they speak vigorously and persuasively against me. Relying on this, Meletus, Anytus, and Lykon have attacked me. Meletus is indignant with me on the part of the poets, Anytus on the part of the artisans and politicians, and Lykon on the part of the orators. And so, as I said at the beginning, I   310
shall be surprised if I am able, in the short time allowed me for my defense, to remove from your minds this prejudice which has grown so strong. What I have told you, Athenians, is the truth: I neither conceal nor do I suppress anything, small or great. Yet I know that it is

just this plainness of speech which rouses indignation. But that is only a proof that my words are true, and that the prejudice against me, and the causes of it, are what I have said. And whether you investigate them now or hereafter, you will find that they are so.   320

What I have said must suffice as my defense against the charges of my first accusers. I will try next to defend myself against Meletus, that "good patriot," as he calls himself, and my later accusers. Let us assume that they are a new set of accusers, and read their indictment, as we did in the case of the others. It runs thus. He says that Socrates is a wrongdoer who corrupts the youth, and who does not believe in the gods whom the state believes in, but in other new divinities. Such is the accusation. Let us examine each point in it separately.   330
Meletus says that I do wrong by corrupting the youth. But I say, Athenians, that he is doing wrong, for he is playing a solemn joke by casually bringing men to trial, and pretending to have a solemn interest in matters to which he has never given a moment's thought. Now I will try to prove to you that it is so.

Come here, Meletus. Is it not a fact that you think it very important that the young should be as good as possible?

Meletus: It is.   340
Socrates: Come then, tell the judges who is it who improves them? You care so much,[7] you must know. You are accusing me, and bringing me to trial, because, as you say, you have discovered that I am the corrupter of the youth. Come now, reveal to the gentlemen who improves them. You see, Meletus, you have nothing to say; you are silent. But don't you think that this is shameful? Is not your silence a conclusive proof of what I say—that you have never cared. Come, tell us, my good man, who makes the young better?   350
Mel: The laws.
Socr: That, my friend, is not my question. What man improves the young, who starts with the knowledge of the laws?
Mel: The judges here, Socrates.
Socr: What do you mean, Meletus? Can they educate the young and improve them?
Mel: Certainly.
Socr: All of them? or only some of them?
Mel: All of them.   360
Socr: By Hera, that is good news! Such a large supply of benefactors! And do the listeners here improve them, or not?
Mel: They do.
Socr: And do the senators?
Mel: Yes.
Socr: Well then, Meletus, do the members of the assembly corrupt the young or do they again all improve them?
Mel: They, too, improve them.   370
Socr: Then all the Athenians, apparently, make the young into good men except me, and I alone corrupt them. Is that your meaning?

---

7. Throughout the following passage Socrates plays on the etymology of the name "Meletus" as meaning "the man who cares."

Mel: Most certainly; that is my meaning.

Socr: You have discovered me to be most unfortunate. Now tell me: do you think that the same holds good in the case of horses? Does one man do them harm and every one else improve them? On the contrary, is it not one man only, or a very few—namely, those who are skilled with horses—who can improve them, while the majority of men harm them if they use them and have anything to do with them? Is it not so, Meletus, both with horses and with every other animal? Of course it is, whether you and Anytus say yes or no. The young would certainly be very fortunate if only one man corrupted them, and every one else did them good. The truth is, Meletus, you prove conclusively that you have never thought about the youth in your life. You exhibit your carelessness in not caring for the very matters about which you are prosecuting me.

Now be so good as to tell us, Meletus, is it better to live among good citizens or bad ones? Answer, my friend. I am not asking you a difficult question. Do not the bad do harm to their associates and the good, good?

Mel: Yes.

Socr: Is there any one who would rather be injured than benefited by his companions? Answer, my good sir; you are obliged by the law to answer. Does any one like to be injured?

Mel: Certainly not.

Socr: Well then, are you prosecuting me for corrupting the young and making them worse, voluntarily or involuntarily?

Mel: For doing it voluntarily.

Socr: What, Meletus? Do you mean to say that you, who are so much younger than I, are yet so much wiser than I that you know that bad citizens always do evil, and that good citizens do good, to those with whom they come in contact, while I am so extraordinarily ignorant as not to know that, if I make any of my companions evil, he will probably injure me in some way, and as to commit this great evil, as you allege, voluntarily? You will not make me believe that, nor anyone else either, I should think. Either I do not corrupt the young at all or if I do I do so involuntarily: so that you are lying in either case. And if I corrupt them involuntarily, the law does not call upon you to prosecute me for an error which is involuntary, but to take me aside privately and reprove and educate me. For, of course, I shall cease from doing wrong involuntarily, as soon as I know that I have been doing wrong. But you avoided associating with me and educating me; instead you bring me up before the court, where the law sends persons, not for education, but for punishment.

The truth is, Athenians, as I said, it is quite clear that Meletus has never cared at all about these matters. However, now tell us, Meletus, how do you say that I corrupt the young? Clearly, according to your indictment, by teaching them not to believe in the gods the state believes in, but other new divinities instead. You mean that I corrupt the young by that teaching, do you not?

Mel: Yes, most certainly I mean that.

Socr: Then in the name of these gods of whom we are speaking, explain yourself a little more clearly to me and to these gentlemen here. I cannot understand what you mean. Do you mean that I teach the young to believe in some gods, but not in the gods of the state? Do you accuse me of teaching them to believe in strange gods? If that is your meaning, I myself believe in some gods, and my crime is not that of complete atheism. Or do you mean that I do not believe in the gods at all myself, and that I teach other people not to believe in them either?

Mel: I mean that you do not believe in the gods in any way whatever.

Socr: You amaze me, Meletus! Why do you say that? Do you mean that I believe neither the sun nor the moon to be gods, like other men?

Mel: I swear he does not, judges; he says that the sun is a stone, and the moon earth.

Socr: My dear Meletus, do you think that you are prosecuting Anaxagoras? You must have a very poor opinion of these men, and think them illiterate, if you imagine that they do not know that the works of Anaxagoras of Klazomenae are full of these doctrines. And so young men learn these things from me, when they can often buy them in the theatre for a drachma at most, and laugh at Socrates were he to pretend that these doctrines, which are very peculiar doctrines, too, were his own. But please tell me, do you really think that I do not believe in the gods at all?

Mel: Most certainly I do. You are a complete atheist.

Socr: No one believes that, Meletus, not even you yourself. It seems to me, Athenians, that Meletus is very insolent and reckless, and that he is prosecuting me simply out of insolence, recklessness and youthful bravado. For he seems to be testing me, by asking me a riddle that has no answer. "Will this wise Socrates," he says to himself, "see that I am joking and contradicting myself? or shall I deceive him and every one else who hears me?" Meletus seems to me to contradict himself in his indictment: It is as if he were to say, "Socrates is a wrongdoer who does not believe in the gods, but who believes in the gods." But this is joking.

Now, my friends, let us see why I think that this is his meaning. Do you answer me, Meletus; and do you, Athenians, remember the request which I made to you at the start, and do not interrupt me with shouts if I talk in my customary manner.

Is there any man, Meletus, who believes in the existence of things pertaining to men and not in the existence of men? Make him answer the question, gentlemen, without these interruptions. Is there any man who believes in the existence of horsemanship and not in the existence of horses? Or in flute playing and not in flute-players? There is not, my friend. If you will not answer, I will tell both you and the judges. But you must answer my next question. Is there any man who believes in the existence of divine things and not in the existence of divinities?

Mel: There is not.

Socr: I am very glad that these gentlemen have managed to extract an answer from you. Well then, you say that I believe in divine things, whether they be old or new ones, and that I teach others to believe in them; at any rate, according to your statement, I believe in divine things. That you have sworn in your indictment. But if I believe in divine things, I suppose it follows necessarily that I believe in divinities. Is it not so? It is. I assume that you grant that, as you do not answer. But do we not believe that divinities are either gods themselves or the children of the gods? Do you admit that? 500

Mel: I do.

Socr: Then you admit that I believe in divinities. Now, if these divinities are gods, then, as I say, you are joking and asking a riddle, and asserting that I do not believe in the gods, and at the same time that I do, since I believe in divinities. But if these divinities are the illegitimate children of the gods, either by the nymphs or by other mothers, as they are said to be, then, I ask, what man could believe in the existence of the children of the gods, and not in the existence of the gods? That would 510 be as absurd as believing in the existence of the offspring of horses and asses, and not in the existence of horses and asses. You must have indicted me in this manner, Meletus, either to test me or because you could not find any crime that you could accuse me of with truth. But you will never contrive to persuade any man with any sense at all that a belief in divine things and things of the gods does not necessarily involve a belief in divinities, and in the gods, and in heroes. 520

But in truth, Athenians, I do not think that I need say very much to prove that I have not committed the crime for which Meletus is prosecuting me. What I have said is enough to prove that. But I repeat it is certainly true, as I have already told you, that I have aroused much indignation. That is what will cause my condemnation if I am condemned; not Meletus nor Anytus either, but that prejudice and resentment of the multitude which have been the destruction of many good men before me, and I think will be so again. There is no fear that I shall be the 530 last victim.

Perhaps some one will say: "Are you not ashamed, Socrates, of leading a life which is very likely now to cause your death?" I should answer him with justice, and say: "My friend, if you think that a man of any worth at all ought to reckon the chances of life and death when he acts, or that he ought to think of anything but whether he is acting rightly or wrongly, and as a good or bad man would act, you are mistaken." According to you, the demigods who died at Troy would be foolish, and 540 among them the son of Thetis, who thought nothing of danger when the alternative was disgrace. For when his mother—and she was a goddess—addressed him, when he was resolved to slay Hector, in this fashion, "My son, if you avenge the death of your comrade Patroclos and slay Hector, you will die yourself, for 'fate awaits you straightway after Hector's death'"; when he heard this, he scorned danger and death; he feared much more to live a coward and not to avenge his friend. "Let me punish the evildoer and straightway die," he said, "that I 550 may not remain here by the beaked ships jeered at, encumbering the earth."[8] Do you suppose that he thought of danger or of death? For this, Athenians, I believe to be the truth. Wherever a man's station is,

8. Homer, *Iliad*, XVIII, 96, 98.

whether he has chosen it of his own will, or whether he has been placed at it by his commander, there it is his duty to remain and face the danger without thinking of death or of any other thing except disgrace.

When the generals whom you chose to command me, Athenians, assigned me my station at Potidaea and 560 at Amphipolis and at Delium, I remained where they stationed me and ran the risk of death, like other men. It would be very strange conduct on my part if I were to desert my station now from fear of death or of any other thing when God has commanded me—as I am persuaded that he has done—to spend my life in searching for wisdom, and in examining myself and others. That would indeed be a very strange thing. Then certainly I might with justice be brought to trial for not believing in the gods, for I should be disobeying the 570 oracle, and fearing death and thinking myself wise when I was not wise. For to fear death, my friends, is only to think ourselves wise without really being wise, for it is to think that we know what we do not know. For no one knows whether death may not be the greatest good that can happen to man. But men fear it as if they knew quite well that it was the greatest of evils. And what is this but that shameful ignorance of thinking that we know what we do not know? In this matter, too, my friends, perhaps I am different from the multitude; and if I were 580 to claim to be at all wiser than others, it would be because, not knowing very much about the other world, I do not think I know. But I do know very well that it is evil and disgraceful to do wrong, and not to be persuaded by my superior, whether man or god. I will never do what I know to be evil, and shrink in fear from what I do not know to be good or evil. Even if you acquit me now, and do not listen to Anytus' argument that, if I am to be acquitted, I ought never to have been brought to trial at all, and that, as it is, you are bound to put me to 590 death because, as he said, if I escape, all your sons will be utterly corrupted by practicing what Socrates teaches. If you were therefore to say to me, "Socrates, this time we will not listen to Anytus; we will let you go, but on this condition that you give up this investigation of yours, and philosophy; if you are found following those pursuits again, you shall die." I say, if you offered to let me go on these terms, I should reply: "Athenians, I hold you in the highest regard and affection, but I will be persuaded by the god rather than you"; and as long as 600 I have breath and strength I will not give up philosophy and exhorting you and declaring the truth to every one of you whom I meet, saying, as I am accustomed, "My good friend, you are a citizen of Athens, a city which is very great and very famous for its wisdom and power— are you not ashamed of caring so much for the making of money and for fame and prestige, when you neither think nor care about wisdom and truth and the improvement of your soul?" And if he disputes my words and says that he does care about these things, I 610 shall not at once release him and go away: I shall question him and cross-examine him and test him. If I think that he does not possess virtue, though he says that he does, I shall reproach him for under-valuing the most valuable things, and over-valuing those that are less valuable. This I shall do to every one whom I meet, young or old, citizen or stranger, but especially to citizens, for they are more closely related to me. For know that the god has commanded me to do so. And I think that no greater good has ever befallen you in the state than my service to the god. For I spend my whole life in going about and persuading you all to give your first and greatest care to the improvement of your souls, and not till you have done that to think of your bodies or your wealth; and telling you that virtue does not come from wealth, but that wealth, and every other good thing which men have, whether in public or in private, comes from virtue. If then I corrupt the youth by this teaching, these things must be harmful; but if any man says that I teach anything else, there is nothing in what he says. And therefore, Athenians, I say, whether you are persuaded by Anytus or not, whether you acquit me or not, I shall not change my way of life: no, not if I have to die for it many times.

Do not interrupt me, Athenians, with your shouts. Remember the request which I made to you, and do not interrupt my words. I think that it will profit you to hear them. I am going to say something more to you, at which you may be inclined to protest, but do not do that. Be sure that if you put me to death, who am what I have told you that I am, you will do yourselves more harm than me. Meletus and Anytus can do me no harm: that is impossible, for I am sure it is not allowed that a good man be injured by a worse. He may indeed kill me, or drive me into exile, or deprive me of my civil rights; and perhaps Meletus and others think those things great evils. But I do not think so: I think it is a much greater evil to do what he is doing now, and to try to put a man to death unjustly. And now, Athenians, I am not arguing in my own defense at all, as you might expect me to do, but rather in yours in order that you may not make a mistake about the gift of the god to you by condemning me. For if you put me to death, you will not easily find another who, if I may use a ludicrous comparison, clings to the state as a sort of gadfly to a horse that is large and well-bred but rather sluggish from its size, and needing to be aroused. It seems to me that the god has attached me like that to the state, for I am constantly alighting upon you at every point to rouse, persuade, and reproach each of you all day long. You will not easily find anyone else, my friends, to fill my place; and if you are persuaded by me, you will spare my life. You are indignant, as drowsy persons are, when they are awakened, and, of course, if you are persuaded by Anytus, you could easily kill me with a single blow, and then sleep on undisturbed for the rest of your lives unless the god in his care for you sends another to arouse you. And you may easily see that it is the god who has given me to your city; for it is not human the way in which I have neglected all my own interests and endured seeing my private affairs neglected now for so many years, while occupying myself unceasingly in your interests, going to each of you privately, like a father or an elder brother, trying to persuade him to care for virtue. There would have been a reason for it, if I had gained any advantage by this, or if I had been paid for my exhortations; but you see

620

630

640

650

660

670

yourselves that my accusers, though they accuse me of everything else without shame, have not had the shamelessness to say that I ever either exacted or demanded payment. To that they have no witness. And I think that I have sufficient witness to the truth of what I say—my poverty.

Perhaps it may seem strange to you that, though I go about giving this advice privately and meddling in others' affairs, yet I do not venture to come forward in the assembly and advise the state. You have often heard me speak of my reason for this, and in many places: it is that I have a certain divine sign, which is what Meletus has caricatured in his indictment. I have had it from childhood. It is a kind of voice which, whenever I hear it, always turns me back from something which I was going to do, but never urges me to act. It is this which forbids me to take part in politics. And I think it does well to forbid me. For, Athenians, it is quite certain that, if I had attempted to take part in politics, I should have perished at once and long ago without doing any good either to you or to myself. And do not be indignant with me for telling the truth. There is no man who will preserve his life for long, either in Athens or elsewhere, if he firmly opposes the multitude, and tries to prevent the commission of much injustice and illegality in the state. He who would really fight for justice must do so as a private citizen, not as an office-holder, if he is to preserve his life, even for a short time.

I will prove to you that this is so by very strong evidence, not by mere words, but by what you value more—actions. Listen then to what has happened to me, that you may know that there is no man who could make me consent to do wrong from the fear of death, but that I would perish at once rather than give way. What I am going to tell you may be a commonplace in the lawcourt; nevertheless it is true. The only office that I ever held in the state, Athenians, was that of Senator. When you wished to try the ten generals who did not rescue their men after the battle of Arginusae, as a group, which was illegal, as you all came to think afterwards, the tribe Antiokhis, to which I belong, held the presidency. On that occasion I alone of all the presidents opposed your illegal action and gave my vote against you. The orators were ready to impeach me and arrest me; and you were clamoring against me, and crying out to me to submit. But I thought that I ought to face the danger, with law and justice on my side, rather than join with you in your unjust proposal, from fear of imprisonment or death. That was when the state was democratic. When the oligarchy came in, the Thirty sent for me, with four others, to the council-chamber, and ordered us to bring Leon the Salaminian from Salamis, that they might put him to death. They were in the habit of frequently giving similar orders to many others, wishing to implicate as many as possible in their crimes. But, then, I again proved, not by mere words, but by my actions, that, if I may speak bluntly, I do not care a straw for death; but that I do care very much indeed about not doing anything unjust or impious. That government with all its power did not terrify me into doing anything unjust; but when we left the council-chamber, the other four

680

690

700

710

720

730

went over to Salamis and brought Leon across to Athens; and I went home. And if the rule of the Thirty had not been overthrown soon afterwards, I should very likely have been put to death for what I did then. Many of you will be my witnesses in this matter. 740

Now do you think that I could have remained alive all these years if I had taken part in public affairs, and had always maintained the cause of justice like a good man, and had held it a paramount duty, as it is, to do so? Certainly not, Athenians, nor could any other man. But throughout my whole life, both in private and in public, whenever I have had to take part in public affairs, you will find I have always been the same and have never 750 yielded unjustly to anyone; no, not to those whom my enemies falsely assert to have been my pupils.[9] But I was never anyone's teacher. I have never withheld myself from anyone, young or old, who was anxious to hear me discuss while I was making my investigation; neither do I discuss for payment, and refuse to discuss without payment. I am ready to ask questions of rich and poor alike, and if any man wishes to answer me, and then listen to what I have to say, he may. And I cannot justly be charged with causing these men to turn out 760 good or bad, for I never either taught or professed to teach any of them any knowledge whatever. And if any man asserts that he ever learned or heard anything from me in private which everyone else did not hear as well as he, be sure that he does not speak the truth.

Why is it, then, that people delight in spending so much time in my company? You have heard why, Athenians. I told you the whole truth when I said that they delight in hearing me examine persons who think that they are wise when they are not wise. It is certainly 770 very amusing to listen to that. And, I say, the god has commanded me to examine men, in oracles and in dreams and in every way in which the divine will was ever declared to man. This is the truth, Athenians, and if it were not the truth, it would be easily refuted. For if it were really the case that I have already corrupted some of the young men, and am now corrupting others, surely some of them, finding as they grew older that I had given them bad advice in their youth, would have come forward today to accuse me and take their revenge. Or if 780 they were unwilling to do so themselves, surely their relatives, their fathers or brothers, or others, would, if I had done them any harm, have remembered it and taken their revenge. Certainly I see many of them in Court. Here is Crito, of my own deme and of my own age, the father of Critobulus; here is Lysanias of Sphettus, the father of Aeschines; here is also Antiphon of Cephisus, the father of Epigenes. Then here are others whose brothers have spent their time in my company— Nicostratus, the son of Theozotides and brother of 790 Theodotus—and Theodotus is dead, so he at least cannot entreat his brother to be silent; here is Paralus, the son of Demodocus and the brother of Theages; here is Adeimantus, the son of Ariston, whose brother is Plato here; and Aeantodorus, whose brother is

Aristodorus. And I can name many others to you, some of whom Meletus ought to have called as witnesses in the course of his own speech; but if he forgot to call them then, let him call them now—I will yield the floor to him—and tell us if he has any such evidence. No, on the 800 contrary, my friends, you will find all these men ready to support me, the corrupter, the injurer, of their relatives, as Meletus and Anytus call me. Those of them who have been already corrupted might perhaps have some reason for supporting me, but what reason can their relatives have who are grown up, and who are uncorrupted, except the reason of truth and justice—that they know very well that Meletus is lying, and that I am speaking the truth?

Well, my friends, this, and perhaps more like this, is 810 pretty much all I have to offer in my defense. There may be some one among you who will be indignant when he remembers how, even in a less important trial than this, he begged and entreated the judges, with many tears, to acquit him, and brought forward his children and many of his friends and relatives in Court in order to appeal to your feelings; and then finds that I shall do none of these things, though I am in what he would think the supreme danger. Perhaps he will harden himself against me when he notices this: it may make him angry, and he may cast 820 his vote in anger. If it is so with any of you—I do not suppose that it is, but in case it should be so—I think that I should answer him reasonably if I said: "My friend, I have relatives, too, for, in the words of Homer,[10] 'I am not born of an oak or a rock but of flesh and blood'"; and so, Athenians, I have relatives, and I have three sons, one of them a lad, and the other two still children. Yet I will not bring any of them forward before you and implore you to acquit me. And why will I do none of these things? It is not from arrogance, Athenians, nor 830 because I lack respect for you—whether or not I can face death bravely is another question—but for my own good name, and for your good name, and for the good name of the whole state. I do not think it right, at my age and with my reputation, to do anything of that kind. Rightly or wrongly, men have made up their minds that in some way Socrates is different from the multitude of men. And it will be shameful if those of you who are thought to excel in wisdom, or in bravery, or in any other virtue, are going to act in this fashion. I have often seen 840 men of reputation behaving in an extraordinary way at their trial, as if they thought it a terrible fate to be killed, and as though they expected to live for ever if you did not put them to death. Such men seem to me to bring shame upon the state, for any stranger would suppose that the best and most eminent Athenians, who are selected by their fellow citizens to hold office, and for other honors, are no better than women. Those of you, Athenians, who have any reputation at all ought not to do these things, and you ought not to allow us to do 850 them; you should show that you will be much more ready to condemn men who make the state ridiculous by these pitiful pieces of acting, than to men who remain quiet.

But apart from the question of reputation, my friends, I do not think that it is right to entreat the judge to acquit

---

9. E.g., Critias, a leader of The Thirty, and Alcibiades.
10. Homer, *Odyssey*, XIX, 163.

us, or to escape condemnation in that way. It is our duty to teach and persuade him. He does not sit to give away justice as a favor, but to pronounce judgment; and he has sworn, not to favor any man whom he would like to favor, but to judge according to law. And, therefore, we ought not to encourage you in the habits of breaking your oaths; and you ought not to allow yourselves to fall into this habit, for then neither you nor we would be acting piously. Therefore, Athenians, do not require me to do these things, for I believe them to be neither good nor just nor pious; and, more especially, do not ask me to do them today when Meletus is prosecuting me for impiety. For were I to be successful and persuade you by my entreaties to break your oaths, I should be clearly teaching you to believe that there are no gods, and I should be simply accusing myself by my defense of not believing in them. But, Athenians, that is very far from the truth. I do believe in the gods as no one of my accusers believes in them: and to you and to god I commit my cause to be decided as is best for you and for me.

[He is found guilty by 281 votes to 220.]

I am not indignant at the verdict which you have given, Athenians, for many reasons. I expected that you would find me guilty; and I am not so much surprised at that as at the numbers of the votes. I certainly never thought that the majority against me would have been so narrow. But now it seems that if only thirty votes had changed sides, I should have escaped. So I think that I have escaped Meletus, as it is; and not only have I escaped him, for it is perfectly clear that if Anytus and Lykon had not come forward to accuse me, too, he would not have obtained the fifth part of the votes, and would have had to pay a fine of a thousand drachmae.

So he proposes death as the penalty. Be it so. And what alternative penalty shall I propose to you, Athenians?[11] What I deserve, of course, must I not? What then do I deserve to pay or to suffer for having determined not to spend my life in ease? I neglected the things which most men value, such as wealth, and family interests, and military commands, and popular oratory, and all the political appointments, and clubs, and factions, that there are in Athens; for I thought that I was really too honest a man to preserve my life if I engaged in these matters. So I did not go where I should have done no good either to you or to myself. I went, instead, to each one of you privately to do him, as I say, the greatest of benefits, and tried to persuade him not to think of his affairs until he had thought of himself and tried to make himself as good and wise as possible, nor to think of the affairs of Athens until he had thought of Athens herself; and to care for other things in the same manner. Then what do I deserve for such a life? Something good, Athenians, if I am really to propose what I deserve; and something good which it would be suitable to me to receive. Then what is a suitable reward to be given to a poor benefactor who requires leisure to exhort you? There is no reward, Athenians, so suitable for him as a public maintenance in the *prytaneum* [town hall]. It is a much more suitable reward for him than for any of you who has won a victory at the Olympic games

with his horse or his chariots. Such a man only makes you seem happy, but I make you really happy; and he is not in want, and I am. So if I am to propose the penalty which I really deserve, I propose this—a public maintenance in the *prytaneum*.

Perhaps you think me stubborn and arrogant in what I am saying now, as in what I said about the entreaties and tears. It is not so, Athenians; it is rather that I am convinced that I never wronged any man voluntarily, though I cannot persuade you of that, for we have discussed together only a little time. If there were a law at Athens, as there is elsewhere, not to finish a trial of life and death in a single day, I think that I could have persuaded you; but now it is not easy in so short a time to clear myself of great prejudices. But when I am persuaded that I have never wronged any man, I shall certainly not wrong myself, or admit that I deserve to suffer any evil, or propose any evil for myself as a penalty. Why should I? Lest I should suffer the penalty which Meletus proposes when I say that I do not know whether it is a good or an evil? Shall I choose instead of it something which I know to be an evil, and propose that as a penalty? Shall I propose imprisonment? And why should I pass the rest of my days in prison, the slave of successive officials? Or shall I propose a fine, with imprisonment until it is paid? I have told you why I will not do that. I should have to remain in prison, for I have no money to pay a fine with. Shall I then propose exile? Perhaps you would agree to that. Life would indeed be very dear to me if I were unreasonable enough to expect that strangers would cheerfully tolerate my discussions and arguments when you who are my fellow citizens cannot endure them, and have found them so irksome and odious to you that you are seeking now to be relieved of them. No, indeed, Athenians, that is not likely. A fine life I should lead for an old man if I were to withdraw from Athens and pass the rest of my days in wandering from city to city, and continually being expelled. For I know very well that the young men will listen to me wherever I go, as they do here; and if I drive them away, they will persuade their elders to expel me; and if I do not drive them away, their fathers and kinsmen will expel me for their sakes.

Perhaps some one will say, "Why cannot you withdraw from Athens, Socrates, and hold your peace?" It is the most difficult thing in the world to make you understand why I cannot do that. If I say that I cannot hold my peace because that would be to disobey the god, you will think that I am not in earnest and will not believe me. And if I tell you that no greater good can happen to a man than to discuss virtue every day and the other matters about which you have heard me arguing and examining myself and others, and that an unexamined life is not worth living, then you will believe me still less. But that is so, my friends, though it is not easy to persuade you. And, what is more, I am not

11. For certain crimes no penalty was fixed by Athenian law, and, having reached a verdict of guilty, the court had still to decide between the alternative penalties proposed by the prosecution and the defense.

accustomed to think that I deserve anything evil. If I had been rich, I would have proposed as large a fine as I could pay: that would have done me no harm. But I am not rich enough to pay a fine unless you are willing to fix it at a sum within my means. Perhaps I could pay you a mina, so I propose that. Plato here, Athenians, and Crito, and Critobulus, and Apollodorus bid me propose thirty minae, and they will be sureties for me. So I propose thirty minae.[12] They will be sufficient sureties to you for the money.

[He is condemned to death.]

You have not gained very much time, Athenians, and, as the price of it, you will have an evil name for all who wish to revile the state, and they will say that you put Socrates, a wise man, to death. For they will certainly call me wise, whether I am wise or not, when they want to reproach you. If you would have waited for a little while, your wishes would have been fulfilled in the course of nature; for you see that I am an old man, far advanced in years, and near to death. I am saying this not to all of you, only to those who have voted for my death. And to them I have something else to say. Perhaps, my friends, you think that I have been convicted because I was wanting in the arguments by which I could have persuaded you to acquit me, if, that is, I had thought it right to do or to say anything to escape punishment. It is not so. I have been convicted because I was wanting, not in arguments, but in impudence and shamelessness—because I would not plead before you as you would have liked to hear me plead, or appeal to you with weeping and wailing, or say and do many other things which I maintain are unworthy of me, but which you have been accustomed to from other men. But when I was defending myself, I thought that I ought not to do anything unworthy of a free man because of the danger which I ran, and I have not changed my mind now. I would very much rather defend myself as I did, and die, than as you would have had me do, and live. Both in a lawsuit and in war, there are things which neither I nor any other man may do in order to escape from death. In battle, a man often sees that he may at least escape from death by throwing down his arms and falling on his knees before the pursuer to beg for his life. And there are many other ways of avoiding death in every danger if a man is willing to say and to do anything. But, my friends, I think that it is a much harder thing to escape from wickedness than from death, for wickedness is swifter than death. And now I, who am old and slow, have been overtaken by the slower pursuer: and my accusers, who are clever and swift, have been overtaken by the swifter pursuer— wickedness. And now I shall go away, sentenced by you to death; and they will go away, sentenced by truth to wickedness and injustice. And I abide by this award as

well as they. Perhaps it was right for these things to be so; and I think that they are fairly balanced.

And now I wish to prophesy to you, Athenians, who have condemned me. For I am going to die, and that is the time when men have most prophetic power. And I prophesy to you who have sentenced me to death that a far more severe punishment than you have inflicted on me will surely overtake you as soon as I am dead. You have done this thing, thinking that you will be relieved from having to give an account of your lives. But I say that the result will be very different. There will be more men who will call you to account, whom I have held back, though you did not recognize it. And they will be harsher toward you than I have been, for they will be younger, and you will be more indignant with them. For if you think that you will restrain men from reproaching you for not living as you should, by putting them to death, you are very much mistaken. That way of escape is neither possible nor honorable. It is much more honorable and much easier not to suppress others, but to make yourselves as good as you can. This is my parting prophecy to you who have condemned me.

With you who have acquitted me I should like to discuss this thing that has happened, while the authorities are busy, and before I go to the place where I have to die. So, remain with me until I go: there is no reason why we should not talk with each other while it is possible. I wish to explain to you, as my friends, the meaning of what has happened to me. An amazing thing has happened to me, judges—for you I am right in calling judges.[13] The prophetic sign has been constantly with me all through my life till now, opposing me in quite small matters if I were not going to act rightly. And now you yourselves see what has happened to me—a thing which might be thought, and which is sometimes actually reckoned, the supreme evil. But the divine sign did not oppose me when I was leaving my house in the morning, nor when I was coming up here to the court, nor at any point in my speech when I was going to say anything; though at other times it has often stopped me in the very act of speaking. But now, in this matter, it has never once opposed me, either in my words or my actions. I will tell you what I believe to be the reason. This thing that has come upon me must be a good; and those of us who think that death is an evil must needs be mistaken. I have a clear proof that that is so; for my accustomed sign would certainly have opposed me if I had not been going to meet with something good.

And if we reflect in another way, we shall see that we may well hope that death is a good. For the state of death is one of two things: either the dead man wholly ceases to be and loses all consciousness or, as we are told, it is a change and a migration of the soul to another place. And if death is the absence of all consciousness, and like the sleep of one whose slumbers are unbroken by any dreams, it will be a wonderful gain. For if a man had to select that night in which he slept so soundly that he did not even dream, and had to compare with it all the other nights and days of his life, and then had to say how many days and nights in his life he had spent better and more pleasantly than this night, I think that a private

---

12. One mina was a trifling sum, Socrates' honest opinion of his just deserts but insulting to the court. A 30-minae fine was comparable to the dowry of a moderately rich man's daughter, as Plato later mentioned, but, by this time, totally unacceptable to the court.

13. The form of address hitherto has always been "Athenians," or "my friends."

person, nay, even the great King[14] himself, would find them easy to count, compared with the others. If that is the nature of death, I for one count it a gain. For then it appears that all time is nothing more than a single night. 1090 But if death is a journey to another place, and what we are told is true—that there are all who have died—what good could be greater than this, my judges? Would a journey not be worth taking, at the end of which, in the other world, we should be delivered from the pretended judges here and should find the true judges who are said to sit in judgment below, such as Minos and Rhadamanthus and Aeacus and Triptolemus, and the other demigods who were just in their own lives? Or what would you not give to discuss with Orpheus and 1100 Musaeus and Hesiod and Homer? I am willing to die many times if this be true. And for my own part I should find it wonderful to meet there Palamedes, and Ajax, the son of Telamon, and the other men of old who have died through an unjust judgment, and in comparing my experiences with theirs. That I think would be no small pleasure. And, above all, I could spend my time in examining those who are there, as I examine men here, and in finding out which of them is wise, and which of them thinks himself wise when he is not wise. What 1110 would we not give, my judges, to be able to examine the leader of the great expedition against Troy, or Odysseus, or Sisyphus, or countless other men and women whom we could name? It would be an infinite happiness to discuss with them and to live with them and to examine them. Assuredly there they do not put men to death for doing that. For besides the other ways in which they are happier than we are, they are immortal, at least if what we are told is true.

And you, too, judges, must face death hopefully, and 1120 believe this as a truth that no evil can happen to a good man, either in life or after death. His fortunes are not neglected by the gods; and what has happened to me today has not happened by chance. I am persuaded that it was better for me to die now, and to be released from trouble; and that was the reason why the sign never turned me back. And so I am not at all angry with my accusers or with those who have condemned me to die. Yet it was not with this in mind that they accused me and condemned me, but meaning to do me an injury. So 1130 far I may blame them.

Yet I have one request to make of them. When my sons grow up, punish them, my friends, and harass them in the same way that I have harassed you, if they seem to you to care for riches or for any other thing more than virtue; and if they think that they are something when they are really nothing, reproach them, as I have reproached you, for not caring for what they should, and for thinking that they are something when really they are nothing. And if you will do this, I myself 1140 and my sons will have received justice from you.

But now the time has come, and we must go away—I to die, and you to live. Which is better is known to god alone.

---

14. Of Persia.

STUDY QUESTIONS

1. The so-called offenses of Socrates were, as mentioned in the text, committed under the old democracy. An amnesty (the Act of Oblivion) forbade any reference to the past, and this set up a tension of unspoken thoughts throughout the trial. The charge of "corruption of the young" was therefore particularly weak, but one can detect its origins by carefully analyzing the defense. What are some examples of Socrates' oblique references to his past actions.
2. Another charge—that of not respecting the gods—was equally vague. What are some of the indications that Meletus, or anyone else, did not know what "impiety" really meant? To what extent was the charge a cover-up for public resentment of Socrates' attacks upon traditional morality and conventional behavior? What, in essence, were the *real* charges and why was Socrates such a problem for the new democracy?
3. Socrates could have saved his life by paying a moderate fine. Why didn't he do this? Paying a fine implies what?
4. Refusing to pay a reasonable rather than a token fine is one thing, but proposing lifetime maintenance at public expense is another matter. Why did Socrates antagonize the court with this proposal? Was he serious?
5. Do you think Socrates would have taken this uncompromising position had he been, say, twenty years younger?

LITERARY SELECTION 9

Republic

Plato

The *Republic* is discussed on pages 157–9. At this point in the dialogue the conversation is mainly between the narrator, Socrates, and Plato's brother, Glaucon. The translation is by F. M. Cornford.

Book IV

For the moment, we had better finish the inquiry which we began with the idea that it would be easier to make out the nature of justice in the individual if we first tried to study it in something on a larger scale. That larger thing we took to be a state, and so we set about constructing the best one we could, being sure of finding justice in a state that was good. The discovery we made there must now be applied to the individual. If it is confirmed, all will be well; but if we find that justice in the individual is something different, we must go back to the state and test our new result. Perhaps if we brought the two cases into contact like flint and steel, we might strike out between them the spark of justice, and in its light confirm the conception in our own minds.

A good method. Let us follow it.

Now, I continued, if two things, one large, the other small, are called by the same name, they will be alike in that respect to which the common name applies. Accordingly, in so far as the quality of justice is concerned, there will be no difference between a just man and a just society.

No.

Well, but we decided that a society was just when each of the three types of human character it contained performed its own function; and again, it was temperate and brave and wise by virtue of certain other affections and states of mind of those same types.

True.

Accordingly, my friend, if we are to be justified in attributing those same virtues to the individual, we shall expect to find that the individual soul contains the same three elements and that they are affected in the same way as are the corresponding types in society.

That follows.

Here, then, we have stumbled upon another little problem: Does the soul contain these three elements or not?

Not such a very little one, I think. It may be a true saying, Socrates, that what is worth while is seldom easy.

Apparently; and let me tell you, Glaucon, it is my belief that we shall never reach the exact truth in this matter by following our present methods of discussion; the road leading to that goal is longer and more laborious. However, perhaps we can find an answer that will be up to the standard we have so far maintained in our speculations.

Is not that enough? I should be satisfied for the moment.

Well, it will more than satisfy me.

Don't be disheartened, then, but go on.

Surely, we must admit that the same elements and characters that appear in the state must exist in every one of us; where else could they have come from? It would be absurd to imagine that among peoples with a reputation for a high-spirited character, like the Thracians and Scythians and northerners generally, the states have not derived that character from their individual members; or that it is otherwise with the love of knowledge, which would be ascribed chiefly to our own part of the world, or with the love of money, which one would specially connect with Phoenicia and Egypt.

Certainly.

So far, then, we have a fact which is easily recognized. But here the difficulty begins. Are we using the same part of ourselves in all these three experiences, or a different part in each? Do we gain knowledge with one part, feel anger with another, and with yet a third desire the pleasures of food, sex, and so on? Or is the whole soul at work in every impulse and in all these forms of behaviour? The difficulty is to answer that question satisfactorily.

I quite agree.

Let us approach the problem whether these elements are distinct or identical in this way. It is clear that the same thing cannot act in two opposite ways or be in two opposite states at the same time, with respect to the same part of itself, and in relation to the same object. So if we find such contradictory actions or states among the elements concerned, we shall know that more than one must have been involved.

Very well.

Consider this proposition of mine, then. Can the same thing, at the same time and with respect to the same part of itself, be at rest and in motion?

Certainly not.

We had better state this principle in still more precise terms, to guard against misunderstanding later on. Suppose a man is standing still, but moving his head and arms. We should not allow anyone to say that the same man was both at rest and in motion at the same time, but only that part of him was at rest, part in motion. Isn't that so?

Yes.

An ingenious objector might refine still further and argue that a peg-top, spinning with its peg fixed at the same spot, or indeed any body that revolves in the same place, is both at rest and in motion as a whole. But we should not agree, because the parts in respect of which such a body is moving and at rest are not the same. It contains an axis and a circumference; and in respect of the axis it is at rest inasmuch as the axis is not inclined in any direction, while in respect of the circumference it revolves; and if, while it is spinning, the axis does lean out of the perpendicular in all directions, then it is in no way at rest.

That is true.

No objection of that sort, then, will disconcert us or make us believe that the same thing can ever act or be acted upon in two opposite ways, or be two opposite things, at the same time, in respect of the same part of itself, and in relation to the same object.

I can answer for myself at any rate.

Well, anyhow, as we do not want to spend time in reviewing all such objections to make sure that they are unsound, let us proceed on this assumption, with the understanding that, if we ever come to think otherwise, all the consequences based upon it will fall to the ground.

Yes, that is a good plan.

Now, would you class such things as assent and dissent, striving after something and refusing it, attraction and repulsion, as pairs of opposite actions or states of mind—no matter which?

Yes, they are opposites.

And would you not class all appetites such as hunger and thirst, and again willing and wishing, with the affirmative members of those pairs I have just mentioned? For instance, you would say that the soul of a man who desires something is striving after it, or trying to draw to itself the thing it wishes to possess, or again, in so far as it is willing to have its want satisfied, it is giving its assent to its own longing, as if to an inward question.

Yes.

And, on the other hand, disinclination, unwillingness, and dislike, we should class on the negative side with acts of rejection or repulsion.

Of course.

That being so, shall we say that appetites form one class, the most conspicuous being those we call thirst and hunger?   140

Yes.

Thirst being desire for drink, hunger for food?

Yes.

Now, is thirst, just in so far as it is thirst, a desire in the soul for anything more than simply drink? Is it, for instance, thirst for hot drink or for cold, for much drink or for little, or in a word for drink of any particular kind? Is it not rather true that you will have a desire for cold drink   150 only if you are feeling hot as well as thirsty, and for hot drink only if you are feeling cold; and if you want much drink or little, that will be because your thirst is a great thirst or a little one? But, just in itself, thirst or hunger is a desire for nothing more than its natural object, drink or food, pure and simple.

Yes, he agreed, each desire, just in itself, is simply for its own natural object. When the object is of such and such a particular kind, the desire will be correspondingly qualified.[15]   160

We must be careful here, or we might be troubled by the objection that no one desires mere food and drink, but always wholesome food and drink. We shall be told that what we desire is always something that is good; so if thirst is a desire, its object must be, like that of any other desire, something—drink or whatever it may be—that will be good for one.[16]

Yes, there might seem to be something in that objection.

But surely, wherever you have two correlative terms,   170 if one is qualified, the other must always be qualified too; whereas if one is unqualified, so is the other.

I don't understand.

Well, "greater" is a relative term; and the greater is greater than the less; if it is much greater, then the less is much less; if it is greater at some moment, past or future, then the less is less at that same moment. The

same principle applies to all such correlatives, like "more" and "fewer," "double" and "half"; and again to terms like "heavier" and "lighter," "quicker" and   180 "slower," and to things like hot and cold.

Yes.

Or take the various branches of knowledge: is it not the same there? The object of knowledge pure and simple is the knowable—if that is the right word—without any qualification; whereas a particular kind of knowledge has an object of a particular kind. For example, as soon as men learnt how to build houses, their craft was distinguished from others under the name of architecture, because it had a unique character,   190 which was itself due to the character of its object; and all other branches of craft and knowledge were distinguished in the same way.

True.

This, then, if you understand me now, is what I meant by saying that, where there are two correlatives, the one is qualified if, and only if, the other is so. I am not saying that the one must have the same quality as the other—that the science of health and disease is itself healthy and diseased, or the knowledge of good   200 and evil is itself good and evil—but only that, as soon as you have a knowledge that is restricted to a particular kind of object, namely health and disease, the knowledge itself becomes a particular kind of knowledge. Hence we no longer call it merely knowledge, which would have for its object whatever can be known, but we add the qualification and call it medical science.

I understand now and I agree.

Now, to go back to thirst: is not that one of these   210 relative terms? It is essentially thirst for something.

Yes, for drink.

And if the drink desired is of a certain kind, the thirst will be correspondingly qualified. But thirst which is just simply thirst is not for drink of any particular sort—much or little, good or bad—but for drink pure and simple.

Quite so.

We conclude, then, that the soul of a thirsty man, just in so far as he is thirsty, has no other wish than to drink. That is the object of its craving, and towards that it is   220 impelled.

That is clear.

Now if there is ever something which at the same time pulls it the opposite way, that something must be an element in the soul other than the one which is thirsting and driving it like a beast to drink; in accordance with our principle that the same thing cannot behave in two opposite ways at the same time and towards the same object with the same part of itself. It is like an archer drawing the bow: it is not accurate to say that his   230 hands are at the same time both pushing and pulling it. One hand does the pushing, the other the pulling.

Exactly.

Now, is it sometimes true that people are thirsty and yet unwilling to drink?

Yes, often.

What, then, can one say of them, if not that their soul contains something which urges them to drink and

---

15. The object of the following subtle argument about relative terms is to distinguish thirst as a mere blind craving for drink from a more complex desire whose object includes the pleasure or health expected to result from drinking. We thus forestall the objection that all desires have "the good" (apparent or real) for their object and include an intellectual or rational element, so that the conflict of motives might be reduced to an intellectual debate, in the same "part" of the soul, on the comparative values of two incompatible ends.

16. If this objection were admitted, it would follow that the desire would always be correspondingly qualified. It is necessary to insist that we do experience blind cravings which can be isolated from any judgment about the goodness of their object.

something which holds them back, and that this latter is a distinct thing and overpowers the other?   240

I agree.

And is it not true that the intervention of this inhibiting principle in such cases always has its origin in reflection; whereas the impulses driving and dragging the soul are engendered by external influences and abnormal conditions.[17]

Evidently.

We shall have good reason, then, to assert that they are two distinct principles. We may call that part of the soul whereby it reflects, rational; and the other, with   250 which it feels hunger and thirst and is distracted by sexual passion and all the other desires, we will call irrational appetite, associated with pleasure in the replenishment of certain wants.

Yes, there is good ground for that view.

Let us take it, then, that we have now distinguished two elements in the soul. What of that passionate element which makes us feel angry and indignant? Is that a third, or identical in nature with one of those two?

It might perhaps be identified with appetite.   260

I am more inclined to put my faith in a story I once heard about Leontius, son of Aglaion. On his way up from the Piraeus outside the north wall, he noticed the bodies of some criminals lying on the ground, with the executioner standing by them. He wanted to go and look at them, but at the same time he was disgusted and tried to turn away. He struggled for some time and covered his eyes, but at last the desire was too much for him. Opening his eyes wide, he ran up to the bodies and cried, "There you are, curse you; feast yourselves on   270 this lovely sight!"

Yes, I have heard that story too.

The point of it surely is that anger is sometimes in conflict with appetite, as if they were two distinct principles. Do we not often find a man whose desires would force him to go against his reason, reviling himself and indignant with this part of his nature which is trying to put constraint on him? It is like a struggle between two factions, in which indignation takes the side of reason. But I believe you have never observed, in   280 yourself or anyone else, indignation make common cause with appetite in behaviour which reason decides to be wrong.

No, I am sure I have not.

Again, take a man who feels he is in the wrong. The more generous his nature, the less can he be indignant at any suffering, such as hunger and cold, inflicted by the man he has injured. He recognizes such treatment as just, and, as I say, his spirit refuses to be roused against it.   290

This is true.

17. Some of the most intense bodily desires are due to morbid conditions, e.g. thirst in fever, and even milder desires are caused by a departure from the normal state, which demands "replenishment."

18. The question whether wisdom rules in the person of one person or of several is unimportant. In the sequel the ideal constitution is called kingship or aristocracy (the rule of the best) indifferently.

But now contrast one who thinks it is he that is being wronged. His spirit boils with resentment and sides with the right as he conceives it. Persevering all the more for the hunger and cold and other pains he suffers, it triumphs and will not give in until its gallant struggle has ended in success or death; or until the restraining voice of reason, like a shepherd calling off his dog, makes it relent.

An apt comparison, he said; and in fact it fits the   300 relation of our Auxiliaries to the Rulers: they were to be like watch-dogs obeying the shepherds of the commonwealth.

Yes, you understand very well what I have in mind. But do you see how we have changed our view? A moment ago we were supposing this spirited element to be something of the nature of appetite; but now it appears that, when the soul is divided into factions, it is far more ready to be up in arms on the side of reason.

Quite true.   310

Is it, then, distinct from the rational element or only a particular form of it, so that the soul will contain no more than two elements, reason and appetite? Or is the soul like the state, which had three orders to hold it together, traders, Auxiliaries, and counsellors? Does the spirited element make a third, the natural auxiliary of reason, when not corrupted by bad upbringing?

It must be a third.

Yes, I said, provided it can be shown to be distinct for reason, as we saw it was from appetite.   320

That is easily proved. You can see that much in children: they are full of passionate feelings from their very birth; but some, I should say, never become rational, and most of them only late in life.

A very sound observation, said I, the truth of which may also be seen in animals. And besides, there is the witness of Homer in that line I quoted before: "He smote his breast and spoke, chiding his heart." The poet is plainly thinking of the two elements as distinct, when he makes the one which has chosen the better course   330 after reflection rebuke the other for its unreasoning passion.

I entirely agree.

The Equality of Women

What I see is that, whereas there is only one form of excellence, imperfection exists in innumerable shapes, of which there are four that specially deserve notice.

What do you mean?

It looks as if there were as many types of character as there are distinct varieties of political constitution.

How many?   340

Five of each.

Will you define them?

Yes, I said. One form of constitution will be the form we have been describing, though it may be called by two names: monarchy, when there is one man who stands out above the rest of the Rulers; aristocracy, when there are more than one.[18]

True.

That, then, I regard as a single form; for, so long as

they observe our principles of upbringing and education, whether the Rulers be one or more, they will not subvert the important institutions in our commonwealth.

Naturally not.

Such, then, is the type of state or constitution that I call good and right, and the corresponding type of man. By this standard, the other forms in which a state or an individual character may be organized are depraved and wrong. There are four of these vicious forms.

What are they?

Here I was going on to describe these forms in the order in which, as I thought, they develop one from another, when Polemarchus, who was sitting a little way from Adeimantus, reached out his hand and took hold of his garment by the shoulder. Leaning forward and drawing Adeimantus towards him, he whispered something in his ear, of which I only caught the words: What shall we do? Shall we leave it alone?

Certainly not, said Adeimantus, raising his voice.

What is this, I asked, that you are not going to leave alone?

You, he replied.

Why, in particular? I inquired.

Because we think you are shirking the discussion of a very important part of the subject and trying to cheat us out of an explanation. Everyone, you said, must of course see that the maxim "friends have all things in common" applies to women and children. You thought we should pass over such a casual remark!

But wasn't that right, Adeimantus? said I.

Yes, he said, but "right" in this case, as in others, needs to be defined. There may be many ways of having things in common, and you must tell us which you mean. We have been waiting a long time for you to say something about the conditions in which children are to be born and brought up and your whole plan of having wives and children held in common. This seems to us a matter in which right or wrong management will make all the difference to society; and now, instead of going into it thoroughly, you are passing on to some other form of constitution. So we came to the resolution which you overheard, not to let you off discussing it as fully as all the other institutions.

I will vote for your resolution too, said Glaucon.

In fact, Socrates, Thrasymachus added, you may take it as carried unanimously.

You don't know what you are doing, I said, in holding me up like this. You want to start, all over again, on an enormous subject, just as I was rejoicing at the idea that we had done with this form of constitution. I was only too glad that my casual remark should be allowed to pass. And now, when you demand an explanation, you little know what a swarm of questions you are stirring up. I let it alone, because I foresaw no end of trouble.

Well, said Thrasymachus, what do you think we came here for—to play pitch-and-toss or to listen to a discussion?

A discussion, no doubt, I replied; but within limits.

No man of sense, said Glaucon, would think the whole of life too long to spend on questions of this importance. But never mind about us; don't be faint-

hearted yourself. Tell us what you think about this question: how our Guardians are to have wives and children in common, and how they will bring up the young in the interval between their birth and education, which is thought to be the most difficult time of all. Do try to explain how all this is to be arranged.

I wish it were as easy as you seem to think, I replied. These arrangements are even more open to doubt than any we have so far discussed. It may be questioned whether the plan is feasible, and even if entirely feasible, whether it would be for the best. So I have some hesitation in touching on what may seem to be an idle dream.

You need not hesitate, he replied. This is not an unsympathetic audience; we are neither incredulous nor hostile.

Thank you, I said; I suppose that remark is meant to be encouraging.

Certainly it is.

Well, I said, it has just the opposite effect. You would do well to encourage me, if I had any faith in my own understanding of these matters. If one knows the truth, there is no risk to be feared in speaking about the things one has most at heart among intelligent friends; but if one is still in the position of a doubting inquirer, as I am now, talking becomes a slippery venture. Not that I am afraid of being laughed at—that would be childish—but I am afraid I may miss my footing just where a false step is most to be dreaded and drag my friends down with me in my fall. I devoutly hope, Glaucon, that no nemesis will overtake me for what I am going to say; for I really believe that to kill a man unintentionally is a lighter offense than to mislead him concerning the goodness and justice of social institutions. Better to run that risk among enemies than among friends; so your encouragement is out of place.

Glaucon laughed at this. No, Socrates, he said, if your theory has any untoward effect on us, our blood shall not be on your head; we absolve you of any intention to mislead us. So have no fear.

Well, said I, when a homicide is absolved of all intention, the law holds him clear of guilt; and the same principle may apply to my case.

Yes, so far as that goes, you may speak freely.

We must go back, then, to a subject which ought, perhaps, to have been treated earlier in its proper place; though, after all, it may be suitable that the women should have their turn on the stage when the men have quite finished their performance, especially since you are so insistent. In my judgment, then, the question under what conditions people born and educated as we have described should possess wives and children, and how they should treat them, can be rightly settled only by keeping to the course on which we started them at the outset. We undertook to put these men in the position of watch-dogs guarding a flock. Suppose we follow up the analogy and imagine them bred and reared in the same sort of way. We can then see if that plan will suit our purpose.

How will that be?

In this way. Which do we think right for watch-dogs:

should the females guard the flock and hunt with the males and take a share in all they do, or should they be kept within doors as fit for no more than bearing and feeding their puppies, while all the hard work of looking after the flock is left to the males?

They are expected to take their full share, except that we treat them as not quite so strong.

Can you employ any creature for the same work as another, if you do not give them both the same upbringing and education?   480

No.

Then, if we are to set women to the same tasks as men, we must teach them the same things. They must have the same two branches of training for mind and body and also be taught the art of war, and they must receive the same treatment.

That seems to follow.

Possibly, if these proposals were carried out, they might be ridiculed as involving a good many breaches of custom.   490

They might indeed.

The most ridiculous—don't you think?—being the notion of women exercising naked along with the men in the wrestling-schools; some of them elderly women too, like the old men who still have a passion for exercise when they are wrinkled and not very agreeable to look at.

Yes, that would be thought laughable, according to our present notions.   500

Now we have started on this subject, we must not be frightened of the many witticisms that might be aimed at such a revolution, not only in the matter of bodily exercise but in the training of women's minds, and not least when it comes to their bearing arms and riding on horseback. Having begun upon these rules, we must not draw back from the harsher provisions. The wits may be asked to stop being witty and try to be serious; and we may remind them that it is not so long since the Greeks, like most foreign nations of the present day, thought it ridiculous and shameful for men to be seen naked.   510
When gymnastic exercises were first introduced in Crete and later at Sparta, the humorists had their chance to make fun of them; but when experience had shown that nakedness is better uncovered than muffled up, the laughter died down and a practice which the reason approved ceased to look ridiculous to the eye. This shows how idle it is to think anything ludicrous but what is base. One who tries to raise a laugh at any spectacle save that of baseness and folly will also, in his serious   520
moments, set before himself some other standard than goodness of what deserves to be held in honour.

Most assuredly.

The first thing to be settled, then, is whether these proposals are feasible; and it must be open to anyone, whether a humorist or serious-minded, to raise the question whether, in the case of mankind, the feminine nature is capable of taking part with the other sex in all occupations, or in none at all, or in some only; and in particular under which of these heads this business of   530
military service falls. Well begun is half done, and would not this be the best way to begin?

Yes.

Shall we take the other side in this debate and argue against ourselves? We do not want the adversary's position to be taken by storm for lack of defenders.

I have no objection.

Let us state his case for him. "Socrates and Glaucon," he will say, "there is no need for others to dispute your position; you yourselves, at the very outset   540
of founding your commonwealth, agreed that everyone should do the one work for which nature fits him." Yes, of course; I suppose we did. "And isn't there a very great difference in nature between man and woman?" Yes, surely." Does not that natural difference imply a corresponding difference in the work to be given to each?" Yes. "But if so, surely you must be mistaken now and contradicting yourselves when you say that men and women, having such widely divergent natures, should do the same things?" What is your answer to   550
that, my ingenious friend?

It is not easy to find one at the moment. I can only appeal to you to state the case on our own side, whatever it may be.

This, Glaucon, is one of many alarming objections which I foresaw some time ago. That is why I shrank from touching upon these laws concerning the possession of wives and the rearing of children.

It looks like anything but an easy problem.

True, I said; but whether a man tumbles into a   560
swimming-pool or into mid-ocean, he has to swim all the same. So must we, and try if we can reach the shore, hoping for some Arion's dolphin or other miraculous deliverance to bring us safe to land.[19]

I suppose so.

Come then, let us see if we can find the way out. We did agree that different natures should have different occupations, and that the natures of man and woman are different; and yet we are now saying that these different natures are to have the same occupations. Is   570
that the charge against us?

Exactly.

It is extraordinary, Glaucon, what an effect the practice of debating has upon people.

Why do you say that?

Because they often seem to fall unconsciously into mere disputes which they mistake for reasonable argument, through being unable to draw the distinctions proper to their subject; and so, instead of a philosophical exchange of ideas, they go off in chase of contradictions   580
which are purely verbal.

I know that happens to many people; but does it apply to us at this moment?

Absolutely. At least I am afraid we are slipping unconsciously into a dispute about words. We have been strenuously insisting on the letter of our principle that different natures should not have the same occupations, as if we were scoring a point in a debate; but we have altogether neglected to consider what sort

---

19. The musician Arion leaped into the sea to escape the treachery of Corinthian sailors and was carried ashore at Taenarum by a dolphin.

of sameness or difference we meant and in what respect these natures and occupations were to be defined as different or the same. Consequently, we might very well be asking one another whether there is not an opposition in nature between bald and long-haired men, and, when that was admitted, forbid one set to be shoemakers, if the other were following that trade.

That would be absurd.

Yes, but only because we never meant any and every sort of sameness or difference in nature, but the sort that was relevant to the occupations in question. We meant, for instance, that a man and a woman have the same nature if both have a talent for medicine; whereas two men have different natures if one is a born physician, the other a born carpenter.

Yes, of course.

If, then, we find that either the male sex or the female is specially qualified for any particular form of occupation, then that occupation, we shall say, ought to be assigned to one sex or the other. But if the only difference appears to be that the male begets and the female brings forth, we shall conclude that no difference between man and woman has yet been produced that is relevant to our purpose. We shall continue to think it proper for our Guardians and their wives to share in the same pursuits.

And quite rightly.

The next thing will be to ask our opponent to name any profession or occupation in civic life for the purposes of which woman's nature is different from man's.

That is a fair question.

He might reply, as you did just now, that it is not easy to find a satisfactory answer on the spur of the moment, but that there would be no difficulty after a little reflection.

Perhaps.

Suppose, then, we invite him to follow us and see if we can convince him that there is no occupation concerned with the management of social affairs that is peculiar to women. We will confront him with a question: When you speak of a man having a natural talent for something, do you mean that he finds it easy to learn, and after a little instruction can find out much more for himself; whereas a man who is not so gifted learns with difficulty and no amount of instruction and practice will make him even remember what he has been taught? Is the talented man one whose bodily powers are readily at the service of his mind, instead of being a hindrance? Are not these the marks by which you distinguish the presence of a natural gift for any pursuit?

Yes, precisely.

Now do you know of any human occupation in which the male sex is not superior to the female in all these respects? Need I waste time over exceptions like weaving and watching over saucepans and batches of cakes, though women are supposed to be good at such things and get laughed at when a man does them better?

It is true, he replied, in almost everything one sex is easily beaten by the other. No doubt many women are better at many things than many men; but taking the sexes as a whole, it is as you say.

To conclude, then, there is no occupation concerned with the management of social affairs which belongs either to woman or to man, as such. Natural gifts are to be found here and there in both creatures alike; and every occupation is open to both, so far as their natures are concerned, though woman is for all purposes the weaker.

Certainly.

Is that a reason for making over all occupations to men only?

Of course not.

No, because one woman may have a natural gift for medicine or for music, another may not.

Surely.

Is it not also true that a woman may, or may not, be warlike or athletic?

I think so.

And again, one may love knowledge, another hate it; one may be high-spirited, another spiritless?

True again.

It follows that one woman will be fitted by nature to be a Guardian, another will not; because these were the qualities for which we selected our men Guardians. So for the purpose of keeping watch over the commonwealth, woman has the same nature as man, save in so far as she is weaker.

So it appears.

It follows that women of this type must be selected to share the life and duties of Guardians with men of the same type, since they are competent and of a like nature, and the same natures must be allowed the same pursuits.

Yes.

We come round, then, to our former position, that there is nothing contrary to nature in giving our Guardians' wives the same training for mind and body. The practice we proposed to establish was not impossible or visionary, since it was in accordance with nature. Rather, the contrary practice which now prevails turns out to be unnatural.

So it appears.

Well, we set out to inquire whether the plan we proposed was feasible and also the best. That it is feasible is now agreed; we must next settle whether it is the best.

Obviously.

Now, for the purpose of producing a woman fit to be a Guardian, we shall not have one education for men and another for women, precisely because the nature to be taken in hand is the same.

True.

What is your opinion on the question of one man being better than another? Do you think there is no such difference?

Certainly I do not.

And in this commonwealth of ours which will prove the better men—the Guardians who have received the education we described, or the shoemakers who have been trained to make shoes?[20]

of the year and controls everything in the visible world, and moreover is in a way the cause of all that he and his companions used to see.

Clearly he would come at last to that conclusion.

Then if he called to mind his fellow prisoners and what passed for wisdom in his former dwelling-place, he would surely think himself happy in the change and be sorry for them. They may have had a practice of honouring and commending one another, with prizes for the man who had the keenest eye for the passing shadows and the best memory for the order in which they followed or accompanied one another, so that he could make a good guess as to which was going to come next. Would our released prisoner be likely to covet those prizes or to envy the men exalted to honour and power in the Cave? Would he not feel like Homer's Achilles, that he would far sooner "be on earth as a hired servant in the house of a landless man" or endure anything rather than go back to his old beliefs and live in the old way?

Yes, he would prefer any fate to such a life.

Now imagine what would happen if he went down again to take his former seat in the Cave. Coming suddenly out of the sunlight, his eyes would be filled with darkness. He might be required once more to deliver his opinion on those shadows, in competition with the prisoners who had never been released, while his eyesight was still dim and unsteady; and it might take some time to become used to the darkness. They would laugh at him and say that he had gone up only to come back with his sight ruined; it was worth no one's while even to attempt the ascent. If they could lay hands on the man who was trying to set them free and lead them up, they would kill him.[25]

Yes, they would.

Application of the Cave Allegory

Every feature in this parable, my dear Glaucon, is meant to fit our earlier analysis. The prison dwelling corresponds to the region revealed to us through the sense of sight, and the fire-light within it to the power of the Sun. The ascent to see the things in the upper world you may take as standing for the upward journey of the soul into the region of the intelligible; then you will be in possession of what I surmise, since that is what you wish to be told. Heaven knows whether it is true; but this, at any rate, is how it appears to me. In the world of knowledge, the last thing to be perceived and only with great difficulty is the essential Form of Goodness. Once it is perceived, the conclusion must follow that, for all things, this is the cause of whatever is right and good; in the visible world it gives birth to light and to the lord of light, while it is itself sovereign in the intelligible world and the parent of intelligence and truth. Without having had a vision of this Form no one can act with wisdom, either in his own life or in matters of state.

So far as I can understand, I share your belief.

Then you may also agree that it is no wonder if those who have reached this height are reluctant to manage the affairs of men. Their souls long to spend all their time in that upper world—naturally enough, if here once more our parable holds true. Nor, again, is it at all strange that one who comes from the contemplation of divine things to the miseries of human life should appear awkward and ridiculous when, with eyes still dazed and not yet accustomed to the darkness, he is compelled, in a law-court or elsewhere, to dispute about the shadows of justice or the images that cast those shadows, and to wrangle over the notions of what is right in the minds of men who have never beheld Justice itself.

It is not at all strange.

No; a sensible man will remember that the eyes may be confused in two ways—by a change from light to darkness or from darkness to light; and he will recognize that the same thing happens to the soul. When he sees it troubled and unable to discern anything clearly, instead of laughing thoughtlessly, he will ask whether, coming from a brighter existence, its unaccustomed vision is obscured by the darkness, in which case he will think its condition enviable and its life a happy one; or whether, emerging from the depths of ignorance, it is dazzled by excess of light. If so, he will rather feel sorry for it; or, if he were inclined to laugh, that would be less ridiculous than to laugh at the soul which has come down from the light.

That is a fair statement.

If this is true, then, we must conclude that education is not what it is said to be by some, who profess to put knowledge into a soul which does not possess it, as if they could put sight into blind eyes. On the contrary, our own account signifies that the soul of every man does possess the power of learning the truth and the organ to see it with; and that, just as one might have to turn the whole body round in order that the eye should see light instead of darkness, so the entire soul must be turned away from this changing world, until its eye can bear to contemplate reality and that supreme splendour which we have called the Good. Hence there may well be an art whose aim would be to effect this very thing, the conversion of the soul, in the readiest way; not to put the power of sight into the soul's eye, which already has it, but to ensure that, instead of looking in the wrong direction, it is turned the way it ought to be.

Yes, it may well be so.

It looks, then, as though wisdom were different from those ordinary virtues, as they are called, which are not far removed from bodily qualities, in that they can be produced by habituation and exercise in a soul which has not possessed them from the first. Wisdom, it seems, is certainly the virtue of some diviner faculty, which never loses its power, though its use for good or harm depends on the direction towards which it is turned. You must have noticed in dishonest men with a reputation for sagacity the shrewd glance of a narrow intelligence piercing the objects to which it is directed. There is nothing wrong with their power of vision, but it has been forced into the service of evil, so that the keener its sight, the more harm it works.

---

25. An allusion to the fate of Socrates.

Quite true. 210

And yet if the growth of a nature like this had been pruned from earliest childhood, cleared of those clinging overgrowths which come of gluttony and all luxurious pleasure and, like leaden weights charged with affinity to this mortal world, hang upon the soul, bending its vision downwards; if, freed from these, the soul were turned round towards true reality, then this same power in these very men would see the truth as keenly as the objects it is turned to now.

Yes, very likely. 220

Is it not also likely, or indeed certain after what has been said, that a state can never be properly governed either by the uneducated who know nothing of truth or by men who are allowed to spend all their days in the pursuit of culture? The ignorant have no single mark before their eyes at which they must aim in all the conduct of their own lives and of affairs of state; and the others will not engage in action if they can help it, dreaming that, while still alive, they have been translated to the Islands of the Blest. 230

Quite true.

It is for us, then, as founders of a commonwealth, to bring compulsion to bear on the noblest natures. They must be made to climb the ascent to the vision of Goodness, which we called the highest object of knowledge; and, when they have looked upon it long enough, they must not be allowed, as they now are, to remain on the heights, refusing to come down again to the prisoners or to take any part in their labours and rewards, however much or little these may be worth. 240

Shall we not be doing them an injustice, if we force on them a worse life than they might have?

You have forgotten again, my friend, that the law is not concerned to make any one class specially happy, but to ensure the welfare of the commonwealth as a whole. By persuasion or constraint it will unite the citizens in harmony, making them share whatever benefits each class can contribute to the common good; and its purpose in forming men of that spirit was not that each should be left to go his own way, but that they 250 should be instrumental in binding the community into one.

True, I had forgotten.

You will see, then, Glaucon, that there will be no real injustice in compelling our philosophers to watch over and care for the other citizens. We can fairly tell them that their compeers in others states may quite reasonably refuse to collaborate: there they have sprung up, like a self-sown plant, in despite of their country's institutions; no one has fostered their growth, and they 260 cannot be expected to show gratitude for a care they have never received. "But," we shall say, "it is not so with you. We have brought you into existence for your country's sake as well as for your own, to be like leaders and king-bees in a hive; you have been better and more thoroughly educated than those others and hence you are more capable of playing your part both as men of thought and as men of action. You must go down, then, each in his turn, to live with the rest and let your eyes grow accustomed to the darkness. You will then see a 270

thousand times better than those who live there always; you will recognize every image for what it is and know what it represents, because you have seen justice, beauty, and goodness in their reality; and so you and we shall find life in our commonwealth no mere dream, as it is in most existing states, where men live fighting one another about shadows and quarrelling for power, as if that were a great prize; whereas in truth government can be at its best and free from dissension only where the destined rulers are least desirous of holding office." 280

Quite true.

Then will our pupils refuse to listen and to take their turns at sharing in the work of the community, though they may live together for most of their time in a purer air?

No; it is a fair demand, and they are fair-minded men. No doubt, unlike any ruler of the present day, they will think of holding power as an unavoidable necessity.

Yes, my friend; for the truth is that you can have a well-governed society only if you can discover for your 290 future rulers a better way of life than being in office; then only will power be in the hands of men who are rich, not in gold, but in the wealth that brings happiness, a good and wise life. All goes wrong when, starved for lack of anything good in their own lives, men turn to public affairs hoping to snatch from thence the happiness they hunger for. They set about fighting for power, and this internecine conflict ruins them and their country. The life of true philosophy is the only one that looks down upon offices of state; and access to power 300 must be confined to men who are not in love with it; otherwise rivals will start fighting. So whom else can you compel to undertake the guardianship of the commonwealth, if not those who, besides understanding best the principles of government, enjoy a nobler life than the politician's and look for rewards of a different kind?

There is indeed no other choice.

STUDY QUESTIONS

1. Women in ancient Greece were generally considered inferior beings who were necessarily subordinate to men, and they are so treated in Plato's works except for the *Republic*. What changes has Plato made in his ideal state that give women equality and equal opportunity to become guardians and philosopher-kings? What does this imply in terms of equal opportunity for today's women?

2. Are Plato's arguments for the equality of women convincing? Would they be persuasive today? How might leaders of NOW (National Organization for Women) state the issues?

3. How would the state function "if philosophers were kings"? What might the problems be? How might they be resolved?

4. In the history of Western civilization have there been any philosopher-kings? Who were they? To what extent were they selfless, wise, virtuous, and, most important, successful?

5. One way to visualize the situation in "The Allegory of the Cave" is to think of people chained in a movie theatre with everyone facing the screen. In the allegory the pictures on the screen are the world of which our senses are aware. "Reality" is the series of moving images on the screen, complete with soundtrack, and the highest reality is the light that projects the images. Another, more depressing situation, would be people chained in front of a television set in which the highest reality would be ABC, CBS, or NBC. Given, say, CBS as the ultimate reality, what would be the implications? To what extent does Plato's allegory apply to life in the electronic age?

6. In "The Allegory of the Cave," why does Plato insist that the one who has come to know the true light must return to the cave, that he or she must partake of the labors and honors of the people in the cave, though these are recognized as foolish?

7. Early in the dialogue Plato wrote that "Mankind censure injustice fearing that they may be the victims of it, and not because they shrink from committing it." Is this generally true? Was Plato being cynical or realistic—or both?

LITERARY SELECTION 10

Poetics

Aristotle (384–322 BC)

Aristotle's *Poetics* is a critical examination of the nature of art and what constitutes good art. Specifically, the treatise is directed to the problems of poetry in the writing of tragedy, which Aristotle feels is the highest form of art. With no word for fine art, the Greek term for art is *techne*, which also translates as "craft" or "skill." Art is therefore the "making" of a thing, which in its highest form is crafted with exceptional skill. The *Poetics* is the first clear statement in the history of **aesthetics** correlating the experience of a work of art with the skill of making the work itself.

For Aristotle, all art is an imitation of nature, and tragedy is

the imitation of an action that is serious and also, as having magnitude, complete in itself; in language with

pleasurable accessories, each kind brought in separately in the parts of the work; in a dramatic, not a narrative form; with incidents arousing pity and fear, wherewith to accomplish a catharsis of such emotions.

The theoretical perfect plot of a tragedy must have a single issue, which should be resolved within a twenty-four-hour day. Further, a good man will be reduced from happiness to misery because of some great error on his part, his so-called "fatal flaw."

The six elements of a tragedy are:

Plot (fable). The action—what happens.
Character. Moral qualities of the agents.
Diction. Metrical structure of the poetry as revealed in speech, recitation, chant, or song.
Thought. Implied themes and theses (universal truths) as exposed by all the elements together.
Spectacle. The stage appearance of set, costumes, movement, dance.
Melody. Aristotle takes this for granted, saying that it is "too completely understood to require explanation."
Melody refers to tunes played on the aulos (see p. 90) and the musical reciting, chanting, and singing of the actors and Chorus. With the statement that "melody is the greatest of the pleasurable accessories of tragedy," Aristotle acknowledges the sensual elements of drama.

The *Poetics* ends with the discussion of tragedy, although Aristotle had earlier said that he would also deal with comedy and other kinds of poetry. Even as an incomplete work, this has been among the most influential of Aristotle's treatises. The abridged translation is by S. H. Butcher.

Tragedy—as also Comedy—was at first mere improvisation. The one originated with the authors of the Dithyramb, the other with those of the phallic songs, which are still in use in many of our cities. Tragedy advanced by slow degrees; each new element that showed itself was in turn developed. Having passed through many changes, it found its natural form, and there it stopped. Aeschylus first introduced a second actor; he diminished the importance of the Chorus, and assigned the leading part to the dialogue. Sophocles   10
raised the number of actors to three, and added scene-painting. Moreover, it was not until late that the short plot was discarded for one of greater compass, and the grotesque diction of the earlier satyric form for the stately manner of tragedy. The iambic measure then replaced the trochaic tetrameter, which was originally employed when the poetry was of the satyric order and had more dancing. Once dialogue had come in, Nature herself discovered the appropriate measure. For the iambic is, of all measures, the most colloquial; we see it   20
in the fact that conversational speech runs into iambic lines more frequently than into any other kind of verse; rarely into hexameters, and only when we drop the colloquial intonation.

Comedy is an imitation of characters of a lower

type—not, however, in the full sense of the word bad, the ludicrous being merely a subdivision of the ugly. It consists in some defect or ugliness which is not painful or destructive. To take an obvious example, the comic mask is ugly and distorted, but does not imply pain. 30

The successive changes through which Tragedy passed, and the authors of these changes are well known, whereas Comedy has had no history, because it was not at first treated seriously. It was late before the Archon granted a comic chorus to a poet; the performers were till then voluntary. Comedy had already taken definite shape when comic poets, distinctively so called, are heard of. Who furnished it with masks, or prologues, or increased the number of actors—these and other similar details remain unknown. 40

Epic poetry agrees with Tragedy, in so far as it is an imitation in verse of characters of a higher type. They differ in that Epic poetry admits but one kind of **meter** and is narrative in form. They differ, again in their length: for Tragedy endeavors, as far as possible, to confine itself to a single revolution of the sun, or but slightly to exceed this limit, whereas the Epic action has no limits of time. This, then, is a second point of difference; though at first the same freedom was admitted in Tragedy as in Epic poetry. 50

Of their constituents some are common to both, some peculiar to Tragedy: Whoever, therefore knows what is good or bad Tragedy, knows also about Epic poetry. All the elements of an Epic poem are found in Tragedy, but the elements of a Tragedy are not all found in the Epic poem.

Of the poetry which imitates in hexameter verse, and of Comedy, we will speak hereafter. Let us now discuss Tragedy, resuming its formal definition, as resulting from what has been already said. 60

Tragedy, then, is an imitation of an action that is serious, complete, and of a certain magnitude; in language embellished with each kind of artistic ornament, the several kinds being found in separate parts of the play; in the form of action, not of narrative; through pity and fear effecting the proper purgation of these emotions. By "language embellished," I mean language into which rhythm, "harmony," and song enter. By "the several kinds in separate parts," I mean, that some parts are rendered through the medium of 70 verse alone, others again with the aid of song.

Now as tragic imitation implies persons acting, it necessarily follows in the first place, that Spectacular equipment will be a part of Tragedy. Next, Song and Diction, for these are the media of imitation. By "Diction" I mean the mere metrical arrangement of the words: as for "Song," it is a term whose sense everyone understands.

Again, Tragedy is the imitation of an action; and an action implies personal agents, who necessarily possess 80 certain distinctive qualities both of character and thought; for it is by these that we qualify actions themselves, and these—thought and character—are the two natural causes from which actions spring, and on actions again all success or failure depends. Hence, the Plot is the imitation of the action—for by Plot I here mean the arrangement of the incidents. By Character I mean that in virtue of which we ascribe certain qualities to the agents. Thought is required wherever a statement is proved, or, it may be, a general truth enunciated. 90 Every Tragedy, therefore, must have six parts, which parts determine its quality—namely, Plot, Character, Diction, Thought, Spectacle, Song. Two of the parts constitute the medium of imitation, one the manner, and three the objects of imitation. And these complete the list. These elements have been employed, we may say, by the poets to a man; in fact, every play contains Spectacular elements as well as Character, Plot, Diction, Song, and Thought.

But most important of all is the structure of the 100 incidents. For Tragedy is an imitation, not of men, but of an action and of life, and life consists in action, and its end is a mode of action, not a quality. Now character determines men's qualities, but it is by their actions that they are happy or the reverse. Dramatic action, therefore, is not with a view to the representation of character: Character comes in as subsidiary to the actions. Hence the incidents and their plot are the end of a tragedy; and the end is the chief thing of all. Again, without action there cannot be a tragedy; there may be 110 without character. The tragedies of most of our modern poets fail in the rendering of character; and of poets in general this is often true. Again, if you string together a set of speeches expressive of character, and well finished in point of diction and thought, you will not produce the essential tragic effect nearly so well as with a play which, however deficient in these respects, yet has a plot and artistically constructed incidents. Beside which, the most powerful elements of emotional interest in Tragedy—*Peripeteia* or Reversal of the 120 Situation, and Recognition scenes—are parts of the plot. A further proof is, that novices in the art attain to finish of diction and precision of portraiture before they can construct the plot.

The plot, then, is the first principle, and, as it were, the soul of a tragedy; Character holds the second place. A similar fact is seen in painting. The most beautiful colors, laid on confusedly, will not give as much pleasure as the chalk outline of a portrait. Thus Tragedy is the imitation of an action, and of the agents mainly with a 130 view to the action.

Third in order is Thought—that is, the faculty of saying what is possible and pertinent in given circumstances. In the case of oratory, this is the function of the political art and of the art of rhetoric: and so indeed the older poets make their characters speak the language of civic life; the poets of our time, the language of the rhetoricians. Character is that which reveals moral purpose, showing what kind of things a man chooses or avoids. Speeches, therefore, which do not make this 140 manifest, or in which the speaker does not choose or avoid anything whatever, are not expressive of character. Thought, on the other hand, is found where something is proved to be or not to be, or a general maxim is enunciated.

Fourth among the elements enumerated comes Diction; by which I mean, as has been already said, the expression of the meaning in words; and its essence is the same both in verse and prose.

Of the remaining elements Song holds the chief place among the embellishments.   150

The Spectacle has, indeed, an emotional attraction of its own, but, of all the parts, it is the least artistic, and connected least with the art of poetry. For the power of Tragedy, we may be sure, is felt even apart from representation and actors. Besides, the production of spectacular effects depends more on the art of the stage machinist than on that of the poet.

These principles being established, let us now discuss the proper structure of the Plot, since this is the   160 first and most important thing in Tragedy.

Now, according to our definition, Tragedy is an imitation of an action that is complete, and whole, and of a certain magnitude; for there may be a whole that is wanting in magnitude. A whole is that which has a beginning, a middle, and an end. A beginning is that which does not itself follow anything by causal necessity, but after which something naturally is or comes to be. An end, on the contrary, is that which itself naturally follows some other thing, either by necessity,   170 or as a rule, but has nothing following it. A middle is that which follows something as some other thing follows it. A well constructed plot, therefore, must neither begin nor end at haphazard, but conform to these principles.

Again, a beautiful object, whether it be a living organism or any whole composed of parts, must not only have an orderly arrangement of parts, but must also be of a certain magnitude; for beauty depends on magnitude and order. Hence a very small animal organism cannot be beautiful; for the view of it is   180 confused, the object being seen in an almost imperceptible moment of time. Nor, again, can one of vast size be beautiful; for as the eye cannot take it all in at once, the unity and sense of the whole is lost for the spectator; as for instance if there were one a thousand miles long. As, therefore, in the case of animate bodies and organisms a certain magnitude is necessary, and a magnitude which may easily be embraced in one view; so in the plot, a certain length is necessary, and a length which can be easily embraced by the memory. The limit   190 of length in relation to dramatic competition and sensuous presentment is no part of artistic theory. For had it been the rule for a hundred tragedies to compete together, the performance would have been regulated by the water-clock—as indeed we are told was formerly done. But the limit as fixed by the nature of the drama itself is this: the greater the length, the more beautiful will the piece be by reason of its size, provided that the whole be perspicuous. And to define the matter roughly, we may say that the proper magnitude is comprised   200 within such limits, that the sequence of events, according to the law of probability or necessity, will admit of a change from bad fortune to good, or from good fortune to bad.

Unity of plot does not, as some persons think, consist in the unity of the hero. For infinitely various are the incidents in one man's life which cannot be reduced to unity; and so, too, there are many actions of one man

out of which we cannot make one action. Hence the error, as it appears, of all poets who have composed a   210 Heracleid, a Theseid, or other poems of the kind. They imagine that as Heracles was one man, the story of Heracles must also be a unity. But Homer, as in all else he is of surpassing merit, here too—whether from art or from natural genius—seems to have happily discerned the truth. In composing the *Odyssey* he did not include all the adventures of Odysseus—such as his wound on Parnassus, or his feigned madness at the mustering of the host—incidents between which there was no necessary or probable connection: but he made the   220 *Odyssey*, and likewise the *Iliad*, to center round an action that in our sense of the word is one. As therefore, in the other imitative arts, the imitation is one when the object imitated is one, so the plot, being an imitation of an action, must imitate one action, and that a whole, the structural union of the parts being such that, if any one of them is disturbed or removed, the whole will be disjointed and disturbed. For a thing whose presence or absence makes no visible difference, is not an organic part of the whole.   230

It is, moreover, evident from what has been said, that it is not the function of the poet to relate what has happened, but what may happen—what is possible according to the law of probability or necessity. The poet and the historian differ not by writing in verse or prose. The work of Herodotos might be put into verse, and it would still be a species of history, with meter no less than without it. The true difference is that one relates what has happened, the other what may happen. Poetry, therefore, is a more philosophical and a higher thing than   240 history: for poetry tends to express the universal, history the particular. By the universal I mean how a person of a certain type on occasion speaks or acts according to the law of probability or necessity; and it is this universality at which poetry aims in the names she attaches to the personages. The particular is, for example, what Alcibiades did or suffered. In Comedy this is already apparent: for here the poet first constructs the plot on the lines of probability, and then inserts characteristic names—unlike the lampooners who write about   250 particular individuals.

But tragedians still keep to real names, the reason being that what is possible is credible: what has not happened we do not at once feel sure to be possible; but what has happened is manifestly possible: otherwise it would not have happened. Still there are even some tragedies in which there are only one or two well-known names, the rest being fictitious. In others, none are well known, as in Agathon's *Antheus*, where incidents and names alike are fictitious, and yet they give none the   260 less pleasure. We must not, therefore, at all costs keep to the received legends, which are the usual subjects of Tragedy. Indeed, it would be absurd to attempt it; for even subjects that are known are known only to a few, and yet give pleasure to all. It clearly follows that the poet or "maker" should be the maker of plots rather than of verses; since he is a poet because he imitates, and what he imitates are actions. And even if he chances to take a historical subject, he is none the less a poet; for there is no reason why some events that have actually happened should not conform to the law of the probable and possible, and in virtue of that quality in them he is their poet or maker.

Tragedy is an imitation not only of complete action, but of events inspiring fear or pity. Such an effect is best produced when the events come on us by surprise; and the effect is heightened when, at the same time, they follow as cause and effect. The tragic wonder will then be greater than if they happened of themselves or by accident; for even coincidences are most striking when they have an air of design. We may instance the statue of Mitys at Argos, which fell upon his murderer while he was a spectator at a festival, and killed him. Such events seem not to be due to mere chance. Plots, therefore, constructed on these principles are necessarily the best.

Plots are either Simple or Complex, for the actions in real life, of which the plots are an imitation, obviously show a similar distinction. An action which is one and continuous in the sense above defined, I call Simple, when the change of fortune takes place without Reversal of the Situation and without Recognition.

A Complex action is one in which the change is accompanied by such Reversal, or Recognition, or by both. These last should arise from the internal structure of the plot, so that what follows should be the necessary or probable result of the preceding action. It makes all the difference whether any given event is a case of propter hoc or post hoc [Lat., "because of this," "after this"].

Reversal of the Situation is a change by which the action veers round to its opposite, subject always to our rule of probability or necessity. Thus in the *Oedipus*, the messenger comes to cheer Oedipus and free him from his alarms about his mother, but by revealing who he is, he produces the opposite effect.

Recognition, as the name indicates, is a change from ignorance to knowledge, producing love or hate between the persons destined by the poet for good or bad fortune. The best form of recognition is coincident with a Reversal of the Situation, as in the *Oedipus*.

There are indeed other forms. Even inanimate things of the most trivial kind may in a sense be objects of recognition. Again, we may recognize or discover whether a person has done a thing or not. But the recognition which is most intimately connected with the plot and action is, as we have said, the recognition of persons. This recognition, combined with Reversal, will produce either pity or fear; and actions producing these effects are those which, by our definition, Tragedy represents. Moreover, it is upon such situations that the issues of good or bad fortune will depend. Recognition, then, being between persons, it may happen that one person only is recognized by the other—when the latter is already known—or it may be necessary that the recognition should be on both sides.

Two parts, then, of the Plot—Reversal of the Situation and Recognition—turn upon surprises. A third part is the Scene of Suffering. The Scene of Suffering is a destructive or painful action, such as death on the stage, bodily agony, wounds, and the like.

As the sequel to what has already been said, we must proceed to consider what the poet should aim at, and what he should avoid, in constructing his plots; and by what means the specific effect of Tragedy will be produced.

A perfect tragedy should, as we have seen, be arranged not on the simple but on the complex plan. It should, moreover, imitate actions which excite pity and fear, this being the distinctive mark of tragic imitation. It follows plainly, in the first place, that the change of fortune presented must not be the spectacle of a virtuous man brought from prosperity to adversity: for this moves neither pity nor fear; it merely shocks us. Nor, again, that of a bad man passing from adversity to prosperity: for nothing can be more alien to the spirit of Tragedy; it possesses no single tragic quality; it neither satisfies the moral sense nor calls forth pity or fear. Nor, again, should the downfall of the utter villain be exhibited. A plot of this kind would, doubtless, satisfy the moral sense, but it would inspire neither pity nor fear; for pity is aroused by unmerited misfortune, fear by the misfortune of a man like ourselves. Such an event, therefore, will be neither pitiful nor terrible. There remains, then, the character between these two extremes—that of a man who is not eminently good and just, yet whose misfortune is brought about not by vice or depravity, but by some error or frailty. He must be one who is highly renowned and prosperous—a personage like Oedipus, Thyestes, or other illustrious men of such families.

A well-constructed plot should, therefore, be single in its issue, rather than double as some maintain. The change of fortune should be not from bad to good, but, reversely, from good to bad. It should come about as the result not of vice, but of some great error or frailty, in a character either such as we have described, or better rather than worse.

A tragedy, then, to be perfect according to the rules of art should be of this construction. Hence they are in error who censure Euripides just because he follows the principle in his plays, many of which end unhappily. It is, as we have said, the right ending. The best proof is that on the stage and in dramatic competition, such plays, if well worked out, are the most tragic in effect; and Euripides, faulty though he may be in the general management of his subject, yet is felt to be the most tragic of the poets.

In the second rank comes the kind of tragedy which some place first. Like the *Odyssey*, it has a double thread of plot, and also an opposite catastrophe for the good and for the bad. It is accounted the best because of the weakness of the spectators; for the poet is guided in what he writes by the wishes of his audience. The pleasure, however, thence derived is not the true tragic pleasure. It is proper rather to Comedy, where those who, in the piece, are the deadliest enemies—like Orestes and Aegisthos—quit the stage as friends at the close, and no one slays or is slain.

Fear and pity may be aroused by spectacular means; but they also result from the inner structure of the piece, which is the better way, and indicates a superior poet. For the plot ought to be so constructed that, even without the aid of the eye, he who hears the tale told will thrill with horror and melt to pity at what takes place. This is the impression we should receive from hearing the story of the *Oedipus*. But to produce this effect by the mere spectacle is a less artistic method and dependent on extraneous aids. Those who employ spectacular means to create a sense not of the terrible but only of the monstrous, are strangers to the purpose of Tragedy; for we must not demand of Tragedy any and every kind of pleasure, but only that which is proper to it. And since the pleasure which the poet should afford is that which comes from pity and fear through imitation, it is evident that this quality must be impressed upon the incidents.

Let us then determine what are the circumstances which strike us as terrible or pitiful.

Actions capable of this effect must happen between persons who are either friends or enemies or indifferent to one another. If an enemy kills an enemy, there is nothing to excite pity either in the act or the intention—except so far as the suffering in itself is pitiful. So again with indifferent persons. But when the tragic incident occurs between those who are near or dear to one another—if, for example, a brother kills, or intends to kill, a brother, a son his father, a mother her son, a son his mother or any other deed of the kind is done—these are the situations to be looked for by the poet. He may not indeed destroy the framework of the received legends—the fact, for instance, that Clytemnestra was slain by Orestes—but he ought to show of his own, and skillfully handle the traditional material. Let us explain more clearly what is meant by skillful handling. The action may be done consciously and with knowledge of the persons, in the manner of the older poets. It is thus too that Euripides makes Medea slay her children. Or, again, the deed of horror may be done, but done in ignorance, and the tie of kinship or friendship be discovered afterwards. The *Oedipus* of Sophocles is an example. Here, indeed, the incident is outside the drama proper; but cases occur where it falls within the action of the play. Again, there is a third case—to be about to act with knowledge of the persons and then not to act. The fourth case is when someone is about to do an irreparable deed through ignorance, and makes the discovery before it is done. These are the only possible ways. For the deed must either be done—or not done—and that wittingly or unwittingly. But of all these ways, to be about to act knowing the persons, and then not to act, is the worst. It is shocking without being tragic, for no disaster follows. It is, therefore, never, or very rarely, found in poetry. One instance, however, is in the *Antigone*, where Haemon threatens to kill Creon. The next and better way is that the deed should be perpetrated. Still better, that it should be perpetrated in ignorance, and the discovery made afterwards. There is then nothing to shock us, while the discovery produces a startling effect. The last case is the best, as when in the *Cresphontes* Merope is about to slay her son, but, recognizing who he is, spares his life. This, then, is why a few families only, as has been already observed, furnish the subjects of tragedy. It was not art, but happy

chance, that led the poets in search of subjects to impress the fragile quality upon their plots. They are compelled, therefore, to have recourse to those houses whose history contains moving incidents like these.

Enough has been said concerning the structure of the incidents, and the right kind of plot.

In respect of Character there are four good things to be aimed at. First and most important, it must be good. Now any speech or action that manifests moral purpose of any kind will be expressive of character: the character will be good if the purpose is good. This rule is relative to each class. Even a woman may be good, and also a slave; though the woman may be said to be an inferior being, and the slave quite worthless. The second thing to aim at is propriety. There is a type of manly valor; but valor in a woman, or unscrupulous cleverness, is inappropriate. Thirdly, character must be true to life: for this is a distinct thing from goodness and propriety, as here described. The fourth point is consistency: for though the subject of the imitation, who suggested the type, be inconsistent, still he must be consistently inconsistent.

As in the structure of the plot, so too in the portraiture of character, the poet should always aim either at the necessary or the probable. Thus a person of a given character should speak or act in a given way, by the rule either of necessity or of probability; just as this event should follow that by necessary or probable sequence. It is therefore evident that the unraveling of the plot, no less than the complication, must arise out of the plot itself; it must not be brought about by the Deus ex Machina—as in the *Medea*, or in the return of the Greeks in the *Iliad*. The Deus ex Machina should be employed only for events external to the drama—for antecedent or subsequent events, which lie beyond the range of human knowledge, and which require to be reported or foretold; for to the gods we ascribe the power of seeing all things. Within the action there must be nothing irrational. If the irrational cannot be excluded, it should be outside the scope of the tragedy. Such is the irrational element in the *Oedipus* of Sophocles.

Again, since Tragedy is an imitation of persons who are above the common level, the example of good portrait painters should be followed. They, while producing the distinctive form of the original, make a likeness which is true to life and yet more beautiful. So too the poet, in representing men who are irascible or indolent, or have other defects of character, should preserve the type and yet ennoble it. In this way Achilles is portrayed by Agathon and Homer.

These then are the rules the poet should observe. Nor should he neglect those appeals to the senses, which, though not among the essentials, are the concomitants of poetry; for here too there is much room for error. But of this enough has been said in our published treatises.

It remains to speak of Diction and Thought, the other parts of tragedy having been already discussed. Concerning Thought, we may assume what is said in the Rhetoric, to which inquiry the subject more strictly belongs. Under Thought is included every effect which has to be produced by speech, the subdivisions being: proof and refutation; the excitation of the feelings, such as pity, fear, anger, and the like; the suggestion of importance or its opposite. Now, it is evident that the dramatic incidents must be treated from the same points of view as the dramatic speeches, when the object is to   520 evoke the sense of pity, fear, importance, or probability. The only difference is that the incidents should speak for themselves without verbal exposition; while effects aimed at should be produced by the speaker, and as a result of the speech. For what were the business of a speaker, if the Thought were revealed quite apart from what he says?

Next, as regards Diction. One branch of the inquiry treats of the Modes of Utterance and of the masters of that science. It includes, for instance, what is a   530 command, a prayer, a statement, a threat, a question, an answer, and so forth. To know or not know these things

involves no serious censure upon the poet's art. For who can admit the fault imputed to Homer by Protagoras—that in the words, "Sing, goddess, of the wrath," he gives a command under the idea that he utters a prayer? For to tell someone to do a thing or not to do it is, he says, a command. We may, therefore, pass this over as an inquiry that belongs to another art, not to poetry.

Concerning Tragedy and imitation by means of action   540 this may suffice.

SUMMARY

Greek civilization began within the shadow of superstition and tradition in ancient times. Slowly those bondages had been pared away until, early in the reign of Pericles, a precarious balance was achieved between the freedom of each individual and the welfare of society. The philosophers, the writers, and the artists of the time took an active interest in politics, and conducted their affairs in the bright sunlight of the Agora.

But change is inevitable. In Athens the knife-edge between individuality and the welfare of the group was apparently too thin, the balance too delicate, for a society to maintain an equilibrium for very long. The skeptical sophists taught that complete individuality was the goal—violating Aeschylus' doctrine of the mean between autocracy and anarchy. The original strength of the city was sapped, but enough vitality remained to give rise to a new and different kind of strength in the broadened horizons of Hellenistic culture. Both Plato and Aristotle (except for their brief efforts to educate a king: Plato as tutor for the Syracusan Dionysius, Aristotle as Alexander's tutor) stood apart from politics and the vigorous life of the time; they deserted the active marketplace. They were contemplatives, aware that something had gone wrong, that the dream had somehow failed, and each in his own way examined himself and his culture to discover what had caused their civilization to falter. Probably nothing had really gone "wrong." Change had simply taken place that led to different patterns of life, new types of exploration into human existence, altered ideas of freedom.

What could have gone "right" was Alexander's dream of turning the ancient world into a kind of United Nations with Greek culture as its unifying and elevating core. This was a monumental task but, had he succeeded, there would have been a functioning world federation over 2,200 years prior to two similar attempts in our own century. However, a critical part of Alexander's vision did survive. Hellenism became the first international culture, flourishing for over seven centuries throughout the Mediterranean and the Near East.

(NOTE: See summary of Greek culture and values on p. 229.)

STUDY QUESTIONS

1. Aristotle contends that the ultimate aim of tragedy is to inspire pity and fear, which will be removed through a catharsis (see p. 157). Does he mean a kind of religious experience that will purge the soul? Or is the implication medical, like cleansing the body of poisons? Is there another explanation? Can the catharsis theory be applied to any one of the three tragedies that are included in chapter 5? Which ones? Why? (NOTE: *Agamemnon* and the *Eumenides* should be considered as the beginning and end of a trilogy, with the catharsis theory applied to the *Eumenides*.)

2. Review the six elements of tragedy and apply them to each tragedy. Which play most closely resembles Aristotle's basic elements?

3. Consider *Oedipus* in terms of Aristotle's "unities." Is there a single, complete issue that is resolved? Does the time span conform to Aristotle's dictum?

4. What is the "fatal flaw" of Oedipus?

5. In the *Poetics* Aristotle uses the phrase "though the woman may be said to be an inferior being, and the slave quite worthless." What does this say about the status of women (and slaves) in Athenian society? Why does he qualify the reference to women, in his wording: "may be said to be"? Is there some doubt in his mind? Could this doubt have something to do with dramatic characters such as Clytemnestra, Antigone, Medea, and Lysistrata?

6. What is the "improbability" in *Oedipus* that Aristotle allows because it is outside the time frame of the play?

CHAPTER 7

The Greek Arts

Life is short, and Art long.
                    Hippocrates

According to Greek mythology, Daidalos (DED-uh-los) was the first and greatest of artists, a legendary Minoan artificer who created amazing figures in wood, bronze, and stone, and even invented the Minoan maze that housed the fabled Minotaur. The myth celebrates Greek commitment to creative activity: to invent, design, sculpt, and build. Daidalean Greeks studied nature and used their discoveries to create dynamic new images and structures radiating the illusion of vitality and life. This urge to create is the hallmark of Greek genius.

The Daidalos story has a tragic ending but it does point to a primary artistic consideration of Greek artists. According to the legend, Icaros, Diadalos' undisciplined son, prevailed upon his father to invent wings made of wax and feathers that enabled the lad to soar birdlike in the air. Disregarding his father's warning not to fly too near the sun, the reckless aviator soared high enough to melt his wings, plummeting him to his death in a sea that now bears his name. A cautionary fabrication that reveals a higher truth, this myth symbolizes Greek respect for the laws of nature. Thus, through Daidalos and his hubristic son we see reflected the Greek search for artistic freedom through the study of nature, invention, and allegiance to reason.

CHRONOLOGICAL OVERVIEW

900–700 BC	Geometric period
700–480 BC	Archaic period
480–323 BC	Classical period
	Early 480–450
	High 450–400
	Late 400–323
323–30 BC	Hellenistic Period

Opposite Sosias painter, *Achilles Bandaging Patroclos' Wound*, detail of fig. 7.14. Photo: B.P.K., Berlin (Ingrid Geske-Heiden).

GREEK CIVILIZATION, CA. 900–30 BC

The principal visual arts of ancient Greece were sculpture, pottery, painting, jewelry, and architecture and the main performing arts were music, poetry, and dance All of the Greek arts continually evolved as artists pursued the ideal of excellence in invention, design, and execution; that does not mean, however, that the nine centuries of Greek civilization reached ever higher levels of quality. The apex in all the arts came during the high classical period, especially the Age of Pericles, and was followed by a very gradual decline throughout the Hellenistic period.

GEOMETRIC PERIOD, CA. 900–700 BC

The invasions of Greek-speaking Dorians (ca. 1100–800 BC) ended Mycenaean dominance, disrupted the lives of all the Hellenes, and greatly affected the once flourishing arts of sculpture and architecture. Military invasions always disturb the arts; political and economic turmoil is not conducive to the commissioning of major works such as temples and life-sized statues. While impoverishing many artists and interfering with technological progress, the waves of Dorian invaders had little impact upon the utilitarian arts of furniture, textiles, glassware, and, above all, pottery. Because most of the pottery produced during these chaotic times emphasized geometric decoration, this is called the Geometric period.

Pottery

Practiced since the Stone Age, the craft of making pots made a great leap forward with the invention (probably in Sumer—Iran—ca. 3250 BC) of the potter's wheel. Introduced into Crete around 2000 BC the wheel enabled Minoan potters to lead the Aegean world in transforming the craft of making utilitarian vessels into an art form that reached its apex with the classic Greek vase.

As early as the ninth century BC, geometric conventions of pottery decoration had evolved into a vocabulary

7.1 *Above   Amphora of the Dipylon.* Ca. 750 BC. Terra-cotta, height 5'1" (1.55 m) with base. National Archaeological Museum, Athens. Photo: Hirmer, Munich.

7.2   Statuette of a youth, "Mantiklos dedicated me . . ." Ca. 700–680 BC. Bronze, height 8" (20.3 cm). Museum of Fine Arts, Boston (Francis Bartlett Donation)

of **meanders**, concentric circles, horizontal bands, wheel patterns, shaded triangles, swastikas, and zigzags. Artisans used abstract animal and figure patterns in two-dimensional form in either full front or profile views. Sophisticated, aesthetically appealing, and utilitarian, the *Amphora of the Dipylon* (fig 7.1) is a masterwork of the potter's art. Once cremation had been abandoned, these monumental vases served as grave markers and as receptacles for liquid offerings, which filtered down to the honored dead through openings in the base. The representational scene is a *prothesis* (PROTH-uh-sis), or lying-in-state of the deceased, flanked by triangulated geometric figures of mourners with their arms raised in grief. Alternating bands separate different versions of the meander motif with a band of grazing antelope highlighting the neck. Created several decades after the inauguration of the Olympic Games in 776 BC, this heroic vase can symbolically mark the beginning of the Homeric Age of ca. 750–700 BC.

Temples

Though it achieved its final form during the archaic period (ca. 600 BC), the Greek temple was apparently known to Homer (*Iliad*, I, 39). Fragmentary **terra-cotta** models from the eighth century display three of the elements of the temple **canon**: rectangular floor plan, enclosed inner shrine, and porch supported by columns. The "canon" (Gk., *kanon*, "rule") of Greek temples refers to fundamental procedures that help convert a concept into reality: buildings that truly look like dwelling-places for the gods.

Statuettes

Among the most popular products of the Greek artisans, statuettes were produced in quantity throughout ancient Greek history. Though not as impressive as life-sized statuary, diminutive figures can be held and examined closely—a very personal relationship. The statuette shown in figure 7.2 is a votive offering, bearing on its thighs the inscription "Mantiklos dedicated me to the Far Darter of the silver bow, as part of his tithe. Do thou, Phoibos, grant him gracious recompense." The geometric elements are obvious but the unknown artist also shows a concern for volume, modeling, and some anatomical details—design elements that place this work on the borderline between the geometric and archaic periods.

On the basis of the surviving pottery and statuettes, it seems that the geometric was a significant interlude between the Mycenaean civilization and the archaic period. Homer's *Iliad* and *Odyssey* were the greatest achievements of this era, which makes one wonder: Did the visual arts lag behind epic poetry, or have some important artworks been lost? In any event, in the geometric the artist began to see and think and create as a Greek, not as an Egyptian, Minoan, or Mycenaean. Borrowings from these civilizations are evident, but the unique forms introduced during the geometric period clearly indicate an elementary process of producing art forms subject to experimentation and invention rather than bound to traditional conventions. Above all, this art was dynamic, never static.

ARCHAIC PERIOD, 700–480 BC

"Archaic" is a term derived from a Greek word meaning "ancient" and is not to be confused with such current definitions as "antiquated, outdated, or old-fashioned." Greek genius blossomed in the sixth century BC with the creation of brilliant works of art. This was one of the most fruitful and imaginative periods in the history of art, a vigorous era that also produced the world's first democracy.

Pursuit of the Ideal

Throughout Greek art, beginning with the archaic period, Greek sculptors evolved new representational modes that differed from all previous artistic conceptions. Fascination with the human body and its complex mechanics led to the creation of fully three-dimensional sculpture, increasingly faithful to the natural world. In a culture that studied the real world and that, above all, valued the individual, the movement toward naturalism seems, in retrospect, to have been inevitable. It was the ideal, the quest for excellence, that impelled Greek artists, just as the philosophers and statesmen sought excellence in a free society. Writing around the time of the Battle of Marathon (490 BC), a Greek poet succinctly described the ideal Greek: "In hand and foot and mind built foursquare without a flaw." And in the twentieth century:

> Greece is in a special category. From the point of view of the present day, the Greeks constitute a fundamental advance on the great peoples of the Orient, a new stage in the development of society. They established an entirely new set of principles for communal life. However highly we may value the artistic, religious, and political achievements of earlier nations, the history of what we can truly call civilization—the deliberate pursuit of an ideal—does not begin until Greece.[1]

Sculpture

Two main subjects preoccupied sculptors throughout the sixth century BC: the standing nude male and the standing fully clothed female. Apparently serving as votive or commemorative statues, these figures were not personalized portraits but rather idealized representations placed

somewhere between humankind and the gods. No one really knows why the men were always nude and the women fully clothed and, moreover, we can apply only vague and unsatisfactory names to these freestanding figures: **kouros** (KOO-rose; "youth") and **kore** (KORE-ay; "maiden"). Probably adapted from Egypt and Mesopotamia, these two subjects were repeated again and again, never exactly duplicated but rather with the competitive drive that leads to constant innovation. The intensity of this ceaseless striving for something different, something better, sets the Greeks apart from all other cultures.

An early work, the *Kore of Auxerre* (fig. 7.3) stands as stiffly as an Egyptian statue, but when compared with

7.3 *Kore of Auxerre*, from France. Ca. 630–600 BC. Limestone with traces of paint, height 29½" (75 cm). Louvre, Paris. Photo: R.M.N., Paris.

1. Gilbert Highet, *Man's Unconquerable Mind* (New York: Columbia University Press, 1954), p. 15.

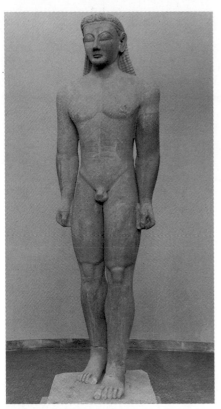

7.4 *Kouros of Sounion*. Ca. 600 BC. Marble, height 10' (3.05 m). National Archaeological Museum, Athens. Photo: Alison Frantz, Princeton.

7.5 Moschophoros, *Calf-Bearer*, detail. Ca. 575–550 BC. Marble, height 5'6" (1.68 m). Acropolis Museum, Athens. Photo: Hirmer, Munich.

Egyptian conventions, it reveals significant differences (see fig. 2.6). Unlike his Egyptian predecessor, the sculptor has cut away some needless stone to outline the figure rather than encasing it. The hair is braided in the geometric manner but the way the wide belt cinches the waist conveys a very human touch. From the light shoulder covering to the swelling hips, there is a skillful contrast between curved and straight lines.

Compare the colossal statue of the *Kouros of Sounion* (fig. 7.4) with the pharaoh (fig. 2.6). The Egyptian figure is "imprisoned" in stone in the manner of a very high relief, whereas the kouros has been liberated from unnecessary stone, except for the hands. The pharaoh stands in repose with his weight on the back foot. The equal distribution of weight of the kouros gives the illusion that he is striding forward, an effect heightened by the taut thigh muscles. Vestiges of geometric ornamentation remain in the rosette hair with meticulous braids and, especially, in the scrolls (**volutes**) that serve as ears. We see the most critical difference between the Egyptian and Greek sculptures in the eyes and facial expression. Displaying the typical relaxed serenity of Egyptian portraiture, the pharaoh gazes dreamily into an undefined distance. Conversely, the *Kouros of Sounion* manifests the characteristic dynamism of Greek art, with tension present in every line of the face. Egyptian figures seem never to have known stress, whereas tension and striving are hallmarks of the restless Greeks. Such were the contrasting views of the cultures in terms of reality and of human values: the pharaoh-gods constituted reality and their subjects lived for eternity; Greek reality was the individual and the time was now. Greek civilization, as Nietzsche said, "was not an effortless growth, but the product of courageous effort sustained by acute tension."

The *Calf-Bearer* (fig. 7.5) was something new in Greek

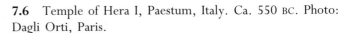

7.6 Temple of Hera I, Paestum, Italy. Ca. 550 BC. Photo: Dagli Orti, Paris.

7.7 *Sacrificial Scene*, votive tablet from the cave of Pitsa near Corinth. Ca. 540 BC. Paint on wood, height 6" (15.2 cm). National Archaeological Museum, Athens.

art, a composition of two figures so unified that neither subject is conceivable without the other. A bearded man with a cloak draped over his upper body is gently balancing a bull calf on his shoulders as he strides confidently forward. With the corners of his mouth lifted in the "archaic smile," he stares ahead with hollow eyes that once contained realistic inlays. Characteristic of the archaic style, his braided hair and close-cropped beard are stylized, contrasting with the naturalistic depiction of the calf.

Architecture

By the sixth century BC, Greek city-states had established colonies in North Africa and from Byzantium (Istanbul) westward to Sicily, Italy, France, and Spain. Magna Graecia (southern Italy) was particularly important; Pythagoras founded his religious brotherhood here (see p. 77) and Parmenides and Empedocles established the Eleatic School of philosophy (see p. 89). One of the better-preserved of the surviving archaic temples is that of Hera I at Paestum (fig. 7.6), the site of two of the religious centers of Magna Graecia. Though employing an unusual nine-column front, this structure has all the elements of the basic Greek temple: rectangular floor plan, columns on four sides, three steps rising from the foundation to the top level on which the columns rest, and an enclosed inner shrine. Apparently the odd number of columns was never tried again. Regularity was an important quality for the Greeks, as exemplified in the six- or eight-column fronts of classical temples (see figs. 7.35 and 7.47). Other archaic features are the heavy, bulging columns that taper sharply as they near the oversize, pillowlike capitals. The whole effect is ponderous, creating a sense of physical strain, unlike the Parthenon (fig. 7.35), which appears light and free of stress.

Painting, Pottery, and Metalwork

Painting was, for the Greeks, one of the supreme art forms, yet very little survives, mainly because pigments are perishable when applied to stone and especially so when painted on wood. The *Sacrificial Scene* (fig. 7.7), found in a grotto near Corinth, presents a small procession of worshipers approaching a bare altar at the right. A dignified woman carrying a pitcher of wine leads, followed, in turn, by a boy leading the sacrificial lamb, a lyre player, an aulos player, and several tranquil women. All wear garlands in an atmosphere of joyful serenity. The placement of the figures has a rhythm analogous to that in vase painting, as if this were a flattened-out vase.

Many more vases than paintings survived because pottery fired in a kiln is virtually indestructible; experts can restore badly fragmented vases to something approaching their original condition. We therefore have enough archaic vases to appreciate the superb achievements of painters who made that art form comparable to the best sculpture and architecture. That the Greeks valued their vases is confirmed by the many painters and potters who signed their creations, which, incidentally, raised the value (and price) of the vase. Artists concentrated on lively interaction between individual gods, goddesses, and heroes. Using an incisive **black-figure technique** (silhouetted figures on a reddish background), vase painters such as Exekias (e-ZEE-ki-as) set an unsurpassed standard (fig. 7.8). In this quiet interlude during the Trojan War we see Achilles (on the left) and Ajax intent on a game of dice. "Balloons" issue from their mouths, with Achilles saying *"tesara"* ("four") and Ajax countering with *"tria"* ("three"). (This does not tell us, however, who is winning the game.) The composition is sparse but elegant, with a sure line sustained by finely incised details in clothing and hair. The scene is quiet and dignified but permeated with dramatic intensity. These warriors are just as determined to win a game as they were on defeating the Trojans. Exekias modeled and painted his

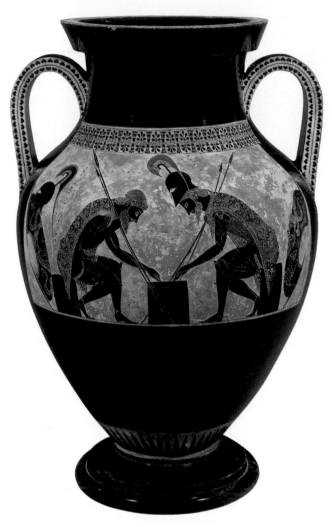

7.8 Exekias, *Amphora with Achilles and Ajax Playing Dice*. Ca. 530 BC. Black-figure pottery, height 24" (61 cm). Musei Vaticani, Rome.

7.9 Krater. Ca. 520 BC. Bronze, height 28¾" (73 cm). National Museum, Belgrade, Serbia.

own vases, eleven of which he signed, but he signed only two paintings. One wonders which he valued more.

The bronze **krater** (fig. 7.9) is a stunning example of the superb metalwork of the archaic period. This was one of the four designs of vessels used specifically for the mixture of wine and water that the Greeks drank on social occasions. (They rarely drank wine straight, which is why, in *Lysistrata*, the rebellious women banned water from their wine.) It was usually filled with wine poured from an **amphora** and water added from a **hydria** (fig. 7.10). The krater's swelling shape is emphasized by the undecorated central surface. There are four horsemen and two Medusas (snake-haired monsters) on the neck and three Medusas on the tripod, each flanked by a dog and a fox. The presence of all these Medusas may suggest that the krater's contents could turn a person to stone, just as viewing Medusa would have a comparable result.

Art and Clothing

By comparing the *Kore in Dorian Peplos* (fig. 7.11) with the *Kore of Auxerre* (fig. 7.3), one can observe a basic continuity while also noting significant changes. This is the last known archaic kore statue to wear the Dorian peplos, a heavy woolen tunic fastened at each shoulder, belted at the waist, and reaching to the ground. It was commonly worn over a light, sleeved tunic called a khiton. There is still a rectangular frontality about this figure but there is no doubt about the presence of a young, nubile body beneath the peplos. With its lovely smile and arched eyebrows, the softly rounded face radiates a serene happiness. The remaining paint on the graceful braids suggests that the young woman was a redhead, a valued hue in ancient Athens.

The Ionian himation worn by the *Kore from Khios* (fig. 7.12) contrasts sharply with the severe Dorian peplos. Made of much lighter material than the peplos, this

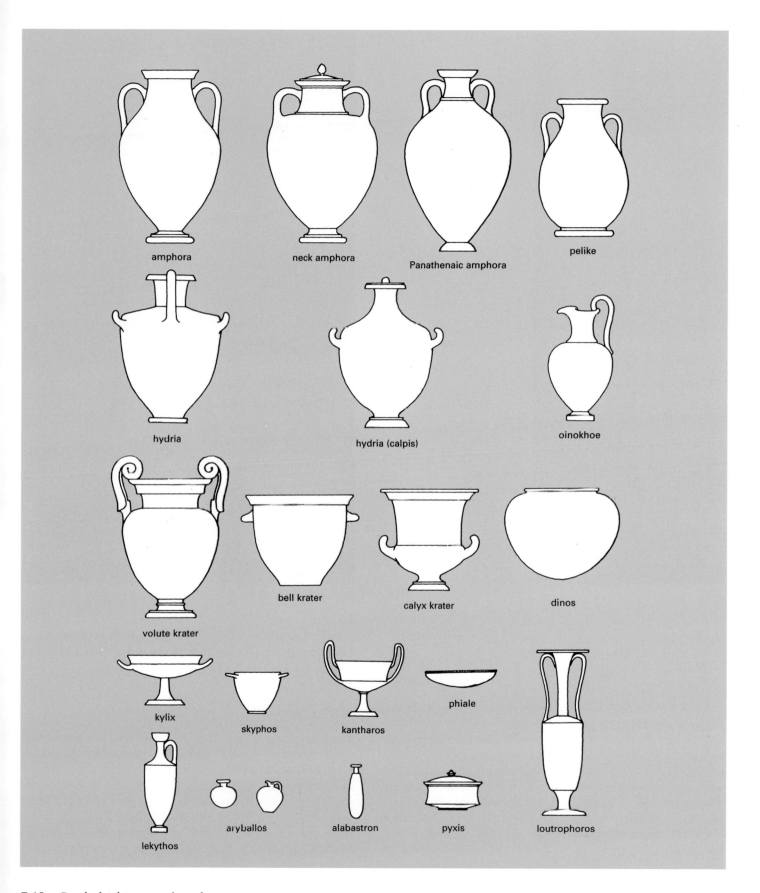

7.10   Greek drinking vessels and vases.

7.11 *Kore in Dorian Peplos*. Ca. 530 BC. Marble with traces of paint, height 4' (1.22 m). Acropolis Museum, Athens. Photo: Hirmer, Munich.

7.12 *Kore from Khios*. Ca. 520 BC. Marble with traces of paint, height 22" (56 cm) (lower part missing). Acropolis Museum, Athens. Photo: Hirmer, Munich.

elegant mantle could be draped over the body in a variety of graceful arrangements. Artists obviously enjoyed sculpting the sinuous lines of the garment, given the many surviving works. Moreover, Athenian women enthusiastically adopted the stylish himation symbolizing the individualistic, pleasure-loving orientation of an Ionian society as compared with the sober peplos and stolid, group-oriented residents of the Dorian city of Sparta. All Greek (and Mesopotamian, Egyptian, and Roman) women were responsible for the production of textiles and clothing. Ionian women were particularly well-known for their elegant, exquisitely decorated fabrics. Some of the sculpted fabrics and vases depicting clothing have survived but very little actual cloth remains from any ancient culture.

Naturalism

The *Anavyssos Kouros* (fig. 7.13), which was placed over the grave of a warrior named Kroisos, signals a major advance toward naturalism, i.e., fidelity to the actual appearance of the natural world. The revolutionary changes already apparent in the *Kouros of Sounion* (see fig. 7.4) are more fully realized in this portrait of the finely tuned body of a youthful wrestler who died on some unknown battlefield. Though the knees and calves are emphasized, following earlier conventions, the muscles of the powerful thighs and taut arms swell with lifelike vitality. Based on an increasing concern with skeletal structure and anatomical details, the sculptor has concentrated on portraying the body as anyone might perceive it. From their very first efforts at monumental sculpture, Greek artists were never interested in portrait busts; their concern was the whole person. This does not imply that the head was secondary—far from it—but rather that Greek artists worked in a culture in which reality was the individual, one who possessed, ideally, a sound mind in a healthy body.

Whatever the reason for portraying men nude and women clothed, it had nothing to do with modesty. Nudity in the context of athletics or gymnastics was commonplace in the Greek world. Near Eastern prejudice against nudity was, for the Greeks, a sure sign of barbarism. Further, the male and female poses were consistently different. The women always stand with feet together, one arm at the side and the other raised (see figs. 7.3, 7.11, and 7.12). The men are always striding forward with the left foot, their hands at their sides (see figs. 7.4 and 7.13). To summarize, we know little of the purpose of these figures and nothing at all about conventional poses or clothing or the lack of it. We know only that their existence enriches our world.

Red-Figure Pottery

Around 530 BC vase painters began working with a color scheme of red figures against a black background, the reverse of black-figure technique. The luminous new **red-figure style** allowed secondary markings such as hair, muscles, details of dress, and even discreet shading. The two styles coexisted for thirty or forty years, but the red-figure technique, with its greater opportunities for delicacy and subtlety, became the dominant style of the classical period. In the red-figure cup by the Sosias painter (fig. 7.14 and p. 188), we see the first known example of eyes painted as they appear in profile. This was a significant advance beyond the Egyptian convention of always depicting the frontal view of eyes. In the painting, Achilles is tending his friend's wound while, in a very human reaction, Patroclos has turned his head away as if he were not a party to this painful event—or wishes he weren't. Differences between red-figure and black-figure technique are readily apparent when one compares this painting with that of Exekias (fig. 7.8). We cannot say that one work is better than the other, only that different techniques lead to diverse styles. Black-figure painting is characteristic of the vigorous archaic period, while red-figure vases typify the serenely confident classical style.

7.13 *Left Anavyssos Kouros.* Ca. 525 BC. Marble with traces of paint, height 6'4" (1.93 m). National Archaeological Museum, Athens. Photo: Alison Frantz, Princeton.

7.14 *Below* Sosias painter, *Achilles Bandaging Patroclos' Wound*, detail of cup, from Vulci. Ca. 500 BC. Red-figure pottery, diameter 12½" (32 cm). Antikenmuseum, Staatliche Museen Preussicher Kulturbesitz, Berlin. Photo: B.P.K., Berlin (Ingrid Geske-Heiden).

CLASSICAL PERIOD, 480–323 BC

Early Classical, 480–450 BC

The year 480 BC marked a critical turning point in Athenian history. Invaded and humiliated by Xerxes' Persian forces, their city ravaged and in ruins, the Athenians and their allies struck back by destroying the Persian fleet at Salamis and defeating the army the following year. A resurgent Athens moved confidently toward power, prosperity, and a legendary Golden Age.

Severe Style

The *Kritios Boy* (fig. 7.15), a prime example of the Severe style of early classicism, was created about the time that Aeschylus was gaining fame as a playwright. Somewhat like the innovations of Aeschylus, this statue represents a new principle in art. Wearing an expression of composed, classical solemnity (compare this with the archaic smile), this is truly a standing figure. Archaic sculptures were generally limited to a striding pose with an equal distribution of weight. Here is a formal composition with a fine balance of tense and relaxed muscles, the head turned slightly, one hip a bit elevated, the weight on one leg with the other at rest. This is how any of us might stand in repose.

Also representing the Severe style is the *Delphi Charioteer* (figs. 7.16 and 7.17), which was once part of a large composition including a chariot and four horses. Chariot races were entered by the owners of racing teams and driven by skilled charioteers, much as professional jockeys ride today's thoroughbred horses. Overlooking the disheveled, dusty condition of a charioteer after a grueling race, the artist idealizes a proud champion, his khiton falling in fluted folds resembling a Doric column (see fig. 7.31).

One of the finest original Greek bronzes, *Poseidon* (*Zeus* according to some; fig. 7.18) stands majestically, prepared to hurl his trident (thunderbolt?). The figure is stridently asymmetrical: arms, legs, even the head, turn in different angles from the torso, which in turn shows the competing muscular strains and tensions. More so than even the most naturalistic archaic statues, this body has muscles rippling beneath taut skin. The concavities and convexities of the bronze surface reflect a shimmering light that further animates the figure. It matters little that if Poseidon's arms were lowered his hands would dangle at the knees; that the eyes are hollow sockets (once filled with colored stones); or that the hair, beard, and eyebrows are stylized; the work exudes a kinetic energy never achieved in earlier sculptures.

7.15 *Kritios Boy*. 481 BC. Marble, height 34" (86.4 cm). Acropolis Museum, Athens. Photo: Hirmer, Munich.

7.17 *Delphi Charioteer*, detail of fig. 7.16. Photo: Hirmer, Munich.

7.16 *Left   Delphi Charioteer.* Ca. 478 or 474 BC. Bronze, height 5'11" (1.81 m). Archaeological Museum, Delphi. Photo: Sonia Halliday, Weston Turville, U.K.

7.18 *Poseidon (Zeus?)*. Ca. 460 BC. Bronze, height 6'10"
(2.08 m). National Archaeological Museum, Athens. Photo:
Dagli Orti, Paris.

7.19 *Poseidon (Zeus?)*, detail of fig. 7.18. Photo: Dagli Orti,
Paris.

7.20 Douris, *Kylix with Youth Making an Offering*. 1st half of
5th century BC. Red-figure pottery, height 3½" (8.9 cm),
diameter 9" (22.9 cm). National Archaeological Museum,
Athens.

The idealism of Greek art—depicting people not as
they were but as they should be—applied also to the gods
(fig. 7.19). Whether Poseidon the earthshaker or Zeus of
the thunderbolt, this is how a god ought to look. Compare
this regal demeanor with the idealized faces of figures 7.21,
7.22, and 7.23 and gauge the difference.

Occupying the borderline between the severe and the
high classical styles, the *Kylix with Youth Making an Offering*
(fig. 7.20) is both restrained and confident. This is one of
thirty-two drinking cups signed by Douris. With an oinokhoe
(OYN-o-koe; "wine jug") in one hand and a **kylix** in the
other (see fig. 7.10), the youth is elegantly caught in mid-
stride. The arrangement of altar, vases, and precisely draped
khiton add up to a meticulous composition that is complex and perfectly balanced; nothing could be added or sub-
tracted. The painting style is severe but the composition
is already high classical.

High Classical, 450–400 BC

More than any other style, the high classical boldly displayed the values of the Athenians of the Golden Age: optimism, freedom, individuality, competitiveness, the
pursuit of excellence, and pride of achievement. This
was the age of Pericles, Sophocles, Euripides, Socrates,

and some of the most extraordinary sculptors, vase painters, metalworkers, and architects in the history of Western civilization.

Sculpture and Vase Painting

Myron's *Discobolus* (*Discus Thrower*; fig. 7.21) is intended to be viewed from the left of the figure, so one becomes totally involved in the moment before explosive action. Though a celebrated classical statue, the figure follows some Egyptian conventions. It is designed on a frontal plane, with head and legs in profile and the upper torso turned toward the front. Balanced by the arc of the arms and the angle of the head and left leg, this is a formal composition with the harmonious proportions characteristic of the classical style. With simplified anatomical details and a stylized pose, all is in readiness for the athlete to wheel about and hurl the discus. Excellence of form counted for half the score with the distance counting for the other half, a procedure comparable to scoring today's competitive diving or gymnastics. An athlete could win the olive wreath with a second-place throw, provided he displayed form comparable to the *Discobolus*. (See also the Olympic Games on pp. 246–7.)

The *Riace Bronze* (ree-AH-chee; fig. 7.22) is one of two original Greek bronzes discovered together in 1972 in the sea off Italy's southern coast and named after Riace township in Calabria. Statue A originally had a shield and a small sword; the eyes are now without pupils; and a tuft of hair is missing. Otherwise, this is a stunning representation of a youthful warrior in the prime of his vigorous life. Bronze is the primary material, but the teeth are silver, the corneas of the eyes ivory and limestone, and the lips, nipples, and eyelashes made of copper. The pose is fascinating; the right turn of the head and the steady far-off gaze express strength and resolution. Thrown-back shoulders strikingly fix the warrior in space.

The creator of this splendid addition to the tiny treasure of original Greek art is unknown. Some scholars say the bronze is worthy of the great Pheidias of Athens (and it is) while others attribute it to the sculptor in Magna Graecia called Pythagoras. It could have been imported from Athens or made in Italy. Stylistically, the warrior stands somewhere between the *Poseidon* (fig. 7.18) and the canon developed by Polykleitos (polly-KLY-toss) of Argos, who is known today only through Roman copies of his work.

This copy of Polykleitos' *Doryphoros* (dory-FOR-os; fig. 7.23) is of sufficiently high quality to demonstrate how it exemplified a "canon" (system of proportions), which became a model for several generations of artists. Displaying the powerful body of a finely conditioned

7.21 *Above* Myron, *Discus Thrower (Discobolus)*. Reconstructed Roman copy of a bronze original of ca. 450 BC. Marble, height 5' (1.52 m). Museo Nazionale Romano, Rome. Photo: Hirmer, Munich.

7.22 *Right* *Riace Bronze* (Statue A). Ca. 460–450 BC. Bronze, height 6' 6" (1.98 m). Museo Nazionale di Reggio Calabria, Italy. Photo: Alinari, Florence.

7.23 Polykleitos, *Spear Bearer (Doryphoros)*. Roman copy of a bronze original of ca. 450–440 BC. Marble, height 6'6" (1.98 m). Museo Nazionale, Naples. Photo: Scala, Florence.

7.24 *Victory Untying Her Sandal*, from the parapet of the Temple of Athena Nike, Acropolis, Athens. Ca. 410 BC. Pentelic marble, height 3'6" (1.07 m). Acropolis Museum, Athens. Photo: Dagli Orti, Paris.

athlete, the young man rests his full weight on the right leg, with the left bent at the knee and his toes lightly touching the ground. With the head barely turned to the right and the right shoulder dropped slightly, we can trace a long S curve from the feet to the head. At rest as no sculpted figure had ever been before, the composition is a dynamic equilibrium of tension and relaxation throughout the body. Harmoniously proportioned and with a classic balance of artistic and natural form, this is the confident style of the Golden Age.

The relief *Victory Untying Her Sandal* (fig. 7.24) illustrates Greek sculpture's wet drapery effect. Sculptors apparently dipped a filmy material in a starchlike substance, draped the nude female model, and arranged the folds for best artistic effect. Portrayed here is a rather awkward human action, but one accomplished so gracefully that the work is a marvel of softly flowing lines in a perfectly balanced design.

In a strikingly different portrait of Nike, goddess of victory (fig. 7.25), we see the goddess descending from the sky. Wearing the diaphanous Ionic himation, Nike is moving so fast that the fabric is almost a second skin.

7.25 Paionios, *Nike*. Ca. 421 BC. Marble, height 6'4¾" (1.95 m) (7'1" [2.16 m] including base). Archaeological Museum, Olympia. Photo: Hirmer, Munich.

Originally balanced by a pair of large wings, the cloth billowing out behind is so skillfully carved that it appears to be undulating drapery. Note also the exceptional artistry that created the illusion of an airborne figure not yet in contact with the ground. Discovered at Olympia in 1875, this is one of the all-too-scarce original marbles from the Periclean Age.

A sculptured gravestone known as the *Stele of Hegesco* (fig. 7.26) shows a serving maid offering her seated mistress, the commemorated deceased, a casket of jewels. Common to sculpture of the classical period is the serenity of the facial expressions, whether the subjects are participating in a procession, a battle, or a meeting of the gods. Note, also, that the heads of the standing servant and seated mistress are close to the same level. This **isocephalic** (i-so-se-FALL-ik) convention, the tradition of keeping all heads on approximately the same level, gives exceptional clarity to Greek relief art. It is so subtly executed that one's sense of rightness remains undisturbed.

Vase painters of this period were just as skilled as the architects and sculptors, and their best work compares favorably with paintings by Renaissance artists such as Raphael or Leonardo da Vinci. Though most artists

7.26 *Stele of Hegesco*, grave relief. Ca. 400–390 BC. Marble, height 4' 10½" (1.49 m). National Archaeological Museum, Athens. Photo: Hirmer, Munich.

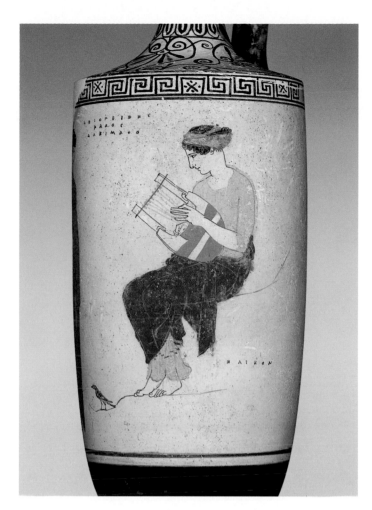

7.27 Achilles Painter, *Muse on Mount Helicon*, detail of lekythos (funerary vase). Ca. 440–430 BC. White-ground pottery, height 14½" (35.5 cm). Glypothek, Munich. Photo: Studio Kopperman, Munich.

preferred red-figure paintings, some used a variety of colors on a white background in what is called the white-ground technique. Before being fired in the kiln, a white clay was added in the area to be decorated and the painting done after firing. Though subject to fading because the color was not baked into the vase as in the red-figure technique, white-ground paintings are similar to easel paintings, but with the additional complication of working on curved surfaces. Some artists chose the permanency of red-figure painting, while others, like the Achilles Painter (fig. 7.27), favored the color range of white-ground decorations. Though he did not sign his work, his distinctive style appears on more than 200 vases. Here, sitting quietly on the sacred mountain of the muses, Polyhymnia, the muse of solemn hymn and religious dance, reverently plucks her seven-string kithara. (See The Greek Muses in box 7.1.) Lightly decorated at top and bottom, there is nothing to draw our attention from the solitary figure with a lone bird at her feet. Graceful line and harmonious composition make this a superb example of the classical style.

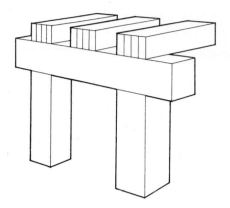

7.28   Post and lintel system.

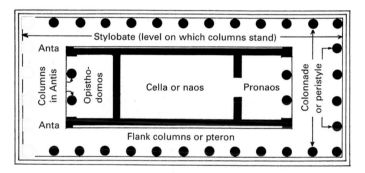

7.29   Typical Greek temple floor plan.

7.30   Typical Greek temple facade.

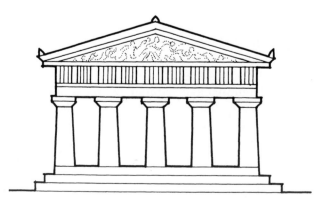

THE GREEK ORDERS

Determining the general mode of the basic temple plan was a problem that was resolved with the inspired conception of the classic Greek orders: **Doric, Ionic,** and **Corinthian** (fig. 7.31). Placed directly on the **stylobate**, the Doric column was about seven times as tall as its diameter, a ratio probably derived from the height of a man in relation to foot size. Fluted to provide visual depth and swelling in subtle convex curves (**entasis**; EN-ta-sis), it rose to a capital (**echinus**; eh-KY-nus), under an **abacus** (AB-a-kus), the square block that joined the **architrave**. Surmounting the columns was a Doric **frieze** of alternating **triglyphs** (TRY-glifs) and **metopes** (MET-o-pays). (See figs. 7.35, 7.46, and 7.47.)

The contrasting Ionic order is lighter than the Doric and more graceful, with a slender shaft about eleven times its diameter (approximately a woman's height in proportion to the size of her foot). Its components are a tiered base, a delicate shaft with softer, spaced fluting, and a capital formed of paired scrolls (volutes) capped by a highly decorated abacus. Usually subdivided into three projecting bands, the Ionic architrave normally consists of a continuous sculptural frieze. (See figs. 7.43 and 7.45.)

A variant of the Ionic, the Corinthian order, adored by the Romans, is considerably more decorative, even opulent. Taller and more slender than the Ionic, its column culminates in an inverted bell shape encrusted with stylized **acanthus** leaves, an ingenious transition from a circular shaft to a rectangular architrave. (See fig. 7.59 for the only Corinthian temple in Greece.)

Like multiple layers of a cake, the columns consisted of stone **drums** that were roughed out in the quarry. After delivery to the site, the drums were fitted with metal pegs coated with lead to resist corrosion and stacked into columns. The assembled columns were then finished under the supervision of the architect, who personally controlled the entire project.

With only one form and three modes of expression, Greek architecture might seem a limited achievement. Not so. The secret is in the limitations. For perfection of proportion and clarity of outline, subtlety of refinement, and visual appearance of solids and spaces in equilibrium, the Greek temple has never been surpassed.

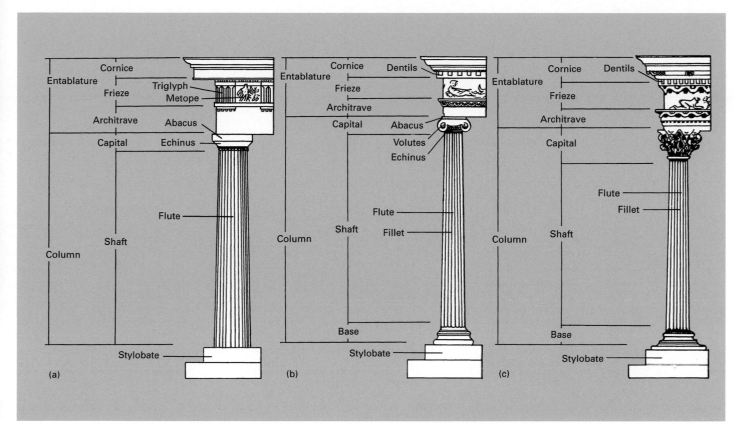

7.31 Greek orders of columns: (a) Doric, (b) Ionic, and (c) Corinthian.

Were the common people of Athens appreciative of these and other great art works? According to Aristotle, there are only two criteria for art: 1) it should entertain and instruct; 2) it should disclose not secrets to the few but treasures to the many. We have ample evidence proving that all the Greek arts served up treasures to a large and appreciative public.

Architecture

As discussed earlier, Greek temples had evolved into their canonical form during the early archaic period (ca. 600 BC). Fundamental to the temple canon is the architectural system of post and lintel (fig. 7.28). After planting a post at all four corners of the space to be enclosed, the builder placed a **lintel** on top of and across the posts. Roof beams (joists) were placed at regular intervals to link the opposite lintels and then covered with a roof. Spaces between the posts were filled, as needed, with walls, windows, and doors. First employed in wood, then in brick, and eventually in stone construction, the post and lintel system was used for all major buildings. Though aware of the greater strength of arches and the arched vault (see Roman Architecture and Engineering, pp. 288–9), architects used this technology for minor projects such as tunnels and sewers.

A typical temple floor plan (fig. 7.29) shows a **cella**, a central room housing the statue of the deity. This basic core was provided with a columned porch at the front and, usually, one at the back, with the latter sometimes enclosed to house a treasury. Large and important temples had exterior columns on all four sides forming a colonnade or **peristyle**.

The plan appears to be simple, but a diagram of a **facade** (fig. 7.30) reveals a progression beyond the basic post and lintel system. Because the Mediterranean area is subject to heavy winter rains, a sloping or saddle-back roof was developed to facilitate drainage. It was covered with terra-cotta or marble tiles, equipped with gutters and rain spouts, and adorned with sculpture. The triangular space at each end, the **pediment**, was usually decorated with large-scale high reliefs or freestanding sculpture.

The architects constructed steps (usually three) on a stone foundation called a stereobate with the top level, the stylobate, forming the floor of the temple. From the stylobate rose columns (shafts with capitals) that supported the lintel, also called an architrave. The ends of the roof joists are called triglyphs, a term derived from the three vertical grooves that had become a decorative stone adaptation of the natural grain of wood joist ends. The spaces between the triglyphs were filled by plain, painted, or relief rectangles called metopes.

7.32 Acropolis (view from the west) Athens. Photo: Sonia Halliday, Weston Turville, U.K.

The Acropolis

Most ancient Greek cities developed around a fortified hill-top (*akra*; "high place"). As cities grew more prosperous and powerful, this "people's high place" (acropolis) became the center of religious and civic activity, suitably adorned with governmental buildings, libraries, and temples dedicated to the gods. According to legend, the Acropolis of Athens (fig. 7.32) was both the burial place of the fabled King Erechtheus and the site where Poseidon and Athena contended for authority over the city.

Under the leadership of Pericles, the Athenians completed a building and art program on the Acropolis surpassing in splendor and artistic quality anything the world had ever seen. It signified the beginning of the Golden Age, in about 460 BC, when Pericles appointed Pheidias overseer of all works on the Acropolis. By 405 the Parthenon, Erechtheion, Propylaia, and Temple of Athena Nike had been built, and the brief period of glory was at an end. These four buildings are identified in the model (fig. 7.33): Temple of Athena Nike, tiny building on the right parapet above the stairs; Propylaia, at the top of the steps; Parthenon, largest building; and Erechtheion, two-part structure at the upper left near the wall. No other buildings have survived.

For half a century this small rocky plateau (ca. 1,000' [305 m] long and 445' [136 m] wide) was a center of

creative activity for the greatest sculptors and architects of the time and the most skillful stonemasons in the Greek world. Entrusted to Athens for protection from Persia, the ample funds of the Delian Treasury were lavished on a building project supposedly dedicated to Athena, but in reality proclaiming Athenian power and glory.

Parthenon Built under the direction of architects Ictinus (ik-TIE-nus) and Callicrates (ka-LIK-kra-teez), the temple of Athena Parthenos or the Parthenon (figs. 7.34 and 7.35) was created as the crowning glory of the Acropolis, complete with sculptural reliefs and a massive gold and ivory statue of Athena created by Pheidias. Although it is the largest Doric temple ever built on the Greek mainland, with refinements so subtle that the building symbolized the Periclean ideal of "beauty in simplicity," its basic plan was still that of the sixth-century archaic temple. Though they invented nothing new, its architects clearly saw just how refined the temple form could be. Despite the great size (228 × 101' [69.54 × 30.8 m] with 34' [10.37 m] columns), this was still a rectangular box surrounded by columns and surmounted by a triangular prism. A temple in which the Doric order achieved perfection, the Parthenon is so unified and harmonious that its immense size belies its lightly poised serenity.

That the building has virtually no straight lines or true right angles is at first surprising. By using slight deviations from mathematical regularity, presumably to correct optical distortions, the architects created the appearance of mathematical precision. This bothered Plato,

7.33 Model of the classical Acropolis. American School of Classical Studies at Athens (Agora Excavations).

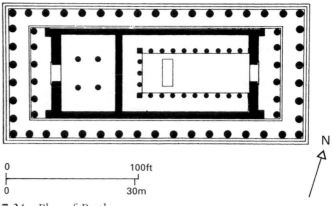

7.34 Plan of Parthenon.

7.35 Ictinus and Callicrates, Parthenon (view from the northwest), Acropolis, Athens. Ca. 447–432 BC. 228 × 101' (69.5 × 39.8 m). Photo: Spectrum, London.

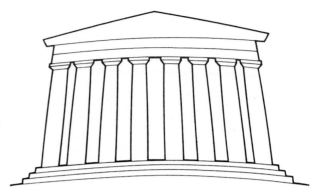

7.37 Schematic drawing of Parthenon refinements.

7.36 *Left* Stereobate and stylobate, Parthenon (north side, looking west). Photo: Lesley and Roy Adkins Picture Library, Langport, U.K.

who could not reconcile the discrepancy between perfection and the illusion of perfection. Thus, the cella walls lean slightly inwards; the stylobate rises 4¼ inches (10.9 cm) at the center of the 228-foot (69.5 m) sides (fig. 7.36) and 2¾ inches (7 cm) at the center of the other two sides.

All columns lean inward about 2½ inches (6 cm), except the corner columns, which lean diagonally inward, so much so that, if extended, all four would meet at a point about a mile (1.6 km) above the temple. Echoing the stylobate, the cornice, frieze, and architrave are all slightly higher in the center. The schematic drawing (fig. 7.37) seems strange but exaggeration illustrates these subtleties.

Further adjustments are found in the greater diameter of the corner columns, each of which is about 24 inches (60 cm) closer to its neighbors than the other columns. Corner columns are seen most directly against the sky, thus the deviations were probably intended to make them seem more supportive. Most Doric buildings show some signs of "correction," for the Doric column always had a slight outward curve called the entasis. In early temples the entasis is a bulge about a third of the way up the column; but the deviation from a straight line is only ¹⁄₁₆ inch (1.7 cm) within the 34-foot (10.4-m) Parthenon column. A long-standing convention, the fluting of Doric columns was not only visually attractive but also made an optical correction; smooth-surfaced columns seem, from a distance, flat, lacking enough substance to perform support functions.

Adorned with some of antiquity's greatest marble carvings, the Parthenon was a visual encyclopedia of activities of the gods and of the Athenians themselves. A reconstruction of the east pediment (fig. 7.38) illustrates the story of the miraculous birth of Athena, who has just emerged from the brow of Zeus. All the gods at the center are astir, but Dionysos (fig. 7.39) is just awakening at the left corner as the sun god, Apollo, drives his chariot onto the scene. At the opposite end, three goddesses (fig. 7.40) are about to hear the good tidings, as Artemis, the moon goddess, begins her nightly travels. Dionysos and the goddesses are freestanding, larger than life-size, and carved in broad, clear planes and sharply delineated lines that made for better viewing at ground level.

A Parthenon metope depicting the *Combat between a Lapith and a Centaur* (fig. 7.41) is a skillfully executed high relief symbolizing the ascendancy of human ideals over human nature's bestial side. Studies of the ninety-two other metopes reveal consistent improvement in quality from the early, rather crude carvings to the exceptional work of such later pieces as the metope of figure 7.41. The stonemasons obviously benefited from some kind of on-the-job training under Pheidias.

The inner frieze, about 3 feet 9 inches (1.1 m) in height and over 500 feet (153 m) in length, ran along the outer walls of the cella. A marble **bas-relief** depicting the Athenians and their gods in the Greater Panathenaea celebration, the frieze portrayed a procession carrying a peplos to the statue of Athena in the Parthenon. Apparently at the very moment that the procession is getting underway, the horsemen (fig. 7.42) ready their mounts to escort the singing

7.38 *Above*   Reconstruction of central section of east pediment of Parthenon. Original height at center ca. 11' (3.35 m). Acropolis Museum, Athens.

7.39 *Right*   *Dionysos*, from east pediment of Parthenon. Ca. 438–432 BC. British Museum, London.

7.40 *Below*   *Three Goddesses: Hestia, Dione, Aphrodite*, from east pediment of Parthenon. Ca. 438–432 BC. Pentelic marble. British Museum, London.

7.41   *Combat between a Lapith and a Centaur*, south metope XXVII from Parthenon. Ca. 447–443 BC. Pentelic marble, height 4'5" (1.35 m). British Museum, London. Photo: Hirmer, Munich.

7.42   *Horsemen*, from north frieze of Parthenon. Ca. 440 BC. Pentelic marble, height ca. 3'6" (1.07 m). British Museum, London. Photo: Hirmer, Munich.

maidens to the temple. With about 600 persons and numerous horses, this scene depicts but one moment of activity; this is simultaneous narration, a sculptural version of the classic unities of Greek drama. The frieze is remarkable for its depiction of hundreds of Athenians on a temple frieze, something unthinkable in other ancient cultures. One has only to think of the dark and forbidden recesses of the Temple at Luxor (see fig. 2.14) to understand some fundamental differences between Egyptian and Greek civilizations.

Erechtheion The complex design of the Erechtheion (AIR-ek-thee-on; fig. 7.43) probably results from both the uneven site and the legendary contest between Athena and Poseidon. As both competed for the guardianship of the city, Poseidon struck a rock with his trident and sea water, symbol of Athenian sea power, gushed forth. Athena then struck the ground with her spear and a full-grown olive tree appeared. Judging olives more important because they were so useful, the other Olympians awarded the city to Athena. The canny Athenians, however, dedicated shrines to both within the same temple, and covered all bets by naming the building after the mythical King Erectheus who had supposedly lived on the site.

The higher (eastern) level of this graceful Ionic temple was dedicated to Athena, while the lower level (right background) was Poseidon's sanctuary. Three **porticos**, each of different design and dimensions, project from three sides. Best known is the south porch (fig. 7.44) with its six **caryatids** (karry-AT-ids; female figures used as columns). Measuring only 10 feet (3 m) deep by 15 feet (4.6 m) wide, the porch has an architrave supported by statues of young women whose drapery suggests the fluting of columns. Grouped as if in a procession toward the Parthenon, three figures on one side bend their right legs while those on the other side bend their left legs to give the illusion of

7.43 *Above* Mnesikles, Erechtheion (view from east), Acropolis, Athens. Ca. 421–405 BC. Height of porch figures ca. 8' (2.44 m). Photo: Hirmer, Munich.

7.44 *Right* Porch of the Maidens (view from southwest), Erechtheion. 10 × 15' (3 × 4.6 m). Photo: Alison Frantz, Princeton.

animation. All columns suggest physical strain; despite the individual beauty of these figures, substituting a human form for a supporting column tends to place an undue burden on our imagination. One might characterize these caryatids as an excellent solution for a less than satisfactory idea. The caryatid to the right of the figure on the left corner is a copy of the figure Lord Elgin carried off to England in 1806 (along with considerable booty from the Parthenon and other buildings) as part of a questionable attempt to "save" Greek art.[2] Compounding the irony, all of the figures were moved to a protected environment and replaced with fiberglass copies, including a copy of the copy. Air pollution, rather than the Turks or an English lord, is the latest and most deadly threat to the Athenian Acropolis.

2. See Theodore Vrettos, *A Shadow of Magnitude: The Acquisition of the Elgin Marbles* (1974), about which the British novelist and poet Lawrence Durrell wrote, "So thoroughly researched and energetically executed, this is the first portrait in depth of that ignoble monomaniac Lord Elgin, who lives in history as the man who despoiled the Parthenon." The Greek government has repeatedly pressed Britain for the return of the Elgin Marbles removed from the Parthenon.

7.45 Callicrates, Temple of Athena Nike, Acropolis, Athens. Ca. 427–424 BC. Pentelic marble, 17'9" × 26'10" (5.4 × 8.2 m). Photo: Alison Frantz, Princeton.

Temple of Athena Nike   A classic example of architectural unity, the exquisite Temple of Athena Nike (fig. 7.45) is a tiny building (17'9" × 26'10" [5.4 × 8.2 m]) of pentelic marble. Though architecture is usually defined as the art of enclosing space, Greek temples embody more than this. Each temple was designed as a series of receding planes from steps to columns to cella wall, with temple reliefs in comparable planes from surface to deepest recesses. Both a strongly defined form and a four-sided sculptural relief, the Greek temple is architectural but it is also a massive sculptural composition. Rather than just enclosing space the temple also fills space, and none any better than the elegant Temple of Nike, goddess of victory. The temple originally housed a statue of the victory goddess with her wings clipped so that she could never leave Athens. Twenty years after the completion of the building Athens fell to Sparta, never to regain her political and military supremacy. Demolished by the Turks in the eighteenth century to build a fort, the Temple of Athena Nike was later reconstructed by retrieving the stones from the wrecked fort. That the temple dedicated to the victory goddess could be restored to its original form symbolizes the enduring quality of a culture that survived invasions by Persians, Spartans, Romans, Venetians, Turks, Italians, and Germans.

Doric Temples—Sicily

Two of the most sophisticated Doric temples of the Periclean age are found not in Greece but in Sicily, the southernmost portion of Magna Graecia. Both the Temple of Concord at Agrigento and the Temple of Segesta are in relatively good condition, but for quite different reasons.

The prosperous Greek city of Akragas (ah-kra-GOSS; "high ground"; modern Agrigento) was built on a plateau overlooking the Mediterranean to the south. Because there was no acropolis, the citizens of Akragas built five Doric temples on the southern slope between the city and the sea. Lined up in a widely spaced "avenue of temples," the buildings provided a cohesive link between the city, the land, and the sea. Seen first when arriving by sea, the temples identified Akragas as a Greek city in a foreign land. One can say that the Greek gods were at home in Greece but they had to be imported into the very different environment of Italy and Sicily.

Temple of Concord   Placed on a high spot midway between the city and the coastal plain, Concord is a hexastyle (six-column front) Doric temple. It has 23-foot (7 m) columns arranged in a thirty-four-column peristyle, with six and eleven on alternate sides (fig. 7.46). Like the Parthenon, it has rising stylobates and entablatures on both sides but the six-column front is set in a straight line. The overall effect is a static front with longitudinal columns moving lightly down each side. When compared with the Parthenon the most significant difference is the hexastyle facade. For most people six columns can be taken in at a glance as a unit. However, one cannot see the eight-column front (octastyle facade) of the Parthenon (see fig. 7.35) as a unit; for most observers the Parthenon insists upon a second or third look. Compare the facade of Concord with that of the Parthenon. The latter appears to be restless and challenging; Concord reflects its name in its serenity, grace, and charm.

The Temple of Concord was, like all Greek temples, a sacred site, probably a sanctuary for Demeter, goddess of fertility, agriculture, and peace. Despite its sacred character, the temple escaped destruction only because it was converted into a Christian church in AD 597. Greek religious architecture used by Christians was always substantially altered but the alternative was the destruction meted out to all other sanctuaries.

Temple of Segesta   Akragas was a very large Greek city (with a population of about 250,000) but Segesta was neither populous nor Greek. Why, then, did it have a large Greek theatre and one of the most interesting of all Doric temples? Located in the mountainous northwest of Sicily, Segesta was within the orbit of Carthaginian influence. Its vulnerable location led it to look to Greece, adopting the language and some of the customs, and eventually reaching an agreement with Athens.

The Temple of Segesta (fig. 7.47) is a hexastyle Doric structure considerably larger than Concord. The columns

7.46 Temple of Concord, Agrigento, Sicily (ancient Akragas, Magna Graecia). Ca. 425 BC. Limestone, ca. 55 × 129' (16.8 × 39.3 m). Photo: Scala, Florence.

7.48 *Above* Stylobate, Temple of Segesta, Sicily. Photo: Ancient Art & Architecture, London.

7.47 *Left* Temple of Segesta, Sicily. Ca. 420s BC. Limestone, ca. 76 × 191' (23 × 58 m). Photo: Scala, Florence.

rise 32 feet (9.8 m) and are arranged in a thirty-six-column peristyle (6 x 12). The temple is sometimes referred to as "anonymous"; no one knows which god it served, only that the god was not Greek. The architect was probably Athenian (maybe even Ictinus) and certainly a knowledgeable and skillful master of the classical style. The architectural historian, Vincent Scully, calls him an "architectural Euripides."

Left in an unfinished condition for unknown reasons, the temple has no roof and no indication that an inner cella was ever planned. The columns are in place awaiting the fluting that never took place. Particularly striking are the stone bosses on the stylobate and stereobate (fig. 7.48) which were never chiseled off. These knobs facilitated the safe transport of heavy slabs from the quarry to this magnificent site.

As in Concord and the Parthenon, the longitudinal stylobate and entablature of Segesta arch upward but much more sharply than in the other two temples (fig. 7.48). The straight, six-column front combined with the swift and tensile longitudinal arc give the building a strange and impressive energy. The architect may have chosen not to flute the columns after he saw their solid mass contributing to the extraordinary power of the structure; maybe the temple

---

7.49 Praxiteles, *Hermes with the Infant Dionysos*. Copy of probable bronze original of ca. 340 BC. Marble, height 6' 1" (1.86 m). Archaeological Museum, Olympia. Photo: Alinari, Florence.

was deliberately left unfinished. That it was not destroyed by invading armies or zealous Christians was due to its isolation in the mountain wilderness of northwestern Sicily.

A comparison of the Temples of Concord and Segesta clearly reveals the range available to an imaginative architect. Both structures are readily classified as Doric by the elements identified in figure 7.31a (except for Segesta's lack of fluting). The aesthetic impact, however, is remarkably different. Concord is serene; Segesta is restless. Concord is graceful; Segesta is massive and muscular. Concord was probably dedicated to Demeter, the Greek goddess of peace. Segesta was intended for an unknown, non-Greek (meaning uncivilized) god. Concord could be transported to an appropriate site in Greece. Segesta is completely at home in the rugged mountains of Sicily. What Concord and Segesta had in common with the Parthenon and all other Greek temples was cogently expressed by an American writer:

> Not magnitude, not lavishness,
> But form—the site;
> Not innovating willfulness,
> But reverence for the archetype.
>
> Herman Melville, 1891

The Golden Age ended with the Spartan defeat of Athens in 404 BC. That Sophocles, Euripides, and Socrates died within a few years of this date further marked the end of an era. Throughout the following century, until the death of Alexander in 323 BC, the classical tradition was maintained, though in a somewhat more theatrical manner. Greek artists prided themselves on adhering to the high standards of the preceding century. Athens no longer ruled the seas but it was still the cultural center of the ancient world.

Late Classical, 400–323 BC

The more pleasing and personal qualities of late classical sculpture and the superbly executed naturalism are largely due to Praxiteles of Athens (prax–SIT–uh–leez), the most celebrated of all Greek sculptors. In his *Hermes with the Infant Dionysos* (fig. 7.49) we see, perhaps, an example of the artist's exceptional skill in working marble. Praxiteles was apparently among the first to exploit the shimmering, translucent quality of marble. There are no sharp angles; everything is smooth, rounded, polished. Compare, for example, the striking clarity of the *Doryphoros* (fig. 7.23) with the softly sensuous treatment of the *Hermes*. Slimmer and more relaxed, the *Hermes* looks positively decadent compared with the earnest *Spear Bearer*. Long regarded as the only surviving original by Praxiteles, this lovely sculpture is in the current expert consensus very likely a Hellenistic copy of what was probably a bronze original. The infant's head is proportionately too small and the rumpled drapery inconsistent with the late classical style. The most telling discrepancy is the marble bar bracing the hip. Greek sculptors usually designed their works to be self-supporting, but a marble copy of an inherently strong bronze original would need bracing.

Definitely a copy, and a good one, the *Aphrodite of Knidos* (fig. 7.50) is a revolutionary work. The single most popular statue in all antiquity, the *Aphrodite* was lavishly praised by the Roman historian Pliny (XXXVI, 20) as the finest statue in the world, so marvelous that it was placed in a shrine to be universally admired. (Pliny was equally enthusiastic about the *Laocoön*—fig. 7.62—and named *it* the world's finest sculpture.) Abandoning the traditional concept of a figure occupying a rectangular space, Praxiteles designed a slender goddess with sinuous lines rising from her feet to the quizzical tilt of her head. The slight outward lean of the right leg increases the sensuous curve of the right hip. Echoing the swelling curve of the hip, the left leg is flexed so that the thighs are pressed gently together with the knees nearly touching. From the knees—the narrowest part of the composition—the figure ascends in an hourglass configuration to the startled reaction of a woman surprised in the act of bathing. In line, pose, proportion, and structure Praxiteles has created an incomparable idealization of femininity, the essence of womanhood. Though nude males were portrayed in a variety of activities, Greek artists invariably depicted women in normal situations that warranted nudity: bathing, making love, functioning as flute girls, or as hetairai.

Looking somewhat like a male version of the *Aphrodite* (fig. 7.50), the original bronze found in the Bay of Marathon (fig. 7.51) was probably derived from the work of Praxiteles. The innate strength of bronze enabled the anonymous artist to dispense with visually irritating supports like the marble bar previously discussed (*Hermes;* fig. 7.49). The lightly poised figure, difficult to achieve in bronze but virtually impossible to reproduce in marble, is similar to the *Hermes,* especially in the modeling of the surfaces and the melting gaze of the eyes (fig. 7.52).

Lysippos, sculptor to the court of Alexander the Great, was probably the most revolutionary artist of the late classical period. His *Apoxyomenos* (a-pox-e-o-MAY-nos; fig. 7.53) was as pivotal in the fourth century as the *Doryphoros* of Polykleitos (fig. 7.23) was a century earlier; both works established new sculptural canons. Departing from the earlier canon, Lysippos introduced new proportions: smaller head, taller and more slender body, and long, lithe limbs. Using an S-shaped tool called a strigil, the athlete is scraping oil, dust, and sweat from his body, a standard procedure following athletic contests. Utilizing the space in front of the body, the extended arms break through the invisible barrier of the frontal plane, violating a convention dating back to Egypt's Old Kingdom art of ca. 2500 BC. There is a new sense of movement with trunk, head, and limbs turned in different directions. This is sculpture conceived, executed, and meant to be viewed in the round—all 360 degrees. As epitomized in the *Apoxyomenos,* these revolutionary ideas were not fully understood until the Italian Renaissance 1,700 years later.

7.50 Praxiteles, *Aphrodite of Knidos*. Roman copy of marble original of ca. 350 BC. Marble, height 6'8" (2.03 m). Musei Vaticani, Rome.

7.51 *Boy from the Bay of Marathon*. Ca. 340–300 BC. Bronze, height 4'3" (1.3 m). National Archaeological Museum, Athens. Photo: Hirmer, Munich.

7.52 *Boy from the Bay of Marathon*, detail of fig. 7.51. Photo: Hirmer, Munich.

7.53 Lysippos, *Scraper (Apoxyomenos)*. Roman copy of bronze original of ca. 330 BC. Marble, height 6'9" (2.06 m). Musei Vaticani, Rome. Photo: Alison Frantz, Princeton. (The museum added the fig leaf).

Jewelry

Jewelry was popular in Greece from Homeric times onward as adornment and as a sign of affluence. Much fine jewelry was made during the early archaic period, especially in Magna Graecia, but comparatively little remains from about 580 to 480 BC, perhaps because of a shortage of gold during that time. Production increased after the Persian wars as Athens moved into its most prosperous era. The Greek general Xenophon noted that men spent their wealth on armor, horses, and houses; women collected expensive clothes and gold jewelry. A well dressed woman would select from her diadems, earrings, necklaces, pendants, brooches, bracelets, and rings. Unlike people of other cultures, Athenians generally preferred elegant gold jewelry without precious or semiprecious stones. This preference is characteristic of a culture that valued moderation and simplicity while also esteeming loveliness. Gemstones did not become popular until the Hellenistic era.

The gold necklace from Tarentum in southern Magna Graecia (fig. 7.54) is a choice example of the skillful goldsmithing of Greek artisans. Generously decorated with delicate filigree, the basic necklace is composed of interlocking rosettes. The pendants consist of flower buds and miniature female heads in two different sizes. The custom of burying favorite jewelry with its owner saved many pieces of fine jewelry, including this necklace.

7.54 Necklace, from Taranto (Tarentum), Italy. 350–330 BC. Gold, length 11" (27.9 cm). British Museum, London.

7.55 *The Dying Gaul*. Roman copy of bronze original from Pergamon, Turkey. Ca. 230–220 BC. Marble, life-size. Museo Capitolino, Rome. Photo: Alison Frantz, Princeton.

HELLENISTIC PERIOD, 323–30 BC

Symbolized by the death of Alexander, the end of the long and enormously productive classical age had arrived. Artists were no longer concerned with idealized portraits and classical harmony, but instead became increasingly interested in actual appearances and in the infinite variety of human nature and experience. In the midst of the rapid disintegration of the Alexandrian empire, the emphasis was upon survival in a world beset by constant sectional strife. However, Alexander had left in his wake Hellenism, the first international culture in which Greek was the common language and which venerated scholarship, education, and the arts.

Sometimes described as decadent, Hellenistic art did indeed include banalities, trivialities, pathos, and empty virtuosity. Greek genius was not yet exhausted, however, for the age also saw the production of exceptional art works that were no less admirable than those of the classical era but which were certainly different.

Sculpture and Architecture

A Celtic tribe that ravaged Asia Minor until subdued by Attalos I of Pergamon, the Gauls were immortalized in the remarkable figure of *The Dying Gaul* (fig. 7.55). Also known as the *Dying Trumpeter* because of the discarded battle trumpet in the right foreground, the hair, facial features, and ornamental neck collar realistically portray a Gallic tribesman. The figure is, however, in the heroic Greek tradition of the nude warrior; the treatment of the vanquished barbarian is sympathetic, portraying a poignant nobility

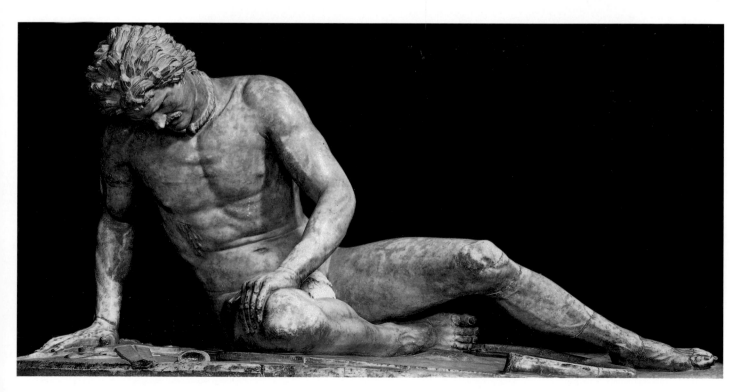

as the dying man braces his right arm against the ground in a futile effort to ward off an ignoble death.

The *Nike of Samothrace* (fig. 7.56) is not only one of the most dramatic and compelling works ever created but a prime example of the continuing power of the classical theme of Nike, the goddess of victory. Attributed to Pythokritos (py-THOCK-ri-toss) and erected in a sanctuary on the island of Rhodes in honor of a naval victory over King Antiochus III of Syria, Victory is portrayed alighting on the symbolic prow of a ship. With her great wings still extended, she is moving into a wind that becomes a tangible presence as it shapes the flowing draperies into deep diagonal folds, carrying our eyes restlessly over the entire surface. Aptly characterized as poetry in motion, Victory communicates both the immediacy of the moment and a feeling for ongoing action in a pervasive atmosphere of wind and sea.

One of the wonders of the ancient world, the great Altar of Zeus (fig. 7.57), was built by the son and successor of Attalos I to commemorate his father's military victories. Though designed as an Ionic structure for an Ionian site, the altar has none of the delicacy of the classic Ionic

7.56 *Above*   Pythokritos of Rhodes, *Nike of Samothrace*. Ca. 190 BC. Marble, height 8' (2.44 m). Louvre, Paris. Photo: Giraudon, Paris.

7.57 *Below*   Altar of Zeus, west front (restored), from Pergamon, Turkey. Ca. 180 BC. Base 100' square (30.5 m²). Staatliche Museen, Berlin. Photo: Marburg.

7.58 *The Battle of the Gods and Giants,* relief segment from the Altar of Zeus, Pergamon. Ca. 180 BC. Height 7'8" (2.34 m). Staatliche Museen, Berlin.

style. With a base 100 feet (30.5 m) square, this monumental altar is intended to impress rather than inspire. The immense frieze around the base is over 400 feet (122 m) long and 7 feet 8 inches (2.34 m) high (fig. 7.58). Using the traditional Greek device of portraying actual historical events in mythological terms, this is an emotional and dramatic work. Here is a world of giants, an exaggeration of physical and emotional force that, in its own way, accomplishes its goals fully as well as the Parthenon frieze (see fig. 7.42). Comparing the friezes defines the significant differences between the classical and Hellenistic styles, thus reflecting the contrast between confident optimism and a constant struggle for survival.

As dramatic as the Altar of Zeus and of equally monumental proportions, Hellenistic public buildings stressed sheer size over classic restraint and harmonious proportions. Even in the scanty remains of the Temple of the Olympian Zeus (fig. 7.59 and p. 64) one can detect some of the grandeur of a temple that originally had 104 columns over 56 feet (17 m) in height. Built in the Corinthian order and entirely of pentelic marble, the temple measured 130 by 340 feet (40 × 104 m), as compared to the 101 by 228 feet (31 × 70 m) of the Parthenon. Though the photograph shows only a few remaining columns, it also reveals the full stylobate of the temple, clearly indicating its enormous size. Affirming the Roman preference for the ornate Corinthian, the architect was Italic and the grandiose project completed by the Roman emperor Hadrian.

Originally part of a full-length statue, the bronze head from Delos (fig. 7.60) is a penetrating study of an apparently unhappy, fleshy-faced man seemingly overwhelmed by doubt and anxiety. Though not limited to the Hellenistic age, private portraits such as this one seem to epitomize the predicament of helpless individuals in a chaotic and often violent world. A comparison of this face with that of the *Doryphoros* (fig. 7.23) sums it up; the Golden Age has receded to the distant past.

The *Piping Satyr* (fig. 7.61) is stylistically close to fourth-century BC sculpture in the proportions, restraint, and carefully rendered muscles. The pose focuses attention on the hands that once clasped the twin tubes of the missing aulos, the instrument of Dionysos and the theatre. One can almost hear the sounds of the pipes and feel the rhythm of the music.

7.59 Cossutius, Temple of the Olympian Zeus, Athens. Ca. 174 BC–AD 131. Pentelic marble, 130 × 340' (40 × 104 m). Photo: © 1989 Loyola University of Chicago (R.V. Schoder, S.J.).

7.60 Portrait Head, from Delos, Greece. Ca. 80 BC. Bronze, height 12¾" (32.4 cm). National Archaeological Museum, Athens. Photo: Scala, Florence.

7.61 *Piping Satyr.* 1st century BC. Hollow cast bronze, height 3'8" (1.12 m). National Museum, Belgrade, Serbia. Photo: Scala, Florence.

The *Laocoön and His Sons* (lay-OK-o-on; fig. 7.62) is an extravagantly dramatic version of the fate of the Trojan priest. Supposedly punished by Poseidon's sea serpents because he warned his people of the Trojan horse scheme, the three Trojans writhe and struggle, their faces distorted with terror (fig. 7.63). Despite his bulging muscles the priest is at the mercy of the god. When discovered in 1506 this work's striking virtuosity made an enormous impression on Michelangelo and other Renaissance artists. The Romans probably imported the *Laocoön* because it represented a vital episode in pre-Roman history. Forewarned of Troy's fall by the priest's punishment, Aeneas escaped from the doomed city to fulfill his destiny as the legendary founder of Rome.

7.62 *Above* Hagesandros, Polydoros, and Athenodoros of Rhodes, *Laocoön and His Sons*. 1st century AD. Marble, height 8' (2.44 m). Musei Vaticani, Rome. Photo: Hirmer, Munich.

BOX 7.1 THE GREEK MUSES

The nine daughters of Zeus and Mnemosyne (nih-MOSS-uh-nee; goddess of memory) presided over literature, the arts, and science. Frequently called the "deities of graceful achievement," the Muses, under the leadership of Apollo, were the source of inspiration for all creative persons. In typically Greek fashion, their names were wonderfully descriptive of each Muse's particular function.

Calliope (kuh-LIE-uh-pea; "beautiful-voiced"), goddess of eloquence and epic poetry.

Clio (KLY-oh; "teller"), goddess of history.

Erato (air-uh-TOE; "loved"), goddess of love poetry.

Euterpe (you-TUR-pea; "charming"), goddess of lyric poetry and music.

Melpomene (mel-POM-uh-nee; "the singing one"), goddess of tragedy.

Ourania (yoo-RAY-nee-uh; "the heavenly one"), goddess of astronomy.

Polyhymnia (polly-HIM-nee-uh; "abounding in songs"), goddess of singing, sacred poetry, religious dance, and oratory.

Terpsichore (turp-SICK-uh-ree; "to delight in dance"), goddess of dance and choral song.

Thalia (tha-LEE-uh; "the blooming one"), goddess of comedy and pastoral poetry.

7.63 *Left* Hagesandros, Polydoros, and Athenodoros of Rhodes, *Laocoön and His Sons*, detail of fig. 7.62. Photo: Alinari, Florence (Anderson).

MUSIC

Music was a requisite for the good life in ancient Greece. The education of the young men of Athens was not complete without extensive instruction in the ethical qualities of music with approximately equal time devoted to music performance. Further, there must be instruction in gymnastics roughly equal to the time and effort expended on music. The question Glaucon posed for Socrates was rhetorical: "After music our youth are to be educated by gymnastics?" For the record the Socratic reply was a terse "Certainly." Music and gymnastics had to be evenly balanced to reach the goal of a sound mind in a healthy body. According to Plato, too much time in the gymnasium makes people "more brutal than they should be," while too much music making causes performers to be "softer than is good for them."

The concept of the balanced regimen apparently originated with Pythagoras, who drew an analogy between a vibrating, finely tuned string and the human mind and body. When stretched to the proper tension and plucked or bowed, the string will produce the exact musical tone that the performer requires. If stretched too tight, the string will break; if the tension is insufficient, the string will be dull and unresponsive. In other words, the mind (musical tone) and the body (tensed string) function best when they are completely in harmony with each other.

The Greek word for music (*mousike;* MOO-si-kay) means "of the Muses": the nine goddesses who presided over the arts, literature, and science (box 7.1). "Music" was therefore an umbrella term, but music as we understand the word was prominent in everyday life in four distinct ways:

1. The arts of singing and of playing a musical instrument. The relationship of poetry and music was symbiotic; rarely did one art form appear without the other.
2. Music in the educational process, that is, performing and listening to music as a vital part of the ethical training that inculcates virtue and "sobriety in the soul" (Plato). This is the doctrine of ethos that figured so prominently in Greek philosophy.
3. The study of the scientific basis of music, emphasizing acoustics (the science of sound) and mathematics.
4. Music and mathematics as a key to understanding the harmony of the universe, the Pythagorean "music of the spheres."

All Athenian citizens were involved in performance, listening, and music education. Plato, Aristotle, and other philosophers dealt with other aspects of music, from the Muses to mathematics to metaphysics.

Musical Instruments

The principal instruments were the lyre, a larger version of the lyre called the kithara, and the aulos. According to mythology the infant Hermes, son of Zeus, killed a turtle and strung gut strings across the hollow shell. That the strings were made from intestines of oxen stolen from his brother Apollo complicated the situation. Hermes craftily avoided further trouble by allowing Apollo to play his lyre. Thus the beginning of the legendary lyre and with it the lyre-playing tradition of the cult of Apollo (fig 7.64).

The seat of the Apollonian cult was the island of Delos and subsequently Delphi. The myths extol the virtues of the early musical life of a Greek mainland untouched by alien influences. Marvelous were the deeds of heroes and of divinely endowed musicians such as Orpheus, Amphion, and others, all with names connected with ancient tribes in the northern part of the mainland. As the tribes migrated they carried their music with them. The Dorians moved to Sparta and as far south as Crete, the Aeolians settled in the eastern Aegean, and the Ionians moved from the west to the east central mainland and to Asia Minor.

The Ionians brought with them their music and their national instrument, the lyre. The influence of Oriental elements synthesized the two cultures which, in turn, led to the founding of Greek classical music, poetry, and dance. Characteristically, mythology depicts the Ionian migration by relating how Orpheus accidentally dropped his lyre, which drifted eastward across the Aegean to the island of

7.64 *Lyre Player of "The Boston Throne."* Ca. 470–450 BC. Three-sided marble relief, height at center 38" (96.5 cm). Museum of Fine Arts, Boston (H. L. Pierce Fund). The lyre was usually played from a sitting position.

Lesbos, the home of Sappho, the famous poet-musician.

The Near East produced the other national instrument, the reed pipe, or aulos (fig. 7.65). The inventors of this pungent-toned instrument (which sounded somewhat like a modern oboe) came from Phrygia in Asia Minor. The aulos was associated with the Phrygian mode and the cult of Dionysos, as contrasted with the lyre, the instrument of the Dorian mode and the cult of Apollo. There was a notable conflict between the two cults. The East did not fully accept the lyre, possibly because its tone quality was too delicate compared to the reedy, nasal quality of the aulos. Legend recounts a musical competition between Olen the Lycian on the lyre and Olympos the Phrygian on the aulos. The results of the contest were inconclusive, indicating that the competing instruments attained a state of parity. The whole of Greek musical culture reflected this kind of balance of power between the Apollonian lyre and the Dionysian aulos, between the intellect and the passions.

The Musicians

The earliest musicians were apparently the blind singers who performed the Homeric epics. Greek legends abound with accounts of singers so full of hubris they challenged the gods. Thamyris was blinded by the Muses because of his boasting. The blind singer Teiresias (as in Sophocles' *Oedipus*) suffered the same penalty for revealing things men should not know.[3] Misenis lost a musical contest to the sea gods and was drowned in the Aegean. The satyr Marsyas was a spectacular loser. First, he picked up the aulos that Athena had discarded because she felt she looked undignified while playing it. She had Marsyas beaten for his impudence. Failing to take the celestial hint, he then challenged Apollo to a playing contest, for which audacity he was flayed alive (fig. 7.66).

The most famous singer-poet was Orpheus, reputedly the son of Apollo and Calliope. The powers attributed to Orpheus were staggering. In order to rescue Eurydice (you-RID-uh-sea), he enchanted the underworld with his lyre (fig. 7.67). He cast spells on all aspects of nature, and he was credited with inventing poetic meter and even the alphabet. The last attribute may refer to the musical notation that was based on the Greek alphabet.

The earliest historical figure to emerge from the legendary past personified by the mythical Olympos is the kithara-player, Terpander of Lesbos (ca. 675 BC). His musical powers were so renowned that the Delphic Oracle ordered him to Sparta to help quell dissension within the state. As the first known musician, Terpander is regarded as the founder of Greek classical music.

7.65 *Aulos Player of the Ludovisi Throne.* Ca. 460 BC. Marble, height 4' (1.2 m). Museo Nazionale Romano, Rome. Photo: Hirmer, Munich.
One of the few known female nudes from the classical period, this lovely work is also notable for the relaxed and casual pose. The aulos could be played standing or sitting.

WORDS AND MUSIC

Most Greek musicians were, like Orpheus, singer-poets (or poet-musicians) who played the accompaniment as they sang their poetry. The first of these **lyric** poets— that is, those who sang with the lyre—was Archilochos (are-ki-LOW-kos; fl. 660 BC) of Paros, a major musical innovator. Before his time each note of music was closely linked to the words. He added "dissenting" notes that were not in unison with the melody, and added embellishments that were improvised on between stanzas. In brief, he made the lyre a solo instrument and a more interesting partner in song. Archilochos was a part-time poet-musician, by occupation a mercenary soldier who died on an unknown battlefield. Later, many poet-musicians, such as Sappho and Simonides, could devote themselves fully to their art.

---

3. Because Teiresias had been both a woman and a man, Zeus asked him which enjoyed sex more. When Teiresias replied that women did, Hera was so angry to have the secret revealed that she struck the poet-musician blind. As partial compensation, Zeus awarded him the gift of prophecy.

7.66 *Above* Workshop of Praxiteles, *Apollo and Marsyas*, from Manitinea. Ca. 400–350 BC. Marble relief, width ca. 4' (1.22 m). National Archaeological Museum, Athens. Photo: Scala, Florence.
Marsyas is on the right, frantically playing, while a slave waits patiently with a knife. Holding a kithara, Apollo sits serenely at the left, waiting to execute the satyr for his hubris.

7.67 *Right* Orpheus painter, *Orpheus Among the Thracians*, detail of krater. Ca. 440 BC. Red-figure pottery, height 24" (60.9 cm). Antikenmuseum, Staatliche Museen Preussischer Kulturbesitz, Berlin. Photo: B.P.K., Berlin (Ingrid Geske-Heiden).
The power of Orpheus' music obviously failed to charm the vulgar Thracians. They murdered him, which tends to confirm the Greek thesis that their music was too sophisticated for barbarians to appreciate.

The illustrious poet-musician Sappho was born on the Aegean island of Lesbos and lived most of her long life there. At a time when Solon was legislating in Athens and Jeremiah was prophesying in Palestine, she was at the height of her fame—and fully aware of her reputation:

> The Muses have made me happy
> And worthy of the world's envy,
> So that even beyond death
> I shall be remembered.

Celebrated in both the Greek and Roman worlds, her poems were preserved until the third century AD by Alexandrian editors but were later almost totally destroyed by zealous Christians along with other pagan literature. The three surviving poems and many fragments remain to testify to the beauty of her lyric poetry, sung to the delicate sounds of the lyre. "Lead off, my lyre,/And we shall sing together."

Sappho's poems focus on her erotic passions and jealousies, but there are also references to two brothers and to her daughter, Kleïs. Though knowledge of her personal life is fragmentary, Sappho certainly enjoyed the social and domestic freedom of a society in which highly educated women mixed freely with men as their equals. Not confined to a subordinate existence like Ionian women or subject to a military discipline like the Dorians of Sparta, Aeolian women were devoted to the arts of beauty—especially poetry, music, and dance (fig. 7.68).

LITERARY SELECTION 11

God's Stunning Daughter

Sappho (fl. 6th century BC)

In the following complete poem, Sappho appeals to Aphrodite to help her win the affections of a reluctant girl. Aphrodite's response is good-natured but a bit impatient; Sappho has made this kind of request before and she will certainly make it again. Moreover, as Aphrodite points out, the girl refuses your gifts today but you will refuse hers tomorrow.

> God's stunning daughter deathless Aphrodite,
> A whittled perplexity your bright abstruse chair,
> Don't blunt my stubborn eye with breathlessness, lady,
> To tame my heart.
>
> But come down to me, as you came before,
> For if ever I cried, and you heard and came,
> Come now, of all times, leaving
> Your father's golden house
>
> In that chariot pulled by sparrows reined and bitted,
> Swift in their flying, a quick blur aquiver,   10
> Beautiful, high. They drew you across steep air
> Down to the black earth;
>
> Fast they came, and you behind them, O
> Hilarious heart, your face all laughter,
> Asking, What troubles you this time, why again
> Do you call me down?
>
> Asking, In your wild heart, who now
> Must you have? Who is she that persuasion
> Fetch her, enlist her, and put her into bounden love?
> Sappho, who does you wrong?   20
>
> If she balks, I promise, soon she'll chase,
> If she's turned from gifts, now she'll give them.
> And if she does not love you, she will love,
> Helpless, she will love.
>
> Come, then, loose me from cruelties.
> Give my tethered heart its full desire.
> Fulfill, and, come, lock your shield with mine
> Throughout the siege.

The next poem is also complete except for the last four words added by the translator. The theme is jealousy, a recital of physical torments brought about by the loved one's interest

---

7.68 *Alkaios and Sappho with Lyres*, detail of vase. Ca. 450 BC. Red-figure pottery, height 20" (50.8 cm). Glypothek, Munich. Photo: Studio Koppermann, Munich. Standing as tall as her colleague, the poet Alkaios, Sappho is depicted as a poised and confident women, fully the equal of a male poet-musician.

Aristotle, the "Golden Mean." However stated, it was the sensible Greek approach to moderation in all things.

The Legacy of Greece

The Greeks of antiquity established a superb foundation for the development of most of Western civilization. They constructed a rational, viable, and humanistic culture in which the emphasis was upon the individual and each person's pursuit of excellence. Their achievements were by no means limited to the arts and philosophy discussed in this text, for they also excelled in commerce, seafaring, medicine, coinage, engraved gems, decorative metalwork, painting and mosaics, glassware, furniture, and textiles. Adding up all of these contributions reveals a marvelously rounded culture that achieved, during the Golden Age, a quality of life never to be seen again. They established standards that serve as thesis or antithesis for contemporary judgments and achievements throughout our cultural life.

> It is important that the great age of Greece came before Christ. The stimulating, even subversive place of Greece comes from belonging within a Western world fundamentally based on Christianity.[7]

Skeptical, resilient, frequently cantankerous, the Greeks celebrated excellence and despised mediocrity. Constantly seeking an understanding of the world and everything in it, they asked not only "Why?" but also "Why not?" And they expected sane and sensible answers. There has never been anyone quite like them.

---

7. Oliver Taplin, *Greek Fire: The Influence of Ancient Greece on the Modern World* (New York: Atheneum, 1990), p. 33.

UNIT 3

Rome:
The
International
Culture

Rome

753 BC–AD 476

	Key Dates	People and Events	Literature	Art and Architecture	Religion, Science, Philosophy
600 BC	753 Founding of Rome (trad.)	606–509 Etruscan period with Tarquin kings			
500	509–27 Roman Republic	509 Tarquins overthrown			
400	450 Romans colonize Italy			ca. 500 *She-Wolf of the Capital* (Etruscan)	
300	343–290 Samnite wars: Rome dominant in Italy	390 Gauls sack Rome	**Theocritus** 310?–250 poet		**Epicurus** 341–2? **Zeno the Stoic** 335?–263?
200	264–241 First Punic War with Carthage; Rome acquires Sicily, Corsica, Sardinia 218–201 Second Punic War; Rome rules western Mediterranean 214–146 Macedonian wars: Rome rules Greece 200–133 Conquest of Near East	287 *Lex Hortensia* ends patrician-plebeian conflict 216 Hannibal invades Italy; defeats Romans at Cannae 202 Scipio Africanus invades Africa	**Plautus** 254?–184 dramatist **Polybius** 205–133 historian		
100	149–146 Third Punic War; Carthage destroyed	146 Corinth destroyed	**Terence** 190?–159 dramatist **Cicero** 106–43 **Caesar** 102–44 *Commentaries*		
0	88–82 BC Civil War: Sulla/Marius 80–43 Age of Cicero 60 First Triumvirate: Pompey, Crassus, Caesar 49 Caesar crosses Rubicon 44 Caesar assassinated by Brutus, Cassius, and others 43 Second Triumvirate: Mark Antony, Lepidus, Octavian (Augustus) 42 BC–AD 17 Augustan golden age 31 Naval battle of Actium	82–79 BC Sulla: dictator 73–71 Slave revolt; Spartacus 63 Cicero as consul 59 Caesar as consul 58–51 Caesar conquers Gaul 48–45 Caesar campaigns in Asia Minor, Egypt (Cleopatra), Spain 27 BC–AD 14 Reign of Caesar Augustus 4 BC? Birth of Christ	**Sallust** 86–34 BC historian **Catullus** 84–54 poet **Virgil** 70–19 *Aeneid* **Horace** 65–8 *Odes* **Livy** 59 BC–AD 17 *History of Rome* **Ovid** 43 BC–AD 17 *Art of Love; Metamorphoses* **Seneca the Younger** 3 BC–AD 65 dramatist	**Vitruvius** ca. 50– ca. AD 10 *De architectura* ca. 50– Villa of the Mysteries, Pompeii 27– Roman Forum, *Ara Pacis*, Baths of Agrippa, Theatre of Marcellus, Rome 20 *Augustus of Primaporta* 20–10 Pont du Gard, Nîmes 19 Maison Carrée, Nîmes	**Lucretius** ca. 96–55 *On the Nature of Things* (Epicureanism)
AD 100	27 BC–AD 476 Roman Empire 27 BC–AD 180 *Pax Romana* AD 17–130 Silver Age 70 Titus destroys Jerusalem and the Temple of Solomon 79 Mount Vesuvius destroys Pompeii and Herculaneum 96–180 The "Good Emperors"	14–37 Reign of Tiberius 37–41 Caligula 41–54 Claudius 54–68 Nero 69 Galba, Otho, Vitellius, Flavian Caesars 69–79 Vespasian 71–81 Titus 81–96 Domitian, Antonine Caesars 96–98 Nerva 98–117 Trajan	**Petronius** d. 66 *Satyricon* **Pliny the Elder** 23–79 naturalist **Quintilian** 35–ca. 100 *Institutes of Oratory* **Lucan** 39–65 poet **Martial** 40–104 *Epigrams* **Plutarch** 46–120 historian **Tacitus** 55–120 historian **Juvenal** 60–140 *Satires* **Pliny the Younger** 62–114 writer **Suetonius** ca. 70–160 *Lives of the Caesars*	54 Roman baths in England 70 *Herakles Discovering the Infant Telephos in Arcadia* 72–80 Colosseum, Rome 81 Arch of Titus, Rome	d. 29? Jesus Christ d. 64? Apostle P[eter] d. 67? Apostle P[aul] **Epictetus** ca. 60–110 Stoic philosopher: *Discourses*
200	180–476 Decline and fall	117–138 Hadrian 138–161 Antoninus Pius 161–180 Marcus Aurelius 180–192 Commodus 193–211 Septimius Severus	**Lucian** ca. 117–180 Greek satirist **Apuleius** fl. 160 *Golden Ass*	106–113 Column, Baths, and Forum of Trajan, Rome 118–125 Pantheon, Rome 135–139 Hadrian's tomb and villa, Tivoli 161–180 Equestrian Statue of Marcus Aurelius, Rome	**Marcus Aurelius** 121–180 *Meditations* **Ptolemy** fl. 126–151 astronomer **Galen** ca. 130–2? physician
300		211–217 Caracalla 222–235 Alexander Severus 235–284 "Barracks Emperors" (25 out of 26 murdered) 284–305 Diocletian		ca. 212 Baths of Caracalla, Rome 298–306 Baths of Diocletian, Rome	**Plotinus** 205–2? founder of Neoplatonism
400	313 Edict of Milan; freedom of worship 330 Constantine establishes Eastern capital in Constantinople 395 Theodosius proclaims Christianity sole permitted state religion	307–337 Constantine I 337–361 Constantius 361–363 Julian 363–364 Jovian 364–378 Valens 379–395 Theodosius I 395–403 Honorius		312–315 Arch of Constantine, Rome 330 *Constantine the Great*	**St. Jerome** 340– **St. Ambrose** 340–397 **St. Augustine** 354–430

The Roman Empire "fell" in 410 with the sack of Rome by the Visigoths or in 476 when the last Roman emperor was deposed.

CHAPTER 8

A Thousand Years of Rome

ROMAN LEGENDS AND VIRTUES

"So great a labor," wrote Virgil, "was it to found the Roman race." And it all began, according to legend, with Romulus and Remus, twin sons of Mars, god of war, and of Rhea Silvia, daughter of King Numitor. It seems that Amulius, Numitor's wicked brother, usurped the throne, forced his niece into service as a Vestal Virgin,[1] and, to secure his rule against future claimants, ordered the infants placed in a flimsy basket and set adrift on the Tiber River. Rescued and suckled by a she-wolf, the ancient symbol of Rome, they were discovered by a shepherd couple and raised to vigorous manhood (fig. 8.1).

Upon learning their identity they demonstrated their straightforward Roman nature by immediately killing Amulius and restoring Numitor to the throne. Ignoring an omen pointing to Romulus as Rome's founder, they resolutely set off to fulfill their destiny: establish a mighty city on the seven hills by the Tiber. The inevitable quarrel between Romulus, the serious twin, and the lighthearted Remus leads to the latter's death, apparently because Remus made fun of a wall constructed by Romulus and fell a victim to his brother's self-righteous wrath. Romulus subsequently raised an army, supplied the soldiers with Sabine wives (the Rape of the Sabines), and, to make a long story short, founded Rome right on schedule in 753 BC. And much as Moses received the tablets of law on the mountain, he accepted the first constitution from the gods and completed his imperative by becoming the first king of the Romans.

Establishing the Roman Republic was the first step; the Roman Empire had its own legendary beginning as related by Virgil (see pp. 248–9 and 252–61) in his epic poem, the *Aeneid*. "It is the nature," boasted Ovid, "of a Roman to do and suffer bravely," and Aeneas (uh–NEE-us) was the prototype of the stoic Roman hero. As Troy fell to the Greeks under Agamemnon, Aeneas and a loyal band of Trojan warriors escaped the debacle and sailed west to confront their destiny. Dumped on a North African shore by a mighty storm, they made their way to nearby Carthage where Queen Dido (DIE-doe) received them with full honors while promptly falling in love with Aeneas. As much as stern duty would allow, Aeneas responded in kind, knowing that he must abandon her to fulfill his sacred mission of founding Rome. A despairing Dido chose suicide and, while she lay on her funeral pyre, still hopeful of a last-ditch rescue, Aeneas sailed resolutely to Sicily and finally to the banks of the Tiber. There he fought and defeated Turnus, married Lavinia the beautiful daughter of King Latinus, and dutifully established the "first among cities, the home of gods, golden Rome" (Ausonius).

Rome was fated to be a city of warriors, grandeur, and glory, and its legends of Romulus and Remus and of Aeneas were self-fulfilling prophecies. Romulus was descended from the god of war and Aeneas was the progenitor of the stalwart city that would restore Trojan honor by conquering the wily Greeks of the wooden horse. Rome was nourished by the forces of nature, symbolized by the she-wolf, and raised to maturity by good people of the soil, the peasant couple who reared the twins. Rome pursued its imperative by seizing the Sabine lands and women, and established its legitimacy with a god-given constitution.

8.1 *The Capitoline She-Wolf.* Wolf, copy of Etruscan original of ca. 500 BC; figures of Romulus and Remus added during the Renaissance. Bronze, height 33½" (85.1 cm). Museo Capitolino, Rome. Photo: Alinari, Florence.

---

1. Selected daughters of the best families served the goddess Vesta in chastity and obedience. Amulius undoubtedly forced Rhea Silvia into the arms of the goddess so that she would not bear a legitimate heir to the throne.

The Romans saw themselves as destined for world leadership; as Cicero (see pp. 249–52) said, "We were born to unite with our fellowmen, and to join in community with the human race." They would triumph because they were a no-nonsense, practical people with the exemplary virtues of thrift, honesty, loyalty, and dedication to hard work. Little interested in abstractions or theory, they had two questions: "Does it work?" and "How can we get the job done?" As Remus discovered, building an illustrious city was no laughing matter; obligations to the city took precedence over everything else, even passion, a lesson lost on the ill-fated Queen of Carthage. Duty to golden Rome was the noblest virtue of all.

Etruscan Influence

The Aeneas legend may have been based on the Etruscans, the mysterious people who emerged in northern Italy during the ninth century BC. Herodotos said they were an advanced culture from the Kingdom of Lydia in western Asia Minor (near Troy), a view today's historians cannot contradict. The Etruscans used letters derived from an archaic Greek alphabet but their language resembles no other tongue, in Lydia or anywhere else. Leaving an immense quantity of art, partially decoded inscriptions, and some undeciphered literature, their origins may never be known.

The Etruscans conquered most of central and northern Italy and ruled Rome itself during the sixth century BC. The decisive battle at Lake Vadimon in 308 BC broke Etruscan political and military power, but the cultural inheritance was exceptionally strong. From Etruscan civilization Rome derived street plans for cities, the idea of the triumphal procession, gladiatorial combat, and the masonry arch, the critical technological contribution. Etruria was densely populated and enjoyed a high standard of living, with large cities surrounded by market towns, villages, and exceptionally productive agricultural areas. Etruscans supported their affluent life-style with the most sophisticated sanitary and civil engineering in the Mediterranean world. Rome's spectacular achievements in engineering and construction were based on the expertise of their conquered enemies.

But Rome did not accept all things Etruscan. Such concerns as life after death, elaborate tombs, and most especially, luxurious living, did not suit sober Roman sensibilities. The pursuit of pleasure shocked the austere and dutiful Romans. Moreover, Etruscan women and men enjoyed about the same rights and liberties, whereas Roman women had scarcely any freedom at all. Etruscan tomb paintings portrayed women drinking wine with men but Roman women couldn't even socialize with men, much less drink with them. The status of Etruscan women so enraged the Romans that they accused them of gross promiscuity, even temple prostitution, judgments that tell us more about self-righteous Romans than it does about Etruscan

morality. Nor were the chauvinistic Greeks any less critical of Etruscan society.

Greek Influence

Rome came under Greek influence very early, in the eighth century BC, when Greek immigrants founded colonies in southern Italy and Sicily in what the Romans called Magna Graecia. Syracuse, Naples, Paestum, Elea, the Pythagoreans of Crotona, the pleasure-loving Greeks of Sybaris—all flourished under the stern gaze of Romans who were always ambivalent about the Greeks. Awed by an obviously superior civilization, they were also hostile, for Greek culture amounted to a reversal of Roman values: urbane, artistic, intellectual, sophisticated, always seeking the good life. Roman enmity was not unexpected from an austere, rigid, and self-righteous society that stressed manly virtues, physical prowess, and duty to the state. From this point of view the Greeks were obviously dissolute and debauched.

THE REPUBLIC, 509–27 BC

Rome was not built in one day.
John Heywood, *Proverbs*, 1546

According to still another Roman tradition, the Republic began in 509 BC with the expulsion of the Etruscan king Tarquin the Proud. Never interested in abstractions or political theory, they pragmatically accepted their kingless state and made adjustments as necessary. We can call it the let's-try-it-this-way-and-see-if-it-stops-hurting philosophy of government. Tarquin's hurried departure left behind an oligarchy (government by the few), which became the basis of the new state. (Plato defined an oligarchy as "A government resting on the valuation of property, in which the rich have power and the poor man is deprived of it.") The oligarchs, the land-owning aristocrats, established a republic with full citizenship reserved for themselves, the patricians (Lat., *pater*, "father"). The other 90 percent or so of the population, the plebeians (pluh-BEE-uns; Lat., *plebs*, "the multitude"), could neither hold office nor marry into the patrician class. They could make money, however, making political adjustments inevitable.

Patricians and Plebeians

The patrician class supplied the executive heads of state, the two consuls who governed with full power for one year (except that each had veto power over the other). Already senators themselves, the consuls appointed patricians to life terms in the 300-member Senate. The other legislative body, the Centuriate Assembly, had less power than the Senate but it did elect the consuls and passed on laws submitted to it by the consuls or Senate. From among the exconsuls the Assembly elected two censors who determined eligibility for military service and ruled on the moral qualifications of Senate nominees.

Consuls were commanders of the army but, in time of war, their mutual veto power could jeopardize the state. Rome invented another adjustment, of course, a dictator, a supreme military commander who received his authority constitutionally and relinquished it at the end of his six-month term. When Julius Caesar had himself elected dictator for life his enemies had their worst fears confirmed.

The Roman oligarchy kept the plebeians in an intolerable situation but their growing financial power did force the Senate to create the new office of tribune, protector of the people. Later in the century (fifth century BC) ever more powerful plebeian forces accused the judges of abusing their office because there were no written laws. The reaction was most uncharacteristic; the Senate sent a commission to Athens to observe Solon's reformed legal system. The commission returned to compose the Twelve Tables of Law, at which point Roman conservatism reasserted itself. The new laws were as harsh as Draco's fierce legal code of nearly two centuries earlier (see p. 71), the very system that Solon's humane reforms had replaced.

Economics and the Military

Roman pragmatists never solved the problem of ownership of the land, a failure that had much to do with the Empire's demise. From the beginning of the Republic absentee landlords controlled a large part of the agricultural market, leaving the working farmer, with his small acreage, struggling to make ends meet. Competition from estate holders plus drought and pestilence forced him into debt and finally into a slavery decreed by the severe Twelve Tables. Large estates grew larger, operating with lower overheads because they used war-booty slaves. The inexorable price for noncompetitive farms was bankruptcy. (There were strikingly similar dilemmas in the American South before the Civil War.) Even after reforms barring debt-slavery and attempts to redistribute land, many farmers ended up as urban poor: landless and unemployed. Unable to work the land their ancestors had farmed for centuries and unfit for employment in a city that relied on slave labor, they became part of the permanent welfare program. By the first century BC about 80 percent of Rome's population was either slave laborers or subsisting on "bread and circuses." The welfare program was a failure because, as Plutarch observed, "The man who first ruined the Roman people was he who first gave them treats and gratuities."

Roman talent for organization was most spectacularly evidenced by their awesome military power. Reducing the ponderous 8,000-man phalanx to 3,600 men armed with javelin and short Roman sword, they created a mobile striking force that could march 24 miles (39 km) in five hours, each man carrying a 60-pound (27-kg) pack. Steely discipline honed a war machine that gave no quarter and asked none.

Some apologists claim that Rome backed into empire, much as England did in the nineteenth century, but this is simply not so. Roman conquest clearly became an end in itself during Republican days. The point at which Rome set out to deliberately conquer the world was probably 146 BC, the final year of the Punic Wars with Carthage (264–146 BC). The First Punic War began when Carthage, the powerful Phoenician colony in North Africa, attempted to expand its trading empire in eastern Sicily. Responding to the appeals of their Greek allies, Roman armies found themselves opposing the Carthaginian navy. Hurriedly building their first fighting fleet, the Romans somehow managed to defeat Carthage while losing more ships through ineptness than to enemy action.

Spain, which had resisted Roman domination for two centuries, became the Carthaginian base for the Second Punic War (218–201 BC). Stating that "we will either find a way or make one," the remarkable general Hannibal crossed the Alps with his elephants and attacked Rome from the rear. Unable to compete with his brilliant tactics, a desperate Rome attacked his vulnerable homeland thus ending Carthage's dominance of the western Mediterranean. The Third Punic War, however, was a different kind of conflict.

Marcus Porcius Cato (Cato the Elder, the Censor; 234–149 BC) was a senator, consul, censor, and writer, and a prime instigator of the final attack on Carthage. Renowned for his devotion to Roman ideals of simplicity, honesty, courage, ability to endure hardship, rigorous sexual morality, and loyalty to Rome and the family, Cato opposed luxury, cultivation of the arts, and extravagance in any form. He hated the Greeks. Believing that fathers should educate their sons in the home, he boasted of teaching his son reading, Roman law and history, and training him in the "arts" of the javelin, riding, armed combat, boxing, and swimming.

Long since recovered from the Second Punic War but not a military threat to Rome, Carthage was a ripe target for Cato and other land-hungry Romans who lusted after her fertile soil and abundant harvests. After returning from a fact-finding mission to Carthage, Cato delivered an impassioned speech in the Senate about a resurgent foe that concluded, as did all his subsequent speeches and writings, with a call to arms: "Delenda est Carthago!" ("Carthage must be destroyed!"). In 149 BC Rome launched an unprovoked attack upon an astonished and unprepared Carthage.

Rome described the conflict with Carthage as preventive warfare, but armed robbery would be a more appropriate term.[2] Carthage was not only captured but demolished and the area sown with salt. The Romans killed the men and sold the women and children into slavery, which prompted Tacitus to write, "they make a desert and call it

2. "From the Punic Wars on, [Rome's] internal history is that of a successful gang of cutthroats quarreling over the division of the swag." Basil Davenport, *The Portable Roman Reader* (Baltimore, Penguin Books, 1977), p. 7.

peace." This was in 146 BC, the fateful year in which another rapacious Roman army administered the same treatment to Corinth, the richest city in Greece. "To the victors belong the spoils" was Ovid's comment, but Seneca wrote: "We are mad, not only individually, but nationally. We check manslaughter and isolated murders; but what of war and the much vaunted crime of slaughtering whole peoples?"

Heading for Civil War

A new and very rich class of war-profiteering contractors, merchants, estate owners, province governors, and generals arose; known as *equites* ("knights"), they could afford to buy equipment for the cavalry, the most expensive branch of the military. The city bulged with plunder, slaves, and increasing numbers of landless, jobless Romans. Reform was long overdue and, in the decade from 130 to 120, the patrician brothers, Tiberius and Gaius Gracchus, attempted to speak for the dispossessed. Although no one knew it then, it was the last opportunity the Senate would have to salvage the integrity of the state. The Senatorial response was to murder Tiberius and force Gaius into suicide, thus unwittingly setting the stage for one-man rule.

The first of the generals to seize power, Marius, won victories against North African and Celtic tribes, but his reorganization of the army was the critical change. He began converting the army from amateurs, who bought their own equipment and farmed between campaigns, to full-time professionals with battle gear provided by the state. With the beginning of Rome's war against King Mithridates in 88 BC, Marius emerged from retirement to claim command. The Senate chose Sulla instead, causing a bloody civil war that ended in 84 BC with Sulla's conquest of Mithridates in Asia Minor. A veteran of Sulla's campaign, the arrogant and ruthless Pompey next rose to power, eventually forming a ruling triumvirate with Crassus and Julius Caesar.

The First Caesar

Gaius Julius Caesar (ca. 102–44 BC)[3] saw himself as the best man to rescue the foundering Republic. Not everyone agreed with him, then or now, and Caesar remains one of history's most controversial figures. A man of enormous energy and even greater ambition, his mastery of power politics made his career a textbook example of how to take over a state. He enjoyed spectacular success in war, politics, oratory, and statesmanship. Caesar's *Commentaries* on the Gallic campaigns were masterpieces of concise and lucid Latin and his social graces were remarkable. Cicero, who hated him, remarked that he would rather spend an evening conversing with Caesar than in any other way.

Family background was important in tradition-minded Rome, and Caesar had impressive credentials; the Julian *gens* ("clan", "family") was among Rome's oldest and most powerful. The patrician Caesar astutely saw the need to side with the foes of an entrenched and unpopular aristocracy and cast his lot with the popular (democratic) party. He passed rapidly through the usual offices, made dazzling orations, and, with a daring speech defending the legal rights of a treasonous conspirator, secured in one bold stroke the enmity of the Senate and the adulation of the people. Caesar added gloss to his growing reputation with a public office in Spain while reducing his staggering debts resulting, it was said, from paying huge bribes to the right people. He married his daughter to Pompey, the most successful general of the time, and completed an unbeatable combination by forming an alliance with Crassus, the richest man in Rome. The next step was by now inevitable: Caesar, Pompey, and Crassus became a ruling coalition called the First Triumvirate, a short-lived association, however, because, as Lucan pointed out, "It is a law of nature that every great man inevitably resents a partner in greatness."

Caesar's self-improvement program was not yet complete because military power was the necessary base for political strength. Appointed governor of the conquered portion of Gaul, his seemingly invincible army overpowered the rest of Gaul and established his reputation as one of history's most successful generals. What Tacitus called "the terror of the Roman name" was confirmed by Caesar: "It is the right of war for conquerors to treat those whom they have conquered according to their pleasure." Though the Gauls thoroughly understood his military prowess Caesar needed strong support back in Rome. His inspired solution was the carefully composed *Commentaries on the Gallic Wars* (what would Latin classes do without Caesar?), which was widely distributed in Rome, becoming a veritable bestseller.

The Die Is Cast

By 49 BC Gaul was secured according to Caesar's pleasure, Crassus was dead in Parthia, Pompey had gone over to the Senate, and Caesar and his loyal army were poised on the banks of the Rubicon in northern Italy. An apprehensive Senate reminded him of the standing order that all field commanders must return to Rome without their troops. Never known for indecisiveness, Caesar observed that "the die is cast," and invaded and conquered all of Italy in several weeks. (With his keen sense of history, Caesar stated his decision in Greek rather than Latin.) Following his triumphant return to a wildly enthusiastic Rome (except the Senate and aristocracy, obviously), he won a war in Spain and defeated his rival, Pompey, in Greece. He further solidified his power and filled his purse by campaigning in Egypt where he stabilized the reign of Cleopatra, Queen of Egypt, fathered a child by her, and guaranteed almost the entire tax revenues of Egypt for himself. In four brilliant years after crossing the Rubicon, Julius Caesar had triumphed in Italy, Spain, Greece, Syria, Egypt, and North Africa,

---

3. All Romans had three names: first name, family name, last name.

strengthening and consolidating the Empire as he went. When he returned to Rome in 45 BC he was undisputed master of the Roman world and a legend in his, and our, time. Less than a year later, on the Ides of March, he died of twenty-three stab wounds on the Senate floor at the base of Pompey's statue. There were about sixty assassins.

The motives for murder ranged from patriotic concerns over constitutional violations to plain jealousy. Moreover, some of Caesar's reforms interfered with corrupt practices of the bloated aristocracy, providing additional incentive for murder. On the other hand, the people, who supported Caesar throughout his meteoric career, considered him a martyr to the ravenous greed of the aristocracy. Saying "the Ides of March have come" when he was attacked, Caesar was obviously aware of the conspiracy but did nothing to protect himself.

Caesar's will left three-quarters of an enormous fortune to his adopted grandnephew, Octavian, but Octavian's true legacy was the opportunity to acquire Rome itself. Though only eighteen when Caesar died (and unaware of the will), Octavian reacted like a veteran politician. He formed a Second Triumvirate with Mark Antony and Lepidus, brutally suppressed all dissent and used terror and the threat of death to raise some fighting money. To his everlasting discredit he failed to stop Mark Antony from having Cicero murdered. He avenged Caesar in Macedonia by defeating and driving to suicide two of his assassins, Brutus and Cassius. (Shakespeare has Brutus say, "Not that I loved Caesar less, but that I loved Rome more.") After he dropped Lepidus from the triumvirate, Antony and Cleopatra tried to use Ptolemy XV (Caesar's son) in their own bid for the empire. After the machinations and intrigue the final showdown was anticlimactic. Octavian won a naval battle off the northwest coast of Greece, near Actium, and the losers returned to Egypt, where Antony committed suicide. Unable to ignite a relationship with Octavian, Cleopatra followed Antony in suicide a year later.

THE EMPIRE, 27 BC–AD 476

Octavian (Caesar Augustus)

Though Octavian is considered Rome's first emperor, he was actually the second, with most Romans never realizing that constitutional government had ended with Caesar. While prudently maintaining the appearance of restoring the Republic, Octavian orchestrated his power by redesigning the creaky governmental machinery to better control the business of empire. Careful to avoid the appellation of emperor, he did accept the Senate titles of *Augustus* ("revered one") and *princeps* ("first citizen"). Though ruling indirectly he had as much control as any titled emperor.

Among many significant innovations, Augustus created a civil service based on merit, endowed a veteran's pension fund from his own capital (secured by the taxes of

---

> ### *CICERO ON LAW, HISTORY, AND PHILOSOPHY*
>
> The people's good is the highest law.
> He used to raise a storm in a teapot.
> Let the punishment match the offense.
> > *De Legibus*, III, 3, 16, 20
>
> History is the witness that testifies to the passing of time; it illumines reality, vitalizes memory, provides guidance in daily life, and brings us tidings of antiquity.
> > *De Oratore*, II, 36
>
> There is nothing so ridiculous but some philosopher has said it.
> > *De Divinatione*, III, 119
>
> I would rather be wrong with Plato than right with such men as these [Pythagoreans].
> > Socrates was the first to call philosophy down from the heavens and to place it in cities, and even to introduce it into homes and compel it to inquire about life and standards and goods and evils.
> > *Tusculanae Disputationes*, I, 17 and V, 4

Egypt), added a sales tax, rebuilt Rome ("I found Rome brick and left it marble"), created the first police and fire departments, overhauled the armed forces, and sponsored army construction of public works projects throughout the Empire. He adjusted the bureaucratic machinery of imperial Rome so it could continue to function under good, mediocre, or incompetent leadership, and even the tenures of such murderous tyrants as Caligula, Nero, Commodus, and Caracalla.

Pax Romana

The **Pax Romana** ("Roman peace") began with Caesar Augustus in 27 BC and ended with the death of Marcus Aurelius in AD 180 (map 8.1). With no major wars in over two centuries, the Roman world was relatively peaceful and the whole Western world stable and orderly for the first time in history. People felt quite safe in their homes and even when traveling over the roads and sea routes of the prosperous Empire. Roman coins (fig. 8.2) replaced the "owls of Athena" (see fig. 5.3) as the monetary standard of the ancient world. All was not rosy, however, because, as Juvenal (see pp. 276–80) observed, "We are suffering the evils of a long peace. Luxury, more deadly than war, broods over the city, and avenges a conquered world."

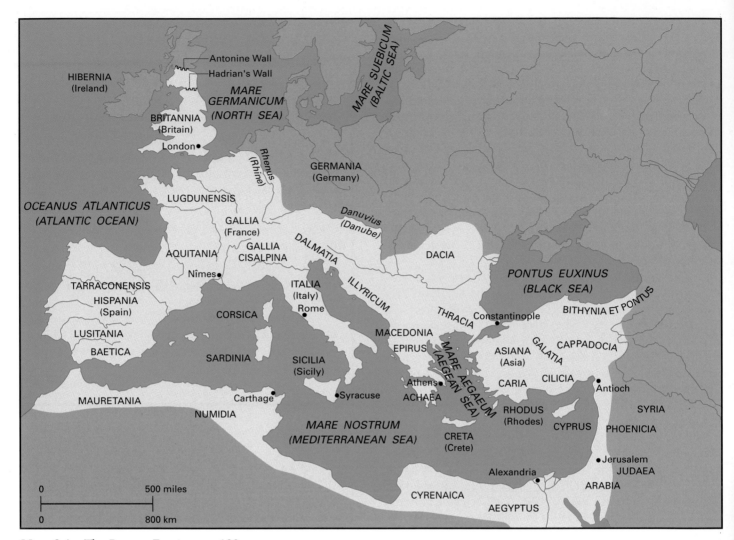

Map 8.1   The Roman Empire, AD 180.

8.2   Roman coin. Obverse: head of Augustus with the inscription "S.P.Q.R.IMP CAESARI." 17 BC. British Library, London.
The reverse features the emperor, Victory, and an elephant standing on a triumphal arch placed on an aqueduct.

Decline and Fall

No one becomes depraved in a moment.
                                                    Juvenal, *Satires*, II, 1.83

After Marcus Aurelius the professional army usually decided the position of emperor, with the legions supporting any general who offered the greatest benefits to the military. The problems all emperors faced were much the same: an increasing national debt because of military expense, a declining population in Italy, a growing disinclination to take public office in the cities outside Rome (the officers were held responsible for paying the cities' taxes to the central government, and with increasing rural poverty no one wanted to bankrupt himself by holding office), and growing rebellion on the borders of the Empire. A vast population movement from the north and east pushed Germanic, Gothic, and Vandal peoples west and south until they overran Italy and Spain.

The century of decline from Commodus to Diocletian (180–284) marked the beginning of the end though Diocletian's reforms temporarily halted the deterioration. The growth of Christianity posed an additional challenge to which Constantine responded with the Edict of Milan (313), granting freedom of worship throughout the Empire. Constantine also divided the Empire into west and east and located the capital of the Eastern Empire in the new city of Constantinople, built on the site of the old Greek colony of Byzantium. Theodosius made Christianity the official religion of the Empire, marking the beginning of vigorous Christian persecution of other religions. As the barbarian invasions intensified, the western emperor Honorius (395–403) moved to Ravenna, leaving the Pope to defend Rome as best he could. Rome was sacked in 410 and again in 455; in 476 the first non-Roman occupied the throne of Caesar and the Roman Empire passed into history. The painfully protracted decline led Emerson to remark that "the barbarians who broke up the Roman Empire did not arrive a day too soon."

ROMAN RELIGIONS AND PHILOSOPHY

Paganism

During the Republic's early years Roman religion encompassed household gods and earthly spirits appropriate to a farmer's simple life. This traditional religion remained viable for those who clung to the land; the word "pagan" (literally, "country dweller") described those who followed the old Roman religion. Agrarian beliefs became inadequate, however, for urban life in an expanding empire, and Rome again looked to Greece for suitable models. The Greek pantheon was adopted and given Roman names, albeit with different characteristics (see box 4.1 on pp. 68–9). For example, playfully amorous Aphrodite, who represented beauty and the pleasures of love, became Venus, the mother of Aeneas, bringer of good fortune and victory and protector of female chastity; Athena, the goddess of wisdom and patroness of the arts, was transformed into Minerva, the goddess of learning and handicrafts; Poseidon, the powerful earthshaker and god of the sea, became Neptune, the god of water.

> Jupiter, tho' called the best and the greatest, he was never, like Zeus, the supreme arbiter of the universe and the governor of the world. Zeus reigned from the heights of Mt. Olympus, Jupiter from a low and easily accessible hill. Zeus belonged to the shining space of the air, while Jupiter, as represented by the Romans, belonged to the earth as much as to the sky. Zeus was free. Jupiter was rigid. When we compare the two gods, we find we are comparing the imagination of the Greeks to the imagination of the Romans; they had almost nothing in common.[4]

4. Robert Payne et al., *Horizon Book of Ancient Rome* (New York: American Heritage Publishing Company, 1966), p. 68.

The practical mind-set of the Romans also manifested itself in their religious practices. The pragmatic Ovid commented that "it is expedient that there should be gods, and as it is expedient, let us believe that they exist." In the interest of efficiency and the glory of the state, the Pantheon (Gk. "of all gods") housed in one sumptuous structure the seven planetary gods (see fig. 9.29). Rome promoted patriotism by elevating the emperors, usually during their lifetime, to godly status. After Caesar Augustus, the Senate deified most emperors and emperor worship became the official religion of the Empire, confirming Seneca's observation: "Religion is regarded by the common people as true, by the wise as false, and by the rulers as useful."

The official religion served the state but did little for the spiritual needs of the common people. The diverse cultures within the Empire led, therefore, to a variety of religions imported to satisfy those needs.

Isis and Cybele

Egypt contributed Isis (fig. 8.3 and p. 2), the mother of Horus and wife of Osiris (fig. 8.4), the dynamic goddess who raised her husband from the dead. Much more than Diana or Minerva, she appealed to Roman women because

8.3 *Isis*, in the Tomb of Horemheb (tomb 57), Valley of the Kings, Egypt. Ca. 1330–1305 BC. Mural painting. Photo: Werner Forman, London (E. Strouhal).

8.4   Priest of Serapis. Ca. AD 170–180. Marble, crystalline with traces of polychrome and gilding, height 31¼" (79.5 cm). J. Paul Getty Museum, Malibu, California. The sacred bull in Egyptian religion, Serapis ruled the underworld and was supposedly the incarnation of Osiris. The diadem and rosette identify the man as a priest.

WHILE ROME BURNED

The fire that destroyed a large part of old Rome in AD 64 burned for six days and seven nights. Historians of the time agree that it was started on orders of Emperor Nero, who vacationed at a seaside resort until Rome was burning lustily. There is no agreement about motive but it was most likely boredom and the desire for a bigger and better royal residence. Returning to his flaming palace, Nero watched the fire from a tower in his garden, reportedly exclaiming about "the beauty of the flames." He then put on a tragedian's costume and sang verses from *The Fall of Troy* while accompanying himself on the lyre. Forbidding anyone to search the rubble for loot because he wanted it all, Nero built a colossal palace with a statue of himself 120 feet (37 m) tall in the entrance hall and a pillared arcade about a mile (1.6 km) long. While moving into the palace he remarked, "Good, now I can at last begin to live like a human being." Four years later he committed suicide, lamenting, while dying, "What an artist the world is losing in me!"

she was a giver of health, beauty, wisdom, and love and, moreover, she needed both priests and priestesses.

Cybele, the Great Mother goddess of Phrygia (in Asia Minor), appeared in Rome during the Second Punic War with Hannibal. According to the legend, she loved the glorious youth Attis, who, like Osiris, was raised from the dead (a standard motif for fertility cults). Her frantic grief over his death and abandoned delirium at his rebirth were followed by his unfaithfulness, at which point she castrated him. All of this dramatic spectacle was echoed in the ecstatic and bloody (including self-castration) rites of Cybele's followers. Aghast at the orgies and blood baths, Rome made periodic attempts to regulate the mayhem.

Mystery Religions and Mithraism

The Eleusinian mysteries and Dionysian rites, both Greek mystery religions, had their Roman adherents, but the vows of silence of both sects have been frustratingly effective; we know so little. Dionysian ritual celebrated the nonrational but the particulars are obscure. The Eleusinian mysteries are particularly intriguing because it appears that the worshipers could overcome their fear of death. Eventually the ceremonies at Eleusis (near Athens) were halted by Christianity; any religion that could conquer humanity's deepest fear had to be suppressed.

Imported from Persia was the resolutely virtuous worship of Mithras, the unconquered intermediary between Ahura-Mazda, lord of life and light, and Ahriman, lord of death and darkness. Mithras was the protector of humanity whose believers had to be courageous and morally pure. Soldiers were strongly attracted to this male-oriented religion which was, in the third century AD, Christianity's greatest rival.

Christianity

Emperor worship as the state religion separated monotheistic Christianity (and Judaism) from all other religions. Viewed as a threat to the state, Christians were traitors who refused to place the emperor above their God. Aristocratic Romans sneered at early Christians as common rabble while the people feared them as radical trouble makers. The Roman historian Tacitus called them criminals which, by law, they were.

As early as AD 64 Christianity was prominent enough for Nero to blame Christian fanatics for the burning of Rome but not until 249 under Decius did systematic persecutions begin. What Christians called persecution the authorities justified as defending the state, except Nero, who needed a convenient scapegoat. Though very sporadic, the attacks created many Christian martyrs and put the church on the defensive. Literally driven underground into the **catacombs** outside Rome, Christianity formed a true community of believers. Rome's efforts to defend the state helped solidify the church while the long periods of tolerance (or indifference) allowed proselytizing throughout Roman society. (Christianity is discussed in detail on pp. 307–15.)

Astrology and Magic

Millions of believers looked to the stars as powerful deities on a par with Jupiter, Isis, and Cybele; astrology was the champion superstition of an age in which countless numbers preferred to believe the movements of heavenly bodies controlled their lives. Originating in Babylonia, astrology was known to Plato (he found it amusing) but it was not until Alexander's conquest of the Middle East that this persistent nonsense penetrated the Greek world and, ultimately, the entire Roman spectrum. The Eastern religions attracted different sectors of the populace but astrology fascinated everyone from slaves to emperors. Greek skeptics asked how it was that people fated to die at different times all went down in the same shipwreck, or how one-twelfth of humankind could share the basic characteristics of a Capricorn, but these rational queries simply bored true believers. (In fact, the earth has rotated on its axis—called precession by astronomers—to a point where the hopelessly outdated astrological signs are now about three weeks too early.) Augustus and Tiberius, never ones to take chances, banned astrologers from Rome, not to curtail larceny, but fearing rivals with horoscopes predicting an enticing throne. Practitioners of magic also did a thriving business. With fraud flourishing on its usual grand scale, spells, charms, incantations, amulets, fetishes, curses, and hexes were sold to an endless procession of fervently gullible Romans.

Epicureanism

Epicureanism and Stoicism, two eminent Athenian schools of philosophy of the third century BC, developed ethical systems that could help individuals feel more secure in an unstable and hostile world. Materialistic and practical, both philosophies suited thoughtful, educated Romans who chose to confront the problems of living an ethical life in a society plagued by dissension, vice, and corruption.

Based on the **materialism** of Democritos (see p. 89), the philosophy of Epicurus (341–270 BC, fig. 8.5) aimed primarily to secure tranquility. He considered pleasure the ultimate good and adhered, with remarkable consistency, to the consequences of this view. "Pleasure," he said, "is the beginning and the end of the blessed life." And further, "I know not how I can conceive the good if I withdraw the pleasures of love and those of hearing and sight. The beginning and the root of all good is the pleasure of the stomach; even wisdom and culture must be referred to this." The mind's pleasure is contemplating the pleasures of the body. Socrates and Plato would disagree of course, but they did not face the uncertainties of a violent age. For Epicurus one acquired virtue by "prudence in the pursuit of pleasure." Justice was not even a virtue but a defense mechanism against pain, a practical matter of behaving without causing fear and resentment in other people.

Epicureanism, like all materialistic philosophies, contained elements of a hedonistic pursuit of physical pleasures, but Epicurus advocated intellectual pleasures as superior to sensual delights and always preferred quiet pleasures to violent joys. Eat moderately for fear of indigestion and drink sparingly for fear of the morning after; avoid politics, love, and other turmoil; do not present hostages to fortune by marrying and having children; above all, avoid fear. Holding public office raised the fear level because envious enemies multiplied as a man achieved power. "The wise man will try to live unnoticed so that he will have no enemies."

Epicurus identified the two greatest sources of fear as religion and dread of death. He believed that the gods, if they even existed, never intervened in human affairs and that the soul perished with the body. Not a consolation but a threat, religion was supernatural interference with nature and a source of terror because immortality denied release from pain. Death was both extinction and liberation.

In his poem, *De Rerum Natura* ("On the Nature of Things"; see pp. 261–4), the Latin poet and philosopher

8.5   Portrait bust of Epicurus. Roman copy, probably after a bronze original of ca. 275–250 BC. Marble, height 15⅞" (40.6 cm). Metropolitan Museum of Art, New York (Rogers Fund, 1911).

This is one of the finest of many copies. The long face, marked by time and poor health, is obviously an actual likeness, but in the wrinkled brow and deep-set eyes we also see "the philosopher."

Lucretius (loo-KREE-shus; ca. 96–55 BC) explained the workings of the universe as seen by the Epicurean: a rational, materialistic interpretation of how all things came to be. The poet Horace (65–8 BC) exemplified an Epicurean life and recorded in his poetry the ethical results of the philosophy. He advocated moderation in all things though he did warn against the inconvenience of poverty; above all, he said, avoid lofty positions because lightning strikes the tallest trees and highest mountains. A sophisticated man with a lively sense of humor, he recognized the foibles of his time, laughed at most of them, and unashamedly participated in a goodly number. As the creed of a cultivated minority, Epicureanism survived about 600 years, though with diminishing vigor.

Stoicism

Stoicism was taught by Zeno the Stoic (335?–263? BC), a Phoenician who lived and taught in Athens. He believed totally in common sense which, in Greece, meant materialism. He trusted his senses and had no patience with metaphysical subtleties. When the skeptic asked Zeno what he meant by the real world the reply was, "I mean solid and material, like this table." "And God," asked the skeptic, "and the soul?" "Perfectly solid," answered Zeno, "more solid than the table." In response to further questioning Zeno added virtue and justice to his list of solid matter. Later Stoics like the Emperor Marcus Aurelius (AD 121–180) abandoned materialism but retained the ethical doctrines in virtually the same form. Stoicism was less Greek than any other doctrine because it was emotionally limited and somewhat fanatical. Moreover, its sober austerity contained religious elements the Greeks seemed unable to supply or endorse. In short, it had qualities that appealed to the Romans.

The main doctrines of Stoicism involve cosmic **determinism** and human freedom. "There is no such thing as chance," said Zeno, "and the course of nature is determined by natural law." The natural world was originated by a Lawgiver, a supreme power called, variously, God or Zeus or Jupiter, who is the soul of the world. Each person has within a part of the Divine Fire. All things are part of a single system called Nature and the individual life is good when in harmony with nature. In one sense, people are in agreement with nature because they cannot violate natural laws, but in the Stoic sense virtue is achieved when the individual will is directed to ends that coincide with nature. The wicked obey God's laws involuntarily, like horses driven by a charioteer.

Virtue is the sole good in an individual's life; health, happiness, possessions are of no account. Because virtue resides in will power, everything good or bad in a person's life depends entirely on that person. A person may be poor but virtuous, or sentenced to death, like Socrates, regarded by Stoics as a patron saint. Other people may have power over externals but virtue, the only true good, is internal.

Everyone can have perfect freedom by freeing themselves from all mundane desires. The doctrine has a non-Greek coldness that condemns not only bad passions but all passions. The Stoic sage does not feel bereft when his wife and children die because his virtue is undisturbed. Friendship is all very well but don't let your friend's misfortunes interfere with your detached calm. Participation in politics is tolerated but helping other people does nothing for virtue.

Stoic doctrine has at least two logical difficulties. If virtue is the only good then the divine lawgiver must promote virtue; why, then, are there more sinners than saints? Also, how can injustice be wrong if, as Stoics liked to suggest, it provided Stoics with more opportunities to endure and thus become ever more virtuous?

The Romans were acquainted with Stoicism mainly through the writings of Cicero, but the three most influential Roman Stoics were Seneca, Epictetus, and Marcus Aurelius: a minister, a slave, and an emperor, in that order. Seneca (ca. 3 BC–AD 65) was Nero's teacher and a multimillionaire, which casts some doubt on both his teaching and his Stoicism. Falsely accused of plotting Nero's assassination, he was ordered to commit suicide. His final words to his grieving family were, "Never mind, I leave you what is far more valuable than earthly riches, the example of a virtuous life."

Epictetus (ep-ik-TEE-tus; ca. AD 60–110) was a Greek and a slave who finally won his freedom. The slave and the emperor, Marcus Aurelius, lived totally different lives but were in nearly complete agreement about the elements of Stoicism. Marcus Aurelius was devoted to Stoic virtue, of which he had great need, for his reign (AD 161–180) saw an endless procession of pestilence, insurrections, wars, and earthquakes. A conscientious ruler, he was mainly unsuccessful and certainly frustrated. Because Christian rejection of the state religion threatened the already besieged empire, he tried, in vain, to stamp out the sect. Epictetus lived a relatively short and uneventful life but his teaching profoundly affected early Christianity. Consider, for example, the implications of the following:

> On earth we are prisoners in an earthly body.
> God is the Father of all men and we are all brothers.
> Slaves are the equal of other men because all are alike
>   in the eyes of God.
> We must submit to God as a good citizen submits to
>   the law.
> The soldier swears to respect no man above Caesar
>   but we are to respect ourselves first of all.
> We must love our enemies.

Late Stoicism, in the philosophy of Epictetus and Marcus Aurelius, emphasized the brotherhood of all humankind. Since the great intelligence (divine spark) is within each person, and each is a necessary part of the rational scheme of things, then all are brothers in the changing universe. Roman law interpreted this as all being equal before the law.

Neoplatonism

Becoming more of a religion than Stoicism, Neoplatonism was the third Greek philosophy to invade Rome. Its vision of an afterlife offered consolation to those who enjoyed little satisfaction or self-fulfillment in their earthly existence. Based on Platonic doctrines, Neoplatonism came to Rome from the **Academy** founded by Plato, the still-flourishing school (until AD 529) in Athens. The Neoplatonists began with the Platonic concept of Ideas as the true reality. But, said the Neoplatonists, ideas in their pure form are unknowable. We can appreciate beauty, for example, as manifested in a beautiful person, or beautiful landscape or picture, but we cannot imagine pure beauty apart from any of these things. Further, we cannot picture pure mind but we can approach a knowledge of the mind as we see people acting according to the dictates of their minds, that is, evidence of the mind at work but not the reality. Similarly, the true reality of Good is something people cannot envision in this life. The goal is to approach as near as possible to an understanding of reality while on earth so that, upon death, one is fit to enter the City of Good and contemplate the True Reality. Neoplatonism initiated the idea of salvation and eternal life for those who lived their earthly lives in contemplation and with a desire for true wisdom. These ideas strongly influenced Christianity, for it was St. Augustine (354–430), a Neoplatonist in his youth, who laid the foundation for the doctrine of the early Christian church in his monumental *The City of God*.

ROME'S ACHIEVEMENTS

Law and Government

Rome's major and most enduring contribution to Western civilization was her legal system: the art and science of law. Administration of justice was an art, while science (jurisprudence) defined justice and injustice. There is no clearer evidence of Roman preference for facts as opposed to abstractions than in a body of law founded, as Cicero stated, "not on theory but on nature." Justice was a process rather than a concept, a way of dealing with everyday problems. "Law is nothing but a correct principle drawn from the inspiration of the gods, commanding what is honest and forbidding the contrary" (Cicero). Venality and rapacity were human characteristics the state had to control so that "the stronger might not in all things have their way" (Ovid). Bertrand Russell wryly said that in his ideal society everyone would be honest and he would be the only thief. Roman law stood guard against the thief in all of us. Rome used its experience of empire to build a body of international law based on a rational appraisal of consistent human behavior in a variable environment.

The legal system worked but that need not imply a government of comparable efficiency. Modern research has shown that the Romans were not masters of the arts of governance. Until the time of Caesar Augustus government was a chaotic mess of corruption and inefficiency caused not by a republic trying to administer an empire but by time-honored inequities and improbabilities. Augustus did make some reforms, but he followed the Roman habit of shuffling parts around when what he needed was a new chariot. Diocletian (reigned 284–305) did design an efficient new system, but by this time it was like harnessing a team of lively horses to a broken-down chariot.

Province management was a permanent problem because there was little governing; the governors were responsible primarily for sending money to Rome. Charging whatever taxes the traffic would bear and rendering "unto Caesar that which is Caesar's," they pocketed the rest. Moreover, Rome's vaunted toleration of provincial cultures was more pragmatic than magnanimous: do nothing that will jeopardize the tax potential of conquered territories. Except for Greece,[5] Rome treated all foreign cultures with equal indifference.

Science

Roman science dealt entirely with empirical data; theoretical science was something left to the Greeks. For example, an Alexandrian Greek named Eratosthenes (air-uh-TOSS-thuh-neez) used reason, empirical data, and math to prove the earth round and measure its circumference within a few miles. Pliny the Elder (see p. 286) observed that the masts of ships approaching shore were visible before he saw the hulls, leading to the deduction that the world had a curved surface. Roman medical science benefited when they combined their organizational talent with their passion for war to produce the field hospital, a predecessor of the general hospital.

Public Projects

A 50,000-mile (80,000-km) network of paved roads linked Rome to all parts of the Empire. All roads did lead to Rome. Originally designed as military highways, they carried the efficient postal service plus peripatetic Romans. Guidebooks, highway patrols, a stable every 10 miles (16 km), and an inn every 30 miles (48 km) made traveling easier and safer than at any other time before the late nineteenth century (fig. 8.6).

Of all societies in western Asia and Europe from antiquity until the nineteenth century, only the Romans set out to build a carefully planned road system, with properly installed and drained surfaces.[6]

---

5. The love-hate relationship with Greece was largely involuntary. As Horace wrote, "Greece, taken captive, captured her savage conqueror, and carried her arts into clownish Latium."
6. Donald Hill, *A History of Engineering in Classical and Medieval Times* (La Salle, Ill: Open Court Publishing Company, 1984), p. 76

8.6 Main thoroughfare, Ostia Antica. Length ca. 4,000'
(1,200 m). Photo: Canali, Brescia.
Leading from Rome to its port city, this three-lane highway
is a typical Roman road. Even today in Europe one can
recognize a Roman route by the way it rolls on and on with
hardly a curve.

Skillful engineering also produced the aqueducts that
supplied the huge amounts of water needed for the luxurious public baths (fig. 8.7) and for the many affluent households that used water for sanitary facilities. Only a few
aqueducts remain, such as the one still serving Segovia in
Spain, and some of the plumbing—in the Pantheon, at

8.7 Great Bath, Roman bath complex, Bath, England.
AD 54. Limestone, ca. 67' 6" × 27' 6" (20.6 × 8.4 m).
Photo: Spectrum, London.
Part of the finest group of Roman remains in England, this
splendid pool is still fed by natural hot springs. Even today
there are more than 6,500 Roman baths in the world.

Pompeii, and at Bath—still works. Almost everything else
has vanished, including the vast irrigation system that
watered productive farms in the northern Sahara and the
300 miles (483 km) of aqueducts that served Rome.

As urbanization gradually supplanted Rome's early
agrarian society, city building became a new specialty. Many
residential units were five- and six-story apartment houses
with such built-in services as nurseries, convenience
markets, and neighborhood snack bars (fig. 8.8). Rome and
other large cities always had extensive **forums** that served
as civic centers (suitable backdrops for Roman pomp and
ceremony) and open-air markets comparable to today's
shopping malls. Rome was not, however, a neat and orderly
city. Except for several thoroughfares there were no names
for the 54 miles (86.4 km) of streets nor any house numbers. (Sample conversation: "See Marius in the leather shop
behind the Pantheon; he knows where your friend, Sepulvius,
lives.") There was pollution ("cease to admire the smoke,
wealth and noise of prosperous Rome."—Horace) and, as
Sallust observed, corruption: "A city for sale and doomed
to speedy destruction, if it finds a purchaser."

City facilities always included public baths, the most
popular of all Roman institutions. Cicero once remarked
that the gong that each day announced the opening of
public baths was "a sweeter sound than the voices of the
philosophers in their schools." Emperors who needed to
improve their public image, which included most of those
who stayed alive long enough, built elaborate facilities
larger than several Grand Central Stations.[7] All the baths
included mixed bathing until Hadrian decreed separate
times for the sexes. These hedonistic temples contained
indoor and outdoor swimming pools, gymnasiums,
libraries, lounges, restaurants, bars, and gardens, with
brothels sometimes included as added attractions. Early
in the Republic the baths facilitated cleanliness but they

8.8 Snack bar, Ostia Antica. Photo: Canali, Brescia.
Across the street from a six-story apartment building, this
bar contained a common room adjoined by a spacious patio.

evolved into what Cicero's gong symbolized: public palaces that made life as pleasant as possible.

The baths soothed and entertained individuals in a variety of ways while mass entertainment was a spectacular Roman specialty. A large amphitheatre, such as the Colosseum, occupied the center of each city, where the favorite spectacle was gladiatorial combat. Other entertainments included wild animal hunts, naval battles, and an occasional gladiator, in a bid for freedom, singlehandedly killing an elephant.

Rome's bequest to the Western world was a curious compound of justice under law, military conquest, the Latin language, and Greek culture. Implicit in the laws that recognized the constitutional rights of citizens was the germinal idea that laws required the consent of the governed. The military conquests were a devastating legacy, but perhaps so was Horace's pious statement, *"dolce et decorum est pro patria mori"* ("it is sweet and glorious to die for one's country").

Rome's finest contributions to Western civilization were law and Greek culture. The Greek temple style was adopted, though mainly the ornate Corinthian order; Greek sculpture was copied so often that most of what we know of Greek work exists in Roman copies. The work of Greek artists, serving Roman tastes, appeared in the frescoes, murals, and mosaics of their houses and public buildings. Greek slaves tutored Roman children in the Greek language and the classics: Homer, Hesiod, and the plays of Aeschylus, Sophocles, and Menander. Roman tourists made the obligatory pilgrimage to Greece to view the centuries-old wonders on the Acropolis and to consult the oracle at Delphi. Rome contributed the language, organization, and law upon which the Church of Rome and medieval civilization were built; at the same time, Rome preserved and transmitted the Greek humanism that sparked the Renaissance and illuminated the Age of Reason.

GREECE, ROME, EUROPE, AND THE UNITED STATES

Rome, with little high culture of its own, absorbed the intellectual and artistic heritage it had conquered, and was in turn conquered by it, as the poet Horace observed. Rome and the Latin language left their mark on everything they touched; but Rome's high culture was derivatively Greek. There is some analogy with the United States in relation to Europe. In Rome, as in America, this produced a tension, since in almost every sphere except culture the Romans were fundamentally dissimilar to the Greeks.[8]

To complete the analogy, the United States inherited European culture but, in general, Americans are just as different from Europeans as the Romans were from the Greeks.

The worlds of classical Greece and Rome deserve our most careful study for two reasons. First, theirs is an extraordinary story, infinitely rich and of worth. And, second, they are the forerunners of the political, social, cultural, economic, and religious traditions of the West, and unless we know something about them, we are adrift in our own world—and at a loss how to manage the future.[9]

CONTRASTING VALUES IN GREECE AND ROME

When Greece and Rome are considered together the reference is to a Graeco-Roman civilization that was literate, rational, and secular, whose high (classical) period dates from ca. 480 BC to ca. AD 180. Taken separately, we can effectively compare the two very different cultures by discussing education and sports.

Education

Roman parents were responsible for their children's education either as teachers or by hiring tutors. As discussed earlier, the elder Cato boasted of teaching his son reading, Roman law and history plus the "arts" of the javelin, riding, swimming, and armed combat. When writing, simple arithmetic, and some Greek and Roman literature are added we have the standard Roman curriculum. This is pragmatic instruction designed to produce Romans useful to the state as citizens and soldiers. The Romans valued education and scorned the uneducated, whether Roman or foreigner. Ignorance, wrote Cicero, condemned these impoverished souls to "the tyranny of the present." While still a slave, Epictetus asserted that "only the educated are free."

Greek parents were also responsible for their children's education. All citizens studied reading and writing, arithmetic, art, poetry recitation, music, dance, and gymnastics. Talented students advanced to instruction in mathematics, rhetoric (oratory), and philosophy. Everyone received ethical education according to the doctrine of ethos. Greek education emphasized imagination, creativity, and, especially, thinking. It was an open-ended process that encouraged excellence in its highly individualistic citizens. Moreover, when teachers followed Plato's advice any talent would be recognized and nourished— "Let early education be a sort of amusement; you will then be better able to find out the natural bent."

Law and history were the two mandatory "academic" subjects in the Roman curriculum, neither of which required much imagination or original thinking. Education

7. The New York landmark was modeled after Rome's Baths of Caracalla.
8. Oliver Taplin, *Greek Fire: The Influence of Ancient Greece on the Modern World* (New York: Atheneum), p. 15.
9. Michael Grant, *Readings in the Classical Historians* (New York: Charles Scribner's and Sons, 1992), p. 1.

reinforced those qualities most highly valued by each culture. Where reality was the State, duty, conformity, discipline, and courage were prime values in a pragmatic society. Individuality, verbal skills, creativity, originality, and imaginative thinking were highly prized in a culture that encouraged diligence in the pursuit of excellence. In neither culture, however, did women have equal educational opportunities; educated Roman and Greek women were a distinct minority. Aristotle summed up the Greek view of education: "Educated men are as much superior to uneducated men as the living are to the dead."

Sports

Let us now consider athletic contests in the ancient world as another way of highlighting the differences. The Olympic Games and gladiatorial combat were both athletic contests, though we might refer to the Olympics as "games" and call battling gladiators something quite different. First we shall describe the games the Greeks played and then look at the Roman versions. By comparing the radically different approaches to athletics (sports), the reader can draw further conclusions about the two cultures.

Olympic Games

Greek festivals featured contests in drama, music, poetry, and athletics, especially athletics. It seems that the cities of Sparta, Elis, and Pisa were always squabbling and, rather than settling their difficulties by fighting, they decided upon a truce built around a footrace to decide superiority. This worked so well that by 776 BC almost the entire Hellenic world was involved in footracing and other contests at the sacred site of Olympia. 776 was considered so significant that the Greeks recorded their subsequent history based on that date. The contests were held every four years (the Olympiad); 776 was the first Olympiad, 772 the second Olympiad, and so on through the 320th Olympiad in AD 392: 1,168 years of Greek history.

From the beginning the critical factor was a truce unique to the Olympic Games. The conditions were simple: no one was to bear arms in Elis (the province of the games); all athletes and spectators were guaranteed safe access to Elis from anywhere in the Greek world; all fighting would cease throughout that world for a period of ten months plus travel time to and from the games. True to style, the Greeks pledged on their honor to abide by these rules. When the Spartans violated the truce the entire Greek-speaking world was called upon to witness their shame; there were no further violations.

Athletic contests were staged throughout Greece with the greatest at Olympia, not just because of the caliber of competition but because Olympia symbolized peace. Sportsmanship and brotherhood were also basic components of the games. Cheating was not tolerated but the Greeks were realistic enough to require an oath of fair play from each athlete. The games recognized the kinship of all Greeks with competition open to all of Greek descent regardless of rank, class, or native city. Brotherhood was national rather than universal, however, because barbarians (foreigners) were barred. The dominating spirit of the games was precisely the same as for all Greek culture: *kalos k'agathos* ("the beautiful and the good").

Selected by competition, the best athletes in each city started training exactly ten months before the festival; no one contestant had an unfair advantage. Because training was forbidden at the sacred site, they held final warm-ups at Elis, after which everyone moved to Olympia for five days of competition dedicated to Zeus and Hera. Because the Olympiad was Greece's top event it was scheduled for both good weather and maximum attendance. Consequently, competition began on the third full moon of summer (in July or August), which placed the festivities after the grain and olive harvests and before fall planting.

The basic events of the games were footraces, primarily because all Greeks took great pride in their speed and stamina as runners.[10] They based the unit of distance (stade) on the length of the stadium at Olympia, which was about 600 feet (183 m). There were sprints of one-stade, two-stade, and so on up to distances of about 3 miles (4.8 km). The Olympics had no second or third place finishes; there was one winner with everyone else an also-ran. The prize, a simple olive wreath,[11] was the most sought after in Greece; though the leaves soon withered and fell, the winner's name was recorded in the roll of the Olympics and, ever after, his descendants would recall his name.

The winner of a footrace in modern track and field is, of course, the first to break the tape, unless disqualified by a foul. The Greeks were more sophisticated; the position of finish counted only 50 percent. The other half was evaluated independently by judges searching for something special: grace, poise, rhythm, what we might call, in a word, style.[12] The Greek word for it is *arete*, which translates as skill, or stylish grace or, more precisely, diligence in the pursuit of excellence.[13] Besides the quality of *arete*, the games differed from the modern version in one other significant respect. Though the Greeks honored tradition they were not bound by the past, preferring instead to live

---

10. Cross-country running was, surprisingly, not one of the Olympic events. The marathon, based on the Marathon-to-Athens run of Phidippides to announce the wondrous victory over the Persians, was introduced at the modern Olympics which began at Athens in 1896.

11. The other games of the sacred circuit awarded the laurel at Delphi (Pythian), pine at Corinth (Isthmian), and wild celery at Nemea (Nemean). The olive branch of the Olympic Games remains as a nearly universal symbol of peace.

12. Athletes competed in the nude so that judges could better evaluate their performance. It should also be noted that women were forbidden to attend the games under penalty of death, a prohibition based on religious reasons rather than the fact of nudity, which was not a problem for the Greeks, who looked upon their readiness to strip in public as one of the traits that separated them from barbarians.

13. Style is a factor in judging such modern Olympic events as diving, gymnastics, and ice skating.

enthusiastically in the present. They kept meticulous records of each Olympiad but they never recorded winning distances or times; athletes competed with each other, not with the past.

Except for chariot racing the ancient Olympic events are still a basic part of the modern Olympics: footracing, broad jump, discus, javelin, and boxing and wrestling (fig. 8.9). The composite event, the pentathlon,[14] featured the kind of individual the Greeks especially admired, a well-rounded person with skills in several areas. The Romans prized specialists but the Greeks preferred generalists.

The high point of the 1,168 years of the Olympic Games was reached, not unexpectedly, during the Age of Pericles. A slight decline in quality and integrity after that time accelerated rapidly beginning in 146 BC, the year in which Carthage and Corinth were razed and the Romans took over Olympia. Typical of the Roman way was Nero's behavior, who had himself declared winner of any event he entered. The games ended in AD 392, after the 320th Olympiad, when, in the name of Christianity, Emperor Theodosios issued an edict forbidding the games because they "promoted the worship of heathen and false gods." No mention was made of the ancient truce when the emperor completed his work by ordering the destruction of the statues and temples. *Arete, kalos k'agathos* ("skill, beauty, and goodness") vanished from the sacred groves of the peaceful river valley at Olympia.

Roman Spectacles

Roman games were originally conceived and produced to honor the gods but, by the time of the Empire, private citizens were sponsoring extravagant spectacles honoring themselves more than the gods. While the Romans had frequent athletic contests the public was far more entranced by the giant spectacles staged in the Colosseum and Circus Maximus (see figs. 9.21, 9.22, and 9.23). These were the *ludi* ("games," from which we get the word *ludicrous*), which referred to five types of extravaganzas produced for immense arenas: chariot races, gladiatorial combats, wild animal hunts, naval battles, and mythological pantomimes. Not concerned with style or beauty, these *ludi* were intended to amuse vast crowds and thus Rome invented mass entertainment.

Romans particularly enjoyed chariot races but gladiatorial combat was on a higher plane. Unique to Roman civilization, it characterized Roman values. There has been a tendency, probably dating from Napoleon, to ascribe the Roman virtues of nobility, courage, and honesty to the austere days of the Republic, and thus blame the Empire for much of the brutality and decadence for which Rome is justly infamous. It was the Republic, however, that bred

gladiatorial combat, beginning in 264 BC, the same Republic that brutally destroyed Carthage and Corinth in 146 BC.

The ritual of mortal combat always began with the ceremonial march of the gladiators into the arena and the famous words to the royal box: *"Ave, Caesar, morituri te salutamus"* ("Hail, Caesar, we who are about to die salute you"). Following the drawing of lots and inspection of arms, a typical match-up would be a Thracian type gladiator versus the *hoplomachi* fighting style. The Thracian wore a heavy helmet and leather and metal armor, and carried a small shield and curved sword. The nearly naked *hoplomachus* wore a heavy helmet and carried a large, oblong shield and a Roman sword. A variety of clothing and armament protected each combatant from disabling minor wounds. The crowd enjoyed a skillful, courageous, and even fight; given this kind of battle, public sentiment tended toward a thumbs-up verdict so the loser could fight another day. The decision, however, lay with the editor, the sponsor of the day's games, and the verdict could just as well be thumbs-down. Of course the crowd expected the loser to display his superb training by presenting his naked throat to his conqueror's sword. Anguish and gore enough it seems, but the Romans further embellished the bloody scene with an actor dressed as a god and brandishing a white-hot staff, which he jabbed into the fallen man to make certain he was dead. The tattered body was then hooked behind a horse and dragged away and the entire arena sprayed with perfume, after which the crowd settled contentedly back for the next contest.

Next were the great crowd pleasers, a *retiarius* and a *secutor*. Possessing neither helmet nor shield, the *retiarius* had a dagger in his belt, while one hand gripped a net and the other a trident. His *secutor* opponent wore a helmet and carried a long rectangular shield and a sword, plus the standard dagger. In a contest pitting a runner against a human tank the *retiarius* had to be very mobile.

The two pairs described above appeared at most spectacles. Other combats included fighting from chariots, dwarf gladiators, female combatants, and whatever else amused the common people in the upper tiers. Staging these extravaganzas was so expensive that the government had to assume responsibility for special schools, which in Rome alone trained and housed some 2,000 gladiators. Amphitheatre combat was probably scheduled only several times a year; this kept expenses down, helped maintain a full complement of gladiators (about 600 pairs fought in each production) and most importantly, heightened expectations for the next spectacular event.

Other spectacles involved elaborately staged hunts, which featured an African jungle, for example, in the Colosseum with hunters and assorted lions and tigers stalking each other, though it is doubtful the frightened creatures wanted anything more than a place to hide from their tormentors. Thousands of wild animals were slaughtered in this manner, so many that whole species were annihilated. Fought in pools built for the occasion, naval battles

---

14. Five events: sprint, broad jump, wrestling and boxing, discus, and javelin. The decathlon (ten events) of the modern Olympics dropped the wrestling and boxing and added shot put, pole vault, high jump, 110-meter hurdles, and 100-, 400-, and 1,500-meter races.

8.9 *Runner at the Starting Point, Two Wrestlers, Javelin Thrower.* Ca. 500 BC. Marble bas-relief, 12¼" × 26½" (31.1 × 67.3 cm). National Archaeological Museum, Athens. Photo: Scala, Florence.
Originally a decoration for the base of a kouros, this illustrates the bound hair and heavily muscled bodies of the athletes who took part in the Olympic Games.

were reenactments of famous engagements, bloody reminders of the power of Roman arms at sea. Finally, there were dramatic pantomimes based on familiar mythological plots and starring condemned criminals in their first and last performance. Treated to mythology in action, audiences witnessed Heracles consumed by flames, Dirce lashed to the horns of a maddened bull, Icaros of the failing wings falling among wild beasts, and other edifying splendors. Roman efficiency prevailed; the mob was entertained; justice was served.

The Roman games were so appallingly brutal that some apologists have tried to rationalize the whole bloody business into justifiable entertainment for potentially dangerous mobs. Others have sought evidence that educated Romans disapproved of the institution; they have looked in vain, however, since Romans of every class and station attended and enjoyed the games, which continued in the Colosseum until they were banned by Honorius in 404.

TO HELEN

Helen, thy beauty is to me
  Like those Nicean barks of yore,
That gently, o'er a perfumed sea,
  The weary, wayworn wanderer bore
To his own native shore.

On desperate seas long wont to roam,
  Thy hyacinth hair, thy classic face,
Thy Naiad airs have brought me home
  To the glory that was Greece
And the grandeur that was Rome.

Edgar Allan Poe (1831)

With the possible exception of Seneca and Pliny the Younger, we know of not one Roman who ever voiced any concerns, humane or otherwise, about the events staged in the Colosseum. Death, in this ancient time, was not a significant consideration for those in power, particularly when the powerless were doing the dying.

> Our critical assumption that the spectators must have been inhuman brutes never occurred to any Roman, philosopher or not. The gladiators brought Rome a strong dose of sadistic pleasure of which people fully approved: pleasure at the sight of bodies and at the sight of men dying."[15]

Ironically, the one event that was vigorously denounced was the *sparsio*, the bonus episode that usually followed the final gladiatorial contest. While the upper class beat a hasty retreat, a machine with a rotating arm that hurled clay or wooden tablets in the general direction of the upper tiers was wheeled into the arena. Whatever the tally depicted was redeemable in kind: a water buffalo, ten pounds of ostrich feathers, an elephant, two lower tier tickets for the next attraction, and so on. Horace spoke for the upper class when he wrote: "I hate the vulgar herd and hold it far."

THE BEST OF THE ROMAN IDEAL

Artistically and creatively, Rome reached its peak during the "golden age" of Caesar Augustus. Augustus had, at long last, won the civil war, bringing peace to an embattled Republic that emerged from the chaos as the mighty Roman Empire. While rebuilding Rome he turned his attention to a literary project perhaps more important than rebuilding a city in gleaming marble—the fabulous history of the city destined to rule the world, Virgil's *Aeneid*.

The *Aeneid*

Augustus selected Virgil (70–19 BC) as his poet of Roman greatness and commissioned him to write an epic poem celebrating the Augustan victory at Actium in 31 BC, depicting the emperor as the noble conqueror of the forces of darkness led by Mark Antony and Cleopatra. The fate of

---

15. Philippe Aries and Georges Duby, gen. eds., *A History of Private Life I—from Pagan Rome to Byzantium* (Cambridge, Mass.: The Belknap Press of Harvard University Press, 1987), p. 20.

the sponsored project was something not only unexpected but infinitely better. Virgil wrote the *Aeneid*.

Virgil saw that much of the greatness of Athens resulted from the tradition provided by Homer's *Iliad* and *Odyssey*. Well versed in Homer's epics, Virgil deliberately patterned his poem upon them to give Rome the same kind of golden past that the Greeks had enjoyed, and to provide inspiration for the creation of great and noble works.

Books I–VI of the *Aeneid*, concerned with the wanderings of Aeneas after his escape from Troy, are based on the *Odyssey*. Books VII–XII are based on the *Iliad* and tell of war and death in Italy as Aeneas follows his destiny. Virgil's major innovation was not writing an adventure story but tackling a noble subject: founding an empire. Reality, for the Romans, was the state; therefore the principal aim of all literature was to stir patriotism. The *Aeneid* is literature and it is also propaganda for a great nation. But what's the matter with propaganda for a noble cause?

Virgil created Aeneas as both Homeric and Roman, ancient and modern, a contemporary of Achilles and Odysseus but also a true Augustan Roman. The story is a bit obviously calculated to create an instant tradition. Somehow the overthoughtful, rather pompous figure of Aeneas falls short of the glory-bound Achilles and Hector, not to mention the clever Odysseus. In Aeneas, the Homeric hero is redefined as a man who can launch a whole civilization, who can write past, present, and future in himself and whose heroism consists in the fact that he can do this and others cannot. In no other person—real or fictional—are the superior qualities of the noble Roman better exemplified.

The hero is middle-aged and has gained the wisdom that sometimes comes with maturity. Aeneas sees clearly that a kind of sadness underlies all heroic acts and that many of people's actions are dictated by external forces. Compared with Homer, Virgil lacks dash; what he offers instead is a sorrowful and chastened wisdom.

Like Stoic philosophy, the *Aeneid* views adherence to duty as the loftiest of all human values. Virgil wonderfully gives Rome its highest creed—its duty to the world—when Anchises tells his son Aeneas:

> Others will cast more tenderly in bronze
> Their breathing figures, I can well believe,
> And bring more lifelike portraits out of marble;
> Argue more eloquently, use the pointer
> To trace the paths of heaven accurately
> And accurately foretell the rising stars.
> Roman, remember by your strength to rule
> Earth's peoples—for your arts are to be these:
> To pacify, to impose the rule of law,
> To spare the conquered, battle down the proud.

This was the highest of Roman ideals. While it sacrificed much in the realm of human value, while it denigrated such qualities as imagination and joy, it provided a noble code of conduct so long as the Romans adhered to it.

LITERARY SELECTION 13

On the Republic
Marcus Tullius Cicero (106–43 BC)

In both his political career and his writing Cicero is the embodiment of the splendid Roman statesman and cultured man of letters. Metaphysics and aesthetics are Greek concerns and of no interest for a patriot committed to the austere occupation of being a Roman. Rather, practicality and devotion to the state are his central concerns; these support a Rome whose duty and destiny are to establish order and to civilize the world.

In his *On the Republic* (54–51 BC), Cicero follows Stoic teaching on promoting the welfare of the state, but adopts some elements from Plato's *Republic*. Though patterned after Plato's "Myth of Er" (*Republic*, Book X), Cicero's "Scipio's Dream" is unequivocally Roman. Plato's myth is a vision of aspiration toward the state as an absolute ideal; Cicero uses a dream device to illustrate duty, honor, and patriotism, for as Scipio is told, "the noblest of pursuits . . . are those undertaken for the safety of your country."

The narrator is Scipio Africanus the Younger, the adopted grandson of Scipio Africanus the Elder, the general who defeated Hannibal at Carthage (Second Punic War, 218–201 BC). Scipio the Younger totally destroyed Carthage at the end of the Third Punic War (149–146 BC). In this essay he is an officer under the consul Manius Manilius, whom he later replaced. Widely read in the Middle Ages, this essay influenced both Chaucer and Dante; one can compare the geography and cosmology of Dante's *Hell* (see pp. 403–13) with Cicero's summary of the science of his day.

From Book VI, "Scipio's Dream"

I served in Africa as military tribune of the Fourth Legion under Manius Manilius, as you know. When I arrived in that country my greatest desire was to meet King Masinissa, who had good reasons to be attached to my family. The old man embraced me tearfully when I called, and presently looked up to heaven and said, "I thank thee, sovereign sun, and ye lesser heavenly beings, that before I depart this life I behold in my realm and beneath my roof Publius Cornelius Scipio, whose very name refreshes my strength, so inseparable from my thought is the memory of that noble and invincible hero who first bore it." Then I questioned him about his kingdom, and he me about our commonwealth, and the day wore away with much conversation on both sides.

After I had been royally entertained we continued our conversation late into the night, the old man talking of nothing but Africanus and rehearsing his sayings as well as his deeds. When we parted to take our rest I fell into a deeper sleep than usual, for the hour was late and I was weary from travel. Because of our conversation, I suppose—our thoughts and utterances by day produce an effect in our sleep like that which Ennius speaks of with reference to Homer, of whom he used frequently to think and speak in his waking hours—Africanus appeared to me, in the shape that was familiar to me from his bust rather than from his own person. I shuddered when I recognized him, but he said: "Courage, Scipio, lay aside your dread and imprint my words on your memory. Do you see yonder city which I forced to submit to Rome but which is now stirring up the old hostilities and cannot remain at rest (from a lofty eminence bathed in brilliant starlight he pointed to Carthage), the city which you have come to attack, slightly more than a private? Within two years you shall be consul and overthrow it, and so win for yourself that which you now bear by inheritance. When you shall have destroyed Carthage, celebrated your triumph, been chosen censor, have traversed Egypt, Syria, Asia, and Greece as ambassador, you will be chosen consul a second time in your absence and will put an end to a great war by extirpating Numantia. But when you shall be borne into the capitol in your triumphal chariot, you shall find the government thrown into confusion by the machinations of my grandson; and here, Africanus, you must display to your country the luster of your spirit, genius, and wisdom.

"But at this period I perceive that the path of your destiny is a doubtful one; for when your life has passed through seven times eight oblique journeys and returns of the sun; and when these two numbers (each of which is regarded as complete, one on one account and the other on another) shall, in their natural circuit, have brought you to the crisis of your fate, then will the whole state turn itself toward thee and thy glory; the senate, all virtuous men, our allies, and the Latins, shall look up to you. Upon your single person the preservation of your country will depend; and, in short, it is your part, as dictator, to settle the government, if you can but escape the impious hands of your kinsmen."—Here, when Laelius uttered an exclamation, and the rest groaned with great excitement, Scipio said, with a gentle smile, "I beg that you will not waken me out of my dream; listen a few moments and hear what followed.

"But that you may be more earnest in the defense of your country, know from me, that a certain place in heaven is assigned to all who have preserved, or assisted, or improved their country, where they are to enjoy an endless duration of happiness. For there is nothing which takes place on earth more acceptable to that Supreme Deity who governs all this world, than those councils and assemblies of men bound together by law, which are termed states; the governors and preservers of these go from hence, and hither do they return." Here, frightened as I was, not so much from the dread of death as of the treachery of my friends, I nevertheless asked him whether my father Paulus, and others, whom we thought to be dead, were yet alive? "To be sure they are alive (replied Africanus), for they have escaped from the fetters of the body as from a prison; that which is called life is really death. But behold your father Paulus approaching you."—No sooner did I see him than I poured forth a flood of tears; but he, embracing and kissing me, forbade me to weep. And when, having suppressed my tears, I regained the faculty of speech, I said: "Why, thou most sacred and excellent father, since this is life, as I hear Africanus affirm, why do I tarry on earth, and not hasten to come to you?"

"Not so, my son," he replied; "unless that God, whose temple is all this which you behold, shall free you from this imprisonment in the body, you can have no admission to this place; for men have been created under this condition, that they should keep that globe called earth which you see in the middle of this temple. And a soul has been supplied to them from those eternal fires which you call constellations and stars, and which, being globular and round, are animated with divine spirit, and complete their cycles and revolutions with amazing rapidity. Therefore you, my Publius, and all good men, must preserve your souls in the keeping of your bodies; nor are you, without the order of that Being who bestowed them upon you, to depart from mundane life, lest you seem to desert the duty assigned you by God. But, Scipio, like your grandfather here, like me who begot you, cherish justice and duty, a great obligation to parents and kin but greatest to your country. Such a life is the way to heaven and to this assembly of those who have already lived, and, released from the body, inhabit the place which you now see" (it was the circle of light which blazed most brightly among the other fires), "which you have learned from the Greeks to call the Milky Way." And as I looked on every side I saw other things transcendently glorious and wonderful. There were stars which we never see from the earth, and all were vast beyond what we have ever imagined. The least was that farthest from heaven and nearest the earth which shone with a borrowed light. The starry spheres were much larger than the earth; the earth itself looked so small as to make me ashamed of our empire, which was a mere point on its surface. As I gazed more intently on earth, Africanus said: "How long will your mind be fixed on the ground? Do you not see what lofty regions you have entered? These are the nine circles, or rather spheres, by which all things are held together. One, the outermost, is the celestial; it contains all the rest and is itself the Supreme God, holding and embracing within itself the other spheres. In this are fixed those stars which ever roll in an unchanging course. Beneath it are seven other spheres which have a retrograde movement, opposite to that of the heavens. Of these, the globe which on earth you call Saturn, occupies one sphere. That shining body which you see next is called Jupiter, and is friendly and salutary to mankind. Next the lucid one, terrible to the earth, which you call Mars. The Sun holds the next place, almost under the middle region; he is the chief, the leader, and the director of the other luminaries; he is the soul and guide of the world, and of such immense bulk, that he illuminates and fills all other objects with his light. He is followed by the orbit of Venus, and that of Mercury, as attendants; and the Moon rolls in the lowest sphere, enlightened by the rays of the Sun. Below this there is nothing but what is mortal and transitory, excepting those souls which are given to the human race by the goodness of the gods. Whatever lies above the Moon is eternal. For the earth, which is the ninth sphere, and is placed in the center of the whole system, is immovable and below all the rest; and all bodies, by their natural gravitation, tend toward it."

When I had recovered from my amazement at these things I asked, "What is this sound so strong and sweet that fills my ears?" "This," he replied, "is the melody which, at intervals unequal, yet differing in exact proportions, is made by the impulse and motion of the spheres themselves, which, softening shriller by deeper tones, produce a diversity of regular harmonies. It is impossible that such prodigious movements should pass in silence; and nature teaches that the sounds which the spheres at one extremity utter must be sharp, and those on the other extremity must be grave; on which account that highest revolution of the star-studded heaven, whose motion is more rapid, is carried on with a sharp and quick sound; whereas this of the moon, which is situated the lowest and at the other extremity, moves with the gravest sound. For the earth, the ninth sphere, remaining motionless, abides invariably in the innermost position, occupying the central spot in the universe. But these eight revolutions, of which two, those of Mercury and Venus, are in unison, make seven distinct tones, with measured intervals between, and almost all things are arranged in sevens. Skilled men, copying this harmony with strings and voice, have opened for themselves a way back to this place, as have others who with excelling genius have cultivated divine sciences in human life. But the ears of men are deafened by being filled with this melody; you mortals have no duller sense than that of hearing. As where the Nile at the Falls of Catadupa pours down from lofty mountains, the people who live hard by lack the sense of hearing because of the cataract's roar, so this harmony of the whole universe in its intensely rapid movement is so loud that men's ears cannot take it in, even as you cannot look directly at the sun, your sense of sight being overwhelmed by its radiance." While I marveled at these things I was ever and anon turning my eyes back to earth, upon which Africanus resumed:

"I perceive that even now you are fixing your eyes on the habitation and abode of men, and if it seems to you diminutive, as it in fact is, keep your gaze fixed on these heavenly things and scorn the earthly. What fame can you obtain from the speech of men, what glory worth the seeking? You perceive that men dwell on but few and scanty portions of the earth, and that amid these spots, as it were, vast solitudes are interposed! As to those who inhabit the earth, not only are they so separated that no communication can circulate among them from the one to the other, but part lie upon one side, part upon another, and part are diametrically opposite to you, from whom you assuredly can expect no glory. You observe that the same earth is encircled and encompassed as it were by certain zones, of which the two that are most distant from one another and lie as it were toward the vortexes of the heavens in both directions, are rigid as you see with frost, while the middle and the largest zone is burned up with the heat of the sun. Two of these are habitable. The southern,

150

160

170

180

190

200

whose inhabitants imprint their footsteps in an opposite direction to you, has no relation to your race. As to this other, lying toward the north, which you inhabit, observe what a small portion of it falls to your share; for all that part of the earth which is inhabited by you, which narrows toward the south and north but widens from east to west, is no other than a little island surrounded by that sea which on earth you call the Atlantic, sometimes the great sea, and sometimes the ocean; and yet with so grand a name, you see how diminutive it is! Now do you think it possible for your renown, or that of any one of us, to move from those cultivated and inhabited spots of ground, and pass beyond that Caucasus, or swim across yonder Ganges? What inhabitant of the other parts of the East, or of the extreme regions of the setting sun, of those tracts that run toward the South or toward the North, shall ever hear of your name? Now supposing them cut off, you see at once within what narrow limits your glory would fain expand itself. As to those who speak of you, how long will they speak?

"Let me even suppose that a future race of men shall be desirous of transmitting to their posterity your renown or mine, as they received it from their fathers; yet when we consider the convulsions and conflagrations that must necessarily happen at some definite period, we are unable to attain not only to an eternal, but even to a lasting fame. Now of what consequence is it to you to be talked of by those who are born after you, and not by those who were born before you, who certainly were as numerous and more virtuous; especially, as amongst the very men who are thus to celebrate our renown, not a single one can preserve the recollections of a single year? For mankind ordinarily measure their year by the revolution of the sun, that is of a single heavenly body. But when all the planets shall return to the same position which they once had, and bring back after a long rotation the same aspect of the entire heavens, then the year may be said to be truly completed; I do not venture to say how many ages of mankind will be contained within such a year. As of old the sun seemed to be eclipsed and blotted out when the soul of Romulus entered these regions, so when the sun shall be again eclipsed in the same part of his course and at the same period of the year and day, with all the constellations and stars recalled to the point from which they started on their revolutions, then count the year as brought to a close. But be assured that the twentieth part of such a year has not yet elapsed.

"Consequently, should you renounce hope of returning to this place where eminent and excellent men find their reward, of what worth is that human glory which can scarcely extend to a small part of a single year? If, then, you shall determine to look on high and contemplate this mansion and eternal abode, you will neither give yourself to the gossip of the vulgar nor place your hope of well-being on rewards that man can bestow. Virtue herself, by her own charms, should draw you to true honor. What others may say of you regard as their concern, not yours. They will doubtless talk about you, but what they say is limited to the narrow regions

210

220

230

240

250

260

which you see; nor does talk of anyone last into eternity—it is buried with those who die, and lost in oblivion for those who come afterward." 270

When he had finished I said: "Truly, Africanus, if the path to heaven lies open to those who have deserved well of their country, though from my childhood I have ever trod in your and my father's footsteps without disgracing your glory, yet now, with so noble a prize set before me, I shall strive with much more diligence."

"Do so strive," replied he, "and do not consider yourself, but your body, to be mortal. For you are not the being which this corporeal figure evinces; but the soul of every man is the man, and not that form which may be 280 delineated with a finger. Know also that you are a god, if a god is that which lives, perceives, remembers, foresees, and which rules, governs, and moves the body over which it is set, just as the Supreme God rules the universe. Just as the eternal God moves the universe, which is in part mortal, so does an everlasting soul move the corruptible body.

"That which is always in motion is eternal; but that which, while communicating motion to another, derives its own movement from some other source, must of 290 necessity cease to live when this motion ends. Only what moves itself never ceases motion, for it is never deserted by itself; it is rather the source and first cause of motion in whatever else is moved. But the first cause has no beginning, for everything originates from the first cause; itself, from nothing. If it owed its origin to anything else, it would not be a first cause. If it has no beginning, it has no end. If a first cause is extinguished, it will neither be reborn from anything else, nor will it create anything else from itself, for everything must 300 originate from a first cause. It follows that motion begins with that which is moved of itself, and that this can neither be born nor die—else the heavens must collapse and nature perish, possessing no force from which to receive the first impulse to motion.

"Since that which moves of itself is eternal, who can deny that the soul is endowed with this property? Whatever is moved by external impulse is soulless; whatever possesses soul is moved by an inner impulse of its own, for this is the peculiar nature and property of 310 soul. And since soul is the only force that moves itself, it surely has no beginning and is immortal. Employ it, therefore, in the noblest of pursuits; the noblest are those undertaken for the safety of your country. If it is in these that your soul is diligently exercised, it will have a swifter flight to this, its proper home and permanent abode. Even swifter will be the flight if, while still imprisoned in the body, it shall peer forth, and, contemplating what lies beyond, detach itself as far as possible from the body. For the souls of those who have 320 surrendered themselves to the pleasures of the body and have become their slaves, who are goaded to obedience by lust and violate the laws of gods and men—such souls, when they pass out of their bodies, hover close to earth, and do not return to this place till they have been tossed about for many ages."

He departed; I awoke from sleep.

LITERARY SELECTION 14

The Aeneid

Virgil (Publius Virgilius Maro; 70–19 BC)

Aeneas, the Trojan hero, has fled from Troy, and, after a great storm at sea, landed on the North African coast. Traveling to Carthage, ruled by Queen Dido, he narrated the last days of the Trojan War. He described how he gathered a group around him including his soon-to-die father, Anchises (an-KI-seez), son Askanius (a-SKAY-nee-us), and the household gods and fled from Asia Minor.

In the meantime Dido has fallen in love with Aeneas, and he, as much as his duty will allow, with her. Fearful of passion that might interfere with duty, Aeneas and his band fled to Sicily, leaving Dido to cast herself on a great funeral pyre. Aeneas left most of his party in Sicily and pushed on to fulfill his destiny—the founding of Rome. The group arrived in Italy after Palinurus (pal-uh-NOOR-us), the steersman, was lost overboard. Long before, Aeneas had been told that on his arrival he should consult the Cumaean Sibyl (kyoo-MEE-an SI-bil), a prophetess of Apollo, and that he should descend to the underworld to meet his father's spirit, a visit presented here in full. After the visit the little group sailed up the Tiber, where Aeneas fulfilled his destiny when he married Lavinia, daughter of King Latinus (la-TIE-nus), and established the Roman Empire.

The selection given here, the pivotal book of the entire poem, is carefully patterned after Homer. In Book XI of the *Odyssey* (see pp. 79–86) Odysseus descended to the underworld primarily to secure Teiresias' prophecy about what the future held for him. Homer took full advantage of the opportunity to introduce many notable figures from Greek history. Virgil used a similar device of presenting past, present, and future but in a significantly different way. Rather than the prophecies of a seer, the future in the *Aeneid* is graphically portrayed.

Aeneas confronts the future—the Romans still to come— in Book VI, and willingly accepts his Roman destiny.

Here he encounters Dido's ghost and attempts a reconciliation, though Dido will never forgive him. This is a prime example of Stoicism. If he must, the Roman hero will tread on others on the road to his destiny but the process is always painful—for the Roman. The hero lives for the future and must therefore deny both past and present. Aeneas is thus sorry for Dido and also for himself as the agent of her destruction. Similarly, Rome destroyed Carthage in the Third Punic War but, in the larger sense, Carthage was fated to be destroyed because Rome was destined to rule the world. Given the belief in the state as the ultimate reality, the manifest destiny of the empire was the only proper course of history.

The Roman view—in particular, Virgil's—was that the opponents of Roman destiny die as they must but their deaths are the necessary price of Roman civilization. Much as we may disagree, it is still a fact that the *Pax Romana* lasted from the reign of Caesar Augustus through that of Marcus Aurelius: two centuries without a major war anywhere in the Roman world.

Since Dante used Virgil as his guide through Hell and Purgatory (see pp. 383–4 and 403–13), there is an obvious influence of Virgil on the *Divine Comedy*. So, the line of influence extends from the *Iliad* and *Odyssey* to the *Aeneid* and all the way to Dante in the final years of the Middle Ages.

The selection was translated by Rolfe Humphries.

From Book VI, "The World Below"

Mourning for Palinurus, he drives the fleet
To Cumae's coast line; the prows are turned, the anchor
Let down, the beach is covered by the vessels.
Young in their eagerness for the land in the west,
They flash ashore; some seek the seeds of flame
Hidden in veins of flint, and others spoil
The woods of tinder, and show where water runs.
Aeneas, in devotion, seeks the heights
Where stands Apollo's temple, and the cave
Where the dread Sibyl dwells, Apollo's priestess,   10
With the great mind and heart, inspired revealer
Of things to come. They enter Diana's grove,
Pass underneath the roof of gold.
                              The story
Has it that Daedalus fled from Minos' kingdom[16]
Trusting himself to wings he made, and traveled
A course unknown to man, to the cold north,
Descending on this very summit; here,
Earth-bound again, he built a mighty temple,
Paying Apollo homage, the dedication
Of the oarage of his wings. On the temple doors   20
He carved, in bronze, Androgeos' death, and the payment
Enforced on Cecrops' children, seven sons
For sacrifice each year: there stands the urn,
The lots are drawn—facing this, over the sea,
Rises the land of Crete: the scene portrays
Pasiphae in cruel love, the bull
She took to her by cunning, and their offspring,
The mongrel Minotaur, half man, half monster,
The proof of lust unspeakable; and the toil
Of the house is shown, the labyrinthine maze   30
Which no one could have solved, but Daedalus

Pitied a princess' love, loosened the tangle,
Gave her a skein to guide her way. His boy,
Icarus, might have been here, in the picture,
And almost was—his father had made the effort
Once, and once more and dropped his hands; he could not
Master his grief that much. The story held them;
They would have studied it longer, but Achates[17]
Came from his mission; with him came the priestess,
Deiphobe, daughter of Glaucus, who tends the
     temple   40
For Phoebus and Diana; she warned Aeneas:
"It is no such sights the time demands; far better
To offer sacrifice, seven chosen bullocks,
Seven chosen ewes, a herd without corruption."
They were prompt in their obedience, and the priestess
Summoned the Trojans to the lofty temple.
     The rock's vast side is hollowed into a cavern,
With a hundred mouths, a hundred open portals,
Whence voices rush, the answers of the Sibyl.
They had reached the threshold, and the virgin cried: 50
"It is time to seek the fates; the god is here,
The god is here, behold him." And as she spoke
Before the entrance, her countenance and color
Changed, and her hair tossed loose, and her heart was
     heaving,
Her bosom swollen with frenzy; she seemed taller,
Her voice not human at all, as the god's presence
Drew nearer, and took hold on her. "Aeneas,"
She cried, "Aeneas, are you praying?
Are you being swift in prayer? Until you are,
The house of the gods will not be moved, nor open   60
Its mighty portals." More than her speech, her silence
Made the Trojans cold with terror, and Aeneas
Prayed from the depth of his heart: "Phoebus Apollo,
Compassionate ever, slayer of Achilles
Through aim of Paris' arrow, helper and guide
Over the seas, over the lands, the deserts,
The shoals and quicksands, now at last we have come
To Italy, we hold the lands which fled us:
Grant that thus far, no farther, a Trojan fortune
Attend our wandering. And spare us now;   70
All of you, gods and goddesses, who hated
Troy in the past, and Trojan glory. I beg you,
Most holy prophetess, in who foreknowing
The future stands revealed, grant that the Trojans—
I ask with fate's permission—rest in Latium
Their wandering storm-tossed gods. I will build a temple,
In honor of Apollo and Diana,
Out of eternal marble, and ordain
Festivals in their honor, and for the Sibyl
A great shrine in our Kingdom, and I will place there   80
The lots and mystic oracles for my people
With chosen priests to tend them. Only, priestess,

---

16. Daedalus (DED-uh-lus) was a mythical artist and inventor. Imprisoned by King Minos of Crete, he constructed wings for himself and his son Icaros (IK-ar-os) and flew away. Icaros flew too near the sun and melted the wax wings. The other pieces of sculpture mentioned here show other incidents in Daedalus' life.
17. Achates (a-KOT-eez) is a companion of Aeneas.

This once, I pray you, chant the sacred verses
With your own lips; do not trust them to the leaves,[18]
The mockery of the rushing wind's disorder."
    But the priestess, not yet subject to Apollo,
Went reeling through the cavern, wild, and storming
To throw the god, who presses, like a rider,
With bit and bridle and weight, tames her wild spirit,
Shapes her to his control. The doors fly open,   90
The hundred doors, of their own will, fly open,
And through the air the answer comes:—"O Trojans,
At last the dangers of the sea are over;
That course is run, but grave ones are waiting
On land. The sons of Dardanus[19] will reach
The kingdom of Lavinia[20]—be easy
On that account—the sons of Dardanus, also,
Will wish they had not come there. War, I see,
Terrible war, and the river Tiber foaming
With streams of blood. There will be another
    Xanthus,   100
Another Simois,[21] and Greek encampment,
Even another Achilles, born in Latium,
Himself a goddess' son. And Juno further
Will always be there: you will beg for mercy,
Be poor, turn everywhere for help. A woman
Will be the cause once more of so much evil,
A foreign bride, receptive to the Trojans,
A foreign marriage. Do not yield to evil,
Attack, attack, more boldly even than fortune
Seems to permit. An offering of safety,—   110
Incredible!—will come from a Greek city."
    So, through the amplifiers of her cavern,
The hollow vaults, the Sibyl cast her warnings,
Riddles confused with truth; and Apollo rode her,
Reining her rage, and shaking her, and spurring
The fierceness of her heart. The frenzy dwindled,
A little, and her lips were still. Aeneas
Began:—"For me, no form of trouble, maiden,
Is new, or unexpected; all of this
I have known long since, lived in imagination.   120
One thing I ask: this is the gate of the kingdom,
So it is said, where Pluto reigns, the gloomy
Marsh where the water of Acheron runs over.
Teach me the way from here, open the portals
That I may go to my beloved father,
Stand in his presence, talk with him. I brought him,
Once, on these shoulders, through a thousand weapons
And following fire, and foemen. He shared with me
The road, the sea, the menaces of heaven,
Things that an old man should not bear; he bore
    them,   130
Tired as he was. And he it was who told me
To come to you in humbleness. I beg you
Pity the son, the father. You have power,
Great priestess, over all; it is not for nothing
Hecate[22] gave you this dominion over
Avernus' groves. If Orpheus could summon
Eurydice from the shadows with his music,
If Pollux could save his brother, coming, going,
Along this path,—why should I mention Theseus,
Why mention Hercules?[23] I, too, descended   140
From the line of Jupiter." He clasped the altar,

Making his prayer, and she made answer to him:
"Son of Anchises, born of godly lineage,
By night, by day, the portals of dark Dis[24]
Stand open: it is easy, the descending
Down to Avernus. But to climb again,
To trace the footsteps back to the air above,
There lies the task, the toil. A few, beloved
By Jupiter, descended from the gods,
A few, in whom exalting virtue burned,   150
Have been permitted. Around the central woods
The black Cocytus glides, a sullen river;
But if such love is in your heart, such longing
For double crossing of the Stygian lake,
For double sight of Tartarus, learn first
What must be done. In a dark tree there hides
A bough, all golden, leaf and pliant stem,
Sacred to Proserpine.[25] This all the grove
Protects, and shadows cover it with darkness.
Until this bough, this bloom of light, is found,   160
No one receives his passport to the darkness
Whose queen requires this tribute. In succession,
After the bough is plucked, another grows,
Gold-green with the same metal. Raise the eyes,
Look up, reach up the hand, and it will follow
With ease, if fate is calling; otherwise,
No power, no steel, can loose it. Furthermore
(Alas, you do not know this!), one of your men
Lies on the shore, unburied, a pollution
To all the fleet, while you have come for counsel   170
Here to our threshold. Bury him with honor;
Black cattle slain in expiation for him
Must fall before you see the Stygian kingdoms,
The groves denied to living men."
                            Aeneas,
With sadness in his eyes, and downcast heart,
Turned from the cave, and at his side Achates
Accompanied his anxious meditations.
They talked together: who could be the comrade
Named by the priestess, lying there unburied?
And they found him on dry sand; it was Misenus,[26]   180
Aeolus' son, none better with the trumpet
To make men burn for warfare. He had been
Great Hector's man-at-arms; he was good in battle
With spear as well as horn, and after Hector

18. The prophecies of this Cumaean Sibyl were usually written on leaves which the winds in the cave might scatter and confuse (v. Book III).
19. The mythical founder of Troy.
20. The daughter of the Italian King Latinus. Aeneas was later to marry her to establish his kingdom.
21. Rivers near Troy that ran with blood during the Trojan War.
22. Hecate (HEK-uh-tee) was believed to be a very powerful goddess who, among many responsibilities, controlled the spirits of the dead. Avernus is a deep pool surrounded by gloomy woods. Its depth and gloom inspired the idea that it led to the underworld.
23. All of these are the names of mythical heroes who had descended into Hades and returned.
24. Dis is another name for the underworld.
25. Proserpine (pro-SUR-pi-nee), as wife of Pluto, is queen of the underworld.
26. (mi-SEEN-us.)

Had fallen to Achilles, he had followed
Aeneas, entering to meaner service.
Some foolishness came over him; he made
The ocean echo to the blare of his trumpet
That day, and challenged the sea-gods to a contest
In martial music, and Triton, jealous, caught him,   190
However unbelievable the story,
And held him down between the rocks, and drowned
    him
Under the foaming waves. His comrades mourned him,
Aeneas most of all, and in their sorrow
They carry out, in haste, the Sibyl's orders,
Construct the funeral altar, high as heaven.
They go to an old wood, and the pine-trees fall
Where wild beasts have their dens, and holm-oak
    rings
To the stroke of the axe, and oak and ash are riven
By the splitting wedge, and rowan-trees come rolling   200
Down the steep mountain-side. Aeneas helps them,
And cheers them on; studies the endless forest,
Takes thought, and prays: "If only we might see it,
That golden bough, here in the depth of the forest,
Bright on some tree. She told the truth, our priestess,
Too much, too bitter truth, about Misenus."
No sooner had he spoken than twin doves
Came flying down before him, and alighted
On the green ground. He knew his mother's birds,[27]
And made his prayer, rejoicing,—"Oh, be leaders,   210
Wherever the way, and guide me to the grove
Where the rich bough makes rich the shaded ground.
Help me, O goddess-mother!" And he paused,
Watching what sign they gave, what course they set.
The birds flew on a little, just ahead
Of the pursuing vision; when they came
To the jaws of dank Avernus, evil-smelling,
They rose aloft, then swooped down the bright air,
Perched on the double tree, where the off-color
Of gold was gleaming golden through the branches.   220
As mistletoe, in the cold winter, blossoms
With its strange foliage on an alien tree,
The yellow berry gilding the smooth branches,
Such was the vision of the gold in leaf
On the dark holm-oak, so the foil was rustling,
Rattling, almost, the bract in the soft wind
Stirring like metal. Aeneas broke it off
With eager grasp, and bore it to the Sibyl.
    Meanwhile, along the shore, the Trojans mourned,
Paying Misenus' dust the final honors.   230
A mighty pyre was raised, of pine and oak,
The sides hung with dark leaves, and somber cypress
Along the front, and gleaming arms above.
Some made the water hot, and some made ready
Bronze caldrons, shimmering over fire, and others
Lave and anoint the body, and with weeping
Lay on the bier his limbs, and place above them
Familiar garments, crimson color; and some
Take up the heavy burden, a sad office,
And, as their fathers did, they kept their eyes   240
Averted, as they brought the torches nearer.

27. Aeneas' mother was Venus.

They burn gifts with him, bowls of oil, and viands,
And frankincense; and when the flame is quiet
And the ashes settle to earth, they wash the embers
With wine, and slake the thirsty dust. The bones
Are placed in a bronze urn by Corynaeus,
Who, with pure water, thrice around his comrades
Made lustral cleansing, shaking gentle dew
From the fruitful branch of olive; and they said
Hail and *farewell!* And over him Aeneas   250
Erects a mighty tomb, with the hero's arms,
His oar and trumpet, where the mountain rises
Memorial for ever, and named Misenus.
    These rites performed, he hastened to the Sibyl.
There was a cavern, yawning wide and deep,
Jagged, below the darkness of the trees.
Beside the darkness of the lake. No bird
Could fly above it safely, with the vapor
Pouring from the black gulf (the Greeks have named it
Avernus, or A-Ornos, meaning *birdless*),   260
And here the priestess for the slaughter set
Four bullocks, black ones, poured the holy wine
Between the horns, and plucked the topmost bristles
For the first offering to the sacred fire,
Calling on Hecate, a power in heaven,
A power in hell. Knives to the throat were driven,
The warm blood caught in bowls. Aeneas offered
A lamb, black-fleeced, to Night and her great sister,
A sterile heifer for the queen; for Dis
An altar in the night, and on the flames   270
The weight of heavy bulls, the fat oil pouring
Over the burning entrails. And at dawn,
Under their feet, earth seemed to shake and rumble,
The ridges move, and bitches bay in darkness,
As the presence neared. The Sibyl cried a warning,
"Keep off, keep off, whatever is unholy,
Depart from here! Courage, Aeneas; enter
The path, unsheathe the sword. The time is ready
For the brave heart." She strode out boldly, leading
Into the open cavern, and he followed.   280
    Gods of the world of spirit, silent shadows,
Chaos and Phlegethon, areas of silence,
Wide realms of dark, may it be right and proper
To tell what I have heard, this revelation
Of matters buried deep in earth and darkness!
    Vague forms in lonely darkness, they were going
Through void and shadow, through the empty realm
Like people in a forest, when the moonlight
Shifts with a baleful glimmer, and shadow covers
The sky, and all the colors turn to blackness.   290
At the first threshold, on the jaws of Orcus,
Grief and avenging Cares have set their couches,
And pale Diseases dwell, and sad Old Age,
Fear, evil-counselling Hunger, wretched Need,
Forms terrible to see, and Death, and Toil,
And Death's own brother, Sleep, and evil Joys,
Fantasies of the mind, and deadly War,
The Furies' iron chambers, Discord, raving,
Her snaky hair entwined in bloody bands.
An el-tree loomed there, shadowy and huge,   300
The aged boughs outspread, beneath whose leaves,
Men say, the false dreams cling, thousands on thousands.

And there are monsters in the dooryard, Centaurs,
Scyllas, of double shape, the beast of Lerna,
Hissing most horribly, Briareus,
The hundred-handed giant, a Chimaera
Whose armament is fire, Harpies, and Gorgons,
A triple-bodied giant. In sudden panic
Aeneas drew his sword, the edge held forward,
Ready to rush and flail, however blindly,   310
Save that his wise companion warned him, saying
They had no substance, they were only phantoms
Flitting about, illusions without body.
    From here, the road turns off to Acheron,
River of Hell; here, thick with muddy whirling,
Cocytus boils with sand. Charon[28] is here,
The guardian of these mingling waters, Charon,
Uncouth and filthy, on whose chin the hair
Is a tangled mat, whose eyes protrude, are burning,
Whose dirty cloak is knotted at the shoulder.   320
He poles a boat, tends to the sail, unaided,
Ferrying bodies in his rust-hued vessel.
Old, but a god's senility is awful
In its raw greenness. To the bank come thronging
Mothers and men, bodies of great-souled heroes,
Their life-time over, boys, unwedded maidens,
Young men whose fathers saw their pyres burning,
Thick as the forest leaves that fall in autumn
With early frost, thick as the birds to landfall
From over the seas, when the chill of the year
        compels them.   330
To sunlight. There they stand, a host, imploring
To be taken over first. Their hands, in longing
Reach out for the farther shore. But the gloomy boatman
Makes choice among them, taking some, and keeping
Others far back from the stream's edge. Aeneas,
Wondering, asks the Sibyl, "Why the crowding?
What are the spirits seeking? What distinction
Brings some across the livid stream, while others
Stay on the farther bank?" She answers, briefly:
"Son of Anchises, this is the awful river,   340
The Styx,[29] by which the gods take oath; the boatman
Charon; those he takes with him are the buried,
Those he rejects, whose luck is out, the graveless.
It is not permitted him to take them over
The dreadful banks and hoarse-resounding waters
Till earth is cast upon their bones. They haunt
These shores a hundred restless years of waiting
Before they end postponement of the crossing."
Aeneas paused, in thoughtful mood, with pity
Over their lot's unevenness; and saw there,   350
Wanting the honor given the dead, and grieving,
Leucaspis, and Orontes, the Lycian captain,
Who had sailed from Troy across the stormy waters,
And drowned off Africa, with crew and vessel,
And there was Palinurus, once his pilot,
Who, not so long ago, had been swept over,
Watching the stars on the journey north from Carthage.
The murk was thick; Aeneas hardly knew him,
Sorrowful in that darkness, but made question:
"What god, O Palinurus, took you from us?   360
Who drowned you in the deep? Tell me. Apollo
Never before was false, and yet he told me

You would be safe across the seas, and come
Unharmed to Italy; what kind of promise
Was this, to fool me with?" But Palinurus
Gave him assurance:—"It was no god who drowned
    me,
No falsehood on Apollo's part, my captain,
But as I clung to the tiller, holding fast
To keep the course, as I should do, I felt it
Wrenched from the ship, and I fell with it, headlong.   370
By those rough seas I swear, I had less fear
On my account than for the ship, with rudder
And helmsman overboard, to drift at the mercy
Of rising seas. Three nights I rode the waters,
Three nights of storm, and from the crest of a wave,
On the fourth morning, sighted Italy,
I was swimming to land, I had almost reached it, heavy
In soaking garments; my cramped finger struggled
To grasp the top of the rock, when barbarous people,
Ignorant men, mistaking me for booty,   380
Struck me with swords; waves hold me now, or winds
Roll me along the shore. By the light of heaven
The lovely air, I beg you, by your father,
Your hope of young Iulus,[30] bring me rescue
Out of these evils, my unconquered leader!
Cast over my body earth—you have the power—
Return to Velia's harbor,—or there may be
Some other way—your mother is a goddess,
Else how would you be crossing this great river,
This Stygian swamp?—help a poor fellow, take me   390
Over the water with you, give a dead man
At least a place to rest in." But the Sibyl
Broke in upon him sternly:—"Palinurus,
Whence comes this mad desire? No man, unburied,
May see the Stygian waters, or Cocytus,
The Furies' dreadful river; no man may come
Unbidden to this bank. Give up the hope
That fate is changed by praying, but hear this,
A little comfort in your harsh misfortune:
Those neighboring people will make expiation,   400
Driven by signs from heaven, through their cities
And through their countryside; they will build a tomb,
Thereto bring offerings yearly, and the place
Shall take its name from you, Cape Palinurus."
So he was comforted a little, finding
Some happiness in the promise.
                              And they went on,
Nearing the river, and from the stream the boatman
Beheld them across the silent forest, nearer,
Turning their footsteps toward the bank. He
        challenged:—
"Whoever you are, O man in armor, coming   410
In this direction, halt where you are, and tell me
The reason why you come. This is the region
Of shadows, and of Sleep and drowsy Night;
I am not allowed to carry living bodies
In the Stygian boat; and I must say I was sorry
I ever accepted Hercules and Theseus

---

28. (KARE-on.)
29. (STICKS.)
30. This is Aeneas' son, also known as Ascanius.

And Pirithous, and rowed them over the lake,
Though they were sons of gods and great in courage.
One of them dared to drag the guard of Hell,
Enchained, from Pluto's throne, shaking in terror,   420
The others to snatch our queen from Pluto's chamber."
The Sibyl answered briefly: "No such cunning
Is plotted here; our weapons bring no danger.
Be undisturbed: the hell-hound in his cavern
May bark forever, to keep the bloodless shadows
Frightened away from trespass; Proserpine,
Untouched, in pureness guards her uncle's threshold.
Trojan Aeneas, a man renowned for goodness,
Renowned for nerve in battle, is descending
To the lowest shades; he comes to find his father.   430
If such devotion has no meaning to you,
Look on this branch at least, and recognize it!"
And with the word she drew from under her mantle
The golden bough; his swollen wrath subsided.
No more was said; he saw the bough, and marveled
At the holy gift, so long unseen; came sculling
The dark-blue boat to the shore, and drove the spirits,
Lining the thwarts, ashore, and cleared the gangway,
And took Aeneas aboard; as that big man
Stepped in, the leaky skiff groaned under the weight,   440
And the strained seams let in the muddy water,
But they made the crossing safely, seer and soldier,
To the far margin, colorless and shapeless,
Grey sedge and dark-brown ooze. They heard the baying
Of Cerberus,[31] that great hound, in his cavern crouching,
Making the shore resound, as all three throats
Belled horribly; and serpents rose and bristled
Along the triple neck. The priestess threw him
A sop with honey and drugged meal; he opened
The ravenous throat, gulped, and subsided, filling   450
The den with his huge bulk. Aeneas, crossing,
Passed on beyond the bank of the dread river
Whence none return.
          A wailing of thin voices[32]
Came to their ears, the souls of infants crying,
Those whom the day of darkness took from the breast
Before their share of living. And there were many
Whom some false sentence brought to death. Here Minos[33]
Judges them once again; a silent jury
Reviews the evidence. And there are others,
Guilty of nothing, but who hated living,   460
The suicides. How gladly, now, they would suffer
Poverty, hardship, in the world of light!
But this is not permitted; they are bound
Nine times around by the black unlovely river;
Styx holds them fast.
          They came to the Fields of Mourning,
So-called, where those whom cruel love had wasted
Hid in secluded pathways, under myrtle,
And even in death were anxious. Procris, Phaedra,
Eriphyle, displaying wounds her son
Had given her, Caeneus, Laodamia,   470
Caeneus, a young man once, and now again
A young man, after having been a woman.
And here, new come from her own wound, was Dido,
Wandering in the wood. The Trojan hero,
Standing near by, saw her, or thought he saw her,

Dim in the shadows, like the slender crescent
Of moon when cloud drifts over. Weeping, he greets
    her:—
"Unhappy Dido, so they told me truly
That your own hand had brought you death. Was I—
Alas!—the cause? I swear by all the stars,   480
By the world above, by everything held sacred
Here under the earth, unwillingly, O queen,
I left your kingdom. But the gods' commands,
Driving me now through these forsaken places,
This utter night, compelled me on. I could not
Believe my loss would cause so great a sorrow.
Linger a moment, do not leave me; whither,
Whom, are you fleeing? I am permitted only
This last word with you."
          But the queen, unmoving
As flint or marble, turned away, her eyes   490
Fixed on the ground: the tears were vain, the words,
Meant to be soothing, foolish; she turned away,
His enemy forever, to the shadows
Where Sychaeus, her former husband, took her
With love for love, and sorrow for her sorrow.
And still Aeneas wept for her, being troubled
By the injustice of her doom; his pity
Followed her going.
          They went on. They came
To the farthest fields, whose tenants are the warriors,
Illustrious throng. Here Tydeus came to meet him,   500
Parthenopaeus came, and pale Adrastus,
A fighter's ghost, and many, many others,
Mourned in the world above, and doomed in battle,
Leaders of Troy, in long array; Aeneas
Sighed as he saw them: Medon; Polyboetes,
The priest of Ceres; Glaucus; and Idaeus
Still keeping arms and chariot; three brothers,
Antenor's sons; Thersilochus; a host
To right and left of him, and when they see him,
One sight is not enough; they crowd around him,   510
Linger, and ask the reasons for his coming.
But Agamemnon's men, the Greek battalions,
Seeing him there, and his arms in shadow gleaming,
Tremble in panic, turn to flee for refuge,
As once they used to, toward their ships, but where
Are the ships now? They try to shout, in terror;
But only a thin and piping treble issues
To mock their mouths, wide-open.
          One he knew
Was here, Deiphobus[34] a son of Priam,
With his whole body mangled, and his features   520
Cruelly slashed, and both hands cut, and ears
Torn from his temples, and his nostrils slit
By shameful wounds. Aeneas hardly knew him,
Shivering there, and doing his best to hide
His marks of punishment; unhailed, he hailed him:—
"Deiphobus, great warrior, son of Teucer,

31. (SIR-bur-us.)
32. Here and about 190 lines later you might compare the sins
    and their punishments with the disposition Dante makes of
    the souls in Hell in Canto XI of the *Inferno* (see p. 409).
33. (MI-nus.)
34. (dee-IF-uh-bus.)

Whose cruel punishment was this? Whose license
Abused you so? I heard, it seems a story
Of that last night, how you had fallen, weary
With killing Greeks at last; I built a tomb,   530
Although no body lay there, in your honor,
Three times I cried, aloud, over your spirit,
Where now your name and arms keep guard. I could
        not,
Leaving my country, find my friend, to give him
Proper interment in the earth he came from."
And Priam's son replied:—"Nothing, dear comrade,
Was left undone; the dead man's shade was given
All ceremony due. It was my own fortune
And a Spartan woman's[35] deadliness that sunk me
Under these evils; she it was who left me   540
These souvenirs. You know how falsely happy
We were on that last night; I need not tell you.
When that dread horse came leaping over our walls,
Pregnant with soldiery, she led the dancing,
A solemn rite, she called it, with Trojan women
Screaming their bacchanals; she raised the torches
High on the citadel; she called the Greeks.
Then—I was worn with trouble, drugged in slumber,
Resting in our ill-omened bridal chamber,
With sleep as deep and sweet as death upon me—   550
Then she, that paragon of helpmates, deftly
Moved all the weapons from the house; my sword,
Even, she stole from underneath my pillow,
Opened the door, and called in Menelaos,
Hoping, no doubt, to please her loving husband,
To win forgetfulness of her old sinning.
It is quickly told: they broke into the chamber,
The two of them, and with them, as accomplice,
Ulysses came, the crime-contriving bastard.
O gods, pay back the Greeks; grant the petition   560
If goodness asks for vengeance! But you, Aeneas,
A living man—what chance has brought you here?
Vagrant of ocean, god-inspired,—which are you?
What chance has worn you down, to come, in sadness,
To these confusing sunless dwelling-places?"
    While they were talking, Aurora's rosy car
Had halfway crossed the heaven; all their time
Might have been spent in converse, but the Sibyl
Hurried them forward:—"Night comes on, Aeneas;
We waste the hours with tears. We are at the cross-
        road,   570
Now; here we turn to the right, where the pathway leads
On to Elysium, under Pluto's ramparts.
Leftward to Tartarus, and retribution,
The terminal of the wicked, and their dungeon."
Deiphobus left them, saying, "O great priestess,
Do not be angry with me; I am going;
I shall not fail the roll-call of the shadows.
Pride of our race, go on; may better fortune
Attend you!" and, upon the word, he vanished.
    As he looked back, Aeneas saw, to his left,   580
Wide walls beneath a cliff, a triple rampart,
A river running fire, Phlegethon's torrent,

Rocks roaring in its course, a gate, tremendous,
Pillars of adamant, a tower of iron,
Too strong for men, too strong for even gods
To batter down in warfare, and behind them
A Fury, sentinel in bloody garments,
Always on watch, by day, by night. He heard
Sobbing and groaning there, the crack of the lash,
The clank of iron, the sound of dragging shackles.   590
The noise was terrible; Aeneas halted,
Asking, "What forms of crime are these, O maiden?
What harrying punishment, what horrible outcry?"
She answered:—"O great leader of the Trojans,
I have never crossed that threshold of the wicked;
No pure soul is permitted entrance thither,
But Hecate, by whose order I was given
Charge of Avernus' groves, my guide, my teacher,
Told me how gods exact the toll of vengeance.
The monarch here, merciless Rhadamanthus,   600
Punishes guilt, and hears confession; he forces
Acknowledgment of crime; no man in the world,
No matter how cleverly he hides his evil,
No matter how much he smiles at his own slyness,
Can fend atonement off; the hour of death
Begins his sentence. Tisiphone, the Fury,
Leaps at the guilty with her scourge; her serpents
Are whips of menace as she calls her sisters.
Imagine the gates, on jarring hinge, rasp open,
You would see her in the doorway, a shape, a sentry,   610
Savage, implacable. Beyond, still fiercer,
The monstrous Hydra dwells; her fifty throats
Are black, and open wide, and Tartarus
Is black, and open wide, and it goes down
To darkness, sheer deep down, and twice the distance
That earth is from Olympus. At the bottom
The Titans crawl, Earth's oldest breed, hurled under
By thunderbolts; here lie the giant twins,
Aloeus' sons, who laid their hands on heaven
And tried to pull down Jove; Salmoneus here   620
Atones for high presumption,—it was he
Who aped Jove's noise and fire, wheeling his horses
Triumphant through his city in Elis, cheering
And shaking the torch, and claiming divine homage,
The arrogant fool, to think his brass was lightning,
His horny-footed horses beat out thunder!
Jove showed him what real thunder was, what lightning
Spoke from immortal cloud, what whirlwind fury
Came sweeping from the heaven to overtake him.
Here Tityos, Earth's giant son, lies sprawling   630
Over nine acres, with a monstrous vulture
Gnawing, with crooked beak, vitals and liver
That grow as they are eaten; eternal anguish,
Eternal feast. Over another hangs
A rock, about to fall; and there are tables
Set for a banquet, gold with royal splendor,
But if a hand goes out to touch the viands,
The Fury drives it back with fire and yelling.
Why name them all, Pirithous, the Lapiths,
Ixion? The roll of crime would take forever.   640
Whoever, in his lifetime, hated his brother,
Or struck his father down; whoever cheated
A client, or was miserly—how many

---

35. Helen of Troy. Virgil believes that she was married to
   Deiphobus after Paris' death.

Of these there seem to be!—whoever went
To treasonable war, or broke a promise
Made to his lord, whoever perished, slain
Over adultery, all these, walled in,
Wait here their punishment. Seek not to know
Too much about their doom. The stone is rolled,
The wheel keeps turning; Theseus forever   650
Sits in dejection; Phlegyas, accursed,
Cries through the halls forever: *Being warned,*
Learn justice; reverence the gods! The man
Who sold his country is here in hell; the man
Who altered laws for money; and a father
Who knew his daughter's bed. All of them dared,
And more than dared, achieved, unspeakable
Ambitions. If I had a hundred tongues,
A hundred iron throats, I could not tell
The fullness of their crime and punishment."   660
And then she added:—"Come: resume the journey,
Fulfill the mission; let us hurry onward.
I see the walls the Cyclops made, the portals
Under the archway, where, the others tell us,
Our tribute must be set." They went together
Through the way's darkness, came to the doors, and
        halted,
And at the entrance Aeneas, having sprinkled
His body with fresh water, placed the bough
Golden before the threshold. The will of the goddess
Had been performed, the proper task completed.   670
    They came to happy places, the joyful dwelling,
The lovely greenery of the groves of the blessed.
Here ampler air invests the fields with light,
Rose-colored, with familiar stars and sun.
Some grapple on the grassy wrestling-ground
In exercise and sport, and some are dancing,
And others singing; in his trailing robe
Orpheus strums the lyre; the seven clear notes
Accompany the dance, the song. And heroes
Are there, great-souled, born in the happier years,   680
Ilus,[36] Assaracus; the city's founder,
Prince Dardanus. Far off, Aeneas wonders,
Seeing the phantom arms, the chariots,
The spears fixed in the ground, the chargers browsing,
Unharnessed, over the plain. Whatever, living,
The men delighted in, whatever pleasure
Was theirs in horse and chariot, still holds them
Here under the world. To right and left, they banquet
In the green meadows, and a joyful chorus
Rises through groves of laurel, whence the river   690
Runs to the upper world. The band of heroes
Dwell here, all those whose mortal wounds were
        suffered
In fighting for the fatherland; and poets,
The good, the pure, the worthy of Apollo;
Those who discovered truth and made life nobler;
Those who served others—all, with snowy fillets
Binding their temples, throng the lovely valley.
And these the Sibyl questioned, most of all
Musaeus,[37] for he towered above the center
Of that great throng:—"O happy souls, O poet,   700
Where does Anchises dwell? For him we come here,
For him we have traversed Erebus' great rivers."

And he replied:—"It is all our home, the shady
Groves, and the streaming meadows, and the softness
Along the river-banks. No fixed abode
Is ours at all; but if it is your pleasure,
Cross over the ridge with me; I will guide you there
By easy going." And so Musaeus led them
And from the summit showed them fields, all shining,
And they went on over and down.   710
    Deep in a valley of green, father Anchises
Was watching, with deep earnestness, the spirits
Whose destiny was light, and counting them over,
All of his race to come, his dear descendants,
Their fates and fortunes and their work and ways,
And as he saw Aeneas coming toward him
Over the meadow, his hands reached out with yearning,
He was moved to tears, and called:—"At last, my son,—
Have you really come, at last? and the long road nothing
To a son who loves his father? Do I, truly,   720
See you, and hear your voice? I was thinking so,
I was hoping so, I was counting off the days,
And I was right about it. O my son!
What a long journey, over land and water,
Yours must have been! What buffeting of danger!
I feared, so much, the Libyan realm would hurt you."
And his son answered:—"It was your spirit, father,
Your sorrowful shade, so often met, that led me
To find these portals. The ships ride safe at anchor,
Safe in the Tuscan sea. Embrace me, father;   730
Let hand join hand in love; do not forsake me."
And as he spoke, the tears streamed down. Three
        times
He reached out toward him, and three times the image
Fled like the breath of the wind or a dream on wings.
    He saw, in a far valley, a separate grove
Where the woods stir and rustle, and a river,
The Lethe,[38] gliding past the peaceful places,
And tribes of people thronging, hovering over,
Innumerable as the bees in summer
Working the bright-hued flowers, and the shining   740
Of the white lilies, murmuring and humming.
Aeneas, filled with wonder, asks the reason
For what he does not know, who are the people
In such a host, and to what river coming?
Anchises answers:—"These are spirits, ready
Once more for life; they drink of Lethe's water
The soothing potion of forgetfulness.
I have longed, for long, to show them to you, name
        them,
Our children's children; Italy discovered,
So much the greater happiness, my son."   750
"But, O my father, is it thinkable
That souls would leave this blessedness, be willing
A second time to bear the sluggish body,
Trade Paradise for earth? Alas, poor wretches,
Why such a mad desire for light?" Anchises
Gives detailed answer: "First, my son, a spirit
Sustains all matter, heaven and earth and ocean,

36. All ancestors of Aeneas, all former kings of Troy.
37. A mythical poet and singer.
38. (LEE-thee.)

The moon, the stars; mind quickens mass, and moves it.
Hence comes the race of man, of beast, of winged
Creatures of air, of the strange shapes which ocean   760
Bears down below his mottled marble surface.
All these are blessed with energy from heaven;[39]
The seed of life is a spark of fire, but the body
A clod of earth, a clog, a mortal burden.
Hence humans fear, desire, grieve, and are joyful,
And even when life is over, all the evil
Ingrained so long, the adulterated mixture,
The plagues and pestilences of the body
Remain, persist. So there must be a cleansing,
By penalty, by punishment, by fire,   770
By sweep of wind, by water's absolution,
Before the guilt is gone. Each of us suffers
His own peculiar ghost. But the day comes
When we are sent through wide Elysium,
The Fields of the Blessed, a few of us, to linger
Until the turn of time, the wheel of ages,
Wears off the taint, and leaves the core of spirit
Pure sense, pure flame. A thousand years pass over
And the god calls the countless host to Lethe
Where memory is annulled, and souls are willing   780
Once more to enter into mortal bodies."
    The discourse ended; the father drew his son
And his companion toward the hum, the center
Of the full host; they came to rising ground
Where all the long array was visible,
Anchises watching, noting, every comer.
"Glory to come, my son, illustrious spirits
Of Dardan lineage, Italian offspring,
Heirs of our name, begetters of our future!
These I will name for you and tell our fortunes: 790
First, leaning on a headless spear, and standing
Nearest the light, that youth, the first to rise
To the world above, is Silvius; his name
Is Alban; in his veins Italian blood
Will run with Trojan; he will be the son
Of your late age; Lavinia will bear him,
A king and sire of kings; from him our race
Will rule in Alba Longa.[40] Near him, Procas,
A glory to the Trojan race; and Capys,
And Numitor, and Silvius Aeneas,   800
Resembling you in name, in arms, in goodness,
If ever he wins the Alban kingdom over.
What fine young men they are! What strength, what
    prowess!
The civic oak already shades their foreheads.
These will found cities, Gabii, Fidenae,
Nomentum; they will crown the hills with towers
Above Collatia, Inuus fortress, Bola,
Cora, all names to be, thus far ungiven.
    "And there will be a son of Mars; his mother
Is Ilia, and his name is Romulus,   810
Assaracus' descendant. On his helmet
See, even now, twin plumes; his father's honor
Confers distinction on him for the world.
Under his auspices Rome, that glorious city,
Will bound her power by earth, her pride by heaven,
Happy in hero sons, one wall surrounding
Her seven hills, even as Cybele, riding

Through Phrygian cities, wears her crown of towers,
Rejoicing in her offspring, and embracing
A hundred children of the gods, her children,   820
Celestials, all of them, at home in heaven.
Turn the eyes now this way; behold the Romans,
Your very own. These are Iulus' children,
The race to come. One promise you have heard
Over and over: here is its fulfillment,
The son of a god, Augustus Caesar, founder
Of a new age of gold, in lands where Saturn
Ruled long ago; he will extend his empire
Beyond the Indies, beyond the normal measure
Of years and constellations, where high Atlas   830
Turns on his shoulders the star-studded world.
Maeotia[41] and the Caspian seas are trembling
As heaven's oracles predict his coming,
And all the seven mouths of Nile are troubled.
Not even Hercules, in all his travels,
Covered so much of the world, from Erymanthus
To Lerna; nor did Bacchus, driving his tigers
From Nysa's summit. How can hesitation
Keep us from deeds to make our prowess greater?
What fear can block us from Ausonian land?   840
    "And who is that one yonder, wearing the olive,
Holding the sacrifice? I recognize him,
That white-haired king of Rome, who comes from Cures,
A poor land, to a mighty empire, giver
Of law to the young town. His name is Numa.
Near him is Tullus; he will rouse to arms
A race grown sluggish, little used to triumph.
Beyond him Ancus, even now too boastful,
Too fond of popular favor. And then the Tarquins,
And the avenger Brutus, proud of spirit,   850
Restorer of the balance. He shall be
First holder of the consular power; his children
Will stir up wars again, and he, for freedom
And her sweet sake, will call down judgment on them,
Unhappy, however future men may praise him,
In love of country and intense ambition.
    "There are the Decii,[42] and there the Drusi,
A little farther off, and stern Torquatus,
The man with the axe, and Camillus, the regainer
Of standards lost. And see those two, resplendent   860
In equal arms, harmonious friendly spirits
Now, in the shadow of night, but if they ever
Come to the world of light, alas, what warfare,
What battle-lines, what slaughter they will fashion,
Each for the other, one from Alpine ramparts
Descending, and the other ranged against him
With armies from the east, father and son
Through marriage, Pompey and Caesar. O my children,
Cast out the thoughts of war, and do not murder
The flower of our country. O my son,   870

---

39. You might compare this with Dante's ideas on the same
    thing. See, for example, *Purgatory*, Cantos XVI and XVIII.
40. One of the earliest of the Italian cities, near Rome.
    Supposedly founded by Ascanius.
41. These names merely signify that the empire will extend
    from one end to the other of the known world.
42. Names of families who produced famous men in Rome's
    history.

Whose line descends from heaven, let the sword
Fall from the hand, be leader in forbearing!
 "Yonder is one who, victor over Corinth,
Will ride in triumph home, famous for carnage
Inflicted on the Greeks; near him another,
Destroyer of old Argos and Mycenae
Where Agamemnon ruled; he will strike down
A king descended from Achilles; Pydna
Shall be revenge for Pallas' ruined temple,
For Trojan ancestors. Who would pass over,   880
Without a word, Cossus, or noble Cato,
The Gracchi, or those thunderbolts of warfare,
The Scipios, Libya's ruin, or Fabricius
Mighty with little, or Serranus, plowing
The humble furrow. My tale must hurry on:
I see the Fabii next, and their great Quintus
Who brought us back an empire by delaying.
Others, no doubt, will better mould the bronze[43]
To the semblance of soft breathing, draw, from marble,
The living countenance; and others plead   890
With greater eloquence, or learn to measure,
Better than we, the pathways of the heaven,
The risings of the stars: remember, Roman,
To rule the people under law, to establish
The way of peace, to battle down the haughty,
To spare the meek. Our fine arts, these, forever."
 Anchises paused a moment, and they marveled,
And he went on:—"See, how Marcellus triumphs,
Glorious over all, with the great trophies
Won when he slew the captain of the Gauls,   900
Leader victorious over leading foeman.
When Rome is in great trouble and confusion
He will establish order, Gaul and Carthage
Go down before his sword, and triple trophies
Be given Romulus in dedication."
 There was a young man going with Marcellus,
Brilliant in shining armor, bright in beauty,
But sorrowful, with downcast eyes. Aeneas
Broke in, to ask his father: "Who is this youth
Attendant on the hero? A son of his?   910
One of his children's children? How the crowd
Murmurs and hums around him! what distinction,
What presence, in his person! But dark night
Hovers around his head with mournful shadow.
Who is he, father?" And Anchises answered:—
"Great sorrow for our people! O my son,
Ask not to know it. This one fate will only
Show to the world; he will not be permitted
Any long sojourn. Rome would be too mighty,
Too great in the gods' sight, were this gift hers.   920
What lamentation will the field of Mars
Raise to the city! Tiber, gliding by
The new-built tomb, the funeral state, bear witness!
No youth from Trojan stock will ever raise
His ancestors so high in hope, no Roman
Be such a cause for pride. Alas for goodness,
Alas for old-time honor, and the arm
Invincible in war! Against him no one,

Whether on foot or foaming horse, would come
In battle and depart unscathed. Poor boy,   930
If you should break the cruel fates; if only—
You are to be Marcellus. Let me scatter
Lilies, or dark-red flowers, bringing honor
To my descendant's shade; let the gift be offered,
However vain the tribute."
 So through the whole wide realm they went together,
Anchises and his son; from the fields of air
Learning and teaching of the fame and glory,
The wars to come, the toils to face, or flee from,
Latinus' city and the Latin peoples,   940
The love of what would be.
                    There are two portals,
Twin gates of Sleep, one made of horn, where easy
Release is given true shades, the other gleaming
White ivory, whereby the false dreams issue
To the upper air. Aeneas and the Sibyl
Part from Anchises at the second portal.
He goes to the ships, again, rejoins his comrades,
Sails to Caieta's harbor, and the vessels
Rest on their mooring-lines.

STUDY QUESTIONS

1. What exactly was Aeneas seeking in the lower world and why?
2. Consider the crimes that condemn people to the lower world. What, for the Romans, are the worst crimes? What do "state" and "duty" mean? What, for example, does "Learn justice; reverence the gods" really mean in practical Roman terms?
3. Consider the statement of Anchises on the Roman "arts": "To pacify, to impose the rule of law, to spare the conquered, battle down the proud." Is this political science? Why do the Romans consider governance an art form?
4. Why did Virgil deliberately pattern his epic poem after the poetry of Homer? What did he hope to achieve? Did he achieve it?

LITERARY SELECTION 15

On the Nature of Things
Titus Lucretius Carus (ca. 96–55 BC)

Nothing is known of Lucretius (Titus Lucretius Carus) beyond his being credited with a poem extolling materialism and the philosophy of Epicurus, under whose disciples he probably studied. This is the most complete exposition of the materialistic basis of Epicureanism, as well as one of the world's celebrated poems.

---

43. These nine lines are probably the best expression of the Roman spirit.

In the following passage Lucretius discusses the rise of ambition, republican forms of government, religions, agriculture, hunting, mining, weaving, singing and dancing, and finally the full development of luxurious civilization. Notice how carefully he suggests a materialistic origin for all these things.

More and more every day men who excelled in intellect and were of vigorous understanding, would kindly show others how to exchange their former way of living for new methods. Kings began to build towns and lay out a citadel as a place of strength and of refuge for themselves, and divided cattle and lands and gave to each man in proportion to his personal beauty and strength and intellect; for beauty and vigorous strength were much esteemed. Afterwards wealth was discovered and gold found out, which soon robbed of their honors strong and beautiful alike, for men however valiant and beautiful of person generally follow in the train of the richer man. But were a man to order his life by the rules of true reason, a frugal subsistence joined to a contented mind is for him great riches; for never is there any lack of a little. But men desired to be famous and powerful, in order that their fortunes might rest on a firm foundation and they might be able by their wealth to lead a tranquil life; but in vain, since in their struggle to mount up to the highest dignities they rendered their path one full of danger; and even if they reach it, yet envy like a thunderbolt sometimes strikes and dashes men down from the highest point with ignominy into noisome Tartarus; since the highest summits and those elevated above the level of other things are mostly blasted by envy as by a thunderbolt, so that far better it is to obey in peace and quiet than to wish to rule with power supreme and be the master of kingdoms. Therefore let men wear themselves out to no purpose and sweat drops of blood, as they struggle on along the straight road of ambition, since they gather their knowledge from the mouths of others and follow after things from hearsay rather than the dictates of their own feelings; and this prevails not now nor will prevail by and by any more than it has prevailed before.

Kings therefore being slain, the old majesty of thrones and proud sceptres were overthrown and laid in the dust, and the glorious badge of the sovereign head bloodstained beneath the feet of the rabble mourned for its high prerogative; for that is greedily trampled on which before was too much dreaded. It would come then in the end to the lees of uttermost disorder, each man seeking for himself empire and sovereignty. Next a portion of them taught men to elect legal officers, and drew up codes, to induce men to obey the laws. For mankind, tired out with a life of brute force, lay exhausted from its feuds; and therefore the more readily it submitted of its own free will to laws and stringent codes. For as each one moved by anger took measures to avenge himself with more severity than is now permitted by equitable laws, for this reason men grew sick of a life of brute force. Thence fear of punishment mars the prizes of life; for violence and wrong enclose all who commit them in their meshes and do mostly recoil on him whom

they began; and it is not easy for him who by his deeds transgresses the terms of the public peace to pass a tranquil and a peaceful existence. For though he eludes God and man, yet he cannot but feel a misgiving that his secret can be kept forever; seeing that many by speaking in their dreams or in the wanderings of disease have often we are told betrayed themselves and have disclosed their hidden deeds of evil and their sins.

And now what cause has spread over great nations the worship of the divinities of the gods and filled towns with altars and led to the performance of stated sacred rites, rites not in fashion on solemn occasions and in solemn places, from which even now is implanted in mortals a shuddering awe which raises new temples of the gods over the whole earth and prompts men to crowd them on festive days, all this is not so difficult to explain in words. Even then in sooth the races of mortal men would see in waking mind glorious forms, would see them in sleep of yet more marvelous size of body. To these then they would attribute sense, because they seemed to move their limbs and to utter lofty words suitable to their glorious aspects and surpassing powers. And they would give them life everlasting, because their face would appear before them and their form abide; yes, and yet without all this because they would not believe that beings possessed of such powers could lightly be overcome by any force. And they would believe them to be preeminent in bliss, because none of them was ever troubled with the fear of death, and because at the same time in sleep they would see them perform many miracles, yet feel on their part no fatigue from the effort. Again they would see the system of heaven and the different seasons of the years come round in regular succession, and could not find out by what cause this was done; therefore they would seek a refuge in handing over all things to the gods and supposing all things to be guided by their nod. And they placed in heaven the abodes and realms of the gods, because night and moon are seen to roll through heaven; moon, day and night, and night's austere constellations and night-wandering of the sky and flying bodies of flame, clouds, sun, rains, snow, winds, lightnings, hail, and rapid rumblings and loud threatful thunderclaps.

O hapless race of men, when that they charged the gods with such acts and coupled with them bitter wrath! What groanings did they then beget for themselves, what wounds for us, what tears for our children's children! No act is it of piety to be often seen with veiled head to turn to a stone and approach every altar and fall prostrate on the ground and spread out the palms before the statues of the gods and sprinkle the altars with much blood of beasts and link vow on vow, but rather to be able to look on all things with a mind at peace. For when we turn our gaze on the heavenly quarters of the great upper world and ether fast above the glittering stars, and direct our thoughts to the courses of the sun and moon, then into our breasts burdened with other ills that fear as well begins to exalt its reawakened head, the fear that we may haply find the power of the gods to be unlimited, able to wheel the bright stars in their varied motion; for lack of power to solve the question troubles the mind with doubts, whether there was ever a birth-time of the world, and whether likewise there is to be any end; how far the walls of the world can endure this strain of restless motion; or whether gifted by the grace of gods with an everlasting existence they may glide on through a neverending tract of time and defy the strong powers of immeasurable ages. Again who is there whose mind does not shrink into itself with fear of the gods, whose limbs do not cower in terror, when the parched earth rocks with the appalling thunder-stroke and rattling runs through the great heaven? Do not people and nations quake, and proud monarchs shrink into themselves smitten with fear of the gods, lest for any foul transgression or overweening work the heavy time of reckoning has arrived at its fullness? When, too, the utmost fury of the headstrong wind passes over the sea and sweeps over its waters the commander of a fleet together with his mighty legions and elephants, does he not draw near with vows to seek the mercy of the gods and ask in prayer with fear and trembling a lull in the winds and propitious gales; but all in vain, since often caught up in the furious hurricane he is borne none the less to the shoals of death? So constantly does some hidden power trample on human grandeur and is seen to tread under its heel and make sport for itself of the renowned rods and cruel axes.[44]

To proceed, copper and gold and iron were discovered and at the same time weighty silver and the substance of lead, when fire with its heat had burnt up vast forests on the great hills, either by a discharge of heaven's lightning, or else because men waging with one another a forest-war had carried fire among the enemy in order to strike terror, or because drawn on by the goodness of the soil they would wish to clear rich fields, and bring the country into pasture, or else to destroy wild beasts and enrich themselves with the booty; for hunting with pitfall and with fire came into use before the practice of enclosing the lawn with nets and stirring it with dogs. Whatever the fact is, from whatever cause the heat of flame had swallowed up the forests with a frightful crackling from their very roots and had thoroughly baked the earth with fire, there would run from the boiling veins and collect into the hollows of the ground a stream of silver and gold, as well as of copper and lead. And when they saw these afterwards cool into lumps and glitter on the earth with a brilliant gleam, they would lift them up attracted by the bright and polished luster, and they would see them to be moulded in a shape the same as the outline of the cavities in which each lay. Then it would strike them that these might be melted by heat and cast in any form or shape soever, and might by hammering out be brought to tapering points of any degree of sharpness and fineness, so as to furnish them with tools and enable them to cut the forests and hew timber and plane smooth the planks, and also to drill and pierce and bore, and they would set about these works just as much with silver and gold at

first as with the overpowering strength of stout copper, but in vain, since their force would fail and give way and not be able like copper to stand the severe strain. At that time copper was in higher esteem and gold would be neglected on account of its uselessness, with its dull blunted edge; now copper lies neglected, gold has mounted up to the highest place of honor. Thus time as it goes round changes the seasons of things. That which was in esteem, falls at length into utter disrepute; and then another thing mounts up and issues out of its degraded state and every day is more and more coveted and blossoms forth high in honor when discovered and is in marvelous repute with men.

And now to find out by yourself in what way the nature of iron was discovered. Arms of old were hands, nails, and teeth, and stones and boughs broken off from the forest, and flame and fire, as soon as they had become known. Afterwards the force of iron and copper was discovered, and the use of copper was known before that of iron, as its nature is easier to work and it is found in greater quantity. With copper they would labor the soil of the earth, with copper stir up the billows of war and deal about the wide gaping wounds and seize cattle and lands; for everything defenseless and unarmed would readily yield to them with arms in hand. Then by slow steps the sword of iron gained ground and the make of the copper sickle became a by-word; and with iron they began to plow through the earth's soil, and the struggles of wavering war were rendered equal . . . .

A garment tied on the body was in use before a dress of woven stuff. Woven stuff comes after iron, because iron is needed for weaving a web; and in no other way can such finely polished things be made, as heddles and spindles, shuttles and ringing yarnbeams. And nature impelled men to work up the wool before womankind; for the male sex in general far excels the other in skill and is much more ingenious; until the rugged countrymen so upbraided them with it, that they were glad to give it over into the hands of the women and take their share in supporting hard toil, and in such hard work hardened body and hands.

But nature parent of things was herself the first model of sowing and first gave rise to grafting, since berries and acorns dripping from the trees would put forth in due season swarms of young shoots underneath; and hence also came the fashion of inserting grafts in their stocks and planting in the ground young saplings over the fields. Next they would try another and yet another kind of tillage for their loved piece of land and would see the earth better the wild fruits through genial fostering and kindly cultivation, and they would force the forests to recede every day higher and higher up the hillside and yield the ground below to tilth, in order to have on the uplands and plains, meadows, tanks, runnels, cornfields, and glad vineyards, and allow a gray-green strip of olives to run between and mark divisions, spreading itself over hillocks and valleys and plains; just as you now see richly dight with varied beauty all the ground which they lay out and plant with rows of sweet fruit-trees, and enclose all round with plantations of other goodly trees.

---

44. A bundle of rods enclosing an axe was the emblem of magisterial authority at Rome.

But imitating with the mouth the clear notes of birds was in use long before men were able to sing in tune smooth-running verses and give pleasure to the ear. And the whistlings of the zephyr through the hollows of reeds first taught peasants to blow into hollow stalks. 240 Then step by step they learned sweet plaintive ditties, which the pipe pours forth pressed by the fingers of the players, heard through pathless woods and forests and lawns, through the unfrequented haunts of shepherds and abodes of unearthly calm. These things would soothe and gratify their minds when sated with food; for then all things of this kind are welcome. Often therefore stretched in groups on the soft grass beside a stream of water under the boughs of a high tree at no great cost 250 they would pleasantly refresh their bodies, above all when the weather smiled and the seasons of the year painted the green grass with flowers. Then went round the jest, the tale, the peals of merry laughter; for the peasant muse was then in its glory; then frolick mirth would prompt to entwine head and shoulders with garlands plaited with flowers and leaves, and to advance in the dance out of step and move the limbs clumsily and with clumsy feet beat mother earth; which would occasion smiles and peals of merry laughter, because all these things then from their greater novelty and 260 strangeness were in high repute, and the wakeful found a solace for want of sleep in this, in drawing out a variety of notes and going through tunes and running over the reeds with curving lip; whence even at the present day watchmen observe these traditions and have lately learned to keep the proper tune; and yet for all this receive not a jot more of enjoyment than erst the rugged race of sons of earth received. For that which we have in our hands, if we have known before nothing pleasanter, pleases above all and is thought to be the best; and as a 270 rule the later discovery of something better spoils the taste for the former things and changes the feelings in regard to all that has gone before. Thus began distaste for the acorn, thus were abandoned those sleeping places strewn with grass and enriched with leaves. The dress too of wild beasts' skin fell into neglect; though I can fancy that in those days it was found to arouse such jealousy that he who first wore it met his death by an ambuscado, and after all it was torn in pieces among them and drenched in blood, was utterly destroyed and 280 could not be turned to any use. In those times therefore skins, now gold and purple plague men's lives with cares and wear them out with war. And in this methinks the greater blame rests with us; but us it harms not in the least to do without a robe of purple, spangled with gold and large figures, if only we have a dress of the people to protect us. Mankind therefore ever toils vainly and to no purpose wastes life in groundless cares, because sure enough they have not learnt what is the true end of getting and up to what point genuine pleasure goes on 290 increasing: this by slow degrees has carried life out into the deep sea and stirred up from their lowest depths the mighty billows of war.

Already they would pass their life fenced about with strong towers, and the land, portioned out and marked off by boundaries, be tilled; the sea would be filled with ships scudding under sail; towns have auxiliaries and allies as stipulated by treaty, when poets began to consign the deeds of men to verse; and letters had not been invented long before. For this reason our age 300 cannot look back to what has gone before, save where reason points out any traces.

Ships and tillage, walls, laws, roads, dress, and all such like things, all the prizes, all the elegancies too of life without exception, poems, pictures, and chiseling of fine-wrought statues, all these things practiced together with the acquired knowledge of the untiring mind taught men by slow degrees as they advanced on the way step by step. Thus time by degrees brings each several thing forth before men's eyes and reason raises it up 310 into the borders of light; for things must be brought to light one after the other and in due order in the different arts, until these have reached their highest point of development.

STUDY QUESTIONS

1. According to Lucretius, what seem to be the positive traits in human nature? The negative traits? What do these characteristics tell us about Lucretius' point of view?
2. Based on the evidence in the poem, what seems to be Lucretius' conception of the good life?

LITERARY SELECTION 16

Poetry

Gaius Valerius Catullus (ca. 84–54 BC)

Catullus, the leading Latin lyric poet, composed his love poetry for the enchanting Clodia (Lesbia in the poems), wife of Quintus Metellus. She became the most notoriously faithless beauty in Rome, while Catullus struggled with a virulent passion for her that slowly shriveled to despair before subsiding into bitter maledictions. Poems 5, 51, 58, 72, and 75 testify to the stages of his infatuation. The first three stanzas of poem 51 are a partial translation by Catullus of a poem by Sappho, the sixth-century Greek poet of Lesbos. Poem 1 is concerned with poets and poetry, while 42 reveals a frustrated poet suffering from writer's block.

1

Who do I give this neat little book to
all new and polished up and ready to go?
You, Cornelius, because you always thought
there was something to this stuff of mine,
and were the one man in Italy with guts enough
to lay out all history in a couple of pages,

a learned job, by god, and it took work.
So here's the book, for whatever it's worth
I want you to have it. And please, goddess,
see that it lasts for more than a lifetime.

5

Let's you and me live it up, my Lesbia,
and make some love, and let old cranks
go cheap talk their damn fool heads off.
Maybe suns can set and come back up again,
but once the brief light goes out on us
the night's one long sleep forever.
First give me a kiss, a thousand kisses,
then a hundred, and then a thousand more,
then another hundred, and another thousand,
and keep kissing and kissing me so many times
we get all mixed up and can't count anymore,
that way nobody can give us the evil eye
trying to figure how many kisses we've got.

42

Calling all syllables! Calling all syllables!
Let's go! I need all the help I can get!
Some filthy whore's playing games with me
and won't give me back my manuscripts with
your pals inside! Are you going to let her?
Who is she, you ask? Well go take a look,
she's over there shaking her ass all around
and flashing smiles like a Pomeranian bitch.
Ready? Okay, line up and let her have it!
"O foul adulteress, O lascivious witch,
give me back my notebooks, you dirty bitch!"
What? Up yours, you say? You slut, tramp,
you've sunk so low you look up to see down!
Still, we can't let her get away like this,
if all else fails, at least let's see whether
we can force a blush from the hard-faced beast.
Try again, fellas, good and loud this time!
"O FOUL ADULTERESS, O LASCIVIOUS WITCH,
GIVE ME BACK MY NOTEBOOKS, YOU DIRTY BITCH!"
No use. It won't work. Nothing moves her.
We've got to switch to different tactics,
almost anything will work better than this.
"O maiden so modest, O virgin so pure . . . ."

51

To me, that man seems to be one of the gods,
or to tell the truth, even more than a god,
sitting there face to face with you, forever
looking, listening

to you laughing sweetly, while poor me, I take
one look at you and I'm all torn up inside,
Lesbia, there's nothing left of me. I can't
make a sound, my tongue's

stuck solid, hot little fire flashes go
flickering through my body, my ears begin
ringing around in my head, my eyes black out,
shrouded in darkness . . .

This soft life is no good for you. Catullus,
you wallow in it, you don't know when to stop.
A soft life's already been the ruin of both
great kings and cities.

58

Caelius, our Lesbia, that Lesbia,
the Lesbia Catullus once loved
more than himself and all he owns,
now works streets and back alleys
groping big-hearted sons of Remus.

72

Time was you said only Catullus could touch you,
that God in heaven couldn't have you before me.
I loved you then, not just as a guy does a girl,
but the way a father loves his sons and grandsons.
Now I know you, Lesbia, and if my passion grows,
you're also much cheaper to me and insignificant.
How's that? Because, hurt a man in love and he
lusts for you more, but the less he really cares.

75

My mind's sunk so low, Lesbia, because of you,
wrecked itself on your account so bad already,
I couldn't like you if you were the best of women,
or stop loving you, no matter what you do.

STUDY QUESTIONS

1. Faced with writing an essay, have you ever had trouble beginning? As you undoubtedly know, this is called "writer's block." How well does Poem 42 express your own frustration in trying to write? Does this poem make you more aware of Catullus as another human being like yourself? What does this say about the nature of poetry?
2. In poems 5, 51, 58, 72, and 75 Catullus seems to have mixed emotions about his Lesbia. What does he love about her? Hate about her? What is romantic love? Can it last?

LITERARY SELECTION   17

Odes

Horace (Quintus Horatius Flaccus; 65–8 BC)

Horace specialized in writing **odes**, such as the two below in modern translations by M. A. Crane. The first is a wry commentary about Pyrrha, his former mistress, while the second is an expression of Horace's Epicurean philosophy.

1

On the bulletin board there's a picture of me
Luckily saved from disaster at sea
Donating my gear to the God of the Ocean.
Tonight, some boy smelling of after-shave lotion
Is making a play for you, Pyrrha, my fair,
Trying that innocent look with your hair.
His turn will come soon to complain of foul weather
If he thinks that after you're going together
You'll stay bland and easy as on this first date.
Until you up anchor, all dinghies look great!

2

The peace that the sailor seeks in the storm
And the rest that's the warrior's aim
Can't be purchased with wealth in any form
Nor, Grosphus, with power or fame.
The pauper who wants only what he can afford
Sleeps soundly. But he who would fly
To new fortunes, although he hastens aboard
Speedy vessels, sees his troubles stand by.
Fools nourish dreams of perfect joy;
I'll take less, having witnessed a hero
Die young and watched rotting old age destroy
Tithonus, reduced to a jibbering zero.
It may be *I* have just those things that *you* need
Amidst your horses, fine clothing, and cattle—
Subsistence, and joy from the poems I read,
And no jealous mob doing me battle.

STUDY QUESTIONS

1. A "conceit" is an extended poetic comparison (**metaphor**) between two unlike things, applying the qualities of one to the other. In Ode 1 what conceit does Horace develop, and to whom or what is it applied?
2. According to the Epicurean philosophy expressed in Ode 2, what is necessary for happiness? Where do material possessions rate on the happiness scale? Why?

"**Satire**" is a general term for any kind of writing that attacks, directly or indirectly, something that is feared or hated. For example, in his *Lysistrata*, the Athenian Aristophanes satirized the sophists and, most especially, the war party. As a definite form of poetry in a clear-cut style, satire first appeared in Rome in the first century BC, most importantly in the works of Horace. Rome was, in fact, preeminent in formal verses that attacked or denounced a variety of people, practices, and institutions. The Romans had a special gift for satirizing in verse the real world with its made-to-order targets.

Horace's satires are effective because they are so low-key. Consistently portraying himself, by name, as urbane and amused, the poet wryly harpoons his targets. The scene of the following satire is the December holiday, the Saturnalia, in which feasting and revelry replace everyday work, duties, and social restraints. Because the world is temporarily turned upside down, slaves are permitted free speech and other indulgences normally forbidden during the rest of the year. (In fact, Horace's father was once a slave.) Horace uses this setting to consider the true nature of freedom as defined by the Stoics. Is the rich man enslaved by his possessions while the Stoic philosopher is free because his mind is unencumbered by material things? Is the slave freer than his master?

LITERARY SELECTION 18

My Slave Is Free to Speak Up for Himself
("Lamdudum ausculto et cupiens tibi dicere servus")

Horace

Davus: I've been listening for quite some time now, wanting to have
A word with you. Being a slave, though, I haven't the nerve.
Horace: That you, Davus?
Davus: Yes, it's Davus, slave as I am.
Loyal to my man, a pretty good fellow: *pretty* good,
I say. I don't want you thinking I'm too good to live.
Horace: Well, come on, then. Make use of the freedom traditionally yours
At the December holiday season. Speak up, sound off!
Davus: Some people *like* misbehaving: they're persistent and consistent.
But the majority waver, trying at times to be good,
At other times yielding to evil. The notorious Priscus   10
Used to wear three rings at a time, and then again, none.
He lived unevenly, changing his robes every hour.
He issued forth from a mansion, only to dive
Into the sort of low joint your better class freedman
Wouldn't want to be caught dead in. A libertine at Rome,
At Athens a sage, he was born, and he lived, out of season.
  When Volanerius, the playboy, was racked by the gout
In the joints of his peccant fingers (so richly deserved),
He hired a man, by the day, to pick up the dice
For him and put them in the box. By being consistent   20
In his gambling vice, he lived a happier life
Than the chap who tightens the reins and then lets them flap.
Horace: Will it take you all day to get to the bottom of this junk,
You skunk?

Davus: But I'm saying, *you're* at the bottom.
Horace: How so, you stinker?
Davus: You praise the good old days, ancient fortunes,
    and manners,
And yet, if some god were all for taking you back,
You'd hang back, either because you don't really think
That what you are praising to the skies is all that superior
Or because you defend what is right with weak
    defenses
And, vainly wanting to pull your foot from the mud,   30
Stick in it all the same. At Rome, you yearn
For the country, but, once in the sticks, you praise to
    high heaven
The far-off city, you nitwit. If it happens that no one
Asks you to dinner, you eulogize your comfortable
    meal
Of vegetables, acting as if you'd only go out
If you were dragged out in chains. You hug yourself,
Saying how glad you are not to be forced to go out
On a spree. But Maecenas *suggests*, at the very last
    minute,
That you be his guest:"Bring some oil for my lamp,
    somebody!
Get a move on! Is everyone deaf around here?" In a
    dither   40
And a lather, you charge out. Meanwhile, your
    scrounging guests,
Mulvius & Co., make their departure from your place
With a few descriptive remarks that won't bear
    repeating
For example, Mulvius admits, "Of course, I'm fickle,
Led around by my stomach, and prone to follow my
    nose
To the source of a juicy aroma, weak-minded, lazy,
And, you may want to add, a gluttonous souse.
But you, every bit as bad and perhaps a bit worse,
Have the gall to wade into me, as if you were better,
And cloak your infamy in euphemism?"
                  What if you're found out   50
To be a bigger fool than me, the hundred-dollar slave?
Stop trying to browbeat me! Hold back your hand,
And your temper, while I tell you what Crispinus'
    porter
Taught me.
          Another man's wife makes you her slave.
A loose woman makes Davus hers. Of us two sinners,
Who deserves the cross more? When my passionate
    nature
Drives me straight into her arms, she's lovely by
    lamplight,
Beautifully bare, all mine to plunge into at will,
Or, turning about, she mounts and drives me to death.
And after it's over, she sends me away neither
    shamefaced   60
Nor worried that someone richer or better to look at
Will water the very same plant. But when you go out
    for it,
You really come in for it, don't you? Turning yourself
    into
The same dirty Dama you pretend to be when you take
    off

Your equestrian ring and your Roman robes, and
    change
Your respectable self, hiding your perfumed head
Under your cape?
                Scared to death, you're let in the house,
And your fear takes turns with your hope in rattling
    your bones.
What's the difference between being carted off to be
    scourged
And slain, in the toils of the law (as a gladiator is),   70
And being locked up in a miserable trunk, where the
    maid,
Well aware of her mistress' misconduct, has stored you
    away,
With your knees scrunched up against your head? Hasn't
    the husband
Full power over them both, and even more over the
    seducer?
For the wife hasn't changed her attire or her location,
And is not the uppermost sinner. You walk open-eyed
Right under the fork, handing over to a furious master
Your money, your life, your person, your good
    reputation.
    Let's assume that you got away: you learned your
    lesson,
I trust, and will be afraid from now on and be careful?   80
Oh, no! You start planning how to get in trouble again,
To perish again, enslave yourself over and over.
But what wild beast is so dumb as to come back again
To the chains he has broken loose from?
                  "But I'm no adulterer,"
You say. And I'm not a thief when I wisely pass up
Your good silver plate. But our wandering nature will
    leap
When the reins are removed, when the danger is taken
    away.
    Are you my master, you, slave to so many
Other people, so powerful a host of other things, whom
    no
Manumission could ever set free from craven anxiety,   90
Though the ritual were conducted again and again?
    And besides,
Here's something to think about: whether a slave who's
    the slave
Of a slave is a plain fellow slave or a "subslave," as you
    masters
Call him, what am I your? You, who command me,
Cravenly serve someone else and are led here and there
Like a puppet, the strings held by others.
                  Who, then, is free?
The wise man alone, who has full command of
    himself,
Whom poverty, death, or chains cannot terrify,
Who is strong enough to defy his passions and scorn
Prestige, who is wholly contained in himself, well
    rounded,   100
Smooth as a sphere on which nothing external can
    fasten,
On which fortune can do no harm except to herself.
    Now which of those traits can you recognize as one
    of yours?

Your woman asks you for five thousand dollars,
    needles you,
Shuts the door in your face and pours out cold water,
Then calls you back. Pull your neck from that yoke!
Say, "I'm free, I'm free!" Come on, say it. You can't! A
    master
Dominates your mind, and it's no mild master who
    lashes
You on in spite of yourself, who goads you and guides
    you.
    Or when you stand popeyed in front of a painting by
      Pausias,   110
You madman, are you less at fault than I am who
    marvel
At the posters of athletes straining their muscles in
    combat,
Striking out, thrusting, and parrying, in red chalk and
    charcoal,
As if they were really alive, and handling these
    weapons?
But Davus is a no-good, a dawdler, and you? Oh,
    MONSIEUR
Is an EXPERT, a fine CONNOISSEUR of antiques, I ASSURE
    you.
    I'm just a fool to be tempted by piping-hot pancakes.
Does your strength of character and mind make much
    resistance
To sumptuous meals? Why is it worse for me
To supply the demands of my stomach? My back will
    pay for it,   120
To be sure. But do you get off any lighter, hankering
After delicate, costly food? Your endless indulgence
Turns sour in your stomach, your baffled feet won't
    support
Your pampered body. Is the slave at fault, who
    exchanges
A stolen scraper for a bunch of grapes, in the dark?
Is there nothing slavish in a man who sells his estate
To satisfy his need for rich food?
                        Now, add on these items:
(1) You can't stand your own company as long as an
    hour;
(2) You can't dispose of your leisure in a decent
    fashion;
(3) You're a fugitive from your own ego, a vagabond
    soul,   130
Trying to outflank your cares by attacking the bottle
Or making sorties into sleep. And none of it works:
The Dark Companion rides close along by your side,
Keeps up with and keeps on pursuing the runaway
    slave.
Horace: "Where's a stone?"
Davus: "What use do you have for it?"
Horace: "Hand me my arrows!"
Davus: The man is either raving or satisfying his
    craving
For creative writing.
Horace: If you don't clear out, instanter,
I'll pack you off to the farm to be my ninth planter.

---

1. Though a slave could be this caustic during Saturnalia, is Davus actually speaking these words or is this a literary device?
2. As Horace's self-portrait, why is the criticism so sharp? What does the poet hope to gain by being so hard on himself? If he is this conscious of his vices, what might be his chances of exercising some virtue? What did the Greeks say about self-knowledge?
3. In reality, which is more free, the Stoic philosopher or Davus?
4. Horace views himself as a connoisseur of art, while Davus likes realistic posters of gladiators. Which man has the greater freedom?
5. Just how difficult is it to write a self-satire? You might try writing a brief dialogue with an outspoken friend to test your ability to examine your own faults and failings.

LITERARY SELECTION 19

The Art of Love

Ovid (Publius Ovidius Naso; 43 BC–AD 17)

Virgil represents the nobility and grandeur of Roman literature while Catullus and Horace are voices of reality who viewed the world with sharply critical eyes. But no one was more forthright than Ovid, the most popular poet of antiquity. The following excerpt is from his *Art of Love*, a sophisticated guide to seduction that also includes deft descriptions of everyday life in Rome. As you read Ovid's "manual" you might ask yourself if times or techniques have really changed.

This is a book for the man who needs instruction in
    loving.
    Let him read it and love, taught by the lines he has read.
Art is a thing one must learn, for the sailing, or rowing, of
    vessels,
    Also for driving a car: love must be guided by art.
Automedon excelled with the reins in the car of Achilles,
    Tiphys in Jason's craft, crafty with rudder and sail;
Thanks be to Venus, I too deserve the title of master,
    Master of Arts,
I might say, versed in the precepts of love.
Love, to be sure, is wild and often inclined to resent me;
Still, he is only a boy, tender and easily swayed.   10
When Achilles was young, Chiron could tame his wild
    spirit,
Even could teach his hands how to move over a lyre.
He, who frightened his foes, and frightened his friends
    just as often,

Dreaded one aged man, so all the ages believe.
He would reach out his hands, submissive and meek, for a
        lashing:
Those were the violent hands Hector was later to know.
Chiron instructed Achilles, and I am Cupid's preceptor,
Each of them savage and rough, each one a goddess's
        son.
Yet, in good time, as bulls accept the yoke and the
        ploughshare,
As the wild horses submit, taking the bridle and bit,   20
So will Love yield to me, though he wounds my heart
        with his arrows,
Whirls his torch in the air, showering sparks from the
        brand.
So much the worse for him: the more he pierces and
        burns me,
I shall avenge all the more all of the wounds he has
        made.
I am no liar to claim that my art has come from Apollo,
Nor am I taught my song by the voices of birds in the air,
Neither has Clio appeared at my side, with all of her
        sisters,
While I was tending my flocks out in some countryside
        vale.
No: I have learned what I know from experience, take
        my word for it.
It is the truth you will hear. Venus, give aid to my song!   30
Keep far away, stern looks and all of modesty's
        emblems,
Headdresses worn by the pure, skirts hiding feet in
        their folds.
What is the theme of my song? A little pleasant
        indulgence.
What is the theme of my song? Nothing that's very far
        wrong.
First, my raw recruit, my inexperienced soldier,
Take some trouble to find the girl whom you really can
        love.
Next, when you see what you like your problem will be
        how to win her.
Finally, strive to make sure mutual love will endure.
That's as far as I go, the territory I cover,
Those are the limits I set: take them or leave them
        alone.   40
While you are footloose and free to play the field at your
        pleasure,
Watch for the one you can tell, "I want no other but
        you!"
She is not going to come to you floating down from the
        heavens:
For the right kind of a girl you must keep using your
        eyes.
Hunters know where to spread their nets for the stag in
        his covert,
Hunters know where the boar gnashes his teeth in the
        glade.
Fowlers know brier and bush, and fishermen study the
        waters
Baiting the hook for the cast just where the fish may be
        found.
So you too, in your hunt for material worthy of loving.

First will have to find out where the game usually goes.   50
I will not tell you to sail searching far over the oceans,
I will not tell you to plod any long wearisome road.
Perseus went far to find his dusky Indian maiden:
That was a Grecian girl Paris took over the sea.
Rome has all you will need, so many beautiful lovelies
You will be bound to say, "Here is the grace of the
        world!"
Gargara's richness of field, Methymna's abundance of
        vineyard.
All the fish of the sea, all the birds in the leaves.
All the stars in the sky, are less than the girls Rome can
        offer;
Venus is mother and queen here in the town of her son.   60
If you are fond of them young, you will find them here
        by the thousands,
Maids in their teens, from whom you will have
        trouble to choose.
Maybe a bit more mature, a little bit wiser? Believe me.
These will outnumber the first as they come trooping
        along.
Take your time, walk slow, when the sun approaches the
        lion.
There are porticoes, marbled under the shade,
Pompey's Octavia's, or the one in Livia's honor.
Or the Danaids' own, tall on the Palatine hill.
Don't pass by the shrine of Adonis, sorrow to Venus,
Where, on the Sabbath day, Syrians worship, and Jews.   70
Try the Memphian fane of the Heifer, shrouded in linen;
Isis makes many a girl willing as Io for Jove.
Even the courts of the law, the bustle and noise of the
        forum,
(This may be hard to believe) listen to whispers of love.
Hard by the marble shrine of Venus, the Appian fountain,
Where the water springs high in its rush to the air.
There, and more than once, your counsellor meets with
        his betters,
All his forensic arts proving of little avail:
Others he might defend; himself he cannot; words fail
        him,
Making objections in vain; Cupid says, *Overruled!*   80
Venus, whose temple is near, laughs at the mortified
        creature,
Lawyer a moment ago, in need of a counsellor now.
Also, the theatre's curve is a very good place for your
        hunting,
More opportunity here, maybe, than anywhere else.
Here you may find one to love, or possibly only have fun
        with,
Someone to take for a night, someone to have and to
        hold.
Just as a column of ants keeps going and coming
        forever,
Bearing their burdens of grain, just as the flight of the
        bees
Over the meadows and over the fields of the thyme and
        the clover,
So do the women come, thronging the festival games.   90
Elegant, smart, and so many my sense of judgment is
        troubled.
Hither they come, to see; hither they come, to be seen.

Take some trouble, at first, to make her handmaiden's
    acquaintance: 250
She, more than any one else, really can lighten your way.
She must be one you can trust, if she knows of the
    tricks you are playing,
Confidante. Wise and discreet, high in her mistress'
    regard.
Spoil her by promising much, and spoil her by pleading a
    little,
What you seek you will find, if she is willing you should.
She will choose the right time—a maid is as good as a
    doctor—
When she is in the right mood, all the more ripe to be
    had.
When she is in the right mood, you will know it because
    she is happy,
Like the flowers in the field, seeming to burst into bloom.
When the hearts are glad, and sorrow does not confine
    them,   260
Then they are open wide, and Venus steals coaxingly in.
Troy, in her days of gloom, was well defended by armor;
When she rejoiced, the horse entered with Greeks in
    its womb.
It is worth making a try when she's grieving because of a
    rival,
Vengeance can quickly be hers if you're conveniently
    there.
While her maid is at work, combing her hair in the
    morning,
Let her keep urging her on, let her add oars to the sail,
Let her say with a sigh, or the softest murmuring
    whisper,
"I don't suppose, after all, there is a thing you can do."
Then let her talk about you, and add some words of
    persuasion,   270
Let her swear that she knows you must be dying of
    love.
Hurry! before the sails are furled and the breezes
    grown milder;
Anger, like brittle ice, dies with a little delay.
"Do you not think it would do any good to seduce the
    maid?" What a question!
Any such notions involve, always, too much of a risk.
One gets up from the bed too anxious, another too lazy,
One aids her mistress's cause, one wants you all for her
    own.
Maybe it works, maybe not: it might be amusing to try it,
Still, my advice would be, let it completely alone.
I would not show you the way over steep and
    precipitous passes,   280
No young man in my school ever will ride for a fall,
Yet, if she seems to please, while giving and taking your
    letters,
By her figure and face, not by her service alone,
Go for the lady first, and let the servant come second;
When you are making love, do not begin with the maid.
One final warning word: if you have any faith in my
    teaching,
If my words are not swept over the sea by the gale,
Either succeed, or don't try—she never will be an
    informer,

If she is guilty herself: how could she tattle on you?
Birds, with the lime on their wings, cannot take flight to
    the heavens,   290
Boars cannot plunge to their dens, caught in the mesh of
    the net.
Don't let your fish get away after the bait has been
    taken:
Press the attack, keep on; don't go away till you've won.
Then she can never betray you, because you were guilty
    together;
All of her mistress's acts, all of her words you will know.
Do not give her away: if she knows you are keeping her
    secrets,
She will be yours any time, knowing and willingly
    known.

STUDY QUESTIONS

1. What characteristics of this excerpt make it clearly Roman rather than Greek?
2. With appropriate changes in names, clothing, places, and activities, is Ovid's description of the dating game a fairly accurate representation of today's practices? What, if anything, has changed?
3. Ovid recommends chariot races for his little games. What might today's equivalent be?

LITERARY SELECTION 20

Epigrams

Martial (Marcus Valerius Martialis; ca. 40–104)

Martial wrote hundreds of epigrams, which are brief poems, often satiric, ending in a surprise twist or climax. His style can be described as terse, sardonic, sparse, acerbic, sarcastic, witty, and, withal, strikingly and delightfully modern.

I, i

Here he is—the one you read,
the one you ask for—Martial,
recognized the world over
for his witty books of epigrams.
Learned reader, you've given him
(while he's still alive to enjoy it)
the glory poets rarely get
after they've turned to ashes.

I, xxxv

You take me to task for writing
poems that aren't as prissy

and prim as they might be, Cornelius.
Not the kind a schoolmaster
would read aloud in the classroom.
But my little books wouldn't satisfy
(anymore than husbands can
their wives) without a little sex.
Would you want me to write a wedding-song
without using the words that wedding-songs   10
always use? Would you cover up
Flora's nymphs with a lot of clothing
or let prostitutes hide their shamefulness
under ladies' robes? There's a rule
that merry songs can't be merry
unless they're a bit indecent.

So forget your prudishness, please,
and spare my jokes and my naughtiness,
and don't try to castrate my poems.
Nothing's worse than Priapus posing   20
as a eunuch of Cybele.

II, xxxvi

I don't say you should curl your hair,
but you could comb it.
I don't say your body should be oiled,
but you could take a bath.
You needn't have a eunuch's beard
or a jailbird's. I don't insist
upon too much manliness,
Pannychus, or too little.
As it is, your legs are hairy
and your chest is shaggy with bristles,
but your mind, Pannychus, is bald.

III, xxxviii

Tell me, what brings you to Rome
so self-confidently, Sextus?
What are you after, and what
do you expect to find there?
"First of all, I'll plead cases
more eloquently than Cicero
himself. There won't be anyone
in the three forums to touch me."
Atestinus and Civis
(you know them both) pled cases,   10
but neither one of them took in
enough to pay the rent.
"Well, if nothing comes of that,
I'll write poems. When you hear them,
you'll say they're Virgil's work."
You're crazy. Wherever you look
you'll see Ovids and Virgils—all of them
shivering in their thin cloaks.
"Then I'll cultivate rich men."
That sort of thing has supported   20
maybe three or four. The rest
of the crowd are pale with hunger.
"What will I do? Advise me.
I'm determined to live in Rome."
Well, Sextus, if you're honest,
you'll be lucky to stay alive.

V, xiii

I'll admit I'm poor, Callistratus,
and always have been. And yet
two Emperors gave me a knighthood
and I'm not altogether unknown,
and my reputation isn't bad.
I've got a great many readers
everywhere in the world who will say
"That's Martial," and recognition
such as few receive after they're dead
has come to me while I'm alive.   10
On the other hand, your house-roof
is supported by a hundred columns,
and your money-boxes contain
a freedman's wealth, and wide fields
near Syene on the River Nile
call you master, and Parma in Gaul
shears its countless flocks for you.
That's what we are, you and I.
But you can never be what I am,
while anyone at all can be like you.   20

VI, xiv

You keep insisting, Labierus,
that you know how to write fine poems.
Then why is it you're unwilling
to try? Knowing how to write
fine poems and never doing it!
What will power, Labierus!

XI, lxvi

You're a spy and a blackmailer,
a forger, a pimp, a pervert,
and a trainer of gladiators,
Vacerra. I can't understand
why you aren't rich.

STUDY QUESTIONS

1. Martial frequently ridicules the person named in the epigram. Who (or what) are his favorite targets?
2. **a.** Try to identify the timeless qualities in Martial's art. For example, substitute the name of some well-known public figures of today in several epigrams; make sure the shoe fits!
   b. Try rewriting several epigrams, altering as necessary, e.g., XI, lxvi:
   You're a fink and a toady,
   a cheat, a liar, a thief,
   and a politician,
   (add appropriate name). I can't understand
   why you aren't rich.

LITERARY SELECTION 21

Discourses of Epictetus

Arrian (b. AD 108)

This lecture of Epictetus (ca. 60–138), as recorded by his student Arrian, together with the meditations of Marcus Aurelius, which follows, presents the Stoic point of view. This philosophy assumes that the great *logos* ("intelligence") pervades the entire world and directs all that happens. Therefore, as will be seen in the selections, it is essentially a stern philosophy of acceptance, duty, and brotherhood of all men.

Book I, Chapter 1: On Things in Our Power and Things Not in Our Power

Of our faculties in general you will find that none can take cognizance of itself; none therefore has the power to approve or disapprove its own action. Our grammatical faculty for instance: how far can that take cognizance? Only so far as to distinguish expression. Our musical faculty? Only so far as to distinguish tune. Does any one of these then take cognizance of itself? By no means. If you are writing to your friend, when you want to know what words to write grammar will tell you; but whether you should write to your friend or should not write grammar will not tell you. And in the same way 10 music will tell you about tunes, but whether at this precise moment you should sing and play the lyre or should not sing nor play the lyre it will not tell you. What will tell you then? That faculty which takes cognizance of itself and of all things else. What is this? The reasoning faculty: for this alone of the faculties we have received is created to comprehend even its own nature; that is to say, what it is and what it can do, and with what precious qualities it has come to us, and to comprehend 20 all other faculties as well. For what else is it that tells us that gold is a goodly thing? For the gold does not tell us. Clearly it is the faculty which can deal with our impressions. What else is it which distinguishes the faculties of music, grammar, and the rest, testing their uses and pointing out the due seasons for their use? It is reason and nothing else.

The gods then, as was but right, put in our hands the one blessing that is best of all and master of all, that and nothing else, the power to deal rightly with our 30 impressions, but everything else they did not put in our hands. Was it that they would not? For my part I think that if they could have entrusted us with those other powers as well they would have done so, but they were quite unable. Prisoners on the earth and in an earthly body and among earthly companions, how was it possible that we should not be hindered from the attainment of these powers by these external fetters?

But what says Zeus? "Epictetus, if it were possible I would have made your body and your possessions 40 (those trifles that you prize) free and untrammelled. But

as things are—never forget this—this body is not yours, it is but a clever mixture of clay. But since I could not make it free, I gave you a portion in our divinity, this faculty of impulse to act and not to act, of will to get and will to avoid, in a word the faculty which can turn impressions to right use. If you pay heed to this, and put your affairs in its keeping, you will never suffer let nor hindrance, you will not groan, you will blame no man, you will flatter none. What then? Does all this seem but 50 little to you?"

Heaven forbid!

"Are you content then?"

So surely as I hope for the gods' favour.

But, as things are, though we have it in our power to pay heed to one thing and to devote ourselves to one, yet instead of this we prefer to pay heed to many things and to be bound fast to many—our body, our property, brother and friend, child and slave. Inasmuch then as we are bound fast to many things, we are burdened by 60 them and dragged down. That is why, if the weather is bad for sailing, we sit distracted and keep looking continually and ask, "What wind is blowing?" "The north wind." What have we to do with that? "When will the west wind blow?" When it so chooses, good sir, or when Aeolus chooses. For God made Aeolus the master of the winds, not you. What follows? We must make the best of those things that are in our power, and take the rest as nature gives it. What do you mean by "nature"? I mean, God's will. 70

"What? Am I to be beheaded now, and I alone?"

Why? Would you have had all beheaded, to give you consolation? Will you not stretch out your neck as Lateranus did in Rome when Nero ordered his beheading? For he stretched out his neck and took the blow, and when the blow dealt him was too weak he shrank up a little and then stretched it out again. Nay more, on a previous occasion, when Nero's freedman Epaphroditus came to him and asked him the cause of his offense, he answered, "If I want to say anything, I 80 will say it to your master."

What then must a man have ready to help him in such emergencies? Surely this: he must ask himself, "What is mine, and what is not mine? What may I do, what may I not do?"

I must die. But must I die groaning? I must be imprisoned. But must I whine as well? I must suffer exile. Can any one then hinder me from going with a smile, and a good courage, and at peace?

"Tell the secret!" 90

I refuse to tell, for this is in my power.

"But I will chain you."

What say you, fellow? Chain me? My leg you will chain—yes, but my will—no, not even Zeus can conquer that.

"I will imprison you."

My bit of a body, you mean.

"I will behead you."

Why? When did I ever tell you that I was the only man in the world that could not be beheaded? 100

These are the thoughts that those who pursue philosophy should ponder, these are the lessons they should write down day by day, in these they should exercise themselves.

Thrasea used to say "I had rather be killed today than exiled tomorrow." What then did Rufus say to him? "If you choose it as the harder, what is the meaning of your foolish choice? If as the easier, who has given you the easier? Will you not study to be content with what is given you?" 110

It was in this spirit that Agrippinus used to say—do you know what? "I will not stand in my own way!" News was brought him, "Your trial is on in the Senate!" "Good luck to it, but the fifth hour is come"—this was the hour when he used to take his exercise and have a cold bath—"let us go and take exercise." When he had taken his exercise they came and told him, "You are condemned." "Exile or death?" he asked. "Exile." "And my property?" "It is not confiscated." "Well then, let us go to Aricia and dine." 120

Here you see the result of training as training should be, of the will to get and will to avoid, so disciplined that nothing can hinder or frustrate them. I must die, must I? If at once, then I am dying: if soon, I dine now, as it is time for dinner, and afterwards when the time comes I will die. And die how? As befits one who gives back what is not his own.

STUDY QUESTIONS

1. What exactly are the "things not in our power"? What is the one thing that is under our control?
2. What is the proper Stoic attitude toward those things we cannot control?

LITERARY SELECTION 22

Meditations

Book II

Marcus Aurelius (121–180)

Begin the morning by saying to thyself, I shall meet with the busybody, the ungrateful, arrogant, deceitful, envious, unsocial. All these things happen to them by reason of their ignorance of what is good and evil. But I who have seen the nature of the good that it is beautiful, and of the bad that it is ugly, and the nature of him who does wrong, that it is akin to me, not only of the same blood or seed, but that it participates in the same intelligence and the same portion of the divinity, I can neither be injured by any of them, for no one can fix on me what is ugly, nor can I be angry with my kinsman, nor hate him. For we are made for cooperation, like feet, 10

like hands, like eyelids, like the rows of the upper and lower teeth. To act against one another then is contrary to nature; and it is acting against one another to be vexed and to turn away.

2. Whatever this is that I am, it is a little flesh and breath, and the ruling part. Throw away thy books; no longer distract thyself: it is not allowed; but as if thou wast now dying, despise the flesh; it is blood and bones 20 and a network, a contexture of nerves, veins, and arteries. See the breath also, what kind of a thing it is, air, and not always the same, but every moment sent out and again sucked in. The third then is the ruling part: consider thus: Thou art an old man; no longer let this be a slave, no longer be pulled by the strings like a puppet to unsocial movements, no longer be either dissatisfied with thy present lot, or shrink from the future.

5. Every moment think steadily as a Roman and a man to do what thou hast in hand with perfect and 30 simple dignity, and feeling of affection, and freedom, and justice; and to give thyself relief from all other thoughts. And thou wilt give thyself relief, if thou doest every act of thy life as it were the last, laying aside all carelessness and passionate aversion from the commands of reason, and all hypocrisy, and self-love, and discontent with the portion which has been given to thee. Thou seest how few the things are, that which if a man lays hold of, he is able to live a life which flows in quiet, and is like the existence of the gods; for the gods 40 on their part will require nothing more from him who observes these things.

9. This thou must always bear in mind, what is the nature of the whole, and what is my nature, and how this is related to that, and what kind of a part it is of what kind of a whole; and that there is no one who hinders thee from always doing and saying the things which are according to the nature of which thou art a part.

11. Since it is possible that thou mayest depart from 50 life this very moment, regulate every act and thought accordingly. But to go away from among men, if there are gods, is not a thing to be afraid of, for the gods will not involve thee in evil; but if indeed they do not exist, or if they have no concern about human affairs, what is it to me to live in a universe devoid of gods or devoid of Providence? But in truth they do exist, and they do care for human things, and they have put all the means in man's power to enable him not to fall into real evils. And as to the rest, if there was anything evil, they would 60 have provided for this also, that it should be altogether in a man's power not to fall into it. Now that which does not make a man worse, how can it make a man's life worse? But neither through ignorance, nor having the knowledge, but not the power to guard against or correct these things, is it possible that the nature of the universe has overlooked them; nor is it possible that it has made so great a mistake, either through want of power or want of skill, that good and evil should happen indiscriminately to the good and the bad. But death 70 certainly, and life, honor and dishonor, pain and pleasure, all these things equally happen to good men and bad, being things which make us neither better nor worse. Therefore they are neither good nor evil.

16. The soul of man does violence to itself, first of all, when it becomes an abscess and, as it were, a tumor on the universe, so far as it can. For to be vexed at anything which happens is a separation of ourselves from nature, in some part of which the natures of all other things are contained. In the next place, the soul   80 does violence to itself when it turns away from any man, or even moves towards him with the intention of injuring, such as are the souls of those who are angry. In the third place, the soul does violence to itself when it is overpowered by pleasure or by pain. Fourthly, when it plays a part, and does or says anything insincerely and untruly. Fifthly, when it allows any act of its own and any movement to be without an aim, and does anything thoughtlessly and without considering what it is, it being right that even the smallest things be done with   90 reference to an end; and the end of rational animals is to follow the reason and the law of the most ancient city and polity.

17. Of human life the time is a point, and the substance is in a flux, and the perception dull, and the composition of the whole body subject to putrefaction, and the soul a whirl, and fortune hard to divine, and fame a thing devoid of judgement. And, to say all in a word, everything which belongs to the body is a stream, and what belongs to the soul is a dream and vapor, and   100 life is a warfare and a stranger's sojourn, and after-fame is oblivion. What then is that which is able to conduct a man? One thing and only one, philosophy. But this consists in keeping the daemon within a man free from violence and unharmed, superior to pains and pleasures, doing nothing without a purpose, nor yet falsely and with hypocrisy, not feeling the need of another man's doing or not doing anything; and besides, accepting all that happens, and all that is allotted, as coming from thence, wherever it is, from whence he himself came; and,   110 finally, waiting for death with a cheerful mind, as being nothing else than a dissolution of the elements of which every living being is compounded. But if there is no harm to the elements themselves in each continually changing into another, why should a man have any apprehension about the change and dissolution of all the elements? For it is according to nature, and nothing is evil which is according to nature.

STUDY QUESTIONS

1. Consider the "ruling part" of human nature; according to Marcus Aurelius, should it be reason, passion, conscience, tradition, authority, or revelation? Why?
2. According to the emperor, what is the proper way to face death?

LITERARY SELECTION 23

Against the City of Rome

Juvenal (Decimus Junius Juvenalis; ca. 60–140)

Juvenal was the last and best of the remarkable Roman satirists. Scarred by abrasive poverty ("It is not easy for men to rise whose qualities are thwarted by poverty," *Satires*, III), he was a brilliant social critic who saw through the glass darkly. The bitter tone, merciless barbs, and blatant prejudices (against the "inferior" sex and all Greeks) are here directed against a Rome he despises because he believes it has become foolish and wicked.

JUVENAL ON . . .

Women
For revenge is always the delight of a mean spirit, of a weak and petty mind! You may immediately draw proof of this—that no one rejoices more in revenge than a woman.

Satires, XIII, 1.189

Greeks
Grammarian, rhetorician, geometrician, painter, trainer, soothsayer, ropedancer, physician, magician—he knows everything. Tell the hungry little Greek to go to heaven; he'll go.

Satires, III, 1.76

Troubled because my old friend is going, I still must commend him
For his decision to settle down in the ghost town of Cumae,[45]
Giving the Sibyl one citizen more. That's the gateway to Baiae
There, a pleasant shore, a delightful retreat, I'd prefer
Even a barren rock in that bay to the brawl of Subura.
Where have we ever seen a place so dismal and lonely?
We'd not be better off there, than afraid, as we are here, of fires,
Roofs caving in, and the thousand risks of this terrible city
Where the poets recite all through the dog days of August?
While they are loading his goods on one little four-wheeled wagon,   10
Here he waits, by the old archways which the aqueducts moisten.
This is where Numa, by night, came to visit his goddess.
That once holy grove, its sacred spring, and its temple,
Now are let out to the Jews, if they have some straw and a basket.

Every tree, these days, has to pay rent to the people.
Kick the Muses out; the forest is swarming with
    beggars.
So we go down to Egeria's vale, with its modern
    improvements.
How much more close the presence would be, were
    there lawns by the water,
Turf to the curve of the pool, not this unnatural marble!
Umbricius has much on his mind. "Since there's no
    place in the city,"   20
He says, "For an honest man, and no reward for his
    labors,
Since I have less today than yesterday, since by
    tomorrow
That will have dwindled still more, I have made my
    decision. I'm going
To the place where, I've heard, Daedalus put off his
    wings,[46]
While my white hair is still new, my old age in the prime
    of its straightness,
While my fate spinner still has yarn on her spool, while
    I'm able
Still to support myself on two good legs, without
    crutches.
Rome, good-bye! Let the rest stay in the town if they
    want to,
Fellows like A, B, and C, who make black white at their
    pleasure,
Finding it easy to grab contracts for rivers and harbors,   30
Putting up temples, or cleaning out sewers, or hauling
    off corpses,
Or, if it comes to that, auctioning slaves in the market.
Once they used to be hornblowers, working the carneys;
Every wide place in the road knew their puffed-out
    cheeks and their squealing.
Now they give shows of their own. Thumbs up! Thumbs
    down! And the killers
Spare or slay, and then go back to concessions for
    private privies.
Nothing they won't take on. Why not?—since the
    kindness of Fortune
(Fortune is out for laughs) has exalted them out of the
    gutter.

"What should I do in Rome? I am no good at lying.
If a book's bad, I can't praise it, or go around ordering
    copies.   40
I don't know the stars; I can't hire out as assassin
When some young man wants his father knocked off for
    a price; I have never
Studied the guts of frogs, and plenty of others know
    better
How to convey to a bride the gifts of the first man she
    cheats with.
I am no lookout for thieves, so I cannot expect a
    commission
On some governor's staff. I'm a useless corpse, or a
    cripple.

45. Cumae was the oldest Greek colony in Italy.
46. Daedalus, according to Virgil, ended his flight at Cumae.

Who has a pull these days, except your yes men and
    stooges
With blackmail in their hearts, yet smart enough to keep
    silent?
"Now let me speak of the race that our rich men dote on
    most fondly.
These I avoid like the plague, let's have no coyness
    about it.   50
Citizens, I can't stand a Greekized Rome. Yet what
    portion
Of the dregs of our town comes from Achaia only?
Into the Tiber pours the silt, the mud of Orontes,
Bringing its babble and brawl, its dissonant harps and its
    timbrels,
Bringing also the tarts who display their wares at the
    Circus.
Here's the place, if your taste is for hat-wearing whores,
    brightly colored!
What have they come to now, the simple souls from the
    country
Romulus used to know? They put on the *trechedipna*
(That might be called, in our tongue, their running-to-
    dinner outfit),
Pin in their *niketeria* (medals), and smell *ceromatic*   60
(Attar of wrestler). They come, trooping from Samos and
    Tralles,
Andros, wherever that is, Azusa and Cucamonga,
Bound for the Esquiline or the hill we have named for
    the vineyard,
Termites, into great halls where they hope, some day, to
    be tyrants.
Desperate nerve, quick wit, as ready in speech as
    Isacus,
Also a lot more long-winded. Look over there! See that
    fellow?
What do you take him for? He can be anybody he
    chooses,
Doctor of science or letters, a vet or a chiropractor,
Orator, painter, masseur, palmologist, tightrope walker.
If he is hungry enough, your little Greek stops at
    nothing.   70
Tell him to fly to the moon, and he runs right off for his
    space ship.
Who flew first? Some Moor, some Turk, some Croat, or
    some Slovene?
Not on your life, but a man from the very center of
    Athens.

"Should I not run away from these purple-wearing
    freeloaders?
Must I wait while they sign their names? Must their
    couches always be softer?
Stowaways, that's how they got here, in the plums and
    figs from Damascus.
I was here long before they were: my boyhood drank in
    the sky
Over the Aventine hill; I was nourished by Sabine olives.
Agh, what lackeys they are, what sycophants! See how
    they flatter
Some ignoramus's talk, or the looks of some horrible
    eyesore,   80

Saying some Ichabod Crane's long neck reminds them of
    muscles
Hercules strained when he lifted Antaeus aloft on his
    shoulders,
Praising some cackling voice that really sounds like a
    rooster's
When he's pecking a hen. We can praise the same
    objects that they do,
Only, they are believed. Does an actor do any better
Mimicking Thaïs, Alcestis, Doris without any clothes on?
It seems that a woman speaks, not a mask; the illusion
    is perfect
Down to the absence of bulge and the little cleft under
    the belly.[47]
Yet they win on praise at home, for all of their talent.
Why?—Because Greece is a stage, and every Greek
    is an actor.   90
Laugh, and he splits his sides; weep, and his tears flow
    in torrents
Though he's not sad; if you ask for a little more fire in the
    winter
He will put on his big coat; if you say "I'm hot," he starts
    sweating.
We are not equals at all; he always has the advantage,
Able, by night or day, to assume, from another's
    expression,
This or that look, prepared to throw up his hands, to
    cheer loudly
If his friend gives a good loud belch or doesn't piss
    crooked,
Or if a gurgle comes from his golden cup when inverted
Straight up over his nose—a good deep swig, and no
    heeltaps!

"Furthermore, nothing is safe from his lust, neither
    matron nor virgin,   100
Nor her affianced spouse, or the boy too young for the
    razor.
If he can't get at these, he would just as soon lay his
    friend's grandma.
(Anything, so he'll get in to knowing the family secrets!)
Since I'm discussing the Greeks, let's turn to their
    schools and professors,
The crimes of the hood and gown. Old Dr. Egnatius,
    informant,
Brought about the death of Barea, his friend and his
    pupil,
Born on that riverbank where the pinion of Pegasus
    landed.
No room here, none at all, for any respectable Roman
Where a Protogenes rules, or a Diphilus, or a
    Hermarchus,
Never sharing their friends—a racial characteristic!   110
Hands off! He puts a drop of his own, or his
    countryside's poison
Into his patron's ear, an ear which is only too willing
And I am kicked out of the house, and all my years of
    long service
Count for nothing. Nowhere does the loss of a client
    mean less.

| **47.** Men played women's roles in Greek-style comedies.

"Let's not flatter ourselves. What's the use of our
    service?
What does a poor man gain by hurrying out in the
    nighttime,
All dressed up before dawn, when the praetor nags at
    his troopers
Bidding them hurry along to convey his respects to the
    ladies,
Barren, of course, like Albina, before any others can get
    there?
Sons of men freeborn give right of way to a rich
    man's   120
Slave; a crack, once or twice, at Calvina or Catiena
Costs an officer's pay, but if you like the face of some
    floozy
You hardly have money enough to make her climb down
    from her high chair.
Put on the stand, at Rome, a man with a record
    unblemished,
No more a perjurer than Numa was, or Metellus,
What will they question? His wealth, right away, and
    possibly, later,
(Only possibly, though) touch on his reputation.
'How many slaves does he feed? What's the extent of
    his acres?
How big are his platters? How many? What of his
    goblets and wine bowls?'
His word is as good as his bond—if he has enough
    bonds in his strongbox.   130
But a poor man's oath, even if sworn on all altars
All the way from here to the farthest Dodecanese island,
Has no standing in court. What has he to fear from the
    lightnings
Of the outraged gods? He has nothing to lose: they'll
    ignore him.

"If you're poor, you're a joke, on each and every
    occasion.
What a laugh, if your cloak is dirty or torn, if your toga
Seems a little bit soiled, if your shoe has a crack in the
    leather,
Or if more than one patch attests to more than one
    mending!
Poverty's greatest curse, much worse than the fact of it,
    is that
It makes men objects of mirth, ridiculed, humbled,
    embarrassed.   140
'Out of the front-row seats!' they cry when you're out of
    money,
Yield your place to the sons of some pimp, the spawn of
    some cathouse,
Some slick auctioneer's brat, or the louts some trainer
    has fathered
Or the well-groomed boys whose sire is a gladiator.
Such is the law of place, decreed by the nitwitted Otho:
*All the best seats are reserved for the classes who have
    the most money.*
Who can marry a girl if he has less money than she
    does?
What poor man is an heir, or can hope to be? Which of
    them ever
Rates a political job, even the meanest and lowest?

Long before now, all poor Roman descendants of
    Romans   150
Ought to have marched out of town in one determined
    migration.
Men do not easily rise whose poverty hinders their
    merit.
Here it is harder than anywhere else: the lodgings are
    hovels,
Rents out of sight; your slaves take plenty to fill up their
    bellies
While you make do with a snack. You're ashamed of
    your earthenware dishes—
Ah, but that wouldn't be true if you lived content in the
    country,
Wearing a dark-blue cape, and the hood thrown back on
    your shoulders.

"In a great part of this land of Italy, might as well face it,
No one puts on a toga unless he is dead. On festival
    days
Where the theatre rises, cut from green turf, and with
    great pomp   160
Old familiar plays are staged again, and a baby,
Safe in his mother's lap, is scared of the grotesque
    mask,
There you see all dressed alike, the balcony and the
    front rows,
Even His Honor content with a tunic of simple white.
Here, beyond our means, we have to be smart, and too
    often
Get our effects with too much, an elaborate wardrobe,
    on credit!
This is a common vice; we must keep up with the
    neighbors,
Poor as we are. I tell you, everything here costs you
    something.
How much to give Cossus the time of day, or receive
    from Veiento
One quick glance, with his mouth buttoned up for fear
    he might greet you?   170
One shaves his beard, another cuts off the locks of his
    boyfriend,
Offerings fill the house, but these, you find, you will pay
    for.
Put this in your pipe and smoke it—we have to pay
    tribute
Giving the slaves a bribe for the prospect of bribing their
    masters.

"Who, in Praeneste's cool, or the wooded Volsinian
    uplands,
Who, on Tivoli's heights, or a small town like Gabii, say,
Fears the collapse of his house? But Rome is supported
    on pipestems,
Matchsticks; it's cheaper, so, for the landlord to shore up
    his ruins,
Patch up the old cracked walls, and notify all the tenants
They can sleep secure, though the beams are in ruins
    above them.   180
No, the place to live is out there, where no cry of *Fire!*
Sounds the alarm of the night, with a neighbor yelling for
    water,

Moving his chattels and goods, and the whole third story
    is smoking.
This you'll never know: for if the ground floor is scared
    first,
You are the last to burn, up there where the eaves of the
    attic
Keep off the rain, and the doves are brooding over their
    nest eggs.

"Yet if Asturicus' mansion burns down, what a frenzy of
    sorrow!
Mothers dishevel themselves, the leaders dress up in
    black,
Courts are adjourned. We groan at the fall of the city, we
    hate
The fire, and the fire still burns, and while it is
    burning,   190
Somebody rushes up to replace the loss of the marble,
Some one chips in toward a building fund, another gives
    statues,
Naked and shining white, some masterpiece of
    Euphranor
Or Polyclitus' chef d'oeuvre; and here's a fellow with
    bronzes
Sacred to Asian gods. Books, chests, a bust of Minerva,
A bushel of silver coins. *To him that hath shall be given!*
The Persian, childless, of course, the richest man in the
    smart set,
Now has better things, and more, than before the
    disaster.
How can we help but think he started the fire on
    purpose?

"Tear yourself from the games, and get a place in the
    country!   200
One little Latian town, like Sora, say, or Frusino,
Offers a choice of homes, at a price you pay here, in one
    year,
Renting some hole in the wall. Nice houses, too, with a
    garden,
Springs bubbling up from the grass, no need for
    windlass or bucket,
Plenty to water your flowers, if they need it, without any
    trouble.
Live there, fond of your hoe, an independent producer,
Willing and able to feed a hundred good vegetarians.
Isn't it something, to feel, wherever you are, how far off,
You are monarch? At least, lord of a single lizard.

"Here in town the sick die from insomnia mostly.   210
Undigested food, on a stomach burning with ulcers,
Brings on listlessness, but who can sleep in a
    flophouse?
Who but the rich can afford sleep and a garden
    apartment?
That's the source of infection. The wheels creak by on
    the narrow
Streets of the wards, the drivers squabble and brawl
    when they're stopped,
More than enough to frustrate the drowsiest son of a
    sea cow.
When his business calls, the crowd makes way, as the
    rich man,

Carried high in his car, rides over them, reading or
   writing,
Even taking a snooze, perhaps, for the motion's
   composing.
Still, he gets where he wants before we do; for all of
   our hurry   220
Traffic gets in our way, in front, around and behind us.
Somebody gives me a shove with an elbow, or two-by-
   four scantling.
One clunks my head with a beam, another cracks down
   with a beer keg.
Mud is thick on my shins, I am trampled by somebody's
   big feet.
Now what?—a soldier grinds his hobnails into my toes.

"Don't you see the mob rushing along to the handout?
There are a hundred guests, each one with his kitchen
   servant.
Even Samson himself could hardly carry those burdens,
Pots and pans some poor little slave tries to keep on his
   head, while he hurries
Hoping to keep the fire alive by the wind of his
   running.   230
Tunics, new-darned, are ripped to shreds; there's the
   flash of a fir beam
Huge on some great dray, and another carries a pine tree,
Nodding above our heads and threatening death to the
   people.
What will be left of the mob, if that cart of Ligurian
   marble
Breaks its axle down and dumps its load on these
   swarms?
Who will identify limbs or bones? The poor man's
   cadaver,
Crushed, disappears like his breath. And meanwhile, at
   home, his household
Washes the dishes, and puffs up the fire, with all kinds
   of a clatter
Over the smeared flesh-scrapers, the flasks of oil, and
   the towels.
So the boys rush around, while their late master is
   sitting,   240
Newly come to the bank of the Styx, afraid of the filthy
Ferryman there, since he has no fare, not even a copper
In his dead mouth to pay for the ride through the muddy
   whirlpool.

"Look at other things, the various dangers of nighttime.
How high it is to the cornice that breaks, and a chunk
   beats my brains out,
Or some slob heaves a jar, broken or cracked, from a
   window.
Bang! It comes down with a crash and proves its weight
   on the sidewalk.
You are a thoughtless fool, unmindful of sudden disaster,
If you don't make your will before you go out to have
   dinner.
There are as many deaths in the night as there are
   open windows   250
Where you pass by; if you're wise, you will pray, in your
   wretched devotions,

People may be content with no more than emptying slop
   jars.
"This is not all you must fear. Shut up your house or your
   store,
Bolts and padlocks and bars will never keep out all the
   burglars,
Or a holdup man will do you in with a switch blade.
If the guards are strong over Pontine marshes and
   pinewoods
Near Volturno, the scum of the swamps and the filth of
   the forest
Swirl into Rome, the great sewer, their sanctuary, their
   haven.
Furnaces blast and anvils groan with the chains we are
   forging:
What other use have we for iron and steel? There is
   danger   260
We will have little left for hoes and mattocks and
   plowshares.
Happy the men of old, those primitive generations
Under the tribunes and kings, when Rome had only one
   jailhouse!

"There is more I could say, I could give you more of my
   reasons,
But the sun slants down, my oxen seem to be calling,
My man with the whip is impatient, I must be on my
   way.
So long! Don't forget me. Whenever you come to
   Aquino
Seeking relief from Rome, send for me. I'll come over
From my bay to your hills, hiking along in my thick boots
Toward your chilly fields. What's more, I promise to
   listen   270
If your satirical verse esteems me worthy the honor."

STUDY QUESTIONS

1. The debate about the relative virtues of rural and
   urban life is as old as cities. What does Juvenal
   detest about Rome? What does he admire about
   the country or small-town life? Why do you think
   he chose to stay in Rome?
2. Twentieth-century cities certainly have their share
   of problems. Which of these seem to be shared by
   ancient Rome?

SUMMARY

The pragmatic Romans cherished their flawed
institutions and their proclivity for war, plunder, and
profits, but they did have the saving grace of being able
to laugh at themselves. Enthusiastically adapting satire

to Roman tastes, they lambasted all they held dear: politics, material possessions, manners, and morals. The Romans were, in the final analysis, rational and (apart from their blood-sports) civilized people, and there is no clearer evidence of this than in their literature. No more given to profundities than their society in general, Roman writers were, collectively, sophisticated, worldly-wise, and often jaded. They sought to entertain and to inform rather than to enlighten, and they accomplished this with great style and a lusty elegance. The literature is consistently entertaining, frequently irreverent, often lewd; it makes lovely reading.

CULTURE AND HUMAN VALUES

The Greeks and the Romans were realists living in a world about which they had few illusions. However, the Greeks were also idealists who believed that people should (and could) be better than they were, that they could achieve freedom, beauty, truth, and justice.

Though not denying the desirability of these ideals, the Romans were total pragmatists. They rejected theory and precedent in favor of practical approaches and expediency. The value of a course of action lay in its observable consequences, the sum of which was its meaning. Serving the Roman state, for example, as a member of a Roman legion brought security, status, discipline, and a reasonable income. The sum of these benefits meant that soldiering was a good life and one that benefited first the state and then the individual. The state rather than the soldier was the true reality, a direct reversal of Greek values that placed the individual above the state. Duty, honor, and patriotism were Roman virtues as opposed to the Greek ideals of freedom, truth, and beauty.

Justice was a deep concern for both cultures, but in very different ways. The Greeks pursued the theory of perfect justice in an ordered society. Roman justice was pragmatic, a process that dealt with practical problems in everyday life. Such human failings as venality and greed were controlled by the state in order to prevent the strong from triumphing over the weak. Roman law implied the consent of the governed, and every citizen, regardless of class, had the right to "appeal to Caesar." Moreover, Roman law was international and based on a pragmatic appraisal of consistent human behavior regardless of the environment. Though we may admire the Greek ideal of justice, it is Roman law that has provided the basic framework of today's body of laws.

The state of balance of the culture-epoch theory was essentially maintained from the beginning of the classical period in Greece to the death of Marcus Aurelius, the sixth and last of the so-called good emperors (480 BC–AD 180). Though ending some eighteen centuries ago, the brilliant Graeco-Roman era set a standard of civilization rarely approached in the ten centuries or so that followed. Most of the so-called progress since that distant age has been technological with little positive effect on the quality of life or the viability of human institutions.

> Those who are most easily depressed about the precarious future of Western civilization are usually people who do not know the full history of its past. They also very generally misunderstand our relation to the Greeks and the Romans. They imagine them as remote peoples whose lives and achievements interest antiquarians alone, and whose languages and thoughts are "dead." Certainly they always conceive the Greeks and Romans as being less than ourselves, instead of being in many ways more mature and more advanced in knowledge and experience.[48]

---

48. Gilbert Highet, *Man's Unconquerable Mind* (New York: Columbia University Press, 1954), p. 15.

CHAPTER 9

Roman Art and Architecture: The Arts of Megalopolis

ETRUSCAN CIVILIZATION

The Etruscans controlled northern Italy for about 400 years and even ruled Rome for nearly a century. Their influence on Roman civilization was considerable but there was almost no mutual exchange. Rome did not impress the Etruscans but Greece did, especially her sculpture, painting, and vases, particularly vases, for much Greek pottery has been recovered from Etruscan tombs.

Despite the strong Greek influence the Etruscans did develop a distinctive kind of art. Provincial, sometimes homespun, with an occasional masterpiece, their work had an earthy vigor that impressed their Roman conquerors. In fact, we know more of Etruscan art than of their culture in general. With an undeciphered literature and little more than some massive stone walls remaining of their fortified hilltop cities, our scanty knowledge of Etruscan culture is based almost entirely on the contents of thousands of tombs found throughout central Italy (map 9.1). Etruscan skill in making terra-cotta objects is exemplified by the funerary sculpture (fig. 9.1) found in the *necropolis* (Gk., "city of the dead") outside Cerveteri, northwest of Rome. A deceased couple is shown resting their left elbows on a couch as if attending a celestial banquet. The smooth bodies, braided hair, and archaic smiles

Map 9.1   Etruscan and Roman Italy.

Opposite   Apollo Slaying the Python, House of the Vettii, Pompeii, detail of fig. 9.9. Ca. AD 65. Mural painting. Photo: Alinari, Florence.

9.1 *Left*   Etruscan sarcophagus, from Cerveteri, Italy. Ca. 510 BC. Painted terra-cotta, length ca. 6'7"(2 m). Museo Nazionale di Villa Giulia, Rome. Photo: Hirmer, Munich.

9.2 *Chimera of Arezzo*, from Italy. Etruscan. Ca. 380–360 BC. Bronze, height 31½" (80 cm). Museo Archeologico, Florence. Photo: Viollet, Paris.

9.3 *Warrior Giving Support to a Wounded Comrade*, finial from a candelabrum. Etruscan. Early 5th century BC. Bronze, height (with base) 5¼" (13.3 cm). Metropolitan Museum of Art, New York (Rogers Fund, 1947.47.11.3).

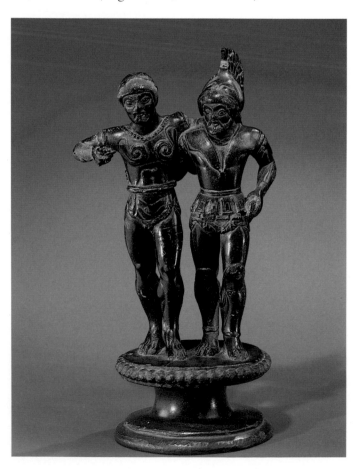

in the Greek manner are typical of the Etruscan style, as is the display of mutual affection and the couple's individualized features. The exact meaning of festive banquet scenes like this and many others is unknown, but continuation of the good life after death is likely.

The remarkable *Chimera* (fig. 9.2) is a masterful monster that radiates the vigor so characteristic of Etruscan art. In Greek mythology a chimera was usually a fire-breathing monster with the head of a lion, body of a goat, and a serpent for a tail. Here the head and tail fit the pattern, but the body is more "lion" than "goat" and the pattern down the backbone seems to be dragonlike. Compounding the four-footed hybrid is the head of a goat protruding from the back with the left horn caught in the fangs of the snake. (A mistake in reconstruction placed the snake's head too low; it should be raised so that its fangs can intimidate observers.) There is no Greek influence here. The Greeks polished off the rough edges of their demons but the Etruscans created a whole company of monsters that specialized in tormenting the dead in the underworld. This seems to reflect the Asiatic origins of the Etruscans, about which Herodotos was so positive. This creature has precedents that go back to Egyptian sphinxes (see fig. 2.2) and the winged, man-faced bulls of Assyria (see fig. 1.19).

The Etruscans were highly skilled workers in precious metals as confirmed by their gold and silver jewelry and bronze sculptures such as the *Chimera* and this sculpture of two warriors (fig. 9.3). Like the Greeks, the Etruscans added ornamentation to common household objects; this is the decorative tip (finial) of a lamp stand. Demonstrating two different but interrelated personalities, a sympathetic comrade supports the wounded soldier. The apprehension of one and the concern of the other are skillfully fashioned into a unified composition.

That the Etruscans were exceptional goldsmiths is shown by the gold disks in figure 9.4. The granulation is extremely fine and the filigree and gold wire work exceptionally delicate. For best effect this figure should be studied with a magnifying glass.

9.4 Etruscan gold disks. Late 6th century BC. Diameter 1¾" (4.4 cm). Antikenmuseum, Staatliche Museen Preussischer Kulturbesitz, Berlin. Photo: B.P.K., Munich (Ingrid Geske-Heiden).

THE ROMAN ARTS,
CA. 753 BC–AD 476

Art for the stern Romans was a dissolute influence that could undermine the moral fiber of the people, especially the Republic's citizen-soldiers. As late as the third century BC Rome was, according to Plutarch, a metropolis devoid of refinement and beauty, a dreary city full of hostages, battle trophies, barbarous weapons, and ostentatious triumphal arches. The penetration of Greek culture, especially Greek art, was a slow process that gathered momentum with Roman triumphs over Greek territories. During the conquest of the luxurious cities of Magna Graecia (southern Italy) in 212 BC, for example, one general returned bearing Greek statues and paintings while another general displayed such "proper" booty as gold and jewels. After the 146 BC conquest of the Greek mainland, a huge volume of confiscated art works flooded the city, overwhelming old guard hostility and establishing Rome as the prime custodian of the Hellenic artistic tradition.

Though much of what we call Roman art is derived from Greek models and often created by Greek artists, the Romans did make some significant contributions with their realistic portrait busts, landscape painting, and, especially, their architecture. Justly famous for the monumental architecture of the imperial period, the Romans must also be credited with developing the "art" of civilized living. During the early days of the Republic more attention was paid to the efficient design of military camps than to the urban planning of Rome and other growing cities of the rapidly expanding Republic. With the shift from a simple rural to an affluent urbanized society, the Romans had to tackle city planning. Taking their cue from Etruscan hill towns, they learned how to design and build the basic requirements for urban life: fortifications; streets; bridges; aqueducts; sewers; town houses; apartment houses; and recreational, shopping, and civic centers.

Pompeii

With no art and very little architecture remaining from the early centuries of the Republic, we begin our study of the arts of Rome with Pompeii, the only surviving city of the Roman Republic. The eruption of Mount Vesuvius in AD 79 buried Pompeii under cinders and ashes that, in effect, preserved the city as a museum of Roman civilization. Probably founded in the sixth century BC, Pompeii was inhabited by Italic Oscans and Samnites, plus some Greeks, until its conquest by Rome in about 80 BC.

City Plan

Containing the earliest extant amphitheatre and public baths, Pompeii was built in a modified Greek grid plan around the most important early forum outside Rome (fig. 9.5). Reflecting Greek influence, the Doric colonnade with

---

ART FORGERIES

Art forgers make objects designed to deceive a potential purchaser, a practice probably as old as collecting art objects. However, the earliest records of fraudulent art date only from ancient Rome. The influx of Greek art after the conquest of the Greek mainland created a demand for Greek paintings and sculpture. Collecting Greek art was a sure sign of taste, breeding, and social position (and money), and enterprising crooks found a ready market for counterfeit Greek art, especially sculpture. Many were the forgeries sold bearing the famous names of Myron, Polykleitos, Pheidias, Praxiteles, and Lysippos, among others. These ancient transactions haunt today's experts who are still puzzling over the authenticity of some Greek sculptures.

---

superimposed Ionic columns was a device later extended to four levels in the Colosseum (see fig. 9.22). There are, in fact, so many different elements of Etruscan, Greek, and Italic contributions to Pompeiian decoration that it is impossible to decide who did what. Measuring 125 by 466 feet (38.2 × 142.2 m), the civic center, or forum, was bordered on the west and east by matching two-story colonnades, ending at arches that flanked the primary city Temple of Jupiter, Juno, and Minerva. One arch and part of the temple base are visible in the right background of figure 9.5. (Also visible in the right background is the looming bulk of Mount Vesuvius.) Combining religious, commercial, and civil functions, forums were the hub of every Roman city, reflecting Roman concerns for centralized authority and control.

9.5 Two sections, west colonnade of the forum, Pompeii, Italy. Whole forum 125 × 466' (38.13 × 142.13 m). Photo: Viollet, Paris.

It was already hot on the morning of 24 August 79. Pliny the Elder and his nephew Pliny the Younger, seeking cooler air, moved to the balcony of their villa overlooking the Bay of Naples. Suddenly they saw a burgeoning cloud across the bay over Vesuvius. The younger Pliny later wrote to Tacitus: "like an immense tree-trunk it was projected into the air, and opened out with branches, sometimes white, sometimes dark and mottled." Seconds later they heard an enormous explosion and felt earth tremors so violent that the nephew and his mother fled their villa and joined a panic-stricken crowd struggling to get out of the debris-filled air. Above the volcano there now "loomed a horrible black cloud ripped by sudden bursts of fire, writhing snakelike and revealing sudden flashes larger than lightning." Ash was falling so thickly that they had to keep moving to avoid being buried in it. The tremors and falling pumice and ash seemed to last several terrifying hours. As darkness gradually lightened to let a dim sun shine through, they could see that the whole top of Vesuvius had been blown away. Where there had once been farms, vineyards, Pompeii, Herculaneum, and Stabiae was now a deadly silent gray carpet of ash. Though the elder Pliny was a writer and lawyer, it was his dedication as a naturalist that compelled him, despite the pleading of his sister and nephew, to investigate this incredible natural wonder. He had set off in a galley for a closer look when he was trapped and died amid clouds of sulfurous fumes.

Domestic Architecture

Because the city-center forum was always closed to vehicular traffic, the network of streets began at the perimeter and expanded outward to the suburbs (fig. 9.6). Much as old Italian towns are today, the streets nearer the forum were lined by shops, which were flanked by houses of shopkeepers and other citizens. The domus, single-family residence, was entered through a front doorway set in a windowless wall that guaranteed privacy and shut out city noise and dirt (fig. 9.7). An entrance hall led to the atrium (fig. 9.8), a typical Italic-Roman design for larger houses and for the still more elaborate villas in the surrounding countryside. A rectangular, windowless court that kept out heat while admitting light and air, the atrium had an inwardly sloping roof that drained rainwater into the pool below, from which it was piped to a cistern. Surrounding the central atrium were the kitchen, and parlors for everyday living. Beyond the atrium were the bedrooms, whose porches fronted on an open courtyard surrounded by a peristyle of, in this case, Doric columns. As was customary with Roman houses, the many blank walls were either brightly painted or decorated with murals. The combination of Roman atrium and Hellenistic Greek peristyle court, which was adopted in the second century BC, makes the Roman house or villa an ideal design for hot Mediterranean summers.

A vivid mythological scene decorates a wall of the

9.6 Plan of Pompeii in AD 79.

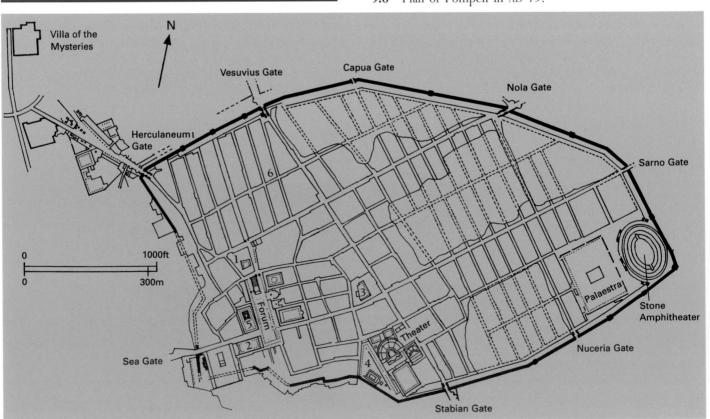

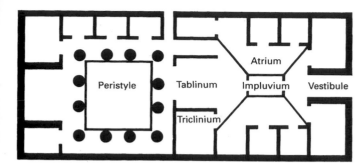

9.7 Plan (*above*) and restoration drawing (*right*) of a Roman patrician house.

garden room of the House of the Vettii (fig. 9.9 and p. 282). Apollo strums his kithara as the vanquished python trails down from an altar where Diana stands at the left with the sacrificial bull. Above the panel is a fantastic architectonic construction under which a goddess plays her cymbals; this may be Euterpe, muse of lyric poetry and music. Left and right of the muse are statues of herms (for Hermes, god of fertility). This is the latest and most elaborate of the four Pompeiian styles.

9.9 *Below Apollo Slaying the Python*, House of the Vettii, Pompeii. Ca. AD 65. Mural painting. Photo: Alinari, Florence.

9.8 *Above* Atrium, House of the Silver Wedding, Pompeii. 1st century AD. Photo: Canali, Brescia.

9.10   Maison Carrée, Nîmes, France. 1st century BC. 59 × 117' (18 × 35.7 m). Photo: Helga Schmidt-Glassner, Stuttgart.

Architecture and Engineering

The Roman Temple

Though no intact Augustan temples remain in Rome, the remarkably well preserved temple nicknamed the Maison Carrée (marble house; fig. 9.10) embodies the qualities advocated by the emperor. Unlike their Greek counterparts, Roman temples stand on high podiums and are entered from the front by a single flight of steps. The open form of the Greek temple, with a walkway and three steps on all four sides, has been converted to the closed form of buildings designed to enclose space. This temple uses the rich Corinthian order (fig. 9.11) favored by most Roman architects and engaged columns attached to the cella walls in a decorative device from Republican days. A small building measuring 59 by 117 feet (18 × 35.7 m) with 30-foot

9.11   Corinthian capital.

(9.2 m) columns, the Maison Carrée became a prototype of temples honoring notable emperors, much as the Jefferson Memorial in Washington memorializes an illustrious president. This building, in fact, inspired Thomas Jefferson to utilize the classic style of Rome in his neoclassic designs of the Virginia State Capitol, the University of Virginia, and his own home of Monticello.

The Roman Arch

Rome made a lasting contribution to the development of the rounded arch and vault as structural architectural principles. Used for centuries in Asia Minor and Greece for lesser works like gates, storage areas, corridors, and sewers, the arch was exploited by Roman engineers on a massive scale. Concerned with spanning and enclosing space, they used arches to build bridges, aqueducts, baths, and basilicas, the secular structures necessary for the efficient operation of Roman cities. A semicircle of stone blocks, or bricks and mortar (fig. 9.12), spanning spaces between **piers** or walls, the arch was better suited to the utilitarian needs of Roman engineering than the post and lintel system. Not intended to bridge large spaces, the lintel is the weaker portion of the system because it can support a limited amount of weight. To bear greater loads it must be enlarged, the columns moved closer together, or both. In the arch, the wedge-shaped blocks called **voussoirs** (voo-SWAHR) curve up to the **keystone** at the apex of the arch,

9.12   (a) Semicircular arch arcade, and (b) barrel or tunnel vault.

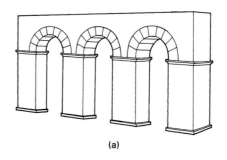

(a)

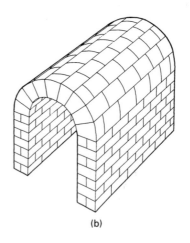

(b)

providing strength and stability because of the mutually supporting pressures from pier to keystone. From the keystone the thrust is transmitted through the voussoirs down through the pier, or wall, to the ground. When the arches are side by side they form an **arcade**, as in the Pont du Gard (fig. 9.13 and p. 231). When extended longitudinally along its axis, the arch is called a **barrel** or tunnel **vault**, as in the Arch of Titus (fig. 9.24).

Aqueducts

Representing Roman engineering and power, aqueducts were a highly visible portion of the network of waterways and roadways that interconnected the Empire. Built by Agrippa, a lieutenant under Augustus, the Pont du Gard (fig. 9.13) is 180 feet (54.9 m) high and in its present condition about 900 feet (275 m) long. It carried water some 25 miles (40 km) from the mountains, across the gorge of the Gard River, and into Nîmes. Spanning over 80 feet (24 m), each massive arch supports an arch of similar dimensions but with much less masonry, which in turn undergirds the watercourse itself. Supported by three small arches for each large one, the water flowed steadily down an approximate 1 percent grade. Using stones weighing up to 6 tons (6,000 kg) each and assembled without mortar, the bridge of the bottom arcade has been in continuous use for 2,000 years.

Sculpture, Painting, and Minor Arts

Maintaining a strong sense of identity was a major concern for Roman families; they preserved collections of wax portrait masks of their ancestors. Recognizable portrayals were therefore required, accounting for the long tradition of starkly realistic marble portrait busts as represented, for example, by the bust of Julius Caesar (fig. 9.14). As the man responsible for the final demise of the embattled Republic, Caesar is depicted as history has revealed him to be: imperious, ruthless, a charismatic leader of men. With their no-nonsense approach to reality, the Romans insisted upon an exactitude that included every wart, pimple, line, and blemish. This bust may have been done from life; if so, Caesar probably relished the portrait, particularly the confident tilt of the head.

Caesar Augustus, 63 BC–AD 14

There are no blemishes on the commanding statue of Caesar Augustus from the Imperial Villa at Primaporta (fig. 9.15). Idealized in the Greek manner, this is Augustus the noble ruler. Based on the *Doryphoros* (see fig. 7.23), with the imperious gesture probably derived from Near Eastern art, this is an official portrait. With his likeness on Roman coins and with thousands of busts distributed throughout the Empire, Augustus created the imperial image of mighty Rome. Augustus' divine origins are revealed in the cupid and the dolphin, symbols of Venus, mother of Aeneas, who was, according to Virgil, the emperor's ancestor. The relief

9.13 Pont du Gard, near Nîmes, France. Ca. 20–10 BC. Height 180' (54.9 m), current length ca. 900' (275 m). Photo: Explorer/Robert Harding, London.

sculpture on the armor details the emperor's road to power. The only realistic elements are the tactile illusions of leather, metal, and cloth that give the feeling of actuality prized by Romans but considered trite by Greeks. Becoming a stock device for depicting kings, emperors, and dictators, this is a superb example of didactic art.

The best-preserved of all Roman funerary memorials, the so-called mausoleum (fig. 9.16) is actually a cenotaph that honors the dead but does not contain the remains.

9.14 Bust of Julius Caesar. 1st century BC. Marble, height 38" (96.5 cm). Museo Archeologico Nazionale, Naples. Photo: Mansell Collection, London.

9.15 *Above Augustus of Primaporta.* Ca. 20 BC. Marble, height 6'9" (2.06 m). Musei Vaticani, Rome. Photo: Scala, Florence.

Erected in honor of two grandsons of Augustus who died in childhood, the three-stage structure has reliefs on the solid base and engaged Corinthian columns flanking the second-level arches. Statues of the two children are within the circular third level. The combination of reliefs, projecting **cornices**, squared-off arches, and rounded forms is eclectic rather than classical and illustrates how far removed Roman excess is from Greek restraint.

Painting

In figure 9.17 we see an example of the continuing interest in classical themes, which formed one of the bridges between Greek and Roman cultures. The powerful Herakles stands before a classically conceived woman representing the mythical Arcadia, where everyone lived at peace with nature and one another. The lion is painted in a vaguely impressionistic manner, while the doe in the left foreground is light and graceful. The disparate figures appear to have been placed in a preexisting space with little concern for their interrelatedness or to the painting's unity. Like much Roman painting, the work does display, however, great technical skill in the manipulation of light, lines, and shapes, and in the illusion of three-dimensional space.

Minor Arts

The citizens of the Republic were as disdainful of such luxury items as jewelry as they were of the visual arts, making surviving examples very rare. However, by the beginning of the Empire in 27 BC, the old austerity had quickly become passé. **Mosaic** work decorated the floors of Roman houses, temples, baths, and other buildings (fig. 9.18). Rome's annexation of the lands of the Hellenistic world included, inevitably, the opulent culture. Essentially a continuation of the Hellenistic style, Roman jewelry was an equally skillful combination of gemstones and precious metals. In figure 9.19 the necklace (second century AD) gold links alternate with emeralds. The hair ornament from Tunis (third century AD) is inlaid with emeralds with a pearl border. The pendant is a sapphire flanked by two pearls. These two pieces in particular symbolize the elegance of the Empire at its height.

The *Cameo of a Victorious Emperor* (fig. 9.20) is a departure from earlier official **cameos** that portrayed serene rulers at ease in a Roman-regulated world. This cameo depicts an emperor fighting ever more threatening barbarians who have disturbed, and will later destroy, the tranquility of the old world of the *Pax Romana*. Though the field is littered with the fallen foe, the emperor seems to be peering ahead at new waves of barbarians flooding the Empire's northern frontiers.

9.16 *Left* Roman mausoleum. Saint-Rémy-de-Provence, France. Ca. AD 40. Height ca 60' (18 m) Photo: Spectrum, London.

9.17 *Herakles Discovering the Infant Telephos in Arcadia*, from Herculaneum, Italy. Roman copy of ca. AD 70 of a Hellenistic original of the 2nd century BC. Mural painting, ca. 7 × 6' (2.1 × 1.9 m). Museo Nazionale, Naples. Photo: Scala, Florence.

9.18 The centerpiece of a Pompeiian mosaic black and white pavement, from the House of the Tragic Poet. Photo: Dagli Orti, Paris.

9.19 Roman jewelry: earrings, brooch in the form of a dog, hair ornament, pendant, and necklace. 1st–4th century AD. Gold with garnets, sapphires, emeralds, and pearls. British Museum, London.

9.20 *Cameo of a Victorious Emperor*. Between AD 325 and 360. Onyx in hues from white to black, height 14⅛" (35.9 cm). National Museum, Belgrade, Serbia. Photo: Scala, Florence.

Greek Theory and Roman Practice

A comparison of the assemblage of visual images of the *Herakles* (fig. 9.17) with the figure of the *Doryphoros* (see fig. 7.23) illustrates some fundamental differences between Greek and Roman cultures. More concerned with practice than theory, the Romans itemized rather than conceptualized. The *Herakles* is a kind of visual catalog of a specific event: Herakles finding his son in Arcadia. The *Doryphoros* is not a specific person but a realization of the ideal athlete, the embodiment of a concept against which individual athletes measured themselves. The Romans portrayed people as they were and the Greeks depicted them as they should be. The Romans were practical, the Greeks theoretical. It is no wonder that the Romans viewed the Greeks with awe, contempt, envy, and suspicion. The Romans accepted the imperfect world as it was; the Greeks wanted something better. The quarreling Greek city-states were forcibly united by Alexander; Rome conquered the world.

The Romans acknowledged Greek culture as generally superior and made Greek literature, art, and architecture basic strands in the fabric of Roman civilization. The Empire was, in fact, administered in two languages—the Latin of the ruling Romans and the Greek of the conquered Hellenes. (Try to imagine Napoleon administering the French Empire in both French and German.) Where the two cultures differed significantly was in sheer size. The population of Athens of the Golden Age was about 100,000; Imperial Rome had a much larger population and greater wealth, but it also endured the endless problems that plague large cities in any culture.

9.21 I Gismondi, Reconstruction of 4th-century Rome. Museo Nazionale Romano, Rome.

The Imperial City

Shown in figure 9.21 is part of the center of a city with over 50 miles (80 km) of streets, almost none with names, and a population in the second century AD of about 1,200,000. Much of this area was constructed by the Flavian emperors (reigned 69–96); the monumental civic structures were completed by Nerva, Trajan, and Hadrian (76–138).

In the far upper left of the model are the Baths of Trajan; with a central complex of thermal, exercise, and dressing rooms surrounded by landscaped grounds, this became the prototype for all subsequent imperial baths. Near the bottom of the figure is the Circus Maximus, the primary stadium for chariot racing and the common meeting ground for all levels of Roman society (see the selection from Ovid on pp. 268–72). Achieving its final form in about AD 329, the stadium enclosed a race course measuring 660 by 1,950 feet (201.3 × 594.8 m). Seating about 150,000 spectators and operating a full racing program on 240 days of the year, the Circus Maximus could total about 8,000,000 admissions a year. This was mass entertainment, Roman style. Directly above the Circus Maximus are the Imperial Forums and the Claudius Aqueduct leading to the Palatine, highest of the seven hills of Rome and urban abode of the aristocracy. At the upper left is the Colosseum, the single most representative building of the Roman Empire, then and now.

The Colosseum

Designed for the staging of battles between various combinations of animals and gladiators, the Colosseum seated about 50,000 spectators around an arena measuring 156 by 258 feet (47.6 × 78.7 m). With underground corridors for gladiators, animals, and technicians, and elaborate stage

GAMES IN A RING

Chariot races (*ludi circenses*; "games in a ring") were staged at six racetracks in and about Rome. Racing was a frenzied and dangerous sport, if one can call driving four-horse chariots on a tight oval track that had only one rule—to the victor go the spoils—a sport. The stakes were high enough; winning drivers made a great deal of money and enjoyed a status comparable to the combined charisma of a pro football star and a Grand Prix champion. There is no contemporary equivalent for a day at the races in Rome's Circus Maximus, which was a combination sports, social, and gambling center. Try to imagine an oval track 2,000 feet (610 m) in circumference, four tense and tough racing teams (blues, greens, whites, reds) and 150,000 fanatical spectators who had millions riding on every race. And some were even betting on who got killed.

9.22 Colosseum, Rome. AD 72–80, 513 × 520' (156 × 189 m), height 161' (49 m). Photo: Alinari, Florence (Lieberman).

9.23 Colosseum, aerial view. Photo: Fototeca Unione, Rome.

equipment for crowd-pleasing effects, the Colosseum was a complete entertainment center. Built on four levels, the exterior is unified by four superimposed orders of columns (fig. 9.22). Beginning with a simplification of the Doric column called Tuscan, the columns mount upward through the Ionic and Corinthian orders to flat Corinthian piers called **pilasters**. Topping the wall are sockets for pennants and for a removable canvas covering that protected against sun and rain. A key design unit in the exterior wall is the characteristic combination of a Roman arch flanked by a Greek order. Called the Roman arch order, the basic elements are a Roman arch set in a Greek post and lintel frame. Used in triumphal arches and other structures, this device was revived in the Italian Renaissance and can be seen today in neoclassic building facades in Europe and the Americas.

The Colosseum is an amphitheatre (Gk., *amphi*, "both"; *theatron*, "theatre"), a structure invented by the Romans as a derivation of Greek theatre design. As the name indicates, this structure is actually two theatres facing each other to form an oval-shaped bowl (fig. 9.23). Brilliantly designed and executed, the Colosseum exemplifies the qualities the Roman architect Vitruvius (first century BC) considered basic for superior design: firmness, commodity, and delight. Structurally sound (firmness), the Colosseum was a spacious arena with eighty portals for easy ingress and egress, comfortable seating, and unobstructed sightlines (commodity). Though not a prime Roman concern, it does have a quality of "delight," an aesthetic appeal that makes a work of art exalted and memorable.

Erected by the Flavian emperors, the Colosseum, also known as the Flavian Amphitheatre, was largely built by prisoners of the Jewish Wars, which had ended in AD 70 with the conquest of Jerusalem and the Temple of Solomon's destruction. Dedicated by Titus in AD 80, the Colosseum opened with inaugural ceremonies that lasted 100 days and

that were, according to contemporary accounts, very successful, costing the lives of some 9,000 wild animals and 2,000 gladiators.

Immediately recognized as an extraordinary achievement, the Colosseum was elevated by Martial to one of the Seven Wonders of the World:

On the Dedication of the Colosseum in Rome

> Barbaric Egypt, boast no more
>   The wonders of your pyramids!
> Babylon, vaunt no longer now
>   The gardens of Semiramis!
> Let not the soft Ionians swell
>   With pride for their great Artemis
> Whose temple splendor long has been
>   The claim and fame of Ephesus.
> Let Delos hide its head in shame
>   And say no more Apollo
> Himself did rear the altar there
>   (A claim both weak and hollow).
> Let not the Carians wildly praise
>   The wondrous, sculptured tomb
> The queen at Halicarnassus raised
>   When Mausolus met his doom.
> Let every wonder of the past
>   Yield now to this great wonder.
> Fame shall cling to this at last,
>   Her applause as loud as thunder.

The Triumphal Arch

Julius Caesar contended that the only truly effective way of controlling conquered people was to execute the entire population. The practical alternative to extermination was the conversion of prisoners of war into a tractable slave labor force. One of the most effective propaganda devices for impressing their bondage on the slaves was the triumphal arch, a symbolic representation of the yoke of oxen.

9.24 Arch of Titus, Rome. AD 81. Marble, height ca. 50' (15 m), width ca. 40' (12 m). Photo: Alinari, Florence.

9.25 Column of Trajan, Rome. Ca. AD 106–113. Marble, height (with base) 125' (38.13 m). Photo: Alinari, Florence.

In a ritualistic dramatization of Roman might, victorious generals marched their prisoners through hastily erected temporary arches to the accompaniment of battle trumpets and drums. What the Romans called the Triumph was meant to be awesome for the spectators and humiliating for the vanquished—and it undoubtedly was.

To commemorate his brother Titus' destruction of Jerusalem in AD 70, Domitian had a permanent version of the triumphal arch erected where the Via Sacra enters the Roman Forum (fig. 9.24). (By the end of the Empire there would be over sixty triumphal arches in Rome and many more throughout the Empire.) Constructed of concrete with a marble facing, the Arch of Titus utilized a Roman arch order similar to that of the Colosseum. Massive piers with dual-engaged columns provided a post and lintel frame for a deep Roman arch vault (see fig. 9.12). With a superstructure called the attic bearing the commemorative inscription, the walls of the vault were decorated with high reliefs depicting Titus' successful campaign against the Jews. Symbolizing a major Roman victory, the arch was also a powerful reminder for all slaves, especially the Jews who labored on the Colosseum, of the futility of opposing the might of Rome.

Trajan's Column

The assassination of Domitian in AD 96 ended the Flavian dynasty and ushered in the era of the so-called good emperors (reigned 96–180): Nerva, Trajan, Hadrian, Antoninus Pius, and Marcus Aurelius. The first non-Italian to occupy the throne, the brilliant Spanish general, Trajan, led Rome to the maximum expansion of its empire. Among the monuments commemorating his phenomenal successes is the Column of Trajan (fig. 9.25), an unprecedented conception. Carved in low relief in 150 scenes, the 658-foot (200 m)

frieze winds twenty-three times around the column as it narrates the highlights of Trajan's two campaigns into Dacia (modern Romania and Hungary). To "read" the story, one walks round and round the column, but it soon becomes impossible to read it without binoculars. How and if this story was read in its entirety has never been satisfactorily explained. Perhaps there were special viewing balconies or perhaps slaves were stationed at the base of the monument delivering illuminating lectures and selling guidebooks.

Though the inspiration for this unusual monument is unknown, it is perhaps significant that it was placed between the Latin and Greek libraries of Trajan; the column is quite similar to library books of the time—*rotuli* ("scrolls"), which were wound on two spindles. The basic inspiration, however, is the "continuous narration" technique, which is so typically Roman, as opposed to Greek "simultaneous narration." The Greek unities of time, place, and action as observed in the Parthenon frieze (see fig. 7.42) were apparently not suitable for the day-to-day world of empire building. Reflected in the Column of Trajan is Roman interest in biography and history; the basic unity is the focus on the leadership of Trajan while history is served by the unfolding scenes of campaigns. A detail from the bottom of the column (fig. 9.26) depicts landscapes as stylized stage sets. Artistic details are minimized, making the soldiers the prime figures of the Roman conquest. Executed under the direction of a single artist, the frieze is a masterpiece of didactic art in the tradition of the *Augustus of Primaporta* (see fig. 9.15). The column was originally topped by a statue of Trajan, which was destroyed during the Middle Ages and since replaced by a sixteenth-century statue of St. Peter. Symbolizing the church's triumph over Rome, the first pope stands above a visual record of two bloody Roman campaigns.

9.26 Column of Trajan, detail. Photo: Fototeca Unione, Rome.

Hadrian, 76–138

Probably the best educated of all Roman emperors and certainly the most cosmopolitan, Hadrian (reigned 117–138) was more interested in improving the cultural life of the Empire than in extending political frontiers. Indicating his style of life, Hadrian lived and worked in Britain, southern France, Spain, Morocco, Asia Minor, Greece (twice), Tunisia, Syria, Palestine, and Egypt. After ten years abroad he finally returned to build Hadrian's Villa at Tivoli near Rome (fig. 9.27). A student of all things Greek, Hadrian was more

9.27 Canopus, Hadrian's Villa, Tivoli, Italy. Ca. AD 135. Photo: Werner Forman, London.

The Canopus is a long pool, named for an Egyptian city on the westernmost mouth of the Nile, which Hadrian decorated with copies of famous sculptures.

9.28 The Pantheon, Rome. Ca. 118–125. Marble, brick, and concrete, portico height 59' (18 m). Photo: Calmann & King, London (Lieberman).

concerned with supporting Greek intellectual life than with whatever took place in Rome's mercantile environment. He did, however, strongly support the most advanced concepts of Roman architects in their interior space designs.

The Pantheon

One of the most revolutionary and authoritative structures ever built, the Pantheon (fig. 9.28) has influenced the architecture of every age from ancient Rome to the present day. The inscription on the frieze, "M. AGRIPPA L.F. COS TERTIUM FECIT" ("Marcus Agrippa, son of Lucius, consul for

the third time, built this"), does not refer to this building but to previous structures erected in 27–25 BC by Agrippa, son-in-law of Augustus. Because the original buildings included baths and a temple called Pantheon, Hadrian, displaying his fine sense of Roman history, had the original inscription repeated on the new temple. With a portico 59 feet (18m) high and measuring 142 feet (43.2 m) in the interior (diameter and height), the Pantheon is topped by one of the largest domes ever constructed. (St. Peter's dome is 139 feet [42.5 m] in diameter.) Twenty feet (6.1 m) thick at the outside edge, the poured concrete dome decreases to less than 5 feet (1.5 m) at the center. Resting on eight enormous piers and providing interior lighting with a circular opening (oculus) 28 feet (8.5 m) in diameter, the dome is coffered (indented panels) to decrease the weight without sacrificing structural strength. Rainwater can be drained away in minutes by a plumbing system that still works. The Pantheon is the best preserved of all Roman buildings because it became a Christian church early in the history of the Church of Rome.

The eight-column front of Corinthian capitals topping polished granite columns is, in effect, a Greek portico opening into a massive drum derived from the circular Greek tholos. The impressiveness of the interior—one of the most astounding spatial accomplishments in architecture—is communicated better by the Panini painting (fig. 9.29) than by any contemporary photograph. Originally painted blue, the hemisphere of concrete was highlighted with rosettes of gilded bronze set into each coffer. Softly colored columns alternate with marble panels, pilasters, and niches, forming a harmonious blend within a single, self-sufficient, uninterrupted space. Dedicated to the worship of the seven planetary gods, the Pantheon is a stunning human version of the sky itself, the Dome of Heaven.

The bronze head of Hadrian (fig. 9.30), which wears a trim beard in the Greek manner, was probably created during the enlightened reign of that remarkable monarch. A combination of the staid portrait style of Republican tradition and the glamorous, more sensuous Hellenistic imperial style, the bust was found in the Thames River under London Bridge. That a masterful portrait of this most urbane of Roman rulers should be found in the outermost reaches of empire symbolizes the international culture of Rome. Writing during the reign of Trajan, the Greek biographer Plutarch remarked, "I am a citizen, not of Athens or of Greece, but of the world."

9.29 Giovanni Paolo Panini, *The Interior of the Pantheon*. Oil on canvas, height 50" (127 cm), width 39" (99 cm). National Gallery of Art, Washington, D.C. (Samuel H. Kress Collection).

Marcus Aurelius, 121–180

The last of the illustrious Antonine emperors,[1] Marcus Aurelius (reigned 161–180) was an unusual combination of distinguished general and Stoic philosopher. Most

9.30 *Portrait Bust of the Emperor Hadrian*. Roman provincial work. Ca. 2nd century AD. Bronze, height 16" (40.6 cm). British Museum, London.
This bust, probably made during Hadrian's reign, shows him wearing a Greek-style beard. It was found in the Thames River, under London Bridge.

un-Roman in his detestation of war, he confined his military activities to defending the borders against barbarian incursions, particularly in the Balkans. It was on that distant frontier that the philosopher-king died in the performance of his Stoic duty. As depicted in the only equestrian statue surviving from the ancient world (fig. 9.31), the emperor wore a beard in the Greek style first adopted by Hadrian. With his right arm extended in the characteristic gesture of a general about to address his troops, the emperor is both commanding and resigned to fulfilling his responsibilities. Vigorous and impatient, the high-spirited warhorse displays the artist's exceptional knowledge of equine anatomy. Mistaken identity assured the survival of the imperial bronze; Christians thought it depicted Constantine.

Rome in Decline

The Empire was in almost continual disruption after the death of Marcus Aurelius in 180. Between 235 and 284 there were no less than twenty-six "barracks emperors" sponsored by various army factions. The accession of Diocletian in 284 replaced anarchy with a rigid despotism under which the Roman Senate lost the last vestige of its by then ephemeral powers. A time of agony and despair, the chaotic third century saw the flourishing of many mystery cults as people sought spiritual salvation in the midst of nihilism. Representative of the malaise of the time, the

1. The very last Antonine was Commodus (reigned 180–192), the son of Marcus Aurelius. Anything but illustrious, he was corrupt, demented, and, ultimately, the victim of a household conspiracy.

9.31 *Equestrian Statue of Marcus Aurelius*, Rome. Ca. AD 161–180. Gilded bronze, height 11'6" (3.5 m). Piazza del Campidoglio, Rome. Photo: Scala, Florence/Art Resource, New York.

Head of a Bearded Man (fig. 9.32) is a study in ambivalence: hopefulness coupled with despair, spiritual aspirations conflicting with the problem of sheer survival. It was the worst of times.

9.32 *Head of a Bearded Man*. Ca. AD 250. Marble, life-size. J. Paul Getty Museum, Santa Monica, California.

9.33   Arch of Constantine, Rome. AD 312–315. Photo: Scala, Florence.

9.35   Head of colossal statue of Constantine, from the Basilica of Constantine, Rome. Ca. AD 330. Marble, height of head as shown 8' 6" (2.6 m) (dimensions of entire statue are not known). Palazzo dei Conservatori, Rome. Photo: Alinari, Florence.

9.34   *Oratio* of Constantine, and the Hadrianic roundels above, on the Arch of Constantine. Height of frieze 3' 4" (1.02 m). Photo: Alinari, Florence.

Constantine, 272–337

Seizing power from his co-regent, Constantine (reigned 312–337) represented the last effective authority in an empire doomed to destruction from external assaults and from internal corruption and decadence.[2] Built to celebrate his assumption of sole imperial power, the Arch of Constantine (fig. 9.33) was wholly dependent on its predecessors for its impressive appearance. In an attempt to recapture the glorious past, the three-arch design was copied from the Arch of Septimus Severus (ca. 203) in the Roman Forum, while the eight Corinthian columns are literally from Domitian's time (reigned 81–96). The free-

2. Constantine himself personified Roman decadence. "Twice married, he murdered Crispus, his son by his first wife, in 326. He had his second wife drowned in the bath; killed his eleven-year-old nephew, then his brother-in-law, after giving his assurance of safe conduct under oath. He murdered his co-regent, Licinius, to become the sole emperor of the West and East." Peter De Rosa, *Vicars of Christ: The Dark Side of the Papacy* (New York: Macmillan Publishing Company, 1988), p. 18.

standing statues, with heads recarved to resemble Constantine, were lifted from monuments to Trajan, Hadrian, and Marcus Aurelius. Despite the borrowed design and transferred columns and statues, there is little trace of the Hellenic tradition. The inferior craftsmanship of the carved reliefs (fig. 9.34) can be explained by a shortage of skilled artists; there had been no official relief sculpture in nearly a century. Despite the technical inadequacies, the shift from classical to a new Constantinian style appears, however, to have been deliberate. Compare, for example, the classical style of the *Augustus of Primaporta* (see fig. 9.15) with the head of Constantine the Great (fig. 9.35). In addition to the notable stylistic differences, it is clear that the latter is intended as a much more obvious symbol of both imperial majesty and spiritual superiority. Part of a colossal statue enthroned in his basilica, the masterful modeling of the head demonstrates a total awareness of the Hellenistic tradition with the significant exception of the extraordinary eyes. Carved even with a marble fleck representing light reflecting from the cornea, these are not the eyes of a mere man; this is an exalted being, unique in authority and vision, with godlike eyes fixed upon infinity. Symbolizing sanctity and sometimes saintliness, oversized eyes become a convention in early Christian and Byzantine art.

Boethius, ca. 475–524

Though a miniature in fact and truly minuscule when compared with the head of Constantine, the *Diptych of Consul Boethius* (bow-E-thi-us; fig. 9.36) is similar to the bust in that the artist has denied the physical reality of Boethius and emphasized instead his authority and spirit. Costume, body, and space are reduced to patterned lines that are more emotional than representational. One of the last Roman consuls and the author of *Consolation of Philosophy* (524), the other-worldliness of Boethius can be compared to the physical reality of the *Augustus of Primaporta*. Both share the commanding arm gesture—a symbol of authority—but all else has changed. In the *Augustus* we see a man with supreme authority and in the *Boethius* there is depicted supreme authority that happens to be a man.

9.36 *Diptych of Consul Boethius*. Ca. 487. Ivory miniature. Museo Romano, Brescia, Italy. Photo: Scala, Florence.

STUDY QUESTIONS

1. The Romans obviously admired Greek art as indicated by so many copies and yet they were frequently uncomfortable with it. Why? Are there any parallels in American attitudes toward twentieth-century art?
2. Roman architecture was generally utilitarian (i.e., responding to public desires and expectations). Was propaganda for the state one of the functions? What do the size, mass, lines, and overall design of triumphal arches, amphitheatres, temples, baths, and the Circus Maximus tell us about the Roman Empire?
3. The style of Roman art shifted during Constantine's reign. Why? Describe the changes and speculate about the significance of the shift.
4. The poem given in a feature box on page 248 by Edgar Allan Poe extols "the glory that was Greece, and the grandeur that was Rome." Explain how this statement applies to the visual arts of the two civilizations.
5. How is the influence of Roman architecture evident in the history and culture of the United States? Consider, for example, government buildings and athletic facilities. What are some prime examples?

SUMMARY

Roman achievements in architecture were notable and still act upon the modern world. The first to achieve mastery of enclosing space, Roman prototypes are visible today in grandiose train stations, monumental public buildings, and the ubiquitous football and soccer stadiums patterned after the Colosseum. With their superbly designed roads, bridges, and aqueducts, Roman engineers made essential contributions to civilizing and humanizing people that were fully as important as their monuments, buildings, and stadiums. Indeed, roads, bridges, and sewers may be as essential for civilized living as art, music, and literature.

Sculpture was as common in the Roman world as billboards are in the United States, but considerably more attractive. Streets, buildings, and homes were filled with portrait busts and freestanding statues or reliefs of the gods of all major and minor religions. Included were masterpieces confiscated from Greece and Egypt and mass-produced copies of Greek works of all periods. Greeks characteristically created while the Romans were often content to copy; Roman artists excelled in portraiture and historical narrative precisely because they copied the world as they saw it.

The little that is left of Roman painting was found mainly in the ruins of Pompeii and Herculaneum (see fig. 9.9), which were buried by the eruption of Vesuvius in AD 79. Excavations that began in the eighteenth century have revealed at least four major styles of painting. Whether this work was accomplished by Greek, Hellenistic, or Roman artists cannot be determined. Furthermore, later development of painting during the enlightened regimes of the Antonines may never be known. Deeply indebted to Greek developments in painting techniques, Roman painters, it is safe to assume, produced works comparable to the Pantheon and the *Augustus of Primaporta*.

CULTURE AND HUMAN VALUES

The Romans were as pragmatic about their art and architecture as with most everything else in their lives. Does it do what it is supposed to do? was a more pertinent question than Is it beautiful? Portrait busts, for example, exactly recalled emperors, statesmen, and ancestors. Their function was to graphically represent a specific person, warts and all, with absolutely no doubt about the subject. The aesthetic quality was of no concern and, indeed, rarely apropos.

Triumphal arches pose a similar problem. Designed to awe and intimidate Rome's conquered foes, they apparently fulfilled their function very well or the Romans wouldn't have built so many. Historically interesting, they are not as artistically inspiring as other structures such as, for example, the amphitheatres.

In fact, roads, bridges, aqueducts, and amphitheatres are consistently more interesting than busts or arches. Why is this so? The answer, in a word, is engineering. An engineer is a problem solver and the Romans produced superb problem solvers. How do I cross the river? Build a bridge. How do I obtain fresh water daily? Construct an aqueduct and plumb the houses and public baths. How do I get from here to there? Design a road.

Roman amphitheatres were designed to solve many problems: large capacity, easy ingress and quick exit, good sightlines, unobtrusive stage equipment, and so forth. The Colosseum is an outstanding example of Roman engineering at its best. All 50,000 spectators could easily see the arena and the sun/rain cover could be cranked into position in a few minutes and retracted just as quickly. After each contest perfume was sprayed throughout the amphitheatre through built-in ducts and the structure could be cleared in five minutes after the last performance. Good architecture, according to the Roman architect Vitruvius, must have firmness, commodity, and delight. The Colosseum is remarkably successful on all counts thanks largely to its sophisticated engineering.

The main point about Roman pragmatism is that it usually worked, which means that, by definition, the Roman virtues of duty, honor, and love of country were true. When combined with Roman practicality and efficiency, the Roman virtues helped build the mightiest empire that the world had yet seen. Theories, concepts, ideas, and ideals may occupy a higher ground but Roman pragmatism made its civilization the dominant way of life in much of Europe, North Africa, and the Middle East.

Judaism
and
Christia

Judaism and Early Christianity

1900 BC–AD 500

	Key Dates	People and Events	Religion	Philosophy and Theology	Art and Literature
1900 BC	**After 1900** Abraham and Israelites migrate from Ur to the Land of Canaan				
1600	**ca. 1600** Israelites follow Joseph into Egypt				
1300	**1300/1200** Moses leads Children of Israel out of Egypt	**ca. 1230** Joshua takes Jericho			
1100	**ca. 1165–1050** Israelite armies battle with Canaanites				
1000		**1020–1000** King Saul defeats Philistines			
900	**933–722** Kingdom of Israel **933–586** Kingdom of Judah	**1000–960** King David **960–933** King Solomon			
800			Prophet: Elijah		
700	**722** Assyria conquers Kingdom of Israel	**722–** "Lost tribes of Israel"	Prophets: Amos, Hosea, Isaiah I, Micah		
600			Prophet: Jeremiah		
500	**586** Nebuchadnezzar II conquers Kingdom of Judah **539–332** Palestine vassal state of Persian Empire	**586–539** Babylonian Captivity	Prophets: Ezekiel, Isaiah II		**ca. 550** Sacred writings in form somewhat like Old Testament
300	**332–63** Palestine vassal state of Alexander and of Egypt				
100					**ca. 100** Old Testament arranged in present form
0	**63 BC** Palestine conquered by Rome; becomes protectorate **ca. 4 BC–AD 29** Jesus Christ	**37–4 BC** Herod, king of Judea **27 BC–AD 14** Reign of Caesar Augustus		**Philo Judaeus** ca. 30 BC–AD 50 Hellenistic Jewish philosopher	**Virgil** 70–19 BC *Aeneid*
AD 100	**50–300** Rise of papacy	**64** Persecution of Christians under Nero **70** Romans destroy Jerusalem and Temple; disperse Jews **93** Persecution of Christians under Domitian	Writing of New Testament (dates approx.): **55** Paul's epistles to Corinthians **60** Acts of Apostles **70** Mark **80–85** Matthew; Luke **93** Revelation **100–120** John	**Epictetus** ca. 60–110 Stoic philosopher, *Discourses*	
200	**180–476** Decline and fall of Rome	**111** Trajan classifies Christians as traitors	**d. 165?** Justin Martyr, *First Apology*	**Tertullian** 160?–240? Latin Father of Church **Origen** 185?–254? Father of Christian theology	
300		**250** Persecution of Christians under Decius	**ca. 200** New Testament becomes canonical Christian text	**Plotinus** 205–270 Founder of Neoplatonism	**ca. 250** Earliest known Christian church, Dura-Europos, Syria; *The Good Shepherd*, Catacombs of St. Callistus, Rome
400	**300–** Growth of monasticism **313** Constantine's Edict of Milan legalizes Christianity throughout Roman Empire **325** First Council of Nicaea condemns Arian heresy **330** Constantine establishes new capital at Constantinople **375–500** Invasions of empire by barbarian tribes **395** Theodosius proclaims Christianity official and only religion of Rome	**302** Persecution of Christians under Diocletian **306–335** Reign of Constantine **314–335** Pope Sylvester I **379–395** Reign of Theodosius I; empire splits into West and East; persecution of non-Christians begins	**ca. 330–379** St. Basil; rules established for Greek church and monasticism **374–397** St. Ambrose as Bishop of Milan	**St. Augustine** 354–430	**ca. 313–** St. John Lateran Basilica, Rome **ca. 330–** Old St. Peter's, Rome **ca. 359** Sarcophagus of Junius Bassus **386–** Basilica of St. Paul's Outside-the-Walls, Rome **397** Augustine, *Confessions*
500	**402** Ravenna new capital of Western Roman Empire **410; 455** Rome sacked by Visigoths and by Vandals **451** Attila the Hun defeated at Battle of Chalons **476** Last Roman emperor deposed **ca. 493–527** Theodoric and Ostrogothic Kingdom; capital at Ravenna	**400–600** Invasions of England by Angles and Saxons **440–461** Pope Leo I the Great; saves Rome from Attila the Hun **St. Benedict** 480–543	**ca. 400** St. Jerome: *Vulgate* (Latin Bible) **413–425** Augustine: *City of God*	**Boethius** ca. 480–524? *The Consolation of Philosophy*	**425–450** Mausoleum of Galla Placidia, Ravenna **430** *Crucifixion*, Church of Santa Sabina, Rome **440–** Basilica of Santa Maria Maggiore, Rome

Hebrew lettering, meaning "Hear O Israel."

CHAPTER 10

The Star and the Cross

Life in the later years of the Roman Empire was marked by increasing pessimism and disillusionment. Epicureanism is grounded on pessimism; Stoicism was at best a resignation to the evils of the world; cults and mystery religions provided little abiding fulfillment. The general malaise was shared by aristocrats, intellectuals and, most especially, the common people. A frequently used Roman epitaph proclaims the melancholy mood of the age:

I was not
I was
I am not
I do not care

One could scarcely go further in apathetic world-weariness.

Of the two conflicting preferences during this period, one was the general disbelief in religion, especially the old Olympian beliefs. The other, paradoxically, was the appeal, however transitory, of mystical religious cults, usually of oriental origin: Mithraism, the worship of Isis, and the cult of Cybele. Whatever the scoffing or indifferent disregard at society's upper level, the poor and uneducated were eager for the emotional appeal of any religiosity that softened their uncertainties and insecurities.

Graeco-Roman culture advocated living according to reason, an intellectual rather than a spiritual existence. For an Aristotle or a Cicero, such a life could be worthwhile and satisfying, but not many men or women in any generation are of such caliber, and even those few are often seen as wanting in human warmth. At best, the God in whom Aristotle found perfection was distant and detached from human affairs, a noble but serenely dispassionate concept.

As important as reason is, it has never been the only human attribute. Call it spirit, emotion, belief, faith—there is something not in the same category. No one can give six good reasons why he or she loves the beloved, for love is not "reasonable," though it is not necessarily contrary to reason; it simply moves in another dimension. The "something" beyond reason may be the compulsion of an ethical ideal or a yearning for spiritual satisfaction. More pronounced in some people than in others, it is rarely totally absent. It is precisely such a range of human experience that the intellectualized traditions of Greece and Rome failed to satisfy.

While the Greek and Roman cultures were developing—cultures devoted to rationalism—an entirely different kind of society had arisen in Palestine. A vast amount of pure intellectual power has gone into the development of Jewish doctrine, but the core of Judaism is faith, as faith is different from but not opposed to reason. The Jewish religion itself, as it has had wider influence through Christianity, wove another strand into the majestic amalgam we call Western civilization.

THE CHOSEN PEOPLE

The Jews would have been just another set of Near Eastern tribes, small in number and lacking talent for art and invention, had it not been for their remarkable religion. Other civilizations have come and gone; Jews have maintained their culture essentially intact for 4,000 years.

The Jews were first called Hebrews (from *Habiru* or *Ibri*; "alien, outcast, nomad"), a descriptive term used mostly by their enemies and still employed today to designate the biblical Jews. Long before the Bible was written, however, these desert nomads had named themselves after the grandson of Abraham, a man originally called Jacob and subsequently named Israel. These, then, were the Israelites, the Children of Israel.

Early Jewish History

Sometime after 1900 BC the Israelites followed Abraham from the Sumerian city of Ur "of the Chaldees," according to the Bible, into the lands northwest of the Euphrates river valley. Several generations later, nomads no longer, they moved west into the Land of Canaan—subsequently called Palestine after the Philistine inhabitants. Sometime after 1600 BC and probably prompted by famine, many Israelites followed Joseph into Egypt, where they prospered along with Joseph, who achieved a position of considerable importance. Time passed until there was a new Pharaoh "who did not know Joseph," according to the Bible. The Children of Israel were reduced to slavery but were finally delivered out of bondage by an Israelite with the Egyptian name of Moses. Leading his people out of Egypt and into Sinai (ca. 1300 BC), Moses gave them the concept of a single tribal god, Yahweh (later mistranslated as Jehovah), and a **covenant** with Yahweh based on their acceptance of the commandments that, according to the Book of Exodus, Moses had carried down the mountain.

Following the death of Moses, after about forty years "in the wilderness," the Promised Land "flowing with milk and honey" was taken by conquest, with the key city of Jericho falling to Joshua around 1230 BC. By 1020 the twelve tribes had been unified and a monarchy forged with Saul as the first king. It was under Saul's leadership that the tenacious Philistines were finally subdued.

The height of Israelite political power was reached with the Twelve Tribes of Israel under King David (1000–960 BC) and his son Solomon (960–933 BC). After Solomon's death the accumulated resentment against his policies of forced labor and high taxes led to the secession of the ten northern tribes to form a separate Kingdom of Israel. The two southern tribes of Judah and Benjamin, though holding to the capital of Jerusalem, were left with the apparently weaker Kingdom of Judah[1] (map 10.1).

Israel did not survive long as a divided kingdom, falling to the Assyrians in 722 BC. Following the standard Assyrian procedure, the kingdom was brutally ravaged and the Ten Tribes dispersed forever, to be known thereafter as the Lost Tribes of Israel. Judah managed to survive until 586 BC, when it was conquered by Nebuchadnezzar II and most of its citizens sent into an exile known to history as the Babylonian Captivity (586–538 BC). The subsequent Persian conquest of Babylon freed the Jews, some of whom returned to Jerusalem where they eventually rebuilt the Temple of Solomon. No longer a commonwealth, they were politically subservient to three successive empires: the Persian (539–332 BC); Alexander and the Ptolemies of Egypt (332–63 BC); and the might of Rome, which proved fatal.

The Romans never knew what to do with the Jews because nothing worked. After their conquest of Palestine in 63 BC, the Romans gave the country a special status as a protectorate. Among other privileges, the Jews were excused from military service and permitted freedom of religion. This was not enough. In AD 66 the Jews launched what turned out to be their most disastrous rebellion against Rome. By AD 70 Jerusalem was totally destroyed and much of the population dead or driven from the land, a Diaspora (dea-AS-po-ra; "scattering") that lasted until the establishment of the State of Israel in 1948.

Four Unique Aspects of Judaism

The Jews' will to resist and to survive was based on their religion, Judaism,[2] four aspects of which were different from all other Near Eastern religions.

1. Monotheism: there was only one God and he came to be viewed as universal.
2. Covenant: God chose Israel to be his people and they accepted him as their God.
3. Graven images: images of God or of any living thing were prohibited.
4. The name of God (Yahweh, meaning "he causes to be" or "the creator") was not to be taken "in vain," i.e., was not to be spoken.

Let us examine each of these concepts. Beginning with the Mosaic period in the Sinai, Yahweh was the primary God among many: "You shall have no other gods before me" (Exodus 20:3). This concept gradually evolved into a monotheism in which there was one Israelite God and, later, one universal God. The first people to insist upon monotheism, the Jews, throughout their history, found this to be their greatest source of strength.

The covenant was a bond with Yahweh that the Hebrews made of their own free will. Moses climbed the mountain and returned with knowledge of God's will—"commandments" inscribed on tablets of stone and subsequently amplified in the **Torah**. In a narrow sense the Torah consists of the first five books of the Bible, the so-called **Pentateuch**, or Books of Moses. The word "torah"

Map 10.1   Palestine, ca. 900 BC.

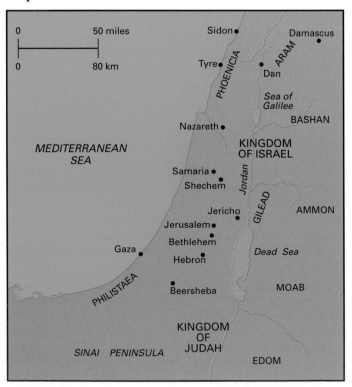

---

1. The inhabitants of Judah (later called Judea) were thereafter known as Jews.
2. A term coined by Greek-speaking Jews to distinguish their religious way of life from that of the Hellenes. Though the term is late, the religion to which it refers goes back to the beginnings of Jewish spiritual life.

means "law" but it also means "teaching" or "direction." In the broad modern sense, Torah refers to the total content of God's unending revelation to and through Israel.

The prohibition of graven images separated Judaism from all other religions, which represented their gods in a variety of ways. This stricture, a defense against idolatry, effectively nullified any significant artistic development. The injunction against using the Lord's name in vain emphasized a reverence unknown to other ancient religions. In sum, Judaism was a People in covenant with God, a Book (the Hebrew Scriptures), a Way of Life, and a Hope grounded in Faith.

Prophecy

The Jewish prophets of the eighth to fifth centuries BC emerged from a tradition of augurs and seers who sought to ascertain the divine will and to forecast the future through dreams, divinations, and induced ecstasy. Eventually these professionals were denounced as "false prophets" and replaced by a succession of preachers, mystics, moralists, and poets who felt they were speaking for Yahweh. Stressing righteousness and justice, prophets such as Amos and Isaiah functioned as restorers and conservators of Israel's inspiring spiritual heritage. Not always accepted by various classes of society, they preached an uncompromising and lofty doctrine: Yahweh was the only god and he demanded the highest ethical standards.

Amos

The first and perhaps most important of the notable eighth-century prophets, Amos preached against luxury, corruption, and selfishness, pointing the way to altruism and a higher form of religion.

> [11]Therefore because you trample upon the poor
>   and take from him exactions of wheat,
> you have built houses of hewn stone,
>   but you shall not dwell in them;
> you have planted pleasant vineyards,
>   but you shall not drink their wine.
> [12]For I know how many are your transgressions,
>   and how great are your sins—
> you who afflict the righteous, who take a bribe,
>   and turn aside the needy in the gate.
> [13]Therefore he who is prudent will keep silent in such a
>   time;
>   for it is an evil time.
> [14]Seek good, and not evil,
>   that you may live;
> and so the LORD, the God of hosts, will be with you,
>   as you have said.
> [15]Hate evil, and love good,
>   and establish justice in the gate;
> it may be that the LORD, the God of hosts,
>   will be gracious to the remnant of Joseph.
>
> Amos 5:11–15

Isaiah

Active around 740–700 BC, Isaiah[3] was the prophet of faith, preaching an abiding trust in the providence of God. A prophet of doom like the other preachers, Isaiah saw that a purging was necessary in the interest of spiritual betterment in a kindlier and more loving world. He was among the first to picture a warless world under the benign rule of a Prince of Peace, a Messiah ("anointed one") descended from the House of David.

> [1]There shall come forth a shoot from the stump of Jesse,
>   and a branch shall grow out of his roots.
> [2]And the Spirit of the LORD shall rest upon him,
>   the spirit of wisdom and understanding,
>   the spirit of counsel and might,
>   the spirit of knowledge and the fear of the LORD.
> [3]And his delight shall be in the fear of the LORD.
> He shall not judge by what his eyes see,
>   or decide by what his ears hear;
> [4]but with righteousness he shall judge the poor,
>   and decide with equity for the meek of the earth;
> and he shall smite the earth with the rod of his mouth,
>   and with the breath of his lips he shall slay the
>   wicked.
> [5]Righteousness shall be the girdle of his waist,
>   and faithfulness the girdle of his loins.
> [6]The wolf shall dwell with the lamb,
>   and the leopard shall lie down with the kid,
> and the calf and the lion and the fatling together,
>   and a little child shall lead them.
> [7]The cow and the bear shall feed;
>   their young shall lie down together;
>   and the lion shall eat straw like the ox.
> [8]The sucking child shall play over the hole of the asp,
>   and the weaned child shall put his hand on the
>   adder's den.
> [9]They shall not hurt or destroy
>   in all my holy mountain;
> for the earth shall be full of the knowledge of the
>   LORD
>   as the waters cover the sea.
>
> Isaiah 11:1–9

> For unto us a child is born,
>   to us a son is given;
> and the government will be upon his shoulder,
>   and his name will be called
> "Wonderful Counselor, Mighty God,
> Everlasting Father, Prince of Peace."
>
> Isaiah 9:6

---

3. The Book of Isaiah contains prophecies attributed to Isaiah or his disciples (chapters 1–35) and those by an unknown prophet of the sixth century called Second Isaiah (Deutero-Isaiah; chapters 40–55). Chapters 56–66 were written still later by a Third Isaiah (Trito-Isaiah). Chapters 36–39 were taken directly from 2 Kings. Two manuscripts of the book were found among the Dead Sea Scrolls.

Ezekiel

During the Babylonian captivity, when his people were far from home, their city and temple destroyed, Ezekiel preached the universality of the faith and of the personal relationship between the individual Jew and his God. God existed wherever the people were; the city and the temple were not indispensable. Each person had the option of selecting good over evil and turning from evil ways to a righteous life.

> [25]"Yet you say, 'The way of the Lord is not just.' Hear now, O house of Israel: Is my way not just? Is it not your ways that are not just? [26]When a righteous man turns away from his righteousness and commits iniquity, he shall die for it; for the iniquity which he has committed he shall die. [27]Again, when a wicked man turns away from the wickedness he has committed and does what is lawful and right, he shall save his life. [28]Because he considered and turned away from all the transgressions which he had committed, he shall surely live, he shall not die. [29]Yet the house of Israel says, 'The way of the Lord is not just.' O house of Israel, are my ways not just? Is it not your ways that are not just?
>
> [30]"Therefore I will judge you, O house of Israel, every one according to his ways, says the Lord GOD. Repent and turn from all your transgressions, lest iniquity be your ruin. [31]Cast away from you all the transgressions which you have committed against me, and get yourselves a new heart and a new spirit! Why will you die, O house of Israel? [32]For I have no pleasure in the death of any one, says the Lord GOD; so turn, and live."
>
> Ezekiel 18:25–32

Isaiah

The celebrated unknown prophet of the exile, generally known as Second Isaiah, was the great architect of Jewish ethical monotheism. Climaxing the prophetic movement, his ethical and religious insight set the sufferings of the Jews against a background of God's eventual redemption of the entire world. He saw the Jews as a people chosen to exemplify in their characters and lives the spiritual presence of the Lord. "A light to the nations" (Isaiah 42:1), their suffering had not been in vain. The world would say of Israel:

> [3]He was despised and rejected by men;
>   a man of sorrows, and acquainted with grief,
> and as one from whom men hide their faces
>   he was despised, and we esteemed him not.
> [4]Surely he has borne our griefs
>   and carried our sorrows,
> yet we esteemed him stricken,
>   smitten by God, and afflicted.
> [5]But he was wounded for our transgressions,
>   he was bruised for our iniquities;

> upon him was the chastisement that made us whole,
>   and with his stripes we are healed.
> [6]All we like sheep have gone astray;
>   we have turned every one to his own way;
> and the LORD has laid on him
>   the iniquity of us all.
>
> Isaiah 53:3–6

They were to return to the New Jerusalem where the work of redemption would be a model for all the world.

> [1]Comfort, comfort my people,
>   says your God.
> [2]Speak tenderly to Jerusalem,
>   and cry to her
> that her warfare is ended,
>   that her iniquity is pardoned,
> that she has received from the LORD'S hand
>   double for all her sins.
> [3]A voice cries:
>   "In the wilderness prepare the way of the LORD,
>   make straight in the desert a highway for our God.
> [4]Every valley shall be lifted up,
>   and every mountain and hill be made low;
> the uneven ground shall become level,
>   and the rough places a plain.
> [5]And the glory of the LORD shall be revealed,
>   and all flesh shall see it together,
>   for the mouth of the LORD has spoken."
> [6]A voice says, "Cry!"
>   And I said, "What shall I cry?"
> All flesh is grass,
>   and all its beauty is like the flower of the field.
> [7]The grass withers, the flower fades,
>   when the breath of the LORD blows upon it;
>   surely the people is grass.
> [8]The grass withers, the flower fades;
>   but the word of our God will stand for ever.
> [9]Get you up to a high mountain,
>   O Zion, herald of good tidings,
> lift up your voice with strength,
>   O Jerusalem, herald of good tidings,
>   lift it up, fear not;
> say to the cities of Judah,
>   "Behold your God!"
>
> Isaiah 40:1–9

The profound insights of Second Isaiah strongly influenced later Judaism but were even more significant for early Christianity. His writings were studied and pondered by those who awaited the coming of the Messiah. In particular the story of the sufferings of Israel (see Isaiah 53:3–6 above) was so specific and individualized that later generations came to believe that he was speaking of a particular person, a Messiah who would redeem the world through his suffering. In Jesus of Nazareth the early Christians found that Messiah.

CHRISTIANITY

Some of the Teachings of Jesus

Jesus was born in the year we now call 4 BC, or possibly 6 BC,[4] a time that was ripe for his message of hope and love. He preached for possibly three years, but in the 2,000 years since that time—whether people have believed his teachings or not, whether they have acted upon them or not—men and women throughout what was once called "Christendom" have been hearing the teachings of Jesus. What are the cardinal points of his teaching? These: that one God (a Personal Spirit, not an abstract idea nor a principle) is not only the Creator but also the loving Father of all humankind; that all people are consequently the children of God, and that as a result all men and women are brothers and sisters; that as children of God, human beings are capable of better lives than they lead; that their human inadequacies, imperfections, and shortcomings can be forgiven if they are repentant; that life is eternal, and death is not extinction; that "all the Law and the Prophets" hangs upon the joint commandment to "Love thy God, and thy neighbor as thyself"; and that the intention—the act of the personality—is of greater importance than the deed—the act of the person.

Not the least of the appeals of Christianity is the joy and hope that it carries with it because of its doctrine of Christ as Redeemer. Theologically, one of several explanations may be stated in this way: because of the sin of Adam, humankind as a whole carried with it the taint of original sin, a sort of moral disease. But God, loving all people, sought to redeem them. This was accomplished through the mystery of **Incarnation** in which God became man, taking to himself all of humankind's inherent guilt. Then, in Christ's death as a mortal, the guilt is atoned, and human beings are set free. The possibility of salvation and eternal life with God, from that moment on, lies before each person. In the world-weary and guilt-ridden time of the late Roman Empire such a possibility could bring hope and joy to the believer.

All of these teachings affect the world of here and now, for Christianity is a "social" religion; its effects are seen in the daily acts of people in society. It is not necessarily a religion in which the believers isolate themselves and seek individual salvation through private contemplation, although some have followed this path. For most Christians their faith entails involvement and commitment. Love must prompt the worshiper to perform acts of love, mercy, and compassion as evidence of an inward change. The three words that Jesus addressed to Peter can summarize his teaching: "Feed my sheep."

---

4. The idea of denominating the years of the Christian era was introduced in AD 525 by Dionysius Exiguus; the BC sequence extending backwards from the birth of Christ was not added until the seventeenth century.

Early Christianity

Jesus left no written record of his work nor are there any surviving accounts contemporary with his ministry. A collection of his sayings, written in Aramaic, disappeared before AD 60, and scholars are still debating some of the references to Jesus in the Dead Sea Scrolls. His life, character, and message inspired hope and joy but without any documentation this was not sufficient basis for a new religion. Christianity is concerned above all with God's relation to human beings. It remained for the followers of Jesus to construct a systematic theology as a solid foundation for the propagation of the new faith.

Written accounts in Greek began to appear several decades after Christ's death: St. Paul's Epistles to the Corinthians (ca. AD 55); the Acts of the Apostles (ca. AD 60); the four Gospels telling the story of Jesus: Mark (ca. AD 70); Matthew and Luke (ca. AD 80–85); and John (ca. AD 100–120). By about AD 200 the texts were revised in Alexandria into a canonical Christian text.

Paul

An upper-class Jew of Orthodox parentage, St. Paul (Saul of Tarsus) was first a persecutor of Christians and later one of the most ardent missionaries of the faith. A Hellenized Jew, Paul took the position that "there is neither Jew nor Greek" (Galatians 3:28). St. Peter at first disagreed, contending that the Christian message was intended only for Jews and converted Gentiles. Paul argued (and Peter later agreed) that the Law was no longer valid, even for Jews; it could only bring people to an understanding of their dependence on Christ in a new covenant with Christ the Savior. Sweeping aside Jewish rituals and practices, Paul, the "apostle to the Gentiles," carried the message of salvation through faith in Christ throughout the eastern Mediterranean and into Rome itself.

An enthusiastic teacher, organizer, and administrator, Paul was neither a theologian nor a logician. Confirmed by his conversion experience on the road to Damascus, Paul believed that faith was a gift of God. Christians had only to accept the discipline of the church and to lead quiet, faithful, and firmly Christian lives.

Logos and John

A synthesis of Judaic, Greek, and Christian ideas, Christian theology developed separately from the work of the Apostle Paul. In his Prologue, which introduces the fourth Gospel, John states that

> [1]In the beginning was the Word, and the Word was with God, and the Word was God. [2]He was in the beginning with God; [3]all things were made through him, and without him was not anything made that was made. [4]In him was life, and the life was the light of men. [5]The light shines in the darkness, and the darkness has not overcome it.
>
> John 1:1–5

In the Greek of the New Testament, "word" is a translation of *logos*, a word as old as the Greek language. Introduced by Herakleitos in the fifth century BC, *logos* was a principle of cosmic interpretation. Constantly changing, the cosmos was a total process becoming controlled by an agency called *logos*. To avoid chaos, change had to conform to fixed patterns; *logos* was thus an intelligent and eternal agent that imposed an orderly process upon change.

Though the concept of *logos* is vague and unspecified in Plato and Aristotle, the Stoics took it from them but used *logos* to designate a divine element present in all men. It remained for Philo Judaeus of Alexandria (ca. 30 BC–AD 50) to go beyond the Stoics and consciously construct a synthesis of Hebraic and Hellenic philosophy. Philo saw *logos* as a mediator between God and man and as a translation of the Hebrew word for "wisdom." As a personal agent of God in the creation of the world, *logos* was not identical with God but distinctly separate from him.

The Prologue of John is thus a creation story; Jesus is a divine being whose existence antedates the world itself. God's relation to this imperfect world was through the intervention of the *logos*; in Christ "the Word became flesh and dwelt among us, full of grace and truth" (John 1:14). It can be said that Herakleitos and Second Isaiah meet in John, representing two contrasting civilizations which are synthesized into a Christian philosophy of history.[5]

WOMEN AND EARLY CHRISTIANITY

The role of women in the early development of the Christian religion has only recently been studied. After the death of Christ women served as missionaries, deaconesses, and ministers. The book of Acts (16:14–15) mentions Lydia, the first Christian convert of Paul's ministry in Macedonia, and the early evangelist Prisca (or Priscilla; 18:18). Numerous letters of the Apostle Paul cite the work of women. Phoebe is identified as a deaconess and Mary and Junia are called "co-workers" by Paul in Romans 16. He also says in Philippians 4:2–3 that Eodia and Syntyche "labored side by side with me in the gospel."

Epiphanius (d. ca. 403), an early Christian writer, argued against women baptizing and performing priestly functions, a sure sign that women were doing these things. As the church grew more formal in its theology, dogma, and rituals, the role of women became ever more constricted. Between the third and fifth centuries they were gradually eliminated from any meaningful participation in official church rites. Tertullian (ca. 160–230) and John Chrysostom (d. ca. 407) were adamant in their hostility to women in the church and their writings reinforced the position adopted by the Church of Rome for the past fifteen centuries.

THE DEAD SEA SCROLLS

First found in caves near the Dead Sea in Jordan in 1947, these were one of the great historical and scholarly discoveries of the century. Written in Hebrew, Aramaic, and Greek, they date from the first century BC to about AD 50 and were left there by the Qumran community, which some scholars identify with the Essenes, a strict ascetic Jewish communal sect. The scrolls were mostly bits and pieces but, when painstakingly assembled, they included many parts of the Old Testament (including two manuscripts of the Book of Isaiah; fig. 10.1), some New Testament, and much non-Biblical Jewish literature. The Old Testament material is much older than any existing manuscripts. Some parallels between the Qumran scrolls and the New Testament led to the much-disputed suggestion that Jesus and John the Baptist were Essenes. The concern that some of this material might contradict or invalidate any part of the Bible has proven, so far, to be unjustified.

10.1 The Great Isaiah Scroll, columns, XLVIII–LI (Chapters 58:6–65:4), from Qumran Cave, Israel. Ca. 100 BC. Parchment, length 24' (7.34 m). Israel Museum, Jerusalem.

5. See chapter 12 for subsequent developments in Christian theology.
6. Christianity was not exclusively a Western development, having been well established in Ethiopia as early as the third century.

THE IMPACT OF CHRISTIANITY

Objective study of the historical Jesus and of the facts about his life and death leaves some basic questions unanswered. Was he the Messiah, "Son of God," "son of man," a religious reformer, prophet, humanitarian, inspired teacher? Or was he, as his Jewish critics claim, a blasphemer and an impostor? Currently available sources have failed to settle the issue, and the multiplicity of Christian beliefs (Roman Catholic, Orthodox, varieties of Protestantism) testifies to the different interpretations of the evidence.

Nevertheless, the Christian emphasis on the importance of the human personality carries a religious sanction weightier than the speculations of the philosophers. The worth and dignity of the individual soul, and its responsibility to itself, has been a shaping influence in Western thought.

As discussed earlier, reality, for the Greeks, was the individual and for the Romans it was the state. What the two cultures had in common was their secular view of the world. Neither the Greeks nor the Romans rejected religion or religious beliefs. There were, in fact, several religions and many believers but religion did not play a central role in the classical world. The rise of Christianity caused a massive shift from a secular to a religious worldview with God as the ultimate reality. The new view of reality caused major changes in values and value systems, which we shall examine in later chapters.

Christianity's expansion was almost in direct proportion to the decline of the Roman Empire, spreading inexorably from an obscure, remote Roman province practically throughout the known world.[6] Its message of hope, joy, salvation, and a merciful and loving God in a world that knew only the sterner aspects of justice in a declining empire made its welcome assured (map 10.2). Encompassing the whole of life, and able to take to itself the good things of any civilization, Christianity could appropriate the best of Greek thought, as well as Rome's most notable products of organization and law. With the passage of time it produced such diverse offshoots as the elegance and beauty of Chartres Cathedral, the terror of witchcraft trials, and the horrors of the Inquisition. Its impact upon the Western world is fundamental.

Map 10.2 The early Christian world.

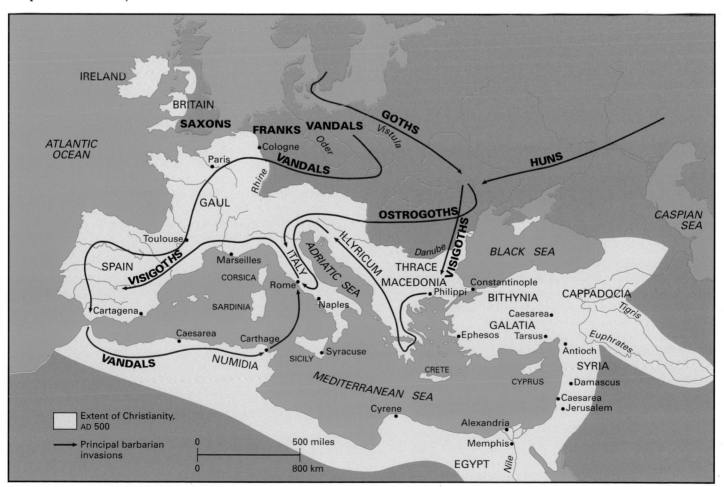

STUDY QUESTIONS

1. What were the significant events that occurred on approximately the following dates? BC: 1900, 1300, 1230, 1000, 933, 586–539, 332–63, 63, 4; AD: 64, 200, 313. What was going on in Egypt and Mesopotamia on or about these dates (through 63 BC)?
2. Four aspects of Judaism differentiated it from all other Near Eastern religions. What were these?
3. How do the Old Testament prophets differ from Greek seers such as Teiresias in *Oedipus the King*?
4. What were the basic teachings of Jesus and how did these differ from the Judaism of his time?

THE BIBLE

The Bible (Gk., *Ta Biblia*, "The Books") has exercised a more profound influence upon Western civilization than any other literary work. Its style alone has burnished the tongues of poets and writers from Chaucer to Shakespeare to Lincoln, and its ethical tenets have become basic to the codes and customs of Western culture. Of its two main divisions, the Old Testament (thirty-nine books in the King James Version) was written almost entirely in Hebrew (with a little Aramaic) from the eleventh to the second century BC. The New Testament (twenty-seven books in the King James Version) was written in Greek from about AD 40 to possibly as late as 150.

Divided into three parts, the Hebrew Scripture (Old Testament) consists of the Law (Pentateuch or Torah), the Prophets, and the Hagiographa ("Sacred writings").

LITERARY SELECTION 24

Psalms of David

The Hagiographa includes the **Psalms**, a hymnal (**Psalter**) reflecting the whole history of Jewish worship. The Psalmists sing Israel's praise of God the creator, intone their sorrow for national guilt and tribulations, and carol the songs of salvation. Following is a Psalm of salvation and glory.[7]

¹Praise the LORD!
Praise God in his sanctuary;
  praise him in his mighty firmament!
²Praise him for his mighty deeds;
  praise him according to his exceeding greatness!

---

7. The translations included in this chapter are all from the American Revised Standard Version (RSV).

³Praise him with trumpet sound;
  praise him with lute and harp!
⁴Praise him with timbrel and dance;
  praise him with strings and pipe!
⁵Praise him with sounding cymbals;
  praise him with loud clashing cymbals!
⁶Let everything that breathes praise the LORD!
Praise the LORD!

Psalm 150

Apparently composed during the Babylonian Captivity (586–538 BC), Psalm 137 is a Lamentation. Though the condition of the Jews in Babylon was relatively favorable, they mourned the destruction of Jerusalem and their separation from the homeland.

This magnificent poem was frequently used in the worship services of American slaves in remembrance of their African homeland.

¹By the waters of Babylon,
there we sat down and wept,
  when we remembered Zion.
²On the willows there
  we hung up our lyres.
³For there our captors
  required of us songs,
and our tormentors, mirth, saying,
  "Sing us one of the songs of Zion!"
⁴How shall we sing the LORD'S song
  in a foreign land?
⁵If I forget you, O Jerusalem,
  let my right hand wither!
⁶Let my tongue cleave to the roof of my mouth,
  if I do not remember you,
if I do not set Jerusalem
  above my highest joy!
⁷Remember, O LORD, against the E'domites
  the day of Jerusalem,
how they said, "Rase it, rase it!
  Down to its foundations!"
⁸O daughter of Babylon, you devastator!
  Happy shall he be who requites you
  with what you have done to us!
⁹Happy shall he be who takes your little ones
  and dashes them against the rock!

Psalm 137

LITERARY SELECTION 25

Ecclesiastes

From the Writings part of the Old Testament, Ecclesiastes (Gk., "the preacher") is representative of pessimistic Oriental wisdom (teaching) literature. It dates from the third century BC and reflects some of the inroads of Greek civilization, but not enough to disturb the basic philosophy that all is vanity and that a young man should enjoy his youth.

[1]For everything there is a season, and a time for every
    matter under heaven:
[2]a time to be born, and a time to die;
 a time to plant, and a time to pluck up what is planted;
[3]a time to kill, and a time to heal;
 a time to break down, and a time to build up;
[4]a time to weep, and a time to laugh;
 a time to mourn, and a time to dance;
[5]a time to cast away stones, and a time to gather stones
    together;
 a time to embrace, and a time to refrain from embracing;
[6]a time to seek, and a time to lose;
 a time to keep, and a time to cast away;
[7]a time to rend, and a time to sew;
 a time to keep silence, and a time to speak;
[8]a time to love, and a time to hate;
 a time for war, and a time for peace.
[9]What gain has the worker from his toil?

[10]I have seen the business that God has given to the sons of men to be busy with. He has made everything beautiful in its time; also he has put eternity into man's mind, yet so that he cannot find out what God has done from the beginning to the end. [11]I know that there is nothing better for them than to be happy and enjoy themselves as long as they live; [13]also that it is God's gift to man that every one should eat and drink and take pleasure in all his toil. [14]I know that whatever God does endures for ever; nothing can be added to it, nor anything taken from it; God has made it so, in order that men should fear before him. [15]That which is, already has been; that which is to be, already has been; and God seeks what has been driven away. [16]Moreover I saw under the sun that in the place of justice, even there was wickedness, and in the place of righteousness, even there was wickedness. [17]I said in my heart, God will judge the righteous and the wicked, for he has appointed a time for every matter, and for every work. [18]I said in my heart with regard to the sons of men that God is testing them to show them that they are but beasts [19]For the fate of the sons of men and the fate of beasts is the same; as one dies, so dies the other. They all have the same breath, and man has no advantage over the beasts; for all is vanity. [20]All go to one place; all are from the dust, and all turn to dust again. [21]Who knows whether the spirit of man goes upward and the spirit of the beast goes down to the earth? [22]So I saw that there is nothing better than that a man should enjoy his work, for that is his lot; who can bring him to see what will be after him?

Ecclesiastes 3

LITERARY SELECTION 26

The Sermon on the Mount

The New Testament contains four sections: (1) the Gospels and Acts of the Apostles, (2) the Epistles of Paul, (3) the pastoral and general Epistles, and (4) the Book of Revelation. Mark's Gospel emphasizes the human aspect of Jesus, while Matthew and Luke include substantial additions dealing mainly with the birth and teaching of Jesus, including the Sermon on the Mount and the parables. The basic ethical teachings of Christ are presented in the Sermon on the Mount, in which the Ten Commandments of Moses are compared with a new ethic. Beginning with the statement "You have heard that it was said to the men of old," Jesus takes each commandment in turn and contrasts it with his own commandment. As presented by Matthew, Jesus is the new Moses expounding a new Torah, which commands a higher righteousness than that found even in the best of Judaism.

5 Seeing the crowds, he went up on the mountain, and when he sat down his disciples came to him. [2]And he opened his mouth and taught them, saying:
    [3]"Blessed are the poor in spirit, for theirs is the kingdom of heaven.
    [4]"Blessed are those who mourn, for they shall be comforted.
    [5]"Blessed are the meek, for they shall inherit the earth.
    [6]"Blessed are those who hunger and thirst for righteousness, for they shall be satisfied.
    [7]"Blessed are the merciful, for they shall obtain mercy.
    [8]"Blessed are the pure in heart, for they shall see God.
    [9]"Blessed are the peacemakers, for they shall be called sons of God.
    [10]"Blessed are those who are persecuted for righteousness' sake, for theirs is the kingdom of heaven.
    [11]"Blessed are you when men revile you and persecute you and utter all kinds of evil against you falsely on my account. [12]Rejoice and be glad, for your reward is great in heaven, for so men persecuted the prophets who were before you.
    [13]"You are the salt of the earth; but if salt has lost its taste, how can its saltness be restored? It is no longer good for anything except to be thrown out and trodden under foot by men.
    [14]"You are the light of the world. A city set on a hill cannot be hid. [15]Nor do men light a lamp and put it under a bushel, but on a stand, and it gives light to all in the house. [16]Let your light so shine before men, that they may see your good works and give glory to your Father who is in heaven.
    [17]"Think not that I have come to abolish the law and the prophets; I have come not to abolish them but to fulfill them. [18]For truly, I say to you, till heaven and earth pass away, not an iota, not a dot, will pass from the law until all is accomplished. [19]Whoever then relaxes one of the least of these commandments and teaches men so, shall be called least in the kingdom of heaven; but he who does them and teaches them shall be called great in the kingdom of heaven. [20]For I tell you, unless your righteousness exceeds that of the scribes and Pharisees, you will never enter the kingdom of heaven.

²¹"You have heard that it was said to the men of old, 'You shall not kill; and whoever kills shall be liable to judgment.' ²²But I say to you that every one who is angry with his brother shall be liable to judgment; whoever insults his brother shall be liable to the council, and whoever says, 'You fool!' shall be liable to the hell of fire. ²³So if you are offering your gift at the altar, and there remember that your brother has something against you, ²⁴leave your gift there before the altar and go; first be reconciled to your brother and then come and offer your gift. ²⁵Make friends quickly with your accuser, while you are going with him to court, lest your accuser hand you over to the judge, and the judge to the guard, and you be put in prison; ²⁶truly, I say to you, you will never get out till you have paid the last penny.

²⁷"You have heard that it was said, 'You shall not commit adultery.' ²⁸But I say to you that every one who looks at a woman lustfully has already committed adultery with her in his heart. ²⁹If your right eye causes you to sin, pluck it out and throw it away; it is better that you lose one of your members than that your whole body be thrown into hell. ³⁰And if your right hand causes you to sin, cut it off and throw it away; it is better that you lose one of your members than that your whole body go into hell.

³¹"It was also said, 'Whoever divorces his wife, let him give her a certificate of divorce.' ³²But I say to you that every one who divorces his wife, except on the ground of unchastity, makes her an adulteress; and whoever marries a divorced woman commits adultery.

³³"Again you have heard that it was said to the men of old, 'You shall not swear falsely, but shall perform to the Lord what you have sworn.' ³⁴But I say to you, do not swear at all, either by heaven, for it is the throne of God, ³⁵or by the earth, for it is his footstool, or by Jerusalem, for it is the city of the great King. ³⁶And do not swear by your head, for you cannot make one hair white or black. ³⁷Let what you say be simply 'Yes' or 'No'; anything more than this comes from evil.

³⁸"You have heard that it was said, 'An eye for an eye and a tooth for a tooth.' ³⁹But I say to you, Do not resist one who is evil. But if any one strikes you on the right cheek, turn to him the other also; ⁴⁰and if any one would sue you and take your coat, let him have your cloak as well; ⁴¹and if any one forces you to go one mile, go with him two miles. ⁴²Give to him who begs from you, and do not refuse him who would borrow from you.

⁴³"You have heard that it was said, 'You shall love your neighbor and hate your enemy.' ⁴⁴But I say to you, Love your enemies and pray for those who persecute you, ⁴⁵so that you may be sons of your Father who is in heaven; for he makes his sun rise on the evil and on the good, and sends rain on the just and on the unjust. ⁴⁶For if you love those who love you, what reward have you? Do not even the tax collectors do the same? ⁴⁷And if you salute only your brethren, what more are you doing than others? Do not even the Gentiles do the same? ⁴⁸You, therefore, must be perfect, as your heavenly Father is perfect.

6 "Beware of practicing your piety before men in order to be seen by them; for then you will have no reward from your Father who is in heaven.

²"Thus, when you give alms, sound no trumpet before you, as the hypocrites do in the synagogues and in the streets, that they may be praised by men. Truly, I say to you, they have their reward. ³But when you give alms, do not let your left hand know what your right hand is doing, ⁴so that your alms may be in secret; and your Father who sees in secret will reward you.

⁵"And when you pray, you must not be like the hypocrites; for they love to stand and pray in the synagogues and at the street corners, that they may be seen by men. Truly, I say to you, they have their reward. ⁶But when you pray, go into your room and shut the door and pray to your Father who is in secret; and your Father who sees in secret will reward you.

⁷"And in praying do not heap up empty phrases as the Gentiles do; for they think that they will be heard for their many words. ⁸Do not be like them, for your Father knows what you need before you ask him. ⁹Pray then like this:

'Our Father who art in heaven,
Hallowed be thy name.
¹⁰Thy kingdom come,
Thy will be done,
    On earth as it is in heaven.
¹¹Give us this day our daily bread;
¹²And forgive us our debts,
    As we also have forgiven our debtors;
¹³And lead us not into temptation,
    But deliver us from evil.'

¹⁴"For if you forgive men their trespasses, your heavenly Father also will forgive you; ¹⁵but if you do not forgive men their trespasses, neither will your Father forgive your trespasses.

¹⁶"And when you fast, do not look dismal, like the hypocrites, for they disfigure their faces that their fasting may be seen by men. Truly, I say to you, they have their reward. ¹⁷But when you fast, anoint your head and wash your face, ¹⁸that your fasting may not be seen by men but by your Father who is in secret; and your Father who sees in secret will reward you.

¹⁹"Do not lay up for yourselves treasures on earth, where moth and rust consume and where thieves break in and steal, ²⁰but lay up for yourselves treasures in heaven, where neither moth nor rust consumes and where thieves do not break in and steal; ²¹for where your treasure is, there will your heart be also.

²²"The eye is the lamp of the body. So, if your eye is sound, your whole body will be full of light; ²³but if your eye is not sound, your whole body will be full of darkness. If then the light in you is darkness, how great is the darkness!

²⁴"No one can serve two masters; for either he will hate the one and love the other, or he will be devoted to the one and despise the other. You cannot serve God and mammon.

²⁵"Therefore I tell you, do not be anxious about your life, what you shall eat or what you shall drink, nor about your body, what you shall put on. Is not life more than food, and the body more than the clothing? ²⁶Look at the birds of the air: they neither sow nor reap nor gather into barns, and yet your heavenly Father feeds them. Are you not of more value than they? ²⁷And which of you by being anxious can add one cubit to his span of life? ²⁸And why be anxious about clothing? Consider the lilies of the field, how they grow; they neither toil nor spin; ²⁹yet I tell you, even Solomon in all his glory was not arrayed like one of these. ³⁰But if God so clothes the grass of the field, which today is alive and tomorrow is thrown into the oven, will he not much more clothe you, O men of little faith? ³¹Therefore do not be anxious, saying, 'What shall we eat?' or 'What shall we drink?' or 'What shall we wear?' ³²For the Gentiles seek all these things; and your heavenly Father

knows that you need them all. ³³But seek first his kingdom and his righteousness, and all these things shall be yours as well.

³⁴"Therefore do not be anxious about tomorrow, for tomorrow will be anxious for itself. Let the day's own trouble be sufficient for the day.

7 "Judge not, that you be not judged. ²For with the judgment you pronounce you will be judged, and the measure you give will be the measure you get. ³Why do you see the speck that is in your brother's eye, but do not notice the log that is in your own eye? ⁴Or how can you say to your brother, 'Let me take the speck out of your eye,' when there is the log in your own eye? ⁵You hypocrite, first take the log out of your own eye, and then you will see clearly to take the speck out of your brother's eye.

⁶"Do not give dogs what is holy; and do not throw your pearls before swine, lest they trample them underfoot and turn to attack you.

⁷"Ask, and it will be given you; seek, and you will find; knock, and it will be opened to you. ⁸For every one who asks receives, and he who seeks finds, and to him who knocks it will be opened. ⁹Or what man of you, if his son asks him for a loaf, will give him a stone? ¹⁰Or if he asks for a fish, will give him a serpent? ¹¹If you then, who are evil, know how to give good gifts to your children, how much more will your Father who is in heaven give good things to those who ask him? ¹²So whatever you wish that men would do to you, do so to them; for this is the law and the prophets.

¹³"Enter by the narrow gate; for the gate is wide and the way is easy, that leads to destruction, and those who enter by it are many. ¹⁴For the gate is narrow and the way is hard, that leads to life, and those who find it are few.

¹⁵"Beware of false prophets, who come to you in sheep's clothing but inwardly are ravenous wolves. ¹⁶You will know them by their fruits. Are grapes gathered from thorns, or figs from thistles? ¹⁷So, every sound tree bears good fruit, but the bad tree bears evil fruit. ¹⁸A sound tree cannot bear evil fruit, nor can a bad tree bear good fruit. ¹⁹Every tree that does not bear good fruit is cut down and thrown into the fire. ²⁰Thus you will know them by their fruits.

²¹"Not every one who says to me, 'Lord, Lord,' shall enter the kingdom of heaven, but he who does the will of my Father who is in heaven. ²²On that day many will say to me, 'Lord, Lord, did we not prophesy in your name, and cast out demons in your name, and do many mighty works in your name?' ²³And then will I declare to them, 'I never knew you; depart from me, you evil-doers.'

²⁴"Every one then who hears these words of mine and does them will be like a wise man who built his house upon the rock; ²⁵and the rain fell, and the floods came, and the winds blew and beat upon that house, but it did not fall, because it had been founded on the rock. ²⁶And every one who hears these words of mine and does not do them will be like a foolish man who built his house upon the sand; ²⁷and the rain fell, and the floods came, and the winds blew and beat against the house, and it fell; and great was the fall of it."

²⁸And when Jesus finished these sayings, the crowds were astonished at his teaching, for he taught them as one who had authority, and not as their scribes.

Matthew 5–7

STUDY QUESTIONS

1. It has been said that this sermon represents the ethics of the Kingdom of Heaven. What sort of moral conduct is expected of citizens who claim to live under the rule of God? That is, what seems to be the general spirit of the behavior that Jesus teaches?
2. Jesus gave only three or four commands whereas Moses began with ten. In what sense, therefore, does Jesus mean that he has "come to fulfill the law"? (Consider the entire message of the sermon.)

LITERARY SELECTION 27

Revelation

For several centuries before and after Christ, there flourished a distinctive writing known as **apocalypse** or revelation. Apocalyptic thought was based on the Jewish eschatological[8] view of history. A portion of the Book of Daniel is an apocalypse, and Paul included several apocalyptic verses in 2 Thessalonians. The last book of the Bible, called Revelation or Apocalypse of John, is the only full apocalypse in the New Testament. Writing to seven besieged churches around AD 93 during Domitian's savage persecution of Christians, John of Patmos declares, in visionary terms, the ultimate triumph over the Roman Empire and his perception of a new heaven, a new earth, and a new Jerusalem after all souls have been raised from the dead for the Last Judgment. In the early church there was a widespread belief that the Second Coming of Christ was imminent.

In the following selection, Christ opens four of the seven seals, releasing the Four Horsemen of the Apocalypse: Conquest, War, Famine, and Death (fig. 10.2).

¹Now I saw when the Lamb opened one of the seven seals, and I heard one of the four living creatures say, as with a voice of thunder, "Come!" ²And I saw, and behold, a white horse, and its rider had a bow; and a crown was given to him, and he went out conquering and to conquer.

³When he opened the second seal, I heard the second living creature say, "Come!" ⁴And out came another horse, bright red; its rider was permitted to take peace from the earth, so that men should slay one another; and he was given a great sword.

⁵When he opened the third seal, I heard the third living creature say, "Come!" And I saw, and behold, a black horse, and its rider had a balance in his hand; ⁶and I heard what

8. Eschatology (Gk., *eschatos*, "furthest") is a branch of theology dealing with the last things, such as death, judgment, resurrection, and immortality.

10.2 *The Fourth Horseman of the Apocalypse*, Angers, France.
Flemish/French. 1373–1380. Wool tapestry, height ca. 8'
(2.4 m). Photo: Scala, Florence.
Woven by Nicolas Bataille in Paris, from a design by
Hennequin de Bruges (Flanders), this is the oldest known
tapestry produced in France.

seemed to be a voice in the midst of the four living creatures
saying, "A quart of wheat for a denarius, and three quarts of
barley for a denarius, but do not harm oil and wine!"

7When he opened the fourth seal, I heard the voice of the
fourth living creature say, "Come!" 8And I saw, and behold,
a pale horse, and its rider's name was Death, and Hades
followed him; and they were given power over a fourth of the
earth, to kill with sword and with famine and with pestilence
and by wild beasts of the earth.

Revelation 6:1–8

Following the Last Judgment, John presents a golden vision
of the world to come:

1Then I saw a new heaven and a new earth; for the first
heaven and the first earth had passed away, and the sea was
no more. 2And I saw the holy city, new Jerusalem, coming
down out of heaven from God, prepared as a bride adorned for
her husband; 3and I heard a great voice from the throne saying,
"Behold, the dwelling of God is with men. He will dwell with
them, and they shall be his people, and God himself will be
with them; 4he will wipe away every tear from their eyes, and
death shall be no more, neither shall there be mourning nor
crying nor pain any more, for the former things have passed
away."

Revelation 21:1–4

SUMMARY

The secular Graeco-Roman world was gradually superseded by two strains of religion, first by Judaism and later by Christianity. The basic strength of the Jews was their religion, the first monotheistic religion of the Western world. Judaism was, briefly stated, the religion of a people who had a covenant with God, a book (the Hebrew Scriptures), a way of life, and a hope based on faith. This sustained them through conquests by Assyrians, Babylonians, Persians, Alexander, and the Romans. They were without a homeland from the Diaspora (scattering) in AD 70 until the reestablishment of the state of Israel in 1948.

The strongest impact upon Rome was that of Christianity, a new faith derived partly from Judaism and based on the teachings of Jesus, recognized by Christians as the Messiah. With its doctrine of Christ as the Redeemer, Christianity was a religion of joy and hope in the jaded days of the late Roman Empire.

CULTURE AND HUMAN VALUES

The rise of Rome caused a shift from the Greek view of the individual as the ultimate reality to one in which reality was the state. With the decline of the Empire and the growth of Christianity the view of reality shifted once again. God became the ultimate reality and the goal of all Christians was to join Him in the Heavenly Kingdom.

The advent of Christianity also caused a major change in values. Prudence, temperance, fortitude, and justice were accepted as the four cardinal virtues (as earlier identified by Plato and the Stoics) to which were added the Christian (theological) virtues of faith, hope, and love. Justice was administered as best they could by courts of justice in the City of Man but only God the Father could dispense infallible justice in the City of God.

CHAPTER 11

The Beginnings of Christian Art

The first two centuries of Christianity had little need for art in any form. Meeting in small groups in private homes, early Christians conducted simple services centered on the **Eucharist**: the consecrated bread and wine commemorating Christ's sacrifice on the cross. Dating from about 250, the earliest known church building is a Greek peristyle house in Dura-Europos, Syria. Suitable for a congregation of no more than sixty, this was a private home converted to liturgical use though it was devoid of decorations or architectural distinction. No Christian art survived from the first two centuries and very little from the third century, and that almost entirely from the catacombs of Rome.

ROMAN CATACOMBS

Initially and during most of the first two centuries, Christians were buried in regular (surface) Roman cemeteries. Rejecting customary cremation because of their belief in resurrection of the body, Christians continued using surface cemeteries, except in the outskirts of Rome, Naples, and Syracuse, where porous stone (tufa) was easily excavated for subterranean tombs. During the late second century Christian communities became increasingly interested in separate areas where they could perform private rites for the dead and safeguard the tombs against vandals. Because Roman law forbade burials within city limits, Christians bought land alongside the major highways leading into Rome, sites that already contained the funerary monuments of wealthy Roman families. Using surface chapels and subterranean passages, these cemeteries suited Christian concerns for seclusion and security as guaranteed by Roman law.[1]

The Roman catacombs had up to five subterranean levels with superimposed niches for sarcophagi eight to ten deep on each level. Each cemetery included small chapels for burial and commemorative services. In the chapels and sometimes over the burial niches are found the earliest examples of Christian figurative art. Executed by artisans working by lamplight in a dark, dank, and undoubtedly malodorous environment, the representations were generally simple, often hastily executed, and aesthetically indifferent. Christians wanted to convey a message or a prayer understood by the Christian community and, above all, by God.

The *Orans*

The most common representation in the catacombs was the *orans* (OR-an; from the Latin word for "praying"; see chapter opener opposite and fig. 11.1), a figure presented frontally, standing with arms raised in prayer or supplication. The *orans* can symbolize the soul of the deceased praying for salvation or reflect the Hellenistic view: a personification in human form of such abstract ideas as resurrection or salvation.

Opposite   Orans, Room of the Veiled Lady. Catacomb of Priscilla, Rome, detail of fig. 11.1. 3rd century. Ceiling fresco. Photo: Scala, Florence.

11.1   *Orans*, Room of the Veiled Lady, Catacomb of Priscilla, Rome. 3rd century. Photo: Canali, Brescia.

---

1. Not used after the sixth century, the catacombs were completely forgotten until rediscovered in the sixteenth century.

11.2 *The Good Shepherd*, Catacombs of St. Callistus, Rome. Ca. 250. Ceiling fresco. Photo: Scala, Florence.

The Good Shepherd

The figure of Jesus as *The Good Shepherd* (fig. 11.2), a commonly used representation throughout the centuries, appears frequently in catacomb frescoes. Not unexpectedly, the "good shepherd" motif itself, as distinguished from Christ, is found in most cultures in which herding sheep is an important occupation. There is, for example, the *Calf-Bearer* (see fig. 7.5) of archaic Greek sculpture and, in the Hebraic tradition, David the shepherd boy, giant-killer, psalmist, and king. Christ as the Good Shepherd symbolized his guardianship of the faithful; further, Jesus was descended from the David who tended sheep in Palestine.

$$
\begin{aligned}
&\text{I}\eta\sigma o\upsilon\varsigma \\
&\text{X}\rho\iota\sigma\tau o\varsigma \\
&\Theta\,\varepsilon o\upsilon \\
&\text{'Y}\iota o\varsigma \\
&\Sigma\,\omega\tau\eta\rho
\end{aligned}
$$

11.3 Acronym derived from Greek for "Jesus Christ, the Son of God, Savior."

CHRISTIAN SYMBOLS

Artistic representation of the concepts inherent in the new religion caused difficulties never dreamed of by Egyptian, Greek, and Roman artists. The Greeks, for example, had created the gods in their own image, thus making the divinities instantly available for artistic representation: Zeus with a thunderbolt symbolizing the power principle, Poseidon with his trident, Aphrodite as the goddess of love, and so forth. How, then, was the Christian artist to depict such abstractions as the Trinity (God the Father, God the Son, God the Holy Spirit), the Eucharist, salvation, redemption, immortality?

In time, artists worked out a variety of solutions using biblical stories, parables, and symbols. Immortality, for example, could be represented through biblical scenes of salvation: Moses leading his people out of Egypt, Jonah released from the whale, Daniel escaping from the lion's den, Lazarus rising from his tomb. The anchor came to represent hope, the dove was peace or the Holy Spirit, and the palm victory through martyrdom. Symbolizing Christ was the chi-rho (KYE-ro) monogram, which superimposes the first two letters of Christ's name (Christos) in Greek: ☧. The first and last letters of the Greek alphabet, Alpha (A) and Omega (Ω), symbolize infinity as in Christ's statement, "I am Alpha and Omega, the Beginning and the End." Multiple meanings are symbolized by the fish: (1) the Last Supper; (2) Christian evangelism, as represented in Christ's exhortation to his fishermen disciples to be "fishers of men"; and (3) an acronym upon a Greek phrase, the initial letters of which form the Greek word *ichthus* ("fish"; fig. 11.3).

The one event not represented in catacomb paintings was the Crucifixion. As the most ignoble and horrible method of Roman execution, crucifixion was reserved for criminals judged guilty of foul and heinous acts. The Romans executed Christ as an "enemy of the state," treason being the worst of all crimes. For early Christians, the simple geometric form of the cross was sufficient to symbolize Christ's sacrifice. Perhaps the earliest extant crucifixion scene produced for a public place is a small, wooden, low-relief panel on a door of the Church of Santa Sabina (fig. 11.4). Set amid a door rich with elaborately carved panels (fig. 11.5) this, the simplest panel, may be a deliberate attempt to tone down the horror of the crucifixion.

CHRISTIAN SCULPTURE

Early Christians refrained from producing sculpture in the round, especially life-size figures. Religious conservatives interpreted God's commandment literally: "Thou shall not make unto thee any graven images." However, early church fathers did recognize and approve the educational value of painting, an attitude summed up by Pope Gregory the Great (reigned 590–604): "Pictures are used in the church in order that those who are ignorant of letters may, merely by

11.4 *Crucifixion*, west door, Church of Sta. Sabina, Rome. Ca. 430. Wooden relief, 11 × 15¾" (28 × 40 cm). Photo: Hirmer, Munich.

11.5 West door, Church of Sta. Sabina, Rome. Photo: Scala, Florence.

CROSSES

The cross is a very old and virtually universal symbol. In preliterate societies the vertical and horizontal arms represented a series of opposing qualities: spiritual and worldly, celestial and terrestrial, positive and negative, active and passive. The four points also symbolized earth, air, fire, and water and the spatial dimensions of height, length, width, and depth. The swastika (1), whose Sanskrit name meant "good luck," was a major symbol of ancient Asian, European, and pre-Columbian American civilizations. For pre-Columbian Americans it represents the wheel of life but Hindus perceive it as a sign of a resigned spirit. Buddhists believe it is emblematic of the Buddha's mind. This ancient left-directed cross is not to be confused with the right-directed swastika that Germany's Nazis mistakenly took for an Aryan symbol.

Christianity has been responsible for over fifty different cross designs, with some of the more important ones illustrated here. The **Latin cross** (2) is the primary symbol of Western Christianity while the **Greek cross** (3) is the principal symbol for Orthodox Christianity. The ankh (4) is an ancient Egyptian symbol of life that later became a Christian symbol. The Tau cross (5) has the shape of the Greek letter *Tau*. According to legend, the Israelites on Passover eve in Egypt marked their doors with blood-drawn Tau crosses to identify themselves as followers of Yahweh. The Maltese cross (6) is associated with the Crusader Knights of Malta and also used as the German military decoration called the Iron Cross. The Celtic or Iona cross (7) developed in medieval Ireland and Scotland while St. Andrew's cross (8) is so named because Andrew, the patron saint of Scotland, was supposedly crucified on a cross of this shape. The cross of Lorraine (9) is usually associated with archbishops and patriarchs but during World War II it was the symbol of the Free French forces led by Charles de Gaulle.

11.6 *Good Shepherd*. Ca. 350. Marble, height 39" (99 cm). Musei Vaticani, Rome. Photo: Islay Lyons, Siena.

11.7 *Christ Enthroned*. Ca. 350–360. Marble, smaller than life-size. Museo Nazionale, Rome. Photo: Hirmer, Munich.

looking at the walls, read there what they were unable to read in books." Supplementing this realistic position was the theological argument that since Jesus was "made flesh and dwelt among us," he had a human likeness and nature that could be represented in art. Conservatives still associated freestanding statues with gods of other religions. This is the primary reason why there was very little monumental sculpture in Europe between the fall of Rome and the tenth century, when new attitudes toward religious art began to emerge.

Despite the rarity of Christian sculptures in fourth-century Rome, two pieces do survive. Classical in pose and reminiscent of the catacomb painting in figure 11.2, the *Good Shepherd* (fig. 11.6) is as carefully detailed as the finest Hellenistic sculpture. Stylistically it still relates to the *Calf-Bearer* (see fig. 7.5) that was created about 1,000 years earlier.

The statue of *Christ Enthroned* (fig. 11.7) depicts Jesus in the guise, perhaps, of a young, clean-shaven philosopher. Features, clothing, and gestures are classical, as is the smooth, idealized face. Though the universal image today, the concept of a bearded Christ was not accepted until later. Because this was art of the spirit rather than the flesh, literal depiction was not the goal; this is Christ the symbol, the Son of God.

Relief sculpture appeared relatively early in the Christian era as a means of decorating sarcophagi. By the middle of the third century important church leaders were being entombed in these stone sarcophagi, but the practice was not widely accepted until Christianity was legalized in the fourth century. At first the subject matter was drawn from the Old Testament but, by the middle of the fourth century, sarcophagi began to emphasize New Testament scenes as shown in the Sarcophagus of Junius Bassus (fig. 11.8). The front panel, illustrated here, is divided into ten reliefs on two levels. The top level includes: (1) the Sacrifice of Isaac, (2) the Arrest of St. Peter, (3) Christ Enthroned between St. Peter and St. Paul, and (4–5) Christ before Pilate. The bottom level shows: (1) the Misery of Job, (2) Adam and Eve after the Fall, (3) Christ's Entry into Jerusalem, (4) Daniel in the Lion's Den, and (5) St. Paul Led to His Martyrdom. Many interpretations are possible for a series this complex: the sacrifice of Isaac is in response to God's command, as is the testing of Job; Daniel, Abraham, and Job represent salvation; the fall of Adam and Eve represents humanity's condition that is redeemed by Christ's sacrifice; the triumphal entry into Jerusalem signals the eternal triumph of the resurrected Christ directly above. To modern eyes the choice of scenes may seem rather odd, but early Christians emphasized the divinity of Christ rather than his earthly existence. His suffering and death are merely suggested in the appearance before Pilate and in the low-keyed martyrdom of St. Paul. All the panels have a detached but controlled air about them; the old classical style was in decline but obviously still influential. The Old and New Testament figures look like Romans of the time and, in fact, the Roman sky god, Caelus, is holding up the firmament on which Christ rests his feet (fig. 11.9).

11.8 *Above* Sarcophagus of Junius Bassus, St Peter's, Rome. Ca. 359. Marble, 3' 10½" × 8' (1.17 × 2.44 m). Photo: Alinari, Florence.

11.9 *Caelus Holding up the Firmament*, detail of fig. 11.8. Photo: Scala, Florence.

11.10   *The Abbot Mena, Protected by Christ*, from Egypt.
Coptic. 5th century. Painted icon. Louvre, Paris. Photo:
R.M.N., Paris.

COPTIC ART

The native Egyptian church was a result of the rivalry
between Alexandria and Constantinople: Egyptian nationalism versus Byzantine imperialism. Though created during Roman domination, most Coptic[2] art reveals the
opposite pulls of the Greek classical tradition and the spirituality of the Christian faith. The icon in figure 11.10 is
one of the best examples of Coptic painting, for it is a skillful synthesis of Greek realism and Christian sanctity. The
realistic facial expressions of the two figures leave no doubt
about who is protecting whom. There are very real bodies
under the artfully draped robes, but the deliberate dis-
proportions of large heads on shortened bodies reflects
the more intellectual orientation of the Hellenistic
(Alexandrian) tradition. The large eyes of both men and
the greater size of the figure of Christ characterize the
Byzantine style of Constantinople. The gold **nimbus** of light
and glory surrounding the heads of Christ and Abbot Mena
first appeared in Christian art in the fifth century but was
known earlier in India and Egypt.

---

2. The word "Copt" is derived from *Kubt*, the Arab version of
   the Greek word *Aigyptios*.

THE AGE OF CONSTANTINE

Christianity made its great leap forward after Constantine proclaimed freedom of religion in the Edict of Milan:

> When we, Constantine Augustus and Licinius Augustus, met so happily at Milan, and considered together all that concerned the interest and security of the State, we decided . . . to grant to Christians and to everybody the free power to follow the religion of their choice, in order that all that is divine in the heavens may be favorable and propitious towards us and towards all who are placed under our authority.
>
> From a rescript issued at Nicomedia
> by Licinius, 13 June, 313.[3]

Though it came soon after the two most severe and methodical persecutions of Christians, by Decius in 249–251 and Diocletian in 303–305, this declaration of religious freedom found organized Christianity ready to build churches and otherwise assume a prominent role in the Empire.

Basilicas

For centuries the Romans had constructed basilicas that served as meeting halls, mercantile centers, and halls of justice. The basilica was a prototype of the large, dignified structure Christians needed for worship services. The basilica at Volubilis (fig. 11.11), for example, originally had five aisles and four rows of arcades like the one pictured here. Only one right-hand aisle remains; the intact building had another right-hand aisle, a central hall, and two left-hand aisles and was about as wide as St. Paul's (see figs. 11.12 and 11.13). Serving as a hall of justice for a large Roman colony, the building has the usual Roman arches with Corinthian pilasters punctuating the heavy columns.

None of the great basilica-type churches built in Constantine's Rome have survived as such. Old St. Peter's was replaced by the present church, and hardly anything original remains of St. John Lateran after many restorations. St. Paul's Outside the Walls was destroyed by fire in 1823 and faithfully reconstructed in 1854, insofar as that was possible. Piranesi drew the original church (fig. 11.12), clearly illustrating a basic Western church design used throughout the medieval period. People entered the secular basilica from its longitudinal sides (see fig. 11.11) but Christians shifted the entrances to a shorter side, usually the western end, thus orienting the building along a longitudinal axis. The interior space was divided into a large area called the **nave**, because it seemed to symbolize a ship (Lat. *navis*, the "ship" of souls), flanked by two aisles on

11.11   Roman basilica, Volubilis, Morocco. 3rd century AD. Photo: Robert C. Lamm, Scottsdale.

each side (fig. 11.13). The nave joins a secondary space, the **transept**, which is placed at right angles to the nave proper and forms an interior Latin cross. Later churches would lengthen the transept so that even the exterior walls assumed a cruciform shape, the most characteristic church design in Western Christendom. Behind the transept is a semicircular space called an **apse** in which the altar is placed on a raised platform. The nave was covered with an A-shaped **truss** roof; at a level well below the nave, lean-to truss roofs topped the aisles so that the **clerestory** (or clearstory) windows could be set in the upper nave wall to illuminate the interior. Corinthian columns connected a nave arcade above which was the triforium, usually painted or covered with mosaics; above that was the clerestory area with alabaster windows. Aesthetically, the basilica interior is complex and stimulating, for there is no single point from which one can comprehend the space. The strong rhythm of the nave arcade seems to march inexorably toward the eastern end and the triumphal arch that frames the ultimate focus of the design: the high altar where the sacraments are celebrated.

An obvious choice for Christian use, the basilica had imperial associations that suited the triumph of Christianity and a spacious interior that could hold thousands of worshipers; Old St. Peter's was said to have a capacity of 40,000. Besides the interior space, large churches like St. Paul's and Old St. Peter's were fronted by an atrium (open courtyard), which was surrounded on three sides by a covered arcade called an ambulatory (walkway). On the fourth side of the atrium was a **narthex** (porch) that led to the front doors of the church. Adapted from Roman house plans, the atrium was later moved to the south side of monastic churches to become the medieval **cloister**.

---

3. Laotantius, *De Mortibus Persecutorum*, xlviii. Constantine did not assume sole leadership of the Empire until 324, when he had Licinius, his co-regent, executed.

11.12   Giambattista Piranesi, *Interior, St. Paul's Outside the Walls*. 1749. Etching.

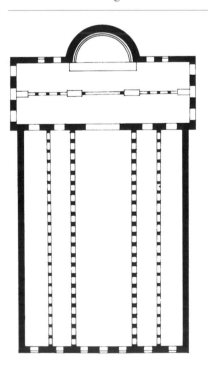

11.13   St. Paul's, Rome, schematic floor plan.

Christian Mosaics

With a deliberately plain exterior of brick or rubble construction, Christian churches reserved glorious interiors—embellished structural materials, marble panels, paintings, and mosaics—for their congregations. (The contrast between exterior and interior serves as a striking allegory for the Christian transport from this world to the next.) Very little of early Christian mural painting has survived, and what remains is not as dazzling as the incredibly beautiful mosaics. Hellenistic and Roman artists created mosaics using small bits of marble called **tesserae** (TES-ser-ay), usually for floor designs. Artists incorporated subtle gradations of color into designs, some of which were reproductions of existing paintings. Early Christian mosaics were, on the other hand, unprecedented. Designed entirely as wall or ceiling decorations, the tesserae were made of bits of glass cubes that had a wide range of color and intensity, including transparent pieces backed with glittering gold leaf. With shiny, irregular glass faces, the tesserae were set into plaster at slightly varying angles, turning a flat wall surface into a shimmering screen of color. Depicting Christ enthroned and raised above the Apostles, the much renovated mosaic of Santa Pudenziana (fig. 11.14) asserts Christ's authority and, by implication, the institutional authority of the church. The background buildings represent the Heavenly Jerusalem, while in the sky are winged

11.14 *Christ Teaching the Apostles in the Heavenly Jerusalem*, apse of Sta. Pudenziana, Rome. Ca. 401–407. Mosaic. Photo: Scala, Florence.

symbols of the four evangelists: the lion of St. Mark, the ox of St. Luke, the eagle of St. John, and the winged man of St. Matthew. Of uncertain origin but widely employed by this time,[4] these evangelical images continued throughout Christian iconography. Not meant to be read as a historical event, this scene is an essay on salvation as assured by Christ's death on the cross, told to us by the evangelists, and available through the church, God's representative on earth.

The oldest cycle (probably) of evangelical and biblical mosaics is found in Rome's fifth-century church of Santa Maria Maggiore. One scene depicts, on two levels, Abraham's encounter with the three celestial visitors at Mamre and his subsequent vision of the Trinity (fig. 11.15). On the lower level Sarah prepares food, which Abraham then sets before the three young men, whose celestial status is marked by halos. On the upper level Abraham bows before his visitors, who now appear in a vision; this time an oval light field called an **aureole** (OR-e-ol) surrounds the central figure of Christ. This manner of representing the Holy Trinity was common in the West into the Gothic period and even in today's Byzantine world.

4. Revelation 4:6–8 describes these same symbols as "four living creatures" that apparently represent the whole of creation: wild and domesticated animals, birds, and humankind. How they came to symbolize the evangelists is not known.

11.15 *Abraham and the Celestial Visitors*, Church of Sta. Maria Maggiore, Rome. 2nd quarter of the 5th century. Mosaic. Photo: Scala, Florence.

RAVENNA AND THE BYZANTINE WORLD

Serving briefly as an imperial city for the Romans, Ostrogoths, and the Byzantine Empire, provincial Ravenna was a most unlikely capital. Located south of Venice in the midst of extensive swamps, the port of Ravenna did provide the Western emperors with an easily defensible site and, perhaps more importantly, a low profile compared with once-mighty Rome, now the target of every barbarian invader. Becoming the capital of the Western Empire under Honorius in 404, Ravenna fell to Odoacer in 476 but emerged as the capital of Theodoric's Ostrogothic kingdom (489–526), and concluded its royal career as the Western capital of Justinian's Byzantine Empire (527–565) (map 11.1). Modern Ravenna contains notable art works from all three imperial periods.

The mausoleum that Empress Galla Placidia, half sister of Honorius, built for members of her family contains some of the best-preserved and most splendid mosaics of the fifth century. Set in a **lunette** (lew-net), a semicircular

---

Map 11.1   The Byzantine world under Justinian, AD 565.

wall of a vaulted room, the mosaic of *The Good Shepherd* (fig. 11.17) depicts a majestic Christ watching over six attentive sheep, who balance him in pyramid formations of three on each side, thus symbolizing the Trinitarian doctrine. The regal pose spirals upward from the right hand, feeding a sheep, to the left hand, which grasps a knob-ended cross signifying the earthly death of the King of Kings. In the Hellenic tradition of classical painting, the forms give the illusion of three-dimensional bulk and appear in a real space. Particularly notable is the rocky landscape, which though increasingly stylized remained in the repertoire of landscape painting throughout the Byzantine tradition and into the late medieval style of such painters as Giotto. Often overlooked are the funnel-shaped tubes along the lower border that represent footlights illuminating a liturgical tableau.

Marking the true beginning of the Byzantine style, the reign of Justinian (reigned 527–565) was notable for artistic production and for the Justinian legal code, plus the dubious distinction of closing, after 1,000 years, Plato's Academy in Athens. Operating from his capitals of Constantinople in the East and Ravenna in the West, Justinian was both an emperor in the Roman tradition and an Oriental potentate in what later became the Byzantine Empire. Except for some architecture in Constantinople, most Byzantine art created before 1204 can be found in

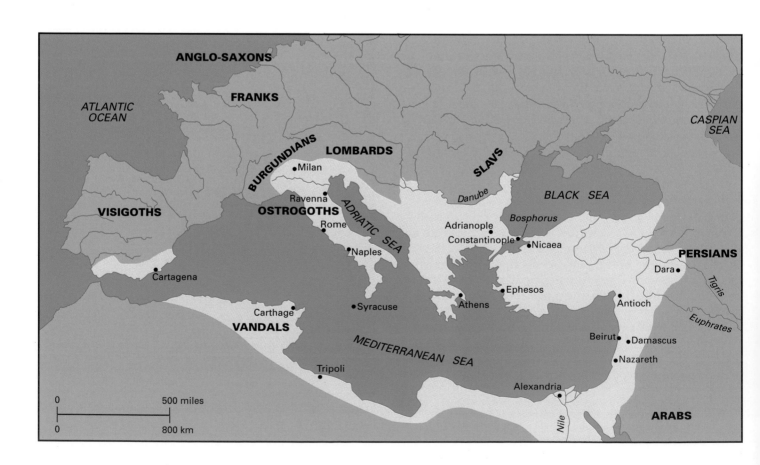

Ravenna. The rape of Constantinople by the Fourth Crusade (1204) destroyed most of the art and much of the city, which was not retaken from the Latins until 1261.

San Vitale

The most "Byzantine" of the many religious buildings in Ravenna is the octagonal, domed church of San Vitale (fig. 11.16), a prototype of the central-plan churches that were to dominate the world of Orthodox Christianity just as the basilica plan prevailed throughout Western Christendom. The brick exterior is a complex and subtle interplay of angular patterns around a central core, marred only by an added Renaissance doorway. The interior is a veritable jewel box (fig. 11.19), with polychromed marble walls, pierced marble screens, hundreds of decorative and pictorial mosaics, marble floor mosaics, and carved alabaster columns. San Vitale is an octagonal structure surmounted by an octagonal drum on which the circular dome rests. The transition from the octagonal drum to the round dome was accomplished by using **squinches**: stone lintels placed diagonally across corners formed by the octagonal walls (fig. 11.18). Topping the aisle surrounding the nave is a vaulted triforium gallery reserved for women, as was customary for Orthodox Christianity. Compact and intimate, San Vitale functioned for the imperial court somewhat like a diminutive, luxurious theatre. The vertical emphasis of the central plan can be seen as a spatial metaphor for the more hierarchal rigidity of the Eastern church while the design also divides the congregation by official rank and gender.

11.18 *Right* Supporting a dome with (a) squinches, and (b) **pendentives**.

11.16 Church of San Vitale, Ravenna. Ca. 526–547. Photo: Canali, Brescia.

11.17 *Above* *The Good Shepherd*, Mausoleum of Galla Placidia, Ravenna, Italy. Ca. 425–450. Mosaic. Photo: Giraudon, Paris.

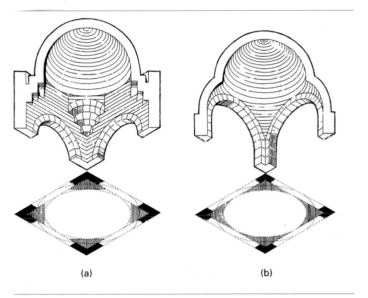

(a)　　　　　　　　(b)

11.19 San Vitale, Ravenna, interior. Photo: Canali, Brescia.

Facing the altar from opposite sides are the two just-ly celebrated mosaics of Emperor Justinian (fig. 11.20) and Empress Theodora (fig. 11.21). Though extensively restored, these ceremonial works are still the best extant examples of early Byzantine mosaics. Illustrating the new ideal of the Byzantine style, all the figures are tall and slim with small feet, solemn faces, and large oval eyes. Frozen in time without a hint of movement, the solemn participants are depicted in full frontality, highly stylized, but still revealing individual differences while clearly showing the distinctions in official rank. Flanked by twelve male companions suggesting the twelve Apostles, Justinian stands in the exact center holding the offering of bread for the **Mass**. He is crowned with both the imperial diadem and a halo, representative of the unity of the spiritual force of the church and of the temporal power of the state. At Justinian's left is Bishop Maximianus, who was responsible for the completion of San Vitale and whose importance is signified by the label over his head. The composition of the work delineates the threefold structure of the Empire:

the six soldiers represent the army, the three staff members the state, and the three clergymen the church. One of the soldiers holds a shield with the Chi-Rho insignia that not only symbolizes the name of Christ but allegorically becomes a combination of the cross and shepherd's crook, suggesting Christ's death and his pastoral mission.

Unlike the emperor, Theodora is depicted in a more specific setting, probably the narthex of San Vitale, thus indicating both her high rank and her inferior position as a woman. About to pass through a doorway to which she is beckoned by one of her female attendants, she is carrying the offering of wine in a gold chalice encrusted with precious stones. With her huge diadem, ropes of pearls, and luxurious ceremonial gown in royal purple, Theodora is portrayed as the strong-willed, intelligent, and beautiful empress history has revealed her to be, and considerably removed from her reputed early career as circus performer and courtesan. Pictured on her gown are the Magi bringing their offerings to the infant Jesus, suggesting a parallel with her gift-bearing activity. Both mosaics achieve some of their clarity by conforming to the Greek isocephalic convention of placing all heads on about the same level. They also underscore the separation of the sexes mandated by Orthodox Christianity.

11.20 *Emperor Justinian and His Courtiers*, San Vitale, Ravenna. Ca. 547. Mosaic. Photo: Gian Carlo Costa, Milan.

THE CITY OF CONSTANTINE

Dedicated by Constantine in 330 as "New Rome," Constantinople, as the city quickly became known, was the sumptuous center of Byzantine civilization for over 1,000 years. The Orthodox faith was totally dominant in this city, but it was still under the aegis of the emperor who built the churches and appointed the patriarch of Constantinople.

Justinian's building program for Constantinople began as a matter of necessity. In 532 the Blues and Greens, rival chariot-racing factions, joined forces in a powerful revolt against the autocratic rule of Justinian and Theodora. Before the imperial troops put down the revolution by slaughtering about 30,000 people, most of the public buildings had been destroyed, including the Basilica of Hagia Sophia (HA-jeh SO-fee-ah; Church of Holy Wisdom). Only the determined resistance of Empress Theodora kept Justinian from fleeing the city. Justinian's reign depended, in fact, on Theodora, whose influence on public policy and the fate of ministers was usually decisive.

11.21 *Empress Theodora and Retinue*, San Vitale, Ravenna. Ca. 547. Mosaic. Photo: Gian Carlo Costa, Milan.

Hagia Sophia

Disdaining the usual procedure of selecting an architect, Justinian appointed the noted mathematician, Anthemius of Tralles, to design the new Hagia Sophia. Assisted by Isidorus of Miletus and possibly Justinian himself, Anthemius invented a revolutionary new design unlike anything in either the Roman or Byzantine world (fig. 11.22). Combining the longitudinal axis of the basilica plan with the domed structure of a central plan, abutted on east and west by half domes, the new Hagia Sophia was a beautiful and inspiring building, truly a majestic architectural achievement. No wonder Justinian supposedly exclaimed as he rode up to the church for its consecration, "O Solomon, I have excelled thee!"

The interior of Hagia Sophia is breathtaking (figs. 11.23 and 11.24) with the dome seemingly floating on light as it rests upon a tightly spaced ring of forty windows. The entire interior is flooded with light from hundreds of windows in the thin, shell-like walls. Adding to the magical effect of all this light were thousands of tesserae that were set into the walls, but later covered with plaster and paint when the Turks converted the building into a mosque. With an interior measuring 233 by 252 feet (71 × 77 m), crowned

11.22 *Above* Anthemius of Tralles and Isidorus of Miletus, Hagia Sophia, Constantinople (Istanbul). 532–537. (The minarets were added later.) Photo: Sonia Halliday, Weston Turville, U.K.

11.24 *Right* Detail of fig. 11.23. Photo: Werner Forman, London.

11.23 *Below* Hagia Sophia, interior. Photo: Explorer, Paris.

by a dome 112 feet (34 m) in diameter and extending to 184 feet (55 m) above the pavement, this is one of the largest space enclosures achieved prior to this century. At the corners of a 100-foot (30.5-m) square area under the dome are 70-foot (21.35-m) piers that support massive arches. They in turn are connected by pendentives (pen-DEN-tivs), which effect the transition from the basic square to the circular rim of the dome. Best described as concave spherical triangles, two of the four pendentives can be seen at the top of figure 11.23 (see also fig. 11.18). A more graceful transition from a square base to a round dome than squinches, pendentives also facilitate the covering of more floor space. Their origin remains unknown and their use on the monumental scale of Hagia Sophia is unprecedented. Subsequently used in most Byzantine architecture, pendentives became standard structural devices from the Renaissance to the present day.

As sometimes happens with highly original buildings, there were some technical problems, the most serious being the collapse of the dome twenty-one years after its completion. The present higher-arched dome solved that problem. Byzantium never produced another structure to equal Hagia Sophia. Though it inspired similar designs seen all over Istanbul, it remains unique—the first and best of its kind. First a church and then a **mosque**, Hagia Sophia is now a museum.

The Iconoclastic Controversy

Brutally terminating the first Byzantine golden age, the Iconoclastic controversy lasted off and on, mostly on, from 726 to 843. Issuing an imperial decree forbidding idolatry, Leo III ordered the destruction of all images of Christ, saints, and prophets. Representations of all sorts, including mosaics in Hagia Sophia, were destroyed along with the entire legacy of pictorial art of Justinian's age, except in Byzantine Italy and on Mount Sinai. Iconoclasts (image-destroyers) mutilated, blinded, tortured, and sometimes executed those trying to protect sacred images. Ostensibly a religious issue based on the commandment forbidding graven images, the controversy was essentially a conflict between church and state. The monastic movement had achieved great wealth and power and won considerable respect from the faithful, much to the consternation of the emperors; furthermore, monasteries were diverting revenue from the state and paying little or no taxes. As principal repositories for sacred images, monasteries were attacked, sometimes confiscated, and their resident monks executed, without, however, stamping out the image-worshiping monks in the West. A later Empress Theodora allowed images again in 843, but the Western and Eastern branches of Christianity were already launched on a parting of the ways, which led, in 1054, to a schism that has yet to be healed. Though the extent of the loss of priceless art works can never be known, the disaster was not total. The controversy did help to spark a renewed interest in

11.25   St Mark's, Venice, facade. Begun 1063. Photo: Camerphoto, Venice.

secular art and late classical motifs, setting the stage for the second Byzantine golden age of ca. 900–1100.

THE SECOND GOLDEN AGE

The largest and most profusely decorated church of the second golden age, St. Mark's of Venice, is also the most ambitious structure outside the Empire. St. Mark's differs from Hagia Sophia in that the Greek cross form is clearly visible from within and that, in addition to the central dome, each arm of the cross is capped by a full dome. From the exterior and especially from the air (figs. 11.25 and 11.26), St. Mark's, with each of its five domes encased in wood covered by gilt copper sheathing and topped by ornate lanterns,

11.26   St. Mark's, Venice, aerial view. Begun 1063. Photo: Alinari, Florence.

is the splendid showcase the republic of Venice intended it to be. As required by law, every ship's captain had to return to Venice with something of value for construction or decoration of the cathedral. Because of the law, many treasures from the 1204 sack of Constantinople found their way to Venice. The Greek cross plan, multiple domes, strong interior lighting, and glittering mosaics make St. Mark's a Byzantine masterpiece (fig. 11.27) despite its Romanesque and Gothic elements.

One of the many treasures in St. Mark's is the sumptuous plaque of the archangel St. Michael (fig. 11.28 and p. 301). On the border polished but uncut gems alternate with **cloisonné** medallions. Other parts are of beaten and painted copper but with a preponderance of gold. The medallion of Christ at the top is flanked by two patriarchs. This colorful masterpiece is so typical of Byzantium that it can be used to define the Byzantine style.

After the victory of the iconophiles (image-lovers) in 843, Byzantine painting and mosaics began to blend the otherworldly beauty of Justinian's time with a renewed interest in classical Greek art. Perhaps the finest examples of art of the second golden age are to be found in the monastery church at Daphne, Greece. In the *Crucifixion* mosaic (fig. 11.29), there are no apostles, soldiers, or thieves, only the grief-stricken Mary looking up at Christ and John

gazing on in sorrow. The suffering is intense but restrained, reflecting an adaptation of classical Greek sculptural elements to the linear Byzantine style. The skull at the base of the cross represents Golgotha, the "place of the skull." Symbolizing the sacraments of the Eucharist and Baptism, the blood spilling from Christ's side also nourishes the flowers, which represent a new life in Christ. Controlled and compassionate, this is not a historical representation but a humanized portrayal of the Passion of Jesus Christ.

Byzantine art was exceptionally splendid under the Macedonian dynasty of the tenth and eleventh centuries. The renewal of classical ideals that emerged in the post-iconoclastic era is particularly notable in the miniature paintings of the period (fig. 11.30). This page from the *Book of Psalms* reveals a style that harks back to the Hellenistic roots of Byzantine civilization. The classical influence can be clearly seen when this painting is compared with the mosaics in San Vitale (figs. 11.20 and 11.21). The Byzantine character of this work is apparent in the elegant, if mannered, fold of the drapery, the courtly pose of the figures, and the mixture of gold and bright colors.

The Byzantine style in painting, architecture, and the decorative arts spread throughout the Balkans, into Russia, and as far west as Sicily. It strongly influenced some of the Western art of the Middle Ages, while continuing to flourish in Eastern Europe for centuries beyond the demise of the Byzantine Empire itself, which fell to the Turks in 1453.

11.27   St. Mark's, Venice, interior. Photo: Camerphoto, Venice.

11.28   *St. Michael*, St. Mark's, Venice. 10th century. Enameled gold plaque. Photo: Werner Forman, London.

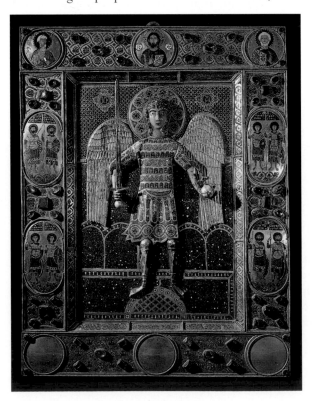

11.29 *Crucifixion*, Monastery Church, Daphne, Greece. Ca. 1100. Mosaic. Photo: Alinari, Florence.

11.30 Byzantine Miniature Painter of the Macedonian Period, *David Between the Personifications of Wisdom and Prophecy*, from the *Vatican Psalter*. 10th century. Tempera on parchment, 13 × 9½" (33 × 24.1 cm). Musei Vaticani, Rome. Photo: Canali, Brescia.

STUDY QUESTIONS

1. Explain what is meant by "squinch" and "pendentive" and what purpose they served.
2. Many animals, birds, flowers, and objects function as symbols in Christian art. What is symbolized by the dove, rose, fish, anchor, lion, peacock, ox, eagle, lily, cup, lamb? What are some of the symbols for salvation, communion, immortality, and peace? Are any of these symbols of pre-Christian or non-Christian origin?
3. Draw floor plans of hypothetical basilica-plan and central-plan churches and identify the areas. Which churches in your community are basilica plan? Central plan? Is there a relationship between certain churches and particular branches of Christianity (Catholic, Greek Orthodox, Baptist, etc.)?
4. Compare the Parthenon, Pantheon, and Hagia Sophia in terms of purpose, size, and style.
5. What exactly is didactic art? Give some examples from early Christianity and some from current magazines and newspapers.
6. How much Christian symbolism do you encounter in everyday life? List, explain, and evaluate religious symbolism as contrasted with governmental (political) symbolism.

SUMMARY

The simple services of the early Christian congregations had no need for art. There were, moreover, two negative factors: (1) the Judaic prohibition of graven images and (2) a basic dislike—even fear—of classical art. However, the explosive growth of the church in the fourth century called for more and more churches, resulting in a need to instruct masses of new converts in the tenets of the faith. The Bible was basic, but artists significantly broadened religious instruction by developing symbols for Christian themes that they used in murals, mosaics, and relief sculptures. By the time of Pope Gregory the Great (reigned 590–604) the church was actively supporting the production of Christian art with special attention to its didactic function.

As the classical age receded further into the past, there was less and less concern with representational art. For the new faith, physical reality was not so important as authority and spirit. Except for the basilica architectural plan, the early Christians rejected virtually the whole of classical culture from styles to ideals. In its place they introduced different sources of inspiration, thereby changing the entire nature of art.

The Byzantine Empire was an outgrowth of the Roman Empire, beginning with Constantine's transfer of his capital to Constantinople in 330. The stream of culture was unbroken from the Hellenistic Age through the ascendancy of Rome to Byzantium itself. The main ingredient of that culture was Greek but the Christian synthesis included Oriental elements. Also Eastern was the absolutism of the emperor, who claimed that his power came directly from God. Eastern features of Byzantium's highly developed art included its abstract nature, its deliberate two-dimensionality, brilliant colors, and elaborate ornamentation.

The Hagia Sophia was one of the great triumphs of Byzantine art, a magnificent conception that influenced Christian and Islamic architecture, especially the latter. A more direct influence on Western art was the mosaics and churches of Ravenna during its glory days as capital of the Western empire. Many of the sacred buildings were built in the Eastern style and most of the pictorial art was created by artisans from Constantinople.

The two basic styles of church architecture were developed during these early centuries. From Rome came the basilica form with a long central hall or nave, and one or two side aisles, usually ending with a semicircular apse at the far end. Byzantium contributed the central-plan building, usually in the shape of a Greek cross, with a central dome over the intersection of the arms of the cross.

The ancient prohibition of graven images returned with a vengeance during the Iconoclastic controversy (726–843) that ended Byzantium's first golden age. The next major shock was the **Great Schism** of 1054 that led to the continuing separation of the Eastern Orthodox churches from the Church of Rome. Inspired by the second golden age (ca. 900–1100), St. Mark's of Venice was constructed as the most elaborate church outside the Byzantine Empire. Byzantine art flourished for centuries after the demise of the Eastern empire in 1453 and is still a force today.

CULTURE AND HUMAN VALUES

During its long decline Rome presided over a world growing increasingly chaotic; the barbarian invasions that contributed to its death throes only added to the confusion. The waning of a strong central authority left a power vacuum gradually filled by the Christian church. The final step in the organization of the church was the establishment of a firm leadership that could assure unity of practice and purpose, and resolve any issue that divided the bishops. For a variety of reasons the Bishop of Rome assumed a place of primary importance in the Christian world. By the fifth century the bishop was calling himself the pope (Lat., *papa*, "father"), Christ's vicar on earth. For members of the Western church he possessed the "keys of the kingdom." Though acknowledged as the Father of the Church in the West, the pope was not regarded as supreme in the East, leading eventually to a schism in 1054 that split the Latin and Greek churches. It was at this time that the pope excommunicated the patriarch of Constantinople and the patriarch excommunicated the pope.

The administrative authority of the church hierarchy was paralleled by the development of biblical authority. The bishops, in fact, used their authority to decide what the Scriptures would and would not include. These determinations were completed near the end of the fourth century, when the pope declared Jerome's Latin translation as the standard text—which it still is today for the Church of Rome.

Although Christian art was concerned with the spiritual world-view of the young church, the dominant concept was authority in any form, from church doctrine to the Bible, the bishops, the pope, Jesus, and God the Father. Representational art of the classical world was rejected; instead, people were depicted in terms of their authority—what they represented rather than how they might look.

Artists also depicted other values, particularly the seven virtues of faith, hope, love, justice, fortitude, temperance, and prudence. The seven deadly sins of pride, envy, anger, avarice, dejection, gluttony, and lust were, supposedly, unfit subjects for art; nevertheless, these attitudes or activities were occasionally graphically depicted as examples of how not to behave.

Christian values dominated Western culture for the next 1,000 years or so. In varying degrees, they retain their importance today for those who adhere to one of various Christian beliefs.

The Age
of Faith

The Middle Ages
500–1453

Key Dates	People and Events	Art, Architecture, Music, Literature	Religion	Philosophy, Science, Education
500 527–565 First Byzantine golden age	527–565 Reign of Emperor Justinian 529 Justinian closes Plato's Academy 533 Legal Code of Justinian 590–604 Pope Gregory the Great; establishes political power, codifies liturgy and chant 597 St. Augustine's mission to England	ca. 500 Early materials of *Ring of the Nibelung* ca. 526–547 San Vitale, Ravenna ca. 530–539 Church of Sant' Apollinare in Classe, Ravenna 532–537 Hagia Sophia, Constantinople (Istanbul)	ca. 529 Benedictine Order founded by St. Benedict at Monte Cassino **Muhammad** 570–632	ca. 500 Origin of Seven Liberal Arts
600 600–800 Irish golden age	622–732 Islamic conquest of Middle East, western Asia, north Africa, Portugal, and Spain	ca. 698–721 *Lindisfarne Gospels*	622 Muhammad's flight from Mecca (the Hegira) 630 Muhammad captures Mecca	
700 750–900 Carolingian Period	732 Battle of Poitiers; Muslim expansion checked by Charles Martel 751– Pepin, King of the Franks 768–814 Reign of Charlemagne (Carolingian Empire)	ca. 740 *Beowulf* ca. 760–820 *Book of Kells* 785–990 Mosque of Córdoba 792–805 Palatine Chapel of Charlemagne, Aachen		781 Charlemagne's Palace School established. Beginning of Carolingian Renaissance
800 800–1100 Development of Feudalism	800 Charlemagne crowned Holy Roman Emperor by Pope Leo III ca. 820 Beginning of Viking raids on England and France, later on Italy and Sicily	806 Germigny des Pres		
900 900–1100 Second Byzantine golden age	955 Invading Magyars stopped by German King Otto 987 Foundation of French monarchy by Hugh Capet		ca. 900 Conversion of Kievan Russia to Orthodox Christianity	
1000 1000–1200 Romanesque Period	ca. 1000 Viking Leif Eriksson reached North America (?) 1042–66 Edward the Confessor, Anglo-Saxon king 1061–91 Norman conquest of Sicily 1066 Norman conquest of England by William the Conqueror	ca. 1000 *Song of Roland* written down 1004–1218 St.-Benoit-sur-Loire 1017– Mont-St.-Michel 1037–67 Abbey of Jumièges 1056– Westminster Abbey, London 1063–1272 Pisa Cathedral 1064 St. Etienne, Caen ca. 1070–80 Bayeux Tapestry 1080– Tower of London 1080–1120 St.-Sernin, Toulouse	1054 Separation of Eastern and Western churches 1095 First Crusade preached by Pope Urban II 1096–1291 Period of major crusades	ca. 1000–1100 Battle of Universals (Realist-Nominalist controversy) **Abelard** 1079–1142 philosopher and theologian
1100 1140–1200 Early Gothic Period	**Eleanor of Aquitaine** 1122–1204 (m. Louis VII of France and Henry II of England) 1152–90 Reign of Frederick Barbarosa, Emperor of Holy Roman Empire 1154–89 Reign of Henry II, first Angevin king of England 1189–99 Reign of Richard the Lion-Heart	ca. 1104–32 Ste.-Madeleine, Vézelay 1140–4 Gothic choir, St.-Denis, near Paris ca. 1160 *Tristan et Iseult* written down 1163–1250 Notre Dame, Paris 1174– Canterbury Cathedral fl. 1183 Pérotin, composer at Notre Dame, Paris 1194–1260 Chartres Cathedral	1147–9 Second Crusade **St. Francis of Assisi** 1182–1226 *Little Flowers of St. Francis* 1198–1216 Pope Innocent III; apex of church political and ecclesiastical power	ca. 1150 Complete works of Aristotle become available from Islam; founding of University of Paris ca. 1163 Founding of Oxford University
1200 1200–1300 High Gothic Period	1215 King John signs Magna Carta 1220–50 Reign of Frederick II, Holy Roman Emperor; royal vs. papal power 1226–70 Reign of Louis IX of France (St. Louis) 1295 Model Parliament of Edward I (Angevin), England	ca. 1200 *Ring of the Nibelung* written down ca. 1220–88 Notre Dame, Amiens ca. 1225– Beauvais Cathedral **Cimabue** 1240–1302 painter 1245–8 Ste.-Chapelle, Paris **Duccio** ca. 1255–1319 painter **Dante Alighieri** 1265–1321 **Giotto** ca. 1266–1337 painter **Philippe de Vitry** 1291–1361 Ars Nova in music	1210 St. Francis founds Franciscan order	**Roger Bacon** ca. 1214–94 scientist **Thomas Aquinas** ca. 1225–74 scholastic philosopher **William of Occam** ca. 1270–1347 Nominalist philosopher
1300 1300–1500s Late Gothic Period: International Style	1322–8 Charles IV, last of Capetian kings of France 1328–50 Philip VI, first Valois king of France 1337–1453 Hundred Years' War: England vs. France 1347–9 Black Death sweeps through Europe 1377–99 Richard II, last Angevin king of England 1399–1413 Henry IV, House of Lancaster, England	*Petrarch 1304–74 *Boccaccio 1313–75 *Decameron* *Chaucer 1340–1400 *Canterbury Tales* 1354–1427 Alhambra, Granada *Christine de Pisan ca. 1365–ca. 1431 writer *Gentile da Fabriano 1370–1427 painter *Brunelleschi 1377–1446 architect *Fra Angelico 1387–1455 painter	1305–76 Papacy at Avignon ("Babylonian Captivity") 1378–1417 Great Schism of the Church of Rome	
1400 1453 Constantinople falls to Ottoman Turks; end of Eastern Roman Empire		ca. 1485 *Everyman*		ca. 1400 Arabs transmit compass and astrolabe to Europe

*These artists and writers represent the Early Renaissance, clearly indicating that a new movement arises as the previous era fades away

CHAPTER 12

Building Medieval Walls

Whether we accept 410 or 476 as the date of the "fall" of Rome makes little difference; the decline of Roman power began in the third century and accelerated throughout the fifth century. Roman civilization, however, never died; many physical remains suffered from vandalism but some were sufficiently intact for Renaissance studies 1,000 years later. Moreover, Roman law, language, organization, and its practical approach to power were incorporated into the fabric of the Church of Rome as it expanded to fill the power vacuum. Formerly (and mistakenly) called the Dark Ages, the Early Middle Ages (ca. 500–ca. 800) saw the steady rise of what is now the oldest major institution in Western civilization.

THE EARLY CHURCH

Christianity originated in the teachings of Christ, but became an institutionalized church largely through the efforts of Paul, Peter, and Augustine. Peter wanted to limit the new faith to Jews, but Paul prevailed with his belief that Christianity had a message for the whole world. Paul preached to the Gentiles but it was Peter, credited with being the first Bishop of Rome and thus the first pope, who placed the leadership of the new church in the best possible setting to inherit what remained of the Roman Empire. Paul, Peter, and a succession of popes worked diligently but the church needed a clear, unified doctrine to become a widely accepted institution for the preservation and propagation of the faith. This task was accomplished in large measure by Augustine.

Augustine the Searcher, 354–430

A North African from Thagaste, Augustine received a fine education followed by further study in Carthage. Always a searcher for a firm belief, the young man considered and rejected the Christian faith of his mother, Monica. He first became a Manichean, an austere religion founded by a third-century Persian named Mani. The religion's core was a dualistic belief (derived in part from Zoroastrianism) in powers of good and evil conflicting in the world and in people. In this ascetic faith the "elect" or "perfect" led a

Spartan life and practiced strict celibacy to ensure immediate happiness after death. Augustine could not accept all of this doctrine—particularly celibacy—and later, in Rome, became a skeptic, a believer in nothing, not even his own existence.

Augustine then considered the Neoplatonists, later crediting this period as the crucial stepping stone to Christianity, for his doctrine incorporated much of Neoplatonism while omitting Greek rationalism. This was in Milan, where he was serving as a municipally appointed teacher and where Bishop Ambrose's preaching had a powerful effect on him. Influenced by Ambrose and by his Christian mother, who had joined his household, he experienced his famous mystical conversion as described in his *Confessions*. Baptized by Ambrose in 387, he led a contemplative life until his appointment as Bishop of Hippo, where he became a powerful advocate of the church against the heresies of the Manicheans and the Arians. But it was the Donatist heresy that he energetically attacked.

Strengthening the Institution

The Arian and Donatist heresies were serious problems for a young institution that would not tolerate dissent. Roman persecution induced some priests to collaborate with authorities by handing over sacred texts. After Constantine's edicts of toleration in 311 and 313, these "handers-over" (*traditores*) resumed their priestly roles only to be challenged by Donatus, Bishop of Carthage. Donatus would punish collaborating priests by declaring their administration of the sacraments invalid, a politically dangerous position because it gave believers a chance to judge priests. Because the controversy was political, Constantine wielded his imperial prerogative by ruling that once the church ordains a priest, his administration of the sacraments remains valid even though his actions may become reprehensible.

The Arian heresy, after Arius, an Alexandrian priest, maintained that God the Son could not be of precisely the same essence as God the Father because the begetter must be superior to and earlier in time than the begotten. This view threatened to diminish the divinity of Christ and demolish the Holy Trinity, as emphasized by Arius' bitter opponent, Athanasius, Bishop of Alexandria. Disdaining logic and espousing mystery, Athanasius and his followers exhorted Christians to accept on faith the Trinity of Father, Son, and Holy Ghost as equal and contemporary. Unable to settle the quarrel, Constantine called, in 325, an ecumenical council (Gk., *oikoumene*, "the inhabited world"), the first meeting involving the whole church. Meeting at Nicaea, across the straits from Constantinople, the assembled bishops backed Athanasius, resulting in the famous Nicene Creed ("I believe in one God"), which Constantine issued with all the force of an imperial decree. It took several centuries, however, to completely suppress the Arian movement.

In his administrative role as Bishop of Hippo Augustine constantly faced the problem of the sacraments (only through which one gained salvation) when performed by heretical or corrupt priests. He decided that the efficacy of the sacraments lay in the priestly office for, if the benefit of the sacraments depended on the quality of the priest, people would be judging God's grace. The resulting doctrine that the priestly office was infallible helped establish the idea of the church as infallible since its power was in its offices. This power, it was argued, descended directly from the apostles, the original bishops of the church. From them it passed to other bishops and on to the priests through the "laying on of hands." This act, which could not be revoked, conferred the power to administer the sacraments.

Theology

Our discussion of Augustine is limited to an overview of his ideas about the nature of God, creation, free will; his philosophy of history; and the infallibility of the church. These beliefs form the backbone for European civilization through the Late Middle Ages.

A New Reality

With the demise of the Roman Empire the time was ripe for a new idea of reality. According to Augustine, God was the only reality, who created the world out of nothingness. This God was a mystic being, not a Neoplatonist intellectual principle; knowledge of God and life in him was available to all human beings, whether or not they were philosophers. Although Augustine regarded his own philosophic speculations as stepping-stones to belief, he felt that his conversion came about not through human efforts but by the grace of God that is available to all people. For Augustine and all believers throughout the Middle Ages, union with God was the only true goal and the only genuine happiness for people, all of which happened in the hereafter.

According to Augustine, the process of creation-from-nothingness took place because of two aspects of the mind of God, roughly corresponding to the Platonic essences, but with significant differences. One such aspect

corresponds to the eternal truths, such as the fact that the sum of the angles of a triangle always equals 180 degrees. Such truths, existing before creation and after the destruction of the world, constitute the basic patterns and harmonies of the universe. Another aspect of God's mind consists of the "seminal [seed] reasons" for created things. These are the patterns that acquire physical substance and form the visible entities: human bodies, trees, earth, and the other myriad things that are apparent to our senses. Such sense-apparent things exist in time; they rise, disintegrate, and pass away, and because of their transitory nature are the least important of God's creations.

Time and Eternity

Implicit in the last statement is Augustine's dualistic concept of time. He believed in a direct flow of time in which humanity's activities moved upward toward eventual perfection, toward the godlike. The flow of time and all the changes that occur within it are characteristic of the temporal world. God, however, with all the attributes of his mind, dwells in eternity, which is really a timeless instant. In this realm past and future have no meaning; all is present.

Augustine reconciled the problem of God's foreknowledge of all events and humanity's free will by asserting that people had free will, even though God knew every event that would take place. How does one avoid fatalism and the idea of predestination if a person's actions are known in advance? The answer is that God's seeing all things as present-time allows for foreknowledge in what we call time, yet the "seeing" of things does not influence them. All events are simultaneous for God, and thus he can know them without influencing them. A person's vision is shackled by past, present, and an inscrutable future, but in the temporal world there is complete free will.

The Material World

Augustine was ambivalent in his attitude toward the body and the material world. If this world is God's creation then it must be good. On the other hand, being overly concerned with the acquisition of worldly goods can turn a person away from God, and that is sinful. The matter of bodily pleasures was especially disturbing. Before his conversion, Augustine had lived a lusty life of fleshly pleasures; his proclivities were dramatized in his famous prayer: "O Lord, make me chaste, but not yet." He shifted to the other extreme after his conversion and condemned sexual pleasure. He included music in this censure because, like the sex act, it kept the mind from contemplating God.

Platonic doctrine strongly influenced Augustine's view of the material world. He believed that the physical things of the world are all passing away and changing. In *The City of God* (426), for example, he notes that many people lost their worldly goods when barbarians sacked Rome in 410, yet Christians remained happy because their "possessions" were spiritual and could not be taken away.

The conclusion is obvious: anxiety about worldly things is a concern over nothing because these things are ephemeral. The only vital consideration is the things of the spirit, which have their existence in eternity. Augustine's position here is not completely dualistic, in that it does not actually despise the flesh and worldly things, yet it tends in that direction. Later on, some Christian thinkers were to turn completely against the world and the flesh, asserting even more strongly than Plato and Augustine that these things were traps for the mind and spirit of humanity. Much of the puritanical thought in the history of Western civilization comes from this reasoning.

Philosophy of History

In the first complete formulation of a Christian philosophy of history, Augustine viewed the story of humanity as a conflict between two cities. (He used the word "city" as we might use the word "community," e.g., "business community.") One was the City of God, the other the City of Man. In the beginning, when time was created, he stated, everything belonged to the good city, yet with the revolt of the angels and Satan's expulsion from heaven, the other city came into being. From that time until the birth of Christ, almost all of humanity belonged to the earthly city. Only a few Hebrews who had faith in the coming of a Savior belonged to the City of God. With Christ's coming for the redemption of mortals, and with the formation of the church, the membership in the two cities was more sharply divided, since all members of the City of God were also members of the church. This, he was careful to assert, did not work conversely; not all members of the church were necessarily members of God's City. The end of history will come with the Last Judgment and the final and complete separation of the two cities. The saved will be reclothed in their perfect bodies and take their place with God; the damned will undergo eternal torture with Satan. Because, according to Augustine, those destined for the good city are already known to God, this can be the basis for the doctrine of predestination, a tenet enunciated by Calvin during the Reformation.

Augustine's philosophy of history has at least one other important consequence. If the original members of the City of God are to be found only among the Hebrews, they alone know truth. Thus all other learning—that of the Greeks, for example—is false and must not be studied. This condemnation of the Graeco-Roman heritage plagued the development of Western civilization for many centuries.

The Church in Rome

Sometime after the death of Augustine the bishops of Rome asserted their supremacy over the other bishops by placing the final authority of the church in Rome. The argument was both pragmatic and biblical. Peter had founded the church in Rome and he was, moreover, Christ's spiritual successor. Biblical authority rested on Christ's words concerning Peter, "Upon this rock [*petras*] will I build my church." Leo, Bishop of Rome (reigned 440–461), first made this claim to ecclesiastical authority, and later, Pope Gregory the Great (reigned 590–604), a skillful diplomat, guaranteed universal acceptance (in the West) of the primacy of the pope. These moves reinforced the stability of an institution that maintained its authority throughout the troubled years of the Early Middle Ages as the only source of order throughout Europe.

FEUDALISM

The Church of Rome replaced imperial Rome as the unifying power of Western civilization but there was no comparable secular authority capable of organizing and governing large territories. Instead, medieval Europe became a patchwork quilt of small fiefdoms. The governmental system, **feudalism**, did not develop fully until the tenth century, but it is discussed here as the slowly evolving political system of the Middle Ages.

Feudalism was, essentially, the division of the former Empire into units small enough for a single man to rule. It also engendered a fighting society, because the lords constantly raided adjoining territories, and all were subject to the forays of the northern tribes from Germany and Scandinavia.

In the wake of Roman civilization many kings lacked enough wealth or power to hold their kingdoms together. To survive, they split their kingdoms among the nobility, starting with the high-ranking barons. In return for land the barons swore allegiance to the monarch and agreed to furnish some fighting men whenever anyone attacked the kingdom. A baron thus became the king's vassal (meaning "servant"). But the barons also lacked sufficient power to administer their lands, leading to the creation of their own vassals and further subdivision of the land. This successive land division continued down to the knight, who owned one demesne (di-MAN): a village and the surrounding farmlands. Each nobleman was thus absolute ruler over the land he controlled, administering justice as he saw fit, and subject only to the oaths of fealty sworn to the lord immediately over him.[1]

MANORIALISM

Coexisting with feudalism on the lowest level of land division was the manorial system. **Manorialism**, as it is also called, regulated the life of rural communities during the Middle Ages. It had its beginnings during late Roman times, when the peasants were forced to stay on the land and

---

1. Feudalism was far from universal in Europe being largely confined to northern France, western Germany, England, the Norman kingdom of Sicily, and northern Spain. Other parts of Europe experienced some feudalism but many areas were never feudalized.

12.1   Aigues-Mortes, France, aerial view. Photo: Lesley and Roy Adkins Picture Library, Langport, U.K.
Located on the Mediterranean coast, this perfectly preserved medieval town was founded as a staging area and supply base for the Crusades. Walls were a common denominator throughout medieval Europe.

SERFDOM

The serf and the lord were obligated to each other by a complex web of interrelationships. The serf pledged labor, loyalty, and some material goods to the lord in return for protection and the use of some land for subsistence farming. Bound to the land, the serf and his descendants were inherited by the lord and his descendants. Though they were not slaves and had certain established rights, serfs were not free to leave the manor. They could buy their freedom, but few managed to save enough money. Another alternative was to flee the manor; those determined ones who could survive in a city for a year and a day were finally rid of all manorial obligations. With increasing prosperity throughout Europe beginning in the eleventh century, more and more serfs could rise above their lowly station to become peasants with only voluntary ties to the land. Although manorialism generally ended in the sixteenth century there were lingering remains. Serfs were not freed in the Austrian Empire until 1781 and it took the 1789 revolution to sweep away remaining pockets of serfdom in France. The czar finally freed Russian serfs in 1861 but, not surprisingly, elements of medieval manorialism survived until the 1917 revolutions.

---

became serfs. It reached its zenith during the tenth and eleventh centuries and then began a long decline that did not end until the modern era.

The manorial system was the totality of the life within one of these villages. Here the lord resided in his manor unless he was away at war. A priest took care of the community's spiritual needs with the church and parish house at the center of the village. Other buildings usually included a community bake-oven, a winepress, and a mill for grinding grain. The farming land (averaging about 1,000 acres [405 hectares]) was divided into three main sections, two of which were planted each year (summer and winter crops) and the third left fallow. The lord retained about half of the land (his demesne, the best part) as his personal property (though serfs farmed it), the priest received a small parcel ("God's acre"), a section was preserved as common woodland, and another as a common meadow. Each serf was given certain strips of land in each of the three fields—each strip was usually an eighth of a mile (0.2 km) in length and about 17 feet (5 m) wide.[2] The serf and his family were "attached" to the land; they could not leave, but neither could they be turned away. The serf gave part of his produce to the lord and was obligated to work a set number of days on the lord's land. The lord, in turn, protected his villagers and provided justice, though he was the only judge in legal disputes and his word was final.

The manorial system ensured a fairly secure but poverty-stricken and almost totally isolated existence. The manor provided the bare necessities and the serf scarcely ever traveled beyond it. There was no news of the outside world except when the lord returned from a war, or when an occasional itinerant peddler happened through. Formal education was unknown, and illiteracy the norm for the serfs and even for many lords. Life on the manor was an endless round of hard work, birth, marriage, and death, with time off only for religious holidays. Existence was maintained at a minimal level behind medieval walls (fig. 12.1), which shut out hostile forces but which also, figuratively speaking, kept out ideas that might disturb the rigid order enforced by the church and the barons. No wonder people regarded the world as a vale of tears as they hopefully anticipated a glorious afterlife in heaven.

---

2. Replacing the scratch plow, a new kind of plow was invented (late seventh century) that was equipped with a vertical knife to cut the furrow, a horizontal plowshare to slice under the sod, and a moldboard to turn it over. Pulled by eight oxen (communally owned), it attacked the land with such violence that cross-plowing was unnecessary and fields tended to be shaped in long strips. Found nowhere else in the world (for centuries to come), this plow marked the beginning of a technological revolution that would transform the European from nature's partner to an exploiter of natural resources, leading, in part, to today's ecological problems.

THE RISE OF ISLAM

Western Christianity, Byzantium, and Islam had the common heritage of Graeco-Roman civilization but the three cultures generally preferred emphasizing their differences. During the Early Middle Ages the West, the most primitive and backward civilization, accused the Muslims of being "infidels" and saw Byzantium as "decadent" and "treacherous." In fact, Eastern and Western Christianity and Islam were monotheistic faiths with their roots deep in Judaism. However reluctant, medieval Europe had much to learn from Islam and Byzantium and, in time, it was strongly influenced by its neighbors as it evolved a unique synthesis of classical, Christian, and Germanic traditions.

For over twelve centuries the relations between Islam and Christianity have ranged from distrust and fear to open warfare; the Muslim conquest of Spain and invasion of France, the Crusades, and the Christian reconquest of Spain are only a few of the major conflicts. Politics and economics, however, cause more alienation and hostility between the two cultures than does ideology. Centuries ago the problems involved Muslim control of Palestine and trade routes to the Far East. Today those problems include Palestine, trade, oil, and Israel.

Islam was the last of the great monotheistic religions, but it made up for lost time with the breathtaking speed of its expansion. Beginning in the Arabian Peninsula in 622, the militant faith, in little more than a century, spread east to the borders of China and west to North Africa and the Iberian Peninsula, an area greater than the Roman Empire at its height (map 12.1).

Pre-Islamic Arabia was a hot, dry, barren, and backward land inhabited mainly by nomadic Bedouin tribes who worshiped trees, stones, and pieces of wood supposedly inhabited by supernatural powers. Human virtues, by their standards, were courage, manliness, loyalty, and generosity. The chief Arabian city was prosperous Mecca, the hub of the lucrative caravan trade and site of the Kaaba, Arabia's holiest shrine. Chief deity of the city was Allah, creator of the universe but still only one of some 300 gods.

Muhammad

Muhammad (or Mohammed or Mahomet) was born in this bustling city in about 570. After supporting himself by tending sheep and then as a merchant, he became an agent for a rich widow in her commercial enterprise and later married her. It was undoubtedly on his business trips for her that he encountered Judaism and Christianity. At about age forty he began his practice of retiring to a mountain cave to meditate where he received spiritual insights that he later compared with "the breaking of dawn." He had visions of an angel and then of a giant Archangel Gabriel. After a second revelation ordering him to "rise and warn" the people, Muhammad began preaching in Mecca in 613. His ministry angered the wealthy and powerful Meccans, and

Map 12.1   Expansion of Islam, 622 to ca. 750.

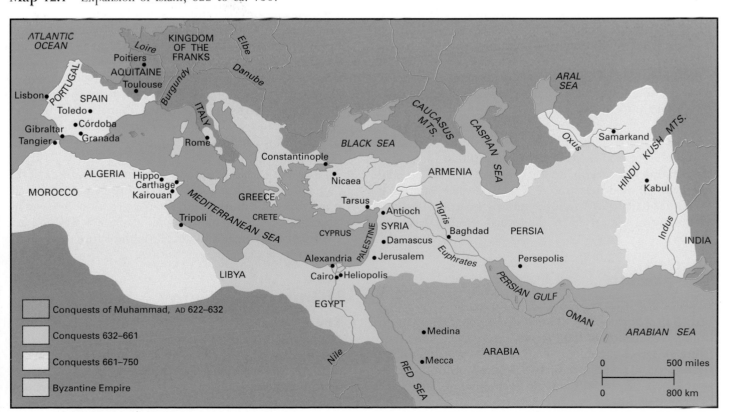

he fled for his life (the Hegira [hi-GYE-rah]) to the city of Yathrib (later called Medina, "City of the Prophet"). This was in 622, which became the first year of the new faith.

Main Articles of Faith

The main articles of that faith are a belief in:

1. Allah, who is the only God;
2. the angels (Gabriel and others);
3. the Prophets (Muhammad, Abraham, Noah, Moses, and Jesus);
4. the sacred books (Old and New Testaments, Psalms of David, and the Koran);
5. the Qadar (God's plan for the collective benefit of all humankind);
6. Resurrection on the Day of Judgment.

The minimum requirement for the religious duties of Muslims is called the Five Pillars of Faith:

1. "There is no God but Allah, and Muhammad is his prophet." This is the Shahadah, which Muslims believe implies all six articles given above. A fundamental part of the religion, this creed needs only to be uttered for any person to be accepted as a Muslim.
2. The obligation of the five daily prayers (dawn, midday, midafternoon, sunset, and nightfall).
3. Giving to the poor (once voluntary, this is now an assessment).
4. Fasting during the month of Ramadan, the ninth month of the Muslim lunar calendar. According to Islamic belief this marks the month in which Allah gave the Koran to Gabriel for revelation to Muhammad.
5. Pilgrimage to Mecca. Though many cannot do this, millions have done so for the experience of mingling as an equal with other believers and for the sense of Islamic unity.

In the early stages of Islam, a sixth duty was required for all able-bodied men: to fight in the **jihad** (holy war). Each caliph ("successor" to Muhammad) felt obligated to reduce the infidel "territory of war" by armed conquest in the name of Allah. With the exception of Spain and Portugal, all territories converted by the sword remain Muslim to this day.

The Koran

Islam is based on the Shahadah, the Koran, which embodies all of Muhammad's teachings, and the Hadith (traditions), a collection of the Prophet's sayings and decisions (some of which are apocryphal). The believer has only to submit to the will of Allah. The Arabic word for submission is "*Islam*," the faith; he who submits is a "*Muslim*," a believer. Submitting unreservedly to an all-powerful God,

believers make up a religious community that follows the Koran's detailed rules for every aspect of daily life. Compiled from the writings of the Prophet some twenty years after his death in 632, the Koran is the only authority, the last word in theology, law, and all social institutions. By far the most important textbook in Muslim universities, the Koran should be read by the faithful in its original language, Arabic, the one language of the faith.

Islamic civilization reached its high point during the tenth century as a kind of Middle Eastern renaissance. The culturally backward Arabs contributed little more than the language, but that was a decisive factor. The language of the Koran is the great unifier of the faith, just as Latin was once the common language of the Church of Rome. The Arabic form of writing was also important, leading, in Islamic art, to the development of an infinite variety of abstract ornament and a remarkable system of linear abstraction that is uniquely Islamic.

Islamic Culture

Islamic culture was a synthesis of Greek, Syrian, Persian, and Indian (Hindu) traditions. But Islam digested as well as borrowed, enriching virtually every field of human endeavor, most significantly in medicine, astronomy, navigation, and mathematics. Omar Khayyam, the Persian astronomer and poet of the *Rubaiyat*, devised a remarkably accurate calendar. Philosophers studied Plato and Aristotle, translating them from Syriac (Syrian scholars had earlier translated the Greek) into Arabic. Trade routes were opened through India and on to China so that material goods and immaterial ideas flowed freely throughout the Islamic world. Learning flourished in the great universities at Cairo and Toledo. The art of gracious living was finely developed, particularly in the luxurious cities of Baghdad and Córdoba. While Western Europe was slogging along in the mud a high culture flourished in the lands of the mosques, the riches of which would not be known until after the Crusades began in the last years of the eleventh century.

Art and architecture were distinctive features of this high culture. National styles of the pre-Islamic era made important contributions but Muslim artistic achievements were not of a particular people or country. Unified and shaped by religion, Islamic art and architecture were among the glories of an entire civilization.

Islamic Architecture

The Mosque

Islam provided direct access to God through prayer; there was no liturgy, sacraments, or priestly class and thus no need for a special kind of architecture. Praying could be done literally anywhere and Muhammad did teach and pray everywhere including his own home. Paradoxically, a religion that had no architectural requirements developed a mosque design that remained essentially the same throughout the vast Muslim world.

The open-court mosque was derived from encampment mosques of the conquering Muslim armies. The "army mosque" was an open field with a ditch and a rustic prayer shelter on the **kibla** side—the wall facing Mecca. Permanent mosques used the basic idea of a large open court enclosed on three sides by covered arcades with a roofed prayer hall on the kibla side. (The arcades provided areas shaded from the torrid desert sun.) Inside the hall a central niche, the **mihrab**, was added to the kibla wall. To the right of the mihrab was the **minibar**, or pulpit, for readings from the Koran and the Friday sermon. A characteristic feature from the earliest days, the **sahn**, a pool for ritual ablutions, was located in the courtyard. Though *muezzins* (mu-EZ-ins; criers) could call the faithful to prayer from any high place, **minarets** or tall, slender towers quickly became standard features of the total mosque design.

The Mosque of Sultan Ahmet I (fig. 12.2, also known as the Blue Mosque) was apparently designed by a student of Koca Sinan, Turkey's greatest architect. Here the original prayer hall of early Islamic architecture has been enlarged into the domed mosque, the finest architectural achievement of the Ottoman Turks. Minarets are placed at the four corners of the mosque and at the two corners of the arcade. There was no mandatory number of minarets; the sole stipulation was that no mosque may have seven minarets like the Great Mosque in Mecca.

To the left of figure 12.2 is Hagia Sophia, the astonishing sixth-century church (now a museum) constructed by Justinian (see figs. 11.22 and 11.23). A comparison of the mosque with the former church reveals the inspiration for Ottoman Turk central-domed mosques. The higher dome and lack of interior decoration give the interior of Hagia Sophia a much different feeling from that of the Blue Mosque. They do represent two very different religious views. Also to the left of figure 12.2 is the site of the Roman Hippodrome, where the chariot races were staged, with a column called the Obelisk of Theodosius that the emperor had moved to Constantinople from the Temple of Karnak. Istanbul has been, in turn, a Greek, Roman, Byzantine, Christian, and Muslim city.

The interior of a mosque (fig. 12.3) illustrates the "dissolution of matter" that was so fundamental to the Islamic style. In the mosque everyone must have a feeling of being equal before Allah. Further, there must be a concern about eternity coupled with a disregard for earthly existence. Highly ornamented surfaces help to disguise and "dissolve" matter. Solid walls are, in effect, camouflaged with tiles and plaster decorated with arabesques and endlessly repetitive designs called "infinite patterns" (fig. 12.4). This feature of Islamic design is very different from ancient Greek architecture, which emphasized the function of architectural members, e.g., the entasis (slight swelling) of columns to suggest their load-bearing function.

HINDU MATHEMATICS

Building on Babylonian and Greek efforts, Hindu mathematicians were even more advanced in their development of arithmetic and algebra than their Chinese counterparts. In addition to the whole numbers and fractions of ordinary arithmetic, algebra involves negative and irrational numbers. Irrational numbers such as *pi* and the square root of 2 that are not expressible as fractions were first discovered by the Greeks in the fifth century BC and used by mathematicians from that time on. Negative numbers were systematically developed in India by Aryabhata in the sixth century AD. This enabled mathematicians to solve such equations as $x + 4 = 2$ in which x is –2.

Babylonian mathematics had lacked a zero symbol which could be used to hold an empty place in a number. This vital concept was introduced into the present base-10 system by the Hindus, who also used "Arabic numerals." By the tenth century all of these innovations had been incorporated into Islamic science; later they were transmitted to Europe through the Moors of Spain.

12.2 Muhammad Ago ibn Ahd al-Muin, Mosque of Sultan Ahmet I, Istanbul, Turkey. 1609–16. Photo: Sonia Halliday, Weston Turville, U.K.

12.4 Mosque of Sultan Ahmet I, arabesques. Photo: Dagli Orti, Paris.

12.3 *Above* Mosque of Sultan Ahmet I, interior. Photo: Spectrum, London.

12.5 Great Mosque (arcades of Abd ar-Rahman I), Córdoba, Spain, interior. Height of columns 9'9" (2.9 m). Photo: Sonia Halliday, Weston Turville, U.K.

The Great Mosque

Begun by Caliph Abd ar-Rahman in the tenth century, the mosque of the caliphs of Córdoba (fig. 12.5) is so large that a sixteenth-century Christian church was built in its midst. With no axis and thus no focus, the forest of columns—856 in all—symbolizes the worshipers, who are as individual as the columns but who are all united in common prayer as part of the great community of believers. The striped arches are a Muslim invention, but the columns themselves were recycled, having been taken from Roman and Christian buildings. In common with mosques throughout the Muslim world, the Great Mosque has no sculpture and no figurative decoration. Although there is no prohibition of figurative art—or even any mention of it—in the Koran, idolatry was expressly prohibited, and to avoid any possibility of this, mosques never contain any representations of living forms. One of the glories of Muslim Spain, the Great Mosque was only one of the wonders of Córdoba, itself the most illustrious center of art and learning in all of Europe until its conquest by Christians in 1236.

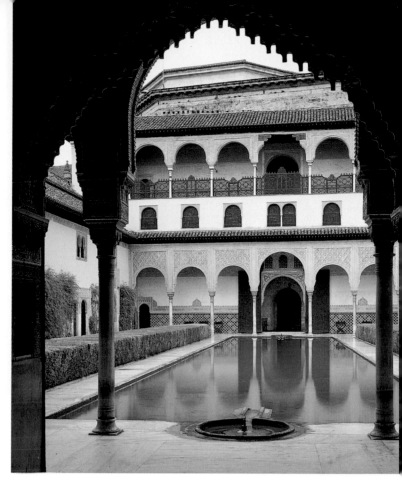

12.6   Court of Myrtles, the Alhambra, Granada, Spain. 1354–91. Photo: Dagli Orti, Paris.

12.7   Court of Lions, the Alhambra. Photo: Dagli Orti, Paris.

AN ORIENTAL PALACE

To the traveler imbued with feeling for the historical and poetical, so inseparably intertwined in the annals of romantic Spain, the Alhambra is as much an object of devotion as is the Caaba to all true Muslims. How many legends and traditions, true and fabulous; how many songs and ballads, Arabian and Spanish, of love and war and chivalry, are associated with this Oriental pile!

1832, Washington Irving (1783–1859), American author

The Alhambra

The ponderous exterior of the palace of the caliphs of Granada, the Alhambra, shields an inner architectural fairyland resonating to the liquid murmur of running water. Because of its desert origins, Islam pictures Hell and Paradise as extensions of the natural environment; Hell is an arid and flaming inferno while Paradise is like an oasis: cool, wet, and luxuriant. Drawing unlimited water from the snows of the Sierra Nevada, the caliphs built an earthly paradise: delicate, intimate, cooled and soothed by playful fountains and the channels of water coursing throughout the palace, the embodiment of an Arabian Nights setting. The main units of the palace are patios framed by architecture. The Court of Myrtles (fig. 12.6) is essentially a reflecting pool with the illusion of floating columns and arches. Multi-colored tiles and plaster casements are decorated with elegant infinite patterns.

The famous Court of Lions (fig. 12.7) is a kind of reverse image of the Court of Myrtles. Here the water runs through the court in slender ribbons, tying the unit

12.8 Abencerrajes Gallery, the Alhambra, interior looking up into the cupola. Photo: Ancient Art and Architecture, London.

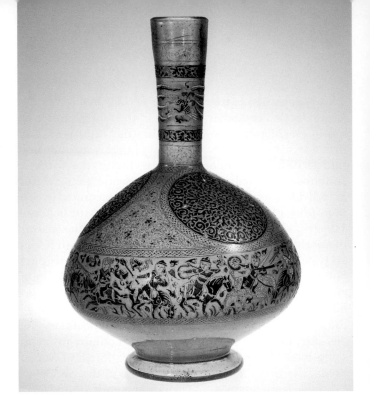

12.9 Bottle, decorated with three arabesques above a wide band of mounted warriors, from Syria. Late 13th century. Free-blown and tooled glass, enameled and gilded, pontil on base, height 17⅛" (43.5 cm). Metropolitan Museum of Art, New York (Rogers Fund, 1941.41.150).

12.10 Junaid, *Bihzad in the Garden*, from the poems of Khwahju Kirmani. Persian. 1396. Illumination. British Museum, London.

together in an intimate arrangement. Fittingly, this is the area reserved exclusively for the ruler, his harem, his family, and the servants. Guarded by sculptures of stylized lions, the fountain adds its bubbling sounds to the flowing waters of a fantastic courtyard of delicate columns and arches decorated with tiles and stucco. Lacy arabesques and airy stuccoed ceilings contribute to what is actually a lucid, rhythmic design. Not one column is perfectly tapered and precisely vertical, thus symbolizing the imperfections of earthly existence. Even this manufactured Eden is but a defective version of the heavenly paradise to come.

The Alhambra contains some of the most elaborate stalactite vaults in all of Islam (fig. 12.8). The Islamic practice of dissolving walls and ceilings has evolved into a fantastic array of stucco stalactites dangling from a huge honeycomb. The star-shaped cupola appears to be lightly floating atop the rhythmic in-and-out undulation of the circle of windows. The last notable structure built in Moorish Spain, the Alhambra fell to Ferdinand and Isabella in the eventful year of 1492.

Islamic Art

From the thirteenth to the sixteenth centuries in Syria and Egypt workers in the decorative arts developed superlative skills. Master craftsmen abounded: potters, ivory and wood carvers, and workers in plaster and metal. This marvelous Syrian bottle (fig. 12.9) has a wealth of ornamentation but all so delicately done that the effect is exquisite. Mongol influence is seen in the warriors of the bottom border and in the Phoenix on the neck band but all else is Muslim from the blue arabesques to the geometric and naturalistic motifs.

Figure 12.10 illustrates an especially beautiful example of Islamic manuscript painting. With the poetic text condensed into the tiny area at the top, the artist has concentrated on nature, from the garden's trees and flowering plants to the star-studded sky. The skillful use of curving lines makes the picture seem to undulate. The use of such colors as pale blue and gold, the soft reds and greens, the deep blue and light rose provide a magical lyrical effect. It was this kind of elegant painting that attracted Henri Matisse (1869–1954) to Persian miniatures.

CHARLEMAGNE AND THE CAROLINGIAN RENAISSANCE

Islam's expansion into France was halted by Charles Martel (688?–741), "mayor of the palace" of the Frankish kingdom of the House of Pepin. Chief official of the kingdom, Martel ("the Hammer") was the first of the Carolingian line (after *Carolus*, Latin for Charles). Facing the **Moors** (also called Saracens) at Poitiers in western France, he used his tightly knit cavalry to drive the enemy back to Spain. Because this was the northernmost Muslim penetration of Europe, the Battle of Poitiers of 732 became a landmark in European history.

Pepin the Short (ruled 751–768), son of Charles Martel, declared himself king of the Franks and vigorously consolidated a kingdom that was subsequently inherited by his son Charlemagne (Charles the Great; ruled 768–814). The most important political and humanistic period of the Early Middle Ages, Charlemagne's reign lit the first bright spark in European culture since the demise of Rome. His Carolingian Renaissance proved that the light of civilization had not been extinguished.

First, Charlemagne expanded and solidified the kingdom of the Franks, fighting the Muslims in Spain, the Norsemen up to the Danish border, and the Germanic Lombards in Italy. The Battle of Roncevaux in 778 in which the Saracens ambushed and killed Charles' knight, Count Roland, furnished the kernel for the great cycle of songs and stories relating to the exploits of Charles. In return for this warring activity against the pagans, and as a shrewd political move, the pope crowned Charles "Emperor of the Romans" on Christmas Day in the year 800.

A Learning Revival

Politics aside, the significant factor is that Charles had a great respect for learning and brought scholars from all over Europe to his court at Aix-la-Chapelle (today's Aachen). The architecture of this court itself is a landmark in Western culture, for Charles had visited Ravenna where he had marveled at the magnificent architecture and gleaming mosaics. The chapel at Aachen (fig. 12.11) is modeled after the Church of San Vitale in Ravenna (figs. 11.16 and 11.19), and it was responsible for introducing Roman stone

MUSLIM INDIA

When British India was subdivided into Pakistan and India in 1947 there were over a million casualties in the ensuing warfare between Hindus and Muslims. Moreover, Muslim Pakistan and secular—but largely Hindu—India have fought two wars since that time. One can hardly believe that India was a Muslim empire from the thirteenth to the nineteenth century, when the British arrived. Things began badly in 1206 when Asian converts to Islam, mainly Turks, Persians, Afghans, and Mongols installed a Delhi Sultanate that persisted through thirty-four sultans despite an unceasing record of tyranny, corruption, and bloodshed. The opposite extreme was reached when the dissolute sultanate was overthrown in 1526 by Babur, a remarkable warrior from Persia and descendant of Mongol conquerors Genghis Khan and Tamerlane. A series of able emperors subsequently added to the glory of the new Mogul dynasty. They developed the administrative machinery that is still basic today and did much to combine Hindu and Muslim motifs in art, architecture, literature, and music. Mogul art and, especially, architecture, which culminated in the Taj Mahal (1630–1648?), have had a lasting impact on Indian culture.

12.11 Odo of Metz, Interior of the Palatine Chapel, Aachen, Germany. 792–805. Photo: Roebild, Frankfurt.

construction and Eastern ideas of beauty to the Western world.

Charles established the Palace (or Palatine) School and imported the English scholar Alcuin from the cathedral school at York to direct it. Alcuin also collected ancient manuscripts and revived the monastic practice of copying manuscripts, both for the palace library and for distribution to other seats of learning. The Palatine School did not generate much original thought, but it was the first center of scholarship since the collapse of Classical civilization and thus crucial for later intellectual development.

Charles brought northern Italy, some of northern Spain, all of France, and western and southern Germany under his rule (map 12.2). Although he did not try to impose a single law code on these diverse people, he did, however, have all of his provinces inspected regularly to ensure good government and the proper administration of justice. Further, he strengthened the power of the church by forcibly Christianizing all conquered people. One consequence of the pope crowning him emperor lay in the idea that the church was superior to secular authority, a belief that was to cause all sorts of trouble in later centuries. Charlemagne

himself foresaw the problem when he remarked that he would not have gone to St. Peter's that Christmas Day had he guessed the pontiff's plan.

After Charlemagne's death in 814, and the brief rule of his ineffective son Louis the Pious, his empire was divided among three weak grandsons who were incapable of continuing the tradition they had inherited. The empire rapidly fell apart, particularly under the invasions of the Norsemen, the Vikings from Scandinavia who ravaged much of Europe and even sailed to the continent later named North America, where they briefly established colonies.

THE ASSIMILATION OF CULTURES

"Middle Ages" is a less than satisfactory term that Renaissance humanists applied to the thousand-year period between the end of Graeco-Roman civilization and the self-conscious "rebirth" of the classical world. For the humanists this middle era was an uninteresting, if extended, interlude between the glories of antiquity and the revival of Graeco-Roman culture. But the humanists failed to see that a new culture had evolved out of the fusion of the Graeco-Romans of the south with the Celto-Germanic peoples of the north.

Map 12.2   The Empire of Charlemagne, AD 814.

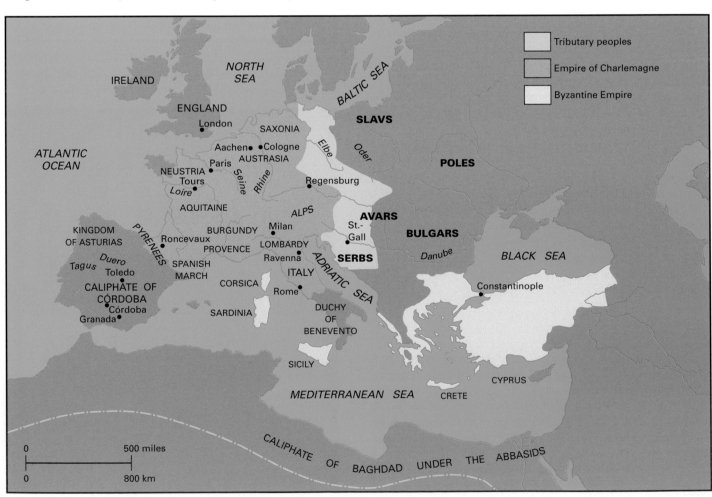

We have already examined the sophisticated, balanced, and intellectual culture of the Graeco-Roman era, whose horizontal-linear architecture and canons of art and architecture testify to a rational civilization. From the third to the sixth centuries many northern people had come into the empire by invitation, infiltration, and military conquest. These were people of a very different character. Primitive and coarse when compared with the cultivated southerners, their architectural line was energetic, vertical, and angular, their decorations intricate, twisted, and unpredictable. Canons of art or architecture were unthinkable.

From around 500 to about 1000 the clashing cultures made this transitional period one full of fear, doubt, confusion, and strife. All was not darkness however. The Church of Rome grew ever stronger, agricultural methods improved and the vital horsecollar was invented, while the sea-worthy Viking ships that could sail the stormy Atlantic became the design of choice. Who were these intrepid sailors who dared to cross the Atlantic to a New World that Columbus "discovered" many centuries later?

The Norsemen

The basic social organization of these northern peoples was the **comitatus**, which was the banding together of a group of fighting men under a warrior chieftain's leadership. The men pledged their loyalty and their strength to the chief and he, in turn, promised to reward them from captured plunder. Thus in the early Anglo-Saxon poem of *Beowulf*, which is based on a Scandinavian legend, both the hero and another leader, Hrothgar, are called "ring-givers" from their roles as leaders distributing gold to their fighting men. The Viking dragonships were fearsome visitors in England and on the Continent because they contained an organized comitatus whose intentions were singleminded: attack, capture, and plunder.

But their religion reveals another aspect of these people. The twentieth-century philosopher Lewis Mumford has described the Graeco-Roman people as "pessimistic of the body and optimistic for the soul," and the Celto-Germanic peoples as "optimistic of the body but pessimistic for the spirit." The distinction is a valid one. The classic and Christian southern peoples regarded earthly existence as a brief period of pain and sorrow followed, they believed, by a joyous afterlife in heaven. The Celto-Germanics ate greatly, drank deeply, killed and raped widely, but were ultimately pessimistic about the afterlife. Theirs was perhaps the only religion that envisions the ultimate defeat of the "good" gods by the forces of evil and darkness.

The Norsemen worshiped a group of anthropomorphic gods who inhabited a celestial residence called Valhalla. Wotan was the king of the gods but the most active was Thor, the god of thunder. Baldur represented the idea of beauty, springtime, and warmth while Loki was the trickster. Even in the heavenly abode the pessimistic nature of these gods emerges for, through a trick of Loki's, Baldur is slain. Norse warriors were promised an afterlife among the gods, but far different from any heaven conceived of by Christians or Muslims, for example. When a warrior died in battle, semidivine maidens (the Valkyrie) swooped over the battlefield to take him to Valhalla, where the hero continued his fighting, eating, and drinking.

An awful fate was predicted, however, for the gods and heroes, for Valhalla was surrounded by the land of the giant Jotuns, who probably represented the cold and darkness of the northern climate. The gods and the Jotuns were engaged in constant petty warfare and trickery. Ultimately, it was believed, a great battle between the two forces would result in victory for the Jotuns and the death of the gods. Thus the ultimate and total pessimism of the spirit of the Celto-Germanic people.

Boethius, ca. 475–524

We have already noted the difference between the Graeco-Roman and Celto-Germanic cultures in their art and architecture. A comparison of their literature is even more revealing. There is no better example of late Graeco-Roman literature than the *Consolation of Philosophy* by Boethius, who served as a Roman consul almost fifty years after the "official" collapse of the Empire. The book is a thoroughly rational dialogue between the author as a man deeply troubled by his unhappy fate, and a vision of philosophy as a stately woman. The discussion includes such subjects as fortune and chance, happiness, the existence of evil, and free will. The entire exchange reads like a Socratic dialogue, and indeed Boethius was heavily indebted to Platonic thought. Although the ideas in the following excerpt are not new, the reader is constantly aware of a classic coolness and dignified withdrawal from the passions of life.

"But it has been conceded that the highest Good is happiness?"

"Yes," I said.

"Therefore," she said, "it must be confessed that God is Happiness itself."

"I cannot gainsay what you premised before," said I, "and I perceive that this follows necessarily from those premises."

"Look, then," she said, "whether the same proposition is not proved more strongly by the following argument: there cannot be two different highest Goods. For it is clear that where there are two different goods the one cannot be the other; wherefore neither one can be the perfect Good while each is wanting to the other. And that which is not perfect is manifestly not the highest; therefore, if two things are the highest Good, they can by no means be different. Further, we have concluded that both God and happiness are the highest Good; therefore the highest

Deity must be identical with the highest happiness."

"No conclusion," said I, "could be truer in fact or stronger in theory or worthier of God."

"Over and above this," she said, "let me give you a corollary such as geometricians are wont to do when they wish to derive a deduction from the propositions they have demonstrated. Since men become happy by attaining happiness, and happiness is identical with divinity, it is plain that they become happy by attaining divinity. And as men become just by attaining justice and wise by attaining wisdom, so by the same reasoning they become God-like by attaining divinity. Every happy man, then, is God-like; but, while there is nothing to prevent as many men as possible from being God-like, only one is God by nature: men are God-like by participation.[3]

NORTHERN HEROIC EPICS

An urbane, civilized discussion such as the selection above would have utterly bewildered the action-oriented northern people. We can get some idea of their very different Celto-Germanic world by considering the hero epics about Beowulf and Roland.

Beowulf

Although it was written down around the year 1000, *Beowulf* probably dates back to ca. 680, according to evidence that emerged in 1939 in a spectacular archaeological discovery at Sutton Hoo in Suffolk, northeast of London. This was a ship-tomb of an East Anglian king dating from the seventh century and containing a harp, ornaments, jewels, and armor like those described in the poem (fig. 12.12). The intricate, skillfully crafted purse cover vividly suggests a dynamic, vigorous culture. The poem even includes a description of a ship-funeral—that of Beowulf himself.

12.12   Purse cover, from the Sutton Hoo ship burial, England. Ca. 655. Gold and enamel, length 7½" (19 cm). British Museum, London.

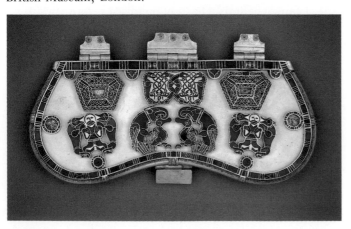

Beowulf is a warrior from southern Sweden who sails to his uncle's court in Denmark where he slays the monster Grendel. As a trophy Beowulf carries home the monster's arm and shoulder that he has wrenched from the giant's torso. Of course there is a great victory feast followed by drunken slumber on the banquet hall floor. After all are asleep Grendel's mother creeps in, kills some of the sleeping men, and carries the bloody "trophy" back to her home, beneath the waters of a dismal swamp.

The next morning Beowulf tracks Grendel's mother to the swamp. Fearlessly he dons his armor and plunges down to the opening of her cave. After a mighty battle with the hag-monster, he kills her with a weapon forged by the giants of old.

The poem's last episode recounts Beowulf's final days when, as chief of his tribe, a dragon threatened his own land. Once more Beowulf sallied forth to slay the dragon but this time he was mortally wounded. The poem ends with his funeral pyre as a Viking chieftain and the construction of his ship-tomb as a landmark for Viking ships at sea.

Beowulf was never tender, never kind, never sympathetic. When his friends die in battle or in the great hall of Heorot, he does not weep for them or extol their virtues. Instead, he swears vengeance and strides forth with sword raised high. He is the mighty warrior, the stalwart adventurer, an authentic Germanic hero.

This was the warrior's world, full of adventure and courage, revenge and death. By the tenth century this ethos had begun slowly to change as the two cultures merged. Many northerners had moved to the south, become Christianized, and given up some of their savage ways. The Angles and Saxons, from Germany, settled in England. Norsemen put down roots in a part of northern France later named for them: Normandy. Throughout Europe the once-restless Germanic people settled on the land. The northern chieftain moved into the evolving feudal system, becoming a baron or a count, a duke or a knight, holding land from his overlord, or suzerain, and granting fiefs to those under him. It was still a warlike society, but a somewhat more settled one, in which the former chieftain gave up his wooden hall for a castle built of stone. The highest virtue continued to be a mutual loyalty between the lord and his vassals.

Song of Roland

The *Song of Roland* is a good example of this new civilization. This minor epic was written in French at about the time of the First Crusade (the 1090s), but the written version simply records a hero-story sung and recited concerning the events that happened, legendarily, three

3. Boethius, *The Consolation of Philosophy*, ed. James J. Buchanan (New York: Frederick Ungar Publishing Co., 1957), pp. 31–2.

centuries before in the days of Charlemagne. The persons of the story are Franks, the Germanic conquerors who gave their name to France; the central figure is Roland, the emperor's nephew. The poem's chief event is the Saracen ambush of the rear guard of Charlemagne's army in a Pyrenees pass at Roncevaux. (Medieval Christians called all Muslims Saracens regardless of nationality. These Saracens were Moors from Spain.) Prompted by envy and revenge, Roland's treacherous kinsman Ganelon arranged the ambush. Roland, his companion Oliver, and the militant Archbishop Turpin are the last survivors of the Frankish host. Facing overwhelming odds, they too are killed. One of the best-known episodes is Roland's stubborn refusal, despite Oliver's urging, to blow his ivory horn (oliphant) to recall Charlemagne's host before the battle begins. When he realizes that he and his fellow Franks are doomed, he at last blows three mighty blasts that Charlemagne hears, 30 leagues (possibly 100 miles or 160 km) away; the emperor returns to rout the Saracens and avenge the death of Roland and his companions. The epic concludes with the trial and punishment of Ganelon.

This is a truly feudal poem, full of the vigorous, active, restless spirit of the northern soldier. Roland is the warrior, a splendid barbarian, courageous in the face of overwhelming odds, loyal to his friends, utterly devoted to God, his spiritual overlord, and to Charlemagne, his temporal one. He is blood brother to his earlier northern kinsman, Beowulf; both heroes represent the all-out, do-or-die, go-for-broke spirit of the heroic age. Following is the 176th stanza, or "laisse," of the poem:

And now Count Roland,　lying beneath a pine,
Has turned his face　to look toward pagan Spain;
And he begins　remembering these things:
The many lands　his valor won the king,
Sweet France, his home,　the men of his own line,
And Charlemagne　who raised him in his house—　2380
The memories　make him shed tears and sigh.
But not forgetting　how close he is to death,
He prays that God　forgive him all his sins:
"O my true Father,　O Thou who never lied,
Thou who delivered　Lazarus from the grave,
Who rescued Daniel　out of the lions' den,
Keep now my soul　from every peril safe,
Forgive the sins　that I have done in life."
Roland, in homage,　offers his glove to God.
Saint Gabriel comes　and takes it from his hand.　2390
His head sinks down　to rest upon his arm;
Hands clasped in prayer,　the count has met his end.
God sends from heaven　the angel Cherubin,
Holy Saint Michael　who saves us from the sea,
And with these two　the Angel Gabriel flies.
Count Roland's soul　they bring to Paradise.

The similarities and differences between this story and that of *Beowulf* are immediately apparent. *Roland*, with its heavy Christian overlay, is more "civilized" than the early

epic, but it is still a savagely militaristic poem, extolling the glories of war, bravery, and loyalty. The role of Archbishop Turpin, an eminent church leader, is notable. Throughout the battle he ranges through the ranks of fighting men, wielding his great mace and breaking heads with the best of them. Churchmen were forbidden a sword that drew blood but not the use of a chain attached to an iron ball studded with spikes. Here is another role of the medieval church: priests active in feudal society, holding land, and as much concerned with battle and secular life, including marriage (until forbidden by Urban II in 1095), as with the religious life. The final act of Roland reveals much of the spirit of the time, for offering his glove to God means pledging loyalty to a feudal lord. Roland, Charlemagne's vassal, has now accepted a new suzerain in God, and Gabriel takes the glove to signify God's approval of Roland as a vassal in the celestial feudal system.

STUDY QUESTIONS

1. In your own words explain how Augustine could believe that people have free will but that God knows the future.
2. Explain how each heresy—Arian and Donatist—differed from the official doctrine of the Church of Rome. Why didn't the church permit several versions of doctrine? What did the church do to eliminate these heresies? Can violence against those labeled as heretics be justified? Why or why not?
3. Describe the key features of a medieval manor. How did it differ from a contemporary American farm community?
4. Review, in your own words, the basic articles and duties of Islam and explain what they mean. Compare these with Roman Catholicism and with some specific Protestant church. What are the critical differences between the three religions? How does Islam compare with Judaism?
5. Explain how and why Islam expanded so rapidly. Can violence in the name of religion be justified? Have Christians ever waged "holy" wars?
6. What, exactly, was the Carolingian Renaissance? Why would a semiliterate king promote a cultural revival?
7. In practical terms, how did a Germanic comitatus work? Was this similar to the feudal system? Why didn't these northern people have manors?
8. Contrast the vision of the hereafter of the Norse religion with the Graeco-Roman tradition and then compare both with medieval Christianity. What are the key differences? What do the differences say about the three cultures?

LITERARY SELECTION 28

Beowulf

Beowulf's Fight with Grendel's Dam

The oldest of English epics, *Beowulf* was written by an unknown author of exceptional talent. The poem is a brilliant exposition of the masculine code, the embodiment of the heroic tradition.[4] In the brief excerpt given below, Beowulf tracks Grendel's hag-mother to her cave in the depths of a swamp where he battles her to the death. The modern translation in alliterative verse is by Charles W. Kennedy; the line numbers are from Klaeber's Old English text.

Beowulf spoke, the son of Ecgtheow:
"Sorrow not, brave one! Better for man
To avenge a friend than much to mourn.
All men must die; let him who may
Win glory ere death. That guerdon is best
For a noble man when his name survives him.
Then let us rise up, O ward of the realm,
And haste us forth to behold the track
Of Grendel's dam. And I give you pledge
She shall not in safety escape to cover,
To earthy cavern, or forest fastness,
Or gulf of ocean, go where she may.
This day with patience endure the burden
Of every woe, as I know you will."
Up sprang the ancient, gave thanks to God
For the heartening words the hero had spoken.

   Quickly a horse was bridled for Hrothgar,
A mettlesome charger with braided mane;
In royal splendor the king rode forth
Mid the trampling tread of a troop of shieldmen.
The tracks lay clear where the fiend had fared
Over plain and bottom and woodland path,
Through murky moorland making her way
With the lifeless body, the best of thanes
Who of old with Hrothgar had guarded the hall.
By a narrow path the king pressed on
                                    1384–1409

Through rocky upland and rugged ravine,
A lonely journey, past looming headlands,
The lair of monster and lurking troll.
Tried retainers, a trusty few,
Advanced with Hrothgar to view the ground.
Sudden they came on a dismal covert
Of trees that hung over hoary stone,
Over churning water and blood-stained wave.
Then for the Danes was the woe the deeper,
The sorrow sharper for Scylding earls,
When they first caught sight, on the rocky sea-cliff,
Of slaughtered Æschere's severed head.

---

4. It is interesting to compare the warrior code of *Beowulf* with the courtly code of the age of chivalry on pp. 399–401 (*The Art of Courtly Love*) and on pp. 447–51 (troubadour-trouvère tradition).

The water boiled in a bloody swirling
With seething gore as the spearmen gazed.
The trumpet sounded a martial strain;
The shield-troop halted. Their eyes beheld
The swimming forms of strange sea-dragons,
Dim serpent shapes in the watery depths,
Sea-beasts sunning on headland slopes;
Snakelike monsters that oft at sunrise
On evil errands scour the sea.
Startled by tumult and trumpet's blare,
Enraged and savage, they swam away;
But one the lord of the Geats brought low,
Stripped of his sea-strength, despoiled of life,
As the bitter bow-bolt pierced his heart.
His watery-speed grew slower, and ceased,
And he floated, caught in the clutch of death.
Then they hauled him in with sharp-hooked boar-spears,
By sheer strength grappled and dragged him ashore,
A wondrous wave-beast; and all the array
                                    1410–1440

Gathered to gaze at the grisly guest.
   Beowulf donned his armor for battle,
Heeded not danger; the hand-braided byrny,
Broad of shoulder and richly bedecked,
Must stand the ordeal of the watery depths.
Well could that corselet defend the frame
Lest hostile thrust should pierce to the heart.
Or blows of battle beat down the life.
A gleaming helmet guarded his head
As he planned his plunge to the depths of the pool
Through the heaving waters—a helm adorned
With lavish inlay and lordly chains,
Ancient work of the weapon-smith
Skillfully fashioned, beset with the boar,
That no blade of battle might bite it through.
Not the least or the worst of his war-equipment
Was the sword the herald of Hrothgar loaned
In his hour of need—Hrunting its name—
An ancient heirloom, trusty and tried;
Its blade was iron, with etched design,
Tempered in blood of many a battle.
Never in fight had it failed the hand
That drew it daring the perils of war,
The rush of the foe. Not the first time then
That its edge must venture on valiant deeds.
But Ecglaf's stalwart son was unmindful
Of words he had spoken while heated with wine,
When he loaned the blade to a better swordsman.
He himself dared not hazard his life
In deeds of note in the watery depths;
And thereby he forfeited honor and fame.
                                    1441–1471

Not so with that other undaunted spirit
After he donned his armor for battle.
Beowulf spoke, the son of Ecgtheow:
"O gracious ruler, gold-giver to men,
As I now set forth to attempt this feat,
Great son of Healfdene, hold well in mind
The solemn pledge we plighted of old,
That if doing your service I meet my death
You will mark my fall with a father's love.

Protect my kinsmen, my trusty comrades,
If battle take me. And all the treasure
You have heaped on me bestow upon Hygelac,
Hrothgar beloved! The lord of the Geats,
The son of Hrethel, shall see the proof,
Shall know as he gazes on jewels and gold,
That I found an unsparing dispenser of bounty,
And joyed, while I lived, in his generous gifts.
Give back to Unferth the ancient blade,
The sword-edge splendid with curving scrolls,
For either with Hrunting I'll reap rich harvest
Of glorious deeds, or death shall take me."
    After these words the prince of the Weders
Awaited no answer, but turned to the task,
Straightway plunged in the swirling pool.
Nigh unto a day he endured the depths
Ere he first had view of the vast sea-bottom.
Soon she found, who had haunted the flood,
A ravening hag, for a hundred half-years,
Greedy and grim, that a man was groping
In daring search through the sea-troll's home.
Swift she grappled and grasped the warrior

1472–1502

With horrid grip, but could work no harm,
No hurt to his body; the ring-locked byrny
Cloaked his life from her clutching claw;
Nor could she tear through the tempered mail
With her savage fingers. The she-wolf bore
The ring-prince down through the watery depths
To her den at the bottom; nor could Beowulf draw
His blade for battle, though brave his mood.
Many a sea-beast, strange sea-monsters,
Tasked him hard with their menacing tusks,
Broke his byrny and smote him sore.
    Then he found himself in a fearsome hall
Where water came not to work him hurt,
But the flood was stayed by the sheltering roof.
There in the glow of firelight gleaming
The hero had view of the huge sea-troll.
He swung his war-sword with all his strength,
Withheld not the blow, and the savage blade
Sang on her head its hymn of hate.
But the bold one found that the battle-flasher
Would bite no longer, nor harm her life.
The sword-edge failed at his sorest need.
Often of old with ease it had suffered
The clash of battle, cleaving the helm,
The fated warrior's woven mail.
That time was first for the treasured blade
That its glory failed in the press of the fray.
But fixed of purpose and firm of mood
Hygelac's earl was mindful of honor;
In wrath, undaunted, he dashed to earth
The jewelled sword with its scrolled design,

1503–1533

The blade of steel; staked all on strength,
On the might of his hand, as a man must do
Who thinks to win in the welter of battle
Enduring glory; he fears not death.
The Geat-prince joyed in the straining struggle,
Stalwart-hearted and stirred to wrath,

Gripped the shoulder of Grendel's dam
And headlong hurled the hag to the ground.
But she quickly clutched him and drew him close,
Countered the onset with savage claw.
The warrior staggered, for all his strength,
Dismayed and shaken and borne to earth.
She knelt upon him and drew her dagger,
With broad bright blade, to avenge her son,
Her only issue. But the corselet's steel
Shielded his breast and sheltered his life
Withstanding entrance of point and edge.
    Then the prince of the Geats would have gone his
      journey,
The son of Ecgtheow, under the ground;
But his sturdy breast-net, his battle-corselet,
Gave him succor, and holy God,
The Lord all-wise, awarded the mastery;
Heaven's Ruler gave right decree.
    Swift the hero sprang to his feet;
Saw mid the war-gear a stately sword,
An ancient war-brand of biting edge,
Choicest of weapons worthy and strong,
The work of giants, a warrior's joy,
So heavy no hand but his own could hold it,
Bear to battle or wield in war.

1534–1563

Then the Scylding warrior, savage and grim,
Seized the ring-hilt and swung the sword,
Struck with fury, despairing of life,
Thrust at the throat, broke through the bone-rings;
The stout blade stabbed through her fated flesh.
She sank in death; the sword was bloody;
The hero joyed in the work of his hand.
The gleaming radiance shimmered and shone
As the candle of heaven shines clear from the sky.
Wrathful and resolute Hygelac's thane
Surveyed the span of the spacious hall;
Grimly gripping the hilted sword
With upraised weapon he turned to the wall.
The blade had failed not the battle-prince;
A full requital he firmly planned
For all the injury Grendel had done
In numberless raids on the Danish race,
When he slew the hearth-companions of Hrothgar,
Devoured fifteen of the Danish folk
Clasped in slumber, and carried away
As many more spearmen, a hideous spoil.
All this the stout-heart had stern requited;
And there before him bereft of life
He saw the broken body of Grendel
Stilled in battle, and stretched in death,
As the struggle in Heorot smote him down.
The corpse sprang wide as he struck the blow,
The hard sword-stroke that severed the head.
    Then the tried retainers, who there with Hrothgar
Watched the face of the foaming pool,
Saw that the churning reaches were reddened,

1564–1594

The eddying surges stained with blood.
And the gray, old spearmen spoke of the hero,
Having no hope he would ever return

Crowned with triumph and cheered with spoil.
Many were sure that the savage sea-wolf
Had slain their leader. At last came noon.
The stalwart Scyldings forsook the headland;
Their proud gold-giver departed home.
But the Geats sat grieving and sick in spirit,
Stared at the water with longing eyes,
Having no hope they would ever behold
Their gracious leader and lord again.
    Then the great sword, eaten with blood of battle,
Began to soften and waste away
In iron icicles, wonder of wonders,
Melting away most like to ice
When the Father looses the fetters of frost,
Slackens the bondage that binds the wave,
Strong in power of times and seasons;
He is true God! Of the goodly treasures
From the sea-cave Beowulf took but two,
The monster's head and the precious hilt
Blazing with gems; but the blade had melted,
The sword dissolved, in the deadly heat,
The venomous blood of the fallen fiend.

1595–1619

STUDY QUESTIONS

1. Literary heroes generally symbolize the virtues valued by the cultures that produce them. Consider the heroic Beowulf and then describe the traits that Germanic culture prized.
2. In American culture, movie and pop stars frequently exemplify the virtues that Americans, at a given time, prize. What do the following personalities tell us about American values—Madonna, Jamie Lee Curtis, Arnold Schwarzenegger, Tom Hanks? You can also consider certain professional football and basketball players, ice skaters, and tennis champions.

LITERARY SELECTION 29

Everyman

Medieval drama began in the tenth century as **liturgical drama** (discussed in detail on pp. 446–7), out of which grew plays in the vernacular called mysteries or mystery plays (a corruption of the Latin *ministerium*, "service"). Performed by trade guilds, mystery plays took the form of cycles depicting the Christian history of humanity from the Fall to the Redemption. The various **guilds** enacted episodes associated with their own craft. Thus the shipwrights' guild was responsible for the building of Noah's ark, the water drawers for the flood, the goldsmiths for the story of the Magi, and so on.

The plays were performed outdoors from dawn to dusk on "pageants" (Lat. *pagina*, "scene of a play"), wagons consisting of roofed platforms on wheels. Scenery was makeshift but costumes often elaborate. Such cycles as *The Second Shepherd's Play* included a large repertoire of acting conventions, comic elaboration, and considerable opportunity for improvisation. During the sixteenth century the plays became more and more secular, with increasing elements of comedy and outright buffoonery until, during the reign of Elizabeth I, they were suppressed. By this time they had been superseded by the plays of playwrights such as Marlowe and Shakespeare.

On the Continent, miracle plays dealt with marvels performed by the saints; in England the term "miracle" was interchangeable with mystery. In a separate category was the morality play, a single work rather than a cycle. Mystery plays dramatized biblical events to show their relevance to everyday life, morality plays were more directly didactic, enacting the conflict between good and evil—the constant struggle within each person between virtue and vice. The contest was presented as an allegory with virtues and vices personified: Patience versus Anger, Pride versus Humility, and so forth. Penance—the recognition and confession of sin to the priest—was a key element, and was followed by absolution, on condition of performing assigned penances. One of the primary themes of the morality play called *Everyman* is the absolute necessity of penitence for sin before death within the discipline of the church.

Everyman was not written down until about 1485, but its ideas and assumptions had long been widely circulated. The English play may be a translation of a Dutch play on the theme, or possibly the Dutch play was a translation from the English. The most famous of its type, *Everyman* actually differs from most morality plays in that it is not a battle between opposites but rather a somber stripping of worldly goods from a man, concentrating on his increasing isolation as he descends into the grave. Only Good-Deeds is left as a mediator between him and Judgment. *Everyman* is a moral allegory of preparation for death, a solemn statement of the human predicament and, just as important, a rigorous exposition of church doctrine.

CHARACTERS

Messenger	**Cousin**	**Strength**
God (Adonai)	**Goods**	**Discretion**
Death	**Good-Deeds**	**Five-Wits**
Everyman	**Knowledge**	**Angel**
Fellowship	**Confession**	**Doctor**
Kindred	**Beauty**	

Here beginneth a treatise how the high father of heaven sendeth death to summon every creature to come and give account of their lives in this world and is in manner of a moral play.

Messenger: I pray you all give your audience,
And hear this matter with reverence,
By figure a moral play—
The *Summoning of Everyman* called it is,
That of our lives and ending shows
How transitory we be all day.
This matter is wondrous precious,

But the intent of it is more gracious,
And sweet to bear away.
The story saith,—Man, in the beginning, 10
Look well, and take good heed to the ending,
Be you never so gay!
Ye think sin in the beginning full sweet,
Which in the end causeth thy soul to weep,
When the body lieth in clay.
Here shall you see how *Fellowship* and *Jollity*,
Both *Strength, Pleasure*, and *Beauty*,
Will fade from thee as flower in May.
For ye shall hear, how our heaven king
Calleth *Everyman* to a general reckoning: 20
Give audience, and hear what he doth say.
God: I perceive here in my majesty,
How that all creatures be to me unkind,
Living without dread in worldly prosperity:
Of ghostly sight the people be so blind,
Drowned in sin, they know me not for their God:
In worldly riches is all their mind,
They fear not my right wiseness, the sharp rod:
My law that I shewed, when I for them died,
They forget clean, and shedding of my blood red: 30
I hanged between two, it cannot be denied:
To get them life I suffered to be dead:
I healed their feet, with thorns hurt was my head:
I could do no more than I did truly,
And now I see the people do clean forsake me,
They use the seven deadly sins damnable;
As pride, covetise, wrath, and lechery,
Now in the world be made commendable;
And thus they leave of angels the heavenly company;
Everyman liveth so after his own pleasure, 40
And yet of their life they be nothing sure:
I see the more that I them forbear
The worse they be from year to year;
All that liveth appaireth[5] fast,
Therefore I will in all the haste
Having a reckoning of Everyman's person
For and I leave the people thus alone
In their life and wicked tempests,
Verily they will become much worse than beasts;
For now one would by envy another up eat; 50
Charity they all do clean forget.
I hoped well that Everyman
In my glory should make his mansion,
And thereto I had them all elect;
But now I see, like traitors deject,
They thank me not for the pleasure that I to them meant
Nor yet for their being that I them have lent;
I proffered the people great multitude of mercy,
And few there be that asketh it heartily;
They be so combered with worldly riches, 60
That needs of them I must do justice,
On Everyman living without fear.
Where art thou, Death, thou mighty messenger?
Death: Almighty God, I am here at your will,
Your commandment to fulfill.
God: Go thou to Everyman,
And show him in my name
A pilgrimage he must on him take,

Which he in no wise may escape;
And that he bring with him a sure reckoning 70
Without delay or any tarrying.
Death: Lord, I will in the world go run over all,
And cruelly outsearch both great and small;
Every man will I beset that liveth beastly
Out of God's laws, and dreadeth not folly:
He that loveth riches I will strike with my dart,
His sight to blind, and from heaven to depart,
Except that alms be his good friend,
In hell for to dwell, world without end.
Lo, yonder I see Everyman walking; 80
Full little he thinketh on my coming;
His mind is on fleshly lusts and his treasure,
And great pain it shall cause him to endure
Before the Lord Heaven King.
Everyman, stand still; whither art thou going
Thus gaily? Hast my Maker forgot?
Everyman: Why askst thou?
Wouldest thou wete?[6]
Death: Yea, sir, I will show you;
In great haste I am sent to thee 90
From God out of his majesty.
Everyman: What, sent to me?
Death: Yea, certainly.
Though thou have forget him here,
He thinketh on thee in the heavenly sphere,
As, or we depart, thou shalt know.
Everyman: What desireth God of me?
Death: That shall I show thee;
A reckoning he will needs have
Without any longer respite. 100
Everyman: To give a reckoning longer leisure I crave;
This blind matter troubleth my wit.
Death: On thee thou must take a long journey:
Therefore thy book of count with thee thou bring;
For turn again thou can not by no way,
And look thou be sure of thy reckoning:
For before God thou shalt answer, and show
Thy many bad deeds and good but a few;
How thou hast spent thy life, and in what wise,
Before the chief lord of paradise. 110
Have ado that we were in that way,
For, wete thou well, thou shalt make none attournay.[7]
Everyman: Full unready I am such reckoning to give.
I know thee not: what messenger art thou?
Death: I am Death, that no man dreadeth.
For every man I rest and no man spareth;
For it is God's commandment
That all to me should be obedient.
Everyman: O Death, thou comest when I had thee
       least in mind,
In thy power it lieth me to save, 120
Yet of my good will I give thee, if ye will be kind,
Yea, a thousand pound shalt thou have,
And defer this matter till another day.
Death: Everyman, it may not be by no way;

5. Is impaired.
6. Know.
7. Mediator.

I set not by gold, silver, nor riches,
Ne by pope, emperor, king, duke, ne princes.
For and I would receive gifts great,
All the world I might get;
But my custom is clean contrary.
I give thee no respite: come hence, and not tarry.   130
Everyman: Alas, shall I have no longer respite?
I may say Death giveth no warning:
To think on thee, it maketh my heart sick,
For all unready is my book of reckoning.
But twelve year and I might have abiding,
My counting book I would make so clear,
That my reckoning I should not need to fear.
Wherefore, Death, I pray thee, for God's mercy,
Spare me till I be provided of remedy.
Death: Thee availeth not to cry, weep, and pray: 140
But haste thee lightly that you were gone the journey.
And prove thy friends if thou can.
For, wete thou well, the tide abideth no man,
And in the world each living creature
For Adam's sin must die of nature.
Everyman: Death, if I should this pilgrimage take,
And my reckoning surely make,
Show me, for saint charity,
Should I not come again shortly?
Death: No, Everyman; and thou be once there,   150
Thou mayst never more come here,
Trust me verily.
Everyman: O gracious God, in the high seat celestial,
Have mercy on me in this most need;
Shall I have no company from this vale terrestrial
Of mine acquaintance that way me to lead?
Death: Yea, if any be so hardy,
That would go with thee and bear thee company.
Hie thee that you were gone to God's magnificence,
Thy reckoning to give before his presence.   160
What, weenest thou thy life is given thee,
And thy worldly goods also?
Everyman: I had wend so, verily.
Death: Nay, nay; it was but lent thee;
For as soon as thou art go,
Another awhile shall have it, and then go therefor
Even as thou has done.
Everyman, thou art mad; thou hast thy wits five,
And here on earth will not amend thy life,
For suddenly I do come.   170
Everyman: O wretched caitiff, whither shall I flee,
That I might scape this endless sorrow!
Now, gentle Death, spare me till to-morrow,
That I may amend me
With good advisement.
Death: Nay, thereto I will not consent,
Nor no man will I respite,
But to the heart suddenly I shall smite
Without any advisement.
And now out of thy sight I will me nie;   180
See thou make thee ready shortly,
For thou mayst say this is the day
That no man living may scape away.
Everyman: Alas, I may well weep with sighs deep;
Now have I no manner of company

To help me in my journey, and me to keep;
And also my writing is full unready.
How shall I do now for to excuse me?
I would to God I had never be gete![8]
To my soul a full great profit it had be;   190
For now I fear pains huge and great.
The time passeth; Lord, help that all wrought;
For though I mourn it availeth nought.
The day passeth, and is almost a-go;
I wot not well what for to do.
To whom were I best my complaint to make?
What, and I to Fellowship thereof spake,
And showed him of this sudden chance?
For in him is all mine affiance;
We have in the world so many a day   200
Be on good friends in sport and play.
I see him yonder, certainly;
I trust that he will bear me company;
Therefore to him will I speak to ease my sorrow.
Well met, good Fellowship, and good morrow!
Fellowship: Everyman, good morrow by this day.
Sir, why lookest thou so piteously?
If any thing be amiss, I pray thee, me say,
That I may help to remedy.
Everyman: Yea, good Fellowship, yea.   210
I am in great jeopardy.
Fellowship: My true friend, show to me your mind;
I will not forsake thee, unto my life's end,
In the way of good company.
Everyman: That was well spoken, and lovingly.
Fellowship: Sir, I must needs know your heaviness;
I have pity to see you in any distress;
If any have ye wronged he shall revenged be,
Though I on the ground be slain for thee—
Though that I know before that I should die.   220
Everyman: Verily, Fellowship, gramercy.
Fellowship: Tush! by thy thanks I set not a straw;
Show me your grief, and say no more.
Everyman: If I my heart should to you break,
And then you to turn your mind from me,
And would not me comfort, when you hear me speak,
Then should I ten times sorrier be.
Fellowship: Sir, I say as I will do in deed.
Everyman: Then be you a good friend at need:
I have found you true here before.   230
Fellowship: And so ye shall evermore;
For, in faith, and thou go to Hell,
I will not forsake thee by the way!
Everyman: Ye speak like a good friend; I believe you
   well;
I shall deserve it, and I may.
Fellowship: I speak of no deserving, by this day.
For he that will say and nothing do
Is not worthy with good company to go;
Therefore show me the grief of your mind,
As to your friend most loving and kind.   240
Everyman: I shall show you how it is;
Commanded I am to go a journey,

| **8.** Been gotten, been born.

A long way, hard and dangerous,
And give a strait count without delay
Before the high judge Adonai.[9]
Wherefore I pray you, bear me company,
As ye have promised, in this journey.
Fellowship: That is matter indeed! Promise is duty,
But, and I should take such a voyage on me,
I know it well, it should be to my pain: 250
Also it make me afeard, certain.
But let us take counsel here as well as we can,
For your words would fear a strong man.
Everyman: Why, ye said, If I had need,
Ye would me never forsake, quick nor dead,
Though it were to hell truly.
Fellowship: So I said, certainly,
But such pleasures be set aside, thee sooth to say:
And also, if we took such a journey,
When should we come again?   260
Everyman: Nay, never again till the day of doom.
Fellowship: In faith, then will not I come there!
Who hath you these tidings brought?
Everyman: Indeed, Death was with me here.
Fellowship: Now, by God that all hath bought,
If Death were the messenger,
For no man that is living today
I will not go that loath journey—
Not for the father that begat me!
Everyman: Ye promised other wise, pardie.   270
Fellowship: I wot well I say so truly
And yet if thou wilt eat, and drink, and make good cheer,
Or haunt to women, the lusty company,
I would not forsake you, while the day is clear,
Trust me verily!
Everyman: Yea, thereto ye would be ready;
To go to mirth, solace, and play
Your mind will sooner apply
Than to bear me company in my long journey.
Fellowship: Now, in good faith, I will not that way.   280
But and thou wilt murder, or any man kill,
In that I will help thee with a good will!
Everyman: O that is a simple advice indeed!
Gentle fellow, help me in my necessity;
We have loved long, and now I need,
And now, gentle Fellowship, remember me.
Fellowship: Whether ye have loved me or no,
By Saint John, I will not with thee go.
Everyman: Yet I pray thee, take the labour, and do so
    much for me
To bring me forward, for saint charity,   290
And comfort me till I come without the town.
Fellowship: Nay, and thou would give me a new gown,
I will not a foot with thee go;
But and you had tarried I would not have left thee so.
And as now, God speed thee in thy journey,
For from thee I will depart as fast as I may.
Everyman: Whither away, Fellowship? Will you forsake
    me?
Fellowship: Yea, by my fay, to God I betake thee.
Everyman: Farewell, good Fellowship; for this my heart
    is sore;
Adieu for ever, I shall see thee no more.   300

Fellowship: In faith, Everyman, farewell not at the end;
For you I will remember that parting is mourning.
Everyman: Alack! shall we thus depart indeed?
Our Lady, help, without any more comfort,
Lo, Fellowship forsaketh me in my most need:
For help in this world whither shall I resort?
Fellowship here before with me would merry make;
And now little sorrow for me doth he take.
It is said, in prosperity men friends may find,
Which in adversity be full unkind.   310
Now whither for succour shall I flee,
Sith that Fellowship hath forsaken me?
To my kinsmen I will truly,
Praying them to help me in my necessity:
I believe that they will do so,
For kind will creep where it may not go,
Where be ye now, my friends and kinsmen?
Kindred: Here be we now at your commandment.
Cousin, I pray you show us your intent
In any wise, and not spare.   320
Cousin: Yea, Everyman, and to us declare
If ye be disposed to go any whither,
For wete you well, we will live and die together.
Kindred: In wealth and woe we will with you hold,
For over his kin a man may be bold.
Everyman: Gramercy, my friends and kinsmen kind.
Now shall I show you the grief of my mind:
I was commanded by a messenger,
That is an high king's chief officer;
He bade me go a pilgrimage to my pain,   330
And I know well I shall never come again;
Also I must give a reckoning straight,
For I have a great enemy, that hath me in wait,
Which intendeth me for to hinder.
Kindred: What account is that which ye must render?
That would I know.
Everyman: Of all my works I must show
How I have lived and my days spent;
Also of ill deeds, that I have used
In my time, sith life was me lent;   340
And of all virtues that I have refused.
Therefore I pray you go thither with me,
To help to make mine account, for saint charity.
Cousin: What, to go thither? Is that the matter?
Nay, Everyman, I had liefer fast bread and water
All this five year and more.
Everyman: Alas, that ever I was bore![10]
For now shall I never be merry
If that you forsake me.
Kindred: Ah, sir; what, ye be a merry man!   350
Take good heart to you, and make no moan.
But one thing I warn you, by Saint Anne,
As for me, ye shall go alone.
Everyman: My Cousin, will you not with me go?
Cousin: No, by our Lady; I have the cramp in my toe.
Trust not to me, for, so God me speed,
I will deceive you in your most need.

9. God.
10. Born.

Kindred: It availeth not us to tice.
Ye shall have my maid with all my heart;
She loveth to go to feasts, there to be nice,   360
And to dance, and abroad to start:
I will give her leave to help you in that journey,
If that you and she may agree.
Everyman: Now show me the very effect of your mind.
Will you go with me, or abide behind?
Kindred: Abide behind? Yea, that I will and I may!
Therefore farewell until another day.
Everyman: How should I be merry or glad?
For fair promises to me make,
But when I have most need, they me forsake.   370
I am deceived; that maketh me sad.
Cousin: Cousin Everyman, farewell now,
For verily I will not go with you;
Also of mine own an unready reckoning
I have to account; therefore I make tarrying.
Now, God keep thee, for now I go.
Everyman: Ah, Jesus, is all come hereto?
Lo, fair words maketh fools feign;
They promise and nothing will do certain.
My kinsmen promised me faithfully   380
For to abide with me steadfastly,
And now fast away do they flee:
Even so Fellowship promised me.
What friend were best me of to provide?
I lose my time here longer to abide.
Yet in my mind a thing there is:—
All my life I have loved riches;
If that my goods now help me might,
He would make my heart full light.
I will speak to him in this distress.—   390
Where art thou, my Goods and riches?
Goods: Who calleth me? Everyman? What haste thou
        hast!
I lie here in corners, trussed and piled so high,
And in chests I am locked so fast,
Also sacked in bags, thou mayst see with thine eye,
I cannot stir; in packs low I lie,
What would ye have, lightly me say.
Everyman: Come hither, Goods, in all the haste thou
        may,
For of counsel I must desire thee.
Goods: Sir, and ye in the world have trouble or
        adversity,   400
That can I help you to remedy shortly.
Everyman: It is another disease that grieveth me;
In this world it is not, I tell thee so.
I am sent for another way to go,
To give a straight account general
Before the highest Jupiter of all;
And all my life I have had joy and pleasure in thee.
Therefore I pray thee go with me,
For, peradventure, thou mayst before God Almighty
My reckoning help to clean and purify;   410
For it is said ever among,
That money maketh all right that is wrong.
Goods: Nay, Everyman, I sing another song,
I follow no man in such voyages;
For and I went with thee

Thou shouldst fare much the worse for me;
For because on me thou did set thy mind,
Thy reckoning I have made blotted and blind
That thine account thou cannot make truly;
And that has thou for the love of me.   420
Everyman: That would grieve me full sore,
When I should come to that fearful answer.
Up, let us go thither together.
Goods: Nay, not so, I am too brittle, I may not endure;
I will follow no man one foot, be ye sure.
Everyman: Alas, I have thee loved, and had great
        pleasure
All my life-days on goods and treasure.
Goods: That is to thy damnation without lesing,
For my love is contrary to the love everlasting
But if thou had me loved moderately during,   430
As, to the poor give part of me,
Then shouldst thou not in this dolour be,
Nor in this great sorrow and care.
Everyman: Lo, now was I deceived or I was ware,
And all I may wyte[11] my spending of time.
Goods: What, weenest thou that I am thine?
Everyman: I had weened so.
Goods: Nay, Everyman, I say no;
As for a while I was lent thee,
A season thou hast had me in prosperity;   440
My condition is man's soul to kill;
If I save one, a thousand I do spill;
Weenest thou that I will follow thee?
Nay, from this world, not verily.
Everyman: I had wend otherwise.
Goods: Therefore to thy soul Goods is a thief;
For when thou art dead, this is my guise
Another to deceive in the same wise
As I have done thee, and all to his soul's reprief.
Everyman: O false Goods, cursed thou be!   450
Thou traitor to God, that has deceived me,
And caught me in thy snare.
Goods: Marry, thou brought thyself in care,
Whereof I am glad,
I must needs laugh, I cannot be sad.
Everyman: Ah, Goods, thou has had long my heartily
        love;
I gave thee that which should be the Lord's above.
But wilt thou not go with me in deed?
I pray thee truth to say.
Goods: No, so God me speed,   460
        Therefore farewell, and have good day.
Everyman: O, to whom shall I make moan
For to go with me in that heavy journey?
First Fellowship said he would with me gone;
His words were very pleasant and gay,
But afterward he left me alone.
Then spake I to my kinsmen all in despair,
And also they gave me words fair,
They lacked no fair speaking,
But all forsake me in the ending.   470
Then went I to my Goods that I loved best,

| **11.** Blame.

In hope to have comfort, but there had I least:
For my Goods sharply did me tell
That he bringeth many into hell.
Then of myself I was ashamed,
And so I am worthy to be blamed;
Thus may I well myself hate,
Of whom shall I now counsel take?
I think that I shall never speed
Till that I go to my Good-Deed,   480
But alas, she is so weak,
That she can neither go nor speak,
Yet will I venture on her now.—
My Good-Deeds, where be you?
Good-Deeds: Here I lie cold on the ground;
Thy sins hath me sore bound,
That I cannot stir.
Everyman: O, Good-Deeds, I stand in fear;
I must you pray of counsel,
For help now should come right well.   490
Good-Deeds: Everyman, I have understanding
That ye be summoned account to make
Before Messias, of Jerusalem King;
And you by me[12] that journey what[13] you will I take.
Everyman: Therefore I come to you, my moan to make;
I pray you, that ye will go with me.
Good-Deeds: I would full fain, but I cannot stand verily.
Everyman: Why, is there anything on you fall?
Good-Deeds: Yea, sir, I may thank you of all;
If ye had perfectly cheered me,   500
Your book of account now full ready had be.
Look, the books of your works and deeds eke;
Oh, see how they lie under the feet,
To your soul's heaviness.
Everyman: Our Lord Jesus, help me!
For one letter here I can not see.
Good-Deeds: There is a blind reckoning in time of
     distress!
Everyman: Good-Deeds, I pray you, help me in this
     need,
Or else I am for ever damned indeed;
Therefore help me to make reckoning   510
Before the redeemer of all thing,
That king is, and was, and ever shall.
Good-Deeds: Everyman, I am sorry of your fall,
And fain would I help you, and I were able.
Everyman: Good-Deeds, your counsel I pray you give
     me.
Good-Deeds: That shall I do verily;
Though that on my feet I may not go,
I have a sister, that shall with you also,
Called Knowledge, which shall with you abide,
To help you to make that dreadful reckoning.   520
Knowledge: Everyman, I will go with thee, and be thy
     guide,
In thy most need to go by thy side.
Everyman: In good condition I am now in every thing,
And am wholly content with this good thing;
Thanked be God my Creator.

12. If you go by me.
13. With.

Good-Deeds: And when he hath brought thee there,
Where thou shalt heal thee of thy smart,
Then go you with your reckoning and your Good-Deeds
     together
For to make you joyful at heart
Before the blessed Trinity.   530
Everyman: My Good-Deeds, gramercy;
I am well content, certainly,
With your words sweet.
Knowledge: Now go we together lovingly,
To Confession, that cleansing river.
Everyman: For joy I weep; I would we were there;
But, I pray you, give me cognition
Where dwelleth that holy man, Confession.
Knowledge: In the house of salvation:
We shall find him in that place,   540
That shall us comfort by God's grace.
Lo, this is Confession: kneel down and ask mercy,
For he is in good conceit with God almighty.
Everyman: O glorious fountain that all uncleanness
     doth clarify,
Wash from me the spots of vices unclean,
That on me no sin may be seen;
I come with Knowledge for my redemption,
Repent with hearty and full contrition;
For I am commanded a pilgrimage to take,
And great accounts before God to make.   550
Now, I pray you, Shrift, mother of salvation,
Help my good deeds for my piteous exclamation.
Confession: I know your sorrow well, Everyman;
Because with Knowledge ye come to me,
I will you comfort as well as I can,
And a precious jewel I will give thee,
Called penance, wise voider of adversity;
Therewith shall your body chastised be,
With abstinence and perseverance in God's service:
Here shall you receive that scourge of me,   560
Which is penance strong, that ye must endure,
To remember thy Savior was scourged for thee
With sharp scourges, and suffered it patiently;
So must thou, or thou scape that painful pilgrimage;
Knowledge, keep him in this voyage,
And by that time Good-Deeds will be with thee.
But in any wise, be sure of mercy,
For your time draweth fast, and ye will saved be;
Ask God mercy, and he will grant truly,
When with the scourge of penance man doth him bind.   570
The oil of forgiveness then shall he find.
Everyman: Thanked be God for his gracious work!
For now I will my penance begin;
This hath rejoiced and lighted my heart,
Though the knots be painful and hard within.
Knowledge: Everyman, look your penance that ye fulfil,
What pain that ever it to you be,
And Knowledge shall give you counsel at will,
How your accounts ye shall make clearly.
Everyman: O eternal God, O heavenly figure,   580
O way of rightwiseness, O goodly vision,
Which descended down in a virgin pure
Because he would Everyman redeem,
Which Adam forfeited by his disobedience:

O blessed Godhead, elect and high-divine,
Forgive my grievous offence;
Here I cry thee mercy in this presence.
O ghostly treasure, O ransomer and redeemer
Of all the world, hope and conductor,
Mirror of joy, and founder of mercy,   590
Which illumineth heaven and earth thereby,
Here my clamorous complaint, though it late be;
Receive my prayers; unworthy in this heavy life,
Though I be, a sinner most abominable,
Yet let my name be written in Moses' table;
O Mary, pray to the Maker of all thing,
Me for to help at my ending,
And save me from the power of my enemy,
For Death assaileth me strongly;
And, Lady, that I may be means of thy prayer   600
Of your Son's glory to be partaker,
By the means of his passion I it crave,
I beseech you, help my soul to save.—
Knowledge, give me the scourge of penance;
My flesh therewith shall give a quittance:
I will now begin, if God give me grace.
Knowledge: Everyman, God give you time and space:
Thus I bequeath you in the hands of our Saviour,
Thus may you make your reckoning sure.
Everyman: In the name of the Holy Trinity,   610
My body sore punished shall be:
Take this, body, for the sin of the flesh;
Also thou delightest to go gay and fresh,
And in the way of damnation thou did me bring;
Therefore suffer now strokes and punishing.
Now of penance I will wade the water clear,
To save me from purgatory, that sharp fire.
Good-Deeds: I thank God, now I can walk and go;
And am delivered of my sickness and woe.
Therefore with Everyman I will go, and not spare;   620
His good works I will help him to declare.
Knowledge: Now, Everyman, be merry and glad;
Your Good-Deeds cometh now; ye may not be sad;
Now is your Good-Deeds whole and sound,
Going upright upon the ground.
Everyman: My heart is light, and shall be evermore;
Now will I smite faster than I did before.
Good-Deeds: Everyman, pilgrim, my special friend,
Blessed be thou without end;
For thee is prepared the eternal glory.   630
Ye have me made whole and sound,
Therefore I will bide by thee in every stound.[14]
Everyman: Welcome, my Good-Deeds; now I hear thy
    voice,
I weep for very sweetness of love.
Knowledge: Be no more sad, but ever rejoice,
God seeth thy living in his throne above;
Put on this garment to thy behove,
Which is wet with your tears,
Or else before God you may it miss,
When you to your journey's end come shall.   640
Everyman: Gentle Knowledge, what do you it call?

Knowledge: It is a garment of sorrow:
From pain it will you borrow;
Contrition it is,
That getteth forgiveness;
It pleaseth God passing well.
Good-Deeds: Everyman, will you wear it for your heal?
Everyman: Now blessed be Jesu, Mary's Son!
For now have I on true contrition.
And let us go now without tarrying;   650
Good-Deeds, have we clear our reckoning?
Good-Deeds: Yea, indeed I have it here.
Everyman: Then I trust we need not fear;
Now, friends, let us not part in twain.
Knowledge: Nay, Everyman, that will we not, certain.
Good-Deeds: Yet must thou lead with thee
Three persons of great might.
Everyman: Who should they be?
Good-Deeds: Discretion and Strength they hight,
And thy Beauty may not abide behind.   660
Knowledge: Also ye must call to mind
Your Five-Wits as for your counsellors.
Good-Deeds: You must have them ready at all hours.
Everyman: How shall I get hither?
Knowledge: You must call them all together,
And they will hear you incontinent.
Everyman: My friends, come hither and be present,
Discretion, Strength, my Five-Wits, and Beauty.
Beauty: Here at your will we be all ready.
What will ye that we should do?   670
Good-Deeds: That ye would with Everyman go,
And help him in his pilgrimage,
Advise you, will ye with him or not in that voyage?
Strength: We will bring him all thither,
To his help and comfort, ye may believe me.
Discretion: So will we go with him all together.
Everyman: Almighty God, loved thou be,
I give thee laud that I have hither brought
Strength, Discretion, Beauty, and Five-Wits; lack I
    nought;
And my Good-Deeds, with Knowledge clear,   680
All be in my company at my will here;
I desire no more to my business.
Strength: And I, Strength, will by you stand in distress,
Though thou would in battle fight on the ground.
Five-Wits: And though it were through the world round,
We will not depart for sweet nor sour.
Beauty: No more will I unto death's hour,
Whatsoever thereof befall.
Discretion: Everyman, advise you first of all;
Go with a good advisement and deliberation;   690
We all give you virtuous monition
That all shall be well.
Everyman: My friends, hearken what I will tell:
I pray God reward you in his heavenly sphere.
Now hearken, all that be here
For I will make my testament
Here before you all present.
In alms half my goods I will give with my hands twain
In the way of charity, with good intent,
And the other half still shall remain   700
In quiet to be returned there it ought to be.

| **14.** Season.

This I do in despite of the fiend of hell
To go quite out of his peril
Ever after and this day.
Knowledge: Everyman, hearken what I say;
Go to priesthood, I you advise,
And receive of him in any wise
The holy sacrament and ointment together;
Then shortly see ye turn again hither;
We will all abide you here. 710
Five-Wits: Yea, Everyman, hie you that ye ready were,
There is no emperor, king, duke, ne baron,
That of God hath commission,
As hath the least priest in the world being;
For of the blessed sacraments pure and benign,
He beareth the keys and thereof hath the cure
For man's redemption, it is ever sure;
Which God for our soul's medicine
Gave us out of his heart with great pine;
Here in this transitory life, for thee and me 720
The blessed sacraments seven there be.
Baptism, confirmation, with priesthood good,
And the sacrament of God's precious flesh and blood,
Marriage, the holy extreme unction, and penance;
These seven be good to have in remembrance,
Gracious sacraments of high divinity.
Everyman: Fain would I receive that holy body
And meekly to my ghostly father I will go.
Five-Wits: Everyman, that is the best that ye can do:
God will you to salvation bring, 730
For priesthood exceedeth all other thing;
To us Holy Scripture they do teach,
And converteth man from sin heaven to reach;
God hath to them more power given,
Than to any angel that is in heaven;
With five words he may consecrate
God's body in flesh and blood to make,
And handleth his maker between his hands;
The priest bindeth and unbindeth all bands,
Both in earth and in heaven; 740
Thou ministers all the sacraments seven;
Though we kissed thy feet thou were worthy;
Thou art surgeon that cureth sin deadly:
No remedy we find under God
But all only priesthood.
Everyman, God gave priests that dignity,
And setteth them in his stead among us to be;
Thus be they above angels in degree.
Knowledge: If priests be good it is so surely;
But when Jesus hanged on the cross with great smart 750
There he gave, out of his blessed heart,
The same sacrament in great torment:
He sold them not to us, that Lord Omnipotent.
Therefore Saint Peter the apostle doth say
That Jesu's curse hath all they
Which God their Saviour do buy or sell,
Or they for any money do take or tell.
Sinful priests giveth the sinners example bad;
Their children sitteth by other men's fires, I have heard;
And some haunteth women's company, 760
With unclean life, as lusts of lechery:
These be with sin made blind.

Five-Wits: I trust to God no such may we find;
Therefore let us priesthood honour,
And follow their doctrine for our souls' succour;
We be their sheep, and they shepherds be
By whom we all be kept in surety.
Peace, for yonder I see Everyman come,
Which hath made true satisfaction.
Good-Deeds: Methinketh it is he indeed. 770
Everyman: Now Jesu be our alder speed.[15]
I have received the sacrament for my redemption,
And then mine extreme unction:
Blessed be all they that counselled me to take it!
And now, friends, let us go without longer respite;
I thank God that ye have tarried so long.
Now set each of you on this rod your hand,
And shortly follow me:
I go before, there I would be; God be our guide.
Strength: Everyman, we will not from you go, 780
Till ye have gone this voyage long.
Discretion: I, Discretion, will bide by you also.
Knowledge: And though this pilgrimage be never so
   strong,
I will never part you fro:
Everyman, I will be as sure by thee
As ever I did by Judas Maccabee.
Everyman: Alas, I am so faint I may not stand,
My limbs under me do fold;
Friends, let us not turn again to this land,
Not for all the world's gold, 790
For into this cave must I creep
And turn to the earth and there to sleep.
Beauty: What, into this grave? Alas!
Everyman: Yea, there shall you consume more and
   less.
Beauty: And what, should I smother here?
Everyman: Yea, by my faith, and never more appear.
In this world live no more we shall,
But in heaven before the highest Lord of all.
Beauty: I cross out all this; adieu by Saint John;
I take my cap in my lap and am gone. 800
Everyman: What, Beauty, whither will ye?
Beauty: Peace, I am deaf; I look not behind me,
Not and thou would give me all the gold in thy chest.
Everyman: Alas, whereto may I trust?
Beauty goeth fast away hie;
She promised with me to live and die.
Strength: Everyman, I will thee also forsake and deny;
Thy game liketh me not at all.
Everyman: Why, then ye will forsake me all.
Sweet Strength, tarry a little space. 810
Strength: Nay, sir, by the rood of grace
Though thou weep till thy heart brast.
Everyman: Ye would ever bide by me, ye said.
Strength: Yea, I have you far enough conveyed;
Ye be old enough, I understand,
Your pilgrimage to take on hand;
I repent me that I hither came.
Everyman: Strength, you to displease I am to blame;
Will you break promise that is debt?

| **15.** Speed in help of all.

Strength: In faith, I care not;   820
Thou art but a fool to complain,
You spend your speech and waste your brain;
Go thrust thee into the ground.
Everyman: I had wend surer I should you have found.
He that trusteth in his Strength
She him deceiveth at the length.
Both Strength and Beauty forsaketh me,
Yet they promised me fair and lovingly.
Discretion: Everyman, I will after Strength be gone,
As for me I will leave you alone.   830
Everyman: Why, Discretion, will ye forsake me?
Discretion: Yea, in faith, I will go from thee,
For when Strength goeth before
I follow after evermore.
Everyman: Yet I pray thee, for the love of the Trinity,
Look in my grave once piteously.
Discretion: Nay, so nigh will I not come.
Farewell, every one!
Everyman: O all thing faileth, save God alone;
Beauty, Strength, and Discretion;   840
For when Death bloweth his blast,
They all run from me full fast.
Five-Wits: Everyman, my leave now of thee I take;
I will follow the other, for here I thee forsake.
Everyman: Alas! then may I wail and weep,
For I took you for my best friend.
Five-Wits: I will no longer thee keep;
Now farewell, and there an end.
Everyman: O Jesu, help, all hath forsaken me!
Good-Deeds: Nay, Everyman, I will bide with thee,   850
I will not forsake thee indeed;
Thou shalt find me a good friend at need.
Everyman: Gramercy, Good-Deeds; now may I true
     friends see;
They have forsaken me every one;
I loved them better than my Good-Deeds alone.
Knowledge, will ye forsake me also?
Knowledge: Yea, Everyman, when ye to death do go:
But not yet for no manner of danger.
Everyman: Gramercy, Knowledge, with all my heart.
Knowledge: Nay, yet I will not from hence depart,   860
Till I see where ye shall be come.
Everyman: Methinketh, alas, that I must be gone
To make my reckoning and my debts pay,
For I see my time is nigh spent away.
Take example, all ye that this do hear or see,
How they that I loved best do forsake me,
Except my Good-Deeds that bideth truly.
Good-Deeds: All earthly things is but vanity:
Beauty, Strength, and Discretion, do man forsake,
Foolish friends and kinsmen, that fair spake,   870
All fleeth save Good-Deeds, and that am I.
Everyman: Have mercy on me, God most mighty;
And stand by me, thou Mother and Maid, holy Mary.
Good-Deeds: Fear not, I will speak for thee.
Everyman: Here I cry God mercy.
Good-Deeds: Short our end, and minish our pain;

Let us go and never come again.
Everyman: Into thy hands, Lord, my soul I commend;
Receive it, Lord, that it be not lost;
As thou me boughtest, so me defend,   880
And save me from the fiend's boast,
That I may appear with that blessed host
That shall be saved at the day of doom.
In manus tuas—of might's most
For ever—*commendo spiritum meum.*[16]
Knowledge: Now hath he suffered that we all shall
     endure;
The Good-Deeds shall make all sure.
Now hath he made ending;
Me thinketh that I hear angels sing
And make great joy and melody,   890
Where Everyman's soul received shall be.
Angel: Come, excellent elect spouse to Jesu:
Hereabove thou shalt go
Because of thy singular virtue:
Now the soul is taken the body fro;
Thy reckoning is crystal-clear.
Now shalt thou into the heavenly sphere,
Unto the which all ye shall come
That liveth well before the day of doom.
Doctor: This moral men may have in mind;   900
Ye hearers, take it of worth, old and young,
And forsake pride, for he deceiveth you in the end,
And remember Beauty, Five-Wits, Strength, and
     Discretion,
They all at the last do Everyman forsake,
Save his Good-Deeds, there doth he take.
But beware, and they be small
Before God, he hath not help at all.
None excuse may be there for Everyman:
Alas, how shall he do then?
For after death amends may no man make,   910
For then mercy and pity do him forsake.
If his reckoning be not clear when he do come,
God will say—*ite maledicti in ignem aeternum.*[17]
And he that hath his account whole and sound,
High in heaven he shall be crowned;
Unto which place God brings us all thither
That we may live body and soul together.
Thereto help the Trinity,
Amen, say ye, for saint Charity.
THUS ENDETH THIS MORALL PLAY OF EVERYMAN.   920

---

16. Into your hands I commend my spirit.
17. Be damned to the eternal fire.

STUDY QUESTIONS

1. Arrange Fellowship, Goods, Knowledge, and the rest of the personified entities in your own rank order of values. How does your system compare with the implied order in *Everyman*?
2. In your own words explain what the "moral" is in the morality play.

LITERARY SELECTION 30

Aucassin and Nicolette

Contrasting sharply with *Everyman*, the *chant-fable* of *Aucassin and Nicolette*[18] points up the conflicts in medieval life represented by the somber morality play and the charming fable of the young lovers. One smiles with pleasure at the sensuous description of Nicolette, or the piling up of ludicrous incidents: Aucassin riding forth to battle like every stereotype of the medieval knight, only to forget what he should be doing, and ending as a captive; or falling off his horse and dislocating his shoulder. Meanwhile, Nicolette hides behind a bush and waits until he drags himself most painfully into her little bower before she gives him love that is more potent than penicillin. Note especially the gracefulness of the verse as opposed to the earnest tone and sober rhythms of *Everyman*. The *chant-fable* not only speaks of the joy of life, it is that joy. The two as a side-by-side contrast ask the question, "Which way is this civilization to go?"

Who will deign to hear the song,
Solace of a captive's wrong,
Telling how two children met,
Aucassin and Nicolette;
How by grievous pains distraught,
Noble deeds the varlet wrought
For his love, and her bright face!
Sweet my rhyme, and full of grace,
Fair my tale, and debonair.
He who lists—though full of care,   10
Sore astonied, much amazed,
All cast down, by men mispraised,
Sick in body, sick in soul,
Hearing, shall be glad and whole,
   So sweet the tale.

Now they say and tell and relate:

How the Count Bougars of Valence made war on Count Garin of Beaucaire, war so great, so wonderful, and so mortal, that never dawned the day but that he was at the gates and walls and barriers of the town, with a hundred knights and ten thousand men-at-arms, on   20
foot and on horse. So he burned the Count's land, and spoiled his heritage, and dealt death to this man. The Count Garin of Beaucaire was full of years, and frail; he had long outworn his day. He had no heir, neither son nor daughter, save one only varlet, and he was such as I will tell you. Aucassin was the name of the lad. Fair he was, and pleasant to look upon, tall and shapely of body in every whit of him. His hair was golden, and curled in little rings about his head; he had gray and dancing eyes,   30
a clear, oval face, a nose high and comely, and he was so gracious in all good graces that nought in him was found to blame, but good alone. But love, that high prince, so utterly had cast him down, that he cared not to become

knight, neither to bear arms, nor to tilt at tourneys, nor yet to do aught that it became his name
to do.

His father and his mother spake him thus, "Son, don now thy mail, mount thy horse, keep thy land, and render aid to thy men. Should they see thee amongst   40
them, the better will the men-at-arms defend their bodies and their substance, thy fief[19] and mine."

"Father," said Aucassin, "why speakest thou in such fashion to me? May God give me nothing of my desire if I become knight, or mount to horse, or thrust into the press to strike other or be smitten down, save only that thou give me Nicolette, my sweet friend, whom I love so well."

"Son," answered the father, "this may not be. Put Nicolette from mind. For Nicolette is but a captive maid,   50
come hither from a far country, and the Viscount of this town bought her with money from the Saracens, and set her in this place. He hath nourished and baptized her, and held her at the font. On a near day he will give her to some young bachelor, who will gain her bread in all honor. With this what has thou to do? Ask for a wife, and I will find thee the daughter of a king, or a count. Were he the richest man in France, his daughter shalt thou have, if so thou wilt."

"Faith, my father," said Aucassin, "what honor of this   60
world would not Nicolette, my very sweet friend, most richly become! Were she Empress of Byzantium or of Allemaigne, or Queen of France, or England, low enough would be her degree, so noble is she, so courteous and debonair, and gracious in all good graces."

Now is sung:

Aucassin was of Beaucaire,
Of the mighty castle there,
But his heart was ever set
On his fair friend, Nicolette.   70
Small he heeds his father's blame,
Or the harsh words of his dame:
"Fool, to weep the livelong day,
Nicolette trips light and gay.
Scouring she from far Carthage,
Bought of Paynims for a wage.
Since a wife beseems thee good,
Take a wife of wholesome blood."
"Mother, nought for this I care,
Nicolette is debonair;   80
Slim the body, fair the face,
Make my heart a lighted place;
Love has set her as my peer,
   Too sweet, my dear."

Now they say and tell and relate:

When the Court Garin of Beaucaire found that in nowise could he withdraw Aucassin his son from the love of Nicolette, he sought out the Viscount of the town, who was his man, and spake him thus, "Sir Count, send Nicolette your godchild straightly from this place. Cursed   90
be the land wherefrom she was carried to this realm; for because of her I lose Aucassin, who will not become knight, nor do aught that it becometh knight to do. Know

---

18. The names are pronounced oh-kah-SAN and ni-koh-LET.
19. Fief—the demesne of the Count.

well that, were she once within my power, I would hurry her to the fire; and look well to yourself for you stand in utmost peril and fear."

"Sire," answered the Viscount, "this lies heavy upon me, that ever Aucassin goes and he comes seeking speech with my ward. I have bought her with my money, and nourished and baptized her, and held her at the font. Moreover, I am fain to give her to some young bachelor, who will gain her bread in all honor. With this Aucassin your son had nought to do. But since this is your will and your pleasure, I will send her to so far a country that nevermore shall he see her with his eyes." 100

"Walk warily," replied the Count Garin, "for great evil easily may fall to you of this." So they went their ways.

Now the Viscount was a very rich man, and had a rich palace standing within a garden. In a certain chamber of an upper floor he set Nicolette in ward, with an old woman to bear her company, and to watch; and he put there bread and meat and wine and all things for their need. Then he placed a seal upon the door, so that none might enter in, nor issue forth, save only that there was a window looking on the garden, strictly close, whereby they breathed a little fresh air. 110

Now is sung:

Nicolette is prisoned fast,
In a vaulted chamber cast,
Shaped and carven wondrous well, 120
Painted as by miracle.
At the marble casement stayed
On her elbow leaned the maid;
Golden showed her golden hair,
Softly curved her eyebrows rare,
Fair her face, and brightly flushed,
Sweeter maiden never blushed.
In the garden from her room
She might watch the roses bloom,
Hear the birds make tender moan; 130
Then she knew herself alone.
"Lack, great pity 'tis to place
Maid in such an evil case.
Aucassin, my liege, my squire,
Friend, and dear, and heart's desire,
Since thou dost not hate me quite,
Men have done me foul despite,
Sealed me in this vaulted room,
Thrust me to this bitter doom.
But by God, Our Lady's Son, 140
Soon will I from here begone.
   So it be won."

Now they say and tell and relate:

Nicolette was prisoned in the chamber, as you have heard and known. The cry and the haro[20] went through all the land that Nicolette was stolen away. Some said that she had fled the country, and some that the Count Garin of Beaucaire had done her to death. Whatever man may have rejoiced, Aucassin had no joy therein, so he sought out the Viscount of the town and spake him 150

20. Protest against injustice.

thus, "Sir Viscount, what have you done with Nicolette, my very sweet friend, the thing that most I love in all the world? Have you borne her off, or hidden her from my sight? Be sure that should I die hereof, my blood will be required of you, as is most just, for I am slain of your two hands; since you steal from me the thing that most I love in all the world."

"Fair sire," answered the Viscount, "put this from mind. Nicolette is a captive maid whom I brought here from a far country. For her price I trafficked with the 160 Saracens, and I have bred and baptized her, and held her at the font. I have nourished her duly, and on a day will give her to some young bachelor who will gain her bread in honorable fashion. With this you have nought to do; but only to wed the daughter of some count or king. Beyond this, what profit would you have, had you become her lover, and taken her to your bed? Little enough would be your gain therefrom, for your soul would lie tormented in Hell all the days of all time, so that to Paradise never should you win." 170

"In Paradise what have I to do? I care not to enter, but only to have Nicolette, my very sweet friend, whom I love so dearly well. For into Paradise go none but such people as I will tell you of. There go those aged priests, and those old cripples, and the maimed, who all day long and all night cough before the altars, and in the crypts beneath the churches; those who go in worn old mantles and old tattered habits; who are naked, and barefoot, and full of sores; who are dying of hunger and of thirst, of cold and of wretchedness. Such as these 180 enter in Paradise, and with them have I nought to do. But in Hell will I go. For to Hell go the fair clerks and the fair knights who are slain in the tourney and the great wars, and the stout archer and the loyal man. With them will I go. And there go the fair and courteous ladies, who have friends, two or three, together with their wedded lords. And there pass the gold and the silver, the ermine and all rich furs, harpers and minstrels, and the happy of the world. With these will I go, so only that I have Nicolette, my very sweet friend, by my side." 190

"Truly," cried the Viscount, "you talk idly, for never shall you see her more; yea, and if perchance you spoke together, and your father heard thereof, he would burn both me and her in one fire and yourself might well have every fear."

"This lies heavy upon me," answered Aucassin. Thus he parted from the Viscount making great sorrow.

Now is sung:

Aucassin departed thus
Sad at heart and dolorous; 200
Gone is she, his fairest friend,
None may comfort give or mend,
None by counsel make good end.
To the palace turned he home,
Climbed the stair, and sought his room.
In the chamber all alone
Bitterly he made his moan,
Presently began to weep
For the love he might not keep.
"Nicolette, so gent, so sweet, 210

Fair the faring of thy feet,
Fair thy laughter, sweet thy speech,
Fair our playing each with each,
Fair thy clasping, fair thy kiss,
Yet it endeth all in this.
Since from me my love is ta'en
I misdoubt that I am slain;
    Sister, sweet friend."

Now they say and tell and relate:

Whilst Aucassin was in the chamber lamenting   220
Nicolette, his friend, the Count Bougars of Valence,
wishful to end the war, pressed on his quarrel, and
setting his pikemen and horsemen in array, drew near
the castle to take it by storm. Then the cry arose and the
tumult; and the knights and the men-at-arms took their
weapons, and hastened to the gates and the walls to
defend the castle, and the burgesses climbed to the
battlements, flinging quarrels[21] and sharpened darts
upon the foe. Whilst the siege was so loud and perilous,
the Count Garin of Beaucaire sought the chamber where   230
Aucassin lay mourning, assotted upon[22] Nicolette, his
very sweet friend, whom he loved so well.

"Ha, son," cried he, "craven art thou and shamed,
that seest thy best and fairest castle so hardly beset.
Know well that if thou lose it, thou art a naked man. Son,
arm thyself lightly, mount the horse, keep thy land, aid
thy men, hurtle into the press. Thou needest not to
strike together, neither to be smitten down, but if they
see thee amongst them, the better will they defend their
goods and their bodies, thy land and mine; and thou art   240
so stout and strong that very easily thou canst do this
thing, as is but right."

"Father," answered Aucassin, "what sayest thou
now? May God give me naught that I require of Him if I
become a knight, or mount to horse, or thrust into the
press to strike knight or to be smitten down, save only
thou givest me Nicolette, my sweet friend, whom I love
so well!"

"Son," replied the father, "this can never be. Rather
will I suffer to lose my heritage, and go bare of all, than   250
that thou shouldst have her, either as woman or as dame."

So he turned without farewell; but when Aucassin
saw him part, he stayed him, saying, "Father, come
now; I will make a true bargain with thee."

"What bargain, fair son?"

"I will arm me, and thrust into the press on such
bargain as this: that if God bring me again safe and
sound, thou wilt let me look on Nicolette, my sweet
friend, so long that I may have with her two words or   260
three, and kiss her only one time."

"I pledge my word to this," said the father. Of this
covenant had Aucassin much joy.

Now is sung:

Aucassin the more was fain
Of the kiss he sought to gain,
Rather than his coffers hold

A hundred thousand marks of gold.
At the call his squire drew near,
Armed him fast in battle gear;   270
Shirt and hauberk donned the lad,
Laced the helmet on his head,
Girt his golden-hilted sword—
Came the war-horse at his word—
Gripped the buckler and the lance,
At the stirrups cast a glance;
Then, most brave from plume to heel,
Pricked the charger with the steel,
Called to mind his absent dear,
Passed the gateway without fear   280
    Straight to the fight.

Now they say and tell and relate:

Aucassin was armed and horsed as you have heard.
God, how bravely showed the shield about his neck, the
helmet on his head, and the fringes of the baldric upon
his left thigh! The lad was tall and strong, slender and
comely to look upon; and the steed he bestrode was
great and speedy, and fiercely had he charged clear of
the gate. Now think not that he sought spoil of oxen and
cattle, nor to smite others and himself escape. Nay, but   290
of all this he took no heed. Another was with him; and
he thought so dearly upon Nicolette, his fair friend, that
the reins fell from his hand, and he struck never a blow.
Then the charger, yet smarting from the spur, bore him
into the battle, amidst the thickest of the foe, so that
hands were laid upon him from every side, and he was
made prisoner. Thus they spoiled him of shield and
lance, and forthwith led him from the field a captive,
questioning amongst themselves by what death he
should be slain.   300

When Aucassin marked their words, "Ha, God!"
cried he. "Sweet Creature, these are my mortal foes
who lead me captive, and who soon will smite off my
head; and when my head is smitten, never again may I
have fair speech with Nicolette, my sweet friend, whom
I hold so dear. Yet have I a good sword; and my horse is
yet unblown. Now if I defend me not for her sake, may
God keep her never, should she love me still!" The varlet
was hardy and stout, and the charger he bestrode
was right fierce. He plucked forth his sword, and smote   310
suddenly on the right hand and on the left, cutting sheer
through nasal and headpiece, gauntlet and arm, making
such ruin around him as the wild boar deals when
brought to bay by hounds in the wood, until he had
struck down ten knights, and hurt seven more, and won
clear of the *mêlée*, and rode back at utmost speed,
sword in his hand.

The Count Bougars of Valence heard tell that his men
were about to hang Aucassin, his foe, in shameful wise,
so he hastened to the sight; and Aucassin passed him   320
not by. His sword was yet in hand, and struck the Count
so fiercely upon the helm that the headpiece was cleft
and shattered upon the head. So bewildered was he by
the stroke that he tumbled to the ground, and Aucassin
stretched forth his hand, and took him, and led him
captive by the nasal of the helmet, and delivered him to
his father. "Father," said Aucassin, "behold the foe who

---

21. Square-headed crossbow-bolt.
22. Infatuated with.

wrought such war and mischief upon you! Twenty years hath this war endured, and none was there to bring it to an end."   330

"Fair son," replied his father, "better are such deeds as this than foolish dreams!"

"Father," returned Aucassin, "preach me no preachings; but carry out our bargain."

"Ha! What bargain, fair son?"

"How now, father, hast thou returned from the market? By my head, I will remember—whosoever may forget—so close is it to my heart! Didst thou not bargain with me, when I armed me and fared into the press, that if God brought me again safe and sound, thou wouldst   340 grant me sight of Nicolette, my sweet friend, so long that I might have with her two words or three, and kiss her once? Such was the bargain; so be thou honest dealer."

"I!" cried the father. "God aid me never, should I keep such terms. Were she here, I would set her in the flames; and thou thyself might well have every fear."

"Is this the very end?" said Aucassin.

"So help me God," said his father, "yea!"

"Certes," said Aucassin, "grey hairs go ill with a lying   350 tongue."

"Count of Valence," said Aucassin, "thou art my prisoner?"

"Sire," answered the Count, "it is verily and truly so."

"Give me thy hand," said Aucassin.

"Sire, as you wish!" So each took the other's hand.

"Plight me thy faith," said Aucassin, "that so long as thou drawest breath, never shall pass a day but thou shalt deal with my father in shameful fashion, either in goods or in person, if so thou canst."   360

"Sire, for God's love make me not a jest, but name me a price for my ransom. Whether you ask gold or silver, steed or palfrey, pelt or fur, hawk or hound, it shall be paid."

"What!" said Aucassin; "art thou not my prisoner?"

"Truly, sire," said the Count Bougars.

"God aid me never," quoth Aucassin, "but I send thy head flying, save thou plight me such faith as I said."

"In God's name," cried he, "I plight such affiance as seems most meet to thee." He pledged his troth; so   370 Aucassin set him upon a horse, and brought him into a place of surety, himself riding by his side.

Now is sung:

When Count Garin knew his son
Aucassin still loved but one,
That his heart was ever set
Fondly on fond Nicolette,
Straight a prison he hath found,
Paved with marble, walled around,
Where in vault beneath the earth   380
Aucassin made little mirth,
But with wailing filled his cell
In such wise as now I tell
"Nicolette, white lily-flow'r,
Sweetest lady found in bow'r,
Sweet as grape that brimmeth up
Sweetness in the spiced cup,

On a day this chanced to you:
Out of Limousin there drew
One, a pilgrim, sore adread—   390
Lay in pain upon his bed,
Tossed, and took with fear his breath,
Very dolent, near to death—
Then you entered, pure and white,
Softly to the sick man's sight,
Raised the train that swept adown,
Raised the ermine-bordered gown
Raised the smock, and bared to him,
Daintily, each lovely limb.
Then a wondrous thing befell.   400
Straight he rose up, sound and well,
Left his bed, took cross in hand,
Sought again his own dear land.
Lily-flow'r, so white, so sweet,
Fair the faring of thy feet,
Fair thy laughter, fair thy speech,
Fair our playing each with each!
Sweet thy kisses, soft thy touch!
All must love thee overmuch.
'Tis for thee that I am thrown   410
In this vaulted cell alone;
'Tis for thee that I attend
Death, that comes to make an end—
For thee, sweet friend!"

Now they say and tell and relate:

Aucassin was set in prison as you have heard tell, and Nicolette for her part was shut in the chamber. It was in the time of summer heat, in the month of May, when the days are warm, long and clear, and the night still and serene. Nicolette lay one night sleepless on her bed, and   420 watched the moon shine brightly through the casement, and listened to the nightingale plain in the garden. Then she bethought her of Aucassin, her friend, whom she loved so well. She called also to mind the Count Garin of Beaucaire, her mortal foe, and feared greatly to remain, lest her hiding-place should be told to him, and she be put to death in some shameful fashion. She made certain that the old woman who held her in ward was sound asleep. So she rose, and wrapped herself in a very fair silk mantle, the best she had, and taking the   430 sheets from her bed and the towels of her bath, knotted them together to make so long a rope as she was able, tied it about a pillar of the window, and slipped down into the garden. Then she took her skirt in both hands, the one before, and the other behind, and kilted her lightly against the dew which lay thickly upon the grass, and so passed through the garden. Her hair was golden, with little lovelocks; her eyes blue and laughing; her face most dainty to see, with lips more vermeil than ever was rose or cherry in the time of summer heat; her teeth   440 white and small; her breasts so firm that they showed beneath her vesture like two rounded nuts. So frail was she about the girdle that your two hands could have spanned her, and the daisies that she brake with her feet in passing showed altogether black against her instep and her flesh, so white was the fair young maiden.

She came to the postern, and unbarring the gate, issued forth upon the street of Beaucaire, taking heed to keep within the shadows, for the moon shone very bright, and thus she fared until she chanced upon the tower where her lover was prisoned. The tower was buttressed with pieces of wood in many places, and Nicolette hid herself amongst the pillars, wrapped close in her mantle. She set her face to a crevice of the tower, which was old and ruinous, and there she heard Aucassin weeping within, making great sorrow for the sweet friend whom he held so dear; and when she had hearkened awhile, she began to speak. 450

Now is sung: 460

Nicolette, so bright of face,
Leaned within this buttressed place,
Heard her lover weep within,
Marked the woe of Aucassin.
Then in words her thought she told:
"Aucassin, fond heart and bold,
What avails thine heart should ache
For a Paynim maiden's sake?
Ne'er may she become thy mate,
Since we prove thy father's hate, 470
Since thy kinsfolk hate me too;
What is left for me to do?
Nothing, but to seek the strand,
Pass o'er sea to some far land."
Shore she then one golden tress,
Thrust it in her love's duress;
Aucassin hath seen the gold
Shining bright in that dark hold,
Took the lock at her behest,
Kissed and placed it in his breast; 480
Then once more his eyes were wet
    For Nicolette.

Now they say and tell and relate:

When Aucassin heard Nicolette say that she would fare into another country, he was filled with anger. "Fair sweet friend," said he, "this be far from thee, for then wouldst thou have slain me. And the first man who saw thee, if so he might, would take thee forthwith and carry thee to his bed, and make thee his leman. Be sure that if thou wert found in any man's bed, save it be mine, I should not need a dagger to pierce my heart and slay me. Certes, no; wait would I not for a knife; but on the first wall or the nearest stone would I cast myself, and beat out my brains altogether. Better to die so foul a death as this than know thee to be in any man's bed, save mine." 490

"Aucassin," said she, "I doubt that thou lovest me less than thy words; and that my love is fonder than thine."

"Alack," cried Aucassin, "fair sweet friend, how can it be that thy love should be so great? Woman can not love man, as man loves woman; for woman's love is in the glance of her eye, and the blossom of her breast, and the tip of the toe of her foot; but the love of man is set deep in the hold of his heart, from whence it can not be torn away." 500

Whilst Aucassin and Nicolette were thus at odds together, the town watch entered the street, bearing naked swords beneath their mantles, for Count Garin had charged them strictly, once she were taken, to put her to death. The warder from his post upon the tower marked their approach, and as they drew near, heard them speaking of Nicolette, menacing her with death. 510

"God," said he, "it is great pity that so fair a damsel should be slain, and a rich alms should I give if I could warn her privily, and so she escape the snare; for of her death Aucassin, my liege, were dead already, and truly this were a piteous case."

Now is sung: 520

Brave the warder, full of guile,
Straight he sought some cunning wile:
Sought and found a song betime,
Raised this sweet and pleasant rhyme.
"Lady of the loyal mind,
Slender, gracious, very kind,
Gleaming head and golden hair,
Laughing lips and eyes of vair!
Easy, Lady, 'tis to tell
Two have speech who love full well.
Yet in peril are they met, 530
Set the snare, and spread the net.
Lo, the hunters draw this way,
Cloaked, with privy knives, to slay.
Ere the huntsmen spy the chase[23]
Let the quarry haste apace
    And keep her well."

Now they say and tell and relate:

"Ah," said Nicolette, "may the soul of thy father and of thy mother find sweetest rest, since in so fair and courteous a manner hast thou warned me. So God please, I will indeed keep myself close, and may He keep me too." 540

She drew the folds of her cloak about her, and crouched in the darkness of the pillars till the watch had passed beyond; then she bade farewell to Aucassin, and bent her steps to the castle wall. The wall was very ruinous, and mended with timber, so she climbed the fence, and went her way till she found herself between wall and moat. Gazing below, she saw the fosse was very deep and perilous, and the maid had great fear. 550

"Ah, God," cried she, "sweet Creature, should I fall, my neck must be broken; and if I stay, tomorrow shall I be taken, and men will burn my body in a fire. Yet were it better to die, now, in this place, than to be made a show tomorrow in the market."

She crossed her brow, and let herself slide down into the moat, and when she reached the bottom, her fair feet and pretty hands, which had never learned that they could be hurt, were so bruised and wounded that the blood came from them in places a many; yet knew she neither ill nor dolor because of the mightiness of her fear. But if with pain she had entered in, still more it cost her to issue forth. She called to mind that it were death 560

| **23.** Quarry.

to tarry, and by chance found there a stake of sharpened wood, which those within the keep had flung forth in their defense of the tower. With this she cut herself a foothold, one step above the other, till with extreme labor she climbed forth from the moat. Now the forest lay but the distance of two bolts from a crossbow, and ran some thirty leagues in length and breadth; moreover, 570 within were many wild beasts and serpents. She feared these greatly, lest they should do her a mischief; but presently she remembered that should men lay hands upon her, they would lead her back to the city to burn her at the fire.

Now is sung:

Nicolette the fair, the fond,
Climbed the fosse and won beyond;
There she kneeled her, and implored
Very help of Christ the Lord.   580
"Father, King of majesty,
Where to turn I know not, I.
So, within the woodland gloom
Wolf and boar and lion roam,
Fearful things, with rav'ning maw,
Rending tusk and tooth and claw.
Yet, if all adread I stay,
Men will come at break of day,
Treat me to their heart's desire,
Burn my body in the fire.   590
But by God's dear majesty
Such a death I will not die;
Since I die, ah, better then
Trust the boar than trust to men.
Since all's evil, men and beast,
    Choose I the least."

Now they say and tell and relate:

Nicolette made great sorrow in such manner as you have heard. She commended herself to God's keeping, and fared on until she entered the forest. She kept upon 600 the fringes of the woodland, for dread of the wild beasts and reptiles; and hiding herself within some thick bush, sleep overtook her, and she slept fast until six hours of the morn, when shepherds and herdsmen came from the city to lead their flocks to pasture between the wood and the river. The shepherds sat by a clear, sweet spring, which bubbled forth on the outskirts of the greenwood, and spreading a cloak upon the grass, set bread thereon. Whilst they ate together, Nicolette awoke at the song of the birds and the laughter, and hastened 610 to the well.

"Fair children," said she, "God have you in His keeping."

"God bless you also," answered one who was more fluent of tongue than his companions.

"Fair child," said she, "do you know Aucassin, the son of Count Garin of this realm?"

"Yes, we know him well."

"So God keep you, pretty boy," said she, "as you tell him that within this wood there is a fair quarry for his 620 hunting; and if he may take her, he would not part with one of her members for a hundred golden marks, nor for

five hundred, nay, nor for aught that man can give."

Then looking upon her steadfastly, their hearts were troubled, the maid was so beautiful. "Will I tell him?" cried he who was readier of words than his companions. "Woe to him who speaks of it ever, or tells Aucassin what you say. You speak not truth but faery, for in all this forest there is no beast neither stag, nor lion, nor boar— one of whose legs would be worth two pence, or three 630 at very best, and you talk of five hundred marks of gold! Woe betide him who believes your story, or shall spread it abroad! You are a fay, and no fit company for such as us; so pass upon your road."

"Ah, fair child," answered she, "yet you will do as I pray; for this beast is the only medicine that may heal Aucassin of his hurt. And I have here five sous in my purse; take them, and give him my message. For within three days must he hunt this chase and if within three days he find not the quarry, never may he cure him of 640 his wound."

"By my faith," cried he, "we will take the money and if he comes this way, will give him your message; but certainly we will not go and look for him."

"As God pleases!" answered she. So she bade farewell to the shepherds, and went her way.

Now is sung:

Nicolette, as you heard tell,
Bade the shepherd lads farewell;
Through deep woodlands warily   650
Fared she 'neath the leafy tree,
Till the grass-grown way she trod
Brought her to a forest road,
Whence, like fingers on a hand,
Forked sev'n paths throughout the land.
There she called to heart her love,
There bethought her she would prove
Whether true her lover's vows.
Plucked she then young sapling boughs,
Grasses, leaves that branches yield,   660
Oak shoots, lilies of the field—
Built a lodge with frond and flow'r—
Fairest mason, fairest bow'r!
Swore then, by the truth of God,
Should her lover come that road,
Nor for love of her who made
Dream a little in its shade,
'Spite his oath, no true love, he
    Nor fond heart, she!

Now they say and tell and relate: 670

Nicolette built the lodge, as you have heard; very pretty it was and very dainty, and well furnished, both outside and in, with a tapestry of flowers and of leaves. Then she withdrew herself a little way from the bower, and hid within a thicket to spy what Aucassin would do. And the cry and the haro went through all the realm that Nicolette was lost; some had it that she was stolen away, and others that Count Garin had done her to death. Whoever had joy thereof, Aucassin had little pleasure. His father, Count Garin, brought him out of his prison, 680 and sent letters to the lords and ladies of those parts bidding them to a very rich feast, so that Aucassin, his son, might cease to dote. When the feast was at its merriest, Aucassin leaned against the musicians' gallery, sad and all discomforted. No laugh had he for any jest, since she whom most he loved was not amongst the ladies set in hall.

A certain knight marked his grief, and coming presently to him, said, "Aucassin, of such fever as yours, I, too, have been sick. I can give you good counsel, if you are willing to listen." 690

"Sir knight," said Aucassin, "great thanks! Good counsel, above all things, I would hear."

"Get to horse," said he; "take your pleasure in the woodland amongst flowers and bracken and the songs of the birds. Perchance (who knows?) you may hear some word of which you will be glad."

"Sir knight," answered Aucassin, "great thanks! This will I do." He left the hall privily, and went downstairs to the stable where was his horse. He caused the charger 700 to be saddled and bridled, then put foot in stirrup, mounted, and left the castle, riding till he entered the forest, and so by adventure came upon the well whereby the shepherd lads were sitting; and it was then about three hours after noon. They had spread a cloak upon the grass, and were eating their bread, with great mirth and jollity.

Now is sung:

Round about the well were set
Martin, Robin, Esmeret— 710
Jolly shepherds, gaily met—
Frulin, Jack, and Aubriet.
Laughed the one, "God keep in ward
Aucassin, our brave young lord—
Keep besides the damsel fair,
Blue of eye and gold of hair,
Gave us wherewithal to buy
Cate and sheath-knife presently,
Horn and quarter-staff and fruit, 720
Shepherd's pipe and country flute;
    God make him well!"

Now they say and tell and relate:

When Aucassin marked the song of the herdboys he called to heart Nicolette, his very sweet friend, whom he held so dear. He thought she must have passed that way, so he struck his horse with the spurs and came quickly to the shepherds.

"Fair children, God keep you!"

"God bless you!" replied he who was readier of tongue than his fellows. 730

"Fair children," said he, "tell over again the song that you told but now."

"We will not tell it," answered he who was more fluent of speech than the others. "Sorrow be his who sings it to you, fair sir!"

"Fair children," returned Aucassin, "do you not know me?"

"Oh, yes; we know that you are Aucassin, our young lord. But we are not your men; we belong to the Count."

"Fair children, sing me the song once more, I pray 740 you!"

"By the Wounded Heart, what fine words! Why should I sing for you if I have no wish to do so? Why, the richest man in all the land—saving the presence of Count Garin—would not dare to drive my sheep and oxen and cows from out his wheatfield or his pasture, for fear of losing his eyes! Wherefore, then, should I sing for you if I have no wish to do so?"

"God keep you, fair children; yet you will do this thing for me. Take ten sous that I have in my purse." 750

"Sire, we will take the money; but I will not sing for you, since I have sworn not to do so. But I will tell it in plain prose, if such be your pleasure."

"As God pleases!" answered Aucassin. "Better the tale in prose than no story at all!"

"Sire, we were in this glade between six and nine of the morn, and were breaking our bread by the well, just as we are doing now, when a girl came by, the loveliest thing in all the world, so fair that we doubted her a fay, and she brimmed our wood with light. She gave us 760 money, and made a bargain with us that if you came here we would tell you that you must hunt in this forest; for in it is such a quarry that if you may take her you would not part with one of her members for five hundred silver marks, nor for aught that man can give. For in the quest is so sweet a salve that if you take her you shall be cured of your wound; and within three days must the chase be taken, for if she be not found by then, never will you see her more. Now go to your hunting if you will, and if you will not, let it go; for truly 770 have I carried out my bargain with her."

"Fair children," cried Aucassin, "enough have you spoken; and may God set me on her track!"

Now is sung:

Aucassin's fond heart was moved
When this hidden word he proved
Sent him by the maid he loved.
Straight his charger he bestrode,
Bade farewell, and swiftly rode
Deep within the forest dim, 780
Saying o'er and o'er to him:
"Nicolette, so sweet, so good,
'Tis for you I search this wood—
Antler'd stag nor boar I chase—
Hot I follow on your trace.
Slender shape and deep blue eyes,
Dainty laughter, low replies,
Fledge the arrow in my heart.
Ah, to find you—ne'er to part!
Pray God give so fair an end, 790
    Sister, sweet friend!"

Now they say and tell and relate:

Aucassin rode through the wood in search of Nicolette, and the charger went right speedily. Do not think that the spines and the thorns were pitiful to him. Truly, it was not so; for his raiment was so torn that the least tattered of his garments could scarcely hold to his body, and the blood ran from his arms and legs and flanks in forty places, or at least in thirty, so that you could have followed after him by the blood which he left upon the 800 grass. But he thought so fondly of Nicolette, his sweet friend, that he felt neither ill nor dolor. Thus all day long he searched the forest in his fashion, but might learn no news of her, and when it drew towards dusk, he commenced to weep because he had heard nothing. He rode at adventure down an old grass-grown road, and looking before him, saw a young man standing, such as I will tell you. Tall he was, and marvelously ugly and hideous. His head was big and blacker than smoked meat; the palm of your hand could easily have gone 810 between his two eyes; he had very large cheeks and a monstrous flat nose with great nostrils; lips redder than uncooked flesh; teeth yellow and foul; he was shod with shoes and gaiters of bull's hide, bound about the leg with ropes to well above the knee; upon his back was a rough cloak; and he stood leaning on a huge club. Aucassin urged his steed towards him, but was all afeared when he saw him as he was.

"Fair brother, God keep you."

"God bless you too," said he. 820

"As God keeps you, what do you here?"

"What is that to you?" said he.

"Truly, naught," answered Aucassin. "I asked with no wish to do you wrong."

"And you, for what cause do you weep?" asked the other, "and make such heavy sorrow? Certainly, were I so rich a man as you are, not the whole world should make me shed a tear."

"Do you know me, then?" said Aucassin.

"Yes, well I know you to be Aucassin, the son of the 830 Count, and if you will tell me why you weep, well, then I will tell what I do here."

"Certes," said Aucassin, "I will tell you with all my heart. I came this morning to hunt in the forest, and with a white grey-hound, the swiftest in the whole world. I have lost him, and that is why I weep."

"Hear him," cried he, "by the Sacred Heart, and you make all this lamentation for a filthy dog! Sorrow be his who shall esteem you more. Why, there is not a man of substance in these parts who would not give you ten or 840 fifteen or twenty hounds—if so your father wishes—and be right glad to make you the gift. But for my part I have full reason to weep and cry aloud."

"And what is your grief, brother?"

"Sire, I will tell you. I was hired by a rich farmer to drive his plough, with a yoke of four oxen. Now three days ago, by great mischance, I lost the best of my bullocks, Roget, the very best ox in the plough. I have been looking for him ever since, and have neither eaten nor drunk for three days; since I dare not go back to the 850 town, because men would put me into prison, as I have no money to pay for my loss. Of all the riches of the world I have nought but the rags upon my back. My poor old mother, too, who had nothing but one worn-out mattress, why, they have taken that from under her, and left her lying on the naked straw. That hurts me more than my own trouble. For money comes and money goes; if I have lost today, why, I may win tomorrow; and I will pay for my ox when pay I can. Not for this will I wring my hands. And you—you weep aloud for a filthy 860 cur. Sorrow take him who shall esteem you more."

"Certes, thou art a true comforter, fair brother, and blessed may you be. What is the worth of your bullock?"

"Sire, the villein demands twenty sous for his ox. I can not beat the price down by a single farthing."

"Hold out your hand," said Aucassin, "take these twenty sous which I have in my purse, and pay for your ox."

"Sire," answered the hind, "many thanks, and God grant you find that for which you seek." 870

So they parted from each other, and Aucassin rode upon his way. The night was beautiful and still, and so he fared along the forest path until he came to the seven crossroads where Nicolette had builded her bower. Very pretty it was, and very dainty, and well furnished both outside and in, ceiling and floor, with arras and carpet of freshly plucked flowers; no sweeter habitation could man desire to see. When Aucassin came upon it, he reined back his horse sharply, and the moonbeams fell within the lodge. 880

"Dear God," cried Aucassin, "here was Nicolette, my sweet friend, and this has she builded with her fair white hands. For the sweetness of the house and for love of her, now will I dismount, and here will I refresh me this night."

He withdrew his foot from the stirrup, and the charger was tall and high. He dreamed so deeply on Nicolette, his very sweet friend, that he fell heavily upon a great stone, and his shoulder came from its socket. He knew himself to be grievously wounded, but he forced 890 him to do all that he was able, and fastened his horse with the other hand to a thorn. Then he turned on his side, and crawled as best he might into the lodge. Looking through a crevice of the bower, he saw the stars shining in the sky, and one brighter than all the others, so he began to repeat—

Now is sung:

Little Star I gaze upon
Sweetly drawing to the moon.
In such golden haunt is set 900
Love, and bright-haired Nicolette.
God hath taken from our war
Beauty, like a shining star.
Ah, to reach her, though I fell
From her Heaven to my Hell!
Who were worthy such a thing,
Were he emperor or king?
Still you shine, oh perfect Star,
    Beyond, afar.

Now they say and tell and relate: 910

When Nicolette heard Aucassin speak these words, she hastened to him from where she was hidden near by. She entered in the bower, and clasping her arms about his neck, kissed and embraced him straitly. "Fair sweet friend, very glad am I to find you."

"And you, fair sweet friend, glad am I to meet." So they kissed, and held each other fast, and their joy was lovely to see.

"Ah, sweet friend," cried Aucassin, "it was but now that I was in grievous pain with my shoulder, but since I 920 hold you close I feel neither sorrow nor wound."

Nicolette searched his hurt, and perceived that the shoulder was out of joint. She handled it so deftly with her white hands and used such skillful surgery, that by the grace of God (who loveth all true lovers) the shoulder came back to its place. Then she plucked flowers, and fresh grass and green leafage, and bound them tightly about the setting with the hem torn from her shift, and he was altogether healed.

"Aucassin," said she, "fair sweet friend, let us take   930 thought together as to what must be done. If your father beats the wood tomorrow, and men take me, whatever may chance to you, certainly I shall be slain."

"Certes, fair sweet friend, the sorer grief would be mine. But so I may help, never shall you come to his hands." So he mounted to horse, and setting his love before him, held her fast in his arms, kissing her as he rode, and thus they came forth to the open fields.

Now is sung:

Aucassin, that loving squire,   940
Dainty fair to heart's desire,
Rode from out the forest dim
Clasping her he loved to him.
Placed upon the saddlebow
There he kissed her, chin and brow,
There embraced her, mouth and eyes.
But she spake him, sweetly wise:
"Love, a term to dalliance;
Since for us no home in France
See we Rome or far Byzance?"   950
"Sweet my love, all's one to me,
Dale or woodland, earth or sea;
Nothing care I where we ride
So I hold you at my side."
So, enlaced, the lovers went,
Skirting town and battlement,
Rocky scaur,[24] and quiet lawn;
Till one morning, with the dawn,
Broke the cliffs down to the shore,
Loud they heard the surges roar,   960
    Stood by the sea.

[From this point Aucassin and Nicolette are separated. After some adventures Aucassin returns to his home where he becomes Count of Beaucaire. Nicolette is taken to Carthage where she is recognized as the king's daughter and is to be married to a Moorish Prince. She runs away, however, and makes her way to Beaucaire disguised as a minstrel.]

Now is sung:

Neath the keep of strong Beaucaire
On a day of summer fair,
At his pleasure, Aucassin
Sat with baron, friend and kin.
Then upon the scent of flow'rs,
Song of birds, and golden hours,
Full of beauty, love, regret,
Stole the dream of Nicolette,   970
Came the tenderness of years;
So he drew apart in tears.
Then there entered to his eyes

Nicolette, in minstrel guise,
Touched the viol with the bow,
Sang as I will let you know.
"Lords and ladies, list to me,
High and low, of what degree;
Now I sing, for your delight,
Aucassin, that loyal knight,   980
And his fond friend, Nicolette.
Such the love betwixt them set
When his kinsfolk sought her head,
Fast he followed where she fled.
From their refuge in the keep
Paynims bore them o'er the deep.
Nought of him I know to end.
But for Nicolette, his friend,
Dear she is, desirable,
For her father loves her well;   990
Famous Carthage owns him king,
Where she has sweet cherishing.
Now, as lord he seeks for her,
Sultan, Caliph, proud Emir.
But the maid of these will none,
For she loves a dansellon,
Aucassin, who plighted troth.
Sworn has she some pretty oath
Ne'er shall she be wife or bride,
Never lie at baron's side   1000
    Be he denied."

Now they say and tell and relate:

When Aucassin heard Nicolette sing in this fashion, he was glad at heart; so he drew her aside, and asked, "Fair sweet friend," said Aucassin, "know you nought of this Nicolette, whose ballad you have sung?"

"Sire, truly, yea; well I know her for the most loyal of creatures, and as the most winning and modest of maidens born. She is daughter to the King of Carthage, who took her when Aucassin also was taken, and   1010 brought her to the city of Carthage, till he knew for certain that she was his child, whereat he rejoiced greatly. Any day he would give her for husband one of the highest kings in all Spain; but rather would she be hanged or burned than take him, however rich he be."

"Ah, fair sweet friend," cried the Count Aucassin, "if you would return to that country and persuade her to have speech with me here, I would give you of my riches more than you would dare to ask of me or to take. Know that for love of her I choose not to have a wife,   1020 however proud her race, but I stand and wait; for never will there be wife of mine if it be not she, and if I knew where to find her I should not need to grope blindly for her thus."

"Sire," answered she, "if you will do these things, I will go and seek her for your sake, and for hers too; because to me she is very dear."

He pledged his word, and caused her to be given twenty pounds. So she bade him farewell, and he was weeping for the sweetness of Nicolette. And when she   1030

---

24. Isolated cliff.

saw his tears, "Sire," said she, "take it not so much to heart; in so short a space will I bring her to this town, and you shall see her with your eyes."

When Aucassin knew this, he rejoiced greatly. So she parted from him, and fared in the town to the house of the Viscountess, for the Viscount, her godfather, was dead. There she lodged, and opened her mind fully to the lady on all the business; and the Viscountess recalled the past, and knew well that it was Nicolette whom she had cherished. So she caused the bath to be   1040 heated, and made her take her ease for fully eight days. Then Nicolette sought an herb that was called celandine, and washed herself therewith, and became so fair as she had never been before. She arrayed her in a rich silken gown from the lady's goodly store, and seated herself in the chamber on a rich stuff of broidered sendal; then she whispered the dame, and begged her to fetch Aucassin, her friend. This she did. When she reached the palace, lo, Aucassin in tears, making great sorrow for the long tarrying of Nicolette, his friend; and   1050 the lady called to him, and said, "Aucassin, behave not so wildly; but come with me, and I will show you that thing you love best in all the world; for Nicolette, your sweet friend, is here from a far country to seek her love." So Aucassin was glad at heart.

Now is sung:

When he learned that in Beaucaire
Lodged his lady, sweet and fair,
Aucassin arose, and came
To her hostel, with the dame;   1060
Entered in, and passed straightway
To the chamber where she lay.
When she saw him, Nicolette
Had such joy as never yet;
Sprang she lightly to her feet,
Swiftly came with welcome meet.
When he saw her, Aucassin
Oped both arms, and drew her in,
Clasped her close in fond embrace,
Kissed her eyes and kissed her face.   1070
In such greeting sped the night,
Till, at dawning of the light,
Aucassin, with pomp most rare,
Crowned her Countess of Beaucaire.
Such delight these lovers met,
Aucassin and Nicolette,
Length of days and joy did win,
Nicolette and Aucassin;
Endeth song and tale I tell
    With marriage bell.   1080

STUDY QUESTIONS

1. The coexistence of morality plays and romances seems to indicate some contradictions between church teachings and actual life. For instance, what differences in attitudes about the body are found in *Everyman* and *Aucassin and Nicolette*? Are there similar contradictions in our own society?

2. What was "love" in the Middle Ages? What did these lovers see in each other? On what was their mutual attraction based? Are today's concepts about attraction and love somewhat different? Considerably different? Account for the differences.

SUMMARY

People of the early Middle Ages built walls around their villages—wooden palisades in the early days; later, the walls were stone and the lord's house and the whole village a fortified enclave. Life paralleled those confining fortifications because people had battlements around their minds, barriers that were reinforced by the church.

Their universe was based on the teachings of the church of Rome, which, in the Middle Ages, allowed no questioning of its tenets or its actions. Further, the church took a dim view of worldly pleasure and repressed any consideration of the physical world. Science as we know it did not exist; the natural world was a closed book, to be interpreted only as a vague shadow of the intention and mind of God. Earthly life was viewed as a brief and transitory journey through a dismal land, with real life and genuine happiness reserved for the next world. Furthermore, as is explicit in the morality play of *Everyman*, the only way to achieve the blissful afterlife lay in the unquestioning acceptance of the doctrines and sacraments of the church.

The economic system of manorialism bound most people to the 1,000 or so acres of the manor itself. There was little chance of escape; the few who left the enclave needed special permission. In fact, the average serf never strayed even a kilometer from the demesne. Food, clothing, and meager physical comforts were limited to what the manor could produce. Not even the mind could escape the narrow confines; reading was almost unknown because most people were illiterate, including many clergymen. Illiteracy and minimal travel meant also that news of the outside world almost never penetrated the closed miniworld of the manor.

The political system of feudalism was equally narrowing. Justice lay entirely in the hands of the feudal lord or, more often, his deputy. Except for the specific obligations of serf to lord and vassal to suzerain, which were generally known and accepted, the law was made up on the spot, and the individual never knew what to expect.

About the only contact feudal society had with the outside world were the bloody incursions of barbarian Norsemen or Magyars, or as victims of Muslim holy wars. Not until the middle of the Middle Ages (ca. 1000) would the Norsemen and Magyars be absorbed by Christian societies and the advanced culture of Islam acknowledged, studied, and drawn into the evolving Western synthesis. Western civilization would not be what it is today without the vital infusion of Islamic culture.

The narrow confines of church, manorialism, and feudalism provided the walls that closed in upon the human spirit. Creativity and freedom of thought were almost unknown. But, with the withdrawal of Roman protection and with all the dangers from bands of marauders, these walls provided protection for the individual. If ordinary serfs could not live well, they could at least live safely.

Perhaps Elinor Wylie's twentieth-century poem "Sanctuary" expresses the basic problem:

This is the bricklayer; hear the thud
Of his heavy load dumped down on stone,
His lustrous bricks are brighter than blood,
His smoking mortar whiter than bone.

Set each sharp-edged, fire-bitten brick
Straight by the plumb-line's shivering length;
Make my marvelous wall so thick
Dead nor living may shake its strength.

Full as a crystal cup with drink
Is my cell with dreams, and quiet, and cool . . .
Stop, old man! You must leave a chink;
How can I breathe? *You can't, you fool!*

But the human spirit is never content with mere security. Particularly with the gaining of a little freedom, as happened in the tenth and eleventh centuries, it clamors more and more for expansion. The seeds that were to germinate and eventually break down medieval walls were already planted. Some of the directions for that growth may be indicated.

First, the human spirit has never long been content *not* to examine the world around it. The varied forms of the world, its beauties, and reason for being demand attention. Both art and science express this quest for an exploration of the sensory world.

Second, the two personality types of Europe, the rational Graeco-Roman and the emotional and energetic Germanic lived side by side but not in unison by the year 1000. Some form of synthesis between these two personality types, almost exactly opposite each other, needed to be found.

Third, a problem limited largely to politics: the question of supremacy of church or state demanded settlement. At a time when the secular power was so weak as to be almost nonexistent, the church could and did assert its authority over kings and lords. But with the growth of the powers of the world a struggle was inevitable, a bitter conflict of church and state that has been waged all over the Western world and which is still not fully resolved.

Fourth, and perhaps most important, people need joy in their lives but this was sternly denied by the church. A desire for immediate physical and intellectual pleasure in life now would necessarily conflict with the doctrine that life here was nothing, the afterlife everything. The pull of life as opposed to the church-dictated pull of death was bound to cleave the human personality until some synthesis could be effected.

These are the latent problems one sees at the end of the Early Middle Ages. Their solutions will be considered in subsequent chapters.

CULTURE AND HUMAN VALUES

The centuries from about 500 to around 1000 were a tumultuous period of transition. The former realities of the Individual and then of the State had been superseded by the vision of God as the true reality and the Church of Rome as the sole possessor of the Keys of the Kingdom. For most people the church was the most easily comprehensible reality. For the faithful it promised salvation and a glorious existence in the afterlife. A sparse and meager existence in this harsh world would be more than made up for by eternal life in the paradise to come. Strict adherence to the church's teaching of the Scriptures and to church doctrine—plus avoidance of sin—virtually assured admission to eternal bliss.

The virtues and vices as specified by the church can be considered from another point of view. The church was the only absolute authority and intended to remain so. Some scholars have suggested that the church-defined virtues and vices also served to reinforce the power and authority of Rome. The first and foremost value was obedience to authority. After this, the seven virtues of faith, hope, love, temperance, prudence, fortitude, and justice would reinforce the dominance of Rome. Condemnation of the sins of pride, lust, envy, anger, avarice, dejection, and gluttony would help guard against any temptation to tinker with the status quo. One should be reminded that justice was the foremost value in ancient Greece, pride was a virtue, and Aphrodite was adored by all. Whatever the interpretation, life during these perilous times was bleak and dismal for most of the population and was to remain so for centuries. There was hope but precious little joy. It must be emphasized that the Early Middle Ages was a difficult transitional period from the chaos of the post-Roman era to the period of balance of the High Middle Ages when a synthesis emerged that emphasized spirituality without sacrificing earthly pleasures.

CHAPTER 13

The Late Middle Ages: Expansion and Synthesis

A NEW CENTURY

There was no single reason for the liberation of a whole social structure, but looking back over the centuries we know it began in eleventh-century Europe. Release from a dreaded Doomsday was one of the many causes of the transformation. Some claimed that the world would end at the dawn of the year 1000, a prophecy believed by some of the peasantry. One must imagine the wonder when people woke up on New Year's morning to discover that they were not only alive but hungry, not for spiritual food, but for a very physical breakfast. Such a reprieve was certainly one of the symbols of the general awakening of Europe. This was still the Middle Ages with God the accepted Reality, but what a difference was soon to be discovered in the lives and thoughts of men and women!

Many were the instruments of change. The shift from feudalism's fierce warrior code to the more cultured ideals of chivalry was a major civilizing influence. The existing church doctrine was widely viewed as austere and remote, which led to the more personal cult of the Virgin, the most popular religious force in the High Middle Ages. Even the Crusades led, however inadvertently, to increasing knowledge of the luxurious Islamic civilization and its priceless hoard of ancient Greek culture. New cities were created while older ones expanded. Universities, destined to influence all of Europe, were founded, supporting a revival of humanistic studies which sparked an intellectual life that had lain dormant for centuries. Perhaps a metaphor for the entire transformation was the philosophic ferment about the nature of reality itself, which culminated in the "Battle of Universals."

The Rise of Cities

New cities and the expansion of existing cities was central to the transformation of Europe. Cities are essential for the development of any civilization; agriculture is the business of rural areas while culture is the business of cities. Of the many reasons for the rise of medieval cities, one lay in the increase of land available for agriculture because of the drainage of swamps, for cities require a guaranteed food supply. Another impetus to the gathering of people was the nobles' need for central military forces for quicker mobilization to fight ever bigger wars. But increasing trade and commerce were probably the most important forces driving urban development.

The itinerant peddler, who traveled from manor to manor, had been a standard fixture of the Early Middle Ages. Sometime during the eleventh century some peddlers-become-merchants set up stalls under the protection of the churches or abbeys. This caused a change comparable to reinventing the wheel: the reintroduction of money in place of bartering as the medium of exchange. For centuries the nobles had received their manorial dues in goods and produce, but money offered far greater freedom in fuelling their ambitions. In return for tax money they granted charters to cities while awarding varying degrees of freedom from feudal responsibilities. Thus they encouraged the growth of urban centers that keyed a general stirring of the human spirit.

Throughout Europe the word went around, "City air is free air." Living in a city for a year and a day made a serf a free man. Here tradesmen organized guilds to regulate the quality and price of their goods and to provide insurance and some social life for the members and their families. As these guilds—first only craft guilds, later also merchant guilds—prospered, grand guildhalls were built flanking the cathedral to form a quadrangle about the open marketplace, a central grouping characteristic of medieval towns and cities.

The Crusades

For a variety of reasons the Crusades were a major force for change. Preached by Pope Urban II in 1095, the First Crusade captured Jerusalem in 1099—the only successful venture in a series of failed Crusades lasting into the Renaissance—and that success was only temporary (map 13.1). The stated intent of the Crusades was to rescue the Holy Land from its Muslim inhabitants so that Christian shrines might become more accessible for Western pilgrims. The hidden agenda included a lust for Middle Eastern lands and riches plus papal attempts to deflect to a foreign foe the increasing criticism of the Holy See. The West justified the Crusades as holy wars freeing biblical lands from infidels but Muslims saw only unprovoked aggression by barbarous heathens. The repercussions have yet to end.

The long-lasting effects of Middle Eastern invasions did, however, include significant benefits. Although Europeans had already encountered Islamic culture in Sicily and Spain, the Crusaders entered the heart of this rich civilization, and what they found there caused substantial changes in virtually every aspect of European life. The luxurious booty carted home by the soldiers, following the ancient custom of all warriors, stoked rising expectations for a better life. First imported as luxuries, such foods as sugar, saffron, rice, citrus, and melon and such manufactured goods as silk, damask, muslin, and cotton soon became necessities. More important than food and textiles, however, was the rich reservoir of Islamic science and the carefully tended heritage of ancient Greece. The way was still long and tortuous but semibarbaric Europe began, finally, to develop the arts of civilized living.

Feudalism and Chivalry

One of the key transformations was the movement from feudalism's warrior ethic to chivalry's more civilized code of behavior. During the later Middle Ages, especially in France, aristocratic women began to assume a more prominent role in shaping the world in which they lived while their husbands were off fighting. They efficiently managed their estates, introduced poetry and music to the courts, and elevated the standards of behavior, dress, and manners.

Epitomizing this metamorphosis was the remarkable Eleanor of Aquitaine (1122–1204), Queen of France and then of England. Insisting on accompanying her first husband, King Louis VII of France, on the Second Crusade in 1147, Eleanor was fascinated by the sophistication of Constantinople and quick to add elements of Byzantine and Muslim culture to her already extensive education. Along with her daughter, Marie of Champagne, and granddaughter, Blanche of Castile, Eleanor established Courts of Love that were to write legal-sounding codes of etiquette. Lyrical love songs composed and performed by aristocratic **troubadours** (fig. 13.1; see also pp. 447–50) replaced epic tales of stalwart heroes fighting bloody battles. This shift in emphasis can be seen clearly in the contrast between Roland's lament over the fallen Franks at Roncevaux, representative of feudal ideals, and the lament over the dead Lancelot, an exemplary knight of the age of chivalry. Surveying the field of death where his comrades in arms lie, Roland says:

Lords and barons, now may God have mercy upon

you, and grant Paradise to all your souls that you may rest among the blessed flowers. Man never saw better men of arms than ye were. Long and well, year in and year out, have ye served me, and many wide lands have ye won for the glory of Charles. Was it to such an end that he nourished you? O France, fair land, today art thou made desolate by rude slaughter. Ye Frankish barons, I see you die through me, yet I can do naught to save and defend you. May God, who knows no lie, aid you!

When Lancelot, the legendary knight of chivalry, lies dead, we hear the following lament from Guinevere:

Thou wert the courtliest knight that ever bare shield, and thou wert the truest friend to thy lover that ever bestrode horse, and thou wert the truest lover among sinful men that ever loved woman, and thou wert the kindest man that ever struck with sword, and thou wert the goodliest person that ever came among the crowd of knights, and thou wert the meekest man and the gentlest that ever are in hall among ladies, and thou wert the sternest knight to thy mortal foe that ever put spear in breast.

Here is a transformation from a fighting code to a humane and courtly standard. Both codes are present in the lament over Lancelot but kindness, love, and humility—never even considered by feudal warriors—are, once again, virtues. Given the vagaries of human nature, the elaborate codes of chivalry were undoubtedly violated about as often as they were observed. They assisted nevertheless in the laborious process of recivilizing Europe.

Powerful women such as Eleanor of Aquitaine were in a position to contribute to the civilizing process, but what of those medieval women who were neither powerful nor royal? With the exception of the Etruscans, Minoans, and the Aegean culture of Lesbos, the role of women in Western civilization was always secondary and subservient. However, determined women could help change the role of their gender in medieval society. Though it was considerably more difficult for women outside a court setting to influence society, Christine de Pisan (ca. 1364–ca. 1431), considered France's first professional writer, was one of the most significant writer/thinkers to do so. An early feminist who was always firm but cheerfully well-mannered within a male-dominated society, she had a voice of reason and restraint—and courage.

Born in Venice, Christine de Pisan spent most of her life in the shadow of the court of Charles V in Paris, where her father was court physician. After ten years of a happy marriage she was suddenly widowed at twenty-five and faced with making her way in a man's world. Utilizing her excellent education, she became so successful as a professional writer that she supported her three children, her mother, and assorted relatives (fig. 13.2 and p. 374). Many of her forty-one works were concerned with the advancement of women, particularly the *Book of the City of Ladies* and *A Medieval Woman's Mirror of Honor: The Treasury of the City of Ladies* (see pp. 401–3).

The Church of Our Lady

Closely allied to chivalry's evolution was the development of beauty and warmth within the church. Church doctrine was an intellectual monument centered on the **Trinity**—Father, Son, and Holy Ghost—a Three who were always One, and administering the uncompromising justice described by Augustine. For guilt-ridden men and women justice was the last thing to be desired. They sought mercy, not justice, turning to the Virgin, the highest of the saints, the Queen of Heaven. She was the essence of purity, an idealized version of love, warmth, and beauty. A manifestation of the polarized medieval view of women, the cult of the Virgin venerated one woman, pure in body and soul, possessor of all the womanly virtues. Her diametric opposite was Eve, Adam's temptress, the "fallen" woman beguiled by Satan, a misogynous concept with disastrous consequences, then and now.

The Virgin was the loving Mother who could mercifully intercede for the faithful, and it was to her that many of the majestic cathedrals were dedicated. Indeed, in France one asks not the way to the cathedral, but how to get to Notre Dame, the church of "Our Lady." The two are almost synonymous. As the nineteenth-century American historian Henry Adams noted in *Mont-St.-Michel and Chartres*:

> The measure of this devotion [to the Virgin], which proves to any religious American mind, beyond possible cavil, its serious and practical reality, is the money it cost. According to statistics, in the single century between 1170 and 1270, the French built 80 cathedrals and nearly five hundred churches of the cathedral class, which would have cost, according to an estimate made in 1840, more than five thousand millions to replace. Five thousand million francs is a thousand million dollars,[1] and this covered only the great churches of a single century . . . . The share of this capital which was—if one may use a commercial figure—invested in the Virgin cannot be fixed . . . but in a spiritual and artistic sense, it was almost the whole . . . .
>
> Expenditure like this rests invariably on an economic idea . . . . In the thirteenth [century] they

trusted their money to the Queen of Heaven—because of their belief in her power to repay it with interest in the life to come.

Therein lay the power of the Virgin in bringing human understanding and sympathy into the remote structure of church doctrine. While theologians wrangled about materialism and spiritualism, the common people were consoled by the presence, in their church, of a beautiful statue representing a person with human sympathy and warmth. Such faith reveals itself in the many stories of the mysteries of the Virgin, including "Our Lady's Juggler" (see pp. 387–8).

Scholasticism

The medieval church insisted upon absolute authority. Despite his early philosophic speculations, St. Augustine finally said, "I believe in order that I may know." Thus faith in the Scriptures and the biblical commentaries of the early church fathers and total submission to these sources was the mandatory first step for the Christian life. Knowledge was secondary; whenever doctrine was inexplicable or contrary to reason, doctrine was believed and intellect denied.

Scholars built the elaborate structure of Christian Scholasticism on this steadfast base. Although Scholasticism was complex the reasoning procedure was simple. A scholar answered any question by studying the Bible and writings of the church fathers to find all passages pertaining to his subject. This was his only source for basic data; exploration of other writings or of the sensory world was forbidden. Secondly, he used Aristotelian logic to work on his source. Such logic is built upon the three-part syllogism: a major premise, *all men are mortal*; a minor premise, *Socrates is a man*; a conclusion, *therefore Socrates is mortal*. The conclusion can then be used as a major or minor premise in further syllogisms until the final, refined answer is found.[2]

Faith and Reason

As early as the ninth century the philosopher Johannes Scotus Erigena had recognized some differences between faith and reason, but he insisted that both reason and the Scriptures had come from God, making conflict "impossible." But the church held to its stand on faith alone, which Anselm of Canterbury reaffirmed in the eleventh century. Late in that century, however, this reaffirmation was challenged by a philosophic dispute that became known as the Battle of Universals. The "battle" was a controversy (greatly simplified here) about the nature of reality. Today's student may consider this an esoteric dispute between ivory-tower philosophers, but the issue was critical. Because a commonly held concept of reality determines the nature of a civilization, any change in the concept will

---

1. This is the money values of 1840. If we multiplied the figure by a hundred, it might still be low for the late twentieth century.
2. Today's students might scoff at this type of reasoning until they are reminded that every culture sets similar limits to its thought processes. In the twentieth century, for example, the searcher for truth investigates the physical world and then uses the scientific method to refine the raw data and gain knowledge about the world in which we live.

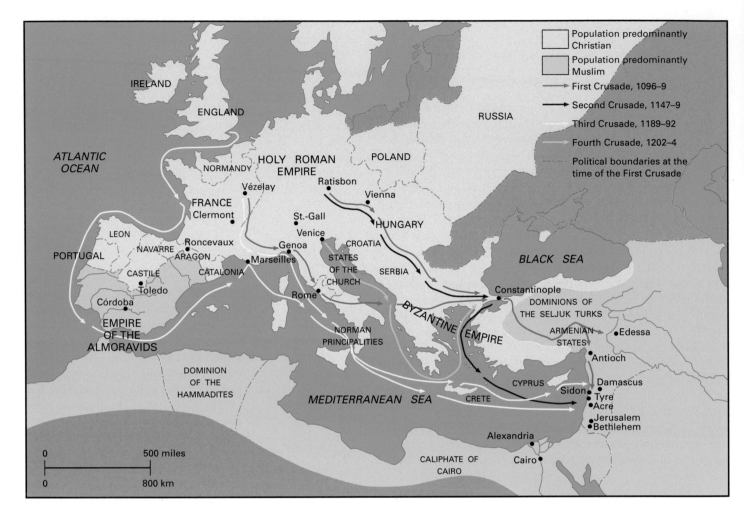

Map 13.1   The major Crusades.

necessarily alter the way people live and think. These philosophers were leading scholars in the central institution of the age, as important in their time as Einstein and Stephen Hawking have been in our century. Any change in the church's position affected everyone from kings to serfs.

The Realist Position

Church doctrine was based on an adaptation of Plato's belief in Forms/Ideas as constituting an ultimate reality that is permanent, unchanging, without material substance, and, according to the church, existing in the mind of God.

13.1 "Music and Her Attendants," from Boethius, *De Arithmetica*. Ca. 14th century. Manuscript illumination. Biblioteca Nazionale, Naples. Photo: Scala, Florence. Holding a portable pipe organ, the elegant lady, who symbolizes the civilized art of courtly music, is surrounded by an ensemble of female court musicians. In the circle at the top King David plays a **psaltery**, an instrument from whose name (of Greek origin) we get the word "psalm."

13.2 "Christine de Pisan Presenting her Poems to Isabel of Bavaria," fol. 3, Harley Ms 4431; detail on p. 374. Manuscript illumination. British Library, London.

Thus physical things, which are subject to change, are only illusory shadows, as described in Plato's "Allegory of the Cave." The human body is to be disregarded and a study of the physical world is wasted time better spent seeking eternal truths. This Neoplatonic/Augustinian doctrine was the Realist position and the position held by the church.

The Nominalist Position

The French philosopher Johannes Roscellinus (ca. 1050–after 1120) first challenged this doctrine with a nominalist position that is close to what many people believe today. Claiming that physical things were the only reality, he stated that, for example, each sense-apparent tree is real and that no higher "treeness" exists. How can we know the idea of tree? We can speak of trees, or people, or elephants, or justice when no specific example is present to our senses. Roscellinus said that these "ideas" were only names (hence the word "nominalist") and that we form the idea as a generalization only after experience with a

number of individual things. We experience, he said, specific examples of elms, oaks, pines, and so forth. We then generalize and form the "idea" tree so that we can discuss the species—and understand each other—in the middle of the ocean with no tree within 1,000 miles.

The two positions in the battle were thus established, as opposite as opposites can be. William of Champeaux (1070–1121) and others stoutly defended the realist position, the standard doctrine of the church. If the defenders should fail, the church itself would be in danger, they said, and indeed it was.

The Conceptualist Position

A middle position was suggested by the brilliant thinker Peter Abelard (1079–1142), probably the most popular teacher in the early University of Paris. Having studied with both Roscellinus and William of Champeaux, Abelard was in a perfect position to propose a compromise. Abelard's conceptualist position anticipated Aristotle's view of the problem even before that whole body of knowledge was known to Europe. The conceptualist view can be stated briefly, for it will become better developed by Thomas Aquinas. Abelard contended that idea is real but that it does not exist either before or after a particular physical thing. That is, reality as idea exists only in the sense-apparent object. Abelard's intellectual daring was condemned by the church but, nevertheless, the battle of the three positions continued until, a century later, Thomas Aquinas formed a synthesis that would become the official dogma of the church.

But the imaginative Abelard was not finished. He tossed a bombshell into religious thought when he published *Sic et non* ("Yes and No"). One remembers that the only valid sources of knowledge then were the Bible and the commentaries of the church fathers. In *Sic et non* Abelard raised a number of important religious questions; then, in opposite columns, he quoted the answers of each father, thus exposing all sorts of contradictions and sending a shudder throughout the church. If this source of knowledge was contradictory then how wrong were the conclusions based on these writings? The sources were faulty and the challenge of authority was inevitable.

Aristotle Rediscovered

Still another blaze broke out in the structure of the church with the late twelfth-century rediscovery of all of Aristotle's works. His logic, his only known work, had been universally used as the only method of reasoning, which made Aristotle the most venerated philosopher of the Early Middle Ages and the Philosopher to one and all.

Everyone appreciated Aristotle, which helps explain the preservation of his work for sixteen centuries and its circuitous route back to Europe. Aristotle had written in Greek, of course, which Syrian scholars translated into Syriac. Translated later into Arabic, his works were brought into Muslim Spain where they were discovered, rendered into Latin, and made available to all of Europe. The discovery of this treasure trove of knowledge revealed, among other things, that the philosopher developed his knowledge by investigating and classifying physical things, not by relying entirely on reason. The church was opposed to such knowledge, yet this man, more revered than some of the saints, had broadened his experience by studying the things of this world. The impact was about as great as if we learned that Einstein made his discoveries by consulting a witch doctor. What was the church to do?

The predictable first reaction was to ban something already too well known for a ban to work, so authorities retreated to "authorized" versions that deleted everything contradicting church doctrine. But the scholars who idolized Aristotle the logician could not be denied and everything became available and avidly studied. Incredibly, the most revered thinker of the Middle Ages had, among many other things, studied anatomy by dissecting animals and classified plants according to their structure. Thus another problem confronted the church, demanding a reasonable solution if the institution was to maintain its authority.

THE UNIVERSITIES

The civilizations of Greece, Rome, Byzantium, and Islam all had centers of learning that predated European universities. The rise of the universities, however, was especially significant in the development of Western civilization. Their origin is obscure, for we have little knowledge of them until their formal charters were issued. In Christian Europe (as distinguished from Muslim Spain) the University of Salerno, specializing in medicine, dated from the eleventh century, but, being situated in southern Italy, it had little influence on the general dawn of culture. The University of Bologna, with its eminent law school, received a formal grant of rights in 1158. The University of Paris was granted a royal charter in 1200 but began much earlier. Its papal license of 1231 reopened a university that had been closed for two years because of a riot between students and city authorities. (Few things are new under the sun!) Oxford had been formed in the twelfth century when some teachers and students seceded from Paris, and Cambridge was founded by a dissident group from Oxford. Growth was so rapid that, by the end of the Middle Ages, some eighty universities were scattered throughout Europe.

Universitas

Universitas is Latin for a corporation such as a trade guild. A university came into being when teachers and students joined together as a legal body. Protected by a charter granted, usually, by the pope or a king, universities were generally freed from local jurisdiction, though they could not avoid "town and gown" conflicts that seem endemic to university communities. Their operation paralleled that of craft guilds, with guild masters (professors) awarding qualifying certificates (degrees) to apprentices (students), who were working to become masters in the teaching corporation (university). Graduation of the apprentices marked their "commencement" as certified teachers.

Flourishing in the largest medieval city (population 300,000), and offering instruction in all recognized fields of knowledge, the University of Paris was the leading institution of the time, with faculties of medicine, law, theology, and liberal arts. As a prerequisite for professional courses, the liberal arts curriculum followed the seven liberal arts pattern of monastic schools: the **trivium** (grammar, rhetoric, logic) and the **quadrivium** (arithmetic, geometry, astronomy, and music, plus the works of Aristotle). In today's terms, trivium subjects were humanistic and those of the quadrivium mathematical.

Studies began with the trivium (including philosophy, literature, and history) but without prescribed hours or units of credit. Comprehensive oral examinations measured achievement with successful candidates awarded the bachelor of arts (B.A.) degree, the prerequisite for studying the quadrivium. Passing the second set of examinations certified the graduate to teach the liberal arts as a master of arts (M.A.). Doctors of law, medicine, or theology were teaching degrees, with the doctor of philosophy (Ph.D.) added later for advanced study in the liberal arts. Usually based on four years of study beyond the M.A., doctorates were awarded to candidates who passed more rigorous examinations and successfully defended a "thesis" (proposition) before a faculty board. The comparative few who survived this ordeal were granted both a doctorate in the appropriate profession and the opportunity to host a banquet for the examiners.

Although Plato's Academy had admitted women and some noted Hellenistic scholars were women, medieval universities were operated by and for men. The assumption that women needed no formal education continued the subordination of women as practiced in the Graeco-Roman world. Woman's inferior position in Christian Europe was, if anything, even more pronounced. The Old Testament expressed the Hebraic view that a wife was a lesser being who was her husband's property. The New Testament offered little improvement and the church fathers were unanimous in their contempt for women, most notably Paul, Jerome, Tertullian, and Augustine. The myth of Eve having originated in Adam's rib was universally believed in an age that accepted biblical stories and myths as facts. The rediscovery of Aristotle's works gave additional ammunition to the church's repression of women, for the still-revered philosopher had called women simply a necessary reproductive adjunct to the superior sex. For medieval universities the end result was the incalculable loss of the brain power of half the human race.

As guilds of teachers and scholars, early universities had neither buildings nor campus. Classes met wherever rooms could be found, usually in churches; regulations specified charges for room and board, the price of books (usually rented because manuscripts were expensive), the minimum number of classes students had to attend to be "official" (usually two a week), and the number of lectures and their length that a professor had to give to collect his fees. Students could fine professors for absences or for lecturing too long and, by not attending their classes, cost them a portion of their fees.

Collegium

The *collegium* (Lat., "community, society") was a residence hall that private benefactors began providing for students too poor to pay for room and board. Robert de Sorbon, royal chaplain to Louis IX, endowed a hall in 1257 called the Collège de Sorbonne, now part of the University of Paris.

Nonexistent in the Early Middle Ages, scholars were a new class, notable for their enthusiasm in the pursuit of all sorts of knowledge and experience. Their motto may well have been Abelard's famous teaching "for by doubting we come to inquiry, by inquiry we discover the truth." Some of these zealous scholars were increasingly restless

in a culture dominated by an authority that allowed no questioning of itself. Here, as in most areas of life in the High Middle Ages, we find a surge of energy, a quickening of the spirit.

SUMMARY

We have seen that medieval men and women sheltered themselves within the narrow walls of the authoritarian church, the rigid structure of feudalism, and manorialism's closed society. Literal and figurative walls provided a measure of physical and psychological safety but left little room for growth. Urban development and the increasing intellectual ferment in the universities helped breach the barriers in the first explorations for knowledge since the end of Graeco-Roman civilization. Virtually overnight the rediscovery of Aristotle raised the intellectual level of Western culture. Most importantly, contacts with more advanced Muslim and Byzantine cultures and the civilizing effects of chivalry and Courts of Love indicated that life on earth could be made immeasurably better.

THE MEDIEVAL SYNTHESIS

The conflicts in the late Middle Ages were between new secular ways of thinking and living and the older religious ways. Where was the art that could bring these together in a new synthesis? Where were the people who could define new relationships between human beings and the universe, human beings and God, the individual and society as a whole? Where were the artists who could suggest new purposes for life now that the old were so sorely challenged?

The new synthesis can be seen in the work of three men, one of them unknown. Thomas Aquinas constructed a new philosophic system that accommodated the divergent positions of the Battle of Universals. The nameless master-builder of Chartres cathedral designed a structure in which form merged with function. In literature, the new balance was represented by Dante Alighieri in *The Divine Comedy*. Let us examine each of these remarkable achievements.

Philosophy: Thomas Aquinas, 1225–74

From the philosophy of Thomas Aquinas (henceforth called Thomism), we focus on his reconciliation of some medieval contradictions. In discussing Thomism one cannot resist borrowing his equilateral triangle as a representation of an individual, a nation, or an empire (fig. 13.3). Aquinas chose this shape deliberately, of course, because it symbolizes the Holy Trinity. For us it suggests both firmness and upward motion—a synthesis of Celto-Germanic energy and Graeco-Roman stability.

PSEUDOSCIENCE

Suppose that you could turn common metals into gold. Suppose, also, that you discovered a panacea, a single cure for all diseases and a way to prolong life indefinitely. The name for these vain pursuits is alchemy. Emerging in both China and Egypt in the third century BC, alchemy sought the secret substance called a "philosopher's stone" that converted base metals into gold and produced a magic elixir that preserved and prolonged life. This pseudoscience merged in Mesopotamia with astrology which fused metals with planetary bodies; the sun was gold, the moon silver, Venus copper, Mars iron and so on. Descending inevitably into further superstition and chicanery, alchemism was revived in the eighth century in Alexandria by the Arabs and transmitted to Europe during the Middle Ages, where it initially received a hearty welcome. Alchemists contributed mystical theories and such practical recipes as how to distill wine, make gunpowder, and construct a telescope. Pragmatic alchemist Paracelsus (1493–1531) turned from pursuing gold to preparing medicinals. Some unfortunates who failed to manufacture gold for sponsoring sovereigns were executed in a variety of unpleasant ways. The mostly incidental chemical facts that accrued over the centuries eventually became the basis for modern chemistry.

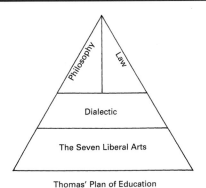

Thomas' Plan of Education

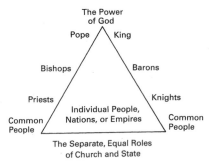

The Separate, Equal Roles
of Church and State

13.3   Thomistic triangles of education and of the separate, equal roles of church and state.

Form and Matter

Thomism reconciled Aristotelian thought with that of the church by accepting the central Aristotelian doctrine that matter and form (or idea) cannot exist separately. Matter has only potentiality—the possibility of being itself—until it is entered into by the idea of the thing; it then becomes that thing. Clay, for example, is not brick, nor is there brick without clay; but when clay, which has only potentiality, is joined with the form or idea of brick, then the brick exists.

Thomism goes on to state that lower forms of existence are merely to be used to create higher forms. Everything is moving, growing, turning into something else. All this movement is toward perfection, which is God. God the First Mover does not move things from behind but is the goal toward which all things are moving. Since things must desire that toward which they move, the motive force is love of God. The First Mover, also called the Unmoved Mover, represents the most important of the five Thomistic proofs of the existence of God. If there is movement then a first attracting power must exist and that power is God. (These proofs could not withstand later analysis but they were accepted in their time.)

In the Thomistic version of reality both form and matter are necessary, thus reconciling the conflict in the Battle of Universals. The question is whether form (idea) has existence *before* or only *in* a specific thing, and whether it exists *after* the specific has vanished. All three says Thomism. The idea exists (as potentiality) before the thing; it exists in the thing; because of its continuing upward progress it exists after the particular thing. Thus, borrowing heavily from the conceptualist view, the three positions are joined in a harmonious whole.

Knowledge and Doctrine

The doctrine of lower and higher forms in motion toward perfection also helped resolve the conflict between worldly knowledge and the church's position that knowledge was useless, a study of nothingness. As illustrated in the Thomistic triangle of education (fig. 13.3), philosophy and law are the highest human studies. Philosophy is a study of the humanly knowable laws for the discipline of the spirit; law is a study of the rules for the governing of our physical nature. According to the Aristotelian-Thomistic concept of reality, both are necessary and equal. To begin a study of these subjects one must first study all forms and all matter. People attain their highest human perfection through knowledge. Or, as Socrates had said eighteen centuries earlier, virtue is knowledge.

Theology, which has its source in God, is, according to Thomism, another realm of knowledge that is complementary to philosophy. However, it can be understood only by revelation, never by learning. The two, however, are not opposed to each other. A knowledge of philosophy leads to the possibility of revelation, and revelation presupposes a knowledge of philosophy. True knowledge, the union with the divine science, comes only after death. It is the duty of everyone to acquire as much natural knowledge as possible so that each is ready to receive the final revelation of God in the afterlife.

Body and Soul

The pull of life and death, perhaps the greatest question of all, was solved, similarly, by the premise that form and matter exist only when together and in each other. Because natural knowledge, gained through the five senses, was necessary for human perfection, it followed that body and soul exist together and equally. Thus Thomism banished the dualism that had existed since Augustine and the cities of God and Man. Henceforward, both body (matter) and soul (form) were considered necessary for earthly perfection.

Church and State

Thomism attempted to reconcile the growing antagonism of church and state. The highest powers of king and pope were judged equal, with both receiving their authority from God. The king would administer God's laws for the physical well-being of his people; the pope and the church would administer the law for the spirit of humankind. An explanation that only justified the uneasy status quo would not stand for long against the escalating forces of nationalism and secularism.

Just as cities were swelling beyond their encircling walls, so this great intellectual synthesis opened the way for people to begin to develop themselves. Science—true science—was expanding, too, with scientific research conducted both within and without the universities. Thomism was an effective synthesis for the increasing numbers of intellectuals but what about the common people?

The Cathedral: "Bible in Stone"

Literally and symbolically the cathedral was central in people's everyday lives. Standing tall at the center of the city, it represented the best of the sacred and secular worlds. Cathedral and civic center, church of Our Lady and theatre, school, court, concert hall, and general meeting place, the Gothic cathedral was a three-dimensional synthesis of church and state and of aspirations both spiritual and worldly.

A Gothic cathedral always thrust strongly upward (see fig. 14.29). Impelled by the dynamic pointed arches, the beholder's gaze moved up its great towers until the spire was reached with its sharp finger pointing toward heaven. Partly because of its architectural sculpture, the cathedral has been called a "Bible in stone." Much of its art is indeed didactic, but a Gothic cathedral is more than the sum of its parts. It is power and glory and spirituality personified. The richly colored light filtered through the stained glass windows, the gliding sound of Gregorian chant, the musky aroma of incense, the pageantry of the celebration of the Mass—all these added beauty, majesty, and joy to people's lives. Building one of these great structures provided a creative outlet for many people for this was a communal effort shared by nobility, burghers, and the common people. In a very real sense the cathedral belonged equally to all who built it and all who used it.

Dante's *Divine Comedy*: An Intellectual Vision

The most significant aspect of the *Divine Comedy* or *Commedia* was the removal of age-old restrictions. The final goal was still the heavenly kingdom but, according to Thomism and Dante, everyone was now relatively free to achieve the blissful afterlife in his or her own way. Morality plays such as *Everyman* no longer applied because God was not an accountant; rather, in Dante's vision, he was perfect wisdom and love. The purpose and goal of humankind, like Aristotle's enteleche, were union with God. For Dante the heavenly state was the ultimate home of humankind which must be ever earned anew because of Adam's fall from grace. While they are alive people cannot fully know the love of God but salvation can be achieved through God's grace. Faith and good works alone will not suffice.

Although people cannot achieve union with God solely by their own efforts, they may prepare for it by gaining the maturity that accompanies the earthly wisdom stressed

A PEASANT GIRL

We know the names of medieval royalty and can identify some of the lords and clergy but the peasants are invariably anonymous—with one exception. This peasant girl was only nineteen when she died for her country but the short life of Joan of Arc (ca. 1412–1431) has been extensively documented and remains endlessly fascinating. She was illiterate, which was normal for her station, but she was well versed in the teachings of the church as she amply demonstrated in a church trial she could not win. Always poised and self-possessed, she convinced the Dauphin of France (later Charles VII) that hers was a divine mission to rid her nation of the British. A remarkably quick learner of military strategy and fighting techniques, she also displayed a solid knowledge of political and military issues as she led French troops to victory over the English at Orléans. Captured by the Burgundians and sold to the English, who turned her over to the church, she was condemned on trumped up charges of heresy and witchcraft and burned at the stake. Within a generation, however, her martyrdom helped inspire the French under Charles VII to expel the English and end the Hundred Years' War. Joan of Arc represents the peasants of France, who would never again be underestimated.

by Thomism. Paradoxically, Dante calls this mature condition innocence: the happy state of Adam and Eve before the Fall. Thus Dante places the Garden of Eden at the top of the mountain of Purgatory, from which God elevates men and women to Paradise.

Hell

What were the choices? The way of God is discipline and order, that of Satan is chaos. God himself is perfect freedom, and the route toward him is marked by an increase in freedom. Sin is the opposite, the loss of free will, which can be illustrated with the simple example of an addiction such as smoking.

At first, with cigarettes, the individual is ignorant, with no firsthand knowledge of the pleasures or problems of smoking. Even after a person smokes a cigarette the act itself is not sinful, nor are subsequent smoking experiences. There comes a time, however, when the smoker has lost the power to say no. One aspect of the freedom of choice has been sacrificed and this, for Dante, is sin. Free will is the ability to say yes, no, or anything in between. Sin is loss of that ability; in Dante's Hell the degree of sin is gauged by the deviation from free will. Those who can no longer choose freely are destined for Hell. Over the mouth of Hell Dante envisions the words "Abandon hope all ye who enter," which express the irreversible state of the condemned. The punishments inflicted on the souls in Hell symbolize what they have made themselves to be. Step by descending step we traverse the cone of Hell, in each lower level viewing the souls ever deeper in sin. Step by descending step we see these souls increasingly enslaved until, at the bottom of the pit, we find Satan immobilized by his sins, forever frozen in ice.

Purgatory

Emerging with Dante at the base of the mountain of Purgatory, we find a very different scene. These souls have strayed from the path of wisdom but they still have hope. Expiating their sins is laborious but they are joyful as they anticipate wisdom, maturity, and the heavenly Paradise. Each soul determines when it is sufficiently purged of sin to ascend to a higher cornice on the mountain. This is explicitly stated when Dante and his guide Virgil encounter the Latin poet Statius, who has just moved up a niche. The mountain is shaken by the momentous occasion while all the souls shout "Gloria in excelsis." The soul has ascended but not until it feels that the stain of former sin is removed, as stated in lines 7–13 of the following:

> "Below that point, there may be small or ample
> tremors; but here above, I know not why,
> no wind concealed in earth has ever caused
> a tremor; for it only trembles here
> when some soul feels it's cleansed, so that it rises
> or stirs to climb on high; and that shout follows.
> The will alone is proof of purity

> and, fully free, surprises soul into
> a change of dwelling place—effectively.
> Soul had the will to climb before, but that   10
> will was opposed by longing to do penance
> (as once, to sin), instilled by divine justice.
> And I, who have lain in this suffering
> five hundred years and more, just now have felt
> my free will for a better threshold: thus,
> you heard the earthquake and the pious spirits
> throughout the mountain as they praised the Lord—
> and may He send them speedily upward."
> So did he speak to us; and just as joy
> is greater when we quench a greater thirst,   20
> the joy he brought cannot be told in words.

Paradise

Finally in Paradise, and guided by Beatrice, Dante receives instruction in theology, the science of God. Here he views the perfect order of the universe, both of humans and of angels. He sees the church and its officers as the guardians of the human spirit and observes the kings' importance to God, for they maintain temporal order on earth. Here, too, he finds freedom, as opposed to the ever-increasing levels of bondage he witnessed in Hell. Though the souls in Paradise are symbolically assigned to different spheres as a result of their different capacities for joy and love, they can pass through all the spheres and approach the throne of God. In the final cantos of the *Paradise* Dante comes as close as any human being can to expressing, as living experience, the mystic union of the soul with God.

Dante Today

What is Dante saying to twentieth-century readers, who may be Catholics, Protestants, Muslims, Buddhists, or **atheists**, or whatever? Like all great literature, the *Commedia* has a universal appeal that speaks to every age. Dante says that we all have free will and that we can choose order and discipline over disorder and chaos. He envisions a life at once balanced and aspiring—one that seeks broad worldly knowledge including a thorough understanding of science. The *Commedia* unites body and soul in a life that men and women must choose for themselves in their contemporary world. In the *Commedia* and its architectural counterpart, the Gothic cathedral, we see the artist proposing answers to the pressing questions of humankind.

Freedom

In the period of balance of the thirteenth and fourteenth centuries what were the extent and nature of freedom? As with all balanced periods this was a typically brief era in which the generally accepted view of reality was mirrored by the values of the High Middle Ages. During these two centuries we see a kind of freedom that might prompt many world-weary people of our time to look back with longing.

The fundamental characteristic of the period was the sense of unity that set rules for human behavior but that provided room for individual values. Rather than a paradox or a contradiction, individual endeavor within a communal solidarity is a special kind of freedom. Consider, for example, the Gothic cathedral, whose basic design was very formalized. It had to be oriented with its altar toward the East so that worshipers could move toward Jerusalem. Its shape had to be cruciform, and its representations included the saints, Jesus, Mary, and Joseph, the Nativity, the Resurrection, and Day of Judgment. Yet consider the freedom of the individual in helping to build a Gothic church, of which no two are even remotely alike. If the stonecutter wanted to carve fat little angels or lively animals he had seen or imagined, that was his decision. One sees this kind of work high on capitals or on the underside of seats in the choir stalls. Here a woodcarver thought it would be fun to carve a pig playing a fiddle. No sooner said than done! Or a carver felt compelled to caricature a local burgher and proceeded to do so. Gothic churches are replete with a variety of images and fantasies.

This kind of freedom within limits existed in all spheres of activity. The craftsman, for example, necessarily belonged to his guild, an association that regulated the quality of his work and the price he could charge. Beyond that, the guild served as an insurance and burial society, a social group, and a dramatic society that participated in the mystery and miracle plays that educated, inspired, and amused the local townsfolk. The guildhall was not only a business center but a social hall where wedding festivities, banquets, and balls were enjoyed by all.

The guild regulated membership and supervised the levels of apprentice, journeyman, and master craftsman, but within these standards the cobbler, say, was absolutely free. When business was slow he could take his family, apprentices, and journeymen for an outing in the country. Every pair of shoes he made was an individual creation in which he took justifiable pride. Whether or not his apprentices did the preliminary work, the master craftsman was totally responsible for the finished product, on which he staked his reputation. In the late twentieth century it is difficult to imagine the satisfaction of someone who exercised total control from inception to production of the finished product.

The story of "Our Lady's Juggler" (see pp. 387–8) exemplifies a similar sort of freedom within an authoritarian religion. The creed was strict and the rules absolute but, given human ingenuity, there was still room for creativity. Dante's concept of freedom as participation in the wisdom, order, and love of God was paramount in the value system of the era. However mistaken some choices might be, the Christian scheme of things viewed any straying from grace as only human. Errors must be purged, of course, but only a deliberate desire to do evil led to eternal damnation.

The idea of freedom in this period of balance was reinforced by the stability, however brief, of the culture. Freedom, individuality, and creativity were available to all who respected the rules of the society. But the balance, like all others we have seen, was too delicate to last. The secular forces that boiled up during the Middle Ages were to triumph, breaking down the still recent designs made by Dante, Thomas Aquinas, and the master builders of the mighty cathedrals. The cathedrals remained, of course, but the fundamental beliefs of medieval culture were to change drastically in a new period of ferment called the Renaissance.

The Church in Turmoil

The supreme irony of the High Middle Ages was the agony of the inner structure of the Church of Rome. Even while cathedrals were rising and Thomism was becoming accepted, the all-powerful and supposedly infallible institution proved, during a century of internal strife and corruption, to be all too fallible. The power struggle between Rome and royalty peaked in the bitter quarrel between Philip IV of France (reigned 1285–1314) and Pope Boniface VIII (reigned 1294–1303), whom Dante had called the "black beast." The corrupt Boniface prevailed but, after his death, a vengeful Philip engineered the election of a subservient pope (Clement V; reigned 1305–14) and transferred the papacy to Avignon in the south of France. Thus began the "Babylonian Captivity" of 1305–78 when French kings controlled the Church of Rome. Newly located in a strange land, the papal court rapidly became notorious for its corruption and decadence. Writing anonymously because he "did not want to be burned," court poet Petrarch described the papacy at a low ebb:

> The shame of mankind, a sink of vice, a sewer where is gathered all the filth of the world. There God is held in contempt, money alone is worshiped and the laws of God and man are trampled underfoot. Everything there breathes a lie: the air, the earth, the houses and above all the bedrooms.

The Babylonian Captivity ended in 1378 with a bad situation made worse by the election, in Rome, of Urban VII. After the new pope managed to alienate just about everyone, the cardinals chose Robert of Geneva (Anti-pope Clement VII), who fled from Urban VII to establish a thoroughly dissolute court in Avignon. This was the Great Schism of 1378–1417 with rival popes in Rome, Avignon, and even Pisa. It was the Pisan anti-pope John XXIII about whom the eighteenth-century English historian Edward Gibbon wrote: "The most scandalous charges were suppressed: The Vicar of Christ was only accused of piracy, murder, rape, sodomy, and incest."[3]

---

3. It was not until 1958 that a pope again chose, quite deliberately, the name of John. Pope John XXIII became one of the greatest popes in the history of the Church of Rome.

Caused, in part, by the French captivity and multiple popes, the view of what constituted the real world began to shift from God as the ultimate reality to the belief that human earthly existence had its own validity. This did not mean that there was any widespread unrest or denial of Christianity; rather, growing resentment over corruption in the church hierarchy led people to question whether this powerful bureaucracy provided the best way to the Kingdom of Heaven. The Great Schism certainly forced many to wonder which of the two or three popes was the true keeper of the keys of the kingdom.

STUDY QUESTIONS

1. Imagine growing up on a medieval manor and then moving to the city. What opportunities might come your way? What new temptations? What new problems? Which aspects of rural life might you miss?
2. What do medieval guilds and modern unions have in common? How do they differ? Why do they differ?
3. Given the European point of view, what were the positive aspects of the Crusades? Negative aspects? Now try answering these two questions from the Muslim point of view.
4. Are the virtues espoused by Courts of Love "feminine" or might they be called "civilized"? Are there any purely masculine or feminine virtues or qualities?
5. Are you a realist, nominalist, conceptualist, or none of the above? Why?
6. Where, in your course of study, are the subjects of the trivium and quadrivium? To what extent do your studies differ from the medieval curriculum? Is every difference necessarily better?
7. The Virgin Mary and Eve, the temptress, represented two extremes of medieval womanhood. What are the extremes today? What is the female ideal of womanhood? The male ideal? Can the values of both sexes be synthesized into a single image?

LITERARY SELECTION 31

Songs of the Wandering Scholars

The pull of life was strong when new ideas were assaulting medieval walls. And students (even the many who were to become learned clergymen) were much the same then as they are now.

Gaudeamus Igitur

Let us live, then, and be glad
  While young life's before us!
After youthful pastime had,
After old age, hard and sad,
  Earth will slumber o'er us.

Where are they who in this world
  Ere we kept, were keeping?
Go ye to the gods above;
Go to hell; inquire thereof;
  They are not; they are sleeping.   10

Brief is life, and brevity
  Briefly shall be ended;
Death comes like a whirlwind strong,
Bears us with his blast along;
  None shall be defended.

Live this university,
  Men that learning nourish;
Live each member of the same,
Long live all that bear its name,
  Let them ever flourish!   20

Live the commonwealth also,
  And the men that guide it!
Live our town in strength and health,
Founders, patrons, by whose wealth
  We are here provided!

Live all gods! A health to you,
  Melting maids and beauteous;
Live the wives and women too,
Gentle, loving, tender, true,
  Good, industrious, duteous!   30

Perish cares that pule and pine!
  Perish envious blamers!
Die the Devil, thine and mine!
Die the starch-neck Philistine!
  Scoffers and defamers!

Lauriger Horatius

Horace with your laurel crowned,
Truly have you spoken:
Time, a-rush with leap and bound,
Devours and leaves us broken.

Where are now the flagons, full
Of sweet wine, honey-clear?
Where the smiles and shoves and frowns
Of blushing maiden dear?

Swift the young grape grows and swells;
So do comely lasses!
Lo, on the poet's head, the snows
Of the Time that passes!

What's the good of lasting fame,
If people think it sinful
Here and now to kiss a dame
And drink a jolly skinful!

LITERARY SELECTION 32

Our Lady's Juggler

This delightful story reveals some of the attraction and charm of the cult of the Virgin, especially for the common people for whom chivalry and philosophy were meaningless (fig. 13.4).

In the days of King Louis there lived a poor juggler by the name of Barnabas, a native of Compiègne, who wandered from city to city performing tricks of skill and prowess.

On fair days he would lay down in the public square a worn and aged carpet, and after having attracted a group of children and idlers by certain amusing remarks which he had learned from an old juggler, and which he invariably repeated in the same fashion without altering a word, he would assume the strangest postures and balance a pewter plate on the tip of his nose. At first the crowd regarded him with indifference, but when, with his hands and head on the ground he threw into the air and caught with his feet six copper balls that glittered in the sunlight, or when, throwing himself back until his neck touched his heels, he assumed the form of a perfect wheel and in that position juggled with twelve knives, he elicited a murmur of admiration from his audience, and small coins rained on his carpet.

Still, Barnabas of Compiègne, like most of those who exist by their accomplishments, had a hard time making a living. Earning his bread by the sweat of his brow, he bore rather more than his share of those miseries we are all heir to through the fault of our Father Adam.

He had never thought much about the origin of wealth nor about the inequality of human conditions. He firmly believed that if this world was evil the next could not but be good, and this faith upheld him. He was not like the clever fellows who sell their souls to the devil; he never took the name of God in vain; he lived the life of an honest man, and though he had no wife of his own, he did not covet his neighbor's, for woman is the enemy of strong men, as we learn by the story of Samson which is written in the Scriptures.

Verily, his mind was not turned in the direction of

13.4 "King David Playing Harp under the Inspiration of the Holy Ghost, While One Attendant Juggles and Others Play the Rebec, Trumpet, and Oliphant." 11th century. Manuscript illumination. British Museum, London. This curious juxtaposition of David the psalm singer with common people juggling and playing musical instruments was a standard medieval theme. The ivory oliphant at the lower right is similar to the one Roland blew (too late) to summon Charlemagne to his rescue. Of Arab origin, the **rebec** (upper right) was an early precursor of the violin (see p. 446).

carnal desire, and it caused him far greater pain to renounce drinking than to forgo the pleasure of women. For, though he was not a drunkard, he enjoyed drinking when the weather was warm. He was a good man, fearing God, and devout in his adoration of the Holy Virgin. When he went into a church he never failed to kneel before the image of the Mother of God and to address her with his prayer:

"My Lady, watch over my life until it shall please God that I die, and when I am dead, see that I have the joys of Paradise."

One evening, after a day of rain, as he walked sad and bent with his juggling balls under his arm and his knives wrapped up in his old carpet seeking some barn where he might go supperless to bed, he saw a monk going in his direction, and respectfully saluted him. As they were both walking at the same pace, they fell into conversation.

"Friend," said the monk, "how does it happen that you are dressed all in green? Are you perchance going to play the part of the fool in some mystery?"[4]

"No, indeed, father," said Barnabas. "My name is Barnabas, and my business is that of juggler. It would be

4. Mystery—one of the religious dramas of the time.

the finest calling in the world if I could eat every day."

"Friend Barnabas," answered the monk, "be careful what you say. There is no finer calling than the monastic. The priest celebrates the praise of God, the Virgin, and the saints; the life of a monk is a perpetual hymn to the Lord." 60

And Barnabas replied: "Father, I confess I spoke like an ignorant man. My estate cannot be compared to yours, and though there may be some merit in dancing and balancing a stick with a denier[5] on top of it on the end of your nose, it is in no wise comparable to your merit. Father, I wish I might, like you, sing the Office every day, especially the Office of the Very Holy Virgin, to whom I am specially and piously devoted. I would willingly give up the art by which I am known from Soissons to Beauvais, in more than six hundred cities and villages, in order to enter the monastic life." 70

The monk was touched by the simplicity of the juggler, and as he was not lacking in discernment, he recognized in Barnabas one of those well-disposed men of whom Our Lord has said, "Let peace be with them on earth." And he made answer therefore: 80

"Friend Barnabas, come with me and I will see that you enter the monastery of which I am the Prior. He who led Mary through the Egyptian desert put me across your path in order that I might lead you to salvation."

Thus did Barnabas become a monk. In the monastery which he entered, the monks celebrated most magnificently the Cult of the Holy Virgin, each of them bringing to her service all the knowledge and skill which God had given him. 90

Perceiving so great a competition in praise and so fine a harvest of good works, Barnabas fell to lamenting his ignorance and simplicity.

"Alas!" he sighed as he walked by himself one day in the little garden shaded by the monastery wall, "I am so unhappy because I cannot, like my brothers, give worthy praise to the Holy Mother of God to whom I have consecrated all the love in my heart. Alas, I am a stupid fellow, without art, and for your service, Madame, I have no edifying sermons, no fine treatises nicely prepared 100 according to the rules, no beautiful paintings, no cunningly carved statues, and no verses counted off by feet and marching in measure! Alas, I have nothing."

Thus did he lament and abandon himself to his misery.

One evening when the monks were talking together by way of diversion, he heard one of them tell of a monk who could not recite anything but the *Ave Maria*. He was scorned for his ignorance, but after he died there 110 sprang from his mouth five roses, in honor of the five letters in the name Maria. Thus was his holiness made manifest.

In listening to this story, Barnabas was conscious once more of the Virgin's beneficence, but he was not consoled by the example of the happy miracle, for his heart was full of zeal and he wanted to celebrate the glory of his Lady in Heaven.

He sought for a way in which to do this, but in vain,

and each day brought him greater sorrow, until one morning he sprang joyously from his cot and ran to the 120 chapel, where he remained alone for more than an hour. He returned thither again after dinner, and from that day onward he would go into the chapel every day the moment it was deserted, passing the greater part of the time which the other monks dedicated to the pursuit of the liberal arts and the sciences. He was no longer sad and he sighed no more. But such singular conduct aroused the curiosity of the other monks, and they asked themselves why Brother Barnabas retired alone so often, and the Prior, whose business it was to know 130 everything that his monks were doing, determined to observe Barnabas. One day, therefore, when Barnabas was alone in the chapel, the Prior entered in company with two of the oldest brothers, in order to watch, through the bars of the door, what was going on within.

They saw Barnabas before the image of the Holy Virgin, his head on the floor and his feet in the air, juggling with six copper balls and twelve knives. In honor of the Holy Virgin he was performing the tricks which had in former days brought him the greatest fame. Not 140 understanding that he was thus putting his best talents at the service of the Holy Virgin, the aged brothers cried out against such sacrilege. The Prior knew that Barnabas had a simple soul, but he believed that the man had lost his wits. All three set about to remove Barnabas from the chapel, when they saw the Virgin slowly descend from the altar and, with a fold of her blue mantle, wipe the sweat that streamed over the juggler's forehead.

Then the Prior, bowing his head down to the marble floor, repeated these words: 150

"Blessed are the pure in heart, for they shall see God."

"Amen," echoed the brothers, bowing down to the floor.

LITERARY SELECTION 33

The Canterbury Tales
Prologue
Geoffrey Chaucer (1340–1400)

Chaucer was exceptionally well read for his time, learned in French, Italian, and Latin literature. Having visited Italy, where he acquired a fair knowledge of Italian, he knew the works of Dante but was more influenced by the collection of stories by Boccaccio called the *Decameron*. This may have inspired him to invent the new scheme of using a pilgrimage as a device to frame his stories and develop the interplay of his characters (fig. 13.5).

Pilgrimages were important features of medieval life (see pp. 419–20). Although primarily religious in purpose, they also had social and cultural dimensions, much as a vacation trip to some exotic locale has today, and the pilgrim returning from Jerusalem, or Santiago de Compostela, or Canterbury enjoyed

---

| **5.** Denier—a small coin.

some prestige in his or her community. The pilgrims in Chaucer's *Tales* are making the relatively short journey from London to Canterbury to view the shrine of St. Thomas à Becket, Archibishop of Canterbury, who had been murdered in his cathedral in 1170 by knights possibly acting for King Henry II (husband of Eleanor of Aquitaine).

In the Prologue we are introduced to a fascinating cast of characters representing a panorama of life in the Late Middle Ages. Note the shrewdness of Chaucer's descriptions—deft touches that reveal the personality of each individual. The modern English translation is by Nevill Coghill (1899–1980).

When the sweet showers of April fall and shoot
Down through the drought of March to pierce the root,
Bathing every vein in liquid power
From which there springs the engendering of the flower,
When also Zephyrus[6] with his sweet breath
Exhales an air in every grove and heath
Upon the tender shoots, and the young sun
His half-course in the sign of the *Ram*[7] has run,
And the small fowl are making melody
That sleep away the night with open eye   10
(So nature pricks them and their heart engages)
Then people long to go on pilgrimages
And palmers[8] long to seek the stranger strands
Of far-off saints hallowed in sundry lands,
And specially, from every shire's end
In England, down to Canterbury they wend
To seek the holy blissful martyr,[9] quick
In giving help to them when they were sick.

It happened in that season, that one day
In Southwark at *The Tabard*, as I lay   20
Ready to go on pilgrimage and start
For Canterbury, most devout at heart,
At night there came into that hostelry
Some nine and twenty in a company
Of sundry folk happening then to fall
In fellowship, and they were pilgrims all
That towards Canterbury meant to ride.
The rooms and stables of the inn were wide;
They made us easy, all was of the best.
And shortly, when the sun had gone to rest,   30
By speaking to them all upon the trip
I was admitted to their fellowship
And promised to rise early and take the way
To Canterbury, as you heard me say.
But none the less, while I have time and space,

6. Zephyr—the west wind: here, the life-giving breath of spring.
7. Ram—the third sign of the zodiac, meaning the date is about mid April.
8. Palmers—pilgrims who had visited the Holy Land bore palms as token of their pilgrimage.
9. Martyr—Thomas à Becket, canonized in 1173. His shrine attracted pilgrims from the Continent, as well as England, and many stories of miraculous cures were told of it.
10. He sat in the seat of honor, at the head of the table—a mark of distinction and worth.
11. Probably he had fought in Latvia or Lithuania, with the Order of Teutonic Knights. Chaucer lists by name other scenes of the Knights' exploits: the main point is, they were associated with fighting for the faith rather than for gain. The Knight is very nearly the ideal knight of chivalry.

Before my story takes a further pace,
It seems a reasonable thing to say
What their condition was, the full array
Of each of them, as it appeared to me,
According to profession and degree,   40
And what apparel they were riding in;
And at a knight I therefore will begin.

There was a *knight*, a most distinguished man,
Who from the day on which he first began
To ride abroad had followed chivalry,
Truth, honor, greatness of heart and courtesy.
He had done nobly in his sovereign's war
And ridden into battle, no man more,
As well in Christian as in heathen places,
And ever honored for his noble graces.   50
He saw the town of Alexandria fall;
Often, at feasts, the highest place of all[10]
Among the nations fell to him in Prussia.
In Lithuania he had fought, and Russia,
No Christian man so often, of his rank.[11]
And he was in Granada when they sank
The town of Algeciras, also in
North Africa, right through Benamarin;
And in Armenia he had been as well
And fought when Ayas and Attalia fell,   60
For all along the Mediterranean coast
He had embarked with many a noble host.
In fifteen mortal battles he had been
And jousted for our faith at Tramissene
Thrice in the lists, and always killed his man.
This same distinguished knight had led the van
Once with the Bey of Balat, doing work
For him against another heathen Turk;
He was of sovereign value in all eyes.
And though so much distinguished, he was wise   70
And in his bearing modest as a maid.
He never yet a boorish thing had said
In all his life to any, come what might;
He was a true, a perfect gentle-knight.
Speaking of his appearance, he possessed
Fine horses, but he was not gaily dressed.
He wore a fustian tunic stained and dark
And smudges where his armor had left mark;
Just home from service, he had joined our ranks
To do his pilgrimage and render thanks.   80

He had his son with him, a fine young *Squire*,
A lover and cadet, a lad of fire
With curly locks, as they had been pressed.
He was some twenty years of age, I guessed.
In stature he was of moderate length,
With wonderful agility and strength.
He'd seen some service with the cavalry
In Flanders and Artois and Picardy
And had done valiantly in little space
Of time, and hoped to win his lady's grace.   90
He was embroidered like a meadow bright
And full of freshest flowers, red and white.
Singing he was, or fluting all the day;
He was as fresh as is the month of May.
Short was his gown, the sleeves were long and wide;

13.5 Pilgrim, fol. 153v, Ellesmere Manuscript of Chaucer's *Canterbury Tales*. Ca. 1410. Huntington Library, San Marino, California.

He knew the way to sit a horse and ride.
He could make songs and poems and recite,
Knew how to joust and dance, to draw and write.
He loved so hotly that till dawn grew pale
He slept as little as a nightingale. 100
Courteous he was, lowly and serviceable,
And carved to serve his father at the table.

    There was a *yeoman* with him at his side,
No other servant; so he chose to ride.
This Yeoman wore a coat and hood of green,
And peacock-feathered arrows, bright and keen
And neatly sheathed, hung at his belt the while
—For he could dress his gear in yeoman style,
His arrows never drooped their feathers low—
And in his hand he bore a mighty bow. 110
His head was like a nut, his face was brown.
He knew the whole of woodcraft up and down.
A saucy brace was on his arm to ward
It from the bow-string, and a shield and sword
Hung at one side, and at the other slipped
A jaunty dirk, spear-sharp and well-equipped.
A medal of St. Christopher he wore
Of shining silver on his breast, and bore
A hunting-horn, well slung and burnished clean,
That dangled from a baldrick of bright green. 120
He was a proper forester I guess.

    There was also a *Nun*, a Prioress;
Simple her way of smiling was and coy.[12]
Her greatest oath was only "By St. Loy!"
And she was known as Madam Eglantyne.
And well she sang a service, with a fine
Intoning through her nose, as was most seemly,
And she spoke daintily in French, extremely,
After the school of Stratford-atte-Bowe;
French in the Paris style she did not know. 130
At meat her manners were well taught withal;
No morsel from her lips did she let fall,
Nor dipped her fingers in the sauce too deep;
But she could carry a morsel up and keep
The smallest drop from falling on her breast.
For courtliness she had a special zest.
And she would wipe her upper lip so clean
That not a trace of grease was to be seen
Upon the cup when she had drunk; to eat,
She reached a hand sedately for the meat. 140
She certainly was very entertaining,
Pleasant and friendly in her ways, and straining
To counterfeit a courtly kind of grace,
A stately bearing fitting to her place,
And to seem dignified in all her dealings.
As for her sympathies and tender feelings,
She was so charitably solicitous
She used to weep if she but saw a mouse
Caught in a trap, if it were dead or bleeding.
And she had little dogs she would be feeding 150
With roasted flesh, or milk, or fine white bread.
Sorely she wept if one of them were dead
Or someone took a stick and made it smart;
She was all sentiment and tender heart.
Her veil was gathered in a seemly way,
Her nose was elegant, her eyes glass-gray;
Her mouth was very small, but soft and red,
And certainly she had a well-shaped head,
Almost a span across the brows, I own;
She was indeed by no means undergrown. 160
Her cloak, I noticed, had a graceful charm.
She wore a coral trinket on her arm,
A set of beads, the gaudies tricked in green[13]
Whence hung a golden brooch of brightest sheen
On which there first was graven a crowned A,
And lower, *Amor vincit omnia*.

    Another *Nun*, the chaplain at her cell,
Was riding with her, and *three Priests* as well.

    There was a *Monk*, a leader of the fashions;
Inspecting farms and hunting were his passions, 170
A manly man, to be an Abbot able,
Many the dainty horses in his stable;
His bridle, when he rode, a man might hear
Jingling in a whistling wind as clear,
Aye, and as loud as does the chapel bell
Where my lord Monk was Prior of the cell.
The rule of good St. Benet or St. Maur[14]
As old and strict he tended to ignore;
He let go by the things of yesterday
And followed the new world's more spacious way. 180
He did not rate that text at a plucked hen

12. In Chaucer's text the word meant "bashful" or "modest."
13. Gauds—the large Paternoster ("Our Father") beads marking off the sections of a rosary.
14. St. Benedict and his disciple Maurus, founders of the Benedictine Order. St. Benedict established the famous monastery at Monte Cassino in 529.

Which says that hunters are not holy men
And that a monk uncloistered is a mere
Fish out of water, flapping on the pier,
That is to say a monk out of his cloister.
That was a text he held not worth an oyster;
And I said I agreed with his opinion;
What! Study until reason lost dominion
Poring on books in cloisters? Must he toil
As Austin[15] bade and till the very soil?   190
Was he to leave the world upon the shelf?
Let Austin have his labor to himself.

    This monk was therefore a good man to horse;
Greyhounds he had, as swift as birds, to course.
Hunting a hare or riding at a fence
Was all his fun, he spared for no expense.
I saw his sleeves were garnished at the hand
With fine gray fur, the finest in the land,
And where his hood was fastened at his chin
He had a wrought-gold cunningly fashioned pin;   200
Into a lover's knot it seemed to pass.
His head was bald and shone as any glass,
So did his face, as if it had been greased.
He was a fat and personable priest;
His bright eyes rolled, they never seemed to settle,
And glittered like the flames beneath a kettle;
Supple his boots, his horse in fine condition.
He was a prelate fit for exhibition,
He was not pale like a tormented soul.
He liked a fat swan best, and roasted whole.   210
His palfrey was as brown as is a berry.

    There was a *Friar*, a wanton one and merry,
A Limiter,[16] a very festive fellow.
In all Four Orders[17] there was none so mellow
As he in flattery and dalliant speech.
He'd fixed up many a marriage, giving each
Of his young women what he could afford her.
He was a noble pillar to his Order.
Highly beloved and intimate was he
With Country folk wherever he might be,   220
And worthy city women with possessions;
For he was qualified to hear confessions,
Or so he said, with more than priestly scope;
He had a special license from the Pope.
Sweetly he heard his penitents at shrift
With pleasant absolution, for a gift.
He was an easy man in penance-giving
Where he could hope to make a decent living;
It's a sure sign whenever gifts are given
To a poor Order that a man's well shriven,[18]   230
And should he give enough he knew in verity
The penitent repented in sincerity.
For many a fellow is so hard of heart
He cannot weep, for all his inward smart.

Therefore instead of weeping and of prayer
One should give silver for a poor Friar's care.
He kept his tippett[19] stuffed with pins for curls,
And pocket-knives, to give to pretty girls.
And certainly his voice was gay and sturdy,
For he sang well and played the hurdy-gurdy.   240
At sing-songs he was champion of the hour.
His neck was whiter than a lily-flower
But strong enough to butt a bruiser down.
He knew the taverns well in every town
And every innkeeper and barmaid too
Better than lepers, beggars and that crew,
For in so eminent a man as he
It was not fitting with the dignity
Of his position dealing with such scum.
It isn't decent, nothing good can come   250
Of having truck with slum-and-gutter dwellers,
But only with the rich and victual-sellers.
But anywhere a profit might accrue
Courteous he was and lowly of service too.
Natural gifts like his were hard to match.
He was the finest beggar of his batch,
And, for his begging-district, payed a rent;
His brethren did no poaching where he went.
For though a widow mightn't have a shoe,
So pleasant was his holy how-d'ye-do   260
He got his farthing from her just the same
Before he left, and so his income came
To more than he laid out. And how he romped,
Just like a puppy! He was ever prompt
To arbitrate disputes on settling days
(For a small fee) in many helpful ways,
Not then appearing as your cloistered scholar
With threadbare habit barely worth a dollar,
But much more like a Doctor or a Pope.
Of double-worsted was the semi-cope   270
Upon his shoulders, and the swelling fold
About him, like a bell about its mold
When it is casting, rounded out his dress.
He lisped a little out of wantonness
To make his English sweet upon his tongue.
When he had played his harp, or having sung,
His eyes would twinkle in his head as bright
As any star upon a frosty night.
This worthy's name was Hubert it appeared.

    There was a *Merchant* with a forking beard   280
And motley dress; high on his horse he sat,
Upon his head a Flemish beaver hat
And on his feet daintily buckled boots.
He told of his opinions and pursuits
In solemn tones, and how he never lost.
The sea should be kept free at any cost
(He thought) upon the Harwich–Holland ranges.
He was expert at dabbling in exchanges.
This estimable Merchant so had set
His wits to work, none knew he was in debt,   290
He was so stately in negotiation,
Loan, bargain and commercial obligation.
He was an excellent fellow all the same;
To tell the truth I do not know his name.

---

15. St. Augustine, Bishop of Hippo, was a great proponent of labor as part of the monastic life.
16. A "Limiter" was a friar licensed to beg within a definite ("limited") region.
17. The Four Orders of mendicant friars: Dominicans, Franciscans, Carmelites, Augustinians.
18. Shriven—confessed all.
19. Tippet—a long scarf and handy substitute for pockets.

There was an *Oxford Cleric* too, a student,
Long given to Logic, longer than was prudent;
The horse he had was leaner than a rake,
And he was not too fat, I undertake,
But had a hollow look, a sober air;
The thread upon his overcoat was bare   300
He had found no preferment in the church
And he was too unworldly to make search.
He thought far more of having by his bed
His twenty books all bound in black and red,
Of Aristotle and philosophy
Than of gay music, fiddles or finery.
Though a philosopher, as I have told,
He had not found the stone for making gold.
Whatever money from friends he took
He spent on learning or another book   310
And prayed for them most earnestly, returning
Thanks to them thus for paying for his learning.
His only care was study, and indeed
Formal at that, respected in the extreme,
Short, to the point, and lofty in his theme.
The thought of moral virtue filled his speech
And he would gladly learn and gladly teach.

A *Sergeant at the Law* who paid his calls,
Wary and wise, for clients at St. Paul's[20]
There also was, of noted excellence.   320
Discreet he was, a man to reverence,
Or so he seemed, his sayings were so wise
He often had been Justice of Azzize[21]
By letter patent, and in full commission.
His fame and learning and his high position
Had earned him many a robe and many a fee.
There was no such conveyancer as he;
All was fee-simple to his strong digestion,
Not one conveyance could be called in question.
Though there was none so busy as was he   330
He was less busy than he seemed to be.
He knew of every judgment, case and crime
Recorded ever since King William's time.[22]
He could dictate defenses or draft deeds;
No one could pinch a comma from his screeds,
And he knew every statute off by rote.
He wore a homely parti-colored coat
Girt with a silken belt of pin-stripe stuff;
Of his appearance I have said enough.

A land-owner, a *Franklin*,[23] had appeared;   340
White as a daisy-petal was his beard.
A sanguine man, high-colored and benign,
He loved a morning sop of cake in wine.
He lived for pleasure and had always done,
For he was Epicurus' very son,
In whose opinion sensual delight

Was the one true felicity in sight.
As noted as St. Julian[24] was for bounty
He made his household free to all the County.
His bread, his ale were finest of the fine   350
And no one had a better stock of wine.
His house was never short of bake-meat pies,
Of fish and flesh, and these in such supplies
It positively snowed with meat and drink
And all the dainties that a man could think.
According to the seasons of the year
Changes of dish were ordered to appear.
He kept fat partridges in coops, beyond,
Many a bream and pike were in his pond.
Woe to the cook whose sauces had no sting   360
Or who was unprepared in anything!
And in his hall a table stood arrayed
And ready all day long, with places laid.
As Justice at the Sessions none stood higher;
He often had been member for the Shire.
A dagger and a little purse of silk
Hung at his girdle, white as morning milk.
As Sheriff he checked audit, every entry.
He was a model among landed gentry.

A *Haberdasher*, a *Dyer*, a *Carpenter*,   370
A *Weaver* and a *Carpet-maker* were
Among our ranks, all in the livery
Of one impressive guild-fraternity.
They were so trim and fresh their gear would pass
For new. Their knives were not tricked out with brass
But wrought with purest silver, which avouches
A like display on girdles and on pouches.
Each seemed a worthy burgess, fit to grace
A guild-hall with a seat upon the dais.
Their wisdom would have justified a claim   380
To make each one of them an alderman;
They had the capital and revenue,
Besides their wives declared it was their due.
And if they did not think so, then they ought;
To be called "*Madam*" is a glorious thought,
And so is going to church and being seen
Having your mantle carried like a queen.

They had a *Cook* with them who stood alone
For boiling chicken with a marrow-bone,
Sharp flavoring-powder and a spice for savor.   390
He could distinguish London ale by flavor,
And he could roast and seethe and broil and fry,
Make good thick soup and bake a tasty pie.
But a great pity, as it seemed to me,
Was that he had an ulcer on his knee.
As for blancmange, he made it with the best.

There was a *Skipper* hailing from far west;
He came from Dartmouth, so I understood.
He rode a farmer's horse as best he could,
In a woolen gown that reached his knee.   400
A dagger on a lanyard falling free
Hung from his neck under his arm and down.
The summer heat had tanned his color brown,
And certainly he was an excellent fellow.
Many a draught of vintage, red and yellow,

---

20. The porch of St. Paul's Cathedral was a traditional meeting
   place for lawyers.
21. Assize: session of the court.
22. The Sergeant knew the law clear back to the Conquest, i.e.,
   the statutes of William the Conqueror.
23. Franklins were landholders of free, but not of noble, birth;
   they ranked below the gentry.
24. St. Julian is the patron saint of hospitality.

He'd drawn at Bordeaux, while the vintner slept.
Few were the rules his tender conscience kept.
If, when he fought, the enemy vessel sank,
He sent his prisoners home; they walked the plank.
As for his skill in reckoning his tides,   410
Currents and many another risk besides,
Moons, harbors, pilots, he had such dispatch
That none from Hull to Carthage was his match.
Hardy he was, prudent in undertaking;
His beard in many a tempest had its shaking,
And he knew all the havens as they were
From Gotland to the Cape of Finisterre,[25]
And every creek in Brittany and Spain;
The barge he owned was called *The Maudelayne*.

A *Doctor* too emerged as we proceeded;   420
No one alive could talk as well as he did
On points of medicine and of surgery,
For, being grounded in astronomy,
He watched his patient's favorable star
And, by his Natural Magic, knew what are
The lucky hours and planetary degrees
For making charms and magic effigies.
The cause of every malady you'd got
He knew, and whether dry, cold, moist or hot;
He knew their seat, their humor and condition.   430
He was a perfect practicing physician.
These causes being known for what they were,
He gave the man his medicine then and there.
All his apothecaries in a tribe
Were ready with the drugs he would prescribe,
And each made money from the other's guile;
They had been friendly for a goodish while.
He was well-versed in Esculapius[26] too
And what Hippocrates and Rufus knew
And Dioscorides, now dead and gone,   440
Galen and Rhazes, Hali, Serapion,
Averroes, Avicenna, Constantine,
Scotch Bernard, John of Gaddesden, Gilbertine.
In his own diet he observed some measure;
There were no superfluities for pleasure,
Only digestives, nutritives and such.
He did not read the Bible very much.
In blood-red garments, slashed with bluish-gray
And lined with taffeta, he rode his way;
Yet he was rather close as to expenses   450
And kept the gold he won in pestilences.
Gold stimulates the heart, or so we're told.
He therefore had a special love of gold.

A worthy *woman* from beside *Bath* city
Was with us, somewhat deaf, which was a pity.
In making cloth she showed so great a bent
She bettered those of Ypres and of Ghent.
In all the parish not a dame dared stir
Towards the altar steps in front of her,
And if indeed they did, so wrath was she   460

As to be quite put out of charity.
Her kerchiefs were of finely woven ground;
I dared have sworn they weighed a good ten pound,
The ones she wore on Sunday, on her head.
Her hose were of the finest scarlet red
And gathered tight; her shoes were soft and new.
Bold was her face, handsome, and red in hue.
A worthy woman all her life, what's more
She'd had five husbands, all at the church door,
Apart from other company in youth;   470
No need just now to speak of that, forsooth.
And she had thrice been to Jerusalem,
Seen many strange rivers and passed over them;
She'd been to Rome and also to Boulogne,
St. James of Compostela and Cologne,
And she was skilled in wandering by the way.
She had gap-teeth, set widely, truth to say.
Easily on an ambling horse she sat
Well wimpled up, and on her head a hat
As broad as is a buckler or a shield;   480
She had a flowing mantle that concealed
Large hips, her heels spurred sharply under that.
In company she liked to laugh and chat
And knew the remedies for love's mischances,
An art in which she knew the oldest dances.

A holy-minded man of good renown
There was, and poor, the *Parson* to a town,
Yet he was rich in holy thought and work.
He also was a learned man, a clerk,
Who truly knew Christ's gospel and would preach it   490
Devoutly to parishioners, and teach it.
Benign and wonderfully diligent,
And patient when adversity was sent
(For so he proved in great adversity)
He much disliked extorting tithe or fee,
Nay rather he preferred beyond a doubt
Giving to poor parishioners round about
From his own goods and Easter offerings.
He found sufficiency in little things.
Wide was his parish, with houses far asunder,   500
Yet he neglected not in rain or thunder,
In sickness or in grief, to pay a call
On the remotest whether great or small
Upon his feet, and in his hand a stave.
This noble example to his sheep he gave,
First following the word before he taught it,
And it was from the gospel he had caught it.
This little proverb he would add thereto
That if gold rust, what then will iron do?
For if a priest be foul in whom we trust   510
No wonder that a common man should rust;
And shame it is to see—let priests take stock—
A shitty shepherd and a snowy flock.
The true example that a priest should give
Is one of cleanness, how the sheep should live.
He did not set his benefice to hire
And leave his sheep encumbered in the mire
Or run to London to earn easy bread
By singing masses for the wealthy dead,
Or find some Brotherhood and get enrolled.   520
He stayed at home and watched over his fold

25. That is, from Sweden to the western tip of France.
26. This impressive list is to indicate that the doctor was
thoroughly versed in all the medical authorities, ancient and
"modern." It seems curious to a modern reader to find
among his qualifications that he is an excellent astrologer.

So that no wolf should make the sheep miscarry.
He was a shepherd and no mercenary.
Holy and virtuous he was, but then
Never contemptuous of sinful men,
Never disdainful, never too proud or fine,
But was discreet in teaching and benign.
His business was to show a fair behavior
And draw men thus to Heaven and their Savior,
Unless indeed a man were obstinate;   530
And such, whether of high or low estate,
He put to sharp rebuke to say the least.
    I think there never was a better priest.
He sought no pomp or glory in his dealings,
No scrupulosity had spiced his feelings.
Christ and His Twelve Apostles and their lore
He taught, but followed it himself before.

    There was a *Plowman* with him there, his brother.
Many a load of dung one time or other
He must have carted through the morning dew.   540
He was an honest worker, good and true,
Living in peace and perfect charity,
And, as the gospel bade him, so did he,
Loving God best with all his heart and mind
And then his neighbor as himself, repined
At no misfortune, slacked for no content,
For steadily about his work he went
To thrash his corn, to dig or to manure
Or make a ditch, and he would help the poor
For love of Christ and never take a penny   550
If he could help it, and, as prompt as any,
He paid his tithes in full when they were due
On what he owned, and on his earnings too.
He wore a tabard smock and rode a mare.

    There was a *Reeve*, also a *Miller*, there,
A College *Manciple* from the Inns of Court,
A Papal *Pardoner* and, in close consort,
A Church-Court *Summoner*, riding at a trot,
And finally myself—that was the lot.
    The *Miller* was a chap of sixteen stone,   560
A great stout fellow big in brawn and bone.
He did well out of them, for he could go
And win the ram at any wrestling show.
Broad, knotty and short-shouldered, he would boast
He could heave any door off hinge and post,
Or take a run and break it with his head.
His beard, like any sow or fox, was red
And broad as well, as though it were a spade;
And, at its very tip, his nose displayed
A wart on which there stood a tuft of hair   570
Red as the bristles in an old sow's ear.
His nostrils were as black as they were wide,
He had a sword and buckler at his side,
His mighty mouth was like a furnace door.
A wrangler and a buffoon, he had a store
Of tavern stories, filthy in the main.
His was a master-hand at stealing grain.
He felt it with his thumb and thus he knew
Its quality and took three times his due—
A thumb of gold, by God, to gauge an oat!   580
He wore a hood of blue and a white coat.

He liked to play his bagpipes up and down
And that was how he brought us out of town.

    The *Manciple*[27] came from the Inner Temple;
All caterers might follow his example
In buying victuals; he was never rash
Whether he bought on credit or paid cash.
He used to watch the market most precisely
And got in first, and so he did quite nicely.
Now isn't it a marvel of God's grace   590
That an illiterate fellow can outpace
The wisdom of a heap of learned men?
His masters—he had more than thirty then—
All versed in the abstrusest legal knowledge,
Could have produced a dozen from their College
Fit to be stewards in land and rents and game
To any peer in England you could name,
And show him how to live on what he had
Debt-free (unless of course the peer were mad)
Or be as frugal as he might desire,   600
And they were fit to help about the Shire
In any legal case there was to try;
And yet this Manciple could wipe their eye.

    The *Reeve*[28] was old and choleric and thin;
His beard was shaven closely to the skin,
His shorn hair came abruptly to a stop
Above his ears, and he was docked on top
Just like a priest in front; his legs were lean,
Like sticks they were, no calf was to be seen.
He kept his bins and garners very trim;   610
No auditor could gain a point on him.
And he could judge by watching drought and rain
The yield he might expect from seed and grain.
His master's sheep, his animals and hens,
Pigs, horses, dairies, stores and cattle-pens
Were wholly trusted to his government.
And he was under contract to present
The accounts, right from the master's earliest years.
No one had ever caught him in arrears.
No bailiff, serf or herdsman dared to kick,   620
He knew their dodges, knew their every trick;
Feared like the plague he was, by those beneath.
He had a lovely dwelling on a heath,
Shadowed in green by trees above the sward.
A better hand at bargains than his lord,
He had grown rich and had a store of treasure
Well tucked away, yet out it came to pleasure
His lord with subtle gifts of goods,
To earn his thanks and even coats and hoods.
When young he'd learnt a useful trade and still   630
He was a carpenter of first-rate skill.
The stallion-cob he rode at a slow trot
Was dapple-gray and bore the name of Scot.
He wore an overcoat of bluish shade
And rather long; he had a rusty blade
Slung at his side. He came, as I heard tell,
From Norfolk, near a place called Baldeswell.
His coat was tucked under his belt and splayed.
He rode the hindmost of our cavalcade.

27. Steward, or purchasing agent.
28. Minor estate official.

There was a *Summoner*[29] with us in the place   640
Who had a fire-red cherubinny face,
For he had carbuncles. His eyes were narrow,
He was as hot and lecherous as a sparrow.
Black, scabby brows he had, and a thin beard.
Children were afraid when he appeared.
No quicksilver, lead ointments, tarter creams,
Boracic, no, nor brimstone, so it seems,
Could make a salve that had the power to bite,
Clean up or cure his whelks of knobby white   650
Or purge the pimples sitting on his cheeks.
Garlic he loved, and onions too, and leeks,
And drinking strong red wine until he was hazy.
Then he would shout and jabber as if crazy,
And wouldn't speak a word except in Latin
When he was drunk, such tags as he was pat in;
He only had a few, say two or three
That he had mugged up out of some decree;
No wonder, for he heard them every day.
And, as you know, a man can teach a jay
To call out "Walter" better than the Pope.   660
But had you tried to test his wits and grope
For more, you'd have found nothing in the bag.
Then "*Questio quid juris*"[30] was his tag.
He was a gentle varlet and a kind one,
No better fellow if you went to find one.
He would allow—just for a quart of wine—
Any good lad to keep a concubine
A twelvemonth, and dispense it altogether!
Yet he could pluck a finch to leave no feather;
And if he found some rascal with a maid   670
He would instruct him not to be afraid
In such a case of the Archdeacon's curse
(Unless the rascal's soul were in his purse)
For in his purse the punishment should be.
"Purse is the good Archdeacon's Hell," said he.
But well I know he lied in what he said;
A curse should put a guilty man in dread,
For curses kill, as shriving brings, salvation.
We should beware of excommunication.
Thus, by mere threat, this fellow could possess   680
The boys and girls of all the Diocese.
He knew their secrets and they went in dread.
He wore a garland set upon his head
Large as the holly-bush upon a stake
Outside an ale-house, and he had a cake,
A round one, which it was his joke to wield
As if it were intended for a shield.

He and a gentle *Pardoner*[31] rode together,
A bird from Charing Cross of the same feather,
Just back from visiting the Court of Rome.   690
He loudly sang "*Come hither, love, come home!*"
The Summoner sang deep seconds to this song,

No trumpet ever sounded half so strong.
The Pardoner had hair as yellow as wax
Hanging down smoothly like a hank of flax.
In driblets fell his locks behind his head
Down to his shoulders which they overspread;
Thinly they fell, like rat-tails, one by one.
He wore no hood upon his head, for fun;
The hood inside his wallet had been stowed,   700
He aimed at riding in the latest mode;
But for a little cap his head was bare
And he had bulging eye-balls, like a hare.
He'd sewed a holy relic on his cap;
His wallet lay before him on his lap,
Brimful of pardons come from Rome all hot.
He had the same small voice a goat has got.
His chin no beard had harbored, nor would harbor,
Smoother than ever chin was left by barber.
I judge he was a gelding, or a mare.   710
As to his trade, from Berwick down to Ware
There was no pardoner of equal grace,
For in his trunk he had a pillow-case
Which he asserted was Our Lady's veil.
He said he had a gobbet of the sail
Saint Peter had the time when he made bold
To walk the waves, till Jesu Christ took hold.
He had a cross of metal set with stones
And, in a glass, a rubble of pigs' bones.
And with these relics, any time he found   720
Some poor up-country parson to astound,
On one short day, in money down, he drew
More than the parson in a month or two,
And by his flatteries and prevarication
Made monkeys of the priest and congregation.
But still to do him justice first and last
In church he was a noble ecclesiast.
How well he read a lesson or told a story!
But best of all he sang an Offertory,
For well he knew that when that song was sung   730
He'd have to preach and tune his honey-tongue
And (well he could) win silver from the crowd.
That's why he sang so merrily and loud.

Now I have told you shortly, in a clause,
The rank, the array, the number and the cause
Of our assembly in this company
In Southwark, at that high-class hostelry
Known as *The Tabard*, close beside *The Bell*.

---

29. Process-server or bailiff for the ecclesiastical court, usually presided over by the archdeacon. Summoned sinners to trial before an ecclesiastical court.
30. "The question is, what part of the law applies?"—a lawyer's technicality.
31. Had authority from the pope to sell pardons and indulgences.

STUDY QUESTIONS

1. The pilgrims can be classified into several groups: the chivalric class, the moneyed class, the corrupt clergy, the sincere clergy, the simple commoners. Name the pilgrims who belong to each group and describe the general traits of each class.
2. Compare this society with our own. What are the differences? The similarities?

The Canterbury Tales

The Reeve's Tale

Chaucer

Just as Chaucer, in his Prologue, gives us a broad cross-section of the people of the Late Middle Ages, so, in the stories that they tell during the pilgrimage, he presents many of the types of literature of the time. "The Reeve's Tale," like the preceding "Miller's Tale," is a fabliau, a type of boisterous and bawdy story popular at the time and, in fact, most any other time. A manager on a large country estate, Oswald the Reeve is shrewd, cunning, and bad tempered. In his early days he was a carpenter, which explains why he becomes incensed by the Miller's tale of a foolish old carpenter who was cuckolded by his young and lively wife. Furthermore, the Reeve is old and, as he says in his Prologue (not given here), is now like everyone else who "knows that when a man no longer has the ability to do a certain thing, he spends his time talking about it." Prodded by the Host to cease his sermonizing, the Reeve begins his story, warning that his language will be just as rough as that used by the Miller. Not surprisingly, the foolish victim of the Reeve's tale is a miller. The modern English translation is by Nevill Coghill.

At Trumpington, not far from Cambridge town,
　A bridge goes over where the brook runs down
And by that brook there stands a mill as well.
And it's God's truth that I am going to tell.
　There was a miller lived there many a day
As proud as any peacock and as gay;
He could play bag-pipes too, fish, mend his gear,
And turn a lathe, and wrestle, and poach deer.
And at his belt he carried a long blade,
Trenchant it was as any sword that's made,　　　　10
And in his pouch a jolly little knife.
No one dared touch him, peril of his life.
He had a Sheffield dagger in his hose.
Round was his face and puggish was his nose;
Bald as an ape he was. To speak more fully,
He was a thorough-going market bully
Whom none dared lay a hand on or come near
Without him swearing that they'd buy it dear.
　He was a thief as well of corn and meal,
And sly at that; his habit was to steal.　　　　20
Simpkin the Swagger he was called in scorn.
He had a wife and she was nobly born;
Her father was the parson of the town;
A dowry of brass dishes he put down
In order to have Simpkin his relation.
The nuns had given her an education.
Simpkin would take no woman, so he said,
Unless she were a virgin and well-bred,
To save the honor of his yeoman stock;
And she was proud, pert as a magpie cock.　　　　30
　It was a proper sight to see the pair

On holidays, what with him strutting there
In front of her, his hood about his head,
And she behind him all decked out in red,
Like Simpkin's hose, for scarlet-red he had 'em.
No one dared call her anything but "Madam,"
And there was no one bold enough to try
A bit of fun with her or wink an eye,
Unless indeed he wanted Sim the Swagger
To murder him with cutlass, knife or dagger,　　　　40
For jealous folk are dangerous, you know,
At least they want their wives to think them so.
And then her birth was smirched to say the least;
Being the daughter of a celibate priest
She must maintain her dignity, of which
She had as much as water in a ditch.
She was a sneering woman and she thought
That ladies should respect her, so they ought,
What with her well-connected family,
And education in a nunnery.　　　　50
　They had a daughter too between them both,
She was a girl of twenty summers' growth;
But that was all except a child they had
Still in the cradle, but a proper lad.
The wench was plump, well-grown enough to pass,
With a snub nose and eyes as gray as glass;
Her rump was broad, her breasts were round and high;
She'd very pretty hair, I will not lie.
The parson of the town, for she was fair,
Intended to appoint the girl as heir　　　　60
To all his property in house and land
And he was stiff with suitors to her hand.
He purposed to bestow her if he could
Where blood and ancient lineage made it good.
For Holy Church's goods should be expended
On Holy Church's blood, so well-descended,
And holy blood should have what's proper to it
Though Holy Church should be devoured to do it.
　This miller levied toll beyond a doubt
On wheat and malt from all the land about,　　　　70
Particularly from a large-sized College
In Cambridge, Solar Hall. 'Twas common knowledge
They sent their wheat and malt to him to grind it.
Happened one day the man who ought to mind it,
The college manciple, lay sick in bed,
And some reported him as good as dead.
On hearing which the miller robbed him more
A hundred times than he had robbed before;
For up till then he'd only robbed politely,
But now he stole outrageously, forthrightly.　　　　80
　The Warden scolded hard and made a scene,
But there! The miller didn't give a bean,
Blustered it out and swore it wasn't so.
　Two poor young Bible-clerks or students, though,
Lived in this College (that of which I spoke).
Headstrong they were and eager for a joke
And simply for the chance of sport and play
They went and plagued the Warden night and day
Just for a little leave to spend the morn
Watching the miller grind their meal and corn,　　　　90
And each was ready to engage his neck
The miller couldn't rob them half a peck

Of corn by trickery, nor yet by force;
And in the end he gave them leave of course.
　　One was called John and Alan was the other,
Both born in the same village, name of Strother,
Far in the north, I cannot tell you where.
　　Alan collected all his gear with care,
Loaded his corn upon a horse he had,
And off he went with John the other lad,　　　　　　　100
Each with his sword and buckler by his side.
John knew the way—he didn't need a guide—
Reaches the mill and down the sack he flings.
　　Alan spoke first: "Well, Simon, lad, how's things?
And how's your canny daughter and your wife?"
Says Simpkin, "Welcome, Alan! Odds my life,
It's John as well! What are you up to here?"
"By God," said John. "Needs-must has got no peer,
And it behooves a man that has nie servant
To work, as say the learned and observant.　　　　　110
Wor Manciple is like enough to dee,
Such aches and torments in his teeth has he;
So Alan here and I have brought wor sack
Of corn for grinding and to bring it back.
Help us get home as quickly as ye can."
"It shall be done," said he, "as I'm a man.
What'll you do while I've the job in hand?"
"By God," said John, "I have a mind to stand
Right by the hopper here and watch the corn
As it gans in. Never since I was born　　　　　　　120
Saw I a hopper wagging to and fro."
　　Alan spoke up: "Eh, John, and will ye so?
Then I shall stand below a short way off
And watch the meal come down into the trough;
I need no more than that by way of sport,
For John, in faith, I'm one of the same sort
And diven't knaa nowt of milling, same as ye."
　　The miller smiled at their simplicity
And thought, "It's just a trick, what they're about
They think that nobody can catch them out,　　　　130
But by the Lord I'll blear their eyes a bit
For all their fine philosophy and wit.
The more they try to do me on the deal,
When the time comes, the more I mean to steal.
Instead of flour they shall be given bran.
'The greatest scholar is not the wisest man,'
As the wolf said in answer to the mare.
Them and their precious learning! Much I care."
　　And when he saw his chance he sidled out
Into the yard behind and looked about　　　　　　140
Without their noticing until at last
He found their horse where they had made him fast
Under an arbor just behind the mill.
　　Up to the horse he goes with quiet skill
And strips the bridle off him there and then.
And when the horse was loose, off to the fen
Through thick and thin, and whinnying "Weehee!"
He raced to join the wild mares running free.
　　The miller then went back, and did not say
A word of this, but passed the time of day　　　　　150
With John and Alan till their corn was ground;
And when the meal was fairly sacked and bound,
John wandered out and found their horse was gone.

"Good Lord! Help! Help! Come quickly!" shouted John,
"Wor horse is lost, Alan! The devil's in it!
God's bones, man, use your legs! Come out this
　　minute!
Lord save us all, the Warden's palfrey's lost."
　　Alan forgot his meal and corn and cost,
Abandoning frugality and care.
"What's that?" he shouted, "Palfrey? Which way?
　　Where?"　　　　　　　　　　　　　　　　160
　　The miller's wife ran clucking like a hen
Towards them, saying, "Gone off to the fen
To the wild mares as fast as he can go.
Curse on the clumsy hand that tied him so!
Should have known better how to knit the reins."
John said, "Bad luck to it. Alan, for Christ's pains,
Put down your sword, man; so will I; let's gan!
We'll rin him like a roe together, man!
God's precious heart! He cannot scape up all!
Why didn't you put the palfrey in the stall?　　　170
You must be daft, bad luck to you! Haway!"
And off ran John and Alan in dismay,
Towards the fen as fast as they could go.
　　And when the miller saw that this was so,
A good half-bushel of their flour he took
And gave it over to his wife to cook.
"I think," he said, "these lads have had a fright.
I'll pluck their beards. Yes. Let 'em read and write,
But none the less a miller is their match.
Look at them now! Like children playing catch.　　180
Won't be an easy job to get him, though!"
　　These foolish Bible-clerks ran to and fro
And shouted, "Woa, lad, stand! . . . Look out behind!
Whistle him up . . . I've got him . . . watch it . . . *mind!*"
But to be brief, it wasn't until night
They caught the palfrey, hunt him as they might
Over the fens, he ran away so fast;
But in a ditch they captured him at last.
　　Weary and wet, like cattle in the rain,
Came foolish John and Alan back again.　　　　　190
Said John, "Alas the day that I was born!
We've earned nowt here but mockery and scorn.
Wor corn is stolen and they'll call us fools,
Warden and all wor meäts in the Schools,
And most of all the miller. What a day!"
　　So back they went, John grousing all the way,
Towards the mill and put the horse in byre.
They found the miller sitting by the fire,
For it was night, too late for going home,
And, for the love of God, they begged a room　　200
For shelter and they proffered him their penny.
"A room?" the miller said. "There isn't any.
There's this, such as it is; we'll share it then.
My house is small, but you are learned men
And by your arguments can make a place
Twenty foot broad as infinite as space.
Take a look round and see if it will do,
Or make it bigger with your parley-voo."
"Well, Simon, you must have your little joke
And, by St. Cuthbert, that was fairly spoke!　　210
Well, people have a proverb to remind them
To bring their own, or take things as they find them,"

Said John. "Dear host, do get us out the cup;
A little meat and drink would cheer us up.
We'll give ye the full payment, on my word.
No empty-handed man can catch a bird;
See, here's the silver, ready to be spent."
        Down into Trumpington the daughter went
For bread and ale; the miller cooked a goose,
And tied their horse up lest it should get loose   220
Again, and in his chamber made a bed
With clean white sheets and blankets fairly spread,
Ten foot from his, upon a sort of shelf,
His daughter had a bed all by herself
Quite close in the same room; they were to lie
All side by side, no help for it, and why?
Because there was no other in the house.
        They supped and talked and had a fine carouse
And drank a lot of ale, the very best.
Midnight or thereabout they went to rest.   230
        Properly pasted was this miller's head,
Pale-drunk he was, he'd passed the stage of red;
Hiccupping through his nose he talked and trolled
As if he'd asthma or a heavy cold.
To bed he goes, his wife and he together;
She was as jolly as a jay in feather,
Having well wet her whistle from the ladle.
And by her bed she planted down the cradle
To rock the baby or to give it sup.
        When what was in the crock had been drunk up,   240
To bed went daughter too, and thereupon
To bed went Alan and to bed went John.
That was the lot; no sleeping-draught was needed.
The miller had taken so much booze unheeded,
He snorted like a cart-horse in his sleep
And vented other noises, loud and deep.
His wife joined in the chorus hot and strong;
Two furlongs off you might have heard their song.
The wench was snoring too, for company.
        Alan the clerk in all this melody   250
Gave John a poke and said, "Are ye awake?
Did ye ever hear sich sang for guidness sake?
There's family prayers for ye among they noddies!
Wild fire come doon and burn them up, the bodies!
Who ever heard a canny thing like that?
The devil take their souls for what they're at!
All this lang neet I shall na get nie rest.
        "But never ye mind, all shall be for the best;
I tell ye, John, as sure as I'm a man,
I'm going to have that wench there, if I can!   260
The law grants easement when things gan amiss,
For, John, there is a law that gans like this:
'If in one point a person be aggrieved,
Then in another he shall be relieved.'
        "Wor corn is stolen, nivvor doubt of that;
Ill-luck has followed us in all we're at,
And since no compensation has been offered
Against wor loss, I'll take the easement proffered.
God's soul, it shall be so indeed, none other?"
        John whispered back to him, "Be careful brother, 270
The miller is a torble man for slaughter;
If he should wake and find ye with his daughter
He might do injury to you and me."

"Injury? Him! I coont him nat a flea!"
        Alan rose up; towards the wench he crept.
The wench lay flat upon her back and slept,
And ere she saw him, he had drawn so nigh
It was too late for her to give a cry.
To put it briefly, they were soon as one.
Now, Alan, play! For I will speak of John.   280
        John lay there still for quite a little while,
Complaining and lamenting in this style:
"A bloody joke . . . Lord, what a chance to miss!
I shall be made a monkey of for this!
My meät has got some comfort for his harms,
He has the miller's daughter in his arms;
He took his chance and now his needs are sped,
I'm but a sack of rubbish here in bed.
And when this jape is told in time to come
They'll say I was a softie and a bum!   290
I'll get up too and take what chance I may,
For God helps those that help theirsels, they say."
        He rises, steals towards the cradle, lifts it,
And stepping softly back again, he shifts it
And lays it by his bed upon the floor.
        The miller's wife soon after ceased to snore,
Began to wake, rose up, and left the room,
And coming back she groped about in gloom,
Missing the cradle, John had snatched away.
"Lord, Lord," she said, "I nearly went astray   300
And got into the student's bed . . . . How dreadful!
There would have been foul doings. What a bed-ful!"
        At last she gropes to where the cradle stands,
And so by fumbling upwards with her hands
She found the bed and thinking nought but good,
Since she was certain where the cradle stood,
Yet knew not where she was, for it was dark,
She well and fairly crept in with the clerk,
Then lay quite still and tried to go to sleep.
John waited for a while, then gave a leap   310
And thrust himself upon this worthy wife.
It was the merriest fit in all her life,
For John went deep and thrust away like mad.
It was a jolly life for either lad
Till the third morning cock began to sing.
        Alan grew tired as dawn began to spring;
He had been hard at work the long, long night.
"Bye-bye," he said, "sweet Molly . . . . Are ye a'right?
The day has come, I cannot linger here,
But ever mair in life and death, my dear,   320
I am your own true clerk, or strike me deid!"
        "Good-bye, my sweet," she whispered, "take good
              heed . . .
But first I'll tell you something, that I will!
When you are riding homewards past the mill
By the main entrance-door, a bit behind it,
There's the half-bushel cake—you're sure to find it—
And it was made out of the very meal
You brought to grind and I helped father steal. . . .
And, dearest heart, God have you in his keeping!"   330
And with that word she almost burst out weeping.
        Alan got up and thought, "Dawn's coming on,
Better get back and creep in beside John."
But there he found the cradle in his way.

"By God," he thought, "I nearly went astray!
My heed is tottering with my work to-neet,
That'll be why I cannot gan areet!
This cradle tells me I have lost my tether;
You must be miller and his wife together."
    And back he went, groping his weary way   340
And reached the bed in which the miller lay,
And thinking it was John upon the bed
He slid in by the miller's side instead,
Grabbing his neck, and with no more ado
Said, "Shake yourself, wake up, you pig's-head, you!
For Christ's soul, listen! O such noble games
As I have had! I tell you, by St. James,
Three times the neet, from midnight into morn,
The miller's daughter helped me grind my corn
While you've been lying in your cowardly way . . . ."   350
"You scoundrel!" said the miller. "What d'you say?
You beast! You treacherous blackguard! Filthy rat!
God's dignity! I'll murder you for that!
How dare you be so bold as to fling mud
Upon my daughter, come of noble blood?"
    He grabbed at Alan by his Adam's apple,
And Alan grabbed him back in furious grapple
And clenched his fist and bashed him on the nose.
Down miller's breast a bloody river flows
Onto the floor, his nose and mouth all broke;   360
They wallowed like two porkers in a poke,
And up and down and up again they go
Until the miller tripped and stubbed his toe,
Spun round and fell down backwards on his wife.
She had heard nothing of this foolish strife,
For she had fallen asleep with John the clerk,
Weary from all their labors in the dark.
The miller's fall started her out of sleep.
"Help!" she screamed. "Holly cross of Bromeholme
    keep
Us! Lord! Into thy hands! To Thee I call!   370
Simon, wake up! The devil's among us all!
My heart is bursting, help! I'm nearly dead,
One's on my stomach, and another's on my head.
Help, Simpkin, help! These nasty clerks are fighting!"
    Up started John, he needed no inciting,
And groped about the chamber to and fro
To find a stick; she too was on the go
And, knowing the corners better than them all,
Was first to find one leaning by the wall;
And by a little shaft of shimmering light   380
That shone in through a hole—the moon was bright—
Although the room was almost black as pitch
She saw them fight, not knowing which was which;
But there was something white that caught her eye
On seeing which she peered and gave a cry,
Thinking it was the night-cap of the clerk.
    Raising her stick, she crept up in the dark
And, hoping to hit Alan, it was her fate
To smite the miller on his shining pate,
And down he went, shouting, "O God, I'm dying!"   390
    The clerks then beat him well and left him lying
And throwing on their clothes they took their horse
And their ground meal and off they went, of course,
And as they passed the mill they took the cake

Made of their meal the girl was told to bake.
    And thus the bumptious miller was well beaten
And done out of the supper they had eaten,
And done out of the money that was due
For grinding Alan's corn, who beat him too.
His wife was plumbed, so was his daughter. Look!   400
That comes of being a miller and a crook!
    I heard this proverb when I was a kid,
"Do evil and be done by as you did."
Tricksters will get a tricking, so say I;
And God that sits in majesty on high
Bring all this company, great and small, to Glory!
Thus I've paid out the Miller with my story!

STUDY QUESTIONS

1. What seems to be the attitude (Chaucer's? society's?) towards "clerks" (students who will become clergy)?
2. Compare the tone of this tale with the morally elevating play *Everyman*. What does this tell you about fourteenth-century England?

LITERARY SELECTION 35

The Art of Courtly Love
Andreas Cappelanus (fl. 1174–1186)

Countess Marie of Champagne established a Court of Love at Troyes, where Andreas was probably chaplain to the court, or so he claimed. Andreas was an accomplished writer whose treatise on love provides us with a vivid and probably accurate picture of courtly life. Specifically, Andreas intended his manual as a portrayal of the Poitiers court of Marie's mother, Queen Eleanor of Aquitaine, as it was between 1170 and 1174.

Undoubtedly commissioned by Countess Marie, the manual is a codification of the etiquette of love. Andreas combines quotations from classic Latin writers (mainly Ovid) and the spirit of lyric love poetry by troubadours such as Bernart de Ventadorn (see p. 449) with his own observation of actual practices, producing a unique work known throughout Europe in a variety of translations.

Book I: Introduction to the Treatise on Love

We must first consider what love is, whence it gets its name, what the effect of love is, between what persons love may exist, how it may be acquired, retained, increased, decreased, and ended, what are the signs that one's love is returned, and what one of the lovers ought to do if the other is unfaithful.

Chapter 1. What Love Is

Love is a certain inborn suffering derived from the sight of and excessive meditation upon the beauty of the opposite sex, which causes each one to wish above all things the embraces of the other and by common desire to carry out all of love's precepts in the other's embrace.

That love is suffering is easy to see, for before the love becomes equally balanced on both sides there is no torment greater, since the lover is always in fear that his love may not gain its desire and that he is wasting his efforts. He fears, too, that rumors of it may get abroad, and he fears everything that might harm it in any way, for before things are perfected a slight disturbance often spoils them. If he is a poor man, he also fears that the woman may scorn his poverty; if he is ugly, he fears that she may despise his lack of beauty or may give her love to a more handsome man; if he is rich, he fears that his parsimony in the past may stand in his way. To tell the truth, no one can number the fears of one single lover.[32] This kind of love, then, is a suffering which is felt by only one of the persons and may be called "single love." But even after both are in love the fears that arise are just as great, for each of the lovers fears that what he has acquired with so much effort may be lost through the effort of someone else, which is certainly much worse for a man than if, having no hope, he sees that his efforts are accomplishing nothing, for it is worse to lose the things you are seeking than to be deprived of a gain you merely hope for. The lover fears, too, that he may offend his loved one in some way; indeed he fears so many things that it would be difficult to tell them.

That this suffering is inborn I shall show you clearly, because if you look at the truth and distinguish carefully you will see that it does not arise out of any action; only from the reflection of the mind upon what it sees does this suffering come. For when a man sees some woman fit for love and shaped according to his taste, he begins at once to lust after her in his heart; then the more he thinks about her the more he burns with love, until he comes to a fuller meditation. Presently he begins to think about the fashioning of the woman and to differentiate her limbs, to think about what she does, and to pry into the secrets of her body, and he desires to put each part of it to the fullest use.[33] Then after he has come to this complete meditation, love cannot hold the reins; but he proceeds at once to action; straightway he strives to get a helper and to find an intermediary. He begins to plan how he may find favor with her, and he begins to seek a place and a time opportune for talking; he looks upon a brief hour as a very long year, because he cannot do anything fast enough to suit his eager mind. It is well known that many things happen to him in this manner. This inborn suffering comes, therefore, from seeing and meditating. Not every kind of meditation can be the cause of love, an excessive one is required; for a restrained thought does not, as a rule, return to the mind, and so love cannot arise from it.

32. Ovid, *Art of Love*, II, 517 ff.
33. Compare Ovid, *Metamorphoses*, VI, 490–93.
34. Compare Cicero, *Tusculan Disputations*, IV.

Book II: Chapter 8

In Chapter 8 (Book II), Andreas presents the Rules of Love as the climax of a properly romantic mission. It seems that a knight of Britain cannot win the love of "a certain British lady" until he has brought her the hawk sitting on a golden perch in King Arthur's court. And, he is told,

> you can't get this hawk that you are seeking unless
> you prove, by a combat in Arthur's palace, that you
> enjoy the love of a more beautiful lady than any man
> at Arthur's court has; you can't even enter the palace
> until you show the guards the hawk's gauntlet, and
> you can't get this gauntlet except by overcoming two
> mighty knights in a double combat.

After defeating the pugnacious keeper of a golden bridge, the Briton then vanquishes a giant and rides on to Camelot where he manfully accomplishes the assigned tasks. While seizing the hawk he discovers a written parchment and is told that "this is the parchment on which are written the rules of love which the King of Love . . . pronounced for lovers. You should take it with you and make these rules known to lovers."

These are the rules.

I. Marriage is no real excuse for not loving.
II. He who is not jealous cannot love.
III. No one can be bound by a double love.
IV. It is well known that love is always increasing or decreasing.
V. That which a lover takes against the will of his beloved has no relish.
VI. Boys do not love until they arrive at the age of maturity.
VII. When one lover dies, a widowhood of two years is required of the survivor.
VIII. No one should be deprived of love without the very best of reasons.
IX. No one can love unless he is impelled by the persuasion of love.
X. Love is always a stranger in the home of avarice.
XI. It is not proper to love any woman whom one would be ashamed to seek to marry.
XII. A true lover does not desire to embrace in love anyone except his beloved.
XIII. When made public love rarely endures.
XIV. The easy attainment of love makes it of little value; difficulty of attainment makes it prized.
XV. Every lover regularly turns pale in the presence of his beloved.
XVI. When a lover suddenly catches sight of his beloved his heart palpitates.
XVII. A new love puts to flight an old one.[34]
XVIII. Good character alone makes any man worthy of love.
XIX. If love diminishes, it quickly fails and rarely revives.
XX. A man in love is always apprehensive.
XXI. Real jealousy always increases the feeling of love.
XXII. Jealousy, and therefore love, are increased when one suspects his beloved.
XXIII. He whom the thought of love vexes eats and sleeps very little.

XXIV.   Every act of a lover ends in the thought of his beloved.

XXV.   A true lover considers nothing good except what he thinks will please his beloved.

XXVI.   Love can deny nothing to love.

XXVII.   A lover can never have enough of the solaces of his beloved.

XXVIII.   A slight presumption causes a lover to suspect his beloved.

XXIX.   A man who is vexed by too much passion usually does not love.

XXX.   A true lover is constantly and without intermission possessed by the thought of his beloved.

XXXI.   Nothing forbids one woman being loved by two men or one man by two women.

These rules, as I have said, the Briton brought back with him on behalf of the King of Love to the lady for whose sake he endured so many perils when he brought her back the hawk. When she was convinced of the complete faithfulness of this knight and understood better how boldly he had striven, she rewarded him with her love. Then she called together a court of a great many ladies and knights and laid before them these rules of Love, and bade every lover keep them faithfully under threat of punishment by the King of Love. These laws the whole court received in their entirety and promised forever to obey in order to avoid punishment by Love. Every person who had been summoned and had come to the court took home a written copy of the rules and gave them out to all lovers in all parts of the world.

STUDY QUESTIONS

1. As the selection indicates, many characteristics of romantic love were first articulated during the Middle Ages. Considering the definition and rules in the text, which concepts are still basic to romantic love?

2. What has changed? Can you explain the changes?

LITERARY SELECTION 36

A Medieval Woman's Mirror of Honor: The Treasury of the City of Ladies

Christine de Pisan (ca. 1364–ca. 1431)

Written specifically for women, this book was intended to help women gain a sense of self-worth, to prepare them to make their own way in the world, whatever problems they might

encounter. As with other medieval writers, de Pisan composes an allegory using the three virtues of Reason, Rectitude, and Justice to guide her. As compared with the sacred virtues of Faith, Hope, and Charity, these are secular qualities that were more appropriate for her world.

Christine de Pisan was not only a successful writer but a famous one. William Caxton, the first English printer, translated and published one of her works, noting that she was "the mistress of intelligence." A contemporary male writer claimed that she was the equal of Cicero for eloquence and Cato for wisdom. De Pisan herself remarked, perhaps ironically, that "women are enhanced by knowledge so it is indeed surprising that some men should oppose it." Certainly her efforts on behalf of women were long overdue, for numerous men had written tracts intended to prepare women for religious or domestic duties or as guides to a suitable marriage, that is, to condition them for a secondary role in a world controlled by men. Nothing had ever been written to help single, married, or widowed women deal with adult situations and problems encompassing every aspect of the everyday world.

Books I and II are addressed mainly to court women and those in religious orders. Book III is directed to all women regardless of class. Her choice of problems to discuss was obviously personal, for the author had to undergo the very experiences she so dispassionately describes. The translation is by Charity Cannon Willard.

Book III.4 Which speaks of widows young and old [ca. 1405]

In order for this work to be more completely profitable to women of all classes, we will speak now to *widows* among the more common people, having already discussed the case of widowed princesses.

Dear friends, we pity each of you in the state of widowhood because death has deprived you of your husbands, whoever they may have been. Moreover, much anguish and many trying problems afflict you, affecting the rich in one manner and those not rich in another. The rich are troubled because unscrupulous people commonly try to despoil them of their inheritance. The poor, or at least, those not at all rich, are distressed because they find no pity from anyone for their problems. Along with the grief of having lost your mate, which is quite enough, you must also suffer three trials in particular, which assault you whether rich or poor.   10

First is that, undoubtedly, you will find harshness and lack of consideration or sympathy everywhere. Those who honored you during the lifetime of your husbands, who may well have been officials or men of importance, now will pay little attention to you and barely even bother to be friendly. The second distress facing you is the variety of lawsuits and demands of certain people regarding debts, claims on your property, and income. Third is the evil talk of people who are all too willing to attack you, so that you hardly know what you can do that will not be criticized. In order to arm you with the sensible advice to protect yourself against these, as well   20 as other overpowering plagues, we wish to suggest some things you may find useful. 30

Against the coldness you undoubtedly will find in everyone—the first of the three tribulations of widowhood—there are three possible remedies. Turn toward God, who was willing to suffer so much for human creatures. Reflecting on this will teach you patience, a quality you will need greatly. It will bring you to the point where you will place little value on the rewards and honors of this world. First of all, you will learn how undependable all earthly things are. 40

The second remedy is to turn your heart to gentleness and kindness in word and courtesy to everyone. You will overcome the hardhearted and bend them to your will by gentle prayers and humble requests.

Third, in spite of what we have just said about quiet humility in words, apparel, and countenance, nevertheless you must learn the judgment and behavior necessary to protect yourself against those all too willing to get the better of you. You must avoid their company, 50 having nothing to do with them if you can help it. Rather, stay quietly in your own house, not involving yourself in an argument with a neighbor, not even with a servingman or maid. By always speaking quietly while protecting your own interests, as well as by mingling little with miscellaneous people if you don't need to, you will avoid anyone taking advantage of you or ruining you.

Concerning the lawsuits that may stalk you, learn well how to avoid all sorts. They damage a widow in many ways. First of all, if she is not informed, but on the 60 contrary is ignorant in legal affairs, then it will be necessary for her to place herself in the power of someone else to solicit on behalf of her needs. Those others generally lack diligence in the affairs of women, willingly deceiving them and charging them eight crown for six. Another problem is that women cannot always *come and go at all hours*, as a man would do, and therefore, if it is not too damaging for her, it may be better to let go some part of what is her due rather than involve herself in contention. She should consider 70 circumspectly any reasonable demands made against her; or if she finds herself obliged to be the plaintiff, she should pursue her rights courteously and should attempt alternatives for achieving her ends. If assailed by debts, she must inform herself of what rights her creditors have and make an appropriate plan of action. Even presupposing there is no official "owing" letter or witness, if her conscience tells her that something is owing, she must not keep anything that really belongs to another. That would burden her husband's soul as well 80 as her own, and God indeed might send her so many additional, expensive misfortunes that her original losses would be doubled.

But if she protects herself wisely from deceitful people who make demands without cause, she is behaving as she should. If, in spite of all this, she is obliged to go to court, she should understand three things necessary for all to take action. One is to act on the advice of wise specialists in customary law and clerks who are well versed in legal sciences and the law. 90

Next is to prepare the case for trial with great care and diligence. Third is to have enough money to afford all this. Certainly if one of these things is lacking, no matter how worthy the cause, there is every danger the case will be lost.

Therefore, a widow in such a situation necessarily must look for older specialists in customary law, those most experienced in various sorts of cases, rather than depending on younger men. She should explain her case to them, showing them her letters and her titles, 100 listening carefully to what they say without concealing anything which pertains to the case, whether in her favor or against her. Counsel can utilize in her behalf only what she tells him. According to his advice, either she must plead steadfastly or accede to her adversaries. If ever she goes to court, she must plead diligently and pay well. Her case will so benefit.

If it is necessary for her to do these things, and if she wishes to avoid further trouble and bring her case to a successful conclusion, she must take on the heart of a 110 *man*. She must be constant, strong, and wise in pursuing her advantage, not crouching in tears, defenseless, like some simple woman or like a poor dog who retreats into a corner while all the other dogs jump on him. If you do that, dear woman, you will find most people so lacking in pity that they would take the bread from your hand because they consider you either ignorant or simple-minded, nor would you find additional pity elsewhere because they took it. So, do not work on 120 your own or depend on your own judgment, but hire always the best advice, particularly on important matters you do not understand.

Thus, your affairs should be well managed among those of you widows who have reached a certain age and do not intend to remarry. Young widows must be guided by their relatives or friends until they have married again, conducting themselves particularly gently and simply so as not to acquire a doubtful reputation that might cause them to lose their prospects and their advantage. 130

The remedy against the third of the three misfortunes pursuing any widow—being at mercy of evil tongues—is that she must be careful in every way possible not to give anyone reason to talk against her because of appearance, bearing, or clothing. All these should be simple and seemly, and the woman's manners quiet and discreet regarding her body, thus giving no cause for gossip. Nor should the widow be too friendly or seemingly intimate with any man who may be observed frequenting her house, unless he is a relative. Even then 140 discretion should be observed, including the presence of a father-in-law, brother, or priest, who should be permitted few visits or none at all. For no matter how devout a woman herself may be, the world is inclined to speak evil. She should also maintain a household where there is no suspicion of great intimacy or familiarity, however fine she knows her staff to be and despite the innocence of her own thoughts. Nor should her household expenses give people opportunity for slandering her. Moreover, to protect her property better, 150 she should make no ostentatious displays of servants, clothing, or foods, for it better suits a widow to be inconspicuous and without any extravagance whatsoever.

Because widowhood truly provides so many hardships for women, some people might think it best for all widows to remarry. This argument can be answered by saying that if it were true that the married state consisted entirely of peace and repose, this indeed would be so. That one almost always sees the contrary   160
in marriages should be a warning to all widows. However, it might be necessary or desirable for the young ones to remarry. But for all those who have passed their youth and who are sufficiently comfortable financially so that poverty does not oblige them, remarriage is complete folly. Though some who want to remarry say there is nothing in life for a woman alone, they have so little confidence in their own good sense that they will claim that they don't know how to manage their own lives. But the height of folly and the greatest   170
of all absurdities is the old woman who takes a young husband: There a joyful song rarely is heard for long. Although many pay dearly for their foolishness, nobody will sympathize with them—for good reason.

STUDY QUESTIONS

1. What does the author mean by "miscellaneous people"?
2. De Pisan comments that some men charge women "eight crown for six." Does this problem still exist? Think, for example, about what some men may charge women for automotive repairs.
3. Why does the writer advocate seeking lawyers who are "older specialists" rather than "younger men"? Does this have something to do with quality work? Do people, in fact, usually get what they pay for? Was this especially important for single women or widows at that time? In our own time?
4. What is meant by taking on the "heart of a *man*"? Is she referring to purely masculine attributes? Or is she describing those qualities that make a person resilient and self-confident regardless of gender? If you had read these words in 1405 what might your reaction have been as a man? As a woman?
5. What is de Pisan's opinion of women who tearfully throw up their hands and give up? Is she justified?
6. At the time of this writing the author was about forty years old, having been a widow for some fifteen years. How would you evaluate her beliefs about the various options available to widows? What was Christine de Pisan's own belief?

Displaying a thoroughly unmedieval concern for renown and influence, de Pisan wrote near the end of the book:

I thought I would multiply this work throughout the world in various copies, whatever the cost might be, and present it in particular places to queens, princesses and noble ladies. Through their efforts, it will be the more honored and praised, as is fitting, and better circulated among other women.

Nineteen manuscripts still exist in addition to three printed editions in French plus a Portuguese translation.

LITERARY SELECTION 37

The Divine Comedy
Dante Alighieri (1265–1321)

Reading the *Divine Comedy* or *Commedia* is no easy task, a fact that Dante himself (fig. 13.6) recognized when, in writing to a friend, he said:

The meaning of this work is not simple . . . for we obtain one meaning from the letter of it, and another from that which the letter signifies; and the first is called *literal*, but the other *allegorical* or *mystical* . . . .
The subject of the whole work, then, taken in the literal sense is "the state of the soul after death straightforwardly affirmed," for the development of the whole work hinges on and about that. But, if, indeed, the work is taken *allegorically*, its subject is: "Man, as by good or ill deserts, in the exercise of his free choice, he becomes liable to rewarding or punishing justice."

On two scores, the rewards of reading the *Commedia* justify the effort. First, it is the finest statement of the medieval synthesis that we have, comparable to Chartres cathedral or the *Summa Theologica* of Thomas Aquinas. Second, and more important, it presents one of the half-dozen most profound insights into the nature and meaning of human life in all of literature or art. It is meaningful to us in the twentieth century not only as a splendid historical document, but as living literature.

Its form represents as tight a discipline as we know in literature, for it is shaped by the number three. It is written in *terza rima*, a form preserved in the translations given below. It consists of three major sections: Hell, Purgatory, and Paradise. Within the Hell is one introductory canto followed by thirty-three more cantos, and thirty-three cantos in each of the following sections. The sum is 100, the perfect and complete number.

Insofar as its meaning is concerned, the poem will speak for itself. We must understand, however, that Dante accepts the idea that all of nature is in motion, following the laws, the love, and the wisdom of God. Of all the orders of being, humans alone have free will and the possibility of turning away from God. Free will dictates the responsibility of choosing and accepting the consequences. People cannot logically argue that they are innocent victims at the mercy of heredity or

13.6   Florentine School, *Allegorical Portrait of Dante*. Ca. 1575–85. Oil on panel, 4' 2" × 3' 11¼" (1.27 × 1.19 m). National Gallery of Art, Washington, D.C. (Samuel H. Kress Collection).

On the open book are inscribed the first forty-eight lines of Canto XXV of *Paradise*, in which Dante yearns to return from exile to be honored by the Florentines. In the right background is the mountain of Purgatory, behind which is the divine glow of Paradise. With his right hand over the dome of Florence cathedral, the poet tries to protect his beloved city from the flames of Hell.

environment. With the gift of intellect and free will, each person must assume the full weight of making choices and must, as well, accept the fact that the choices are critical decisions that can affect and influence other people.

This verse translation, considered by many scholars as the best available, is by the poet and scholar Allen Mandelbaum.

Hell

Canto I

The Story

The voyager-narrator astray by night in a dark forest. Morning and the sunlit hill. Three beasts that impede his ascent. The encounter with Virgil, who offers his guidance and an alternative path through two of the three realms the voyager must visit.

When I had journeyed half of our life's way,
I found myself within a shadowed forest,
for I had lost the path that does not stray.

Ah, it is hard to speak of what it was,
that savage forest, dense and difficult,
which even in recall renews my fear:

so bitter—death is hardly more severe!
But to retell the good discovered there,
I'll also tell the other things I saw.

I cannot clearly say how I had entered   10
the wood; I was so full of sleep just at
the point where I abandoned the true path.

But when I'd reached the bottom of a hill—
it rose along the boundary of the valley
that had harassed my heart with so much fear—

I looked on high and saw its shoulders clothed
already by the rays of that same planet
which serves to lead men straight along all roads.

At this my fear was somewhat quieted;
for through the night of sorrow I had spent,   20
the lake within my heart felt terror present.

And just as he who, with exhausted breath,
having escaped from sea to shore, turns back
to watch the dangerous waters he has quit,

so did my spirit, still a fugitive,
turn back to look intently at the pass
that never has let any man survive.

I let my tired body rest awhile.
Moving again, I tried the lonely slope—
my firm foot always was the one below.   30

And almost where the hillside starts to rise—
look there!—a leopard, very quick and lithe,
a leopard covered with a spotted hide.

He did not disappear from sight, but stayed;
indeed, he so impeded my ascent
that I had often to turn back again.

The time was the beginning of the morning;
the sun was rising now in fellowship
with the same stars that had escorted it

when Divine Love first moved those things of
          beauty;   40
so that the hour and the gentle season
gave me good cause for hopefulness on seeing

that beast before me with his speckled skin;
but hope was hardly able to prevent
the fear I felt when I beheld a lion.

His head held high and ravenous with hunger—
even the air around him seemed to shudder—
this lion seemed to make his way against me.

And then a she-wolf showed herself; she seemed
to carry every craving in her leanness;   50
she had already brought despair to many.

The very sight of her so weighted me
with fearfulness that I abandoned hope
of ever climbing up that mountain slope.

Even as he who glories while he gains
will, when the time has come to tally loss,
lament with every thought and turn despondent,

so was I when I faced that restless beast,
which, even as she stalked me, step by step
had thrust me back to where the sun is speechless.   60

While I retreated down to lower ground
before my eyes there suddenly appeared
one who seemed faint because of the long silence.

When I saw him in that vast wilderness,
"Have pity on me," were the words I cried,
"whatever you may be—a shade, a man."

He answered me: "Not man; I once was man.
Both of my parents came from Lombardy,
and both claimed Mantua as native city.

And I was born, though late, *sub Julio*,   70
and lived in Rome under the good Augustus—
the season of the false and lying gods.

I was a poet, and I sang the righteous
son of Anchises who had come from Troy
when flames destroyed the pride of Ilium.

But why do you return to wretchedness?
Why not climb up the mountain of delight,
the origin and cause of every joy?"

"And are you then that Virgil, you the fountain
that freely pours so rich a stream of speech?"   80
I answered him with shame upon my brow.

"O light and honor of all other poets,
may my long study and the intense love
that made me search your volume serve me now.

You are my master and my author, you—
the only one from whom my writing drew
the noble style for which I have been honored.

You see the beast that made me turn aside;
help me, O famous sage, to stand against her,
for she has made my blood and pulses shudder."   90

"It is another path that you must take,"
he answered when he saw my tearfulness,
"if you would leave this savage wilderness;

the beast that is the cause of your outcry
allows no man to pass along her track,
but blocks him even to the point of death;

her nature is so squalid, so malicious
that she can never sate her greedy will;
when she has fed, she's hungrier than ever.

She mates with many living souls and shall   100
yet mate with many more, until the Greyhound
arrives, inflicting painful death on her.

That Hound will never feed on land or pewter
but find his fare in wisdom, love, and virtue;
his place of birth shall be between two felts.

He will restore low-lying Italy
for which the maid Camilla died of wounds,
and Nisus, Turnus, and Euryalus.

And he will hunt that beast through every city
until he thrusts her back again to Hell,   110
from which she was first sent above by envy.

Therefore, I think and judge it best for you
to follow me, and I shall guide you, taking
you from this place through an eternal place,

where you shall hear the howls of desperation
and see the ancient spirits in their pain,
as each of them laments his second death;

and you shall see those souls who are content
within the fire, for they hope to reach—
whenever that may be—the blessed people.   120

If you would then ascend as high as these,
a soul more worthy than I am will guide you;
I'll leave you in her care when I depart,

because that Emperor who reigns above,

since I have been rebellious to His law,
will not allow me entry to His city.

He governs everywhere, but rules from there;
there is His city, His high capital:
O happy those He chooses to be there!"

And I replied: "O poet—by that God   130
whom you had never come to know—I beg you,
that I may flee this evil and worse evils,

to lead me to the place of which you spoke,
that I may see the gateway of Saint Peter
and those whom you describe as sorrowful."

Then he set out, and I moved on behind him.

Canto II

The Story

The following evening. Invocation to the Muses. The narrator's questioning of his worthiness to visit the deathless world. Virgil's comforting explanation that he has been sent to help Dante by three Ladies of Heaven. The voyager heartened. Their setting out.

Canto III

The Story

The inscription above the Gate of Hell. The ante-Inferno, where the shades of those who lived without praise and without blame now intermingle with the neutral angels. He who made the great refusal. The River Acheron. Charon. Dante's loss of his senses as the earth trembles.

THROUGH ME THE WAY INTO THE SUFFERING
   CITY,
THROUGH ME THE WAY TO THE ETERNAL PAIN,
THROUGH ME THE WAY THAT RUNS AMONG THE
   LOST.

JUSTICE URGED ON MY HIGH ARTIFICER;
MY MAKER WAS DIVINE AUTHORITY,
THE HIGHEST WISDOM, AND THE PRIMAL LOVE.

BEFORE ME NOTHING BUT ETERNAL THINGS
WERE MADE, AND I ENDURE ETERNALLY.
ABANDON EVERY HOPE, WHO ENTER HERE.

These words—their aspect was obscure—I read   10
inscribed above a gateway, and I said:
"Master, their meaning is difficult for me."

And he to me, as one who comprehends:
"Here one must leave behind all hesitation;
here every cowardice must meet its death.

For we have reached the place of which I spoke,
where you will see the miserable people,
those who have lost the good of the intellect."

And when, with gladness in his face, he placed
his hand upon my own, to comfort me,   20
he drew me in among the hidden things.

Here sighs and lamentations and loud cries
were echoing across the starless air,
so that, as soon as I set out, I wept.

Strange utterances, horrible pronouncements,
accents of anger, words of suffering,

and voices shrill and faint, and beating hands—
all went to make a tumult that will whirl
forever through that turbid, timeless air,
like sand that eddies when a whirlwind swirls.   30

   And I—my head oppressed by horror—said:
"Master, what is it that I hear? Who are
those people so defeated by their pain?"

   And he to me: "This miserable way
is taken by the sorry souls of those
who lived without disgrace and without praise.

   They now commingle with the coward angels,
the company of those who were not rebels
nor faithful to their God, but stood apart.

   The heavens, that their beauty not be lessened,   40
have cast them out, nor will deep Hell receive them—
even the wicked cannot glory in them."

   And I: "What is it, master, that oppresses
these souls, compelling them to wail so loud?"
He answered: "I shall tell you in few words.

   Those who are here can place no hope in death,
and their blind life is so abject that they
are envious of every other fate.

   The world will let no fame of theirs endure;
both justice and compassion must disdain them;   50
let us not talk of them, but look and pass."

   And I, looking more closely, saw a banner
that, as it wheeled about, raced on—so quick
that any respite seemed unsuited to it.

   Behind that banner trailed so long a file
of people—I should never have believed
that death could have unmade so many souls.

   After I had identified a few,
I saw and recognized the shade of him
who made, through cowardice, the great refusal.   60

   At once I understood with certainty:
this company contained the cowardly,
hateful to God and to His enemies.

   These wretched ones, who never were alive,
went naked and were stung again, again
by horseflies and by wasps that circled them.

   The insects streaked their faces with their blood,
which, mingled with their tears, fell at their feet,
where it was gathered up by sickening worms.

   And then, looking beyond them, I could see   70
a crowd along the bank of a great river;
at which I said: "Allow me now to know

   who are these people—master—and what law
has made them seem so eager for the crossing,
as I can see despite the feeble light."

   And he to me: "When we have stopped along
the melancholy shore of Acheron,
then all these matters will be plain to you."

   At that, with eyes ashamed, downcast, and fearing
that what I said had given him offense,   80
I did not speak until we reached the river.

   And here, advancing toward us, in a boat,
an aged man—his hair was white with years—
was shouting: "Woe to you, corrupted souls!

   Forget your hope of ever seeing Heaven:
I come to lead you to the other shore,
to the eternal dark, to fire and frost.

And you approaching there, you living soul,
keep well away from these—they are the dead."
But when he saw I made no move to go,   90

   he said: "Another way and other harbors—
not here—will bring you passage to your shore:
a lighter craft will have to carry you."

   My guide then: "Charon, don't torment yourself:
our passage has been willed above, where One
can do what He has willed; and ask no more."

   Now silence fell upon the wooly cheeks
of Charon, pilot of the livid marsh,
whose eyes were ringed about with wheels of flame.

   But all those spirits, naked and exhausted,   100
had lost their color, and they gnashed their teeth
as soon as they heard Charon's cruel words;

   they execrated God and their own parents
and humankind, and then the place and time
of their conception's seed and of their birth.

   Then they forgathered, huddled in one throng,
weeping aloud along that wretched shore
which waits for all who have no fear of God.

   The demon Charon, with his eyes like embers,
by signaling to them, has all embark;   110
his oar strikes anyone who stretches out.

   As, in the autumn, leaves detach themselves,
first one and then the other, till the bough
sees all its fallen garments on the ground,

   similarly, the evil seed of Adam
descended from the shoreline one by one,
when signaled, as a falcon—called—will come.

   So do they move across the darkened waters;
even before they reach the farther shore,
new ranks already gather on this bank.   120

   "My son," the gracious master said to me,
"those who have died beneath the wrath of God,
all these assemble here from every country;

   and they are eager for the river crossing
because celestial justice spurs them on,
so that their fear is turned into desire.

   No good soul ever takes its passage here;
therefore, if Charon has complained of you,
by now you can be sure what his words mean."

   And after this was said, the darkened plain   130
quaked so tremendously—the memory
of terror then, bathes me in sweat again.

   A whirlwind burst out of the tear-drenched earth,
a wind that crackled with a bloodred light,
a light that overcame all of my senses;
   and like a man whom sleep has seized, I fell.

Canto IV

The Story

*Dante's awakening to the First Circle, or Limbo,
inhabited by those who were worthy but lived before
Christianity and/or without baptism. The welcoming of
Virgil and Dante by Homer, Horace, Ovid, Lucan. The
catalogue of other great-hearted spirits in the noble
castle of Limbo.*

The heavy sleep within my head was smashed
by an enormous thunderclap, so that
I started up as one whom force awakens;
     I stood erect and turned my rested eyes
from side to side, and I stared steadily
to learn what place it was surrounding me.
     In truth I found myself upon the brink
of an abyss, the melancholy valley
containing thundering, unending wailings.
     That valley, dark and deep and filled with mist,   10
is such that, though I gazed into its pit,
I was unable to discern a thing.
     "Let us descend into the blind world now,"
the poet, who was deathly pale, began;
"I shall go first and you will follow me."
     But I, who'd seen the change in his complexion,
said: "How shall I go on if you are frightened,
you who have always helped dispel my doubts?"
     And he to me: "The anguish of the people
whose place is here below, has touched my face   20
with the compassion you mistake for fear.
     Let us go on, the way that waits is long."
So he set out, and so he had me enter
on that first circle girdling the abyss.
     Here, for as much as hearing could discover,
there was no outcry louder than the sighs
that caused the everlasting air to tremble.
     The sighs arose from sorrow without torments,
out of the crowds—the many multitudes—
of infants and of women and of men.   30
     The kindly master said: "Do you not ask
who are these spirits whom you see before you?
I'd have you know, before you go ahead,
     they did not sin; and yet, though they have merits,
that's not enough, because they lacked baptism,
the portal of the faith that you embrace.
     And if they lived before Christianity,
they did not worship God in fitting ways;
and of such spirits I myself am one.
     For these defects, and for no other evil,   40
we now are lost and punished just with this:
we have no hope and yet we live in longing."
     Great sorrow seized my heart on hearing him,
for I had seen some estimable men
among the souls suspended in that limbo.
     "Tell me, my master, tell me, lord," I then
began because I wanted to be certain
of that belief which vanquishes all errors,
     "did any ever go—by his own merit
or others'—from this place toward blessedness?"   50
And he, who understood my covert speech,
     replied: "I was new-entered on this state
when I beheld a Great Lord enter here;
the crown he wore, a sign of victory.
     He carried off the shade of our first father,
of his son Abel, and the shade of Noah,
of Moses, the obedient legislator,
     of father Abraham, David the king
of Israel, his father, and his sons,
and Rachel, she for whom he worked so long,   60
     and many others—and He made them blessed;

and I should have you know that, before them,
there were no human souls that had been saved."
     We did not stay our steps although he spoke;
we still continued onward through the wood—
the wood, I say, where many spirits thronged.
     Our path had not gone far beyond the point
where I had slept, when I beheld a fire
win out against a hemisphere of shadows.
     We still were at a little distance from it,   70
but not so far I could not see in part
that honorable men possessed that place.
     "O you who honor art and science both,
who are these souls whose dignity has kept
their way of being, separate from the rest?"
     And he to me: "The honor of their name,
which echoes up above within your life,
gains Heaven's grace, and that advances them."
     Meanwhile there was a voice that I could hear:
"Pay honor to the estimable poet;   80
his shadow, which had left us, now returns."
     After that voice was done, when there was silence,
I saw four giant shades approaching us;
in aspect, they were neither sad nor joyous.
     My kindly master then began by saying:
"Look well at him who holds that sword in hand,
who moves before the other three as lord.
     That shade is Homer, the consummate poet;
the other one is Horace, satirist;
the third is Ovid, and the last is Lucan.   90
     Because each of these spirits shares with me
the name called out before by the lone voice,
they welcome me—and, doing that, do well."
     And so I saw that splendid school assembled,
led by the lord of song incomparable,
who like an eagle soars above the rest.
     Soon after they had talked awhile together,
they turned to me, saluting cordially;
and having witnessed this, my master smiled;
     and even greater honor then was mine,   100
for they invited me to join their ranks—
I was the sixth among such intellects.
     So did we move along and toward the light,
talking of things about which silence here
is just as seemly as our speech was there.
     We reached the base of an exalted castle,
encircled seven times by towering walls,
defended all around by a fair stream.
     We forded this as if upon hard ground;
I entered seven portals with these sages;   110
we reached a meadow of green flowering plants.
     The people here had eyes both grave and slow;
their features carried great authority;
they spoke infrequently, with gentle voices.
     We drew aside to one part of the meadow,
an open place both high and filled with light,
and we could see all those who were assembled.
     Facing me there, on the enameled green,
great-hearted souls were shown to me and I
still glory in my having witnessed them.   120
     I saw Electra with her many comrades,
among whom I knew Hector and Aeneas,

and Caesar, in his armor, falcon-eyed.
I saw Camilla and Penthesilea
and, on the other side, saw King Latinus,
who sat beside Lavinia, his daughter.
I saw that Brutus who drove Tarquin out,
Lucretia, Julia, Marcia, and Cornelia,
and, solitary, set apart, Saladin.
When I had raised my eyes a little higher,   130
I saw the master of the men who know,
seated in philosophic family.
There all look up to him, all do him honor:
there I beheld both Socrates and Plato,
closest to him, in front of all the rest;
Democritus, who ascribes the world to chance,
Diogenes, Empedocles, and Zeno,
and Thales, Anaxagoras, Heraclitus;
I saw the good collector of medicinals,
I mean Dioscorides; and I saw Orpheus,   140
and Tully, Linus, moral Seneca;
and Euclid the geometer, and Ptolemy,
Hippocrates and Galen, Avicenna,
Averroës, of the great Commentary.
I cannot here describe them all in full;
my ample theme impels me onward so:
what's told is often less than the event.
The company of six divides in two;
my knowing guide leads me another way,
beyond the quiet, into trembling air.   150
And I have reached a part where no thing gleams.

Canto V

The Story

*The Second Circle, where the Lustful are forever
buffeted by violent storm. Minos. The catalogue of
carnal sinners. Francesca da Rimini and her brother-in-
law, Paolo Malatesta. Francesca's tale of their love and
death, at which Dante faints.*

So I descended from the first enclosure
down to the second circle, that which girdles
less space but grief more great, that goads to weeping.
There dreadful Minos stands, gnashing his teeth:
examining the sins of those who enter,
he judges and assigns as his tail twines.
I mean that when the spirit born to evil
appears before him, it confesses all;
and he, the connoisseur of sin, can tell
the depth in Hell appropriate to it;   10
as many times as Minos wraps his tail
around himself, that marks the sinner's level.
Always there is a crowd that stands before him
each soul in turn advances toward that judgment;
they speak and hear, then they are cast below.
Arresting his extraordinary task,
Minos, as soon as he had seen me, said:
"O you who reach this house of suffering,
be careful how you enter, whom you trust;
the gate is wide, but do not be deceived!"   20
To which my guide replied: "But why protest?

Do not attempt to block his fated path:
our passage has been willed above, where One
can do what He has willed; and ask no more."
Now notes of desperation have begun
to overtake my hearing; now I come
where mighty lamentation beats against me.
I reached a place where every light is muted,
which bellows like the sea beneath a tempest,
when it is battered by opposing winds.   30
The hellish hurricane, which never rests,
drives on the spirits with its violence:
wheeling and pounding, it harasses them.
When they come up against the ruined slope,
then there are cries and wailing and lament,
and there they curse the force of the divine.
I learned that those who undergo this torment
are damned because they sinned within the flesh,
subjecting reason to the rule of lust.
And as, in the cold season, starlings' wings   40
bear them along in broad and crowded ranks,
so does that blast bear on the guilty spirits:
now here, now there, now down, now up, it drives
   them
There is no hope that ever comforts them—
no hope for rest and none for lesser pain.
And just as cranes in flight will chant their lays,
arraying their long file across the air,
so did the shades I saw approaching, borne
by that assailing wind, lament and moan;
so that I asked him: "Master, who are those   50
who suffer punishment in this dark air?"
"The first of those about whose history
you want to know," my master then told me,
"once ruled as empress over many nations.
Her vice of lust became so customary
that she made license licit in her laws
to free her from the scandal she had caused.
She is Semíramis, of whom we read
that she was Ninus' wife and his successor:
she held the land the Sultan now commands.   60
That other spirit killed herself for love,
and she betrayed the ashes of Sychaeus;
the wanton Cleopatra follows next.
See Helen, for whose sake so many years
of evil had to pass; see great Achilles,
who finally met love—in his last battle.
See Paris, Tristan . . ."—and he pointed out
and named to me more than a thousand shades
departed from our life because of love.
No sooner had I heard my teacher name   70
the ancient ladies and the knights, than pity
seized me, and I was like a man astray.
My first words: "Poet, I should willingly
speak with those two who go together there
and seem so lightly carried by the wind."
And he to me: "You'll see when they draw closer
to us, and then you may appeal to them
by that love which impels them. They will come."
No sooner had the wind bent them toward us
than I urged on my voice: "O battered souls,   80
if One does not forbid it, speak with us."

Ca

Th

The
wit
pur
sco
Jas
exc

ma
as

is a
wh

and
its

in c
the

and
righ

rur
tho

wh
he

I s
filli

to
be

co
tha

up
an

sa
wl

the
a :

of
"I

m
ar

by
fo

m

Even as doves when summoned by desire,
borne forward by their will, move through the air
　with wings uplifted, still, to their sweet nest,
those spirits left the ranks where Dido suffers,
approaching us through the malignant air;
　so powerful had been my loving cry.
　"O living being, gracious and benign,
who through the darkened air have come to visit
our souls that stained the world with blood, if He   90
　who rules the universe were friend to us,
then we should pray to Him to give you peace,
for you have pitied our atrocious state.
　Whatever pleases you to hear and speak
will please us, too, to hear and speak with you,
　now while the wind is silent, in this place.
　The land where I was born lies on that shore
to which the Po together with the waters
that follow it descends to final rest.
　Love, that can quickly seize the gentle heart,   100
took hold of him because of the fair body
taken from me—how that was done still wounds me.
　Love, that releases no beloved from loving,
took hold of me so strongly through his beauty
that, as you see, it has not left me yet.
　Love led the two of us unto one death.
Caïna waits for him who took our life."
These words were borne across from them to us.
　When I had listened to those injured souls,
I bent my head and held it low until   110
the poet asked of me: "What are you thinking?"
　When I replied, my words began: "Alas,
how many gentle thoughts, how deep a longing,
had led them to the agonizing pass!"
　Then I addressed my speech again to them,
and I began: "Francesca, your afflictions
move me to tears of sorrow and of pity.
　But tell me, in the time of gentle sighs,
with what and in what way did Love allow you
to recognize your still uncertain longings?"   120
　And she to me: "There is no greater sorrow
than thinking back upon a happy time
in misery—and this your teacher knows.
　Yet if you long so much to understand
the first root of our love, then I shall tell
my tale to you as one who weeps and speaks.
　One day, to pass the time away, we read
of Launcelot—how love had overcome him.
We were alone, and we suspected nothing.
　And time and time again that reading led   130
our eyes to meet, and made our faces pale,
and yet one point alone defeated us.
　When we had read how the desired smile
was kissed by one who was so true a lover,
this one, who never shall be parted from me,
　while all his body trembled, kissed my mouth.
A Gallehault indeed, that book and he
who wrote it, too; that day we read no more."
　And while one spirit said these words to me,
the other wept, so that—because of pity—   140
I fainted, as if I had met my death.
　And then I fell as a dead body falls.

Cantos VI–XI

The Story

*Dante finds the Gluttonous in the Third Circle, where
they are flailed by cold and filthy rain. In the Fourth Circle
the Avaricious and the Prodigal endlessly roll weights in
circles while, in the Fifth Circle, the Wrathful and Sullen
are tormented by the River Styx. The two poets are
rowed across the Styx to the City of Dis but cannot enter
without divine intervention. The Furies appear and
threaten to unloose Medusa. Dante is frightened but a
Heavenly Messenger appears to open the city gates.
They go into the Sixth Circle where they see the burning
tombs of the Heretics.*

Canto XII

The Story

*The Seventh Circle, First Ring: the Violent against their
Neighbors. The Minotaur. The Centaurs, led by Chiron,
who assigns Nessus to guide Dante and Virgil across the
boiling river of blood (Phlegethon). In that river, Tyrants
and Murderers, immersed, watched over by the Centaurs.*

　The place that we had reached for our descent
along the bank was alpine; what reclined
upon that bank would, too, repel all eyes.
　Just like the toppled mass of rock that struck—
because of earthquake or eroded props—
the Adige on its flank, this side of Trent,
　where from the mountain top from which it thrust
down to the plain, the rock is shattered so
that it permits a path for those above:
　such was the passage down to that ravine.   10
And at the edge above the cracked abyss,
there lay outstretched the infamy of Crete,
　conceived within the counterfeited cow;
and, catching sight of us, he bit himself
like one whom fury devastates within.
　Turning to him, my sage cried out: "Perhaps
you think this is the Duke of Athens here,
who, in the world above, brought you your death.
　Be off, you beast; this man who comes has not
been tutored by your sister; all he wants   20
in coming here is to observe your torments."
　Just as the bull that breaks loose from its halter
the moment it receives the fatal stroke,
and cannot run but plunges back and forth,
　so did I see the Minotaur respond;
and my alert guide cried: "Run toward the pass;
it's better to descend while he's berserk."
　And so we made our way across that heap
of stones, which often moved beneath my feet
because my weight was somewhat strange for them.   30
　While climbing down, I thought. He said: "You
　　wonder,
perhaps, about that fallen mass, watched over
by the inhuman rage I have just quenched.
　Now I would have you know: the other time

the arch until the bridge's highest point.

This was the place we reached; the ditch beneath
held people plunged in excrement that seemed
as if it had been poured from human privies.

And while my eyes searched that abysmal sight,
I saw one with a head so smeared with shit,
one could not see if he were lay or cleric.

He howled: "Why do you stare more greedily
at me than at the others who are filthy?"
And I: "Because, if I remember right,   120

I have seen you before, with your hair dry;
and so I eye you more than all: you are
Alessio Interminei of Lucca."

Then he continued, pounding on his pate:
"I am plunged here because of flatteries—
of which my tongue had such sufficiency."

At which my guide advised me: "See you thrust
your head a little farther to the front,
so that your eyes can clearly glimpse the face

of that besmirched, bedraggled harridan   130
who scratches at herself with shit-filled nails,
and now she crouches, now she stands upright.

That is Thaïs, the harlot who returned
her lover's question, 'Are you very grateful
to me?' by saying, 'Yes, enormously.'

And now our sight has had its fill of this."

Cantos XIX–XXXIII

The Story

*The Simonists are in the Eighth Circle (including Pope
Nicholas III), as are the Diviners, Astrologers, and
Magicians, each of the latter with their heads turned
backwards. Further on in the same circle they see
Swindlers plunged in boiling pitch, Hypocrites clothed in
lead cloaks, Thieves bitten by serpents, and the
Fraudulent Counselors (including Ulysses and Diomedes)
clothed in eternal flames. The Sowers of Scandal and
Schism (including Mohammed and Ali), Alchemists
plagued by scabs, Counterfeiters, and Liars occupy the
remainder of the circle. The poets pass to the final circle,
the Ninth, and gaze down into the central pit of Hell. Two
giants lower them to the icy floor, where they see
Traitors to their Kin and Traitors against their Guests.*

Canto XXXIV

The Story

*The Ninth Circle, Fourth Ring, called Judecca, where
Traitors against their Benefactors are fully covered by
ice. Dis, or Lucifer, emperor of that kingdom, his three
mouths rending Judas, Brutus, and Cassius. Descent of
Virgil and Dante down Lucifer's body to the other,
southern hemisphere. Their vision of the stars.*

"Vexilla regis prodeunt inferni
toward us; and therefore keep your eyes ahead,"
my master said, "to see if you can spy him."

Just as, when night falls on our hemisphere

or when a heavy fog is blowing thick,
a windmill seems to wheel when seen far off,
so then I seemed to see that sort of structure.
And next, because the wind was strong, I shrank
behind my guide; there was no other shelter.

And now—with fear I set it down in meter—   10
I was where all the shades were fully covered
but visible as wisps of straw in glass.

There some lie flat and others stand erect,
one on his head, and one upon his soles;
and some bend face to feet, just like a bow.

But after we had made our way ahead
my master felt he now should have me see
that creature who was once a handsome presence;

he stepped aside and made me stop, and said:
"Look! Here is Dis, and this the place where you   20
will have to arm yourself with fortitude."

O reader, do not ask of me how I
grew faint and frozen then—I cannot write it:
all words would fall far short of what it was.

I did not die, and I was not alive;
think for yourself, if you have any wit,
what I became, deprived of life and death.

The emperor of the despondent kingdom
so towered from the ice, up from midchest,
that I match better with a giant's breadth   30

than giants match the measure of his arms;
now you can gauge the size of all of him
if it is in proportion to such parts.

If he was once as handsome as he now
is ugly and, despite that, raised his brows
against his Maker, one can understand

how every sorrow has its source in him!
I marveled when I saw that, on his head,
he had three faces: one—in front—bloodred;

and then another two that, just above   40
the midpoint of each shoulder, joined the first;
and at the crown, all three were reattached;

the right looked somewhat yellow, somewhat white;
the left in its appearance was like those
who come from where the Nile, descending, flows.

Beneath each face of his, two wings spread out,
as broad as suited so immense a bird:
I've never seen a ship with sails so wide.

They had no feathers, but were fashioned like
a bat's; and he was agitating them,   50
so that three winds made their way out from him—

and all Cocytus froze before those winds.
He wept out of six eyes; and down three chins,
tears gushed together with a bloody froth.

Within each mouth—he used it like a grinder—
with gnashing teeth he tore to bits a sinner,
so that he brought much pain to three at once.

The forward sinner found that biting nothing
when matched against the clawing, for at times
his back was stripped completely of its hide.

"That soul up there who has to suffer most,"   60
my master said: "Judas Iscariot—
his head inside, he jerks his legs without.

Of those two others, with their heads beneath,
the one who hangs from that black snout is Brutus—

see how he writhes and does not say a word!
That other, who seems so robust, is Cassius
But night is come again, and it is time
for us to leave; we have seen everything."
Just as he asked, I clasped him round the neck;   70
and he watched for the chance of time and place,
and when the wings were open wide enough,
he took fast hold upon the shaggy flanks
and then descended, down from tuft to tuft,
between the tangled hair and icy crusts.
When we had reached the point at which the thigh
revolves, just at the swelling of the hip,
my guide, with heavy strain and rugged work,
reversed his head to where his legs had been
and grappled on the hair, as one who climbs—   80
I thought that we were going back to Hell.
"Hold tight," my master said—he panted like
a man exhausted—"it is by such stairs
that we must take our leave of so much evil."
Then he slipped through a crevice in a rock
and placed me on the edge of it, to sit;
that done, he climbed toward me with steady steps.
I raised my eyes, believing I should see
the half of Lucifer that I had left;
instead I saw him with his legs turned up;   90
and if I then became perplexed, do let
the ignorant be judges—those who can
not understand what point I had just crossed.
"Get up," my master said, "be on your feet:
the way is long, the path is difficult;
the sun's already back to middle tierce."
It was no palace hall, the place in which
we found ourselves, but with its rough-hewn floor
and scanty light, a dungeon built by nature.
"Before I free myself from this abyss,   100
master," I said when I had stood up straight,
"tell me enough to see I don't mistake:
Where is the ice? And how is he so placed
head downward? Tell me, too, how has the sun
in so few hours gone from night to morning?"
And he to me: "You still believe you are
north of the center, where I grasped the hair
of the damned worm who pierces through the world.
And you were there as long as I descended;
but when I turned, that's when you passed the point   110
to which, from every part, all weights are drawn.
And now you stand beneath the hemisphere
opposing that which cloaks the great dry lands
and underneath whose zenith died the Man
whose birth and life were sinless in this world.
Your feet are placed upon a little sphere
that forms the other face of the Judecca.
Here it is morning when it's evening there;
and he whose hair has served us as a ladder
is still fixed, even as he was before.   120
This was the side on which he fell from Heaven;
for fear of him, the land that once loomed here
made of the sea a veil and rose into
our hemisphere; and that land which appears
upon this side—perhaps to flee from him—
left here this hollow space and hurried upward."

There is a place below, the limit of
that cave, its farthest point from Beelzebub,
a place one cannot see: it is discovered
by ear—there is a sounding stream that flows   130
along the hollow of a rock eroded
by winding waters and the slope is easy.
My guide and I came on that hidden road
to make our way back into the bright world;
and with no care for any rest, we climbed—
he first, I following—until I saw,
through a round opening, some of those things
of beauty Heaven bears. It was from there
that we emerged, to see—once more—the stars.

Dante's Ultimate Vision

Dante has ascended the Mountain of Purgatory and, led
by Beatrice, has moved through the spheres of the
heavens, where he has been instructed in the nature of
God's order for the universe; in his own spirit he has
experienced this love, order, and wisdom. Finally they
have reached the Empyrean, beyond the last sphere of
the heavens, which is the place of God and of souls who
have experienced the joy of salvation. Here St. Bernard,
the special devotee of the Virgin, becomes Dante's
guide.

Paradise

Canto XXXIII

The Story

*Still the Tenth Heaven: the Empyrean. Prayer of St.
Bernard to the Virgin. Her acknowledgment of his prayer.
Dante sees the Eternal Light. The three circles of the
Trinity. The mystery of the Incarnation. The flashing light
that fulfills Dante's vision. His desire and will at one with
Love.*

"Virgin mother, daughter of your Son,
more humble and sublime than any creature,
fixed goal decreed from all eternity,
you are the one who gave to human nature
so much nobility that its Creator
did not disdain His being made its creature.
That love whose warmth allowed this flower to bloom
within the everlasting peace—was love
rekindled in your womb; for us above,
you are the noonday torch of charity,   10
and there below, on earth, among the mortals,
you are a living spring of hope. Lady,
you are so high, you can so intercede,
that he who would have grace but does not seek
your aid, may long to fly but has no wings.
Your loving-kindness does not only answer
the one who asks, but it is often ready
to answer freely long before the asking.
In you compassion is, in you is pity,
in you is generosity, in you   20
is every goodness found in any creature.

This man—who from the deepest hollow in
the universe, up to this height, has seen
the lives of spirits, one by one—now pleads
    with you, through grace, to grant him so much virtue
that he may lift his vision higher still—
may lift it toward the ultimate salvation.
    And I, who never burned for my own vision
more than I burn for his, do offer you
all of my prayers—and pray that they may not   30
    fall short—that, with your prayers, you may disperse
all of the clouds of his mortality
so that the Highest Joy be his to see.
    This, too, O Queen, who can do what you would,
I ask of you: that after such a vision,
his sentiments preserve their perseverance.
    May your protection curb his mortal passions.
See Beatrice—how many saints with her!
They join my prayers! They clasp their hands to you!"
    The eyes that are revered and loved by God   40
now fixed upon the supplicant, showed us
how welcome such devotions are to her;
    then her eyes turned to the Eternal Light—
there, do not think that any creature's eye
can find its way as clearly as her sight.
    And I, who now was nearing Him who is
the end of all desires, as I ought,
lifted my longing to its ardent limit.
    Bernard was signaling—he smiled—to me
to turn my eyes on high; but I already   50
was doing what he wanted me to do,
    because my sight, becoming pure, was able
to penetrate the ray of Light more deeply—
That Light, sublime, which in Itself is true.
    From that point on, what I could see was greater
than speech can show: at such a sight, it fails—
and memory fails when faced with such excess.
    As one who sees within a dream, and, later
the passion that had been imprinted stays,
but nothing of the rest returns to mind,   60
    such am I, for my vision almost fades
completely, yet it still distills within
my heart the sweetness that was born of it.
    So is the snow, beneath the sun, unsealed;
and so, on the light leaves, beneath the wind,
the oracles the Sibyl wrote were lost.
    O Highest Light, You, raised so far above
the minds of mortals, to my memory
give back something of Your epiphany,
    and make my tongue so powerful that I   70
may leave to people of the future one
gleam of the glory that is Yours, for by
    returning somewhat to my memory
and echoing awhile within these lines,
Your victory will be more understood.
    The living ray that I endured was so
acute that I believe I should have gone
astray had my eyes turned away from it.
    I can recall that I, because of this,
was bolder in sustaining it until   80
my vision reached the Infinite Goodness.
    O grace abounding, through which I presumed

to set my eyes on the Eternal Light
so long that I spent all my sight on it!
    In its profundity I saw—ingathered
and bound by love into one single volume—
what, in the universe, seems separate, scattered:
    substances, accidents, and dispositions
as if conjoined—in such a way that what
I tell is only rudimentary.   90
    I think I saw the universal shape
which that knot takes; for, speaking this, I feel
a joy that is more ample. That one moment
    brings more forgetfulness to me than twenty-
five centuries have brought to the endeavor
that startled Neptune with the Argo's shadow!
    So was my mind—completely rapt, intent,
steadfast, and motionless—gazing; and it
grew ever more enkindled as it watched.
    Whoever sees that Light is soon made such   100
that it would be impossible for him
to set that Light aside for other sight;
    because the good, the object of the will,
is fully gathered in that Light; outside
that Light, what there is perfect is defective.
    What little I recall is to be told,
from this point on, in words more weak than those
of one whose infant tongue still bathes at the breast.
    And not because more than one simple semblance
was in the Living Light at which I gazed—   110
for It is always what It was before—
    but through my sight, which as I gazed grew
        stronger,
that sole appearance, even as I altered,
    seemed to be changing. In the deep and bright
essence of that exalted Light, three circles
appeared to me; they had three different colors,
but all of them were of the same dimension;
    one circle seemed reflected by the second,
as rainbow is by rainbow, and the third
seemed fire breathed equally by those two circles.   120
    How incomplete is speech, how weak, when set
against my thought! And this, to what I saw
is such—to call it little is too much.
    Eternal Light, You only dwell within
Yourself, and only You know You; Self-knowing,
Self-known, You love and smile upon Yourself!
    That circle—which, begotten so, appeared
in You as light reflected—when my eyes
had watched it with attention for some time,
    within itself and colored like itself,   130
to me seemed painted with our effigy,
so that my sight was set on it completely.
    As the geometer intently seeks
to square the circle, but he cannot reach,
through thought on thought, the principle he needs,
    so I searched that strange sight: I wished to see
the way in which our human effigy
suited the circle and found place in it—
    and my own wings were far too weak for that.
But then my mind was struck by light that flashed   140
and, with this light, received what it had asked.
    Here force failed my high fantasy; but my

desire and will were moved already—like
a wheel revolving uniformly—by
   the Love that moves the sun and the other stars.

STUDY QUESTIONS

One way to understand Dante's Hell more clearly is
to convert his allegorical meanings into modern
terms. Following are just a few examples:

1. What is actually meant by the "shadowed forest"?
2. What might the leopard, lion, and she-wolf stand
   for? Consider these clues. Cantos III–VIII
   describe sins of incontinence such as lust,
   gluttony, and hoarding. Cantos IX–XXVII cover
   sins of violence such as heresy and suicide. The
   remaining cantos are about sins of malicious
   fraud such as pandering, seducing, thieving, and
   treason.
3. Translate the inscription above the Gate of Hell
   into modern English.

SUMMARY

The eleventh century marked the beginning of a new era
we call the High Middle Ages. Cities began to grow and
develop. The walls behind which men and women had
sheltered themselves—the authoritarian church, the
rigid structures of feudalism and manorialism—began to
crumble. International trade began not long after the
first Crusader entered Jerusalem in 1099. Even more
importantly, contact with the civilized Middle East
tapped the reservoir of Islamic science, medicine, and
mathematics plus the culture of ancient Greece that
Islamic scholars had carefully preserved.

Partly because of the increasing influence of
important women, feudalism began to give way to the
more civilized code of chivalry. Running parallel to this
was the cult of the Virgin, in whose honor hundreds of
magnificent churches were erected.

The tenets of Scholasticism, the dominant mode of
Christian thought, were challenged by the Battle of
Universals that marked the beginning of a conflict
between faith and reason. The rediscovery of the
complete works of Aristotle also challenged the
theologians. Further, the proliferation of medieval
universities led inevitably to intellectual challenges of the
monolithic church.

In philosophy, the synthesis of the High Middle
Ages was made by Thomas Aquinas, who merged
Christian and Aristotelian thought. Dante's *Divine
Comedy* delineated the options available to humankind.

The goal was still heaven but people were free to pursue
it under their own power and through the discipline of
their own will. In Gothic religious architecture—notably
in the great cathedrals—the world of the senses and the
world of the spirit were triumphantly united.

CULTURE AND HUMAN VALUES

The period of balance of the High Middle Ages was
glorious, an era of magnificent achievements in art,
architecture, literature, music, and philosophy. Although
Christian doctrine remained central, there was a
discernible shift in attitudes and values in the ever-
growing educated class. Church teachings that had been
accepted for centuries were increasingly questioned. The
issue was not just the faith but the hierarchy. This is not
to say that there was widespread unrest, but the Avignon
papacy (Babylonian Captivity) and Great Schism had
exposed an all too fallible power structure. The church
preached obedience to authority, but what if that
authority were corrupt?

In looking back on the volatile fourteenth century,
one can perceive the beginning of the restless stirring
that would eventually lead to the Renaissance, the
Reformation, and the modern world. Call it 20–20
hindsight, but the ingredients were there: the rise of
science; the proliferating universities; the rediscovery of
Aristotle, followed by ancient Greek culture as preserved
in the Islamic world.

A new value emerged during the age, a marvelous
rediscovery called knowledge. Monasteries had
preserved and endlessly copied what the church deemed
important from the classical past, but there had been no
real search for knowledge since the expiration of Graeco-
Roman civilization. Thomism had responded to the new
movement by justifying the acquisition of knowledge as
a prerequisite for philosophy, law, and divine
understanding. Whether the thirst for knowledge
prompted the founding of universities or whether the
universities sparked the search cannot be known.
Whatever the case, there arose a need for knowledge for
its own sake—a burning desire to know everything about
the physical world. This ceaseless drive accounts for the
rise of science, for "whatever scientists do, the most
significant thing they do is to try to find out things that
are not known."[35] Science investigates the material
world; and so began a slow but inexorable shift from the
spirituality of the Middle Ages to the materialism of the
modern world.

35. Dennis Flanagan, *Flanagan's Version: A Spectator's Guide to
    Science on the Eve of the 21st Century* (New York: Alfred A.
    Knopf, 1988), p. 13.

onginned   godpell   apt   matheuf
IICIPIT euaggeli   um secundum matthei..
                        cnifter

Th
lu
lu

untedlice
rucð pæf
cnifteef ncu
pe ro

godlice

cynnpeccenife t cneupefu   ruceð dur   pieh   mið þr

RATIONILIBRATCM

pær   bi poeddes t beboden t bepeurtnud t betæht

EXEIEOSBOLIXAIA

moðer   luf

MATEREIUSMARICCIOSEBR

rogemar
nalleh t
banne.

abiatha
ðe-aldoy
pær inð
tið inhr
ralem p
byrcob.h
beoð ma
ioyephi
gemenn
tobegieo
annt n
claenn

CHAPTER 14

The Medieval Synthesis in Art

The giants of medieval art are comparable to Dante and Chaucer but few names have come down to us. For one thing, the creation rather than the creator was much more important in the God-centered world of the Middle Ages; the cathedral dedicated to Our Lady and built for the greater glory of God far transcended the identity of the master builder who supervised its construction. Moreover, individual personalities were generally submerged in the groups of artists who labored on such cooperative projects as illuminated manuscripts, tapestries, stained glass windows, architectural sculpture, and, especially, the majestic Romanesque and Gothic churches and cathedrals that rose all over Europe.

The complexity of that art and architecture and the sheer length of the era we are examining—from the seventh through the fifteenth centuries—make it necessary (and prudent) to divide this chapter into the following periods or styles (all dates approximate):

CHRONOLOGICAL OVERVIEW

600–800	Hiberno-Saxon Style
750–900	Carolingian Art
1000–1150/1200	Romanesque Style
1140–1200	Early Gothic Style
1200–1300	High Gothic Style in France
	Gothic Style Elsewhere in Europe
1300–1500s	Late Gothic Style

Opposite Bishop Eadfrith (?), "X–P Page," fol. 29, *Lindisfarne Gospels*. Ca. 698. Illuminated manuscript, 13½ × 9¾" (34.3 × 24.8 cm). British Library, London.

HIBERNO-SAXON PERIOD, CA. 600–800

Though never part of the Roman Empire, Ireland was known to the Romans, who called it *Hibernia*. This later became *Ivernin* in Old Celtic and then *Erin* in Old Irish. Occupied by Celts and Christianized by St. Patrick of Gaul, Ireland was cut off from the continent by the Anglo-Saxon conquest of England. This isolation led to the development of a unique form of Christian monasticism patterned after the solitary hermits of Egypt rather than the urbanized Roman version of Christianity. Founding monasteries in the countryside, Irish monks cultivated a strict ascetic discipline and, unlike the desert saints, a deep devotion to scholarship. Preempting the power of the bishops, Irish monasteries sponsored a remarkable missionary program in England and western Europe resulting in a spiritual and cultural ascendancy fittingly called the Irish Golden Age (ca. 600–ca. 800).

Manuscripts were produced in abundance to supplement these missionary activities, especially numerous copies of the Bible, all elaborately decorated to signify the supreme importance of the sacred texts. Displaying little interest in the figurative art of Roman Christianity, monks synthesized Celtic and Germanic elements to produce a richly decorated art based on geometric designs and organic abstractions derived from plant and animal forms. Created at a monastery on the island of Lindisfarne off the east coast of England, the *Lindisfarne Gospels* is a superb example of Hiberno-Saxon decorative art. As meticulous as printed electronic circuitry, the "X–P (chi-rho) Page" (see chapter opener opposite) is lovely testimony to the masterful use of color to enhance but not compete with either the linear composition or importance of the gospel text. Inside the letters is a miniature maze of writhing shapes and mirror-image effects. With details so fine they are best studied with a magnifying glass, one wonders how this work was accomplished.

The last of the remarkable Hiberno-Saxon illuminated manuscripts, the *Book of Kells* is also the most elaborately decorated. On one page the Greek letters XPI (khri), an abbreviation of the name of Christ, dominate a design swirling with animal and abstract interlaces and

geometric decoration (fig. 14.1). Whorls within circles within larger circles dazzle the eye, but closer study reveals two human faces and, on the left vertical of the X, three human figures depicted from the waist up. Near the bottom and to the right of the same vertical is a playful **genre** scene featuring two cats and four mice.

Hiberno-Saxon manuscripts typify the early period of intricate and painstaking northern craftsmanship, which included metalworking, woodworking, jewelry, ivory carving, stone carving, and by the eleventh century stained glass, a tradition that led to spectacular achievements in the Gothic age and, eventually, to machine design and the industrial revolution. An important factor in the development of northern crafts may have been climate, for these are mainly indoor activities that could be carried on despite inclement weather and long, bleak winters.

14.1 "XPI Page," fol. 34, *Book of Kells*. Ca. 760–820. Illuminated manuscript, 13 × 10" (33 × 25 cm). Library of Trinity College, Dublin.

14.2 "St. Mark," fol. 18v, *Gospel Book of Archibishop Ebbo of Reims*. 816–35. Illuminated manuscript, ca. 10 × 8" (25.4 × 20.3 cm). Bibliothèque Municipal, Epernay, France. Photo: Giraudon, Paris.

CAROLINGIAN ART, CA. 750–900

Ruling from 768 to 814 as a Frankish king, Charlemagne saw himself as a successor to the Caesars of Rome, a notion reinforced in 800 when the pope crowned him Emperor of the Holy Roman Empire. To his capital at Aachen (formerly Aix-la-Chapelle), in present-day Germany, Charlemagne brought scholars, artists, and craftsmen to help revive the civilization of classical antiquity. Short-lived, but vital for later developments, the Carolingian Renaissance drew upon Celto-Germanic and Mediterranean traditions to produce a Carolingian art that combined classic forms with Christian symbols and subject matter.

Societies tend to develop an architecture based on the availability of building materials, and at that time the vast forests of northern Europe provided an endless supply of wood for the timber-frame construction of private and public buildings. Charlemagne, however, preferred impressive palaces and churches built in the Roman manner. He imported southern techniques of building in stone and southern masons to work the stone and instruct northern craftsmen. This educational process was to culminate in the expert stonework of the great medieval cathedrals.

One of the few buildings to survive intact from the age of Charlemagne, the chapel of his palace at Aachen (see fig. 12.11) is an impressive example of northern European stone construction. As might be expected during this early period, the columns and most of the capitals were simply taken from existing Roman buildings. One suspects that Charlemagne fancied using columns of the Caesars for his personal chapel.

Painted shortly after Charlemagne's death, the "St. Mark" (fig. 14.2) derives from a classic model. The Hiberno-Saxon influence is discernible in the draperies swirling about the torso in lines as dynamic as those in an Irish manuscript. Rather than a scholar writing a book, Mark is a man inspired by divine guidance, a transmitter of the sacred text. This follows the ancient view that poets—Homer

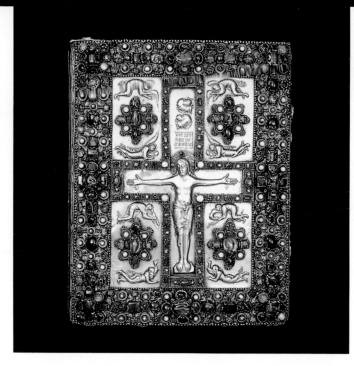

14.3 "Crucifixion Cover," *Lindau Gospels.* Ca. 870. 13¾ × 10½" (34.9 × 26.7 cm). Pierpont Morgan Library, New York.

14.4 St.-Martin-du-Canigou, near Vernet-les-Bains, France, interior of upper church. 1001–26. Photo: Giraudon, Paris.

for example--are divinely inspired and possess super-human powers.

Influenced possibly by Byzantine decorative arts, Carolingian book covers were made of precious metals and richly ornamented with jewels. Created during the waning influence of the Carolingian dynasty, the "Crucifixion Cover" of the *Lindau Gospels* is made of gold, with the figures of Christ and angels delineated in graceful, sinuous lines (fig. 14.3). The artist outlined the golden Greek cross with gold beads and precious and semiprecious stones, then echoed the cross motif with jeweled crosses in the four panels and all around the border. Major stones are set above the gold surface so that reflected light can add to their brilliance. No one could doubt the importance of the text within such a cover.

After the remarkable reign of Charlemagne the Holy Roman Empire declined in power and influence. Nevertheless, the revival of Greek and Roman learning sparked a synthesis of classical civilization and Celto-Germanic culture, elements of which are still discernible in modern Europe and America.

ROMANESQUE STYLE,
CA. 1000–1150/1200

By about AD 1000 virtually all of Europe had been Christianized, and, after centuries of ferocious attacks, the barbaric Vikings and Magyars had finally been assimilated by their erstwhile victims. Major building programs began all over Europe to replace damaged structures and to construct new churches and monasteries. With at least one new church in every hamlet, village, town, and city, architecture and architectural sculpture became the dominant art forms of this vigorous new age.

Vaulted Churches

Located high in the French Pyrenees, the tiny monastic church of St.-Martin-du-Canigou is one of the earliest structures with a complete barrel vault of cut stone (fig. 14.4). Vaulted stone roofs became the rule for Romanesque churches in place of the wooden truss roofs of earlier buildings; whether accidental or caused by hostile invaders, fire was a constant danger. Stone roofs relieved that difficulty but brought about another: how to support the heavy roof. The solution included thick walls supported by evenly spaced columns alternating with massive piers and connected by semicircular arches. Dimly lit because large windows weaken supporting walls, Romanesque churches are characteristically heavy and solid, giving a feeling of protective walls shutting out a hostile world. Intended for the exclusive use of the religious community, the monastic church shielded the monks from all outside influences.

A new monastery founded in 910 at Cluny in French Burgundy became the mother house of a reformed order that spread throughout Europe, building 1,000 churches within a century. The enormous mother church at Cluny was destroyed by peasant rebellions but a smaller version in the Cluniac style was erected under the direction of St. Hugues, Abbot of Cluny (fig. 14.5). Of great simplicity, with two square towers surmounting the narthex and supported by powerful buttresses, the restrained design has a serene, majestic dignity. Originally dedicated to the Virgin Mary, the abbey church was raised to the level of a basilica in 1875 and consecrated to the Sacred Heart of Jesus.

Christians had been making pilgrimages to scenes of Christ's life since the third century and, since Charlemagne's time, in ever-increasing numbers. By the tenth century it was commonly believed that viewing sacred relics of Christ and the saints secured God's pardon for sins, a belief encouraged by the churches containing such relics. One of these

14.5 Basilica of the Sacred Heart, Paray-le-Monial, Burgundy, France. 1090–1109. Photo: James Austin, Cambridge, U.K.

14.6 St.-Benoit-sur-Loire, France, nave, looking east. End of 11th century. Photo: B.P.K., Berlin.

COMMUNITIES OF WOMEN

Most women in the medieval world could look forward to marriage, raising a family, and requisite domestic chores with little opportunity for anything else—with one exception. They could join an abbey (monastery, later called a convent) where they could acquire an education and learn a variety of skills as they dedicated their life to God. Because abbeys were usually independent institutions run by an abbess, they had to be self-supporting, with nuns trained in the tasks that kept the order functioning.

The nuns had to import a priest to say Mass and hear confessions, but they performed all other duties, including the preservation of knowledge through manuscript copying and research. Some abbeys became prominent centers of learning staffed with notable intellectuals. Hrotsvit, abbess of Gandersheim (ca. 930–90), wrote histories and plays. Hildegard of Bingen (1098–1179) was a composer, scientist, and theologian. Herrad of Landsberg, abbess at Hohenberg (1165–95), assisted by her nuns, wrote the *Hortus Deliciarum* (*Garden of Delights*), an encyclopedia of knowledge and world history (see fig. 15.3). Beginning in the thirteenth century, universities began replacing abbeys as educational institutions while women's education became virtually nonexistent for the next five or six centuries.

was the Abbey of Fleury (now St.-Benoit-sur-Loire). Claiming to contain the bones of St. Benedict, the abbey became one of the prime destinations for organized parties of pilgrims. Rebuilt in the eleventh and twelfth centuries after brutal Viking raids in the ninth century, St.-Benoit-sur-Loire is another fine example of the Cluniac style. Its nave has a barrel vault with ornamental ribs (fig. 14.6). The clerestory windows, which admit considerable light for a Romanesque church, are set above a blind arcade that decorates the upper wall. Adorned only with architectural details, the masonry walls are supported by majestic columns connected by Roman (semicircular) arches. The interiors of French Romanesque churches are always restrained, depending for their effect on a unity of basic design and discreet architectural embellishment without recourse to wall mosaics, murals, frescoes, or similar pictorial decorations. The result is a rational design of awesome power.

Many pilgrimage churches were monastic. An important stop on the pilgrimage road from Italy and Provence to Spain's Santiago de Compostela, the Basilica of St.-Sernin in Toulouse is a superb example of the Romanesque style and of the influence of pilgrimages on church architecture. The barrel vault is punctuated by nonstructural transverse arches evenly distributed down the nave (fig. 14.7), which is flanked by double aisles to accommodate the many pilgrims. Constructed on the module of the **crossing** square under the tower, the size of each compartment between the columns, called a **bay**, is exactly half the area of the crossing square under the central tower (fig. 14.8). In the side aisles each square is one-quarter of the module (the crossing). The piers with their attached compound columns are two stories high with arches supporting a gallery that runs above the side aisles and that was probably used by some of the pilgrim throngs. Minus the triumphal arch of early Christian churches, the evenly spaced columns and identically sized bays lead inexorably down the nave to the focal point of the altar. St.-Sernin is a classic example of French Romanesque design, unified and lucid.

Now one of the most imposing ruins in France, the Abbey of Jumièges, in Normandy, was built in the eleventh century on the site of a seventh-century building which had been destroyed by Vikings in the ninth. It was reconsecrated in 1067 in the presence of William the Conqueror, himself a descendant of Viking marauders (fig. 14.9). With its 141-foot (43-m) twin towers and projecting porch, Jumièges represents the impressive Norman style of Romanesque that was established in England (where it is called, simply, Norman) by the conquerors. The present state of Jumièges typifies the fate of French monasteries during the French Revolution. After the monks were dispersed, the abbey was auctioned off in 1793 to a timber merchant who quarried and sold many of the stones. The ruins now belong to the nation.

Another fine example of Norman Romanesque is the Church of St.-Etienne (fig. 14.10) in Caen. It formed part of the Abbaye aux Hommes (Abbey for Men), which, along

14.7 *Above* Basilica of St.-Sernin, Toulouse, France, nave. Ca. 1080–1120. Length of nave 377' 4" (115 m). Photo: Dagli Orti, Paris.

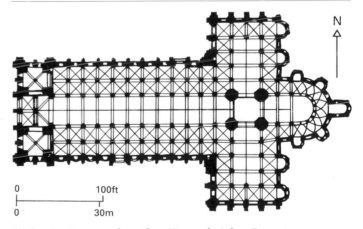

14.8 St.-Sernin, plan after Kenneth John Conant.

14.9 Abbey of Jumièges, near Rouen, France, west facade. 1037–67. Photo: James Austin, Cambridge, U.K.

14.10 St.-Etienne (Abbaye aux Hommes), Caen, France, from the southeast. 1064–1135. Photo: James Austin, Cambridge, U.K.

14.11 "The Battle Rages," detail of the Bayeux Tapestry. Ca. 1070–80. Wool embroidery on linen, height ca. 20" (51 cm), entire length 231' (70.5 m). Musée de l'Evêche, Bayeux. Photo: Scala, Florence.

with the Abbaye aux Dames, was built by William the Conqueror as an act of penance for having married a distant cousin named Matilda. The characteristic twin towers of Norman architecture reach 295 feet (90 m) with the aid of later Gothic spires. The seven towers are a vigorous contribution to the design as well as symbols of the Holy Trinity plus the four evangelists. With the Conqueror's tomb before the high altar, St.-Etienne still stands as the royal church of the Norman king.

The Bayeux Tapestry

Probably designed by a woman and embroidered on linen by Saxon women, the Bayeux Tapestry is the most precise medieval document that has survived intact, providing daily life scenes and details of clothes, customs, and weapons. The rivalry between King Harold of England and Duke William of Normandy for the English throne is depicted in fifty-eight scenes, culminating in the Battle of Hastings (fig. 14.11). In the episode shown, the English, identified by their mustaches, are beginning to succumb to the superior numbers and better equipment of the Normans. At the far left in the battle scene a rider protects himself with a large shield while brandishing his lance. Unlike the British, the Norman cavalry had stirrups in which they stood as they relentlessly mowed down the enemy with their deadly lances. The tripartite design features an ornamental band above the violent battle scene and a lower band depicting the casualties. Despite the stylized design, the details are brutally realistic; warriors and horses have died in agony.

Ste.-Madeleine, Vézelay

The Abbey Church of Ste.-Madeleine in the village of Vézelay is intimately associated with another kind of warfare: holy war. Originally scheduled for Vézelay, the First Crusade was preached by Pope Urban II from Clermont in 1095, calling on all Christians to free the Holy Land from the Saracens. In 1146 Vézelay was the site for St. Bernard's Second Crusade and, in 1190, King Richard the Lion-Hearted of England and King Phillip Augustus of France departed from Vézelay on the Third Crusade, a disastrous failure, as was every Crusade from the Second to the Eighth.

One of the most distinctive of all Romanesque interiors, the nave of Ste.-Madeleine (fig. 14.12) is high—about 90 feet (27 m)—with unusual transverse arches of white and pinkish brown stone, probably inspired by such Islamic buildings as the Great Mosque in Córdoba (see fig. 12.5). The tunnel, or barrel, vault was no longer used because of its inherent drawback: an unbroken series of arches pressed back to back can be lighted or opened only on the opposite ends. Any and every opening in the supporting wall weakens the entire structure. One of the earliest French churches to abandon the barrel vault, Ste.-Madeleine's uses a vault that is intersected at right angles by another vault to form a **groin** or cross **vault** (fig. 14.13).

Note that at this high level the groin vaults of Vézelay permit considerable illumination from the clerestory windows. Close study of the interior also reveals that the architect used groin vaults that were too heavy for the exterior wall, vaults so massive that the upper walls are pushed outward. External flying **buttresses** (see an example of the principle in fig. 14.27) had to be added to balance the **thrust** of the vaults, thus stabilizing this lovely nave.

A striking architectural sculpture at another Burgundian church portrays the most powerful subject in Christendom. *The Last Judgment* **tympanum** at Autun (fig. 14.14) exemplifies the revived relationship of architecture and sculpture in the Romanesque style. Set between the arch and lintel, the tympanum is a compendium of sermons warning the faithful about the terrors of Hell. Staring straight forward, the imposing figure of the final Judge holds his hands out as in a set of scales. Along the lower edge the dead are rising from their graves. On the left the saved are passing into Heaven, and on the right the damned are being thrust into Hell by hideous devils and demons. Heated by a fervent faith, the Romanesque imagination knew no bounds in graphic warnings to transgressors.

The medieval love of embellishment touched all of the fine and decorative arts, from sculpture to manuscripts, liturgical vestments, and such ceremonial objects as crosses, chalices, incense burners, candlesticks, and reliquaries. A casket containing a sacred object, a **reliquary** was invariably made of precious materials and highly decorated. The

14.12 *Above* Basilica of Ste.-Madeleine, Vézelay, Burgundy, France, nave. Ca. 1104–32. Photo: Lonchampt-Delehaye, C.N.M.H.S./© DACS 1995.

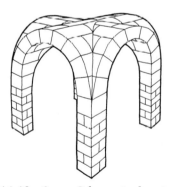

14.13 *Above* Schematic drawing of a cross vault.

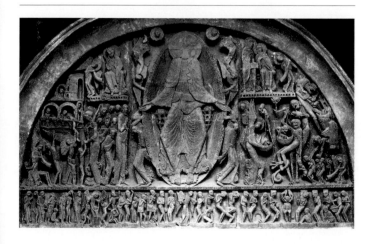

14.15 *Below* Reliquary in the shape of a head. Rhenish. Early 12th century. Silver. British Museum, London.

14.14 *Left* Gislebertus, *The Last Judgment*, tympanum of the central portal, Cathedral of St.-Lazare, Autun, France. Ca. 1130. Photo: Viollet, Paris.

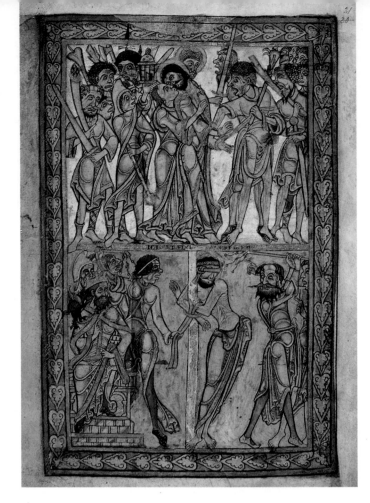

14.16 "Capture of Christ and the Flagellation," fol. 21, *Psalter of St. Swithin*. Ca. 1250. Illuminated manuscript. British Library, London.

silver Rhenish reliquary in the shape of a head (fig. 14.15) is quite restrained for the period, particularly in the classical style of the hair. **Embossed** and incised silver figures of the twelve Apostles surround the base of what the twentieth century would label a three-dimensional composite work or "combine." In the twelfth century it was not even regarded as sculpture but as a reliquary, pure and simple.

The restless linear style of the Autun tympanum is also prominent in this scene from the *Psalter of St. Swithin* (fig. 14.16). In both the upper and lower scenes, elegant arabesques outline the figures, thus emphasizing the grotesque faces of the brutal soldiers in comparison to the resigned passivity of Christ. Beauty and horror are effectively combined to convey a powerful spiritual message.

Tuscan Romanesque

The basic Romanesque style of Roman (round) arches and vaults, heavy walls, and alternating square piers and columns spread throughout western Europe, always

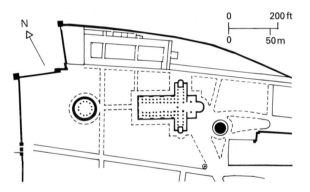

14.18 Pisa baptistery, cathedral, and campanile, plan.

14.17 Buscheto, Pisa Cathedral and campanile. 1063–1272. Photo: Alinari, Florence.

14.19 Pisa Cathedral with baptistery, view from campanile. Photo: Robert Harding, London (Walter Rawlings).

displaying, however, certain variations depending on regional conventions and traditions. In Tuscany and other parts of northern Italy, the style adhered closely to the basilica plan of early Christian churches, and also evidenced an increased interest in classical art, a heritage that had never been totally forgotten. The most distinguished complex in the Tuscan Romanesque style is the cathedral group at Pisa (fig. 14.17). Constructed of readily available white marble, the cathedral resembles an early Christian basilica, but with Romanesque characteristics: the dome over the crossing; the superimposed arcades on the west front; the blind arches encircling the entire building. The extended transepts with an apse at each end add to the poise and serenity of the design, which makes the famous Leaning Tower, the **campanile**, all the more striking. Begun in 1174 by Bonanno Pisano on an unstable foundation, the tower began to tilt well before its completion in 1350. The three upper sections were adjusted slightly in the north in an attempt to compensate for the southward incline. Now 16 feet 6 inches (5 m) off the perpendicular, the tower—whose bells haven't rung in decades—is apparently no longer moving. In May 1992 two steel bands were wrapped around it and covered with stucco to match the rest of the tower. Also added was a counterweight of 800 pounds (363 kg) of lead. Eventually, engineers will add a total of eighteen bands as they check to see if the tower is stabilized.

The view from the top of the campanile reveals the **cruciform** plan of the cathedral with its clerestory windows and upper level of blind arcades (figs. 14.18 and 14.19). The massive baptistery, topped with a dome 115 feet (35 m) in diameter, was built between 1153 and 1278 and later embellished at the upper level with Gothic details, the only discordant note in an otherwise harmonious design.

Mont-St.-Michel

In all its manifestations, Romanesque art finds its unity in architecture; the church is the Fortress of God where the apocalyptic vision is ever called to mind. No more vivid representation of this idea exists than the Abbey of Mont-St.-Michel in the Sea of Peril (fig. 14.20), which rises in awesome majesty off the coast of Normandy. The abbey was begun about 1020 by Abbot Hildebert and Richard II, Duke of Normandy, grandfather of William the Conqueror. Its building spanned five centuries, as abbot succeeded abbot and style succeeded style. Mont-St.-Michel summarizes medieval architecture, a glorious mixture of Norman, Norman Romanesque, Early, High, and Late Gothic styles.

14.21 *Right* Gargoyle, Notre Dame, Paris. Stone. Photo: Viollet, Paris.

1. Known initially as the "French style," the term Gothic was not used until the sixteenth century.

14.20 Mont-St.-Michel. Ca. 1017–1144; 1211–1521. Photo: Robert C. Lamm, Scottsdale. This view also illustrates the stormy weather so typical of this portion of the northern coast of France.

EARLY GOTHIC STYLE,
CA. 1140–1200

Mankind was never so happily inspired as when it made a cathedral.

Robert Louis Stevenson (1850–94)

Erected usually in the countryside as part of monastic communities, Romanesque churches were built by and for "regular" clergy, those who lived under the rule (*regula*) of a religious order. The rise of the great cities on the Continent was paralleled by the development of the new Gothic style (map 14.1).[1] Staffed by the "secular" clergy, priests who lived "in the world" (*in saecula*), Gothic churches were urban—designed to serve city parishes. Each city's glory and chief community center, the Gothic cathedral was not only the seat (*cathedra*) of the bishop but a theatre, classroom, concert hall, court, and general meeting place.

Symbolic of the Gothic age is the gargoyle perched high

14.22 *Above*   Cathedral of St.-Denis, near Paris, interior. 1140–4. Photo: C.N.M.H.S./© DACS 1995.

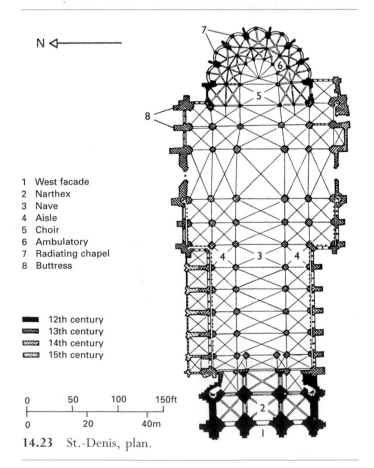

N ◄—

1   West facade
2   Narthex
3   Nave
4   Aisle
5   Choir
6   Ambulatory
7   Radiating chapel
8   Buttress

▬▬ 12th century
▨▨ 13th century
▨▨ 14th century
▨▨ 15th century

0   50   100   150ft
0   20   40m

14.23   St.-Denis, plan.

above the sprawl of modern Paris (fig. 14.21). The former represents prevailing medieval superstitions while the latter was, and is, one of the foremost cultural centers of Europe.

Gothic Vaulting

Though the basic structural elements of Gothic architecture were developed and used during the Romanesque period, it remained for an unknown architectural genius to put it all together at St.-Denis, just north of Paris (fig. 14.22). It was carried out under Abbot Suger, who left a detailed account of his administration (1122–51), and his goals. Suger wished to give the church a new choir and ambulatory, one that would be full of light—symbolic of the presence of God (fig. 14.23). The cramped, dark ambulatory of the existing church, with its thick walls between chapels, was to be replaced with walls of colored glass. To achieve this, the architect supported the weight of the vaults with pointed arches, which are more stable than semicircular ones. The arch principle is one of mutual support; the two halves lean against each other so that the force (gravity) that would cause either to fall actually holds them in place. However, the flatter the arch the greater the lateral thrust at the springline, that is, the outward push where the arch begins (fig. 14.24). This thrust is significantly reduced when the pointed arch is used because the springline is angled more nearly downward. Hence, the more pointed the arch, the less the tendency to push its supporting pier outward, thus reducing the need for massive supports.

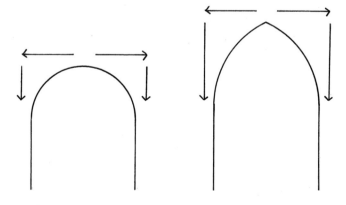

14.24 *Above*   Romanesque and Gothic arch thrusts.

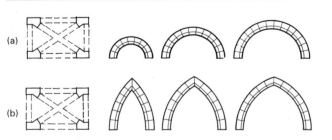

14.25   (a) Cross vault of semicircular arches over an oblong bay, (b) cross vault of pointed arches over an oblong bay.

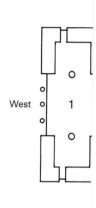

West

1 Narthex
2 Nave
3 Bay
4 Aisle
5 Crossing

14.28 Crucifor

parts of the chu
designs. The or
shipers enter
Jerusalem in th
low this geograp
minology.) In th
three in each tr

HIGH GOT
CA. 1200–1

After a disastro
which left intac
unfinished cath
commenced im
structure comp
drals took deca
and probably b
never fully com
added or elabo:

Chartres C

The first mast
Cathedral has l
epitome of Got
Gothic but un
begins with a

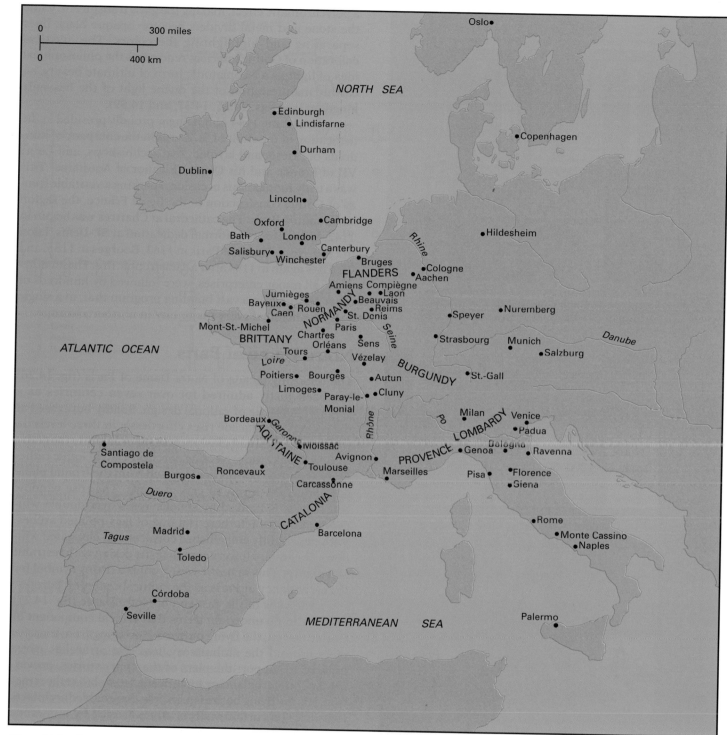

Map 14.1 Romanesque and Gothic sites in Western Europe.

The round arch has a fixed radius because it is always half of a circle. Since it has no unalterable diameter, the pointed arch can rise to almost any height and span virtually any space (fig. 14.25). In the illustration the first rounded arch spans the short side, the second the long side, and the third the diagonal, necessitating piers of different heights. With their identical height, pointed arches sim-

plify the engineering and improve the aesthetic effect with slender columns topped by capitals at a uniform height.

The most striking difference at St.-Denis is the marked increase in light. Stained glass windows function as light converters, transforming the interior into a hazy luminosity of shifting colors. The windows are subdivided first by **mullions** (carved stone posts), then by stone **tracery** to form still smaller glass panels, and finally by thin lead strips to hold in place the individual pieces of colored glass. The light penetrating the stained glass creates

14.31   Notre Dame, Chartres, tympanum of Royal Portal. Photo: James Austin, Cambridge, U.K.

14.30 *Left*   Notre Dame, Chartres, central doorway of Royal Portal. Ca. 1140–50. Photo: Kersting, London.

14.26 *Above*
1163–1250:

14.27 No
Photo: Jan

the octagonal shape of the fourth level. From here the graceful spire soars to a height of 344 feet (105 m), the characteristic "finger pointing to God" of the Gothic age. The elaborate north tower, which was not completed until well into the Northern Renaissance, lacks the effortless verticality of the south tower. Verticality was a hallmark of Gothic; cities competed in unspoken contests to erect cathedrals with the highest vaults and the tallest towers. An inspiring House of God was also a symbol of civic achievement. With a facade 157 feet (48 m) wide and measuring 427 feet (130 m) in length, Chartres cathedral is as prominent a landmark today as when it was built, thanks in part to modern zoning ordinances that control building heights throughout the village.

Incorporated into the facade when the cathedral was rebuilt, the Royal Portal (western doorways) of the earlier church emphasizes the Last Judgment theme of Romanesque portals but with significant differences (figs. 14.30 and 14.31). Rather than the harsh Damnation of the Last Judgment, the theme is now the Second Coming with its promise of salvation. No longer is there the inventive freedom of the Romanesque; all is unified and controlled. The outer frame is provided by the twenty-four elders of the Apocalypse on the **archivolts** and the lower row of twelve Apostles. Surrounded by symbols of the four Evangelists, the now benign figure of Christ raises an arm in benediction in the manner of Caesar Augustus (see fig. 9.15). Beneath the tympanum are the **jamb figures**, a wholly new idea in architectural sculpture. Conceived and carved in the round, the figures were very likely fashioned after live models rather than copied from manuscripts, a further indication of the emerging this-worldly spirit of the age.

The most significant manifestation of the new age was the dedication of the cathedrals themselves. Named after apostles and saints in previous eras, the new churches were almost invariably dedicated to Our Lady (Notre Dame). Mary was Queen of Heaven, interceding for her faithful who, sinners all, wanted mercy, not justice. This was the Cult of the Virgin Mary, the popular spiritual movement of the Gothic age. The Romanesque was the style of the age of feudalism and conflict; the more cultivated Gothic represented the Age of Chivalry, as derived from Courts of Love sponsored by powerful women like Eleanor of Aquitaine. With the development of cathedral schools such as those at Paris and Chartres, Mary was viewed much like Athena, as patroness of arts and science. The right doorway of the Chartres Royal Portal includes portraits of Aristotle, Cicero, Euclid, Ptolemy, Pythagoras, and symbols of the seven liberal arts. In fact the school associated with Chartres cathedral was a renowned center of classical learning, and this portal, like the Gothic cathedral itself, represents the medieval synthesis of spiritual and secular life at its best.

The nave of Notre Dame of Chartres is 53 feet (16 m) wide, the most spacious of all Gothic naves. The total length is 130 feet (40 m) and the height 122 feet (37 m)—the loftiest vault of its day (fig. 14.32). Around the apse are the tall pointed arches of the arcade and above them, the **triforium**, an arcaded passageway. Five huge windows, dedicated to the Virgin, flood the choir with colored light.

Chartres has six bays in the nave and two in each transept, a single aisle in the nave, and a double aisle in the choir and apse (fig. 14.33). Figure 14.34a depicts a full bay (center) and the three levels of the nave wall. The diagram of the vaulting (fig. 14.34b) gives some idea of the complexity of the exterior support system.

One of the chief glories of Gothic interiors is the kaleidoscopic color cascading from the mighty stained glass windows. Retaining most of its original windows, Chartres is a treasure house of the art, with clerestory windows 44 feet (13.4 m) high, all in all some 20,000 square feet (1,858 m²) of medieval glass. Located at the north end of the transepts, the northern rose is like a gigantic multicolored jewel set above the five figurative **lancet windows** (fig.

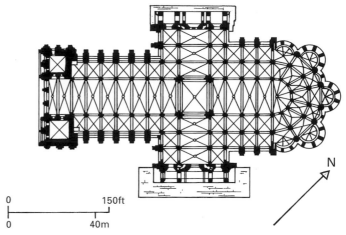

14.33 Notre Dame, Chartres, floor plan after Dehio.

14.32 *Left* Notre Dame, Chartres, nave. Photo: Giraudon, Paris.

14.35 Notre Dame, Chartres, northern rose and lancets. Early 13th century. Diameter of rose window ca. 42' (12.8 m). Photo: Sonia Halliday, Weston Turville, U.K.

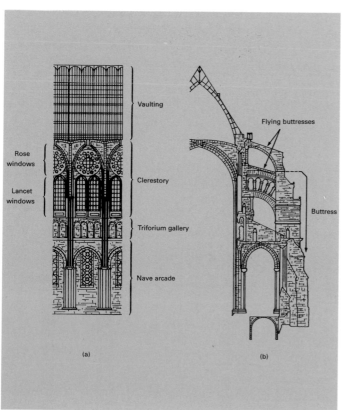

14.34 Goubert, Drawings of Notre Dame, Chartres. (a) Section of nave wall, (b) diagram of vaulting.

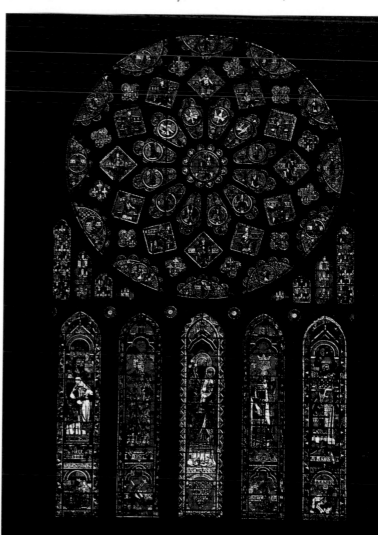

14.35). As a northern exposure window the color leans toward the cool part of the spectrum with a preponderance of blue. Its counterpart, the southern rose (not illustrated), transmits the warmer colors: red, orange, and yellow. Contrary to what one might expect, direct sunlight on any of the windows upsets their chromatic balance for they were designed to function best under the even, cool light characteristic of northern France.

Other French Cathedrals

Designed originally by Robert de Luzarches, one of the first known master builders, the Cathedral of Notre Dame of Amiens marks the culmination of the best ideas of the French Gothic style. Modeled after that of Notre Dame in Paris, the west front (fig. 14.36) is not as controlled and majestic as its model, but its grandeur is overwhelming. Looking like one gigantic and intricate work of sculpture, the west front is dominated by its incomparable portals. The imposing entrances thrusting outward from the facade proclaim the interior in unmistakable terms; the central portal announces the lofty nave and the two flanking door-ways the side aisles. As in other French Gothic cathedrals, the inner structure is prefigured by the exterior design.

14.36 Notre Dame, Amiens, France, west facade. Ca. 1220–88. Photo: Hirmer, Munich.

14.37 Notre Dame, Amiens, nave. Completed 1236. Photo: Jean Feuillie, C.N.M.H.S./© DACS 1995.

14.38 Robert de Luzarches, Notre Dame, Amiens. (a) Plan and (b) vaulting.

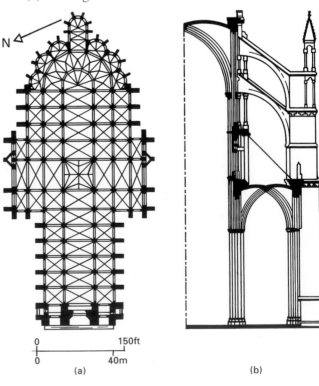

```
0         150ft
0    40m
(a)            (b)
```

Patterned after Chartres, the nave of Amiens is even more integrated, soaring in one breathtaking sweep to 144 feet (44 m) above the pavement (fig. 14.37). Unfortunately minus its stained glass, the interior is nevertheless the culmination of the High Gothic style: lofty arcades with slender columns rising to the ribbed vaults. Once thought to have functioned as structural supports for the vault, the ribs are actually decorative extensions of columns carrying the design to the apex of the vault, which is completely self-supporting (fig. 14.38). Amiens represents the ultimate phase of the High Gothic style in France called **rayonnant** ("radiant") because of the emphasis on line and space: soaring columns, ribs, and vaults and vast areas of stained glass.

Reims Cathedral is the traditional site for the consecration of French kings for it was here, in 496, that Bishop Remi baptized Clovis, leader of the conquering Franks. The inspiring interior is both beautiful and delightful. The gorgeous rose window within the pointed arch is crowned by an even more dazzling rose at the top of the 125-foot (38-m) vaulting (fig. 14.39). The most remarkable aspect of Reims is its homogeneous design. The four master builders who followed the original design of Jean d'Orbais (master until 1231) left the nation a priceless legacy: the majestic Coronation Church of France.

Completed in less than thirty-three months for Louis IX of France, later St. Louis, Sainte Chapelle is today a small chapel set in the midst of the Palais de Justice. With virtually no stone walls, the structure is a set of piers supporting stained glass curtains. Topped by a spire reaching 246 feet (75 m) into the sky, the upper chapel, with its 49-foot (15-m) windows, rests on a lower level intended for the use of servants. With almost 6,700 square feet (622 m²) of glass containing 1,134 scenes, the upper chapel is a triumph of the *rayonnant* style: a jewelbox of color dominated by brilliant reds and luminous blues (fig. 14.40). Because there are no side aisles, there are no flying buttresses to impede the penetration of light into a building whose walls are about 75 percent glass. Rivaling Chartres in the extent and quality of its original glass, Sainte Chapelle managed to survive the Revolution; damaged and neglected, it became a storage area for old government files. Restored in the nineteenth century to an approximation of its original condition, the remarkable fact is that its basic structure is so flawless, so perfectly engineered that it survived intact for seven centuries.

With the building of the cathedral at Beauvais, the competition to build the highest vault came crashing to an end (fig. 14.41). The vault, which reached the amazing height of 157 feet (48.9 m), was a wonderment to all until its collapse in 1284; only the apse was left standing. Rebuilt

14.39 *Above* Notre Dame, Reims, France, interior looking west. Begun 1210. Photo: Bulloz, Paris.

14.40 Sainte Chapelle, Paris, upper level of interior. 1245–8. Photo: Jean Feuillie, C.N.M.H.S./© DACS 1995.

14.41 Cathedral of St. Pierre, Beauvais, France, aerial view of choir. Begun ca. 1225. Photo: Bernard, Paris.

over a period of forty years, the choir remains today as a testament both to Gothic vertical aspirations and to the waning of enthusiasm for building enormously expensive churches. The money ran out along with the spirit. Previously it was thought that stone simply could not support such a lofty vault as that of Beauvais, but modern engineering research[2] points to a design flaw in an exterior pier, the deterioration of which was not detected. The nature of the 1284 disaster ironically confirmed the nature of Gothic engineering, in which the stability of the vaulting depends on the proper functioning of all components. When the single pier failed due to undetected weathering, it was only the choir vaults that came tumbling down; the structurally independent apse remained standing. Interestingly enough, the design flaw in the defective pier was corrected during the rebuilding program, meaning that the entire cathedral could then have been completed as originally planned. Today, looking at the magnificent choir, one wonders what might have been at Beauvais.

Gothic Style Elsewhere in Europe

By the second half of the thirteenth century the Gothic style had been accepted throughout most of Europe, though Italy was less than enthusiastic. Regional variations gave each area its own brand of Gothic. Taking to Gothic as if they had invented it, the English built in the style with enthusiasm, but showed a clear intention to give it their own stamp. Whereas French cathedrals are marked by verticality, their English counterparts are noted for their length, often including double sets of transepts. The choir end is

usually squared off rather than curved, and includes a Lady chapel, devoted to the Virgin. The clean lines of French verticality were abandoned at the outset in favor of a profusion of patterns—reflected in the name applied to mature English Gothic of the late thirteenth and fourteenth centuries: Decorated. Veritable forests of ribs adorn the vaults of many English cathedrals, as we can see in that of Winchester (fig. 14.42). It is the vault, rather than the arcading, that is of primary interest here. Another difference is that many English cathedrals were built over a longer time span than French ones and incorporated more diversity of styles including, often, some Norman (Romanesque) features. Although the total effect lacks the serene harmony of French Gothic, it offers much visual and historic interest. Unfortunately, little remains of English medieval stained glass, most of which was destroyed by iconoclastic Protestants during the sixteenth and seventeenth centuries. The English see French interiors as cold and impersonal while viewing their version of Gothic as warmly intimate and hospitable. Different styles suit different folks.

Salisbury Cathedral (fig. 14.43) was the only English cathedral built on a virgin site, to a uniform plan, and completed (apart from the spire) without interruption. Started the same year as Amiens (1220), this is a very different structure. For one thing, it was (like several other English cathedrals) connected to a monastery and thus has a cloister—an exceptionally beautiful one—to one side of the nave. It is set within a spacious "close" of well-tended lawn, which gives it, even today, a sense of pastoral tranquility, whereas Amiens is closely surrounded by its bustling city.

It has, typically, a much lower vault: 84 feet (25.6 m), compared to Amiens' 140 feet (42.7 m). But Salisbury's lower profile is complemented by its crowning glory, the central tower and spire by Master Richard of Fairleigh, completed in 1380. Rising 404 feet (123 m) the stone spire displays a convincing sense of scale with its alternation of plain and diagonally embellished segments. Several centuries later, when Christopher Wren was aked to correct the slight tilt of the tower, his recommendation was not to tamper with visual perfection.

Italy took up the Gothic style slowly and with reservations; Italians were, after all, the people who had, in the sixteenth century, labeled the "French style" as a barbaric creation of northern Goths. Distinctly unclassical, a Gothic cathedral is restless, unsettled, always unfinished, whereas a classical temple is serenely complete. Nevertheless, the Gothic spirit was on the move in Italy, becoming part of the classical and Romanesque traditions.

For all its Gothic elements, the west front of the cathedral at Siena (fig. 14.44) has square doorways, triangular pediments, and a balanced design reminiscent of the classical past. Gothic features include a rose window, but without stained glass, the unobtrusive Gothic towers, lacy blind arcading, and the three portals. Most of the statuary has been liberated from its architectural bondage and the

---

2. Robert Mark, *Experiments in Gothic Structure* (Cambridge, Mass.: MIT Press, 1982), pp. 58–77.

14.42 Winchester Cathedral, England, nave. Begun 1079. Photo: E.T. Archive, London.

14.43 Salisbury Cathedral, England. Begun 1220. Photo: British Tourist Authority/Mirror Syndication, London.

tympanums display colorful mosaics. Faced with multicolored marble, the facade is a lively ensemble of Gothic and Tuscan Romanesque elements, all in all a notable example of Italian reaction to the Gothic spirit.

Whatever its regional variations, the Gothic cathedral epitomizes the explosive creativity and intellectual boldness of the High Middle Ages. Never completely finished, a process rather than an end product, it stood at the center of the storm of changes that would sweep away the medieval synthesis. It represents both the triumphant climax of the Age of Faith and the end of the Middle Ages. The German author Heinrich Heine (1797–1856) succinctly characterized the Middle Ages: "People in those old times had convictions; we moderns only have opinions. And it needs more than a mere opinion to erect a Gothic cathedral."

Decorative Arts

Although architecture was the dominant art of the High Middle Ages, the so-called minor, or decorative, arts were notable for both quality and quantity. The page from the *Psalter of St. Louis* is a stunning example of Gothic **illumination** (fig. 14.45). It shows three angels appearing to Abraham and, on the right, Abraham and Sarah serving supper to the angels. Vibrating with color, the two scenes are separated by a marvelously decorative oak tree. By comparing it with a mosaic of the same subject (fig. 11.17), one can see the difference between Byzantine and medieval styles of representational art. Notice the architectural

14.44 Giovanni Pisano, Siena Cathedral, facade. Begun ca. 1285. Photo: Spectrum, London.

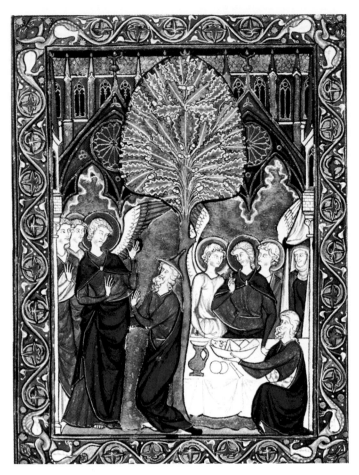

14.45 *Abraham and the Three Angels*, from the *Psalter of St. Louis*. 1253–70. Illuminated manuscript, 8½ × 5½" (21 × 14.5 cm). Bibliothèque Nationale, Paris.

14.46 Clasp from the workshop of Nicolas of Verdun. Ca. 1210. Gilt-bronze, 2 × 3" (5.1 × 7.6 cm). Metropolitan Museum of Art, New York. (Cloisters Collection, 1947.47.101.48)

setting of the later scene; Gothic features such as vaults, arcading, and tracery are incorporated into many medieval works of art, reflecting the primacy of architecture in this period. Reliquaries, in particular, often resemble Gothic churches or chapels. (Conversely, the Sainte Chapelle is, in effect, a large reliquary.)

Representing both sculpture and metalworking, the gilt-bronze clasp in figure 14.46 exemplifies the superb craftsmanship of medieval jewelers. Usually confined to brooches and rings, medieval jewelry also included such utilitarian items as belt buckles and mantle clasps. The freshness and grace of this clasp illustrate the lively spirit of the Middle Ages.

Cameos are precious or semi-precious stones that are carved in relief, a technique not developed until the Hellenistic period of ancient Greece. This is the exact opposite of the far older process of engraved stones (intaglio) widely used in signet rings. The "Noah" cameo (fig. 14.47), one of the great masterpieces of this art form, depicts Noah and his family leaving the Ark. The most impressive aspect of this extraordinary work is the feeling of optimistic vitality as the family strides forth into a brave new world.

Medieval manuscripts, being mainly of a religious nature, were customarily illuminated with a variety of sacred scenes and events. However, the *Beatus* page from the *Peterborough Psalter* (fig. 14.48) illustrates how important the secular world had become. This is the beginning of Psalm I, but one would be hard pressed to discover a single figure or object related to the text. Instead, we see a broad selection of scenes from everyday life, all done in a realistic and sometimes whimsical style.

14.47 "Noah" cameo, from the court of Frederick II Hohenstaufen, Sicily or southern Italy. Ca. 1204–50. Onyx within gold frame, width 2" (5.1 cm). British Museum, London.

14.48 *Beatus* page, fol. 14r from the *Peterborough Psalter*. 1300. Illuminated manuscript. Bibliothèque Royale, Brussels.

14.49 Reliquary of the Holy Thorn, Notre Dame, Reims, France. 11th-century vase with 15th-century setting. Rock crystal, gold, pearl, ruby, enamel, 10 × 37 × 31½" (25.5 × 94 × 80 cm). Photo: Giraudon, Paris.

LATE GOTHIC STYLE, CA. 1300–1500s

The extraordinary richness and sensuosity of the *Beatus* page, painted in 1300, brings us to the period when medieval art was in full flower: confident, exuberant, and, in many cases, unashamedly pretty. It was also a period in which large-scale painting (as contrasted with manuscript illumination) began, slowly, to be revived.

Created in the Late Gothic age, the Reliquary of the Holy Thorn (fig. 14.49) is splendidly luxurious at a time when this kind of opulence was expected in a sacred vessel. The gold armature and base are abundantly embellished with large pearls and pink rubies. Bearing a golden crown of thorns, the exquisitely sculpted angel has an enameled robe and wings. The interior of the vase holds a tiny golden angel gripping a thorn supposedly taken from Christ's crown of thorns. The overall effect is both secular and sacred, a vase fit for royalty surmounted by the most elegant of angels.

An integral part of Gothic architecture, stained glass windows and relief sculpture served the pictorial purposes once provided by mosaics, murals, and frescoes. Virtually nonexistent in the Gothic north, large-scale paintings were still done in Italy, which had maintained its contact with Byzantium. It was Italian painters who synthesized Byzantine and Gothic styles to create new procedures crucial to the future development of Western painting.

Cimabue

Renowned for his skill as a fresco and **tempera** painter,[3] the Florentine Cimabue (chee-ma-BOO-uh; 1240?–1302) introduced features that were incorporated into the developing Italian style. His *Madonna Enthroned* (fig. 14.50) illustrates the new characteristics of strong, forceful figures in a serene setting. The human scale of the lower figures emphasizes the towering dignity of the Madonna holding the mature-looking child. Distinguished from Byzantine icons by its much greater size, the gable shape and solid throne are also Gothic in origin as is the general verticality. The rigid, angular draperies and rather flat body of the Madonna are from the Byzantine tradition, but the softer lines of the angels' faces and their lightly hung draperies were inspired by works from contemporary Constantinople.

Giotto

Cimabue's naturalistic, monumentally scaled work had a profound influence on his purported pupil Giotto (JOT-toe; ca. 1267–1337), the acknowledged "father of Western

---

3. Fresco paintings are made on fresh wet plaster with pigments suspended in water; tempera uses pigments mixed with egg yolk and applied, usually, to a panel. Because the drying time for both techniques is very fast, corrections are virtually impossible without redoing entire areas. Therefore, artists had to work rapidly and with precision.

14.50 *Above* Cimabue, *Madonna Enthroned*. Ca. 1280–90. Tempera on wood, 12' 7½" × 7' 4" (3.85 × 2.24 m). Galleria degli Uffizi, Florence. Photo: Scala, Florence.

14.51 Giotto, *Madonna Enthroned*. Ca. 1310. Tempera on wood, 10' 8" × 6' 8" (3.25 × 2.03 m). Galleria degli Uffizi, Florence. Photo: Dagli Orti, Paris.

painting." Giotto was a one-man revolution in art. He established the illusionary qualities of space, bulk, movement, and human expression—all features of most pictorial art for the next six centuries. His indebtedness to Cimabue is obvious in his *Madonna Enthroned* (fig. 14.51), but there are significant changes that make it not necessarily better but certainly different. Giotto abandoned the Byzantine tradition and patterned his work after Western models, undoubtedly French cathedral statues. His solid human forms occupy a three-dimensional space surrounded by an architectural framework. His *Madonna Enthroned* is highlighted by the protruding knee of the Madonna, indicating a tangible body underneath the robe, a figure of monumental substance. When compared with Cimabue's angels, we see that Giotto's angels, especially the kneeling ones, are placed firmly at the same level on which the base of the Gothic throne rests. The ethereal quality of Byzantine painting has been supplanted by the illusion of tangible space occupied by three-dimensional figures.

Giotto's reputation, imposing in his own time, rests mainly on his frescoes, most notably the celebrated Arena Chapel biblical scenes (fig. 14.52). In his *Lamentation* (fig.

14.52 *Left* Arena Chapel, Padua, with *The Last Judgment* by Giotto, ca. 1304–13, over the door. Photo: Scala, Florence.

14.53 Giotto, *Lamentation*, Arena Chapel, Padua. 1305–6. Fresco, 7' 7" × 7' 9" (2.32 × 2.37 m). Photo: Scala, Florence.

14.53) the artist has staged a pictorial Greek tragedy. The mourning tableau is placed in the foreground so that the picture space is at eye level, involving us in the tragedy, our concern heightened by the wonderfully expressive backs of the two anonymous mourners. Grief is individualized, with each participant mourning according to his or her personality. The emotional range is vast, from the controlled intensity of the earth-bound figures to the tortured grief of the writhing angels. Giotto's achievements are summarized in this one powerful work: the creation of subtle illusions of tactile qualities; existence and movement in space; a deep psychological understanding of subject and viewer; and the establishment of a continuity of space between viewer and painting. To all of these achievements he brought a profound awareness of human emotions. Difficult as it is to realize today, Giotto's contemporaries saw these works as ultimate reality, so "real" you could walk into them. We can understand this view by comparing Giotto's work with that of his contemporaries, and by remembering also that reality, or the illusion of reality, changes from epoch to epoch.

Two Artists from Siena

Two Sienese artists, whose work was unlike that of either Cimabue or Giotto, established the International Style, the first international movement in Western art. Duccio (DOOT-cho; ca. 1255–1319) painted Byzantine-type faces except for the eyes, but in a style comparable to northern Gothic manuscripts and ivories. The most elegant painter of his time, his *Rucellai Madonna* (fig. 14.54) is highly decorative, with sinuous folds of background drapery and a remarkable delicacy of line for so large a work. Contrasting with the Byzantine-style flatness of the Madonna, the kneeling angels are portrayed much more in the round, combining the Hellenistic-Roman naturalistic tradition with that of Gothic architectural sculpture. This one work is a virtual encyclopedia of the International Style synthesis of Mediterranean and northern cultures.

In his *Calling of the Apostles Peter and Andrew* (fig. 14.55), Duccio depicts a world of golden sky and translucent greenish sea where the commanding yet elegant figure of Christ beckons gently to the slightly puzzled fishermen. It is a lovely creation, the world of Duccio, and this is the style the popes at Avignon and the northern kings and queens admired and encouraged their artists to emulate.

14.54 *Above* Duccio, *Rucellai Madonna*, after restoration, 1989. 1285. Tempera on wood, 14' 9" × 9' 6" (4.5 × 2.9 m). Galleria degli Uffizi, Florence. Photo: Dagli Orti, Paris.

Serving the pope's court in Avignon, Duccio's pupil Simone Martini (1284–1344) combined the grace of the Sienese school with the exquisite refinement of Late Gothic architecture. His *Annunciation* (fig. 14.56) epitomizes the courtly style. Completely Gothic, the frame is replete with **crockets**, or ornamental leaves and flowers, and finials, or carved spires; signifying eternity, the gold-leaf background is Byzantine. Delineated in graceful curved-lines, the Angel Gabriel kneels before the Virgin to proclaim "Hail Mary, full of grace . . . ." As the words travel literally from his lips, she draws back in apprehension, her body arranged in an elaborate S-curve and covered by a rich blue robe. Between the two figures is an elegant vase containing white lilies symbolic of Mary's purity. As delicately executed as fine jewelry, the artistic conception is aristocratic and courtly, comparable to the polished **sonnets** of Petrarch, who also served the papal court at Avignon.

With its combined classical, Byzantine, and Gothic attributes, the International Style was promulgated throughout the religious and secular courts of Europe. It found an enthusiastic response wherever wealthy clients prized grace, delicacy, and refinement in art, music, dress, and manners. Aesthetic pleasure was the goal, not spiritual enlightenment.

14.56 Simone Martini, *Annunciation*. 1333. Tempera on wood, 8' 8" × 10' (2.64 × 3.05 m). (Saints in side panels by Lippo Memmi.) Galleria degli Uffizi, Florence. Photo: Scala, Florence.

14.55 *Left* Duccio, *The Calling of the Apostles Peter and Andrew*. 1308–11. Tempera on panel, 17⅛ × 18⅛" (43.5 × 46 cm). National Gallery of Art, Washington, D.C. (Samuel H. Kress Collection).

STUDY QUESTIONS

1. What exactly was the purpose of "pilgrimage churches"? How were they supported? Would merchants have wanted a pilgrimage church in their town?
2. Explain the differences between Romanesque and Gothic architecture. Then explain why Gothic developed on the Continent as an urban art form when Romanesque was essentially a rural style.
3. Medieval churches were very expensive, but many hundreds of them were built, indicating that they were highly valued by society. Which of the following are most valued by our society?

Museums	Sports facilities
Airports	Scientific facilities
Office buildings	Nuclear power plants
Educational buildings	Other
Military bases	

   What does this tell us about modern American values?
4. Architectural historians still argue about which building is better (greater, more beautiful, more inspired): the Parthenon or Chartres cathedral. Pick one and defend your choice.

SUMMARY

A curious backwater during Roman times, Christianized Ireland launched missionary activities that led to a golden age highlighted by the production of exquisite manuscripts in the Hiberno-Saxon style. Establishing a tradition of meticulous northern craftsmanship, the *Lindisfarne Gospels* and the *Book of Kells* were among the first and best of a long history of illuminated manuscripts.

Charlemagne seized the opportune moment to create the Holy Roman Empire and launch the Carolingian Renaissance. Importing technology and stonemasons from the Mediterranean area, he set in motion the forces that would produce the Romanesque style and climax in the Gothic Age.

The year AD 1000 marked the Christianization of virtually all of Europe and the launching of a vast building program of monasteries and churches. Inspired by Roman models, builders constructed stone-vaulted churches such as the pilgrimage churches of St.-Benoit-sur-Loire, St.-Sernin, Toulouse, and Ste.-Madeleine, Vézelay. Notable among the numerous monasteries built during the period were Jumièges and Mont-St.-Michel.

Inspired by the revolutionary design of the choir of St.-Denis, which launched the Gothic style, French master builders erected some of the most sublime buildings ever conceived by humankind, most notably the cathedrals of Chartres, Amiens, and Reims. The style spread to other European countries, where it acquired various regional variations. It also influenced decorative arts, such as jewelry and manuscript illumination.

Though relatively immune to Gothic architecture, Italian artists synthesized classical, Byzantine, and Gothic elements to create the first International Style in art. A medieval man like Dante and his friend and fellow Florentine Giotto carried medieval art to its final consummation. Indeed, Dante's work marks the end of the Middle Ages and sets the stage for the Renaissance.

CULTURE AND HUMAN VALUES

Of the many significant artistic achievements of the Middle Ages, the Gothic cathedral would have to rank as the crowning glory. These amazing structures represented, simultaneously, inspired engineering, breathtaking architecture, appropriate settings for Christian worship, and notable symbols of civic pride. The church ranked pride among the seven deadly sins but pride—a sense of one's own dignity and value—was a vital factor in artistic achievement, as well as stimulating the competitive drive in commerce. The striving for excellence was matched by the vying for position, profit, or prizes.

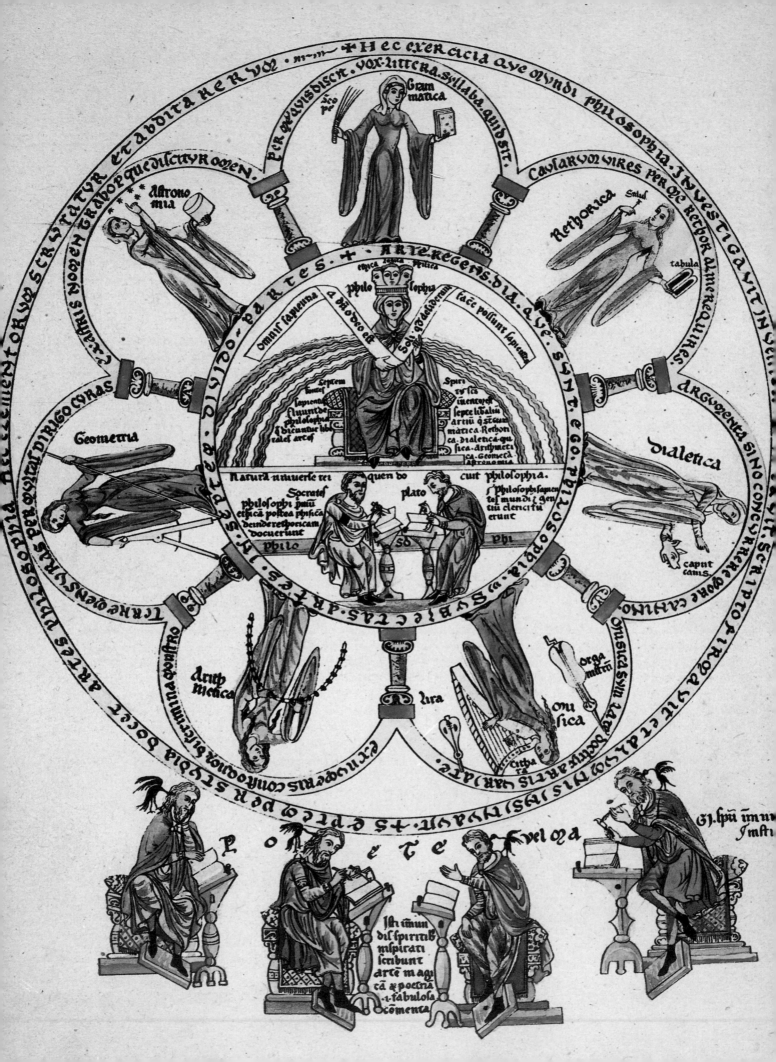

CHAPTER 15

Medieval Music and Dance: Sacred and Secular

The line today between secular music and music used for religious purposes is often very fuzzy, with some of the same music turning up on both sides of the line. Inherently, music is neither sacred nor secular, but it is used for sacred and secular purposes, which is the only way to tell the difference. We can't even say, for example, that "dance music" doesn't belong in church because people do dance in some churches and, conversely, anyone can pray in a nightclub or at a football game. What this adds up to, of course, is that we live in a secular society, and have ever since this country was founded.

Medieval Europe was not a secular society. To be sure, what took place out of sight of the authorities was probably no different than everyday life today. Nevertheless, the society was structured and it was rigid, with everyone knowing his or her place from the village cobbler through the millers, squires, yeomen, knights, earls, barons, kings, monks, priests, bishops, and on and on. Music also knew its place. Only in certain strictly defined ways could it appear in church. It was sacred music and it had to serve God. The service was dictated, of course, by the church, for it made the rules.

SACRED MUSIC

Throughout the world, the oldest type of music is **monophonic**, a single melodic line with no other parts or accompaniment. This kind of unadorned melody line became the liturgical (officially authorized) music of the Church of Rome. The music is monophonic in a style called **Gregorian chant**, or **plainsong**.

Opposite Abbess Herrad von Landsberg, "The Seven Liberal Arts," fol. 32 from the *Hortus Deliciarum* (modern reconstruction; see fig. 15.3). Original ca. 1170. Manuscript. Photo: A.K.G., London.

Gregorian Chant

According to legend, Pope Gregory the Great (reigned 590–604; fig. 15.1) ordered a body of liturgical music organized, priests trained in singing the music, and a common liturgy disseminated throughout the Western church. He did reorganize the church, but the chant that bears his name reached its final form during and shortly after the reign of Charlemagne (reigned 768–814). Consisting today of nearly 3,000 melodies, Gregorian chant is a priceless collection of subtle and sophisticated melodies.

Gregorian chant is monophonic, **a cappella** (unaccompanied), and sung by male or female voices (solo and chorus) in Latin. The authorized texts determine the note values and musical accents, that is, the rhythm of the music

15.1 "King David as Organist *[left]* and Pope Gregory the Great," fol. 5v, Codex Lat. 17403, Bayerische Staatsbibliothek, Munich. 1241. Illuminated manuscript. The Psalms, many of which are attributed to David, formed a large part of the Gregorian repertoire. Inspired by the dove of the Holy Spirit and holding a **monochord**, (an instrument for measuring the mathematical relations between musical tones), Gregory is depicted in his legendary role as codifier of liturgical chant.

15.2 "Guido d'Arezzo," fol. 35v, Codex 51, Vienna Staatsbibliothek. 12th century. Illuminated manuscript. Seated at the left, Guido is demonstrating on a monochord the two-octave scale (A–B–C–D–E–F–G, etc.) which was converted to neumes and placed on the staff.

matches the rhythm of the words. There is no steady pulsation or beat, no division into regular accents as there is in a march or waltz. The undulating melodies flow smoothly, resonating through the cavernous stone churches, weaving a web of sound, and evoking in the worshipers feelings of awe and reverence.

Like secular music, Gregorian chant existed for centuries as a purely oral tradition. The precise musical notation of the ancient Greeks had been lost, and it was not until the eighth century that a new notational system began to evolve. Symbols for musical pitches, called **neumes**, were at first vague about the precise pitch, leading the monk Guido of Arezzo (ca. 990–1050) to remark that, "In our times, of all men, singers are the most foolish." He blamed the lack of precise musical notation for

1. Simple musical notation is used on a modest scale throughout this text; once you understand how to read this, it will make your listening more meaningful and enjoyable. See the Appendix, "Music Listening and Notation," for the basic principles of reading music.
2. CD1, track 3.

"losing time enough in singing to have learned thoroughly both sacred and secular letters." To solve this problem Guido invented a four-line musical **staff** on which neumes could symbolize precise pitches (fig. 15.2).

Many Gregorian melodies were adapted from Jewish synagogue chant, especially the **Alleluias** (Hebrew, *Hallelujah*, "praise ye the Lord"). The seventh item of the Christian Mass (see table 15.1), Alleluias are characteristically **melismatic**, with many notes sung to one syllable. Following is an Alleluia from the Mass for Epiphany (the visit of the Magi).

Listening Example 2
GREGORIAN CHANT

Anonymous, "Alleluia Vidimus stellam"
Codified 590–604[1]
Alleluia. We have seen his star in the East, and have come with gifts to worship the Lord. Alleluia.

Time: 1:04
Cassette 1, track 2[2]

Alleluia, Vidimus stellam   **Anonymous (codified 590–604)**

The Mass

The two basic types of Catholic services are the Mass and the Daily Hours of Divine Services, usually called **Office Hours**. The latter are celebrated eight times a day in religious communities such as monasteries and convents. The Mass, also celebrated daily, is the principal act of Catholic worship. In form this sacrament is an elaborate reenactment of the Lord's Supper and its climax is the consecration of the bread and the wine and the partaking of these elements by the congregation. Everything else in the service is either preparation for Communion (the Eucharist, Gk., "thanksgiving") or a postscript to this commemorative act.

In a "low Mass," the words are enunciated by the priest in a low (speaking) voice in front of a silent congregation. In a "high Mass," the service is recited and sung in a high (singing) voice using either Gregorian chant or a combination of chant and other music.

The Mass consists of the proper, in which the texts vary according to the **liturgical** calendar, and the ordinary, which uses the same texts throughout the church year. Both proper and ordinary have texts that are recited or chanted by the celebrants (clergy) or sung by the choir.

The complete Mass is outlined in table 15.1 (italics indicate the sung portions of the text). Although modernization of the Mass permits the use of indigenous modern language, increased lay participation, and congregational singing, the essential structure remains unchanged.

TABLE 15.1   THE MASS

Ordinary (same text)	Proper (changing texts)
	1. *Introit*
2. *Kyrie*	
3. *Gloria*	
	4. Oratio (prayers, collect)
	5. Epistle
	6. Gradual
	7. *Alleluia* (or *Tract* during Lent)
	8. Gospel
9. *Credo*	
	10. *Offertory*
	11. Secret
	12. Preface
13. *Sanctus*	
14. Canon	
15. *Agnus Dei*	
	16. *Communion*
	17. Postcommunion
18. *Ite missa est* (or *Benedicamus Domino*)	

Tropes

A **trope** (Lat., *tropus*, "figure of speech") is a textual addition to an authorized text, an interpolation in the chant. Sentences or even whole poems were inserted between words of the original text. Sometimes, added words were fitted to preexisting notes; at other times both words and music were injected together into the established text. For example, the chant *Kyrie eleison* ("Lord have mercy upon us"), with an interpolated trope, might read: Lord, *omnipotent Father, God, Creator of all,* have mercy upon us.

The practice of troping could have resulted from boredom, a desire for creativity, an inability to remember the notes, or varying combinations of all three. The authorized texts had not only remained the same for centuries but many of them—particularly the texts of the ordinary—were sung countless times. More positively, troping permitted exercises in creativity that could enliven the unvarying liturgical music without unduly disturbing the authorities.

Sequences

The oldest form of trope was that inserted into the last syllable, the "ia" (ja) of the Alleluia (see the example of an Alleluia given above). Many Alleluias, because of their Eastern origin, ended with an exotic and elaborate melisma on the final syllable. New poetry was added to this melisma and then, in time, the last section was detached from the Alleluia to become a separate composition called a **sequence**—that which follows. After this separation had occurred, composers felt free to alter the melodic line—a chance, finally, to move beyond the church-imposed formulas for sacred music.

The sequence marked the beginnings of musical composition for its own sake, a new development that would lead eventually to the works of such composers as Palestrina, Beethoven, and Stravinsky. Composing sequences was a first step away from the rigidity of a prescribed musical repertoire. Composers began to explore ever more musical innovations and thus to breach and, ultimately, to break down medieval walls.

The proliferation of sequences threatened for a time to dominate traditional Gregorian chant—a development that alarmed some churchmen. The Council of Trent (1545–63), formed to oppose the Reformation, abolished sequences, which caused such a furor that four sequences were returned to the repertoire. Following is the oldest of the surviving sequences, the so-called Easter Sequence by Wipo of Burgundy (WEE-po; ca. 1024–50), chaplain to the Holy Roman Emperor Henry III. This melody also served later as the basis for a Lutheran Easter **chorale**, "Christ Lay in the Bonds of Death," with text by Martin Luther.

Listening Example 3
SEQUENCE

Wipo of Burgundy, "Victimae paschali laudes"
11th century

Time: 1:42
Cassette 1, track 3

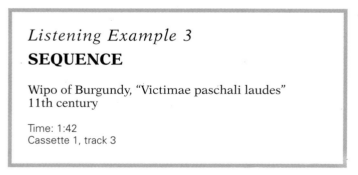

Victimae paschali laudes   **Wipo of Burgundy (11th century)**

Vic - ti - mae pas - cha - li lau - des   im - mo - lent Chri - sti - a - ni.
(Let Christians dedicate their praises to the Easter victim.)

Liturgical Drama

Religious ceremonies, such as the Mass, extend themselves into the realm of the theatre. The dramatic reenactment of the Last Supper in the Mass led, in time, to the development of medieval drama. The impulse was somewhat similar to that which saw classical Greek drama evolve from the cult of Dionysos. There were notable differences, however. Greek tragedy dealt with ethical choices made under stress; illiterate medieval peasants were concerned with representations of the Nativity, the Shepherds, the Three Wise Men, and other specific events connected with their religion. Apparently the earliest surviving complete liturgical drama (words and music) was written by Hildegard (1098–1179), abbess of Bingen, who told the story of a contest between the devil and a human soul (*anima*).

At first the actors were priests and the plays episodes from the life of Christ, particularly the Christmas and Easter stories. During the liturgy, priests interpolated paraphrased dialogues from the Gospels, frequently using tropes. But these miniature dramas were too brief and too abstract for the unlettered congregation. Gradually the actors (clergy) gave priority to the Scriptures by using Latin for the formal sections and the vernacular for the dialogues. Eventually whole plays were performed in the native language, which in the early plays was French. Dramas were originally enacted in front of the altar; as vernacular elements were added performances were moved to the church portal and acting parts taken by laypeople who, in time, formed their own confraternities or societies of actors.

Liturgical dramas were mainly musical, relying for their effects on singing and on a rich variety of accompanying instruments. Of the dozens of instruments available, favorites included the **organ**, **harp**, lyre, **horn**, **trumpet**, **recorder**, rebec (precursor of **viols** and then violins), drums, and other **percussion** instruments (fig. 15.3).

The following opening dialogue (sung in Latin) is from *The Play of the Three Kings*, which dates from the late eleventh century. Some of the melodies were borrowed from plainsong, but much of the music was undoubtedly composed for the occasion. This recorded performance is *a cappella*, but instruments could have been added to underscore the Oriental origins of the Magi.

15.3   Abbess Herrad von Landsberg, fol. 32 from the *Hortus Deliciarum*. Ca. 1170. Manuscript fragment. Photo: Marburg.

Formerly in the town library of Strasbourg, the manuscript was destroyed in the 1870 Franco-Prussian War. Hanging at the right is a rebec, a bowed string instrument of Arab origin. The female performer holds a harp, and, at the left, there hangs a wheel-lyre (organistrum). This instrument has three strings set in motion by a revolving wheel operated by a hand crank and is an ancestor of the hurdy-gurdy.

Listening Example 4

LITURGICAL DRAMA

Anonymous, "Infantem vidimus"
11th–12th century; excerpt
Shepherds
Infantem vidimus
(We have seen the Infant.)
Boys
Qui sunt hi, quos stella ducit nos adeuntes, inaudita ferentes?
(Who are those whom the star leads, approaching us and bearing strange things?)
Magi
Nos sumus quos cernites reges Tharsis et Arabum et Saba, dona offerentes Christo Reginato Domino.
(We are those whom you see—the kings of Tharsis, Arabia, and Sheba, offering gifts to Christ the King, the new-born Lord.)

Time: 1:08
Cassette 1, track 4

Conductus

The conductus was a processional used to "conduct" important characters on and off the stage. One of the most familiar of these was the "Song of the Ass,"[3] which was often used to describe Mary's flight into Egypt riding on a donkey. This song is shown as it was used in the twelfth-century *Play of Daniel*. Accompanying the Virgin as she rides into the church on a donkey, the conductus, as befits its function as processional music, is metrical. It has four beats to each **measure** in the manner of a solemn march. Only one of the seven verses is given here.

3. G. M. Dreves, *Analecta hymnica* xx, 217, 257; H. C. Greene, *Speculum vi*.

Play of Daniel: "Song of the Ass," Verse 1   **Anonymous (12th century)**

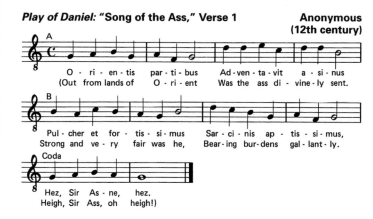

O - ri - en - tis par - ti - bus   Ad - ven - ta - vit a - si - nus
(Out from lands of   O - ri - ent   Was the ass di - vine - ly sent.

Pul - cher et for - tis - si - mus   Sar - ci - nis ap - tis - si - mus,
Strong and ve - ry fair was he,   Bear - ing bur - dens gal - lant - ly.

Coda

Hez, Sir As - ne, hez.
Heigh, Sir Ass, oh heigh!)

Beginning in the fourteenth century, liturgical drama developed into mystery plays (Lat., *ministerium,* "service") performed entirely in the vernacular under secular sponsorship. Using music only for processions, fanfares, and dances, these dramatic portrayals of biblical stories (the Creation, the life of Jesus, and so forth) were the forerunners of modern European drama.

SECULAR MUSIC

Goliards

The **goliards** of the tenth through thirteenth centuries were a motley collection of rebellious vagabonds: disenchanted students, defrocked priests, minstrels, rascals, artists, and dreamers. Generally dissatisfied with established values and entrenched institutions, they took their name from a "Bishop Golias," whom they claimed as a patron—a very tolerant patron.

The goliards' songs treat many subjects: love, drinking, springtime, and more love, and include material both moral and immoral. Generally light-hearted and frequently obscene, their songs reflect, according to contemporary accounts, the licentious conduct of the goliards themselves.

Though little of their music is extant, many of their poems have survived, including those quoted on page 386 and a thirteenth-century manuscript published as *Carmina Burana.* Selections from this collection have been set to music by the modern German composer Carl Orff (1895–1982). A sampling of the opening lines from this poetry indicates some basic themes.

"Were the world all mine from the sea to the Rhine, I would gladly forsake it all if the Queen of England were in my arms."

"In rage and bitterness I talk to myself."

"I am the Abbot of Cluny, and I spend my time with drinkers."

"When we are in the tavern we don't care who has died."

"The God of Love flies everywhere."

"Sweetest boy I give myself completely to you."

The licentious conduct of the goliards and their assault upon established values led inevitably to conflicts with the church. However, the movement died out, not because of clerical opposition, but due to the rise of universities, which replaced wandering students with resident ones. However, conflict between the church and the universities, between authority and knowledge, became ever more strident.

Jongleurs

The **jongleurs** of France (and the *Gauklers,* their German counterparts) were generally not as educated as the goliards. Appearing first during the ninth century, these wandering men and women were seldom composers but always entertainers. They played music and sang songs that others had written, did tricks with trained animals, and generally helped to brighten weddings and other special events. Though some of them were sufficiently talented to be socially acceptable, many were considered disreputable as far as a despairing clergy was concerned.

The jongleurs' repertoire included **chansons de geste,** epic chronicles of the valorous deeds of heroes such as Charlemagne and Roland. Because the melodies consisted of easily remembered tunes, there was no real need to write down the music and thus very little of it has survived. In a twelfth-century manuscript of the *Chanson de Roland* there are musical fragments that were apparently used to sing of the exploits of Roland and his horn. The chantfable, part prose and part verse, was similar to the chanson de geste but with a slightly different form. The best-known chant-fable is *Aucassin and Nicolette* (see pp. 363–72).

Troubadours and Trouvères

A manifestation of the age of chivalry, the troubadours of Provence and their later followers in northern France, the **trouvères,** produced the finest repertoire of lyric song of the Middle Ages. These educated aristocrats, both men and women, composed love poetry in the tradition of Ovid, whose love poems and *Art of Love* (see pp. 268–72) were known to the cultured nobles of the south of France. The repertoire is large (2,600 troubadour poems, about 300 melodies; 4,000 trouvère poems, 1,400 melodies) and covers many subjects: the Crusades, travel, adventure, and, above all, romantic love. Despite the relative paucity of surviving melodies, all of the poems were meant to be sung. According to the troubadour Folquet of Marseilles (ca. 1155–1231), "A verse without music is a mill without water."

The earliest known troubadour, Duke William IX of Aquitaine (1071–1126), was a Crusader, poet, and performer, whose lusty life and romantic pursuits are reflected in his poetry, of which eleven poems and one melody have survived. The boldly masculine attitude in the following poem is comparable to Ovid's most aggressive style.

LITERARY SELECTION 38

Troubadour Songs
Duke William IX of Aquitaine

1. Friends, I'll write a poem that will do:
   But it'll be full of fun
   And not much sense.
   A grab-bag all about love
   And joy and youth.

2. A man's a fool if he doesn't get it
   Or deep down inside won't try
   To learn.
   It's very hard to escape from love
   Once you find you like it.   10

3. I've got two pretty good fillies in my corral:
   They're ready for any combat—
   They're tough.
   But I can't keep 'em both together:
   Don't get along.

4. If I could tame 'em the way I want,
   I wouldn't have to change
   This set-up,
   For I'd be the best-mounted man
   In all this world.   20

5. One's the fastest filly up in the hills,
   And she's been fierce and wild
   A long, long time.
   In fact, she's been so fierce and wild,
   Can't stick her in my pen.

6. The other was born here—Confolens way—
   And I never saw a better mare,
   I swear
   But she won't change her wild, wild ways
   For silver or gold.   30

7. I gave to her master a feeding colt;
   But I kept myself a share
   In the bargain too:
   If he'll keep her one whole year,
   I will a hundred or more.

8. Knights, your advice in this affair!
   I was never so troubled by
   Any business before.
   Which of these nags should I keep:
   Miss Agnes? Miss Arsen?   40

9. I've got the castle at Gimel under thumb,
   And over at Nieul I strut
   For all the folks to see.
   Both castles are sworn and pledged by oath:
   They belong to me!

Considerably more subtle, the next poem is designed to create a romantic, seductive atmosphere.

1. I'm going to write a brand-new song
   Before the wind and rain start blowing.
   My lady tries and tests me
   To see the way I love her.
   Yet despite the trials that beset me,
   I'd never break loose from her chain.

2. No, I put myself in her bondage,
   Let her write me into her charter.
   And don't think that I'm a drunkard
   If I love my good lady thus,   10
   For without her I couldn't live.
   I'm so hungry for her love.

3. O, she's whiter than any ivory statue.
   How could I worship any other?
   But if I don't get reinforcements soon
   To help me win my lady's love,
   By the head of St. George, I'll die!—
   Unless we kiss in bower or bed.

4. Pretty lady, what good does it do you
   To cloister up your love?   20
   Do you want to end up a nun?
   Listen: I love you so much
   I'm afraid that grief will jab me
   If your wrongs don't become the rights I beg.

5. What good will it do if I'm a monk
   And don't come begging round your door?
   Lady, the whole world's joy could be ours,
   If we'd just love each other.
   Over there at my friend Daurostre's
   I'm sending this song to be welcomed and sung.   30

6. Because of her I shake and tremble,
   Since I love her with the finest love.
   I don't think there's been a woman like her
   In the whole grand line of Lord Adam.

William's son governed the duchy for a few years, followed by his granddaughter, the celebrated Eleanor of Aquitaine (1122–1204), who established a court of love in Poitiers in 1170. Eleanor sponsored several troubadours and trouvères, the most notable of whom was Bernart de Ventadorn (d. 1195). Dante conferred the title of master singer on Arnaut Daniel and consigned another troubadour, Bertran de Born, to Hell but modern critics have ceded the palm to the poet-musician from Ventadorn as the finest lyric poet of the age.

Forty poems, eighteen with music, by Bernart de Ventadorn are known today. Lively, witty, and eminently singable, the subject is immutable: love rewarded, unrequited, noble, sacred, or profane, but always love. In the following canso (love song; **chanson** in northern France) the first of six verses is given in both Provençal, the language of the troubadours, and in English.

Listening Example 5
TROUBADOUR CANSO

Bernart de Ventadorn, "Be m'an perdut"
12th century; excerpt
Be m'an perdut lai enves Ventadorn tuih meo amic,
(I am indeed lost from the region of Ventadorn / To all
my friends,)
*pois ma domna no m'ama; et es be dreihz que jamais lai
no torn*
(for my lady loves me not; With reason I turn not back
again,)
c'a des estai vas me salvatj' egrama.
(For she is bitter and ill-disposed toward me.)
Veus per quem fai semblan irat emorn;
(See why she turns a dark and angry countenance to
me;)
car en s'amor me deleih e'm sojorn!
(Because I take joy and pleasure in loving her!)
ni de ren als no's rancura ni's clama.
(Nor has she ought else with which to charge me.)

Time: 0:52
Cassette 1, track 5[4]

"Be m'an perdut"   **Ventadorn (d. 1195)**

After her divorce from the king of France, Eleanor
married, in 1152, Henry II, Duke of Normandy and, later,
King of England. The next poem implies that Bernart has
followed her to England and that the haughty highborn
lady is either Eleanor herself or a member of her court.

LITERARY SELECTION 39

Lancan vei per mei la landa

Bernart de Ventadorn

1.   Whenever I see amid the plain
     The leaves are drifting down from trees
     Before the cold's expansion,
     And the gentle time's in hiding,
     It's good for my song to be heard,
     For I've held back more than two years
     And it's right to make amends.

2.   It's hard for me to serve that woman
     Who shows me only her haughty side,
     For if my heart dares make a plea,   10
     She won't reply with a single word.
     Truly this fool desire is killing me:

I follow the lovely form of Love,
     Not seeing Love won't attend me.

3.   She's mastered cheating, trickery,
     So that always I think she loves me.
     Ah, sweetly she deceives me,
     As her pretty face confounds me!
     Lady, you're gaining absolutely nothing:
     In fact, I'm sure it's toward your loss   20
     That you treat your man so badly.

4.   God, Who nurtures all the world,
     Put it in her heart to take me,
     For I don't want to eat any food
     And of nothing good I have plenty.
     Toward the beautiful one, I'm humble,
     And I render her rightful homage:
     She can keep me, she can sell me.

5.   Evil she is if she doesn't call me
     To come where she undresses alone   30
     So that I can wait at her bidding
     Beside the bed, along the edge,
     Where I can pull off her close-fitting shoes
     Down on my knees, my head bent down:
     If only she'll offer me her foot.

6.   This verse has been filled to the brim
     Without a single word that will tumble,
     Beyond the land of the Normans,
     Here across the wild, deep sea.
     [Apparently England.]
     And though I'm kept far from Milordess,   40
     She draws me toward her like a magnet:
     God, keep that beauty ever safe!

7.   If the English king and the Norman duke
     Will it, I'll see her soon
     Before the winter overtakes us.

8.   For the king I remain an English-Norman,
     And if there were no Lady Magnet,
     I'd stay here till after Christmas.

A number of female troubadours have been identified, including Azalais of Porcairagues, Maria of Ventadorn,
Lombarda, and the Countess Garsenda of Provence. The
most notable poet-musician, whose work is comparable to
that of any male troubadour, was the Countess of Dia
(present-day Die), who lived in the Drôme valley in southern France during the twelfth century and was known as
Beatritz. Her voice is as distinctive as that of Sappho (see
pp. 225–6). In the following dialogue song the lady sweeps
aside male rationalizations and exacts a pledge of loyalty,
devotion, and a love to be shared equally.

4. C. Appel, *Bernart von Ventadorn* (Halle, 1915), Plate ix (citing
    Milan manuscript *Chansonnier G*, folio 14). The form is AAB
    (see p. 460).

LITERARY SELECTION 40

Troubadour Songs

Beatritz, Countess of Dia

1. Friend, I stand in great distress
Because of you, and in great pain;
And I think you don't care one bit
About the ills that I'm enduring;
And so, why set yourself as my lover
Since to me you bequeath all the woe?
Why can't we share it equally?

2. Lady, love goes about his job
As he chains two friends together
So the ills they have and the lightness too   10
Are felt by each—in his fashion.
And I think—and I'm no gabber—
That all this deep-down, heartstruck woe
I have in full on my side too.

3. Friend, if you had just one fourth
Of this aching that afflicts me now,
I'm sure you'd see my burden of pain;
But little you care about my grief,
Since you know I can't break free;
But to you it's all the same   20
Whether good or bad possess me.

4. Lady, because these glozing spies,
Who have robbed me of my sense and breath,
Are our most vicious warriors,
I'm stopping: not because desire dwindles.
No, I can't be near, for their vicious brays
Have hedged us in for a deadly game.
And we can't sport through frolicsome days.

5. Friend, I offer you no thanks
Because my damnation is not the bit   30
That checks those visits I yearn for so.
And if you set yourself as watchman
Against my slander without my request,
Then I'll have to think you're more "true-blue"
Than those loyal Knights of the Hospital.

6. Lady, my fear is most extreme
(I'll lose your gold, and you mere sand)
If through the talk of these scandalmongers
Our love will turn itself to naught.
And so I've got to stay on guard   40
More than you—by St. Martial I swear!—
For you're the thing that matters most.

7. Friend, I know you're changeable
In the way you handle your love,
And I think that as a chevalier
You're one of that shifting kind;
And I'm justified in blaming you,
For I'm sure other things are on your mind,
Since I'm no longer the thought that's there.

8. Lady, I'll never carry again   50
My falcon, never hunt with a hawk,
If, now that you've given me joy entire,
I started chasing another girl.
No, I'm not that kind of shyster:
It's envy makes those two-faced talk.
They make up tales and paint me vile.

9. Friend, should I accept your word
So that I can hold you forever true?

10. Lady, from now on you'll have me true,
For I'll never think of another.   60

More direct than much of the poetry of her male counterparts, the following song leaves no doubt about the lady's fiery passion. The slighting reference to the husband may have amused the Count, for this is, after all, a fictional account of a woman who has much in common with the Wife of Bath in Chaucer's *Canterbury Tales*.

1. I've suffered great distress
From a knight whom I once owned.
Now, for all time, be it known:
I loved him—yes, to excess.
His jilting I've regretted,
Yet his love I never really returned.
Now for my sin I can only burn:
Dressed, or in my bed.

2. O, if I had that knight to caress
Naked all night in my arms,
He'd be ravished by the charm   10
Of using, for cushion, my breast.
His love I more deeply prize
Than Floris did Blancheflor's.
Take that love, my core,
My sense, my life, my eyes!

3. Lovely lover, gracious, kind,
When will I overcome your fight?
O, if I could lie with you one night!
Feel those loving lips on mine!   20
Listen, one thing sets me afire:
Here in my husband's place I want *you*,
If you'll just keep your promise true:
Give me everything I desire.

By the middle of the twelfth century, troubadour influences had spread to northern France, where notable trouvères included Blondel de Nesles (b. ca. 1155), minstrel to Richard the Lionhearted (reigned 1189–99 and himself a trouvère). Like troubadour cansos, trouvère chansons were monophonic with accompaniment an option depending on available instruments. The following **virelai** is a trouvère form that begins with a refrain that repeats after each verse. Composed by an unknown trouvère, this is a superb example of the sophisticated style of northern France.

Listening Example 6

TROUVERE VIRELAI

Anonymous,"Or la truix"
12th–13th century; excerpt
Or la truix trop durete, voir, voir! A ceu k'elle est simplete.
(I find it hard to woo her, indeed! Because she is so simple.)
Trop por outrecuidiés me taius, cant je cudoie estre certains
(Much too presumptuous did I act, e'en though it seem'd I was so sure)
de ceu ke n'averaides mois, oix, oix! C'est ceu ke plus me blece.
(of that which I shan't have so soon, alas! 'Tis mostly that which hurts me.)
Or la truix trop durete, voir, voir! A ceu k'elle est simplete.
(I find it hard to woo her, indeed! Because she is so simple.)

Time: 1:00
Cassette 1, track 6[5]

"Or la truix"   Anonymous (12th–13th century)

In 1208 Pope Innocent III preached a crusade against the Albigensian heresy (latter-day Manicheans; see p. 337), stating that the church must "use against heretics the spiritual sword of excommunication, and if this does not prove effective, use the material sword." His army killed 12,000 Christians in a single day. Exploiting the Albigensian Crusade as an excuse to plunder the south of France, nobles, the French crown, and the papacy destroyed the high culture that had fostered the troubadour tradition, chivalry, and the Courts of Love.

POLYPHONIC MUSIC

The high point of medieval music was the development of **polyphony**. Polyphony (Gk., *poly-phonos*, "many sounds") is a style of music in which two or more melodies are played and/or sung together. "Row, Row, Row Your Boat," when sung as a **round**, is an example of one kind of polyphonic music in which the same melody is sung at different times. "Jesu, Joy of Man's Desiring," by J. S. Bach, combines three different melodies.

5. Bodleian Oxford, Douce 308, folios 226 and 237. The form is ABAA.

Related to polyphonic music is a style that evolved in the late seventeenth and early eighteenth centuries, and is called **homophonic** (Gk., *homo-phonos*, "like sounds"). Homophonic music consists of a single melody plus accompaniment or, to put it another way, melody and **harmony**. For example, "The Star Spangled Banner" and "The Battle Hymn of the Republic" are homophonic.

Polyphonic and homophonic styles of music are closely related with neither style usually existing in a pure form. Music that emphasizes two or more melodies of roughly equal importance is termed polyphonic. Homophonic music, on the other hand, emphasizes a predominant melody accompanied by harmony that enriches the melodic line. The two styles may be illustrated as follows:

Homophonic (3-part)

Melody

Harmony

Polyphonic (3-part)

Melody 1

Melody 2

Melody 3

Non-Western music (from the Middle and Far East and Africa) has not developed polyphonic or homophonic styles of music. Although polyphony may occur in the music of these cultures, it is spontaneous rather than planned, the result of accidental conjunctions of melodies rather than a premeditated polyphonic composition, as we find in Western music.

It is this multi-voiced quality (both polyphonic and homophonic) that makes Western music unique. The development of polyphony during the Middle Ages was thus a crucial step leading to the enormous proliferation of musical styles: those of Bach, Beethoven, Bob Dylan, and Bruce Springsteen; the blues, ragtime, jazz, country-western, rock, and all the others.

The earliest medieval polyphony drew on the rich treasury of monophonic chants. Early attempts at multiple melodies, beginning in the tenth century, were quite literal: another voice was added at a fixed interval from the original chant (parallel **organum**). Later, in free organum, the two voices generally moved in contrary motion. That is, when one voice went up the other would go down. Still later, in melismatic organum, one voice moved slowly on prolonged notes (the original chant) while the other traced elaborate melismas.

Listing Example 7

EARLY POLYPHONY: ORGANUM

Parallel: "Rex caeli, Domine"[6]
Free: Trope, "Agnus Dei"[7]
Melismatic: "Benedicamo Domino"[8]

Time: 2:29
Cassette 1, track 7[9]

"Rex caeli, Domine"   Anonymous (900–1150)

Rex cae - li Do - mi - ne ma - ris un - di - so - ni.
(King of the hea - vens, Lord of the wave - sound - ing sea.)

"Agnus Dei"   Anonymous (900–1150)

"Benedicamo Domino"   Anonymous (900–1150)

Be -   -   -   ne   -

Cantus Firmus

Eventually the chant melody was consistently placed in the lowest voice and referred to as the **cantus firmus** ("fixed song"). The chant was identified by quoting the initial phrase of the Latin text. The cantus firmus was also called the **tenor** (Lat. *tenere*, "to hold") because it held (retained) the original chant.

All polyphonic compositions of the medieval period were based on a cantus firmus, usually assigned to the tenor voice. The practice of using authorized liturgical music (plainsong) as a foundation for composing original music is comparable to basing a sermon on a scriptural quotation. Both procedures quoted an approved source as the prerequisite for what was essentially an exercise in creativity.

Polyphonic writing developed rapidly during the twelfth century due, in part, to the invention of rhythmic notation by composers of the school of music associated with the Cathedral of Notre Dame in Paris. The Paris composers wanted the larger sound of more voices for the cavernous nave of Notre Dame. They began writing three- and four-part compositions after they discovered how to synchronize the different voices, how to keep the singers moving together to the right notes at the right time. This Notre Dame notation (now called rhythmic modes) was based on the poetic meters such as iambic, dactylic, trochaic, and so forth. These were patterns of long and short sounds that were transformed into musical notation. The remarkable thing about rhythmic notation was that "it represented the first symbolic manipulation of measured time—time independent of motion and detached from the environment."[10] The Notre Dame composers were the first to discover how to measure time.

Following is a three-part organum by Pérotin, the foremost composer of the **Notre Dame school**. The beginning measures are given in musical notation so that the two voice parts plus instrumental line can be seen as well as heard. The music is now "measured" with a **time signature** and bar lines separating the measures. Any of the melodies can be sung, whistled, or played on an instrument. The complexity of polyphony results from the simultaneity of, in this case, uncomplicated melody lines.

Listening Example 8

THREE-PART ORGANUM

Pérotin, "Alleluya" (Nativitas)
12th century; excerpt

Time: 1:35
Cassette 1, track 8[11]

"Alleluya"   Pérotin (12th century)

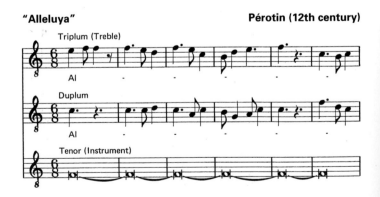

6. M. Gerbert, *Scriptores* (St. Blaise, France, 1784) Vol. I, p. 167.
7. Besseler, *Die Musik des Mittelalters* (Potsdam, 1931), p. 95.
8. F. Ludwig, *Handbuch der Musikgeschichte* (Frankfurt am Main, 1924), p. 148.
9. CD 1, track 4.
10. Szamosi, Geza, "The Origin of Time: How Medieval Musicians Invented the Fourth Dimension." *The Sciences* 26 (September/October 1986): 33–7.
11. Y. Rokseth, *Polyphonies du XIIIe siècle* (Paris, 1935).

The **motet**, one of the most important forms of sacred music, was developed in the thirteenth century. This polyphonic form was based originally on a passage of plainsong, which was used as the cantus firmus. Above this, the composer wrote one, two, or more melodic lines, each with its own set of words. The first of these was called the motetus (Fr., *mot*, "word"). A third voice added to the cantus firmus and the motetus was called the triplum; a fourth voice, the quadruplum.

The motet offered enormous scope for variation. Not only could the different voices sing different words, but they might be in different languages: the cantus firmus being in Latin, for example, and the upper voices being in the vernacular. It was not long before secular poetry was being used for the upper voices, at which point the sacred Latin text of the cantus firmus was often dropped and this line performed instrumentally. This type of secular motet is illustrated by the following example, in which the upper voices sing variations on a French love song. Its title contains, as was customary, the first few words of each line, those of the tenor line serving only to identify the original chant. Here again, the opening measures of notation illustrate the uncomplicated nature of the individual melodies.

Listening Example 9

MOTET

Anonymous, "En non Diu! Quant voi; Eius in Oriente"
13th century; excerpt

Time: 1:07
Cassette 1, track 9[17]

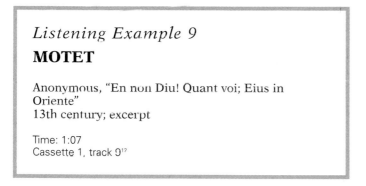

"En non Diu! Quant voi; Eius in Oriente"　　**School of Notre Dame (13th century)**

---

12. Y. Rokseth, *Polyphonies du XIIIe siècle* (Paris, 1935).
13. CD 1, track 5.

The earliest extant piece of music in six parts is the "Reading Rota," a double round found at Reading Abbey and set to a Middle English text: "Sumer is icumen in." The top melody is sung by four voices as a four-part round. One voice begins alone, the second voice begins when the first has gotten to the asterisk, and so on. At the same time the lower two voices sing a two-part round to the words "sing cuccu."

Listening Example 10

DOUBLE ROUND

Anonymous, "Sumer is icumen in"
Ca. 1240

Time: 1:42
Cassette 1, track 10[13]

"Sumer is icumen in"　　**Anonymous (ca. 1240)**

Polyphonic Mass

Musical styles developed very rapidly during the High Middle Ages, and some composers acquired international reputations (in contrast to the great master builders of Gothic cathedrals, most of whom remain anonymous). Guillaume de Machaut (ca. 1300–77), equally proficient as poet and as a composer of both sacred and secular music, was the most acclaimed of the gifted artists of the Late Middle Ages (fig. 15.4). He was the first to write a polyphonic setting of all five movements of the ordinary of the Mass, a practice that was subsequently followed by every major composer through the sixteenth century and by many composers up to the present day.

The following "Agnus Dei" is sung by the upper three voices and accompanied by an instrument on the *contratenor* part, as indicated by the absence of text. The tenor, now the next lowest voice, still sings the cantus firmus. The polyphonic Mass, as distinguished from a motet, uses the Latin text of the monophonic chant. The beginning of the movement is notated here in an open score (one staff for each part) so that the more complex movement of the melodies can be compared with the examples previously given of an organum and a motet.

15.4 Master of Bocqueteaux, "Machaut Receiving Honors of Royalty and Clergy." Miniature. Bibliothèque Nationale, Paris.
This first known portrait of a Western composer is indicative both of Machaut's reputation and of the status of a creative artist in late medieval France.

Listening Example 11
POLYPHONIC MASS

Machaut, "Agnus Dei," Mass of Notre Dame
1364

Time: 1:02
Cassette 1, track 11[14]

14. CD 1, track 7. H. Besseler, *Die Musik des Mittelalters und der Renaissance* (Bucken, *Handbuch der Musikwissenschaft*) (Potsdam, 1931), p. 149.

MEDIEVAL DANCE
Sacred Dance

Although the Church of Rome officially disapproved of dance in worship because of its non-Christian associations, dancing as a glorification of God was widely accepted in some Christian communities up until the High Middle Ages, when it was universally banned. Especially popular was the "Hymn of Jesus," a round dance (or ring dance) with twelve dancers representing the twelve disciples and the twelve signs of the zodiac. The idea of zodiac dancing to restore order to the cosmos can be traced as far back as the ancient Egyptians. However, a direct influence was probably the Pythagorean concept of the music of the spheres. This ring dance was also called the Ring Dance of Angels or simply Angel Dance.

The tripudium dated from early Christianity and was one of the few dance steps to survive into the medieval period. A tripudium was a three-step dance with two steps forward and one step backward. The dance symbolized both the Holy Trinity and, possibly, the concept of two (spiritual) steps forward and one step (of human frailty) backward.

"The Way to Jerusalem" was a stately dance that symbolized a pilgrimage to the Holy City. The dance was executed on the design of a labyrinth inlaid in the nave floor of some cathedrals. A chosen leader determined the pace and the steps that matched the pattern of the floor tiles. This was a slow, spiraling dance that coordinated the dance steps with an accompanying chant. To make it all the way to Jerusalem, the leader had to arrive at the center of the labyrinth at the precise moment that the final syllable of the chant was sung. The dance was usually performed on a labyrinth modeled after the Cretan version in the Knossos Labyrinth. The labyrinth in the cathedral of Chartres dates from the twelfth century and is 40 feet (12.2 m) in diameter.

Choreomania, a kind of dance mania, probably first appeared in England in the twelfth century. It was characterized by group psychosis and frenzied, even demented dancing. The Dance of Death (*Danse Macabre*) was a phenomenon that appeared during the Black Death. Enacting the superstition that the dead danced on their graves to lure the living, some plague victims did their Dance of Death in the cemetery.

Secular Dance

Little is known of dancing in the Early Middle Ages, but by the eighth or ninth centuries social dancing was a universal activity enjoyed by people at every level of society. The frequent fairs and festivals, with the attendant vigorous dancing, enabled the peasantry to forget temporarily their generally bleak and meager existence.

The earliest form of European social dancing was

THE BLACK DEATH

No pestilence to date has been more devastating than the Black Death of the Middle Ages. Active in Central Asia in 1338, the plague infiltrated every European country with a port city and killed about a third of the population—75 million people. Spread by fleas who had fed on the blood of infected rodents, the disease traveled aboard rat-infested ships. Symptoms included vomiting, delirium, muscular pain, and swollen lymph nodes called buboes, thus "bubonic plague," with death certain 60 to 90 percent of the time. Inhaling droplets from a victim whose disease had spread to the respiratory system caused pneumonic plague, when death was literally in the air, swift and virtually inevitable. What caused the sickness was unknown but Christians blamed non-Christians and sinners, who were supposedly reaping God's punishment. Scapegoats were everywhere: cripples, lepers, Arabs, and Jews—especially Jews, who were massacred in Germany, southern France, the Low Countries, and parts of Spain. The Jews in Basel, Switzerland, were locked in wooden buildings and burned alive. Ironically, a non-Christian civilization had already found the answer in the fifth century AD, when the Indian physician Susrata noted the relationship of malaria to mosquitoes and of plague to rats. Plague is still a menace and still kills if antibiotics are not started within hours of the first symptoms. The disease is apparently not as virulent as the earlier strain but the emergence of AIDS signals a plague that could surpass the medieval killer.

the right, then backward, then forward, then backward once more, and then began the pattern all over again.

Following is a two-part estampie with the parts labeled simply as cantus superior and cantus inferior. They were to be played by any available instruments. To get a sense of what it was like to dance in a medieval court, try executing the steps of the estampie to an accompaniment of the cassette or any two or more different percussion instruments like the drum, tambourine, bells, or triangle.

Listening Example 12
ESTAMPIE

Anonymous, "Instrumental Dance"
13th century; excerpt

Time: 1:26
Cassette 1, track 12[15]

"Instrumental Dance"   Anonymous (13th century)

STUDY QUESTIONS

1. Hearing an authentic performance of music that has been sung for 1,000 years or more is a moving and exhilarating experience. Find a vocal group in your area that sings Gregorian chant, possibly in a Catholic church or monastery or a college music department.

2. How does a Protestant service (Presbyterian, Methodist, Baptist, and so on) differ from the Catholic Mass? (NOTE: The several denominations also differ considerably from each other.) What do the Mass and various forms of Protestant services have in common?

3. What, if anything, do rock lyrics have in common with troubadour songs? You might want to look up additional troubadour songs for better comparisons.

performed by a group of people arranged either in a ring or in a chain. One of the most popular early dances was the **branle**, which was danced in an arc or in a closed circle, moving in a clockwise direction, interrupted by occasional steps to the right, producing a swaying effect. Like many other dances, the branle was taken up by the nobility, who used its basic steps to devise more refined and complex dances. Some of these new aristocratic dances were performed by couples—a development that may have first taken place in twelfth-century Provence. The earliest known couple dance, called the **estampie** (Provençal, *estamper*, "to stamp"), remained the most popular dance through the High Middle Ages. The music for the estampie was in triple meter and consisted of short, rotating phrases that were repeated many times during the course of the dance. To begin the dance, couples stood side by side in a semicircle. The first part of the dance began with both starting on the same foot with a step, close, step, close to first position with heels together. The dancers moved first to

15. Wooldridge, *Early English Harmony* (London, 1897), p. 19.

SUMMARY

The first medieval music to be written down was composed for the church. This was monophonic music of a form known as Gregorian chant or plainsong, performed by monks or nuns without accompaniment as part of the Mass or the Divine Office. In time, these chants were elaborated by the introduction of tropes and sequences—extra words and notes that varied the pattern in interesting ways. These embellishments led, in turn, to the development of liturgical drama as part of the Mass, and then to spoken drama in the form of mystery plays.

Medieval secular music consisted at first of songs, performed by various groups of musicians, from the vagabond goliards and jongleurs to the aristocratic troubadours and trouvères of Provence and northern France, respectively, who composed their own songs, mainly about love.

Beginning in the tenth century, composers began to experiment with polyphony ("many sounds"), adding one or more melodic lies to an existing chant. In time, such experiments were to lead to a rich variety of musical textures, using several melodies together and, in other cases, a single melody supported by harmony—called homophonic music. The High Middle Ages produced some wonderfully complex polyphonic music, including the first polyphonic Mass, by Guillaume de Machaut.

Early medieval dance included some forms intended for worship, but this practice came to an end in the High Middle Ages. Peasant dances, originally performed in a ring or a chain, were refined and elaborated by the aristocracy into couple dances such as the estampie.

CULTURE AND HUMAN VALUES

The history of medieval music is much more than the study of the musical practices of a cultural period. Music of any era, in the playing and the singing, reflects and expresses the hopes, aspirations, frustrations, and fears of people of all classes and stations in life. Music is still the nearest equivalent to an international language that humans have yet devised.

Medieval music, when properly performed, is an aural time machine. It can bring alive the vast panorama of medieval musical life, from Gregorian chant to liturgical drama, from troubadour love songs to peasant dances. Because its sound is so different from that of music we normally hear, it seems to conjure up the whole world that produced it.

The sound of the music has a correlation with the architectural styles of the period. Gregorian chant, for example, was intended for participating worshipers—monks or nuns—rather than for an audience. It is therefore most effective and persuasive heard in a church or, better still, a monastery or convent, with its narrow windows, heavy walls, and pervasive quietude.

The development of more complex forms in music during the Middle Ages was paralleled by the increasing complexity of architecture. The spare line of monophonic chant is complemented by the equally austere forms of early Romanesque churches. Each has a simplicity and purity capable of refreshing the spirit. Similarly, the development of polyphony reflects—and is reflected by—the flowering of the Gothic style of architecture, with its intricate structures of rib vaults and flying buttresses, its delicate tracery and glittering stained glass windows. Both the music and the architecture of the High Middle Ages display a love of elaboration and a delight in scaling the heights of creativity.

The High Middle Ages achieved the first period of balance since Graeco-Roman civilization, a long and torturous trek up the mountain of culture. The Church of Rome reached its pinnacle of power at the same time, only to see its formidable structure begin to crack with the "Babylonian Captivity" in Avignon and the Great Schism, while the Renaissance and Reformation waited impatiently in the wings. Even as the medieval synthesis settled into place, the forces that were to hurl Europe into the chaos of the Renaissance were already undermining the foundations of society: science, universities, Aristotle, humanism, burgeoning commerce and trade, and rising nationalistic expectations. There was, however, an enormous difference between the fall of Rome and the waning of the Middle Ages. Rome's extended demise left a vacuum that was largely filled by the barbarians within and those at the gates. The vibrant Gothic age was gradually supplanted by another version of reality that bred new values and goals. Rather than taking a step backward, European civilization was poised at its medieval apex as its leaders, artists, and intellectuals sought new directions in a rapidly changing world.

Music Listening and Notation

Music listening is always enriched by a basic knowledge of how it is constructed. This appendix aims to provide such knowledge. It should, ideally, be studied for content and used, along with the glossary, as often as necessary in conjunction with the material on music.

CHARACTERISTICS OF MUSICAL SOUNDS

Musical tones are sounds of definite pitch and duration, as distinct from noises and other less identifiable sounds. Musical tones have the four characteristics of pitch, intensity, tone color, and duration, which may be described as follows:

Pitch The location of musical sound from low to high or high to low.
Intensity Relative degree of softness or loudness.
Tone color The quality of a sound that distinguishes it from other musical sounds of the same pitch and intensity; for example, the different tone quality of a flute as contrasted with a clarinet. Also called timbre.
Duration The length of time a tone is audible.

THE FOUR ELEMENTS OF MUSIC

Rhythm, melody, harmony, and tone color are the essential elements of music. Composers and performers are concerned with each, while for the listener, they are experienced as a web of sound that often makes it difficult to single out any one element. Each can, however, be considered in isolation as a guide to understanding.

Rhythm

There is rhythm in the universe: our heartbeat, the alternation of day and night, the progression of the seasons, waves crashing on a beach. Artificially produced rhythm can be heard in train wheels clicking on rails, a ping-pong game, or the clacking castanets of a Spanish dancer. Although little is known about prehistoric music, the earliest music was probably the beating out of rhythms long before the existence of either melody or speech.

Essentially, rhythm is the organization of musical time—that is, everything that takes place in terms of sound and silence, accent and non-accent, tension and relaxation. Rhythm can also be defined as the "melody of a monotone"; music can often be recognized just by hearing its rhythm. For example, tapping out the rhythmic patterns of "Dixie" can bring that familiar melody to mind.

Rhythm is not to be confused with beat, which results from a certain regularity of the rhythmic patterns. Beat, or pulse, can be compared with the heartbeat or the pulse rate. The beat will usually be steady, but it may temporarily speed up or slow down. It may be explicit (the uniform thump of a bass drum in a marching band) or implicit (resulting from combinations of rhythmic patterns). As soon as one note follows another, there will be rhythm but not necessarily beat. Certain types of music (such as Gregorian chant) do not produce the regular pulsation called beat.

When beats are produced by the music in a repeating pattern of accents, the result is meter. Metered music is measured music, with groupings of two, three, or four beats (or combinations of these) in each measure, or bar.

Time Signatures

When there is a regular pattern of accented and unaccented beats, it is customary to use a time signature. This looks like a fraction, in which the upper figure indicates the number of beats in a measure and the lower figure the unit of beat; that is, the note value the composer has selected to symbolize one beat. For example:

2/4 = two beats per measure (duple meter)
= ♩ unit of beat (quarter note receives one beat)

3/8 = three beats per measure (triple meter)
= ♪ unit of beat (eighth note receives one beat)

Melody and Harmony

A melody is a horizontal organization of pitches or, simply, a succession of musical tones. Harmony is a vertical organization of pitches in which two or more tones are sounded together. The following example illustrates melody on the upper staff and harmony on the lower staff.

"Old Folks at Home"

Tone Color

Sometimes called timbre (TAM-ber), tone color is to music what color is to the painter. It is tone color that enables us to distinguish between a flute, a clarinet, and an oboe. A soprano voice differs from a bass voice not only by its higher pitch, but also by its different tone color. Through experience, people learn to recognize the unique colors of many instruments. Further study leads to finer discriminations between similar instruments such as violin and viola, oboe and English horn, and so on. Composers select instruments for expressive purposes based largely on their coloration, whether singly or in combination. The full sound of a Beethoven symphony differs from a work by Richard Strauss, for example, because Strauss uses a wider range of instrumental colors.

MUSICAL LITERACY

The most abstract of the arts, music is sound moving in time. Factual information about music certainly helps the listener, but all the facts in the world can only assist the listening process; information can never replace the sound of music. One extremely useful method of learning to understand music is to study major themes and ideas in musical notation while listening to the music itself.

A practical approach to intelligent listening must include some instruction in musical literacy sufficient to read a single line of music. This is a simple process that can be quickly learned by young children and can be taught to an adult in a few minutes. The strangely prevalent attitude that musical notation is "too hard" or "too technical" has no foundation in fact, and probably refers to reading music as a performer—a very different matter that need not concern us here. As basic to music as the ABC's of written language, musical notation is an indispensable guide for music listeners.

Learning to pick out musical themes will turn abstract sounds into intelligible tunes, thus giving oneself an opportunity to anticipate the themes as they emerge in the music. Equally valuable is the repetition of themes after the listening experience. To summarize, picking out melodies on the page is an aid to understanding, a helpful preview of music to be listened to, and a reminder of music already heard.

Try to approach the following material not with apprehension but with anticipation. Master the principles of musical notation with the positive attitude that this not only will materially assist in a better understanding of the music in this text but also lead, in time, to a lifetime of pleasurable listening.

MUSICAL NOTATION

Pitch

The essential elements of our notational system were devised some ten centuries ago and subsequently altered and augmented to become a reasonably efficient means of communicating the composer's intentions to a performer. The system is based on the first seven letters of the alphabet and can best be illustrated on a piano keyboard. The pitches range from low to high, from A through G in a repeating A–G pattern.

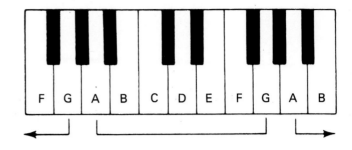

In order to know which of the eight A's available on the piano is the intended note, you will need to do the following:

1. Use a musical staff (also called a stave) of five lines and four spaces.
2. Use a symbol for a musical pitch, i.e., a note.

   𝅝

3. Place the notes on the lines or in the spaces of the staff.

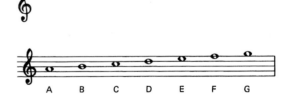

4. Indicate by means of a clef sign the names of the notes.

The word "clef" (French, "key") implies that the key to precise placement of the notes is the establishment of the letter name of one of the lines or spaces of the staff. There are two clefs in common use. Both are ornamental symbols, one derived from the letter G and one from F. The solid lines below are the present clef signs and the dotted lines their original form:

The clefs are placed on the staff to indicate the location of the letters they represent. The spiral portion of the G clef curls around the second line to fix the location of G; the two dots of the F clef are placed above and below the fourth line to show that this is the F line.

Once the five-line staff has received its pitch designation of G or F, the staff is subsequently identified as a treble or a bass staff.

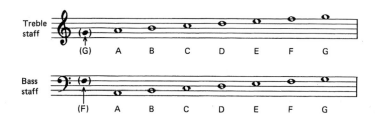

Not all melodies are composed so that they can be played on the white notes only of the piano. Sometimes another key, or different set of pitches, is used, as demonstrated in the following examples:

In the second version, below, the key signature indicates that all the F's and C's have been raised a half step to the next closest note—on a piano the adjacent black keys to the right. A symbol called a sharp (#) indicates raised notes.

The other common symbol that changes a note is the flat (♭), which lowers a note a half step to the next closest note. Following is the same melody written in the key of B♭. As indicated by the key signature, all the B's and E's have been lowered to B♭ and E♭. Key signatures can include up to seven sharps or flats.

You will see that the staff just given has an added short line, a ledger line, used to accommodate the last two notes.

On a piano keyboard the black keys are grouped in alternating sets of two and three. The white note, or key, immediately to the left of the two black keys is always C. There are eight C's; the C closest to the center is called middle C. It is from this C that you can locate the notes of the themes.

Below is a guide to the chromatic scale, which includes all the black and white keys, twelve in all, in one octave.

Duration

The notation of the length of time of musical sounds (and silences) was developed, more or less, in conjunction with the notation of pitch. The modern note-value system consists of fractional parts of a whole unit, or whole note (o), expressed in mathematical terms as 1/1. A half note (♩) is one-half the whole unit, or 1/2; a quarter note (♪) is one-quarter the unit, or 1/4; and so on.

The name of the note value indicates the number of notes in the whole-note unit. There are four quarter notes (4 × 1/4 = 1/1), eight eighth notes (8 × 1/8 = 1/1), etc.

With note values smaller than the whole note, the relationships remain constant. There are two quarter notes in a half note (2 × 1/4 = 1/2), two eighth notes in a quarter note (2 × 1/8 = 1/4), etc.

Rhythmic notation is both relative and fixed. The duration of a whole note is dependent on the tempo (speed) and notation of music. It may have a duration of one second, eight seconds, or something in between. The interior relationships, however, never vary.

A whole note has the same duration as two half notes, four quarter notes, and so forth. The mathematical relationship is fixed and precise. See table A.1 for an outline of the system.

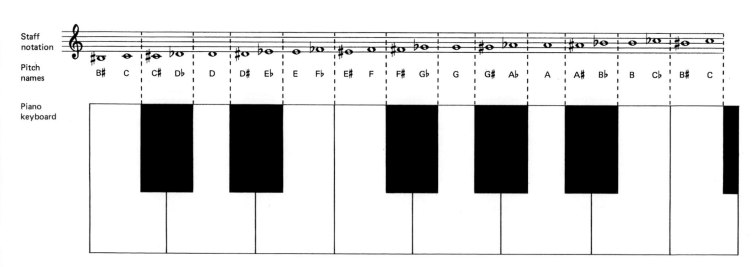

VOICES AND INSTRUMENTS

Choral ensembles are usually divided into four voice parts ranging from high to low: soprano and alto (women) and tenor and bass (men).

TABLE A.1 NOTE AND REST VALUES

Note value	Symbol
Whole note (basic unit)	𝅝
Half note	𝅗𝅥
Quarter note	𝅘𝅥
Eighth note	𝅘𝅥𝅮
Sixteenth note	𝅘𝅥𝅯

Rest value	Symbol
Whole (note) rest	𝄻
Half rest	𝄼
Quarter rest	𝄽
Eighth rest	𝄾
Sixteenth rest	𝄿

Instruments of the symphony orchestra and other ensembles are grouped by family, from highest pitch to lowest:

Strings	Woodwinds	Brass	Percussion
violin	piccolo	trumpet (and cornet)	snare drum
viola	flute	French horn	timpani
cello	oboe	trombone	bass drum
bass	clarinet	tuba	cymbals
	bassoon		(many others)

Keyboard instruments include piano, harpsichord, and organ. The piano, originally called *pianoforte* (It., "soft" "loud"), is based on the principle of hammers striking the strings; the harpsichord has a mechanism that plucks the strings. Organs are built with two or more keyboards called manuals. The traditional organ uses forced air to activate the pipes; some modern organs use an electronic reproduction of sound.

MUSICAL TEXTURE

The words for the three kinds of musical texture are derived from Greek and are virtually self-explanatory:

    monophonic (one sound)
    homophonic (same sound)
    polyphonic (many sounds)

Monophonic music has a single unaccompanied melodic line. Much of the world's music—including Chinese and Hindu music and, in Western civilization, Gregorian chant and troubadour songs—is monophonic. Homophonic music has a principal melodic line accompanied by harmony, sometimes referred to as chordal accompaniment. Although homophony is relatively unknown outside Western culture, it comprises the bulk of our music, including nearly all popular music. Polyphonic music has two or more melodies sounding simultaneously. Familiar rounds such as "Three Blind Mice" and "Row, Row, Row Your Boat" are polyphonic, as is most Renaissance music. The music of Baroque composers such as Bach, Handel, and others is basically polyphonic too.

MUSICAL FORM

Briefly stated, form in music is a balance of unity and variety. Too much unity becomes boring, whereas excessive variety leads to fragmentation and even chaos. Understanding form in music is essential to its appreciation. As German composer Robert Schumann remarked, "Only when the form is quite clear to you will the spirit become clear to you."

The smallest unit of form is the motive. This is a recurring combination of at least two notes with an identifiable rhythmic pattern. The principal motive in the first movement of Beethoven's Fifth Symphony has two different pitches in a four-note rhythmic pattern:

Symphony No. 5,   **Beethoven**
First movement   **(1770–1827)**

A musical phrase is a coherent group of notes roughly comparable to a literary phrase and having about the same function. Two related phrases form a period, analogous to a sentence. In the period illustrated below, the first phrase has a transitional ending called a half cadence, and the second phrase ends solidly with a full cadence. Note also the extreme unity; the first three measures of each phrase are identical.

"Ode to Joy"   **Beethoven**

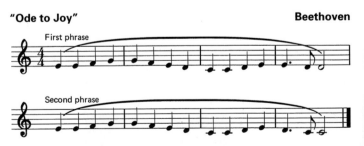

In large works the musical periods are used in various combinations to expand the material into sections comparable to paragraphs, and these are then combined to make still larger units.

Musical structure can be comprehended only after the music has arrived at wherever the composer intends it to go. Look again at "Ode to Joy" (from Beethoven's Ninth Symphony). You can "see" its form only because the music is notated, which is why learning some notation is so important. When the music is played, your ear follows the line to the half cadence, which is then heard as a statement that demands completion. As the second phrase begins, there is aural recognition of its relationship to the first phrase. When the second phrase concludes with a gratifying full cadence, there is a kind of flashback to the memory of the first phrase. In other words, the conclusion of the second phrase is satisfying because it completes the thought of the still-remembered first phrase. The music conforms to its own inner logic; that is, the second phrase is a logical consequence of the first.

As a general rule, most music is constructed around two different but logically related musical ideas. We can call one idea A and the other B. One common musical form is two-part (binary), or simply AB. An even more common form is three-part (ternary), or ABA. In two-part form the composer makes a musical statement (A), which is followed by a new section (B), which is sufficiently different to provide variety but not so different as to destroy the balance. The following hymn tune is a complete composition in two-part form, with two phrases in each section. Section B has the same rhythm as Section A, but the melody is a kind of inversion of the melody in A. The inner logic is maintained through the similarities.

"St. Anne"

The following complete hymn tune has a form related to two-part form: AA'B, called A, A prime, B. Part A is followed by another A that is varied going into the cadence. Part B is properly different but related to A and A' by the similarity of measures 2, 6, and 10. In terms of measures, the structure of the piece can be diagrammed as:

	A 2 + 2	A' 2 + 2	B 2 + 2

"Regent Square"

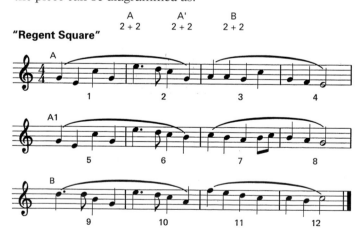

Three-part form operates on the principle of closing with the melody that began the piece, a rounding off of the material: ABA. The following example can be analyzed as AA'BA' and diagrammed as:

	A 4 + 4	A' 4 + 4	B 4 + 4	A' 4 + 4

This is the thirty-two-measure form most commonly used for popular songs.

"In the Gloaming"

There are, of course, other variants of AB and ABA forms, as well as several other structures. However, the examples given illustrate the principle of a balance between unity and variety, of which unity is paramount. Perhaps because of its fluid nature, music, more than any other art, emphasizes repetition, restating the material again and again, but mixing it with enough variety to maintain interest. The forms illustrated can also be heard in the larger context of longer compositions. For example, "In the Gloaming" has thirty-two measures in a basic ABA form; a large symphonic work could have, say, 200 measures and be diagrammed as follows:

A	B	A	or	A	B	A'	or	A	B	A'
aba	aba	aba		aba'	aba	a'ba'		aa'ba	aba	aa'ba

THE LISTENING EXPERIENCE

Listening to music begins with the question, *What do you hear?* This is an objective question that has nothing whatever to do with a story you may imagine the music is telling, random associations the music happens to trigger, or any meaning that may be attributed to the music. The idea, rather, is to objectively identify the sounds to determine how the sounds are produced, and to try to determine how the sounds are organized.

Composers do not pour out notes as if emptying a can of beans on a tabletop. They arrange their sounds in a sort of container in a manner that molds the receptacle to the material it holds. Learning to comprehend the musical structure leads to the ability to anticipate the next melody, cadence, section, or other development. Being able to anticipate what is to happen next means that you are tuned in to the web of sound, listening along with the pace of the music. Almost everyone has already acquired the ability to follow the progress of popular music and to anticipate what comes next in favorite recordings. The larger world of classical music lies only a step beyond this level of listening ability. It is an inspiring and enriching stride into one of the greatest achievements of Western civilization.

Glossary

A

Abacus   The flat slab on top of a *capital.

Abstract Art   Term covers many kinds of non-representational art, e.g., action painting, works by Kandinsky, the Cycladic sculptures.

Academy   Originally derived from the *Akademeia*, the grove in which Plato taught his seminars.

Acanthus   A plant whose thick leaves are reproduced in stylized form on *Corinthian capitals (see fig. 9.11).

A cappella (ah ka-PELL-ah; Lat.)   Originally unaccompanied music sung "in the chapel." Term now applies to choral music without instrumental accompaniment.

Acoustics   The science of sound.

Aerial perspective   See *perspective.

Aesthetic   Concerned with a sensitivity to the pleasurable and the beautiful; the opposite of anaesthetic.

Aesthetics   The study or philosophy of beauty; theory of the fine arts and human responses.

Agnosticism (Gk., *agnostos*, "unknowing")   The impossibility of obtaining knowledge of certain subjects; assertion that people cannot obtain knowledge of God.

Agora   In ancient Greece, a marketplace or public square.

Allegory   A literary mode with a literal level of meanings plus a set of meanings above and beyond themselves. This second level may be religious, social, political, or philosophical, e.g., *The Faerie Queen* by Spenser is an allegory about Christian virtues.

Alleluia   Latinization of the Hebrew *Halleluyah* ("Praise ye the Lord"). Third item of the Proper of the *Mass.

Altarpiece   A painted (or sculptured) panel placed behind an altar.

Ambulatory   A passageway around the *apse of a church (see fig. 14.28).

Amphora   Greek vase, usually quite large, with two handles, used to store food staples (see fig. 7.8).

Apocalypse   Prophetic revelation given through a symbolic vision of the future. Apocalyptic literature concerns the final period of world history and depicts the final confrontation between God and the powers of evil, as described, for example, in the Book of Revelation in the New Testament.

A posteriori (a-pos-TEER-e-or-e; Lat., "following after")   Reasoning from observed facts to conclusions; inductive; empirical.

A priori (a-pree-OAR-e; Lat., "coming before")   Reasoning from general propositions to particular conclusions; deductive; nonempirical.

Apse   A recess, usually semicircular, in the east wall of a Christian church or, in a Roman *basilica, at the wall opposite to the general entrance way.

Arabesque   Literally Arab-like. Elaborate designs of intertwined flowers, foliage, and geometric patterns used in Islamic architecture.

Arcade   A series of connected *arches resting on *columns (see fig. 9.12).

Arch   A curved structure (semicircular or pointed) spanning a space, usually made of wedge-shaped blocks. Known to the Greeks, who preferred a *post and lintel system, but exploited by the Romans.

Archetype (Gk., *arche*, "first"; *typos*, "form")   The original pattern of forms of which things in this world are copies.

Architrave   The lowest part of an *entablature, a horizontal beam or *lintel directly above the *capital (see fig. 7.31).

Archivolt   In architectural sculpture, the decorative molding carried around an arched wall opening.

Ars antiqua (Lat., "old art")   Music of the late twelfth and thirteenth centuries.

Ars nova (Lat., "new art")   Music of the fourteenth century. Outstanding composers were Machaut (France) and Landini (Italy).

Atheism (Gk., *a*, "no"; *theos*, "god")   The belief that there is no God; also means "not theistic" when applied to those who do not believe in a personal God.

Atrium   The court of a Roman house, roofless, and near the entrance (see fig. 9.8). Also the open, colonnaded court attached to the front of early Christian churches.

Aulos (OW-los)   A shrill-sounding oboelike instrument associated with the Dionysian rites of the ancient Greeks. Double-reed instrument normally played in pairs by one performer (see fig. 7.65).

Aureole   A circle of light or radiance surrounding the head or body of a representation of a deity or holy person; a halo.

Avant-garde (a-vahn-gard)   A French term meaning, literally, "advanced guard," used to designate innovators and experimentalists in the various arts.

B

Babylonian Captivity   The exile of the Jews, 586–538 BC; also the Church of Rome in Avignon rather than in Rome, 1305–78.

Baldachino (ball-da-KEEN-o)   A canopy over a tomb or altar of which the most famous is that over the tomb of St. Peter in St. Peter's in Rome designed by Bernini.

Ballad (Lat., *ballare*, "to dance")   Originally a dancing song. A narrative song, usually folk song, but also applied to popular songs.

Ballade   Medieval *trouvère song. In the nineteenth and twentieth centuries dramatic piano pieces, frequently inspired by Romantic poetry.

Balustrade   A railing plus a supporting row of posts.

Banjo   Instrument of the *guitar family, probably introduced into Africa by Arab traders and brought to America on the slave ships. The body consists of a shallow, hollow metal drum with a drumhead on top and open at the bottom. It has four or more strings and is played with fingers or plectrum.

Barrel vault   See *vault.

Basilica   In Roman architecture, a rectangular public building used for business or as a tribunal. Christian churches that use a *cruciform plan are patterned after Roman basilicas (see fig. 11.11). Though basilica denotes an architectural style, the Church of Rome designates a church a basilica if it contains the bones of a saint.

Bas-relief   A sculptural term (low relief) used to describe an object with a design slightly projecting from the surface. The opposite of high relief in which the design appears to be almost wholly detached.

Bay   In Romanesque and Gothic churches the area between the *columns (see fig. 14.28).

Black-figure technique   Greek vase painting in which the subject is incised in black on a light, usually orange, background. In what is essentially silhouette painting, the effect can be very powerful and compelling. Exekias (active 545–525 BC) is the foremost Greek painter of the black-figure technique.

Blank verse   Unrhymed *iambic pentameter* (see *meter) in the English language, much used in Elizabethan drama.

Bourgeoisie   The middle class; in Marxist theory, the capitalist class, which is opposed to the proletariat, the lower or industrial working class.

Branle   (bruhn-l; Fr., *branler*, "to sway") Originally, in the Middle Ages, a step in the Basse Danse.

Buttress   Exterior support used to counter the lateral thrust of an *arch or *vault. A *pier buttress* is a solid mass of masonry added to the wall; a *flying buttress* is typically a pier standing away from the wall from which an arch "flies" from the pier to connect with the wall at the point of outward thrust (see fig. 14.27).

C

Cadence   Term in music applied to the concluding portion of a phrase (temporary cadence) or composition (permanent cadence).

Cameo   In jewelry, a technique of engraving in relief on a gem or other stone, especially with layers of different hues, leaving the raised design with one color and the background with another.

Campanile   Italian for bell tower, usually freestanding. The Leaning Tower of Pisa is a campanile (see fig. 14.17).

Canon   (Gk., "law, rule") 1. A body of principles, rules, standards, or norms. 2. In art and architecture, a criterion for establishing proportion, measure, or scale. 3. In music, in which a melody is imitated strictly and in its entirety by another voice. Canons that have no specified way to end but keep going around are called "rounds," for example, "Three Blind Mice."

Cantata   (It., *cantare*, "to sing") A "sung" piece as opposed to a "sound" (instrumental) piece, for example, sonata. The term is now generally used for secular or sacred choral works with orchestral accompaniment, which are on a smaller scale than *oratorios.

Cantilever   A self-supporting projection that needs no exterior bracing; e.g., a balcony or porch can be cantilevered.

Cantus firmus   (Lat., "fixed song") A preexisting melody used as the foundation for a *polyphonic composition. *Plainsong melodies were used for this purpose, but other sources included secular songs, Lutheran *chorales, and *scales. Any preexisting melody may serve as a cantus firmus.

Capital   The top or crown of a *column (see fig. 7.31).

Cartoon   A full-size preliminary drawing for a pictorial work, usually a large work such as a *mural, *fresco, or tapestry. Also a humorous drawing.

Caryatid   (care-ee-AT-id) A female figure that functions as a supporting *column; male figures that function in a like manner are called *atlantes* (at-LAN-tees; plural of Atlas; see fig. 7.44).

Catacombs   Subterranean Christian cemeteries, e.g. those in the outskirts of Rome, Naples, and Syracuse.

Catharsis   (Gk., "purge, purify") Purification, purging of emotions effected by tragedy (Aristotle).

Cella   The enclosed chamber in a classical temple that contained the cult statue of the god or goddess after whom the temple was named.

Chanson   (Fr., "song") A major part of the *troubadour-*trouvère tradition, dating from the eleventh through the fourteenth centuries. Also a generic term for a song with a French text.

Chanson de geste   A genre of Old French epic poems celebrating deeds of heroic or historical figures.

Chevet   (sheh-vay; Fr., "pillow") The eastern end of a church, including *choir, *ambulatory, and *apse.

Chiaroscuro   (kee-AR-oh-SKOOR-oh; It., "light-dark") In the visual arts the use of gradations of light and dark to represent natural light and shadows.

Choir   That part of the church where the singers and clergy are normally accommodated; usually between the *transept and the *apse; also called chancel (see fig. 14.28).

Chorale   A *hymn tune of the German Protestant (Lutheran) church.

Chord   In music the simultaneous sounding of two or more tones.

Chromatic   (Gk., *chroma*, "color") The use of notes that are foreign to the musical *scale and have to be indicated by a sharp, flat, natural, etc. The *chromatic* scale is involved in these alterations. It consists of twelve tones to an octave, each a semitone apart.

Cire perdue   (seer pair-due; Fr., "lost wax") A metal-casting method in which the original figure is modeled in wax and encased in a mold; as the mold is baked the wax melts and runs out, after which the molten metal is poured into the mold.

Clavichord   The earliest type of stringed keyboard instrument (twelfth century). Probably developed from the *monochord. It is an oblong box, 24 by 48 inches (61 x 132 cm) with a keyboard of about three octaves. The strings run parallel to the keyboard, as opposed to harpsichords and pianos, in which the strings run at right angles to the keyboard. The keys are struck from below by metal tangents fastened to the opposite ends of elongated keys. The tone is light and delicate but very expressive because the performer can control the loudness of each note. It was sometimes called a "table *clavier" because it was portable.

Clavier   Generic term for any instrument of the stringed keyboard family: *clavichord, harpsichord, and piano.

Clef   (Fr., "key") In music a symbol placed on the staff to indicate the pitches of the lines and spaces. There are three clefs in use today: G, F, and C. The G clef is used to indicate that the note on the second line is G (treble clef). The F clef is usually used to indicate that F is on the fourth line (bass clef). (See Appendix.)

Clerestory   In a *basilica or church, the section of an interior wall that rises above the roof of the side aisles and which has numerous windows.

Cloisonné   Enamel used for artistic purposes and painted on metal bases. Thin wires of gold, silver, or copper are soldered onto a base plate of the same metal. After these *cloises* (compartments) are filled with powdered glass, the object is baked in an oven until the glass fuses. Additional powdered glass or metal may be enameled for subsequent firings.

Cloister   (Lat. *claustrum*, "hidden") An inner court bounded by covered walks; a standard feature of monastery architecture.

Colonnade   A series of spaced *columns, usually connected by *lintels (see fig. 7.28).

Column   A vertical support, usually circular, which has a base (except in *Doric style), shaft, and *capital (see fig. 7.31).

Comedy   A play or other literary work in which all ends well, properly, or happily. Opposite of *tragedy.

Comitatus   Early Anglo-Saxon society was organized in families and clans and centered on the warrior and a system of reciprocity (mutual loyalty) called *comitatus*.

Corinthian   The most ornate style of Greek architecture, little used by the Greeks but preferred by the Romans; tall, slender, channeled *columns topped by an elaborate *capital decorated with stylized *acanthus leaves (see fig. 9.11).

Cornice   The horizontal, projecting member crowning an *entablature.

Cosmology   Philosophical study of the origin and nature of the universe.

Couplet   In poetry two successive rhymed lines in the same meter.

Covenant   A legal concept often used in the Bible as a metaphor describing the relationship between God and humankind. This idea lies at the heart of the Bible and explains the selection of the word "testament," a synonym for covenant, in naming the two parts of the Bible.

Crocket   In Gothic architecture, an ornamental device shaped like a curling leaf and placed on the outer angles of *gables and pinnacles (see fig. 14.56).

Crossing   In a church, the space formed by the interception of the *nave and the *transepts.

Cruciform   The floor plan of a church in the shape of a *Latin cross (see fig. 14.28).

Cuneiform   A writing system of ancient Mesopotamia consisting of wedge shapes.

Cupola   A rounded roof or ceiling; a small *dome.

D

Determinism (Lat., *de*, "from," *terminus*, "end")   The doctrine that all events are conditioned by their causes and that people are mechanical expressions of heredity and environment; in short, we are at the mercy of blind, unknowing natural laws in an indifferent universe.

Deus ex machina (DAY-oos ex ma-KEE-na; Lat.)   In Greek and Roman drama a deity who was brought in by stage machinery to resolve a difficult situation; hence, any unexpected or bizarre device or event introduced to untangle a plot.

Dialectic   Associated with Plato as the art of debate by question and answer. Also dialectical reasoning using *syllogisms (Aristotle) or, according to Hegel, the distinctive characteristic of speculative thought.

Diorite   A dense igneous rock, ranked in hardness between gabbro and granite.

Dome   A hemispherical *vault; may be viewed as an *arch rotated on its vertical axis.

Doric   The oldest of Greek temple styles, characterized by sturdy *columns with no base and an unornamented cushionlike *capital (see fig. 7.31).

Drum   The circular sections that make up the shaft of a *column; also the circular wall on which a *dome is placed.

Dualism   In *metaphysics, a theory that admits two independent substances, e.g., Plato's dualism of the sensible and intelligible worlds, Cartesian dualism of thinking and extended subjects, Kant's dualism of the noumenal and the phenomenal.

E

Echinus   The highest part of the shaft of a Greek *column immediately below the *abacus. It is wider at the top and narrower at the bottom and contains whatever decorative elements the column may have.

Elegy   A meditative poem dealing with the idea of death.

Elevation   The vertical arrangements of the elements of an architectural design; a vertical projection.

Embossing   In metalworking, the adding of decorative relief designs.

Empiricism   The view that the sole source of knowledge is experience, that no knowledge is possible independent of experience.

Engaged column   A non-functional form projecting from the surface of a wall; used for visual articulation (see fig. 9.10).

Engraving   The process of using a sharp instrument to cut a design into a metal plate, usually copper; also the print that is made from the plate after ink has been added.

Entablature   The part of a building of *post and lintel construction between the *capitals and the roof. In classical architecture this includes the *architrave, *frieze, and *cornice (see fig. 7.31).

Entasis (EN-ta-sis)   A slight convex swelling in the shaft of a *column.

Epic   A lengthy narrative poem dealing with protagonists of heroic proportions and issues of universal significance, e.g., Homer's *Iliad*.

Epicurean   One who believes that pleasure, especially that of the mind, is the highest good.

Epistemology   A branch of philosophy that studies the origin, validity, and processes of knowledge.

Eschatology (Gk., *eschata*, "death")   That part of theology dealing with last things: death, judgment, heaven, hell.

Estampie (es-tahm-pea)   A dance form popular during the twelfth to fourteenth centuries. Consists of a series of repeated sections, for example, aa, bb, cc, etc.

Etching   A kind of *engraving in which the design is incised into a wax-covered metal plate, after which the exposed metal is etched by a corrosive acid; the print made from the plate is also called an etching.

Ethos   In ancient Greek music, the "ethical" character attributed to the various modes. The Dorian was considered strong and manly; the Phrygian, ecstatic and passionate; the Lydian, feminine, decadent, and lascivious; the Mixolydian, mournful and gloomy. (See pp. 156–7.)

Eucharist (Gk., *eucharistia*, "thanksgiving")   The sacrament of Communion, the taking of Christ's body and blood, that Christ instituted at the Last Supper.

F

Facade   In architecture the face of a building; one or more of the exterior walls of a building, especially the one containing the main entrance.

Fenestration   The arrangement of windows or other openings in the walls of a building.

Feudalism   A medieval contractual arrangement by which a lord granted land to his vassal in return for military service. Feudalism was further characterized by the localization of political and economic power in the hands of lords and their vassals.

Fiddle   Colloquialism for the violin. Also used to designate the bowed ancestors of the violin, particularly the medieval instrument used to accompany dances.

Finial   In Gothic architecture an ornament fitted to the peak of an *arch; any ornamental terminating point, such as the screw-top of a lamp (see fig. 9.3).

Flamboyant   Late Gothic architecture of the fifteenth or sixteenth centuries, which featured wavy lines and flamelike forms.

Flèche (flesh; Fr., "arrow")   In architecture a slender exterior spire above the intersection of the *nave and *transepts (see fig. 14.27).

Flute   A woodwind instrument made of wood (originally), silver, gold, or preferably platinum. It is essentially a straight pipe with keys, is held horizontally and played by blowing across a mouthpiece.

Fluting   The vertical grooves, usually semicircular, in the shaft of a *column or *pilaster.

Foot   A metrical unit in poetry such as the iamb ‿— (see *meter).

Foreshortening   Creating the illusion in painting or drawing that the subject is projecting out of or into the frontal plane of a two-dimensional surface.

Forum   The public square and/or marketplace of an ancient Roman city.

Fresco (It., "fresh")   Painting on plaster, usually wet plaster, into which the colors sink as the plaster dries so that the fresco becomes part of the wall.

Frieze   In architecture, a decorated horizontal band, often embellished with carved figures and molding; the portion of an *entablature between the *architrave and the *cornice above (see fig. 7.31).

G

Gable   In architecture, the triangular section at the end of a pitched roof, frequently with a window below.

Genre (zhan-re)   In the pictorial arts, a depiction of scenes of everyday life. In literature, the type of work—epic, novel, and so on.

Gnosticism   The doctrines of certain early Christian cults (particularly in Egypt) that valued inquiry into spiritual truth above faith.

Goliards   Wandering scholars of the tenth through the thirteenth centuries: students, young ecclesiastics, dreamers, and the disenchanted.

Gospels   In the Bible, New Testament accounts (Matthew, Mark, Luke, and John) of the life and teachings of Christ.

Gouache (goo-ahsh; Fr.)   Watercolor made opaque by adding zinc white.

Graphic arts   Visual arts that are linear in character: drawing, engraving, printing, printmaking, typographic, and advertising design.

Great Schism   Separation of Eastern Orthodox Churches from the church of Rome in 1054; rival popes of the Church of Rome in Rome, Avignon, and Pisa, 1378–1417.

Greek cross   A cross in which the four arms are of equal length.

Gregorian chant   See *plainsong.

Groin   In architecture the edge (groin) formed by the intersection of two *vaults (see fig. 14.13).

Guild   An association of persons of the same trade, pursuits, or interests, formed for their mutual aid and protection and the maintenance of standards; in the Middle Ages a society of merchants or artisans.

Guitar   A plucked string instrument with a flat body and six strings (modern guitar). Brought into Europe during the Middle Ages by the Moorish conquest of Spain.

H

Harmony   In music the simultaneous combination of notes in a chord.

Harp   Musical instrument consisting of upright, open triangular frame with forty-six strings of graduated length.

Hatching   A series of closely spaced

parallel lines in a drawing or print giving the effect of shading.

Hedonism The doctrine that pleasure or pleasant consciousness are intrinsically good; that pleasure is the proper—and the actual—motive for every choice.

Heroic couplet Two successive lines of rhymed iambic pentameter, used, e.g., in Pope's *Essay on Man*.

Hieratic (hye-uh-RAT-ik) Of or used by priests; priestly.

Hieroglyphics Symbols or pictures giving written form to syllables or sounds; writing system of ancient Egyptians.

Homophonic (Gk., "same sound") Music in which a single melodic line is supported by chords or other subordinate material (percussion instruments).

Horn Wind instrument made of brass.

Hubris (HU-bris) Tragic flaw, i.e., excessive pride or arrogance that harms other people and brings about the downfall of the person with the flaw.

Hue The name of a color. The chief colors of the spectrum are: red, yellow, blue (primary); green, orange, violet (secondary).

Hydraulis Ancient Greek pipe *organ, probably invented in the Middle East 300–200 BC. Air for the pipes was provided by hydraulic pressure and the pipes activated by a keyboard. Originally the tone was delicate and clear, but the Romans converted it into a noisy outdoor instrument by a large increase in air pressure.

Hydria Greek vase designed to hold water (see fig. 7.10).

Hymn A poem of praise, usually, but not necessarily, sacred. The music accompanying a hymn is called the hymn tune.

I

Icon (EYE-kon; Gk., "image") Two-dimensional representation of a holy person; in the Greek church a panel painting of a sacred personage (see fig. 11.29).

Iconography Visual imagery used to convey concepts in the visual arts; the study of symbolic meanings in the pictorial arts.

Illumination Decorative illustrations or designs, associated primarily with medieval illuminated manuscripts (see fig. 14.1).

Impasto (It., "paste") A painting style in which the pigment is laid on thickly, as in many of van Gogh's paintings.

Incarnation Denotes the embodiment of a deity in human form, a frequent idea in mythology. Vishnu is believed by Hindus to have had nine incarnations. For Christians the incarnation is a central dogma referring to the belief that the Son of God, the second of the Trinity, became man in the person of Jesus Christ.

Intaglio (in-TAL-yo) A graphic technique in which the design is incised; used on seals, gems, and dies for coins and also for the kinds of printing and printmaking that have a depressed ink-bearing surface.

Ionic A style of Greek classical architecture using slender, *fluted *columns and *capitals decorated with scrolls and *volutes (see fig. 7.31).

Isocephaly (I-so-SEPH-uh-ly) In the visual arts a convention that arranges figures so that the heads are at the same height (see fig. 7.26).

J

Jamb figure Sculpted figure flanking the portal of a Gothic church (see fig. 14.30).

Jihad Muslim holy war; a Muslim crusade against unbelievers.

Jongleurs (zhō-gleur) French professional musicians (minstrels) of the twelfth and thirteenth centuries who served the *troubadours and *trouvères.

K

Keystone The central wedge-shaped stone in an *arch; the last stone put in place, it makes the arch stable.

Kibla The point toward which Muslims turn when praying, toward Mecca.

Kithara (KITH-a-ra) The principal stringed instrument of the ancient Greeks. Essentially a larger version of the *lyre, it has a U-shaped form and usually seven to eleven strings running vertically from the cross-arm down to the sound-box at the base of the instrument. The legendary instrument of Apollo (see fig. 7.66).

Kore Archaic Greek sculpture of a standing, clothed female figure (see fig. 7.11).

Kouros Archaic Greek sculpture of a standing, usually nude, male figure (see fig. 7.13).

L

Lancet arch In architecture, a narrow arch pointed at the top like a spear.

Lancet window In architecture a tall, narrow window set in lancet arch.

Lantern In architecture, a small decorative structure that crowns a *dome or roof.

Lapis lazuli Long valued as a deep blue ornamental gem and the source of ultramarine pigment, lapis lazuli is a contact metamorphic rock that varies in composition and physical property. It is distinguished from jasper by tiny flecks of gold and the absence of the colorless quartz crystals present in jasper.

Latin cross A cross in which the vertical member is longer than the horizontal arm it bisects.

Libretto (It., "little book") The text or words of an *opera, *oratorio, or other extended vocal work.

Lintel In architecture, a horizontal crosspiece over an open space, which carries the weight of some of the superstructure (see fig. 7.28).

Lithography A printmaking process that uses a polished stone (or metal plate) on which the design is drawn with a crayon or greasy ink. Ink is chemically attracted only to the lines of the drawing, with a print made by applying paper to the inked stone.

Liturgical Pertaining to public worship, specifically to the organized worship patterns of Christian churches.

Liturgical drama Twelfth- and thirteenth-century enactments of biblical stories, frequently with music. Developed into the "mystery plays" of the fourteenth through sixteenth centuries.

Lituus (Lat.) Bronze *trumpet used by the Roman armies. Shaped like the letter *J*.

Logos (Gk., *logos*, "speech, word, reason") Cosmic reason, considered in Greek philosophy as the source of world intelligibility and order.

Lost-wax process See *cire perdue.

Lunette In architecture, a crescent-shaped or semicircular space, usually over a door or a window.

Lute Plucked stringed instrument with a pear-shaped body and a fingerboard with frets. It had eleven strings tuned to six notes (five sets of double strings plus a single string for the highest note). It was the most popular instrument during the Middle Ages and Renaissance.

Lyre (or Lyra) Ancient Greek instrument, a simpler form of the *kithara. The sound-box was often made of a tortoise shell. Used mainly by amateurs. The larger kithara was used by professional musicians (see fig. 7.64).

Lyric Poetry sung to the accompaniment of a *lyre (Greek); *troubadour and *trouvère poetry intended to be sung; short poems with musical elements.

M

Madrigal Name of uncertain origin that refers to fourteenth-century vocal music or, more usually, to the popular sixteenth-century type. Renaissance madrigals were free-form vocal pieces (usually set to love lyrics) in a *polyphonic style with intermixed *homophonic sections. Flemish, Italian, and English composers brought the madrigal to a high level of expressiveness in word painting and imagery. Madrigals were sometimes accompanied but mostly *a cappella.

Magi The Magi (singular Magus) were the priestly hierarchy of Zoroastrianism. Like the Brahmans of India, they were keepers of the cult and of sacrificial power and exercised considerable political influence when Zoroastrianism was the Persian state religion. Christians honor them as the first Gentiles to believe in Christ and celebrate their visit to Bethlehem, as told in the Bible, by the feast of the Epiphany.

Manorialism The economic, social, and administrative system that prevailed in medieval Europe. Originating in the fourth century, it peaked in the twelfth century and then began a long decline that ended only in modern times.

Mass The central service of public worship of some Christian churches, principally the Church of Rome.

Materialism The doctrine that the only reality is matter; that the universe is not governed by intelligence or purpose but only by mechanical cause and effect.

Meander The Greek fret or key pattern

used in art or architecture. From a winding, turning course, like a river.

Measure   In music, the metrical unit between two bars on the *staff; a bar.

Melisma   A melodic unit sung to one syllable; *plainsong has frequent *melismatic* passages.

Metaphor   A form of figurative language that compares dissimilar objects (e.g., publicity is a two-edged sword; the moon is blue).

Metaphysics   Philosophic inquiry into the ultimate and fundamental reality; "the science of being as such."

Meter   In music, a grouping of beats into patterns of two, three, or four beats or combinations thereof; in English poetry the basic rhythmic pattern of stressed (—) and unstressed (˘) syllables. Metrical patterns include: iambic (˘ —), trochaic (— ˘), anapestic (˘ ˘ —), and dactylic (— ˘ ˘).

Metope   (MET-o-pay)   In classical architecture the panel between two *triglyphs in a *Doric *frieze; may be plain or carved. The Parthenon metopes are all carved (see fig. 7.41).

Mihrab   A niche inserted in the wall of a mosque indicating the direction of Mecca so that all worshipers may face Mecca.

Minaret   A tall, slender tower attached to a Muslim mosque from which a muezzin calls the faithful to prayer (see fig. 11.22).

Minibar   The high pulpit from which the Islamic preacher delivers the sermon. Originally used by judges administering the law.

Modes, rhythmic   A thirteenth-century system of music rhythmic notation based on the patterns of poetic meter. Rhythmic modes give the characteristic flavor to thirteenth-century *organum and *motets because of the constant repetition of the same rhythmic patterns. All modes were performed in so-called "perfect" *meter, that is, triple.

Monism   (Gk., *mones*, "single")   The philosophical position that there is but one fundamental reality. The classical advocate of extreme monism was Parmenides of Elea; Spinoza is a modern exponent.

Monochord   A device consisting of a single string stretched over a soundboard with a movable bridge. Used to demonstrate the laws of acoustics, especially the relationships between intervals and string lengths and the tuning of *scales (see fig. 15.2).

Monophonic   (Gk., "one sound")   A single line of music without accompaniment or additional parts, as in *plainsong, *troubadour-*trouvère-minnesinger songs, and some folk songs.

Monotheism   The religious conception of a single, transcendent god. It contrasts with polytheism (belief in many gods) and pantheism (belief in God as synonymous with the universe). Judaism, Christianity, and Islam are the principal monotheistic religions.

Montage   (moan-tahzh)   A composition made of existing photographs, paintings, or drawings; in cinematography the effects achieved by superimposing images or using rapid sequences.

Moor   The term Moor (Sp., *moro*) is derived from "Mauretania," the Roman name for present-day Morocco and Algeria. As the Islamic tide swept across Africa it was joined by the Berbers of this region, who invaded Spain in 711, where they remained in power for eight centuries.

Mosaic   The technique of embedding bits of stone, colored glass, or marble in wet concrete to make designs or pictures for walls or floors. To achieve a complex interplay of light and shadows, the bits are set in the holding material with minute differences in the angles, as in the mosaics of San Vitale in Ravenna (see figs. 11.20 and 11.21).

Mosque   A place of public worship in the Islamic religion. The term is from the Arabic *masjid*, "a place to prostrate one's self [in front of God]."

Motet   (from Fr., *mot*, "word")   The most important form of early *polyphonic music (ca. thirteenth to seventeenth centuries). *Medieval motet* (thirteenth to fourteenth centuries). Usually three parts (triplum, motetus, tenor). The tenor "holds" to a *cantus firmus and the upper two voices sing different texts (sacred and/or secular).

Mullion   A vertical member that divides a window into sections; also used to support the glass in stained glass windows.

Mural   A painting on a wall; a *fresco is a type of mural.

Mythology   Collections of stories explaining natural phenomena, customs, institutions, religious beliefs, and so forth of a people. Usually concerned with the supernatural, gods, goddesses, heroic exploits, and the like.

N

Narthex   A porch or vestibule of a church through which one passes to enter the *nave (see fig. 14.28).

Naturalism   The view that the universe requires no supernatural cause or government, that it is self-existent, self-explanatory, self-operating, and self-directing, and that it is purposeless, deterministic, and only incidentally productive of humanity. In relation to literature sometimes defined as "realism on all fours." The dominant traits of literary naturalism are biological determinism (people are what they must be because of their genes) and environmental determinism (people are what they are because of how they are brought up).

Nave   The main central space of a church running from the entrance to the *crossing of the *transepts; typically flanked by one or two side aisles. Name derived from *naval* because the barrel *vault ceiling has the appearance of the inside hull of a ship (see fig. 14.28).

Neume   (From Gk., *pneuma*, "breath")   Sign used in notation of medieval *plainsong.

Nimbus   In Christian iconography, a device symbolizing sanctity, usually a radiance or a bright circle.

Notre Dame school   The composers of the twelfth- and thirteenth-century cathedral school at Notre Dame de Paris, most notably Léonin and Pérotin. The Notre Dame school invented rhythmic notation for *polyphonic music.

O

Oboe   (From Fr., *haut bois*, "high wind," that is, high-pitched instrument)   A double-reed, soprano-range instrument with a conical bore (slightly expanding diameter from reed to bell). It has a nasal, but mellow and poignant, tone.

Octave   In music, the interval of eight diatonic degrees between tones, one of which has twice as many vibrations per second as the other.

Ode   A formal lyric on a usually dignified theme, in exalted language, e.g., works by Horace.

Office hours   In the Church of Rome, the services (usually observed only in monastic churches) that take place eight times a day (every three hours): Matins, Lauds, Prime, Terce, Sext, None, Vespers, and Compline. Musically the important services are Matins, Vespers, and Compline.

Oligarchy   (Gk., "rule by the few")   A form of government in which a small group of people holds the ruling power. Some political theorists believe that even democratic governments can end up in the hands of an oligarchy ("iron law of oligarchy").

Ontology   (Gk., *on*, "being," *logos*, "logic")   Philosophic inquiry into the ultimate nature of things, what it means to be.

Open score   In music, one voice part per *staff.

Opera   (From It., *opera in musica*, "works in music")   A play in which the text is generally sung throughout to the accompaniment of an orchestra. Modern opera had its beginnings in Florence in the late sixteenth century when some musicians, poets, and scholars attempted a revival of Greek drama, which they assumed to have been sung throughout.

Oratorio   A musical setting of a religious or epic theme for performance by soloists, chorus, and orchestra in a church or concert hall. Originally (early seventeenth century) it was similar to an *opera (sacred opera) with staging, costumes, and scenery. It is now usually presented in concert form, for example, *Messiah* by G. F. Handel.

Orchestra   (From Gk., *orcheisthai*, "to dance")   In ancient Greek theatres the circular or semicircular space in front of the stage used by the chorus; group of instrumentalists performing ensemble music, e.g., symphony orchestra.

Organ, pipe organ   An instrument (see *Hydraulis) of ancient origin consisting of from two to seven keyboards (manuals) and a set of pedals (usually thirty-two notes) for the feet.

Organum   (OR-ga-num; Lat.)   The name given to the earliest types of *polyphonic music.

P

Pantheism (Gk., *pan*, "all," *theos*, "god") As a religious concept, the doctrine that God is immanent in all things.

Patrician Member of the hereditary aristocratic class of ancient Rome and entitled to privileges denied other citizens. By the third century BC the plebeians substantially diminished the patricians' privileged position. The distinction between the two classes became blurred during the empire and "patrician" eventually became an honorific title.

Pax Romana The period from the rule of Caesar Augustus through Marcus Aurelius (27 BC–AD 180) in which there were no major wars anywhere in the Roman Empire.

Pediment In classical architecture, a triangular space at the end of a building framed by the *cornice and the ends of the sloping roof (*raking cornices). (See fig. 7.31.)

Pendentive In architecture, a concave triangular piece of masonry, four of which form a transition from a square base to support the circular rim of a *dome (see fig. 11.18).

Pentateuch The first five books of the Bible, the so-called "Books of Moses": Genesis, Exodus, Leviticus, Numbers, and Deuteronomy.

Percussion Instruments that are played by striking, shaking, scraping, etc.

Peristyle A series of *columns that surround the exterior of a building or the interior of a court, e.g., the Parthenon has a peristyle (see fig. 7.35).

Perspective The illusion of a three-dimensional world on a two-dimensional surface. *Linear perspective* uses lines of projection converging on a vanishing point, with objects appearing smaller the further from the viewer. *Aerial (atmospheric) perspective* uses diminished color intensity and blurred contours for objects apparently deeper in space.

Pier A mass of masonry, usually large, used to support *arches or *lintels; more massive than a *column and with a shape other than circular.

Pietà (pyay-TA; It., "pity, compassion") Representations of the Virgin mourning the body of her Son.

Pilaster A flat vertical *column projecting from the wall of a building; usually furnished with a base and *capital in the manner of an *engaged column, which is rounded rather than rectangular like the pilaster (see fig. 9.22).

Plainsong The term generally used for the large body of nonmetrical, *monophonic, *liturgical music of the Church of Rome; also called Gregorian chant.

Polyphony (po-LIF-o-nee) *Polyphonic* (pol-ly-PHON-ik), that is, "many-voiced" music having melodic interest in two or more simultaneous melodic lines. Examples of polyphonic music would be *canons and *rounds.

Polytheism The belief in and worship of many gods.

Portico A porch or walkway with a roof supported by *columns.

Post and lintel A structural system in which vertical supports or *columns support horizontal beams. The *lintel can span only a relatively short space because the weight of the superstructure centers on the mid-point of the horizontal beam. In a structural system using *arches the thrust is distributed to the columns supporting the bases of the arches, thus allowing for a greater span. The lintel is also called an *architrave. (See fig. 7.28.)

Pragmatism (Gk., *pragma*, "things done") Philosophic doctrine that the meaning of a proposition or course of action lies in its observable consequences and that its meaning is the sum of its consequences. In everyday life the favoring of practical means over theory; if something works, it's good; if not, it's bad.

Primary colors The *hues of red, yellow, and blue with which the colors of the spectrum can be produced. Primary colors cannot be produced by mixing.

Program music Music intended to depict ideas, scenes, or other extramusical concepts.

Proscenium (Gk., *pro*, "before," *skene*, "stage") In traditional theatres the framework of the stage opening.

Psalm A sacred song, poem, or *hymn; the songs in the Old Testament book of Psalms.

Psalter Vernacular name for the book of Psalms.

Psaltery Ancient or medieval instrument consisting of a flat soundboard over which a number of strings are stretched. A psaltery is plucked with the fingers. The harpsichord is a keyed psaltery. (See fig. 13.1.)

Q

Quadrivium The higher division of the seven liberal arts in the Middle Ages: arithmetic, astronomy, geometry, and music.

Quatrain A stanza of four lines, either rhymed or unrhymed.

R

Raking cornice The end *cornice on the sloping sides of a triangular *pediment.

Rayonnant (Fr., "radiant") The ultimate phase of High Gothic architecture that emphasizes soaring lines and vast expanses of stained glass walls (see fig. 14.36).

Rebec A small, bowed medieval string instrument adapted from the Arabian *rehab*. One of the instruments from which the violin developed during the sixteenth century (see fig. 15.3).

Recorder A straight, end-blown *flute, as distinct from the modern side-blown (transverse) flute. It was used from the Middle Ages until the eighteenth century and has been revived in the twentieth century.

Red-figure style Incised, shaded orange figures against a jet black background. The technique was capable of infinite

subtleties. Euphronios (fl. 520–505 BC) was probably the greatest painter in the style, though many artists were noteworthy.

Refrain Recurring section of text (and usually music), e.g., verse-refrain.

Relief In sculpture, carvings projecting from a background that is a part of the whole. Reliefs may be high (almost disengaged from the background) or low (*bas-relief*, slightly raised above the background).

Reliquary (Fr., "remains") A receptacle for storing or displaying holy relics (see fig. 14.15).

Round In music a commonly used name for a circle *canon. At the conclusion of a melody the singer returns to the beginning, repeating the melody as often as desired. Examples: "Brother James," "Three Blind Mice," and "Row, Row, Row Your Boat."

S

Sahn A ritual pool in mosque courtyards in which the faithful make their ablutions.

Sanctuary A sacred or holy place set aside for the worship of a god or gods; a place of refuge or protection.

Sarcophagus A stone coffin.

Satire An indictment of human foibles using humor as a weapon, e.g., the relatively mild satires of Horace and the bitter ones of Juvenal and Jonathan Swift.

Scale (Lat., "ladder") The tonal material of music arranged in a series of rising or falling pitches. Because of the variety in the world's music there are many different scales. The basic scale of European music is the diatonic scale (C-D-E-F-G-A-B-C), i.e., the white keys of the piano. This arrangement of tones is also called a major scale, in the example given, a C major scale. (See Appendix.)

Scholasticism The philosophy and method of medieval theologians in which speculation was separated from observation and practice, revelation was regarded as both the norm and an aid to reason, reason respected authority, and scientific inquiry was controlled by theology.

Secondary colors Those *hues located between the *primary colors on a traditional color wheel: orange, green, and violet.

Sequence A type of chant developed in the Early Middle Ages in which a freely poetic text was added to the long *melisma at the end of the *Alleluias. Subsequently separated from the Alleluias, the sequences became independent syllabic chants. The composition of many original sequences finally led to the banning of all but five sequences by the Council of Trent (1545–63).

Simile A comparison between two quite different things, usually using "like" or "as."

Skene (SKAY-nuh) The Greek stage building, originally of wood, at the rear of the orchestra.

Schein, Seth L. *The Mortal Hero: An Introduction to Homer's ILIAD*. Berkeley: University of California Press, 1984. A clear presentation for nonspecialists.

Vivante, Paolo. *Homer*. New Haven: Yale University Press, 1985. An enthusiastic introduction for the general reader.

Warner, Rex. *The Stories of the Greeks*. New York: Farrar, Straus, & Giroux, 1961. Fascinating accounts of heroes and gods.

General Studies of Greek Culture
These works cover the whole period through the Hellenistic age and will not be listed again.

Barr, Stringfellow. *The Will of Zeus; A History of Greece from the Origins of Hellenic Culture to the Death of Alexander*. Philadelphia: J. B. Lippincott, 1961. Whenever possible Barr lets the Greeks tell their own tale. No one can tell it better.

Bulfinch, Thomas. *Bulfinch's Mythology*. New York: HarperCollins, 1991. The age of fable, the age of chivalry, legends of Charlemagne. The recognized standard work, originally published in three separate volumes.

Bury, J. B. *History of Greece*. New York: St. Martin's Press, 1975. Still the standard history and for all the right reasons.

Chamoux, François. *The Civilization of Greece*. New York: Simon & Schuster, 1965. A handsome cultural history with fine illustrations.

Eliot, Alexander. *The Horizon Concise History of Greece*. New York: Horizon Press, 1973. Packed with information; fascinating reading.

Finley, M. I., *The Legacy of Greece: A New Appraisal*. New York: Oxford University Press, 1981. After a lifetime of study a noted classicist offers his mature assessment of the Greek achievement.

Translations of Original Material
Fitzgerald, Robert. *The Iliad of Homer*. Garden City, N.Y.: Doubleday, 1975. *The Odyssey of Homer*. Garden City, N.Y.: Doubleday, 1961. Each generation should have its own translation of Homer, and these are superb.

Hogan, James C. *A Guide to the Iliad; based on the translation by Robert Fitzgerald*. Garden City, N.Y.: Doubleday, 1979.

NOTE: The latest archeological evidence about Aegean civilizations can be found in periodicals such as: *National Geographic, Smithsonian, Science News, Archeology, Nature*.

5   Hellenic Athens: The Fulfillment of the Good Life

Fantham, Elaine, et al. *Women in the Classical World*. New York: Oxford University Press, 1994.

Grant, Michael. *Readings in the Classical Historians*. New York: Charles Scribner's Sons, 1992. An exceptionally useful introduction to Greek and Roman historians by a noted classical scholar.

Hill, Donald. *A History of Engineering in Classical and Medieval Times*. La Salle, Ill.: Open Court Publishing, 1984. Includes an important reevaluation of the role of technology in ancient Greece.

Knox, Bernard. *The Oldest Dead White European Males and Other Reflections on the Classics*. New York: W. W. Norton, 1993. Despite all the sound and fury about not being "politically correct," the title of this latest book by a noted

classicist states what cannot be denied: this is where, for the most part, Western civilization came from.

Pomeroy, Sarah. *Goddesses, Whores, Wives and Slaves: Women in Classical Antiquity*. New York: Schocken, 1975. Valuable study.

Robertson, Charles A., Jr. *Athens in the Days of Perikles*. Norman, Okla.: University of Oklahoma Press, 1971. Fine study of the great leader.

Rose, H. J. *A Handbook of Greek Literature from Homer to the age of Lucian*. New York: Dutton, 1960. London: Methuen, 1948. A standard reference work in the field.

Sagan, Eli. *The Honey and the Hemlock; Democracy and Paranoia in Ancient Athens and Modern America*. New York: Basic Books of HarperCollins, 1991. Remarkable insights into the parallels between ancient and modern democracies.

Scarisbrick, Diana, et al. *Jewellery: Makers, Motifs, History, Techniques*. London: Thames & Hudson, 1989. Possibly the best one-volume history of this ancient craft.

Taplin, Oliver. *Greek Fire: The Influence of Ancient Greece on the Modern World*. New York: Atheneum, 1990. Fascinating. Very highly recommended. The opening line foretells the contents: "Not back to the Greeks, but forward with the Greeks."

Thucydides. *History of the Peloponnesian War*. Trans. Richard Crawley. New York: Random House, 1981. Objective, thorough, a highly readable book by one of the most distinguished of the ancient Greek historians.

Translations and Studies of Greek Drama
Bates, William N. *Euripides: A Student of Human Nature*. New York: Russell & Russell, 1969. The dramatist as a realist.

Cook, Albert. *Oedipus Rex: A Mirror for Greek Drama*. Belmont, Calif.: Wadsworth, 1964. A broad, general approach to Greek drama and highly recommended.

Fitts, Dudley, and Robert Fitzgerald. *The Oedipus Cycle*. New York: Harcourt, Brace, Jovanovich, 1967. Brilliant translations that are both faithful and poetic.

Grene, David, and Richard Lattimore. *Greek Tragedies*. 3 vols. Chicago: University of Chicago Press, 1960. Excellent modern translations of the more important plays of Aeschylus, Sophocles, and Euripides.

Hogan, James C. *Aeschylus: A Commentary on the Complete Greek Tragedies*. Chicago: University of Chicago Press, 1985. General introduction to Aeschylean drama plus detailed discussion of the seven surviving plays.

McLeish, Kenneth. *The Theatre of Aristophanes*. New York: Taplinger, 1980. Fascinating discussion of style and content.

O'Brien, Michael J., ed. *Twentieth Century Interpretations of Oedipus Rex: A Collection of Critical Essays*. Englewood Cliffs, N.J.: Prentice Hall, 1968. Contemporary scholars present varied views of this inexhaustibly challenging play.

Solomos, Alexis. *The Living Aristophanes*. Ann Arbor: University of Michigan Press, 1974. Good background information.

6   Greece: From Hellenic to Hellenistic World

General Studies of the Hellenistic World
Burn, Andrew R. *Alexander the Great and the Hellenistic World*. New York: Macmillan,

1974. Alexander's role in spreading Greek culture.

Bury, J. B. *The Hellenistic Age*. New York: W. W. Norton, 1970. A fine treatment by the eminent Greek historian.

Grant, Michael. *From Alexander to Cleopatra: The Hellenistic World*. New York: Charles Scribner's Sons, 1982. Comprehensive overview.

Hamilton, J. R. *Alexander the Great*. Pittsburgh: University of Pittsburgh Press, 1974. Excellent biographical study.

Philosophy and Social Issues
Else, Gerald F. *Greek Homosexuality*. New York: Random House, 1980. Behavior and attitudes as revealed in vase paintings, poetry, Plato, lawcourt speeches, and the comedies of Aristophanes.

————. *Plato and Aristotle on Poetry*. Chapel Hill: University of North Carolina Press, 1986. Examination of Plato's attacks on poetry and Aristotle's defense of poets and poetry.

Huby, Patricia. *Plato and Modern Morality*. Atlantic Highlands, N. J.: Humanities Press, 1972. Assessment of Plato's enduring relevance.

Long, A. A. *Hellenistic Philosophy: Stoics, Epicureans, Sceptics*. New York: Charles Scribner's Sons, 1974. Important currents after Plato and Aristotle.

Randall, John Herman. *Aristotle*. New York: Columbia University Press, 1960. Authoritative study.

Taylor, A. E. *Plato: The Man and His Work*. New York: World Publishing, 1966. Outstanding and comprehensive.

Waithe, Mary Ellen, ed. *A History of Women Philosophers: Volume 1, Ancient Women Philosophers, 600 BC–AD 500*. Boston: Martinus Nijhoff, 1987.

Translations of Original Material
Aristotle. *Aristotle: Selections from Seven Books*. Ed. Philip Wheelwright. Indianapolis: Odyssey Press, 1951. Significant selections.

————. *Aristotle's Poetics*. Trans. James Hutton. New York: W. W. Norton, 1982. Includes helpful introduction and notes.

————. *The Ethics of Aristotle: The Nichomachean Ethics*. Ed. Hugh Tredinnick, trans. J. A. Thompson. Baltimore: Penguin, 1977. The discussion of happiness is particularly accessible.

Plato. *Great Dialogues of Plato*. Trans. W. H. D. Rouse. New York: New American Library, 1956. The standard one-volume work.

Fiction
Renault, Mary. *Fire from Heaven*. New York: Pantheon, 1970. The first in her Alexandrian trilogy: *Alexander's Youth*. *The Persian Boy* (1972) recounts his life from age twenty-six to his death. *Funeral Games: The Combat of Alexander's Heirs* (1981) concludes the trilogy.

————. *The Mask of Apollo*. New York: Bantam, 1974. A lively picture of Plato's times.

7   The Greek Arts

Art and Architecture
Hampe, Roland, and Erika Simon. *The Birth of Greek Art: From the Mycenaean to the Archaic Period*. New York: Oxford University Press, 1981. Detailed and thorough.

Lawrence, A. W. *Greek Architecture*. Rev. ed. New York: Viking, 1984. A comprehensive study.

Lullies, Reinhard, and Max Hirmer. *Greek Sculpture*. New York: Harry N. Abrams, 1960. Includes 282 magnificent photographs by Hirmer.

Richter, Gisela M. A. *Handbook of Greek Art*. 7th ed. New York: Dutton, 1980. Concise and well illustrated. Includes minor arts.

Robertson, Martin. *A History of Greek Art*. 2 vols. New York: Cambridge University Press, 1975. Detailed and interesting. Abridged edition available in paperback as *A Shorter History of Greek Art*. New York: Cambridge University Press, 1981.

Scully, Vincent. *The Earth, the Temples, and the Gods*. New Haven: Yale University Press, 1979. Fascinating study of the landscape of Greek sacred architecture.

Dance and Music
Georgiades, Thrasybulos. *Greek Music, Verse, and Dance*. Reprint. New York: Da Capo Press, 1973. The interrelationships in Greek culture.

Sorell, Walter. *Dance in Its Time*. Garden City, N.Y.: Doubleday, 1981. Dance in its cultural contexts throughout history.

Poetry
Bowra, C. M. *Greek Lyric Poetry*. 2nd ed. New York: Oxford University Press, 1961. Written by a noted classicist, this is regarded as the standard discussion of the topic.

Duban, Jeffrey M. *Ancient and Modern Images of Sappho: Translations and Studies in Archaic Greek Love Lyrics*. Lanham, Md.: University Press of America, 1984. An illuminating focus on the great poet.

8   A Thousand Years of Rome

Auguet, Roland. *Cruelty and Civilization: The Roman Games*. London: Allen & Unwin, 1972. Excellent survey of a subject both fascinating and repulsive.

Brantlinger, Patrick. *Bread and Circuses: Theories of Mass Culture as Social Decay*. Ithaca: Cornell University Press, 1985. The "decline and fall" motif from Greece and Rome to the present day.

Cary, Max, and H. H. Scullard, *A History of Rome*. New York: St. Martin's Press, 1975. One of the finest short histories.

Casson, Lionel. *The Horizon Book of Daily Life in Ancient Rome*. New York: American Heritage, 1975. Outstanding series that also includes Ancient Egypt, the Middle Ages, the Renaissance, and Victorian England.

Gardiner, E. N. *Athletics in the Ancient World*. Chicago: University of Chicago Press, 1978. The single most useful source on the interrelationship of athletics and religion in Greece and Rome.

Luck, Georg. *Arcana Mundi: Magic and the Occult in the Greek and Roman Worlds*. Baltimore: Johns Hopkins University Press, 1985.

Nicolet, Claude. *The World of the Citizen in Republican Rome*. Berkeley: University of California Press, 1980. Probably the finest study of social and political life in the Republic.

Petit, Paul. *Pax Romana*. Trans. James Willis. Berkeley: University of California Press, 1976. Excellent study of the Roman world order.

Rostovzeff, Mikhail. *Social and Economic History of the Roman Empire*. New York: Oxford University Press, 1957. The standard work.

Wellard, James. *The Search for the Etruscans*. New York: Saturday Review Press, 1973. A review of theories while the search continues.

Translations and Interpretations of Original Material
Translations of all Roman authors are available in the Loeb Classical Library series published by Harvard University Press. Excellent translations of standard works are also published by the Indiana University Press, Bloomington, Indiana. The following works are also recommended:

Davenport, Basil, ed. *The Portable Roman Reader*. New York: Viking, 1959. The best cross section of Roman literature in a single volume.

Graves, Robert. *Suetonius: The Lives of the Twelve Caesars*. Baltimore: Penguin, 1957. The author of *I, Claudius* is also a superb translator.

Hammond, N. G., and H. H. Scullard, *Oxford Classical Dictionary*. Oxford: Clarendon Press, 1970. The definitive reference work for Greek and Roman culture.

Mulls, Barriss. *Epigrams from Martial: A Verse Translation*. Lafayette: Purdue University Press, 1969. Skillful contemporary translation.

Sesar, Carl. *Selected Poems of Catullus*. New York: Mason & Lipscomb, 1974. Idiomatic, profane, erotic, and scatalogical and, thus, very close to the style and spirit of the original.

Turner, Paul. *Plutarch's Lives*. Carbondale: Southern Illinois University Press, 1963. Good translation of a standard work.

9   Roman Art and Architecture: The Arts of Megalopolis

Boethius, Axel, and J. B. Ward-Perkins. *Etruscan and Early Roman Architecture*. Baltimore: Penguin, 1979. Comprehensive.

Brown, Frank E. *Cosa: The Making of a Roman Town*. Ann Arbor: University of Michigan Press, 1980. Case study of civic planning.

Grant, Michael. *The Art and Life of Pompeii and Herculaneum*. New York: Newsweek, 1979. A popular and picturesque account.

Henig, Martin, ed. *A Handbook of Roman Art: A Comprehensive Survey of All the Arts of the Roman World*. Ithaca: Cornell University Press, 1983.

MacDonald, William L. *The Pantheon: Design, Meaning, and Progeny*. Cambridge, Mass.: Harvard University Press, 1976.

Merrifield, Ralph. *London: City of the Romans*. Berkeley: University of California Press, 1983. A reconstruction of Roman London.

Sear, Frank. *Roman Architecture*. Ithaca: Cornell University Press, 1983. Comprehensive overview of 1,000 years of Rome.

Toynbee, Jocelyn M. *Animals in Roman Life and Art*. Ithaca: Cornell University Press, 1973. Animal motifs in Roman art.

10   The Star and the Cross

Judaism: General History and Culture
Albright, William F. *From the Stone Age to Christianity*. Baltimore: Johns Hopkins University Press, 1957. A standard work that traces the rise of monotheism.

Beltz, Walter. *God and the Gods*. Trans. Peter Heinegg. New York: Penguin, 1983. Relates biblical stories to religious traditions of surrounding cultures.

Bright, John. *A History of Israel*. Philadelphia: Westminster Press, 1972. Excellent survey by a noted biblical scholar.

Miller, Madeleine S., and J. Lane Miller. *Harper's Encyclopedia of Bible Life*. New York: Harper & Row, 1978. Solid information on everyday life and culture in the biblical period.

Christianity: General History and Culture
Johnson, Paul. *A History of Christianity*. New York: Atheneum, 1976. A detailed survey from the apostolic and patriarchal ages to the present.

Meeks, Wayne A. *The First Urban Christians: The Social World of the Apostle Paul*. New Haven: Yale University Press, 1983. What it was like to be an ordinary Christian in the Roman Empire.

Papini, Giovanni. *Life of Christ*. Trans. Dorothy Canfield Fisher. New York: Harcourt, Brace, & World, 1951. A vivid, powerful biography by a foremost Italian man of letters.

Pelikan, Jaroslav. *Jesus Through the Centuries: His Place in the History of Culture*. New Haven: Yale University Press, 1985. A stimulating, informative, and illustrated study of the changing role of Christ in cultural movements of Western civilization.

Wilken, Robert L. *The Christians as the Romans Saw Them*. New Haven: Yale University Press, 1985. A fascinating account of the Christian movement from a non-Christian perspective.

Translations and Expositions of the Bible
Bruce, F. F. *The English Bible: A History of Translations from the Earliest English Versions to the New English Bible*. New York: Oxford University Press, 1961.

Fiorenza, Elizabeth Schussler. *In Memory of Her—A Feminist Theological Reconstruction of Christian Origins*. New York: Crossword Publishing Company, 1989.

Friedman, Richard Elliot. *Who Wrote the Bible?* New York: Summit, 1987. A noted biblical scholar documents the Pentateuch as written by four different authors and combined into one narrative by an editor. He also identifies significant contradictions between the creation stories in Genesis 1 and Genesis 2.

Frye, Northrop. *The Great Code: The Bible and Literature*. New York: Harcourt, Brace, Jovanovich, 1982. A renowned critic examines the continuing significance of the Bible as the single most important influence in the imaginative tradition of Western art and literature.

Gastor, Theodor H. *The Dead Sea Scrolls*. Garden City, N.Y.: Anchor, 1976. Assesses the significance for biblical studies of this modern find of ancient manuscripts.

Kraemer, Ross Shepard. *Her Share of the Blessings—Women's Religions Among Pagans, Jews and Christians in the Greco-Roman World*. New York: Oxford University Press, 1992.

Laymon, Charles M., ed. *The Interpreter's One-Volume Commentary on the Bible*. New York: Abingdon Press, 1971. The most authoritative one-volume reference work, with scholarly introductions and commentary on each book, including the Apocrypha.

Pritchard, J. B., ed. *Ancient Near Eastern Texts Relating to the Old Testament*. Princeton: Princeton University Press, 1955. Mesopotamian and Egyptian documents that exhibit provocative parallels with biblical texts.

Stendahl, K. *The Bible and the Role of Women*. Philadelphia: Fortress Press, 1966.

11   The Beginnings of Christian Art

Beckwith, John. *Early Christian and Byzantine Art*. Pelican History of Art Series. New York: Penguin, 1980. A good introduction in a fine series.

Demus, Otto. *Byzantine Mosaic Decoration: Aspects of Monumental Art in Byzantium*. New Rochelle, N.Y.: Aristide E. Caratzas, 1976. An illuminating study of a long tradition.

Hulme, F. Howard. *Symbolism in Christian Art*. Atlantic Highlands, N.J.: Humanities Press, 1971. A classic study of the subject.

Mango, Cyril. *Art of the Byzantine Empire*. Englewood Cliffs, N.J.: Prentice Hall, 1972. A wide-ranging survey.

————. *Byzantine Architecture*. History of World Architecture Series. New York: Harry N. Abrams, 1976. Excellent study in a consistently good series.

12   Building Medieval Walls

General

Aland, Kurt. *A History of Christianity: From the Beginnings to the Threshold of the Reformation*. Philadelphia: Fortress Press, 1985. A fine study utilizing recent scholarship.

Bishop, Morris. *The Middle Ages*. Magnolia, Mass.: Peter Smith, 1983. A graceful and witty account of the 1,000 years between Rome and the Renaissance.

Gies, Joseph, and Frances Gies. *Life in a Medieval Castle*. New York: Harper & Row, 1979. Everyday life in a castle.

Peterson, Karen, and J. J. Wilson. *Women Artists—Recognition and Reappraisal, From the Early Middle Ages to the Twentieth Century*. New York: Harper & Row, 1976.

Strayer, J. R. *Western Europe in the Middle Ages*. Glenview, Ill.: Scott, Foresman, 1982. Perhaps the best short introduction to the political and cultural history of this period.

Literature

Brentano, Robert, ed. *The Early Middle Ages: 500–1000*. New York: Macmillan, 1964. Excellent anthology of Western Christian sources.

Rexroth, Kenneth, and Ling Chung. *The Orchid Boat—Women Poets of China*. New York: McGraw Hill, 1973.

Terry, Patricia. *The Song of Roland*. Indianapolis: Bobbs-Merrill Educational Publishing, 1965. Considered the best available translation and the one used in this chapter.

Trapp, J. B., ed. *Medieval English Literature*. New York: Oxford University Press, 1973. Fine anthology which includes *Beowulf*, *Sir Gawain and the Green Knight*, Chaucer, and other classics.

13   The Late Middle Ages: Expansion and Synthesis

Barber, Richard. *The Knight and Chivalry*. New York: Harper & Row, 1982. An overview of a fascinating subject.

Durrell, Lawrence. *Pope Joan*. New York: Penguin, 1974. The persistent legend of the Joan who became Pope John, engagingly retold by a renowned novelist.

Gies, Frances. *Joan of Arc: The Legend and the Reality*. New York: Harper & Row, 1981.

————. and Joseph Gies. *Life in a Medieval City*. New York: Harper & Row, 1981. An engaging popular account with a focus on thirteenth-century Troyes.

Gies, Joseph, and Frances Gies. *Women in the Middle Ages*. New York: Barnes & Noble, 1980. The status and roles of women.

Gimpel, Jean. *The Medieval Machine: The Industrial Revolution of the Middle Ages*. New York: Penguin, 1977. Significant technological developments in late medieval times.

Heller, Julek, and Deirdre Headon. *Knights*. New York: Schocken, 1982. Rich illustrations capture the romance of legendary knights: Lancelot, Galahad, Tristan, Roland.

Hildegard of Bingen. *Scivias*. Trans. Columba Hart and Jane Bishop. New York: Paulist Press, 1990.

Howarth, David. *1066: The Year of Conquest*. New York: Penguin, 1981. Exciting re-creation of the Norman invasion of England.

Lopez, Robert. *The Commercial Revolution of the Middle Ages: 950–1350*. New York: Cambridge University Press, 1976. Explores another area for which the Middle Ages has received insufficient credit.

Mayer, Hans Eberhard. *The Crusades*. Trans. John Gillingham. New York: Oxford University Press, 1972. The idealism, realism, and barbarism of the Crusades in what is acclaimed as the best one-volume survey.

Translations and Studies of Original Material

Gray, Douglas, ed. *The Oxford Book of Late Medieval Verse and Prose*. New York: Oxford University Press, 1985. The period from Chaucer's death to the reign of Henry VIII.

Kibler, William, ed. and trans. *Chrétien de Troyes: Lancelot, or the Knight of the Cart*. New York: Garland Publishing, 1981. A superb translation of one of the finest medieval romances.

Loomis, Laura H., and Roger S. Loomis, eds. *Medieval Romances*. New York: Random House, 1965. The best of the genre.

Power, Eileen. *Medieval Women*. Cambridge, U.K.: Cambridge University Press, 1975.

Radice, Betty, trans. *The Letters of Abelard and Heloïse*. New York: Penguin, 1976. The correspondence from the most famous love affair of the Middle Ages.

Richards, Earl Jeffrey, trans. *The Book of the City of Ladies by Christine de Pizan*. New York: Persea Books, 1982. First published in 1405, this is a delightful book by a gifted writer.

Wilhelm, James J., and Laila Zamuelis Gross, eds. *The Romance of Arthur: An Anthology*. Arthurian material in modern translation.

Yenal, Edith. *Christine de Pisan; A Bibliography of Writings by Her and About Her*. Metuchen, N.J.: Scarecrow Press, 1982.

14   The Medieval Synthesis in Art

Brown, Peter, ed. *The Book of Kells: A Selection from the Irish Medieval Manuscripts*. New York: Alfred A. Knopf, 1980. Reproductions from one of the world's most beautiful books.

Calkins, Robert. *Illuminated Books of the Middle Ages*. Ithaca, N.Y.: Cornell University Press, 1983. Includes exquisite color plates.

Duby, Georges. *The Art of the Cathedrals: Art and Society, 980–1420*. Trans. Eleanor Levieux and Barbara Thompson. Chicago: University of Chicago Press, 1981. Changing attitudes as reflected by art and architecture.

Kraus, Henry. *The Living Theatre of Medieval Art*. Philadelphia: University of Pennsylvania Press, 1967. Examines the controversial aspects of medieval art and their popular impact.

Male, Emile. *Art and Artists in the Middle Ages*. Trans. Sylvia Lowe. Redding Ridge, Conn.: Black Swan, 1981. Fine illustrations with a text by a noted French art historian.

Simson, Otto von. *The Gothic Cathedral*. New York: Harper & Row, 1964. Classic coverage of the origins and philosophy of the Gothic cathedral.

Smart, Alastair. *The Dawn of Italian Painting, 1250–1400*. Ithaca, N.Y.: Cornell University Press, 1978. Late medieval developments leading toward the Renaissance.

15   Medieval Music and Dance: Sacred and Secular

Collins, Fletcher, Jr. *The Production of Medieval Church Music-drama*. Charlottesville: University of Virginia Press, 1972. Both historical and practical.

Drinker, Sophie. *Music and Women: The Story of Women in Their Relation to Music*. New York: Coward McCann, 1948, reprinted 1980. Influential women in music, art, poetry, and politics from the ancient world to the modern era.

Harksen, Sibylle. *Women in the Middle Ages*. New York: Abner Schram, 1975. From anonymous women in everyday life to those in art, music, professions, and positions of power.

Whigham, Peter, ed. *The Music of the Troubadours*. Santa Barbara: Ross-Erikson, 1979. Good collection of words and music.

Wilhelm, James J. *Seven Troubadours: The Creators of Modern Verse*. University Park: Pennsylvania State University Press, 1970. Engaging study of some fascinating troubadours.

Credits

CHAPTER 1

Page 17: Excerpt from *The Epic of Gilgamesh* reprinted by permission of Princeton University Press from James B. Pritchard, ed., *Ancient Near East: An Anthology of Texts and Pictures*. Copyright © 1958, renewed 1986, by Princeton University Press.

Pages 26–7: Scripture quotations are from the *Revised Standard Version Bible*, copyright © 1946, 1951, 1972 by the Division of Education and Ministry of the National Council of the Churches of Christ in the USA. Used by permission.

CHAPTER 4

Page 72: Untitled poem by Solon is from *Greek Lyrics*, 2nd ed., trans. Richmond Lattimore. Copyright © 1949, 1955, 1960 by Richmond Lattimore, The University of Chicago Press, Chicago, Ill. Reprinted by permission.

Page 79: From the *Odyssey* by Homer, trans. R. Fitzgerald. Copyright © 1961, 1963 by Robert Fitzgerald and renewed 1989 by Benedict R. C. Fitzgerald. Reprinted by permission of Vintage Books, a Division of Random House, Inc.

CHAPTER 5

Pages 100 and 112: *Agamemnon and Eumenides* from *The Laurel Classical Drama: Aeschylus* by Robert Corrigan, ed., trans. George Thomson. Translation copyright © 1965 by Dell, a division of Bantam Doubleday Dell Publishing Group, Inc. Used by permission of Dell Books, a division of Bantam Doubleday Dell Publishing Group, Inc.

Page 116: *Pericles' Memorial Oration*—Source: *Thucydides History of the Peloponnesian War*, trans. Benjamin Jowett, in *The Greek Historian*, ed. F. R. B. Godalphin. Copyright © 1942 Random House, Inc., New York, N.Y.

Page 117: *The Oedipus Rex of Sophocles: An English Version* by Dudley Fitts and Robert Fitzgerald, copyright 1949 by Harcourt Brace Jovanovich, Inc. and renewed 1977 by Cornelia Fitts and Robert Fitzgerald, reprinted by permission of the publisher. CAUTION: All rights, including professional, amateur, motion picture, recitation, lecturing, public reading, radio broadcasting, and television are strictly reserved. Inquiries on all rights should be addressed to Harcourt Brace Jovanovich, Inc., Orlando, Fla. 32887.

Page 135: "Lysistrata: An English Version" from *Aristophanes: Four*

Comedies by Dudley Fitts, copyright 1954 by Harcourt Brace & Company and renewed 1982 by Cornelia Fitts, Daniel M. Fitts, and Deborah W. Fitts, reprinted by permission of the publisher. CAUTION: Professionals and amateurs are hereby warned that all titles included in this volume, being fully protected under the copyright laws of the United States of America, the British Empire, including the Dominion of Canada, and all other countries which are signatories to the Universal Copyright Convention and the International Copyright Union, are subject to royalty. All rights, including professional, amateur, motion picture, recitation, lecturing, public reading, radio broadcasting, television and the rights of translation into foreign languages are strictly reserved. Inquiries on professional rights should be addressed to Lucy Kroll Agency, 390 West End Avenue, New York, N.Y. 10024; inquiries on amateur and translation rights should be addressed to Harcourt Brace & Company, Permissions Department, Orlando, Fla. 32887–6777.

CHAPTER 6

Page 161: From *Euthyphro, Apology, and Crito*, trans. F. J. Church and R. D. Cumming. Copyright © 1956 by Bobbs-Merrill Company, Inc. Reprinted by permission.

Page 171: Reprinted from *The Republic of Plato* translated by F. M. Cornford (1941) by permission of Oxford University Press, Oxford, England.

CHAPTER 7

Pages 225 and 226: Poems by Sappho are from *Archilochos Sappho Alkman: Three Lyric Poets of the Late Greek Bronze Age*, trans. and ed. Guy Davenport. Copyright © 1980 The University of California Press, Berkeley, Calif. Reprinted by permission of the author and publisher.

Page 226: Source: Untitled poem by Simonides, trans. Richard Lattimore in *The Horizon Book of Ancient Greece*. Copyright © 1965 American Heritage Publishing Co., New York.

CHAPTER 8

Page 249: From *The Basic Works of Cicero*, ed. M. Hadas. Copyright © 1957 by Random House, Inc. Reprinted by permission of the publisher.

Page 253: Book VI of the *Aeneid* of Virgil: *The Aeneid of Virgil*, trans. Rolfe Humphries. Copyright © 1951 Charles Scribner's Sons, New York, N.Y. Reprinted by permission.

Page 262: From *The Stoic and Epicurean Philosophers* by Whitney J. Oates. Copyright © 1940 by Random House, Inc. Reprinted by permission of Random House, Inc.

Page 264: From *Selected Poems of Catullus*, trans. Carl Sesar. Copyright

© 1974 Mason and Lipscomb. Reprinted by permission.

Page 266: *Odes of Horace:* Translation reprinted by permission of Maurice A. Crane.

Page 266: From Horace, "My Slave is Free to Speak Up For Himself," in *The Satires and Epistles of Horace*, trans. Smith Palmer Bovie. Copyright © 1959 The University of Chicago Press, Chicago, Ill. Reprinted by permission.

Page 268: From Ovid, *The Art of Love*, trans. Rolfe Humphries. Copyright © 1957 by Indiana University Press, Bloomington, Indiana. Reprinted by permission.

Page 272: *Epigrams from Martial*, trans. Barriss Mills, Purdue University Press, copyright © 1969 Purdue Research Foundation, West Lafayette, Ind. 47907. Reprinted with permission.

Page 274: Arrian's *Discourses of Epictetus*: Reprinted by permission of the publishers and The Loeb Classical Library from *Epictetus: Volumes I and II*, trans. W. A. Oldfather, Cambridge, Mass.: Harvard University Press, 1925, 1928.

Page 275: Marcus Aurelius, excerpts from *Meditations, Book II*, from *The Stoic and Epicurean Philosophers* by Whitney J. Oates. Copyright © 1940 by Random House, Inc. Reprinted by permission of Random House, Inc.

Page 276: *Against the City of Rome* by Juvenal is reprinted from *The Satires of Juvenal*, trans. Rolfe Humphries. Copyright © 1958 Indiana University Press, Bloomington, Ind. Reprinted by permission.

CHAPTER 9

Page 293: "On the Dedication of the Colosseum in Rome" trans. Barriss Mills, Purdue University Press, copyright © 1969 Purdue Research Foundation, West Lafayette, Ind. 47907. Reprinted by permission.

CHAPTER 10

Page 305: Scripture quotations in the chapter are from *Revised Standard Version Bible*, copyright © 1946, 1951, 1972 by the Division of Education and Ministry of the National Council of the Churches of Christ in the USA. Used by permission.

CHAPTER 12

Page 349: Selection from Boethius is from *The Consolation of Philosophy*, ed. James J. Buchanan. Copyright © 1957 and 1963 Crossroad Publishing Company, New York, N.Y. Reprinted by permission.

Page 351: Source: Trans. Leslie Dae Lindou.

Page 352: From *Beowolf, The Oldest English Epic*. Translated into Alliterative Verse with a Critical

Introduction by Charles W. Kennedy. Copyright 1940 by Oxford University Press, Inc.; renewed 1968 by Charles W. Kennedy. Reprinted by permission of Oxford University Press, Inc.

Page 363: *Auccassin and Nicolette*, trans. Eugene Mason, copyright © 1910 Everyman's Library. Reproduced by permission of David Campbell Publishers Ltd., London.

Page 373: "Sanctuary" is from the *Collected Poems of Elinor Wylie* by Elinor Wylie. Copyright © 1921 by Alfred A. Knopf, Inc. and renewed 1949 by William Rose Benet. Reprinted by permission of Alfred A. Knopf, Inc.

CHAPTER 13

Page 386: Poems from *The Wandering Scholars* by Helen Waddell are used by permission of Mary M. Martin, and Constable Publishers, London, England.

Page 387: Source: "Our Lady's Juggler," trans. Barrett H. Clark, *Great Short Stories of the World*.

Page 389: Nevil Coghill, "The Prologue" from Chaucer's *Canterbury Tales* (Penguin Classics, 1951, 4th edn rev. 1977). Copyright © Nevill Coghill 1951, 1958, 1960, 1975, 1977. Reproduced by permission of Penguin Books Ltd.

Page 396: Nevil Coghill, "The Reeve's Tale" from Chaucer's *Canterbury Tales* (Penguin Classics, 1951, 4th edn rev. 1977). Copyright © Nevill Coghill 1951, 1958, 1960, 1975, 1977. Reproduced by permission of Penguin Books Ltd.

Page 399: From Andre, Le Chapelain, *The Art of Courtly Love by Andreas Capellanus*, trans. John Jay Parry. Copyright © 1969 W. W. Norton & Company, Inc. Reprinted by permission of Columbia University Press, New York, N.Y.

Page 401: Selections from *A Medieval Woman's Mirror of Honor: The Treasury of the City of Ladies* by Christine de Pisan, trans. Charity Cannon Willard, copyright © 1989 by Bard Hall Press and Persea Books, Inc. Reprinted by permission of Persea Books.

Page 404: Excerpts from *The Divine Comedy of Dante Alighieri: Inferno and Paradiso*, trans. Allen Mandelbaum. Copyright © 1982 by Allen Mandelbaum, on the English translation. Used by permission of Bantam Books, a division of Bantam Doubleday, Dell Publishing Group, Inc.

CHAPTER 15

Pages 448–50: Troubadour songs— From James J. Wilhelm, *Seven Troubadours: the Creators of Modern Verse*, pp. 43–6, 125–6, and 134–7. Copyright © 1970 by The Pennsylvania State University, University Park and London. Reproduced by permission of the publisher.

Index